The Bloomsbury Handbook of Popular Music, Space and Place

The Bloomsbury Handbook of Popular Music, Space and Place

Edited by Geoff Stahl and
J. Mark Percival

BLOOMSBURY ACADEMIC
NEW YORK · LONDON · OXFORD · NEW DELHI · SYDNEY

BLOOMSBURY ACADEMIC
Bloomsbury Publishing Inc
1385 Broadway, New York, NY 10018, USA
50 Bedford Square, London, WC1B 3DP, UK
29 Earlsfort Terrace, Dublin 2, Ireland

BLOOMSBURY, BLOOMSBURY ACADEMIC and the Diana logo are trademarks
of Bloomsbury Publishing Plc

First published in the United States of America 2022
Paperback edition published 2024

Copyright © Geoff Stahl and J. Mark Percival, 2022
Each chapter copyright © the contributor, 2022

Cover design: Louise Dugdale
Cover photograph by Dean Lewins

All rights reserved. No part of this publication may be reproduced or transmitted
in any form or by any means, electronic or mechanical, including photocopying,
recording, or any information storage or retrieval system, without prior
permission in writing from the publishers.

Bloomsbury Publishing Inc does not have any control over, or responsibility for, any
third-party websites referred to or in this book. All internet addresses given in this book
were correct at the time of going to press. The author and publisher regret any
inconvenience caused if addresses have changed or sites have ceased
to exist, but can accept no responsibility for any such changes.

A catalog record for this book is available from the Library of Congress.

ISBN: HB: 978-1-5013-3628-7
PB: 978-1-5013-9067-8
ePDF: 978-1-5013-3630-0
eBook: 978-1-5013-3629-4

Typeset by Integra Software Services Pvt. Ltd.

To find out more about our authors and books visit www.bloomsbury.com
and sign up for our newsletters.

Contents

List of contributors viii

Introduction *Geoff Stahl and J. Mark Percival* 1

Section I Theory and method

1. **Music, space, place and non-place** *Geoff Stahl* 7
2. **Rhythmanalysis and circulation** *Will Straw* 21
3. **Global, local, regional and translocal: Towards a relational approach to scale in popular music** *Hyunjoon Shin and Keewoong Lee* 31
4. **Sociological perspectives on music and place** *Andy Bennett* 45
5. **Ethnomusicology and place** *Kimberly Cannady* 57
6. **Political economies of urban music** *Shane Homan* 67
7. **Sensobiographic walking and ethnographic approach of the Finnish school of soundscape studies** *Helmi Järviluoma* 83

Section II Space, place and consumption

8. **At home with Sinatra** *Keir Keightley* 101
9. **Music radio** *J. Mark Percival* 117

10 **The record shop** *Nabeel Zuberi* 129

11 **The nightclub** *Hillegonda C Rietveld* 139

12 **The live venue** *Robert Kronenburg* 153

13 **Mobile listening cultures** *Raphaël Nowak* 165

Section III Space, place, production and performance

14 **In the city: Glasgow** *Martin Cloonan* 177

15 **Bedroom production** *Emília Barna* 191

16 **The studio** *Ruth Dockwray* 205

17 **The virtual studio** *Martin K. Koszolko* 217

18 **The space of the record: Something happening somewhere** *Simon Zagorski-Thomas* 229

19 **The live gig** *Sam Whiting* 241

Section IV Cities, suburbs, nations and beyond

20 **Suburban breakout: Nomadic reverie in British pop** *Andrew Branch* 257

21 **Sounding South African township life** *Kathryn Olsen* 271

22 **Funk: A musical symbol of Rio de Janeiro's favelas** *Vincenzo Cambria* 281

23 **Postcolonial noise: How did French rap (re)invent 'the banlieue'?** *Christina Horvath* 291

24 **Music and the nation** *Melanie Schiller* 301

25 **Transnational music** *Simone Krüger Bridge* 315

Section V Selling, celebrating, representing space and place

26 Music, heritage and place *Catherine Strong* 331

27 Music and tourism *Leonieke Bolderman* 341

28 Festivals *Chris Anderton* 357

29 Cinematic places: Popular music soundtracks and the charge of the real *Kate Bolgar Smith* 369

Index 381

List of contributors

Chris Anderton is Associate Professor in Cultural Economy, with a particular focus on the music industries, music culture and music history. His research examines a range of topics including the live music and festivals industries, the development and representation of music genres, the management and marketing of popular music, and the intersection of fan practices and intellectual property law. Chris's books include *Understanding the Music Industries* (Sage 2013) and *Music Festivals in the UK: Beyond the Carnivalesque* (Routledge 2019). His research has appeared in such journals as *Rock Music Studies* and *Popular Music and Society*.

Emília Barna is a sociologist and popular music scholar. She is Assistant Professor at the Department of Sociology and Communication, Budapest University of Technology and Economics, and head of the Cultural Industries MA specialization. She completed a Popular Music Studies PhD programme in 2011 at the University of Liverpool. Her main research areas are music scenes and technology; the music industries and digitization; popular music and gender; and cultural labour. With Tamás Tófalvy, she has co-edited the books Made in Hungary: Studies in Popular Music (2017, Routledge) and Popular Music, Technology, and the Changing Media Ecosystem: From Cassettes to Stream (2020, Palgrave). She is a member of the International Association for the Study of Popular Music (IASPM) and the Working Group for Public Sociology "Helyzet".

Andy Bennett is Professor of Cultural Sociology in the School of Humanities, Languages and Social Science at Griffith University. He has written and edited numerous books including *Popular Music and Youth Culture*, *Music, Style and Aging*, *British Progressive Pop 1970–1980* and *Music Scenes* (co-edited with Richard A. Peterson). He is Faculty Fellow of the Yale Center for Cultural Sociology, International Research Fellow of the Finnish Youth Research Network, founding member of the Consortium for Youth, Generations and Culture and founding member of the Regional Music Research Group.

Leonieke Bolderman is Assistant Professor of Cultural Geography in the Faculty of Spatial Sciences at the University of Groningen, The Netherlands. Her books include *Contemporary Music Tourism. A Theory of Musical Topophilia* (Routledge 2020) and *Locating Imagination in Popular Culture: Place, Tourism, Belonging* (Routledge 2021). Her work appears in such journals as *Journal of Virtual Exchange*, *European Journal of Cultural Studies* and *Tourist Studies*.

Kate Bolgar Smith completed her doctoral research at SOAS, funded by the AHRC, with a thesis that focused on the soundtracks of films made by diasporic and migrant filmmakers in London and Paris. Broadly, her research explores the interactions between sound and space, often through the lens of film. While completing her thesis, she also lectured in African film history and film curation at SOAS. Since completing her PhD she moved to Melbourne for a couple of years, where she worked at Monash University and had her first child. She now owns a bookshop in Edinburgh, and is working on a new writing project.

Andrew Branch is Senior Lecturer in Media and Communication in the School of Arts and Creative Industries at the University of East London. His writing has appeared in journals such as *Popular Music* and *Punk and Post Punk*, as well as publications from The Subcultures Network. His current research on the cultural tastes and political values of working-class people, and the extent to which these are shaped by experiences of formal education, is indebted to both the conceptual framework developed by Pierre Bourdieu and the conjunctural analysis pioneered by the founders of British Cultural Studies. Andrew is co-founder of the Cultural Engine Research Group (CERG), whose public engagement activity facilitates knowledge exchange.

Vincenzo Cambria holds a PhD in Ethnomusicology from Wesleyan University (USA) and he is now Professor of Ethnomusicology at the Federal University of the State of Rio de Janeiro (UNIRIO), Brazil. He has done research on the music of Bahian *candomblé* and *blocos-afro*. His current research deals with issues such as music and violence, *favelas*, participatory research methodologies, urban ethnomusicology, racism and decolonial studies. On these issues, he has published articles and book chapters. From 2015 to 2017 served as President of the Brazilian Association for Ethnomusicology (ABET).

Kimberly Cannady is Senior Lecturer in ethnomusicology and programme director of music studies at Te Herenga Waka/Victoria University of Wellington, Aotearoa/New Zealand. Kimberly specializes in traditional and popular music of the Nordic region with a focus on music in Iceland, Greenland and the Faroe Islands. Her current major research project explores the legacy of emotions in traditional Icelandic vocal music and is based on long-term ethnographic research. She is also interested in the history of popular music in Aotearoa/New Zealand, and the growth of the local recording industry in Aotearoa and the wider Pacific region. Kimberly earned her PhD in ethnomusicology at the University of Washington in Seattle.

Martin Cloonan is Director of the Turku Institute for Advanced Studies (TIAS) at the University of Turku in Finland. Prior to this he was Professor of Popular Music Politics at the University of Glasgow. Martin's research interests span the political economy of the music industries and issues of freedom of expression.

Ruth Dockwray is Associate Professor of Popular Music at the University of Chester, UK. Ruth is a research network lead for the Department of Performing Arts and her research interests include theory of music production, sonic spatialization and use of surround sound, video game music and the music of Queen. She has contributed to a number of collections, including *The Routledge Companion to Screen Music and Sound* (2017), *Mixing Music: Perspectives on Music Production* (Routledge 2016) and *Living Stereo: Histories and Cultures of Multichannel Sound* (Bloomsbury 2015). Her research has appeared in such journals as *Popular Music: In Practice, Leonardo Music Journal* and *Twentieth-Century Music*.

Shane Homan is Associate Professor in the School of Media, Film and Journalism at Monash University, Melbourne, Australia. His most recent publications are *The Music Export Business: Born Global* (Routledge 2021) with Stephen Chen, Richard Vella and Tracy Redhead; and *Melbourne Music City: Urban Cultures, Histories and Policy* (with Seamus O'Hanlon, Catherine Strong and John Tebbutt) (Bloomsbury 2022). He is the editor of the *Bloomsbury Handbook of Popular Music Policy* (2022).

Christina Horvath is Reader in French Literature and Politics at the University of Bath. Her research addresses urban representations in literature and film, with emphasis on artistic expressions of advanced marginality such as contemporary French 'banlieue narratives' and favela literature in Brazil. She has published widely on contemporary French and Francophone literature, banlieues and postcolonial France. Since 2014 she has worked on the conceptualization of 'Co-Creation' defined as an art-based method to promote social justice in disadvantaged urban areas.

Helmi Järviluoma is a Finnish sound, music, and cultural scholar and writer. She is Professor of Cultural Studies at the University of Eastern Finland, and Principal Investigator of ERC AdG project Sensory Transformations. Among her 180 publications, *Acoustic Environments in Change* (2009) together with Simon Fraser University, and *Gender and Qualitative Methods* (Sage 2003/2010) continue to draw attention. She has written and directed altogether six radio features for Finnish Broadcasting Company YLE; three alone and two in cooperation with Steven Feld, and one with Noora Vikman. She belonged to the first group of members in Réseau International Ambiances, and has cooperated with atmosphere researchers of CRESSON for twenty years.

Keir Keightley is Associate Professor of Media Studies at the University of Western Ontario, Canada. His work has appeared in collections including *The Cambridge Companion to Pop and Rock, The Sage Handbook of Popular Music* and *Good Vibrations: Brian Wilson and the Beach Boys in Critical Perspective*, and in journals such as *Musical Quarterly, Journal of Popular Music Studies* and *Modernism/Modernity*. He is currently completing a book about the emergence of New York's 'Tin Pan Alley' as an epitome of modern mass media culture, entitled *Tin Pan Allegory: Music, Media, Modernity*.

Martin K. Koszolko is a recognized expert in remote music collaboration. He has presented at national and international seminars and conferences and has published in the fields of collaborative music production and mobile music innovation. His practice-led PhD project investigated the impact of remote music collaboration software on music production. He is consulting for companies producing cloud-based and collaborative software for music makers and is the founder of School of Music Collaboration, an educational portal for disseminating collaborative music strategies and technologies. Martin is an award-winning music producer known for his creative work under the *KOshowKO*, *Philosophy of Sound* and *iubar project* monikers. He has extensive experience as a composer, performing musician, remixer, music and video producer and is the vice-president of Clan Analogue Recordings, the record label arm of Australia's longest running electronic music collective. He has contributed music to over fifty releases on several record labels.

Robert Kronenburg is Roscoe Professor of Architecture at the University of Liverpool. His research focuses on the history of innovative design and its impact on human experience, identifying how environments, locales and objects can profoundly influence how people understand and feel about their place in the world. His book *This Must Be the Place: An Architectural History of Popular Music Performance Venues* was published in 2019 by Bloomsbury. He has contributed to a number of collections, including *Sound Spaces: Pop Music Concerts and Festival Stages in Urban Environments* (Bloomsbury 2020) and *From Shed to Venue: The Arena Concert Event Space* (Bloomsbury 2015).

Simone Krüger Bridge is Reader in Music in the School of Humanities and Social Science at Liverpool John Moores University. Her research interests are at the intersection between cultural sociology, ethnomusicology and popular music studies. Her monographs are *Trajectories and Themes in World Popular Music: Globalization, Capitalism, Identity* (Equinox 2018) and *Experiencing Ethnomusicology* (Ashgate 2009). She has edited *The Globalization of Musics in Transit: Music, Migration and Tourism* (Routledge 2014) and *Ethnomusicology in the Academy: International Perspectives* (Verlag 2011), and has been published in numerous journals and edited collections.

Keewoong Lee is Research Professor at Institute for East Asian Studies, SungKongHoe University, South Korea. His research interests lie in Asian pop, urban culture and migration. He has published in Korean, English and Chinese on a wide array of topics. His publications include *Assembling Pop Records in Twentieth Century Korea: A Double Is Twice as Good as a Single*; *Great Albums, Greedy Collectors and Gritty Sounds? A View from 'Snobbish Connoisseurs' on the Canonization and Archivalism of Korean Pop-Rock*; and *Gentrification Effects: The Flow of Cultural Refugees and Making Alternative Places in the Vicinities of Hongdae* (in Korean). Recently, he published a book on COVID-19 pandemic titled *Beyond the New Normal: Affect and Response to the Pandemic in Indonesia* (in Korean).

Raphaël Nowak is Lecturer in Sociology at the University of York (UK). His research is in cultural sociology and specifically explores issues regarding the contemporary distribution and consumption of music, cultural taste and practices, and cultural heritage. He is the author of *Consuming Music in the Digital Age* (Palgrave 2016), co-editor with

Andrew Whelan of *Networked Music Cultures* (Palgrave 2016) and co-author with Sarah Baker and Lauren Istvandity of *Curating Pop* (Bloomsbury 2019). His work has also featured in journals such as *Cultural Sociology, The European Journal of Cultural Studies, The British Journal of Sociology, Popular Communication, The International Journal of Social Research Methodology, Young, The International Journal of Heritage Studies* and *Leisure Sciences.*

Kathryn Olsen is Lecturer in Ethnomusicology, Musicology and Popular Music Studies at the University of KwaZulu-Natal, South Africa. She has a broad interest in all types of music and in cultural studies generally. Dr Olsen regards music research as a dialogue between the musical and the social aspects of performance practice. Her research on maskanda published in *Music and Social Change: Maskanda Past and Present* (Temple University Press 2014) is a comprehensive analysis of maskanda performance in the context of the social, political and economic power struggles that are peculiar to different periods in maskanda's development. Kathryn Olsen is concerned not only with what constitutes 'the music' but also with how it operates as a system of meaning-making that both gives and reflects the identities and experiences of those who lay claim to it as their own. She is currently working on a project funded by NHISS titled 'Intersecting Ideologies: A Study of the Interaction between Music-Making Strategies (Particularly But Not Exclusively, Maskanda Music), and Spiritual Belief Systems in the Context of Institutionalized Economic and Legal Platforms'.

J. Mark Percival is Senior Lecturer in Media at Queen Margaret University, Edinburgh. He leads the Creative Industries group at the QMU Centre for Communication, Cultural and Media Studies. His doctoral thesis at the University of Stirling, *Making Music Radio*, focused on the social dynamics of the relationship between record industry pluggers and music radio programmers in the UK. Mark has written about Scottish indie music production, popular music and identity, mediation of popular music and punk rock as heritage culture. He has contributed to collections including *The Bloomsbury Handbook of Music and Policy* (2022), *Rock for Change* (Rowan and Littlefield 2022), *DIY Cultures and Underground Music Scenes* (2019) and *Comics and Popular Culture* (University of Texas Press 2019). His work has appeared in such journals as *Popular Music History, Popular Music and Society*, and *Volume!*

Hillegonda C. Rietveld is Professor of Sonic Culture at London South Bank University (UK) and was Chief Editor of *IASPM Journal* between 2011 and 2017. During the 1980s, she recorded for Manchester's Factory Records and was closely involved in its nightclub The Haçienda, FAC51. She has published extensively on electronic dance music and DJ cultures, including a co-edited collection for Bloomsbury Academic, *DJ Culture in the Mix: Power, Technology, and Social Change in Electronic Dance Music,* and a co-edited special issue for *Dancecult: Journal of Electronic Dance Music Culture*. She additionally publishes research in concomitant aspects of electronic popular music, as well as in the nascent field of game music studies.

Melanie Schiller is Assistant Professor of media studies and popular music at the Department for Arts, Culture and Media at the University of Groningen (The Netherlands), and the author of *Soundtracking Germany – Popular Music and National Identity* (Rowman and Littlefield 2018 and 2020). Schiller is on the executive board and national representative of the International Association for the Study of Popular Music (IASPM) Benelux branch, and was a member of the academic advisory committee of the German Society for Popular Music Studies (GfPM). Her current research focuses on popular music and populism in Europe and Sweden in particular, in the international research project *Popular Music and the Rise of Populism in Europe* (funded by the Volkswagen Foundation 2019–22).

Hyunjoon Shin is Professor in the Faculty of Social Sciences and the Institute for East Asian Studies (IEAS) at Sunkonghoe University. Having received his PhD with a thesis on the transformation of the Korean music industry, he has carried out broader research on popular culture, international migration, and urban spaces in South Korea and East Asia. Since the mid-2000s, he wrote some academic papers in English for journals such as *Inter-Asia Cultural Studies, Popular Music, City, Culture and Society*. He has worked as a freelance writer, and has supported 'subcultural activism' since the mid-1990s until recently.

Geoff Stahl is Senior Lecturer in Media & Communication at Te Herenga Waka/Victoria University of Wellington, Aotearoa/New Zealand. His research areas include scenes and subcultures, urban studies and semiotics. His publications include co-authoring *Understanding Media Studies* (Oxford University Press 2009), editing *Poor, But Sexy: Reflections on Berlin Scenes* (Peter Lang 2014) and co-editing (with Shelley Brunt) *Made in Australia and Aotearoa/New Zealand: Studies in Popular Music* (Routledge 2018), *Mixing Pop & Politics*, with Catherine Hoad and Oli Wilson (Routledge 2021), as well as articles on urban musical culture in Berlin, Montreal and Wellington.

Will Straw is James McGill Professor of Urban Media Studies at McGill University in Montreal, where he teaches within the Department of Art History and Communications Studies. He is the author of *Cyanide and Sin: Visualizing Crime in 50s America* (Andrew Roth Gallery 2006) and co-editor of several volumes including *The Cambridge Companion to Rock and Pop* (with Simon Frith and John Street 2001), *Circulation and the City: Essays on Urban Culture* (with Alexandra Boutros 2010), *Formes Urbaines* (with Anouk Bélanger and Annie Gérin 2014) and *The Oxford Handbook of Canadian Cinema* (with Janine Marchessault 2019). He has published widely on cultures of the urban night and is the author of over 160 articles on music, cinema and urban culture.

Catherine Strong is Senior Lecturer in the BA (Music Industry) at RMIT University. Her work focuses on heritage and memory, and gender issues in music, with a specialization in music careers that has emerged out of extensive industry engagement. She is the author of *Grunge: Music and Memory* (Ashgate), and co-editor of *Death and the Rock Star* (Routledge), *The Routledge Companion to Popular Music History and Heritage*, and

Towards Gender Equality in the Music Industry (Bloomsbury), and is the co-editor of the journal *Popular Music History*.

Sam Whiting is Lecturer in Creative Industries at the University of South Australia. His research is focused primarily on music scenes and the music industries, specifically the role of venues in the live music ecology. Previous published papers of Sam's have explored issues of access, identity, gender, heritage, live music, capital and cultural production as they relate to popular music studies. His PhD focused on the social and cultural value of small live music venues and was awarded by RMIT University in 2019. Sam is currently working on a book about small venues for Bloomsbury Academic.

Simon Zagorski-Thomas is Professor of Music at the London College of Music, University of West London, Co-chair of the Association for the Study of the Art of Record Production and Director of the Art of Record Production Conference. He is also founder and convenor of the 21st Century Music Practice Research Network. He worked for 25 years as a composer, sound engineer and producer and is, at present, conducting research into twenty-first-century music practice and the musicology of record production. In 2015 he was the Principal Investigator in the AHRC-funded Classical Music Hyper-Production and Practice as Research project and in 2012 he was awarded a visiting fellowship at the University of Cambridge and was the Principal Investigator in the AHRC-funded network on Performance in the Recording Studio. His book *The Art of Record Production*, which he co-edited with Simon Frith, was published by Ashgate Press in 2012 and his monograph *The Musicology of Record Production* for Cambridge University Press was published in 2014 and won the IASPM Book Prize in 2015.

Nabeel Zuberi is Associate Professor of Media and Screen at the University of Auckland, Aotearoa/New Zealand. Nabeel's publications include *Sounds English: Transnational Popular Music* (University of Illinois Press 2001), *Media Studies in Aotearoa New Zealand 1 & 2* (co-edited with Luke Goode, Pearson 2004; 2010) and *Black Popular Music in Britain since 1945* (co-edited with Jon Stratton, Ashgate/Routledge 2014). A monograph *Music, Race and Media after 9/11* about hip hop, punk, bass culture and electronic music genres in the UK and the United States during the War on Terror is forthcoming with Bloomsbury. Since 2004, Nabeel has co-hosted 'The Basement', a weekly music show with Nick Fitzherbert on BASE FM Auckland.

Introduction
Popular music, space and place

Geoff Stahl and J. Mark Percival

The relationship between popular music, space and place is a rich and varied one, and occupies a great deal of real estate in popular music studies (as well as other disciplines). We envisioned this volume as offering as broad a spectrum as possible, and although it has not been possible to address every aspect of the popular music studies field, we are confident it provides readers with a variety of approaches that neatly sums up, as well as hopefully provokes, wider debates and discussions. There are many different takes here, in terms of methodologies, theories, perspectives and disciplines, encompassing a diversity of genres and geographies, together speaking to the rich and central role that space and place play in popular music studies.

This project has spanned some years, and its latter stages unfolded during the global pandemic, aspects of which are captured in some of the chapters collected here. The spaces and places that make up the production, distribution and consumption of popular music have been indelibly affected by COVID. Many venues and performance spaces have disappeared, others have atrophied, and yet many others have found ways to adapt and carry on. While hesitant to employ neoliberal terms such as 'resilience', 'pivoting' or 'agility' to describe how some of these latter places and spaces have fared, popular music has in many of these contexts persevered. The situation has brought into view how music continues to matter and mean, not without struggle, but in ways that underpin how people work to try to ground themselves through the experiences afforded in and through popular music. In spaces and places of isolation, lockdown or in physically distanced settings, popular music persists. The sociomusical experience during the pandemic has been warped, its affective power recalibrated and rechannelled, and the ways in which things musical are done have been reimagined through a multitude of online workarounds and as many offline gigs. Consequently, we have had to rethink and reflect upon the spaces and places of popular music in our lives, as musicians, fans and scholars, and we trust this volume can in some modest way help serve that purpose.

We have divided the volume into five parts: 'Theory and Method'; 'Space, Place and Consumption'; 'Space, Place, Production and Performance'; 'Cities, Suburbs, Nations and Beyond'; and 'Selling, Celebrating, Representing Space and Place'. Our opening part, 'Theory and Method', provides different conceptual and methodological approaches to popular music, space and place; Geoff Stahl's opening chapter considers some of the key points of debate and discussion around space and place; Will Straw draws upon Henri Lefebvre and Catherine Régulier's rhythmanalytic project to consider the nature of circulation, with a particular emphasis on the city and its distinctive spatio-temporal ratios and examples drawn from Montreal and Dakar, among others; Hyunjoon Shin and Keewoong Lee survey debates and discussions about globalization, transnationalism and regionalism, with an emphasis on the case in East Asia, Korea specifically, advocating for a move away from the global/local binary and challenging more recent models of glocal and hybridity; Andy Bennett presents an overview of significant debates around the sociology of place, which includes a discussion of different social forms, including subcultures and scenes, the relationship between the private and the public, and constructions of cultural memory; Kimberly Cannady covers a number of distinct ethnomusicological approaches to music and place, highlighting some of the important theoretical groundings and their divergences; Shane Homan considers the nature of policy as a factor shaping music, space and place in the city, including how regulatory regimes impact the sociomusical experience in the city; and, tying this section up, Helmi Järviluoma invites us on a personal soundscape walk as a way of illustrating this unique perspective, through the lens of what she refers to here as *sensobiography*, as it has been undertaken in the Finnish context.

Part Two, 'Space, Place and Consumption', examines a host of different sites where music is consumed, as well as different modes of consumption, working across a number of different scales from the very local to the global. Keir Keightley analyses the virtual tourism enabled through the travel-exoticizing long-playing high-fidelity records of the 1950s and in particular the work of Frank Sinatra and the LP, *Come Fly With Me*; J. Mark Percival looks at how both publicly funded and commercial sector broadcasters in Canada and the UK construct, reconstruct and navigate national terrains in relation to radio; Nabeel Zuberi gives us an engaging overview of the record store, its changing role in the history of popular music and the issues it now faces; Hillegonda C. Reitveld examines the history and changing nature of the dancefloor, alongside significant shifts in DJ culture and changes in urban night-time economies; Robert Kronenburg looks at the different architectures of the live venue; and Raphaël Nowak finishes the section with a chapter on the role that mobile technologies play in altering the experience of space and place.

The third part, 'Space, Place, Production and Performance', considers scenes and performance spaces, in online and offline contexts. Martin Cloonan draws upon personal experience of Glasgow, Scotland, to reflect upon the city's indie music scene; Emília Barna looks at bedroom production, through the lens of lo-fi music production, noting how these spaces are gendered, as well as how they can offer challenges to hierarchies that exist in the more mainstream commercial music industry; Ruth Dockwray considers the ways in which the recording studio can be both a real, physical place in which music is practised and also a site at which virtual spaces are created, manipulated and used to inscribe meaning; Martin Koszolko appeals to personal experience to explore the spaces associated with virtual performance and live online collaboration; Simon Zagorski-Thomas explores and develops ideas around theories of record production and spatialization; and finally, Sam Whiting, using the notion of the scene, explores the implications of regulation and gentrification and its impact on the live venue and gigs for musicians, publicans and punters alike.

Part Four, 'Cities, Suburbs, Nations and Beyond', considers distinctive spaces at different scales. Andrew Branch, for example, analyses the much-maligned suburbs, drawing upon the work of Pierre Bourdieu to consider what 'suburban pop' has come to mean, as well how perceptions of it are changing; Kathryn Olsen gives us a welcome analysis of South African townships and the role music such as kwaito, among other local genres, serves to ground communities in place even under the horrors of apartheid, acting as resource and refuge; Vincenzo Cambria uses funk in Rio de Janeiro to consider how a genre gets localized and politicized and along the way becomes a defining sound of a place; Christina Horvath uses rap in France's *banlieues* to examine how issues around race, ethnicity, immigration and postcolonialism play out in the sounds of the French suburbs; Melanie Schiller examines the role of music in fostering nationalism in different countries, ranging from the perspective of the protectionist politics of cultural and broadcasting policy to the recent rise of ethno-nationalism; Simone Krüger Bridge closes this section with an examination of transnationalism and how music is taken up and transformed up by diasporic, migrant and refugee communities, particularly in Liverpool, but also using looking at how reggae took shape in the UK through its Caribbean connections and how hip-hop as a global genre was inflected when taken up in France and China.

Our final part, 'Selling, Celebrating, Representing Space and Place Music', assembles chapters dedicated to scrutinizing the policies and practices associated with marketing, place promotion and the politics of representation with a shared emphasis on how popular music is put to use in cities, both in branding exercises and how it plays out on screen. Catherine Strong looks at the complex politics associated with heritage and place particularly around the politics of curating and nominating what aspects of popular music are worth preserving; Leonieke Bolderman continues with the role played by popular music in tourist campaigns and the implications for local musicians and others, considering how tourism can be both beneficial and detrimental in certain contexts; Chris Anderton examines the evolution of music festivals and how some places have seen entire local infrastructures reworked to accommodate festivals, the ways in which festivals are seen as branding tools but also as sites that can combine transgression and commercialism in complex fashion; and our volume concludes with Kate Bolgar Smith cinematic places, utilizing Paris and Jamaica as a case studies in relation to hip-hop and reggae as they are heard on film, suggesting that the marriage of music and mise-en-scène produces an ethical charge on the screen and in the viewer.

We would like to thank our authors for their contributions to this volume. Individually, they have provided us with insights and approaches we think neatly capture where things have been and where they are in thinking about space and place. Collectively, they have mapped out aspects of the field of popular music studies in such a way as to produce a cartographic density we think captures the nature of space and place in engaging and invigorating ways.

Section I

Theory and method

1

Music, space, place and non-place

Geoff Stahl

Introduction

Space, as Henri Lefebvre notes in *The Production of Space* (1991 [1968]), is not neutral; it is produced. More importantly, it is socially produced: 'There is an ideology of space. Because space, which seems homogeneous, which appears as a whole in its objectivity, in its pure form, such as we determine it, is a social product' (171). It has a history, bound to a mode of production, and as such generates certain ideological effects. This can lead to discussions of spatial consequences in that how and who produces a given space, whose interests are served by a given mode of spatial production, shapes the individual and collective experience had in that space. Alongside its ideological dimension, the production of space has social, symbolic and material effects. It is possible then to consider that cultural products and social forms are types of spatialized expression, manifestations of a mode of spatial production that under closer scrutiny can tell us a great deal about a society at a given point in time. And while Lefebvre touches only lightly upon music in this particular study (later work does more with music, particularly through his notion of rhythmanalysis; see Lefebvre 1996, and Straw this volume), it goes without saying that music too produces spaces, comforting, complicated, contradictory, as well as contested, spaces. As a result, when we consider music and space and place, we are faced with trying to account for many different scales and dimensions the relationship between them engenders. These extend anywhere from spaces of performance and listening, the spaces notes fill and the spaces between the notes, and the spaces associated with production, distribution and consumption of music, many of which are covered in more detail in this volume. In this chapter, I will outline some of the overarching aspects of the relationship of music and space, place and non-place as related but distinct aspects of popular music that exist as unique kinds of spatial productions.

Music and space

One formulation of the production of space that Lefebvre stresses is that its production is a 'realistic illusion' of 'natural simplicity' (Lefebvre, 29). Many of the spaces associated with popular music aspire to this notion of the illusion, masking its production. For example, the space of the song, the text at the centre of popular music, uses production and recording techniques to create the illusion of a single musical performance that can then evoke different sorts of spatial relationships. Here, there is also the intimate, communicative space found between listener and artist, an interpellative invitation often established by the use of 'you' in a lyric, the spaces evoked through the tropes used in a song (from specific sites, such as a street, a bar, a dancefloor, a bedroom, a house, a highway, a city and a country), the manner in which instruments are understood to have their 'own space', to the way recording techniques are used to create the illusion of particular sonic space. Peter Doyle (2005), on this latter point, notes how echo and reverb were used to de- and re-territorialize (in Deleuze and Guattari's terms) in the recording and production of country music, conjuring up a range of sonic landmarks of *here* and *there* that generates a distinctive terrain of the 'imaginary West' for the listener (Doyle: 94). Similarly, studio techniques and recording technologies can also create the illusion of proximity. The introduction of the microphone in the 1920s, for example, appeared to collapse the space between the singer and the listener, introducing a new feeling of intimacy that changed how popular songs were henceforth constructed. This put the singer at the centre of the song, where they could now express their innermost emotional truths through the very grain of their voice and the intertwinement of pop song and singer emerges, with Bing Crosby as a 'crooner' being its most significant progenitor (see Lockheart 2003).

As these examples illustrate, music moves us or, better yet, transports us, taking us to other affective or emotional states. It also works to create a sonic topography carved out in a song or an evocative sound, and at the same time helps us transcend places and circumstances. It can do this in more mundane ways, making routine tasks bearable or it can be employed as a prompt for recalling better times and places, all part of the emotional toolkit employed as part of our identity work (DeNora 2000). Or this can also be much more complicated, where transport and transcendence may serve to reproduce other kinds of spatial divides. Keir Keightley (1996), for example, has written about how the hi-fi explosion in the in the 1950s and early 1960s retrenched gender divides in the suburban home, where men could enjoy new innovations in playback technologies secreted away from their wives and children, at the same time that the recording industry was capitalizing on 'exotic' sounds of elsewhere, allowing these same men to 'explore' distant locales from the safety of their own segregated homes (a point he explores in more detail in this volume).

Music, space and social forms

There have been a number of terms employed by scholars trying to capture music's sociospatial dimensions. Paul Lopes (2002), for example, provides us with a rich study on the emergence of a jazz art world, viewed through a distinctly Bourdieusian lens, exploring how a genre gains legitimacy courtesy an interlaced network of media forms and institutions in the United States (for a broader take on art worlds with some discussion of music, see Becker 2008). There is also the shadowy realm of bohemia, which Bernard Gendron (2002) makes good use of in his mapping out of the relationship between popular music and the avant-garde, a trans-continental journey that begins in post-First World War Europe and extends to the no-wave world of late 70s New York. However, two terms in particular have come to dominate discussions of space and social forms in relation to music: subcultures and scenes. The former, in its British cultural studies incarnation (Hall and Jefferson 1993 [1976]; Hebdige 1978), emerges through discussion of working-class youth culture where the rituals associated with musical consumption are key markers of social distinction. These rituals, which include music gigs, hanging out at record shops, etc., are examples of what Hall and colleagues refer to as 'winning space', a temporary counter-hegemonic zone that enables a consolidation of a collective identity against a dominant group or class (in this case it was both the middle and upper classes as well as their parents). That space at its core was a creative one, a demarcation of social difference and solidarity of which music was a crucial binding agent. These exemplify what Lefebvre would refer to as 'differential spaces', sites that eluded or challenged authority, imagining and putting into practice alternative sociomusical worlds that had music as one of their key organizing principles. Notably, these spaces were highly gendered, and it would take the work of Angela McRobbie (1978) and others, to consider other kinds of spaces (such as bedrooms), where, for instance, young women were consuming music, privately, away from what had appeared in the scholarly literature up to that point as 'heroically' counter-hegemonic public social spaces the masculine biases of which were rarely interrogated.

Continuing in the sociological tradition, the term 'scene' had by the 1990s begun to displace 'subculture' as the preferred social descriptor. Trying to capture some of the less formal elements of cultural activity, scene was taken up by Andy Bennett (2004) and others as a concept that did not appear as wedded to the subcultural homologies of the past, where musical spaces, and the sociality and, more pointedly, the cultural identities associated with them, were more porous. Another formulation of the concept was put forward by Will Straw (1991), where a music scene is conceived of as a space that plays host to and enables a range of musical activities to manifest themselves, fostering forms of 'cross-fertilization' that give these spaces an attractive form of social energy and also allow for certain generic changes. Scenes in this latter sense are at once profoundly local, but also produce a space looking to absorb other outside influences (in this respect, as Straw notes, they are different from musical communities which tend to be bound more to local musical traditions and histories). The term is quite germane to popular music studies, as he notes, for a number of reasons:

> The production and consumption of music lend themselves more easily to a mobile urban sociability than does involvement in other cultural forms. Antoine Hennion has noted the intimate relationship of music to multiple forms of social mediation: 'musical activity inscribes itself within bodies, within collectivities, within ways of doing things, within movement'.
>
> (Straw 2004: 413)

As with the term 'subculture', the term 'scene' has also been the subject of much scrutiny. Dave Hesmondhalgh has noted that 'scene has gone beyond the point where such metaphorical associations can aid in the analysis of the spatial dimensions of popular music… used for too long in too many different and imprecise ways' (Hesmondhalgh 2005: 30). Here, the concept's flexibility, seen by some as a virtue, is also its fundamental weakness with regard to what it can account for in terms of the cultural analysis of popular music. However, this has not diminished its ongoing appearance in studies of popular music, and Straw (2015) has revisited and refined it in ways that have encouraged new insights into the social dimensions of musical spaces (among other cultural spaces).

Music, space, nations and borders

We can build out from the granularity of cultural spaces to the more expansive space of culture and music's role in shaping it, when we move to consider music in relation to larger social groups, where ethnic spaces and music come together. If scenes are marked more by exclusivity rather than exclusion, these larger groups can offer the inverse, exclusion over exclusivity. As Melanie Schiller (2018) has argued, among others, music and its relation to a politics of exclusion works on different levels, extending from the (seemingly) banal jingoism of national anthems to the more visceral, and sometimes violence-generating, football chant. Both are about conjuring up what Benedict Anderson (1996) calls 'imagined communities', where music and song are used to consolidate affective allegiances around a notion of shared but demarcated space. Music is the partitioning device, which acting as a galvanizing force can mobilize people in ways that mark out territories, boundaries and borders.

Musical displays, storage space and their spatial effects

One of the more intriguing and increasingly germane discussions around music and space has emerged out the issue of storage, which we can think of in both the material culture associated with music (which extends from wax cylinders to CDs to various ephemera, such as gig posters, zines and magazines) to the impact the 'dematerialisation' of music has had in terms of popular music's ecological footprint. Of the first aspect, around the world, the spaces associated with the storage of music's material culture have evolved and expanded from record stores (new and second-hand) to museums and galleries (Leonard 2010), libraries (Clark and Linehan 1987) and archives (Baker et al. 2016). Many of these latter spaces have dedicated themselves to the preservation (and remediation through digitization in many cases), curation and display of a region's musical heritage. Some are organized with the intent to educate and/or entertain, which can catalyse discussions around which sort of musical artefacts and histories are deemed worthy of being highlighted or celebrated, and those that are not, for locals and tourists alike. Similarly, as Leonieike Bolderman and Stijn Reijnders (2017) have noted, urban areas can be musealized as part of the cityscape, with musical tours, in this case of Liverpool (The Beatles, et al) and Bayreuth (Wagner), used to illustrate how cities can reimagine their musical heritage as a resource from which different kinds of value (cultural, economic, historical) can be extracted and celebrated. Places around the globe have come to recognize the cultural value associated with local musical cultures and even specific genres. Sarah Daynes, for instance, has noted that reggae in Jamaica has become the island nation's premier brand, where, citing the Jamaican Tourist Board it is referred to as 'the heartbeat of our people' (Daynes 2009), and Berlin marketers and place-promoters mobilize its club scene as the pre-eminent marker of its distinction in a marketplace crowded with 'entrepreneurial cities' (see also Rapp 2010; Stahl 2014).

While the institutionalization of musical histories in museums and galleries may provide opportunities to correct the musical record of a place (allowing historically marginalized voices, women, immigrants, indigenous peoples, to be re-centred), there is also the danger that the same stories get told and re-told, in ways that can often tyrannize contemporary music-makers. Discussing the accumulation of cultural textures in places, Rolf Lindner (2006) reminds us that in generating out of these textures 'mythographies' being in thrall to them can also function as a trap of sorts. Oli Wilson and Michael Holland (2020) have considered these issues in relation to Dunedin, Aotearoa/New Zealand, as a city still beholden to the legacy of the 'Dunedin Sound'. A particular grouping of post-punk and indie bands associated with the early 80s music scene in that city (noting that many bands and artists were not from Dunedin specifically), it is an idea of the place that has been musealized through the city council and it is part of the city's urban brand. Contemporary Dunedin indie bands must continually perform in the shadow of the 'sound', a persistent reference point and evaluative mechanism, such are the lingering associations of this particular musical myth.

Outside of the more altruistic and virtuous intentions of these institutions, the musical artefacts of popular music enter into other circulatory flows, which present us with other, increasingly salient, issues regarding the spatialization of music. Will Straw (1999–2000: 162) shows that undesirable vinyl records tend to circulate almost endlessly in secondary economies where, even though their value is exhausted, they accumulate in 'museums of failure' in which 'their bulk nevertheless functions almost monumentally' (Devine 2015: 378). While not enshrined in the hallowed halls of museums, where they are imbued with the aura of a sacred object, used cultural commodities like vinyl LPs, cassettes and CDs take their place among other second-hand, abject things to be combed and picked over by collectors, connoisseurs and DJs, among others. As Devine stresses, this points to another aspect of space that has only recently been discussed in relation to popular music: its ecological footprint. The production, distribution and discarding of these cultural commodities has profound spatial consequences, from the extraction of the crude materials for their production, to the various delivery infrastructures underpinning their distribution regionally and across the globe, as well as the space needed to house/dispose of these artefacts once they are no longer wanted. Devine is quite pointed in reminding us of the political ecology of popular music:

> [W]hile the material intensity of recording is only one part of a larger set of problems, music is nevertheless mentioned quickly and frequently in environmental criticism as a phenomenon that symbolises the worst excesses of development, consumption and waste.
> (Devine, 384)

The so-called 'de-materialisation' of music, associated with digitization and more recently streaming, does not solve the issue of space; rather it further displaces it, moving it out of sight and out of mind. With the rise of streaming services and other online musical platforms, Devine and others have made very clear that the immense size of the servers, as well as the amount of energy needed to run them, does not absolve the music industry or consumers from the spatial consequences of having convenient access to music 24/7. As the source of music is disarticulated to a point of such an abstraction, woven into an ideology bound up in digital fantasies of convenience, immediacy and access, it becomes harder to fathom, but at the same time even more urgent to consider, the deleterious impact these sorts of storage spaces have on the world beyond the 'mere' enjoyment of music.

Music and place

Place in relation to music can be associated with emotional or affective registers, tied to memories, which can be individual as well as communal. Music and place are intimately bound up in this respect to identity, personal and collective, through heritage, culture and tradition, the way in which music connects individuals and groups to sites through a sense of embeddedness or emplacement. The scholarly move towards deeper conceptions of the relationship between place and music gained traction in the 1990s, as part of the larger 'spatial turn' in the humanities and social sciences. Humanistic and cultural geographers were at the vanguard of analysing music and place and produced numerous articles, monographs and edited collections (see, for example, Leyshon et al.; Skelton and Valentine 1998; Connell and Gibson 2003), and the spatial turn was also marked by popular music scholars themselves, resulting in the volume *Music, Space and Place: Popular Music and Cultural Identity* (Whiteley, Bennett and Hawkins 2004). The publishing boom that ensued was summed up at the end of the decade quite neatly by George Carney (1998), who provides a taxonomy of the various studies of music and place, which tended to fall into one (or more) of the following ten categories:

1. The delimitation of music regions and interpretation of regional music.
2. The evolution of a music style with place, or place-specific music.
3. The origin (culture hearth) and diffusion of music phenomena.
4. The spatial dimensions of music dealing with human migration, transportation routes, and communication networks.
5. The psychological and symbolic elements of music pertinent to shaping the character of a place – image of place, sense of place, and place consciousness.
6. The effect of music on the cultural landscape.
7. The spatial organization of the music industry and other music phenomena.
8. The relationship of music to the natural environment.
9. The function of 'nationalistic' and 'anti-nationalistic' music.
10. The interrelationships of music with other culture traits in a spatial sense.
    (Carney, 3–4)

This litany of approaches captures just how wide the catchment can be when considering music and place, from the material, to the symbolic, to the discursive, to the psychological, to the sociological, to the environmental, etc. Leyshon et al. remind us, however, that we need to consider the music and place and the place of music as not just its geographical location 'but to allow a purchase on the rich aesthetic, cultural, economic and political geographies of musical language' (425), an understanding that Sara Cohen echoes, stating that musics 'originate within, interact with, and are inevitably affected by, the physical, social, political and economic factors which surround them' (Cohen 1991: 342). Places can be prompts and resources, informing how music is made, circulated and consumed. They are pathways, to use Ruth Finnegan's useful term (2007), across space and over time, where careers are mapped out and new sorts of skills acquired. These pathways are about movement through places and over time, providing the cultural ballast and strengthening the social affinities that elsewhere Lawrence Grossberg has referred to as mattering and meaning maps (Grossberg, 2014). These maps overlap to form complex emotional and existential cartographies of places that matter. Ola Johannson also that notes:

> Popular music, in this sense, is a cultural form that actively produces geographic discourses and can be used to understand broader social relations and trends, including identity, ethnicity, attachment to place, cultural economies, social activism, and politics.
> (Ola Johansson 2016: 2)

As a cultural form, popular music can come to represent places, with the term 'represent' having a double meaning in a genre such as hip-hop. Here the music and artist acts as an ambassador for/speaking on behalf of. Murray Forman (2002), as Johansson and Bell note, in considering the discourses hip hop, points to how it constructs places, both metaphorical and material, such as the 'ghetto', 'the 'hood' and the 'inner city', where '[t]hese spaces, as socio-spatial symbols, provide especially African-Americans with an identity both on an individual and a collective level, and they have become central to hip hop authenticity' (cited in Johansson and Bell 2016: 19).

Music, place and genre

As the example of hip-hop in the United States also reminds us, music, musical practices and sounds can also be tied to places generically: Germany and *Schlager* (Currid 2000), Brazil and bossa nova (McGowan and Pessanha 1998), Jamaica and reggae (Rhiney and Cruse 2012), New Orleans and jazz (Hardie 2002), Japan and karaoke (Yano 1996), France and *chanson* (LeBrun 2016), Seattle and grunge (Bell 1998), among countless others. Mooring a musical form to a place, with sounds sedimenting out over time, creates the cultural ballast through which musical communities coalesce, traditions become embedded in musical memories and reproduced in practice.

Globalization and the different ways in which music moves across the world raises a number of issues with regard to place. Migrants and refugees take their music with them, in very different ways and under very different circumstances, but both groups can rely on music to create a form of 'diasporic belonging' (De Martini 2020). Indigenous peoples use music to mark their places (see, for example, Marcus Breen on Aboriginal Australians 1989). Katherine Kirbort, in a discussion of contemporary indigenous artists such as the First Nations group A Tribe Called Red, notes:

> [s]ubaltern peoples everywhere are engaged in anti-colonial forms of resistance, fighting to reclaim their identities. The use of music videos on platforms like YouTube help these nations reclaim rhetorical and visual sovereignty and engage both their own people and broader audiences in discussions of media representation, colonial struggles, and the future they will build for themselves. It is this aspect that makes the music video 'medicine' to communities that bridge the divide between modern and traditional ways of living.
>
> (Kibort 2020: 8–9)

Here virtual spaces become places charged with meaning and affect such that they become shared resources, where indigeneity finds musical expression and helps to formulate new forms of communal identity, creating places where decolonizing practices can manifest themselves in creative as well as politically efficacious ways.

As these examples indicate, music's relation to a politics of place is notable for illuminating issues having to do with cultural imperialism and (de)colonization, and cultural appropriation, engendering debates among musicians and fans alike. Certain genres travel widely and take their politics with them, tailored to suit local needs, making up a political pastiche that serves a local or regional purpose. Hip-hop has been especially mobile in this regard, encouraging otherwise marginalized or disenfranchised voices to be heard. In another formulation that troubles concerns around cultural appropriation of music, where authenticity and musical traditions are often at play, Tony Mitchell has described how hip hop has found a home in France, Italy and Aotearoa/New Zealand, domesticating it through localized lens both linguistically and socioeconomically whereby the politics of that place is more clearly enunciated (Mitchell 1996). Others have suggested that music, particularly popular music, produces a space in which the boundaries between insiders and outsiders blur. It is a

> 'promiscuous' enterprise which encourages cross fertilization and discourages the idea of cultural purity. Of course, this can raise another problem, that of 'cultural appropriation'. When the music of the subaltern catches the ears of the dominant group (or more often their children) it is rarely the subaltern that reaps the benefits. Still, artistic production is often the place where ethnic boundaries can be reimagined, where outsiders become insiders and hybridity and genre blurring can produce some of their most widely appreciated results.
>
> (Kasinitz and Martiniello 2019: 858)

Others may borrow musical sounds from elsewhere and syncretize them within local musical traditions. The contemporary Japanese band Minyo Crusaders, for example, flit between cumbia, reggae, bossa nova and other genres on a single album, inflected through the locally distinct 'Okinawa Sound' (see Gillan 2009), creating a musical hybrid that references multiple geographically dispersed genres that come from elsewhere but are now 'japanised'. The latter is a term Shuhei Hosokawa employs to describe the way in which Haroumi Hosono (solo artist as well as founding member of Yellow Magic Orchestra) uses a form of 'strategic ambiguity' to evoke a sense of 'Japan-ness' through sounds and technology, as a way of ironizing and satirizing Western models of orientalism (Hosokawa 1999: 116). Similarly, Julio Mendivil (2020) has discussed how German music, notably Schlager as well as other German folk musics, have taken root in Blumenau, a city in the southern part of Brazil. These examples, among others, often raise concerns about cultural appropriation or attempt to problematize these issues, pointing to the complexities of popular music and how as a cultural form it tends towards the elision of borders, both generic and geographic, providing unique places to encounter difference.

Music and non-place

The relationship between music, mobility and place as exemplified in the previous sections takes on another valence of meaning, or lack of meaning in some cases, when it is considered in terms of some other formulations of music, space and place. For Anahid Kassabian (2013), the reduction of music to almost pure functionality, to a form of what she has called sometimes nothing more than 'phatic communication in late capitalism', brings us to its complicated role in what anthropologist Marc Augé (1995) has referred to as 'non-places'. Augé uses this term to describe places of transit or 'meaningless' spaces, such as motorways, waiting rooms and airports, sites or contexts to which people have little or no affective affinity. They are, paradoxically, spaces of disconnection but also spaces that connect other points of meaning (home, work, away). Non-places are often the 'voids' people traverse to get to these places of meaning, empty of meaning themselves but with the potential to be inscribed with meaning, where music becomes one of the tools of inscription. Music here is often a distraction, 'filling' empty time and empty spaces with other meanings. In thinking about the space of the airport, for example, Brian Eno described his album, *Ambient 1: Music for Airports* (1978) as designed to 'accommodate many levels of listening attention without enforcing one in particular; it must be as ignorable as it is interesting'. It is the background music in cafés, supermarkets and malls (in North America this is often referred to as 'elevator music' or under its corporate moniker, 'Muzak'. See Lanza 1991), often instrumental music that unobtrusively lubricates these contexts to better ease consumption. In waiting rooms, its pleasant middling tones are meant to allay any anxiety about an impending diagnosis or dental work. It is music designed to distract at best, or be 'wallpaper' at worst.

For Kassabian, and others, the ubiquity of music in everyday life runs the risk of draining music of its affective charge, bent increasingly to serve the interests of late-stage capitalism. The music is not meant to connect us to these places but rather interpellates us as consumers, which is troubled further in her formulation of the link between ubiquitous musics and subjectivities. If music and place are one of the ways in which a cultural identity is articulated to a place, here she questions notions of identity as tied to a singular, physically grounded notion of place in her discussion of ubiquitous music, that is, music of the sort that is everywhere and seems to come from nowhere in particular, where source and performance are disarticulated. The background music at malls (in North America referred to as Muzak) or the kinds of musical medleys one could find at coffee chains like Starbucks positions listeners as 'distributed subjects', by which Kassabian means they are now part of 'a field of ebbs and flows that can appear and be engaged at any expanse, from the molecular to the social, from pipe organs to ethnicities' (2013: 111). This she suggests renders identity less stable, 'less predictable' (2013). The sort of emplacement that music usually grants a listener is undermined in these sorts of consumer-centred soundscapes.

Music and mobility

The idea of non-place finds another iteration through the ubiquity of mobile listening devices, such as Walkmans, iPods and smartphones. Michael Bull's (2005, 2013) work on both is significant, drawing from Raymond Williams's notion of 'mobile privatization' and the pleasures afforded listeners who can now craft their own soundtracks to listen to during their commute through the city, or at the gym, or while wandering its streets, where its own unique soundscape is rendered inaudible, the listener curating their own aestheticized, privatized experience of urban space. For Bull, Kassabian and others, the rise of mobile technologies and listening devices troubles the relationship of people to place. Music has always had the ability to transport as much as transcend the here and now. Smartphones and streaming services accentuate this, but differently transform how people engage or disengage from spaces (and one another), a networked subjectivity. These individuated sonic bubbles, mobile spheres of private space have been characterized as a 'stimulus shield' against 'hyperstimulation' of the city (Groening 2014), earbuds and headphones a signifier of an algorithmic asociality, keeping not only other sounds out but also other people, a form of what Bull calls 'solipsistic aestheticization' (Bull 2013: 500).

As Stephen Groening (2014) reminds us, part of the pleasure of these devices is their portability, the mobility they enable and the immateriality and invisibility of processes, which combined underpin a certain fantasy of constant communication, always on, always available, always accessible. Here we have the materiality of device coupled with the disappearance of infrastructure which allows these new media technologies appear transcendent, evoking what Vincent Mosco has referred to as the 'digital sublime' (2005), the production of another kind of space that says a great deal about the contemporary moment and the distinctive spaces, places and non-places it has produced.

References

Anderson, B. (1996), *Imagined Communities*, London, Verso.
Augé, M. (1995), *Non-places: Introduction to an Anthropology of Supermodernity*, London: Verso.
Baily, J. and Collyer, M. (2006), 'Introduction: Music and Migration', *Journal of Ethnic and Migration Studies*, 32 (2): 167–82.

Baker, S., Doyle, P., and Homan, S. (2016), 'Historical Records, National Constructions: The Contemporary Popular Music Archive', *Popular Music and Society*, 39 (1): 8–27.
Becker, H. S. (2008), *Art Worlds: Updated and Expanded*, Berkeley: University of California Press.
Bell, T. (1998), 'Why Seattle? An Examination of an Alternative Rock Culture Hearth', *Journal of Cultural Geography*, 18 (1): 35–47.
Bennett, A. (2004), Consolidating the Music Scenes Perspective. *Poetics*, 32 (3–4): 223–34.
Bolderman, L., and Reijnders, S. (2017), 'Have You Found What You're Looking For? Analysing Tourist Experiences of Wagner's Bayreuth, ABBA's Stockholm and U2's Dublin', *Tourist Studies*, 17 (2): 164–81.
Breen, M. (1989), *Our Place, Our Music*, Australian Institute of Aboriginal Studies.
Brovig-Hanssen, R. and Danielsen, A. (2016), *Digital Signatures: The Impact of Digitization on Popular Music Sound*, Cambridge: MIT Press.
Bull, M. (2005), 'No Dead Air! The iPod and the Culture of Mobile Listening', *Leisure Studies*, 24 (4): 343–55.
Bull, M. (2013), 'iPod Use: An Urban Aesthetics of Sonic Ubiquity', *Continuum*, 27 (4): 495–504.
Carney, G. (1998), 'Music Geography', *Journal of Cultural Geography*, 18 (1): 1–10.
Clark, C., and Linehan, A. (1987), 'Popular Music in British Libraries', *Brio*, 24 (1): 30–7.
Cohen, S. (1991), Popular Music and Rrban Regeneration: The Music Industries of Merseyside. *Cultural Studies*, 5 (3): 332–46.
Cohen, S. (2017), *Decline, Renewal and the City in Popular Music Culture: Beyond the Beatles*, New York: Routledge.
Connell, J., and Gibson, C. (2003), *Sound Tracks: Popular Music, Identity and Place*, New York: Routledge.
Currid, B. (2000), 'A Song Goes Round The World': The German Schlager, as an Organ of Experience', *Popular Music*, 19 (2): 147–80.
Daynes, S. (2009). 'A Lesson of Geography, on the Riddim: The Symbolic Topography of Reggae Music', in Johansson, O., & Bell, T. L. (eds), *Sound, Society, and th Geography of Popular Music*, 91–106, London: Ashgate.
De Martini U. N. (2020), 'Music-Making and Forced Migrants' Affective Practices of Diasporic Belonging', *Journal of Ethnic and Migration Studies*, 1–18.
DeNora, T. (2000), *Music in Everyday Life*, London: Cambridge University Press.
Devine, K. (2015), 'Decomposed: A Political Ecology of Music', *Popular Music*, 34 (3): 367–89.
Doyle, P. (2005), *Echo and Reverb: Fabricating Space in Popular Music* Recording, *1900–1960*, Middletown, CT: Wesleyan University Press.
Eno, B. (1978), Ambient 1: Music for Airports (liner notes). Brian Eno. PVC Records. PVC 7908 (AMB 001). Retrieved 23 October 2020.
Finnegan, R. (2007), *The Hidden Musicians: Music-Making in an English Town*, Middletown: Wesleyan University Press.
Forman, M. (2002). The 'Hood Comes Rirst: Race, Space, and Place in Rap and hip-hop, Middletown, CT: Wesleyan University Press.
Gendron, B. (2002), *Between Montmartre and the Mudd Club: Popular Music and the Avant-Garde*, Detroit: University of Chicago Press.
Gillan, M. (2009), 'Imagining Okinawa: Japanese Pop Musicians and Okinawan Music', *Perfect Beat*, 10 (2), 177–95.
Groening, S. (2014), 'New Immaterialities towards a Meteorology of the Media', *Transformations*, 25.

Grossberg, L. (2014), 'Is Anybody Listening? Does Anybody Care?: On Talking about the State of Rock', in A. Ross and T. Rose (eds), *Microphone Fiends*, 41–58, New York: Routledge.

Hall, S., and Jefferson, T., eds (1993 [1976]), *Resistance through Rituals: Youth Subcultures in Post-War Britain*, vol. 7, London: Psychology Press.

Hardie, D. (2002), *Exploring Early Jazz: The Origins and Evolution of the New Orleans Style*, Lincoln, NE: iUniverse.

Hebdige, D. (1978), *Subculture: The Meaning of Style*, London: Methuen, 1979.

Hesmondhalgh, D. (2005). 'Subcultures, Scenes or Tribes? None of the Above'. *Journal of Youth Studies*, 8 (1): 21–40.

Hosokawa, S. (1999), 'Soy Sauce Music: Haruomi Hosono and Japanese Self-orientalism', in P. Hayward (ed.), *Widening the Horizon: Exoticism in Post-War Popular Music*, 114–44, Bloomington: Indiana University Press.

Hudson, R. (2006), 'Regions and Place: Music, Identity and Place', *Progress in Human Geography*, 30 (5): 626–34.

Johansson, O. and Bell, T. L., eds (2016), *Sound, Society and the Geography of Popular Music*, London: Ashgate.

Kasinitz, P. and Martiniello, M. (2019), 'Music, Migration and the City', *Ethnic and Racial Studies*, 42 (6): 857–64.

Kassabian, A. (2013), *Ubiquitous Listening: Affect, Attention, and Distributed Subjectivity*, Berkeley: University of California Press.

Keightley, K. (1996), '"Turn it Down!"She Shrieked: Gender, Domestic Space, and High Fidelity, 1948–59 ', *Popular Music*, 15 (2), 149–77.

Kibort, K. (2020), 'An "Electric Pow Wow": Indigenous American Use of Music Videos to Discuss Identity and Reclaim Visual Sovereignty', *Ethnographic Encounters*, 10 (2): 1–11.

Kruse, H. (2010), 'Local Identity and Independent Music Scenes, Online and Off', *Popular Music and Society*, 33 (5), 625–39.

Lanza, J. (1991), 'The Sound of Cottage Cheese (Why Background Music Is the Real World Beat!)', *Performing Arts Journal*, 13 (3): 42–53.

Lebrun, B. (2016), *Protest Music in France: Production, Identity and Audiences*, New York: Routledge.

Lefebvre, H. (1991), *The Production of Space*, London: Wiley Blackwell.

Lefebvre, H. (1996), *Writings on Cities*, trans. E. Kofman and E. Lebas. London: Blackwell.

Leonard, M. (2010), 'Exhibiting Popular Music: Museum Audiences, Inclusion and Social History', *Journal of New Music Research*, 39 (2): 171–81.

Leyshon, A., Matless, D. and Revill, G. (1995), 'The Place of Music:[Introduction]', *Transactions of the Institute of British Geographers*, 20 (4): 423–33.

Lindner, R. (2006), 'The Cultural Texture of the City', *Cities and Media*: 53–8.

Lockheart, P. (2003), 'A History of Early Microphone Singing, 1925–1939: American Mainstream Popular Singing at the Advent of Electronic Microphone Amplification', *Popular Music and Society*, 26 (3): 367–85.

Lopes, P. (2002), *The Rise of a Jazz Art World*, Cambridge, UK: Cambridge University Press.

Magaña, M.R. (2021), 'The Politics of Black and Brown solidarities: Race, Space, and hip-hop Cultural Production in Los Angeles', *Ethnic and Racial Studies*, 1–24.

McGowan, C., and Pessanha, R. (1998), *The Brazilian Sound: Samba, Bossa Nova, and the Popular Music of Brazil*, Philadelphia: Temple University Press.

McRobbie, A. (1978), *Jackie: An Ideology of Adolescent Femininity*, Centre for Cultural Studies: University of Birmingham.

Mendívil, J. (2020), 'Hallo Blumenau, bom dia Brasil!: German Music beyond Germany', in O. Seibt, M. Ringsmut, D-E Wickström (eds), *Made in Germany*, 154–62, London: Routledge.

Mitchell, T. (1996), *Popular Music and Local Identity: Rock, Pop and Rap in Europe and Oceania*, London: Leicester University Press.

Mosco, V. (2005), *The Digital Sublime: Myth, Power, and Cyberspace*, Cambridge: MIT Press.

Pearce, R. and Lohman, K. (2019), 'De/constructing DIY Identities in a Trans Music Scene', *Sexualities*, 22 (1–2): 97–113.

Rapp, T. (2010), *Lost and Sound: Berlin, Techno and the Easyjet Set*, Innervisions: Berlin.

Rhiney, K. and Cruse, R. (2012). '"Trench Town Rock": Reggae Music, Landscape Inscription, and the Making of Place in Kingston, Jamaica', *Urban Studies Research*, 1–12.

Schiller, M. (2018), *Soundtracking Germany: Popular Music and National Identity*, New York: Rowman & Littlefield.

Skelton, T. and Valentine, G., eds (1998), *Cool Places: Geographies of Youth Cultures*, New York: Psychology Press.

Stahl, G. (2014), 'Getting by and Growing Older: Club Transmediale and Creative Life in the New Berlin', G. Stahl (ed.), *Poor, but Sexy: Reflections on Berlin Scenes*, 191–210, Berlin: Peter Lang.

Straw, W. (1991), 'Systems of Articulation, Logics of Change: Communities and Scenes in Popular Music', *Cultural Studies*, 5 (3): 368–88.

Straw, W. (2004), 'Cultural Scenes', *Loisir et société/Society and Leisure*, 27 (2): 411–22.

Straw, W. (2015), 'Some Things a Scene Might Be: Postface', *Cultural Studies*, 29 (3): 476–85.

Whiteley, S., Bennett, A., and Hawkins, S., eds (2004), *Music, Space and Place: Popular Music and Cultural Identity*, Burlington: Ashgate.

Wilson, O., and Holland, M. (2020), 'Not our "Dunedin Sound": Responses to the Historicisation of Dunedin Popular Music', *Popular Music*, 39 (2): 187–207.

Yano, C. (1996), 'The Floating World of Karaoke in Japan', *Popular Music & Society*, 20 (2): 1–17.

Discography

Brian Eno (1978), *Ambient 1: Music for Airports*, Polydor AMB 001, 2310647.

2
Rhythmanalysis and circulation

Will Straw

Introduction

In a perceptive account of life in the city in which I live, Julien Besse writes of the ways in which Pop Montreal, an annual festival of music and culture, replicates the everyday rhythms of Montreal experience. 'As Pop Montreal melts into a sense of the everyday', Besse muses, one can't help asking the question: '[what] if life was like this all the time?' (Besse 2015: 113). In fact, he suggests, the year-round experience of living in Montreal is, indeed, very much like that of attending Pop Montreal (if you are a young twenty-or-thirty-something who spends their time going to music shows and other kinds of cultural events). Rather than disrupting the flow of city life, in a carnivalesque, transgressive overturning of habits or rhythms, the Pop Montreal festival simply draws temporary parentheses around events and behaviours typical of the endless routines of Montreal life. 'All through the year', Besse writes, 'the Pop Montreal attendee goes to conferences and exhibits, eats locally, freely practices the sexualities of their choice, attends talks and participates in debates' (116; my translation). The Pop Montreal festival itself is little more than a lightly augmented version of Montreal life as it is lived on a daily basis.

We find, intertwined in this analysis (even if they are not named), the notions of rhythm and circulation which are the focus of this chapter. As a festival, Pop Montreal might be expected to disrupt or at least interrupt the normal rhythms of Montreal life. As French geographer Luc Gwiazdzinski suggests in his account of urban festivals, such events – through their 'transitory and cyclical character, through their capacity to metamorphose all parts of a city, to rewrite its pathways, its orientations and its [sense of] centralities' – invite a city's residents to experience the city's rhythms in new ways, to imagine other ways of living and moving through it (Gwiazdzinski 2011: 332–3; my translation). Besse's argument, however, is that this is not the case with Pop Montreal. As a festival which proposes particular pathways of movement through the city, from venue to venue and event to event, Pop Montreal imposes itself lightly upon the circulatory patterns of ordinary cultural experience.

Music festivals and the 'rhythmanalytic project'

In what follows, I will discuss rhythm and circulation in turn, before offering some tentative remarks on their possible reconciliation. If I will continue to take festivals as my privileged example, this is because they pose the relationship of music to time and space at so many levels. Festivals, like other musical events, form part of what Henri Lefebvre and Catherine Régulier (2004: 73), in their plan for a 'Rhythmanalytic Project', called 'the concrete modalities of social time'. City life, they note, is made up of multiple, overlapping rhythms – of movement, of sounds, of activities and routines. This multiplicity of rhythms produces the *polyrhythmia* – the co-existence of multiple rhythms – which is a feature of any city. The task of the *rythmanalyst* is not simply to catalogue this multiplicity, but to chart the ways in which different rhythms operate together in harmonious or conflictual ways. If cultural life in Montreal is marked, as it seems to be for Besse, by an ongoing, low-level pleasantness, we might say that this is because the rhythms of special events like Pop Montreal are often in a relationship of *eurythmia* (or harmonization) with the normal flow of experience. That festival thus fails, in the terms offered by Lefebvre and Régulier, to produce an *arrythmia*, a radical interruption of rhythms which might make the event a utopian tear in the ongoing flow of city life, a glimpse of other possibilities of the sort described by Gwiazdzinski.

A music festival is both the container of what we might call internal rhythms, which organize its succession of events and experiences, and a participant within the larger rhythmic fluctuations of urban life. The internal rhythms of a musical festival are many. They include, for example, the fluctuating and sequential affectual states of those who attend them. This affectual economy unfolds across the states of arrival, waiting, engagement, intensity, attentiveness, distraction and disengagement which are part of any popular musical experience but repeated over and over in the duration of a festival. In live musical performance, the succession of these states has become standardized within those routines which Lefebvre and Régulier might call 'concrete modalities': the dimming of lights to suggest a performance is about to begin, the sequence of appearances of band members on stage, the delaying of favourite musical pieces to produce a sense of anticipation (or the early performances thereof to get them out of the way), and the complicated set of performative and technological gestures by which it is made clear that a show has conclusively ended. The rhythms of these affectual states are only broadly predictable: they will vary with the degree of professionalism of an event or performer, and according to gestures by which performers perform their acquiescence or challenge to well-entrenched expectations. (The various ways in which a concert may end – through ceremonial words of gratitude and goodbye, a silent departure from the stage, or a raucous encore in which audience involvement is solicited – are common examples of this variety.)

These features of musical performance might further invite a comparative analysis with other events and routines. Festival concerts, like air travel and restaurant dining, involve a significant activity of waiting, in relation to norms and schedules whose reliability is never absolutely certain. The duration of a festival concert, like that of a theatrical play or religious ceremony, is subject to the vagaries of live human performance and technological functioning, but while the first may involve significant, improvised changes in the intended sequence of words and sounds, this is much less likely in the case of the other two. Like mall shopping, a large festival will offer simultaneous alternatives to accommodate the rhythms of fluctuating interest or attention; like conventions, festivals offer multiple spaces for those who prioritize open-ended socializing over adherence to a scheduled programme.

In their interaction with a broader context, the rhythms of festivals join and overlap with other means of marking time, which provide its frame and context (and to which a festival contributes). The most important of these are those which divide months and seasons from each other. Pop Montreal is both one of the last of Montreal's summer musical festivals and a way of sneaking summer-like pleasure into those days, at summer's end, marked by a return to the routine of work and school. In Montreal, as in many other cities, the end of summer is marked by a shift in journalistic attention from popular music to other art forms, typically of higher cultural esteem, like literature, theatre and cinema, which launch new titles or productions and hold their own festivals.

This distribution of cultural forms and events across the twelve-month cycle of seasons is one possible focus of a rhythmanalysis, one with particular pertinence in countries like Canada in which the meteorological distinction between seasons is strong. At the same time, cultural festivals participate in the slow and partial displacement of older systems for the organization of musical performance, such as lengthy 'seasons' of classical music concerts or the musical venue's schedule of bookings. While both of these persist, the model of the festival, which condenses musical abundance and variety within a brief window of musical bingeing, is expanding as these other models retract.

The scheduling of cultural events may thus enforce or challenge a city's ways of organizing time. Benjamin Pradel, in a study of the relationship of natural to cultural rhythms in cities, suggests that present-day cities have come to accord natural seasons ever greater importance in the differentiation of cultural experiences. Urban beaches, open-air cinemas, Christmas markets, and, in Montreal, outdoor winter electronic music festivals (like Igloofest) are attempts to exploit the distinct identities of natural seasons, counter-acting any tendency of urban life to become disengaged from the rhythms of meteorological seasonality (Pradel 2013: 24). Alternatively, cities may seek to disrupt the normal sequencing of cultural events within the twenty-four-hour cycle. They may pull musical performance out of the night and into the daytime (through such events as lunch-time raves or afternoon tea dances). Inversely, through *nuits blanches* and 'museum nights', they may pull the day-time activity of visiting arts institutions deeper into the night.

The rhythmanalysis of cities and the musical analogy

A rhythmanalysis, cultural theorist Ben Highmore suggests, is not methodologically rigorous. Rather, it is 'an attitude, an orientation, a proclivity: it is not "analytic" in any positivistic or scientific sense of the term. It falls on the side of impressionism and description, rather than systematic data collecting' (Highmore 2005: 150; see also Revol 2016). A rhythmanalysis of cities, in other words, must take leave of the claims to formal rigour and systematicity with which those who analyse music speak in formal terms of measures and beats. While Highmore's designation of rhythmanalysis as impressionistic describes most examples of the practice, we may note the growing tendency in recent work to employ statistical methods and large data sets in the mapping of urban rhythms, offering an image of greater scientificity. The rhythms of certain behaviours (such as tweeting or photo-posting) are being mapped on the basis of millions of examples (e.g. Neuhaus 2015), and the graphic representations of rising and falling frequencies suggest analogies between patterns of urban behaviour and the musical score.

The very notion of a rhythmanalysis draws on the musical analogy, but there is variation in the extent to which its application to urban life requires a view of the city as somehow musical. In her book *Musical Cities*, urban designer Sara Adhitya maps a series of possible relationships between music, rhythmanalysis and cities. In what I take to be the first of her analytic moves, she follows Lefebvre's call to be attentive to all the audible, interwoven and overlaid sounds of the city, from our heartbeat through the music and noise which surround us. Music itself is thus absorbed within a broader soundscape. This soundscape – already an example of *polyrhythmia* – will itself, in a second move, be caught up in other sorts of rhythms which are not necessarily audible or sonic: those produced by the tempo of human movement or by such cycles as those created by the changing of traffic lights change or the rapidity with which urban dwellers walk. In an even further move, Adhitya invites us to turn our attention to the rhythms frozen within static structures – to the ways in which, for example, the built environment contains both intervals and unbroken lines, and thus produces variations of emptiness and fullness which we might consider rhythmic. All of these phenomena together enact what Adhitya, quoting geographer Anne Buttimer, calls 'the orchestration of various time-space rhythms' (Adhitya 2017: 7), a designation which returns us to the over-arching model of music.

Adhitya's own practice, in urban design and architecture, is directed towards producing what she calls a Sonified Urban Masterplan, 'an audio-visual tool for the representation of the urban masterplan, which allows us to play the composition of the city like a piece of music' (2017: 44). This tool is a means of translating visual data into sounds, so as to register, in sonic form, intensities and rhythms implicit in phenomena which are typically inaudible. It is also intended to make us conscious of the extent to which, in however unintended and uncoordinated a fashion, a city is 'composed'.

This notion of cities as 'composed', through an analogy with music, recalls the various attempts over the years to think of cities as in some way 'written' or 'spoken', in practices modelled on textuality or speech. In an efficient summary of such attempts, Paul Connerton quotes Roland Barthes's suggestion that, by moving through urban space, 'we speak our city'; he further invokes Michel de Certeau's well-known claim that 'the act of walking is to the urban system what the act of speaking is to the language system' (Connerton 2009: 115). In these models, however, the emphasis is on the individual's appropriation of the city's constituent features. Those who pursue the analogy with music, in contrast, typically have little to say about the individual performance of urban rhythms – there are few claims that to move through the city is, somehow, to 'play' it like an instrument, in the way de Certeau's urban dweller 'writes' the city by walking through it. Rather, attention is focused on the city's capacity to 'compose' itself in the interweaving of its various rhythmic elements.

For a nuanced critique of the 'composed' city, we might turn to the work of Ato Quayson, who challenges the notion that sound and rhythm unproblematically fill (or organize) the space of cities:

> the measure of music is also a metronome of our emotional responses to it, and that is what allows it to be pleasant or unpleasant to the listener. Space, on the other hand, is populated both by objects, whether these objects be trees, pylons, and so forth, and the more labile and ephemeral human social interactions that also come to fundamentally define our experience of it. Thus there is a physical- cum-social interactional materiality to space that distinguishes it from the sonic (materialities?) of music.
>
> (Quayson 2014: 28)

Across the variety of writings seeking to elaborate a rhythmanalysis of cities, we may distinguish between two poles of theoretical affinity. At one of these, analysts will quickly depart from the musical dimensions of rhythm, focusing on cycles of collective movement and finding their inspiration in such fields as time-geography, studies of urban infrastructure (such as transportation systems) or human kinesics. At the other pole, music persists as the conceptual centre and privileged analogy of a rhythmanalysis, inspiring work which builds upon metaphors of orchestration and composition.

For the first of these, a politics of urban rhythms in relation to music might take the prosaic form of proposals to synchronize concert times with the needs of an early-rising work force, or late-night transit with the closing hours for clubs. Music, from such a perspective, is no more privileged than other urban activities in its relationship to the cycles and schedules of city life. At the second conceptual pole, music is, in contrast, privileged as the model by which the city might be lived and experienced. From this point of departure, a rhythmanalytic politics of the city might seek to instil a sensitivity to all its rhythmic features, propagating something like a 'deep listening' to the city of the sort theorized within music and sound studies. Such a politics might, as well, be attentive to the role played by musical rhythms in producing social relations of cohesion or fragmentation. Johan Fornas, writing earlier in this century, offered the argument that then-new mobile technologies for music listening (like the iPod) enclosed the human subject in an isolated space from which the world was experienced as a highly individualized rhythmic unity. 'In Lefebvre's classical rhythm-analysis', Fornas argues, 'urban experience was understood as polyrhythmic, whereas iPods tend to let every-thing move in step with you as you move in step with the music, erecting sensory gates around sound ghettoes, in line with the growth of gated communities' (Fornas 2006: 16). This new individualism detached the iPod-wearer from any engagement with a city's polyrhythmia, its shared and collective sonic dimension.

If this rhythmic unity, for Fornas, was the basis of an intense individuality, others have offered examples of shared rhythms serving as the basis of solidarities and group identities.

Drawing on the notion of 'speedtribes' developed by theorist and music label owner Steve Goodman, Alex de Jong and Marc Schuilenberg argue for a broader conception of 'sound communities', to define those clusters of social relations which emerge through a collective commitment to specific categories of 'sounds and rhythms' (2006: 102–3). Sound communities would include those which gather around club-based music genres distinguished by particular narrow ranges of beats-per-minute, or by particular operations to interrupt or otherwise subvert dominant rhythmic patterns. If this notion of rhythm as the basis of community recalls many of the claims of ethnomusicological work on the deep rhythmic foundations of collective life in non-urban communities of the Global South (e.g. Stewart 2010), the *speedtribes* or sound communities discussed by de Jong and Schuilenberg are the shifting, transitory clusters of affinity more typical of the contemporary city. A rhythmanalysis of urban music might be seen as interweaving this interest in 'sound communities' or *speedtribes* with an attentiveness to the broader notion of 'temporal communities' theorized a few years earlier by Boulin and Muckenberger (1999: 55). Such communities are distinguished by the ways in which they 'occupy' distinctive temporalities of city life.

Circulation

In the summer of 2019, as the Lil Nas X track 'Old Town Road' concluded its nineteen-week run at the top of *Billboard*'s Hot 100 chart, music journalist Jason Lipshutz speculated as to some of the reasons for its success (Lipshutz 2019). Others had noted how the track's brevity (at less than two minutes) inspired listeners to keep hitting the replay button on media platforms hosting the track (Hinz 2019), thus pushing it up the charts that register such plays. Lipshutz himself, however, tied its success to the variety of spaces, both on-line and off-line, through which 'Old Town Road' circulated. Early on, the track had gathered momentum through innumerable uses on the platform TikTok, where it served as soundtrack for short video clips which each followed its own trajectory of sharing and viewing. As re-mixes, new video clips and a series of guest vocalists multiplied the media instantiations of 'Old Town Road', they extended both its commercial lifecycle in time and the sequence of cultural spaces across which it could be seen to circulate.

For our purposes, the most interesting development in the lifecycle of 'Old Town Road' was its popularity in elementary schools, where young people knew the words, sang them in groups on breaks and performed the dance moves which had come to gather around the track. The cultural lifecycle of 'Old Town Road' saw it move between digital and non-digital spaces, between media platforms and school years, with re-enactments in the latter filmed and posted on the former, stimulating further re-enactments in what became a series of complex feedback loops. This take-up and re-performance of mediated music in physical spaces has been typical of musical culture since the early days of sheet music, as we know. In 2019, the recording industry took Little Nas X's success as proof that physical spaces like the schoolyard and street had now been reinvigorated as sites for the accumulation of musical popularity. The track's circulation across an ongoing series of platforms and non-digital spaces produced the rhythms of re-versioning and renewal by which its incredible success was assured.

Most of the time, music is caught up in an almost infinite variety of circulations, from those which send music tracks up and down popularity charts to the patterns of human migration which have moved musical styles around the world. Attempts to effectively capture the circulation of music often unravel in the face of the magnitude of the challenge, and due to the variety of processes which might be considered circulatory. At the same time, while notions of circulation would seem to bear intimate affinities with the project of a rhythmanalysis, they are generally applied separately from each other. Typically, circulation is set against rhythm as space is opposed to time. In a political economy of music, circulation is one name for the distribution of musical commodities. In ethnomusicology, it stands for those processes by which musical forms travel across space, losing or retaining their original features, resisting or nourishing processes of musical syncretism. In both cases, a rhythmic dimension figures only implicitly, as the repetition of certain patterns – the sales arcs of musical commodities, for a political economy, and the recurrent cycles of emergence, up-rooting and hybridization, for an ethnomusicology.

The circulation of people, objects and cultural expression may be organized rhythmically, of course – one need only think of the fixed cycles of daily distribution of newspapers in the twentieth century, or the regularized arrival of musical recordings in retail stores on particular days of the week. People circulating through cities will encounter a variety of different rhythms of all kinds and experience the relationships of polyrhythmia, eurythmia and arrythmia elaborated by Léfebvre and Régulier. The jarring arrhythmic transitions in cities, as one moves between the muzak of one retail store and the electronic club music of another, divide up the rhythms of a city, just as the eurythmia of automobile horns and loud car radios collaborates in producing a sense of vibrant urbanity. Both experiences fuel our broader perception of urban space as polyrhythmic, as a particular complex set of rhythmic relationships through which we circulate.

Tomas Fouquet's rich account of the lives of young women in the Senegalese city of Dakar offers an effective example of the interweaving of rhythmic patterns and circulatory routes in the weekend night-time behaviour of this social group. Fouquet begins by noting, as have others before him, that night may be considered a space-time (*espace-temps*). Night is a segment of the 24-hour temporal cycle, of course, but in a variety of discourses (touristic, regulatory, economic and so on) it is spatialized, presented as a territory to be visited, governed or exploited. For the young women of Dakar whom Fouquet studies, the night is a time in which life acquires greater speed and in which the horizons of possibility are opened up. The day, in contrast, is associated with a slowness and confinement whose causes are the inertial features of collective life, which restrict movement and enforce the boundaries of gender, class and age (Fouquet 2017: 91). In Fouquet's analysis, the circulatory pathways of Dakar women who go out on the town at night pull them into 'global rhythms', evoking other cities whose levels of prosperity and opportunity are perceived as greater. These global rhythms are experienced as liberating escapes from the atrophied rhythm (*rythme atrophié*) of their own society. Collective movement through the night, then, is a form of circulation within urban space. It is also a process of disengagement from rhythmic complexes in which multiple features of colonial history, social structure and individual possibility have become encrusted.

To return briefly to the example of Pop Montreal, with which we began, we may note how the organization of an 'event' (an annual festival) as a set of routes to be travelled accomplishes that spacing of time and timing of space which have been a prominent interest of geographers over the last four decades or more (e.g. Parkes and Thrift 1975). Time becomes spatialized when the rhythms of musical experience (the passage from commercial club to after-hours venue, for example) trace lines of circulation across the city. Space becomes temporalized when movements across urban space 'stick' to particular swaths of time – when, for example, the late-night fast-food venue becomes the space in which a late-night of clubbing or concert-going is concluded. Rhythm and circulation become necessarily intertwined once one recognizes that every fluctuation in speed or duration shapes the meaning of the spaces in which it is felt, just as every movement in space bears a temporality which feeds the broader rhythms of urban life.

References

Adhitya, S. (2017), *Musical Cities*, London: UCL Press.
Barnett, C. (2008), 'Convening Publics: The Parasitical Spaces of Public Action', in K. Cox, M. Low and J. Robinson (eds), *The Sage Handbook of Political Geography*, London: Sage.
Besse, J. (2015), 'Pop Montréal, le festival quotidien', *Audimat*, 3: 101–18.
Boulin, J-Y. and Mückenberger, U. (1999), 'Temps de la ville et qualité de vie', *Best: Études Européennes sur le temps*, 1: 55.
Connerton, P. (2009), *How Modernity Forgets*, Cambridge and New York: Cambridge University Press.
De Jong, A. and Schuilenberg, M. (2006), *Mediapolis: Popular Culture and the City*, Rotterdam: 010 Publishers.
Fornas, J. (2006), 'Introducing MediaCities', in J. Fornas (ed), *Cities and Media: Cultural Perspectives on Urban Identities in a Mediatized World*, Linköping, Sweden: Linköping University Electronic Press.
Fouquet, T. (2017), 'La nuit urbaine, un 'espace potentiel '? Hypothèses dakaroises', *Cultures & Conflits*, 105–106: 83–97. Available online: http://conflits.revues.org/19452 (accessed 8 September 2019).
Gwiazdzinski, L. (2011), 'La ville par intermittence: du temps de la fête à un urbanisme des temps', *Cidades*, 18 (3): 317–35.
Highmore, B. (2005), *Cityscapes: Cultural Readings in the Material and Symbolic City*, Basingstoke and New York: Palgrave.
Hinz, L. (2019), 'How Lil Nas X's Never-Ending "Old Town Road" Rollout Changed The Game', *hnhh*, July 29. Available online: https://www.hotnewhiphop.com/how-lil-nas-xs-never-ending-old-town-road-rollout-changed-the-game-news.86731.html (accessed 1 September 2019.)

Lefebvre, H. and Régulier, C. (2004), 'The Rhythmanalytical Project', in *Rhythmanalysis: Space, Time and Everyday Life*, trans. Stuart Elden and Gerald Moore, London and New York: Continuum. Originally published 1992.

Lipshutz, J. (2019), 'Lil Nas X's "Old Town Road": 5 Things The Music Industry Should Learn From Its Record- Setting Run', *Billboard*, August 21. Available online: https://www.billboard.com/articles/columns/hip-hop/8527857/lil-nas-x-old-town-road-5-music-industry-takeaways (accessed 28 August 2019).

Neuhaus, F. (2015), *Emergent Spatio-temporal Dimensions of the City: Habitus and Urban Rhythms*, Heidelberg, New York, Dordrecht and London: Springer.

Parkes, D. N. and N. J. Thrift (1975), 'Timing Space and Spacing Time', *Environment and Planning A*, 7: 651–70.

Pradel, B. (2013), 'La mise en scène événementielle des saisons dans la ville', in A. Guez and H. Subremon (eds), *Saisons des Villes*, Paris: Editions donner lieu.

Quayson, A. (2014), *Oxford Street, Accra City Life and the Itineraries of Transnationalism*, Durham, NC: Duke University Press.

Revol, C. (2016), 'Rythmes et urbanisme. Pour une approche esthétique du dynamisme urbain', *Rhuthmos*, September 17. Available online: http://rhuthmos.eu/spip.php?article493. (accessed 1 September 2019).

Stewart, J. (2010), 'Articulating the African Diaspora through Rhythm: Diatonic Patterns, Nested Looping Structures, and the Music of Steve Coleman', *Intermédialités / Intermediality*, 16: 167–84. Available online: https://doi.org/10.7202/1001961ar. (accessed 15 July 2019).

Straw, W. (2017), 'Circulation', in I. Szeman, S. Blacker and J. Sully (eds), *A Companion to Critical and Cultural Theory*, Hoboken, NJ: Wiley.

3

Global, local, regional and translocal: Towards a relational approach to scale in popular music

Hyunjoon Shin and Keewoong Lee

Introduction: Asia into global?

More than twenty years ago, Keith Negus wrote, 'Japan is an important global market, whereas India is not' (Negus 1999: 157) with respect to 'global marketing' of the music industry. He went on to say that 'the "global" is imagined in terms of a series of very particular criteria' (Negus 1999) and the criteria are epitomized in 'copyright legislation and highly priced CDs' (Negus 1999). 'Highly priced CDs' need to be replaced with something else or something more complex, but the logic of the industry remains the same.

Perhaps it would have been more apposite had he chosen China and South Korea (hereafter 'Korea') instead of India, since not only Japan but also China and Korea established themselves as parts of 'global music market' in the most recent report by International Federation of the Phonographic Industry (IFPI 2021). Japan, Korea and China took the second, sixth and seventh places in the ranking of 'Top 10 music markets' and there are no other non-Western countries in the chart as of 2020.

One should, of course, bear in mind that in defining what is 'global' or not, IFPI uses its own criteria and that, therefore, one should examine IFPI's numbers with a critical eye. Thus, what has been going on behind the simple numbers should be further examined and critically assessed. Yet, the report that has eagerly included Asia in its own map of the world provides a good reason to reflect on the global from the perspective of Asia as a region.

If the global–local binary has long served as a key conceptual framework to examine culture in globalization, the meaning of the couplet and the relationship between the pair have never been clear. The binary is even becoming problematic, if Asia or East Asia cannot 'merely' be called as one of the regions, let alone the locals. Actually, uncritical or not, Korean pop a.k.a. K-pop is safely and happily called as being global at least in its home country and, probably, across the world.

A chapter that deals with the issue of scale, the next section tackles these conceptual ambiguities and uncertainties concerning the global and local in popular music. It also necessitates reiteration of related concepts such as glocal, hybrid, regional and translocal. All these will be discussed in depth in the following sections one after another.

The global: From strategy to network

The diverse usages of the terms 'global' and 'local' justify the late Jan Fairley's lament that '"global" and "local" are ill-defined terms, offering multiple vantage points' (Fairley 2001: 272). From this perspective, it would be relevant to start from one of Simon Frith's early 1990s articles on globalization. Frith's argument is summed up in the statement, 'the cultural imperialist model – nation versus nation – must be replaced by a post-imperial model of an infinite number of local experiences of (and responses to) something globally shared' (Frith 1991: 267–8). The argument suggests that the timespace of cultural imperialism and Anglo-American hegemony was fading in the early 1990s with the end of the Cold War and the advent of the single European monetary market. The influential 'center-periphery' model was increasingly irrelevant and rapidly discredited. The model of interconnectedness, interdependence and transnational flows emerged as the new dominant paradigm of the era.

Frith's argument has been further developed and elaborated by fellow British scholars, especially, Keith Negus (1996, 1999) and David Hesmondhalgh (1998, 2000, 2002). They made significant contributions to the study of globalization in popular music based on their analyses of global strategies of the music industry. Hesmondhalgh even claims 'neither cultural imperialism nor globalization theory is adequate to assess spatial and geographical changes in the cultural industries across the world' (Hesmondhalgh 2002: 197).

While Negus and Hesmondhalgh share a critical viewpoint towards the global stemming from their focus on music industry strategy, other authors have taken a more positive approach to it and tried to develop an analytical tool for explaining the changing environment of popular music. For example, David Laing uncovers 'new music networks' forming beyond the boundaries of what he calls (Anglo-American) 'rock formation' (Laing 1997). On the other hand, Jason Toynbee follows Laing and shows 'global networks' that replace the 'hegemonic center' (Toynbee 2002). In the same vein, Jan Fairley adopted a network approach to rethink the global–local binary in her discussion of world music (Fairley 2001). Here, the concept of network appears to have a distinct benefit of revealing ambiguous, complex and unintentional characteristics of the Anglo-American hegemony in popular music.

These two approaches to the global, that is, strategy versus network, are neither mutually exclusive nor diametrically opposite. However, they still constitute two disparate positions in debate which leads up to following three points:

Firstly, globalization means the spatial reach and flow of popular music come to encompass virtually the entire globe. This change has had a radical impact on the music industry which was pushed to go through a near-wholesale transformation. Yet, it is difficult to argue that the newly established global order was in any way of a more horizontal, egalitarian or democratic nature like the network approach suggested.

Secondly, the global–local could be conceived of as geographical scales. However, these are not politically innocent categories but charged with values and political connotations. Here, the global appears large, macro and important whereas the local is associated with small, micro and trivial.[1] Applying to popular music, these epithets point not only to differences in size and value but also to different economies, practices and institutional arrangements.

Thirdly, the global is not a thing but, to borrow the term from Anna Tsing, aggregate practices of 'scale-making' (Tsing 2000: 342, 348) by multiple actors. The space of music making is simultaneously that of sense and affect making. The logic of capitalist global economy is insufficient to explain this cultural dimension. Rather, it is more effective to approach it as a product of complex cultural practices, strategic actions, and struggles and negotiations by diverse and heterogeneous actors, human and non-human, such as musicians, intermediaries, music industry workers, consumers, technologies, laws and regulations as well as capital dispersed across the world.

In this respect, it is not surprising that situated empirical studies have proliferated in popular music studies, particularly since the mid-2000s. Thanks to the increase in researchers with diverse cultural and ethnic backgrounds as well as the normalization of reflexive deconstruction of the US- or Western-centric perspective, the imaginary geography of the West and the Rest has largely subsided in academic discourses. Once the hierarchical binary conceptualization of the global–local declined, popular music from the non-Western world no longer appears backward or inferior and, thus, can be treated more fairly and equally.

'Global versus local' or 'glocal hybrid'

Since the mid-1990s, the global–local dichotomy has appeared in virtually every publication of popular music studies. Among them, two books seem exemplary in revealing some crucial shortcomings in the concepts: one is *Global Pop: World Music and World Markets* (Taylor 1997), and the other *Popular Music and Local Identity: Rock, Pop and Rap in Europe and Oceania* (Mitchell 1996). While Taylor focuses on the 'global' nature of the music produced in or influenced by the global South, mainly sub-Saharan Africa and South Asia, Mitchell, attends to the 'local' identities of popular music in non-hegemonic regions, mainly continental Europe and Australasia. The contrasting conceptualizations of the global and local disclose certain arbitrariness of categorization.

At this point, it is important to emphasize that understanding music-making requires consideration of both interconnection, dialogue and communication on the global level, and inequalities, hierarchies and asymmetries[2] between places at the local level. However, it should be pointed out that Taylor's classification of world music as global *pop* sounds rather premature in hindsight as the genre has taken a different route from the conventional pop genre in its subsequent development, although it is still 'mass-mediated' (McKay 2013: 6). Indeed, later studies on world music tend to avoid its association with popular music despite continuing to use the term 'global'. One example is Elijah Wald, whose book *Global Minstrels* (Wald 2006) touches on this very issue. Another work by Tony Mitchell embraces the term 'global' when he collects a series of studies on non-American rap and hip-hop under the title, *Global Noise* (Mitchell 2001).

It is interesting that Toynbee adopted the term 'glocal rap' (Toynbee 2002: 159) for the cases similar to what Mitchell called 'global noise'. The term 'glocalization' became influential from the moment it appeared as a keyword in Roland Robertson's work in which the concept was defined as the simultaneous process of both cultural homogenization and heterogenization (Robertson 1995). Another popular concept in a similar vein is 'hybridization', famously advocated by Jan Nederveen Pieterse (Pieterse 1995). Both concepts, from different theoretical traditions and with different emphases, reject the idea of globalization as homogenization.

Even before the advent of globalization, there were terms to depict diverse forms of cultural diffusion such as indigenization, domestication and transculturation. In popular music studies, these concepts have been widely applied to describe local appropriation and (re)creation of the Anglo-American pop-rock. In one of early definitions, world music was distinguished from 'pop' music, and the latter did not only mean Anglo-American pop and rock mainstream but also included local adoption of it (see Shuker 1998: 311–12).

However, the introduction of glocalization and hybridization to academic vernacular made this line of work more complex and rich. A great number of studies on popular music have employed at least one of these concepts to reimagine and reposition what has become called thereafter in various ways 'national popular music' (Biddle and Knights 2007) or 'ethno-national pop-rock' (Regev 2007a, 2007b) or 'global pop and local language' (Berger and Carroll 2003).

Deliberately or not, all these efforts contributed aggregately to deconstruct the dominant conception of the global–local binary. The anxieties about the supposedly deleterious effects of media globalization widespread since the 1970s as seen in the famous words 'The media are American' by Jeremy Tunstall (1977). But they were slowly replaced by the optimism for local cultural forms in the millennium. Non-Anglo-American contemporary pop, rather than folk and traditional music in the name of world music, began to be circulated on a global scale, (re)discovered, (re)valued and repackaged both within and without its country of origin. As the empowerment of local popular music gathers pace, it became increasingly difficult to sustain the once-prevailing hierarchy of the global–local. At the very least, a radical reconfiguration of the order, particularly its implied synonymy with the West and the rest, was urgently called for.

However, the global–local is not the only problematic concept. The glocal and hybrid are also in need of scrutiny. The latter has been of particular concern for those studying Asian popular music. For instance, Jeroen de Kloet, in his studies on Chinese rock, argues, 'it is important not to get caught in a global versus local opposition here, or to read rock in China as hybrid (or, indeed, glocal)' (De Kloet 2010: 31). On the other hand, Emma Baulch, who has researched Indonesian popular music for decades, argues 'the "homogenous-hybrid" dialectic can blind observers to more complex interplays of power and nuances of meaning at the local level' (Baulch 2008: 7). These critiques debunk that the categories of the glocal and the hybrid are inherently limited in addressing the non-Anglo-American pop since the local here is deprived of its autonomy and depends on the global for its existence. In the glocal/hybrid framework, therefore, the local appears meaningless unless it is touched by the global. Methodologically, it requires researchers to focus on tracing how the global is translated in a particular cultural context, which restricts investigation on local creativity.[3]

The question of cultural geography also needs to be mentioned here. It is difficult to find popular music literature that applies the term 'glocal' to the music from countries like the United States, the United Kingdom, Ireland, Canada, Australia and Aotearoa/New Zealand. It is a tacit assumption that these Anglophone countries share the same popular music culture, and thus are given the position of the global without qualification. In contrast, the music of non-Anglophone Western European countries such as France, Germany and Italy is sometimes attached with the adjective, particularly when it comes to locally developed contemporary pop genres like French hip-hop, German techno and Italo disco respectively, since these countries are not considered quite as hegemonic. Then again, all these countries are thrown into the category of 'the West' in a certain context claiming a hegemonic position vis-à-vis the rest of the world. It raises the question of the position of 'the East' in the world of popular music.

The regional and the inter-Asian: Alternative to the global–local?

The regional as an intermediate scale between the global and the local was developed by some pioneering scholars in the late 1990s and the early 2000s. The 'regional bloc' by David Laing (1997: 124–6) and the 'geocultural market' by David Hesmondhalgh (2002: 179–80) are some of the influential works of the era. These concepts were the inspirations behind the concerted efforts to construct East Asia as a cultural region since the late 1990s.

Despite the almost complete lack of institutional infrastructure and political backing, regional cultural flows between East Asian countries have been growing by leaps and bounds thanks mainly to committed individuals such as those academics seeking to produce regional knowledge and the cultural entrepreneurs in search of greater market opportunities.[4] Coincidentally, it was the time of power shift in the region as Japan was in decline and China was on the rise as the regional hegemon. This cataclysm made the regional integration a highly decentred and unpredictable process.

In this context, popular culture emerged as an unexpected but potent source of common identity. The works of Chua Beng Huat and Koichi Iwabuchi are of particular importance in initiating academic interests in East Asian popular culture previously only studied as discrete national cultures. Their agenda of 'de-Westernizing' and 'mutual referencing' (Iwabuchi 2014: 44–57) of the newly emerging regional culture is evident in the statements '"global" still tends to be exclusively associated with the West' and 'A dynamic interaction among countries in the non-West has been seriously under-explored' (Iwabuchi, Muecke and Thomas 2004: 9).

After the research on 'pop culture China' by Chua (2001) and 'popular culture and Japanese transnationalism' by Iwabuchi (2002) resulted in the collaboration between the two (Chua and Iwabuchi eds. 2008). It redraws the cultural map of East Asian pop culture that far exceeds one from a Chinese- or Japanese-centred outlook. Although they, confusingly, used both the conventional 'East Asia' and then-new 'inter-Asia' or 'trans-Asia', their efforts produced an imagination that the region is not simply the sum of disparate national or cultural entities, but an ongoing process of construction through interplays of various flows across national borders. Thus, it could be said that the regional/inter-Asian is at the same time a perspective and a process.

This is one of the main reasons why the postcolonial concept of hybridity does not work very well in the field of East Asian popular music.[5] The concept has been successfully applied to the case of world music which implicates North–South musical flows. However, East Asian pop, most notably the recently flourishing country name-branded popular music such as J-pop, K-pop, C-pop and V-pop, cannot be neatly categorized as world music in spite of it also being music from the 'rest'. This is not music thriving on Western validation but on sizeable and enthusiastic following in the region and beyond. In terms of the market, the audience and production, East Asian pop, led by hugely successful K-pop, shows the characteristics of bona fide global pop rather than a niche genre of world music. Furthermore, there has been growing tendency to refuse the tag world music among practitioners and scholars of popular music in the region for its underlying logic of othering and exploitative intent (see for example, Fermont and Faille 2016).

However, the regional/inter-Asia does have its shortcomings too. Theoretically speaking, the relation between regional and national runs the risk of reproducing the very impasse that has restricted the theoretical potential of the global–local. In a recent article on 'inter-Asian pop culture', Christopher Wan-ling Wee contrasts 'a vision of a regional market with a newfound interdependence' with 'the great modern ideology of nationalism' (Wee 2021: 118). While Wee is in favour of the former as he considers it as advancement over the latter, he seldom expresses concerns regarding inequality and injustice inherent in capitalist marketization, and its incongruity with the vision of East Asia as an equal and mutually beneficial region. One case in point for Wee is K-pop which is considered to be domesticated in the high-income countries like Singapore and Japan. However, this view could face a challenge from those who consider that K-pop and the Korean Wave 'carry threats of cultural imperialism' (Nguyen 2016: 43) in countries like Vietnam and (possibly) Mongolia, where it signifies the hierarchical nature of regional market organization despite the emphasis on interdependence.

In popular music studies, recent studies on regional/inter-Asian pop tend to focus on big sounds or commercial pop such as K-pop. What is called 'manufactured pop' is not specific to the region, and the commercial mainstream has always been a major research area in popular music studies. However, it has often been warned that, thanks to its enormous popularity throughout the Asian continent, 'K-pop idol', often conceived of as a variant of electronic dance pop performed by boy bands or girl group, could wash away all the other 'genre music'[6] from the popular music business. Consequently, it becomes urgent to develop a conceptual tool to handle small sounds or marginal genres properly.

Before moving on to the next topic, it is necessary to discuss, briefly, the question of local in the inter-Asia context. The concept of the local has been very often associated with the national. However, it is problematic in that the category would ignore any difference between super-states like China and mini-states like Singapore. Moreover, there are numerous non-state territories such as Taiwan, Hong Kong and Okinawa that are not eligible for the category, even though they have played crucial roles in the evolution of regional popular music. Even Korea, the current powerhouse of East Asian pop, is a divided nation, which would make her half a local. For these reasons, the concept of the local is urgently in need of redefinition.

Translocal: Widely dispersed but closely encountered

In a study on diaspora and migration, the prefix 'trans' is said to signify 'lasting relationships and repeated movements across borders', and its agents are 'not states or nations, but individual actors or associations' (Kokot, Tölölyan and Alfonso 2004: 3–4). Therefore, when the agent is states or nations, their relationships transient, and movements intermittent, 'inter' rather than 'trans' would be more suitable. More often than not, trans- implies that the relationship in question is multilateral than bilateral, and the movements multidirectional than unidirectional.

Traditionally, the local has been closely associated with the notion of place conceived of as fixed concrete space with lasting attributes. However, the local in translocal is far from the place in the traditional sense that is the site of cohesion, organicity, community, roots and authenticity. In order to reconceptualize the local, it is useful to rework the concept of place. Geographer Doreen Massey has provided a good starting point when she contends that local place is 'open,' 'porous' and 'provisional' space (Massey 1994: 121, 168). In her view, place is a shifting and transient event rather than a bounded and permanent entity. In a similar vein, anthropologist Anna Tsing argues 'places are made through their connections with each other, not their isolation' (Tsing 2000: 330). In short, these authors call upon a processual and relational approach to place hence the local.

In a way, Massey's 'global sense of place' and Tsing's 'global situation' are products of their times, when the term 'global' was in vogue in academia. However, these expressions could have been more effective if global were replaced by translocal. This was exactly the point Andy Bennet and Richard A. Peterson raised when they criticized Keith Kahn-Harris's use of global (Peterson and Bennett 2004: 8–9).[7] The links and networks that hold together dispersed music scenes are better described as translocal since it attends to the relational aspect of the collective rather than the global's macro entity. It could avoid confusion from scalar mix up such as the 'global network of local scenes' by sticking to what Manuel DeLanda (DeLanda 2002) called 'flat ontology' which 'attempts to break down classificatory schema […] that result in hierarchical or binary modes of thinking' (Ash 2020: 347).

It seems that, thus far, Peterson and Bennett's edited volume *Music Scenes: Local, Translocal, and Virtual* provided arguably the most satisfying account of the translocal in popular music. Here, the authors explain that 'a particular kind of music are in regular contact with similar local scenes in distant places' (Peterson and Bennett 2004: 8). According to their account, scenes are primarily local, place-bound but 'also connected with groups of kindred spirits many miles away' (Peterson and Bennett 2004: 8). The book provides a rich array of case studies – such as those on riot grrrls, goths and anarcho-punks – to support the claim. Other than geographical/technological traits of contacts, and networks, there are also emotional properties of closeness and intimacy, and social attributes of regularity and reciprocity constitute the characteristics of the translocal.

Despite containing some of the most advanced scholarships in popular music studies of the time, *Music Scenes* appears a kind of a missed opportunity, as, in the end, the book is entirely constituted of studies on transatlantic music scenes. It is certainly not the case that translocal scenes do not exist outside the region. Eric Ma's study on the Hong Kong rap metal band LazyMuthaFucka (LMF) is a good and pioneering case in point. Ma stresses distanced connection as a crucial component of scene building in East Asia as he says, 'connectivity is also maintained and recharged by translocal tours and mediated encounters' (Ma 2002: 144).

Translocal networks cut across not only the binary of dominant West and the subaltern East but also that of the former colonizer and the former colonized. Yoshitaka Mori and Hyunjoon Shin showed this in their investigation of the 'transnational exchanges' or 'transnational flows' between Japan and Korea (Mōri 2000; Shin 2009). It should be noted here that transnational in these studies is in fact translocal as the authors did not fully differentiate two concepts at the time. Both scholars are critical of the international, in this case Japan–Korea, perspective particularly its inadequacy in dealing with popular cultural flows. For example, the exchange between Shibuya in Tokyo (Japan) and Hongdae in Seoul (Korea) since the 1990s is difficult to grasp from the international perspective as nation as a unit of analysis is too sparse to capture the dynamics of mostly informal, often under-the-radar cultural exchanges between two micro localities or places within two metropolises. In popular culture, or narrowly in popular music, this sort of translocal *and* inter-Asia cultural flows have always been in action and, thanks to the wide penetration of mobile technology in the region, almost become a norm in recent years.

The concept of translocal has not stayed still but kept evolving. Another example is Adam Kielman's recent study on the musical blending of Yunnan folk and reggae/ska in Southern China. In his research, Kielman focuses on physical mobility, the forms of connectedness, and the ways in which independent musicians and music business practitioners imagine space. In doing this, he proposes a novel definition of translocal, that is 'a capacity to belong to multiple places and a mode of existence in between places' (Kielman 2018: 9). Here, translocal becomes a capacity, which represents a marked shift from the objective movement in space to a subject-making agency.

The question of language is one that remains to be discussed. While translocal flow and exchange have gathered pace, language has been one of the main hindrances to connections, dialogues and mutual understandings. It is particularly pertinent in the region in which national languages are not only diverse but also virtually incommensurable. For this reason, English has become the closest thing to a common language despite the fact that it is still spoken by a small minority. What is more important is the culture of translocal in which English speaking has become a taken-for-granted assumption. Sender Dovchin's work on 'English as translocal language' in Mongolian popular music gives a fresh insight on this issue. She argues, the 'flows of English resources in the local context are often relocalized to make new local meanings' (Dovchin 2018: 9). While English has become increasingly hegemonic as a language of the translocal, there emerged a few contenders such as Japanese, Chinese (Mandarin) and Korean in recent years thanks largely to popular cultural flows in the region. It all points to complexities and instabilities in construction of regional culture in which the establishment of common language assumes simultaneously global and local characteristics in the form of localized English mingled with various local languages in the region.

Conclusion

After decades of hyper-exploitation, the categories of global and globalization do not seem to have anything left to offer. Indeed, it has been more than a decade since we saw a theoretical debate about globalization. While 'global' has become a ubiquitous adjective to all kinds of events, products and practices, the word has increasingly become devoid of meaning since it was associated with so many different, sometimes contradictory things. Thus, it is now difficult to tell what global popular music is, and whether it is meaningful to talk about it, particularly when any song on social network platforms has a potential to go viral on a global scale. The divide between global and local pop is progressively disappearing.

Motti Regev's book *Pop-rock Music: Aesthetic Cosmopolitanism in Late Modernity* (2013) is one of the last attempts to regenerate global and globalization in popular music studies. In this book, Regev is keen to integrate what could be considered translocal aesthetics into the notion of globalization. He is particularly interested in 'actors who aspire to participate as equals in what they perceive to be the cultural modernity' (Regev 2013: 11). These actors are the creators, producers, intermediaries and consumers of, in his words, 'ethno-national pop-rock.' Regev's arguments should produce long lasting affective resonance in readers who share the desire and aspiration of his actors. However, two points need to be made: one is that cosmopolitanism is not singular but has many different guises; and the other is that, among those guises, what Shin called 'subaltern cosmopolitanism' (Shin 2016) also has a diversity of forms.[8] By tweaking the concepts in this way, Regev's theory could provide a foundation for a richer and more insightful account of translocal pop and its cosmopolitanism.

Take Superorganism, the online-based indie pop band, for example. The band started as a recording project whose eight members were spatially dispersed across four continents. They met online and spent their early days co-creating music remotely. While seven members have united and based themselves in the UK since, one member remains living apart and joins others virtually from Sydney. This technologically enabled, place-defying, ethnically diverse band presents a model of twenty-first-century music making. Superorganism operates on multiple bases integrating various cultural elements from those localities while maintaining the established international aesthetics of ramshackle indie music. In this sense, the music of Superorganism represents neither the global nor the local. Instead, theirs is a sound of flat ontology, a product of ongoing translocal flow and exchange of ideas, affects and experiments. The substantial international following the band garnered with their music indicates this placeless music is capturing the zeitgeist.

This chapter is a substantially revised version of 'The Question of Geographic Scale in Asian Popular Music: Global, Local, Regional, and Translocal' published in 2020 in the *Korean Journal of Popular Music* 25.

Keewoong Lee acknowledges that this work was supported by the Ministry of Education of the Republic of Korea and the National Research Foundation of Korea (NRF-2018S1A6A3A01080743)

Notes

1. See Latour (1999/2014) Farías (2009).
2. Asymmetry is a key concept in Michael Fuhr's analysis of K-pop. See Fuhr (2017: 19–20).
3. In K-pop scholarship, the concepts of glocal and hybrid have often been used uncritically or to promote state agenda. One author argues that globalization is 'high quality localization that is meant to be re-exported to other countries' (Oh 2017: 160). An opposing view on hybridity is seen in Kim (2017).
4. For a 'constructivist' view on Asian regionalization that argues 'East Asian regionalism is widely acknowledged to rely on informal market institutions more than on formal political arrangements' (Katzenstein 2006: 18). Yet, we doubt that this international relations theory pays enough attention to sub-national entities.
5. Below is a list of works that applies the concept glocal or hybrid to popular music in Asia. For Japan, see Bourdaghs (2012); for Japan and Korea, see Mōri (2009); for Hong Kong, see Chow and de Kloet (2013); for Taiwan, see Moskowitz (2010); for Vietnam, see Olsen (2008).
6. About genre music, see Simon Frith (2001: 50). Yet, it should be discussed whether the classification of 'authentic' genres in Anglo-American popular music should be taken for granted.
7. For the case of the translocal scene of heavy metal, see Harris (2000) and Hecker (2010).
8. If given the opportunity, the term subaltern should be replaced by subdominant in the case of K-pop.

References

Ash., J. (2020), 'Flat Ontology and Geography', *Dialogues in Human Geography*, 10 (3): 345–61.
Baulch, E. (2008), *Making Scenes: Reggae, Punk, and Death Metal in 1990s Bali*, Durham: Duke University Press.
Berger, H. M. and Carroll, M. T., eds (2003), *Global Pop, Local Language*, Jackson: University Press of Mississippi.
Biddle, I. and Knights, V. (2007), 'National Popular Musics: Betwixt and beyond the Local and Global', in I. Biddle and V. Knights (eds), *Music, National identity and the Politics of Location: Between the Global and the Local*, 1–15, London: Routledge.
Born, G. and Hesmondhalgh, D. (2000), 'Introduction: On Difference, Representation and Appropriation in Music', in G. Born and D. Hesmondhalgh (eds), *Western Music and Its Others: Difference, Representation and Appropriation in Music*, 1–58, Berkeley and Los Angeles: University of California Press.
Bourdaghs, M. K. (2012), *Sayonara Amerika, Sayonara Nippon: A Geopolitical Prehistory of J-Pop*, New York: Columbia University Press.
Chow, Y. F. and De Kloet, J. (2013), 'Blowing in the China Wind: Engagements with Chineseness in Hong Kong's *Zhongguofeng* Music Videos', in Kwok-bun Chan (ed), *Hybrid Hong Kong*, 77–94, London and New York: Routledge, 2013.
Chu, Y. -W. (2017), *Hong Kong Cantopop: A Concise History*, Hong Kong: Hong Kong University Press.
Chua, B. H. (2001), 'Pop Culture China', *Singapore Journal of Tropical Geography*, 22 (2): 113–21.
Chua, B. H. (2012), *Structure, Audience and Soft Power in East Asian Pop Culture*, Hong Kong: Hong Kong University Press.
Chua, B. H. and Iwabuchi, K., eds (2008), *East Asian Pop Culture: Analysing the Korean Wave*, Hong Kong: Hong Kong University Press.
De Kloet, J. (2010), *China with a Cut: Globalisation, Urban Youth and Popular Music*, Amsterdam: Amsterdam University Press.
DeLanda, M. (2002), *Intensive Science and Virtual Philosophy*, London: Continuum.
Dovchin, S. (2018), *Language, Media and Globalization in the Periphery: The Linguascapes of Popular Music in Mongolia*, New York and London: Routledge.
Fairley, J. (2001), 'The "Local" and "Global" in Popular Music', in S. Frith, W. Straw, and J. Street (eds), *The Cambridge Companion to Pop and Rock*, 272–89, Cambridge: Cambridge University Press.
Farías, I. (2009), 'Interview with Nigel Thrift', in I. Farías and T. Bender (eds), *Urban Assemblages: How Actor-Network Theory Changes Urban Studies*, 109–19, London and New York: Routledge.
Featherstone, S. (2008), *Englishness: Twentieth-Century Popular Culture and the Forming of English Identity: Twentieth-Century Popular Culture and the Forming of English Identity*, Edinburgh: Edinburgh University Press.
Fermont, C. and Della Faille, D. (2016), *Not Your World Music: Noise in South East Asia – Art, Politics, Identity, Gender, and Global Capitalism*, Berlin: Hushush.
Frith, S. (1991), 'Anglo-America and Its Discontents', *Cultural Studies*, 5 (3): 263–9.
Frith, S. (2001), 'The Popular Music Industry', in S. Frith, W. Straw, and J. Street (eds), *The Cambridge Companion to Pop and Rock*, 26–52, Cambridge: Cambridge University Press.

Fuhr, M. (2017), *Globalization and Popular Music in South Korea: Sounding out K-pop*, New York and London: Routledge.

Harris, K. (2000), '"Roots?" The Relationship between the Global and the Local within the Extreme Metal Scene', *Popular Music*, 19 (1): 13–30.

Hecker, P. (2010), 'Heavy Metal in the Middle East: New Urban Spaces in a Translocal Underground', in A. Bayat and L. Herrera (eds), *Being Young and Muslim: New Cultural Politics in the Global South and North*, 325–39, Oxford: Oxford University Press.

Hesmondhalgh, D. (1998), 'Globalisation and Cultural Imperialism: A Case Study of the Music Industry', in R. Kiely and P. Marfleet (eds), *Globalisation and the Third World*, 163–84, London and New York: Routledge.

Hesmondhalgh, D. (2002), *The Cultural Industries*, London: Sage.

IFPI (2021), *IFPI Global Music Report*. 23 Mar 2021. Available online: https://www.ifpi.org/wp-content/uploads/2020/03/GMR2021_STATE_OF_THE_INDUSTRY.pdf (accessed 30 June 2021).

Iwabuchi, K. (2002), *Recentering Globalization: Popular Culture and Japanese Transnationalism*, Durham: Duke University Press.

Iwabuchi, K. (2014), 'De-Westernisation, Inter-Asian Referencing and beyond', *European Journal of Cultural Studies*, 17 (1): 44–57.

Iwabuchi, K., Muecke, S. and Thomas, M. (2004), 'Introduction: Siting Asian Cultural Flows', in K. Iwabuchi, S. Muecke and M. Thomas (eds), *Rogue Flows: Trans-Asia Cultural Traffic*, 1–9, Hong Kong: Hong Kong University Press.

Katzenstein, P. J. (2006), 'East Asia – Beyond Japan', in P. J. Katzenstein and T. Shiraishi (eds), *Beyond Japan: The Dynamics of East Asian Regionalism*, 1–33, Ithaca, NY: Cornell University Press.

Kielman, A. (2018), 'Sonic Infrastructures, Musical Circulation and Listening Practices in a Changing People's Republic of China', *Sound Studies*, 4 (1): 19–34.

Kim, G. (2017), 'Between Hybridity and Hegemony in K-Pop's Global Popularity: A Case of Girls' Generation's American Debut', *International Journal of Communication*, 11: 2367–86.

Kokot, W., Tölölyan, K. and Alfonso, C. (2004), 'Introduction', in W. Kokot, K. Tölölyan and C. Alfonso (eds), *Diaspora, Identity and Religion: New Directions in Theory and Research*, 1–9, London: Routledge.

Laing, D. (1997), 'Rock Anxieties and New Music Networks', in A. McRobbie (ed), *Back to Reality?: Social Experience and Cultural Studies*, 115–32, Manchester: Manchester University Press.

Latour, B. (1999/2014), 'On recalling ANT', *The Sociological Review*, 47 (S1): 15–25.

Ma, E. K. -W (2002), 'Translocal Spatiality', *International Journal of Cultural Studies*, 5 (2): 131–52.

Massey, D. (1994), *Space, Place, and Gender*, Minneapolis: University of Minnesota Press.

McKay, G. (2013), *Shakin' All Over: Popular Music and Disability*, Ann Arbor: University of Michigan Press.

Mitchell, T. (1996), *Popular Music and Local Identity: Rock, Pop, and Rap in Europe and Oceania*, London: Leicester University Press.

Mitchell, T., eds (2001), 'Introduction: Another Root: hip-hop outside the USA', in T. Mitchell (ed), *Global Noise: Rap and hip-hop Outside the USA*, 1–38, Middleton, CT: Wesleyan University Press.

Mōri, Y. (2000), 'Reconsidering Hybridity: Transnational Exchanges of Popular Music in-between Korea and Japan', in C. Berry, N. Liscutin and J. D. Mackintosh (eds), *Cultural Studies and Cultural Industries in Northeast Asia: What a Difference a Region Makes*, 213–30, Hong Kong: Hong Kong University Press.

Morra, I. (2013), *Popular Music, and National Identity: The Making of Modern Britain*, London: Routledge.

Moskowitz, M. L. (2010), *Cries of Joy, Songs of Sorrow: Chinese Pop Music and Its Cultural Connotations*, Honolulu: University of Hawaii Press.

Negus, K. (1996), 'Globalization and the Music of the Public Spheres', in A. Gebesmair and A. Smudits (eds), *Globalization, Communication and Transnational Civil Society*, 179–96, Cresskill, NJ: Hampton Press.

Negus, K. (1999), *Music Genres and Corporate Cultures*, London: Routledge.

Nguyen, D. H. P. (2016), 'Korean Wave as Cultural Imperialism: A Study of K-pop Reception in Vietnam', master thesis, Leiden University.

Oh, I. (2017), 'From Localization to Glocalization: Contriving Korean Pop Culture to Meet Glocal Demands', *Kritika Kultura*, 29: 157–67.

Olsen, D. A. (2008), *Popular Music of Vietnam: The Politics of Remembering, The Economics of Forgetting*, New York: Routledge.

Peterson, R.A. and Bennett, A. (2004), 'Introducing Music Scenes', in A. Bennett and R. A. Peterson (eds), *Music Scenes: Local, Translocal, and Virtual*, Nashville: Vanderbilt University Press.

Pieterse, J. N. (1995), 'Globalization as Hybridization', in M. Featherstone, R. Robertson and S. Lash (eds), *Global Modernities*, 45–68, London: Sage.

Regev, M. (2007a), 'Cultural Uniqueness and Aesthetic Cosmopolitanism', *European Journal of Social Theory*, 10 (1): 123–38.

Regev, M. (2007b), 'Ethno-National Pop-Rock Music: Aesthetic Cosmopolitanism Made from Within', *Cultural Sociology*, 1 (3): 317–41.

Regev, M. (2013), *Pop-Rock Music: Aesthetic Cosmopolitanism in Late Modernity*, Cambridge: Polity Press.

Robertson, R. (1995), 'Glocalization: Time-Space and Homogeneity-Heterogeneity', in M. Featherstone, R. Robertson and S. Lash (eds), *Global Modernities*, 25–44, London: Sage.

Shin, H. (2009), 'Reconsidering Transnational Cultural Flows of Popular Music in East Asia: Transbordering Musicians in Japan and Korea Searching for "Asia"', *Korean Studies*, 33: 101–23.

Shin, H. (2016), 'K-pop, the Sound of Subaltern Cosmopolitanism?', in K. Iwabuchi and E. Tsai (eds), *Routledge Handbook of East Asian Popular Culture*, London and New York: Routledge.

Shuker, R. (1998), *Key Concepts in Popular Music*, London: Routledge.

Taylor, T. D. (1997), *Global Pop: World Music, World Markets*, New York and London: Routledge.

Toynbee, J. (2002), 'Mainstreaming, from Hegemonic Centre to Global Networks', in D. Hesmondhalgh and K. Negus (eds), *Popular Music Studies*, 149–63, Oxford: Oxford University Press.

Tsing, A. (2000), 'The Global Situation', *Cultural Anthropology*, 15 (3): 327–60.

Tunstall, J. (1977), *The Media Are American*, New York: Columbia University Press.

Wald, E. (2006), *Global Minstrel: Voices of World Music*, New York and London: Routledge.

Wee, C. W. -L. (2021), 'East Asian Pop Music and an Incomplete Regional Contemporary', in M. Bourdaghs, P. Iovene and K. Mason (eds), *Sound Alignments: Popular Music in Asia's Cold Wars*, 93–127, Durham: Duke University Press.

4
Sociological perspectives on music and place

Andy Bennett

Sociological interest in music's relationship to place essentially began to develop from the 1950s onwards, a period when music's significance as a mediated form and connections between, music, fashion, visual appearance and other forms of cultural consumerism became increasingly visible across the industrialized world. Research in the fields of sociology and, more recently, cultural sociology has offered rich accounts of music's spatial qualities that range from the mapping of connections between music and place as distinctly local, and often characterized by distinctive scenes or 'subcultures', to identifying trans-local links between clusters of musicians, music industry workers and audiences. More recently, sociologists have also considered the significance of cultural memory in the narrativization of music and place. A vivid example of memory's role in this respect is seen in stories of musical origin and the evolution of place-based sounds. Such stories are often grounded in a vernacular context and evolve through the prism of collective belief that places 'own' music by dint of the fact that a particular sound, or even a whole genre of music, appeared to grow in a particular place at a particular time. The purpose of this chapter is to consider the contributions that sociological research in the field of music has made to the understanding of music's connections to and interaction with place in contemporary social settings. The chapter begins by offering some general reflections on the conceptualization of place as a social construct, an interpretation that has informed much of the sociological research subsequently discussed in the chapter. This is followed by a consideration of how sociologists have used particular conceptual tools, such as scene and subculture, in understanding connections between music and place. As will be illustrated, such research has gradually broadened from a focus on specific local examples of scenes and subcultures to consider trans-local and global connections. The chapter then turns to a consideration of the importance of the complex relationship between macro/public and micro/private dimensions of place as these have been analysed in relation to musical affect. Finally the chapter looks at more recent sociological work on music, memory and place.

Place as a 'social' construct

The concept of place as a social construct acquired critical currency through the work of cultural geographers, such as Doreen Massey (1993) and Michael Keith and Steven Pile (1993). Key to the work of these theorists was the notion of place as subject to appropriation and (re)narrativization by different social groups with differing and often-conflicting interests. Through such a conceptual lens, the meaning of place in its fixed, physical sense gave way to a more complex array of what Keith and Pile referred to as 'spatialisations', whereby the concept of space is recast as a series of ideologically framed discourses that inform practices whereby individuals collectively understand and situate themselves within particular spaces and places, essentially claiming them in the process. Such perspectives contributed to a significant rethinking of space and place as entities that transcended physical, geographic definitions to encompass culturally encoded meanings. Such work has fundamentally shifted the way that space and place, particularly, though not exclusively, in urban settings is now conceptualized and understood. Such interpretations of space, however, are not without precedent in earlier eras of social theory. Indeed, during the late nineteenth-century German sociologist Georg Simmel (1957) observed how urban spaces were giving rise to new forms of lifestyle based on patterns of leisure and consumption that manifested through forms of fashion and other aspects of external appearance. These aspects of Simmel's work were extended in the writings of Weber (1919/1978) and Veblen (1994 [1924]) whose respective coining of the terms 'leisure classes' and 'status groups' further consolidated the sociological understanding of space and place as dialectically connected with emergent and evolving forms of social life in urban settings. Following the Second World War, when consumption and leisure became more commonplace across the social strata, a generation of theorists also begun to contemplate what Stahl (1999) terms the 'winning of space' in a body of work that would serve as an important foundation for sociological studies of music, space and place. Thus, during the late 1960s and early 1970s British subcultural researchers embarked on a form of what could be referred to as proto-spatialization study of post-war British cityscapes. through work that mapped a connection between post-war 'spectacular' subcultures, such as Teddy Boys and Skinheads, and an identification with territory or turf. In their reading of this connection, subcultural theorists varied in their interpretation of motive for youth subcultural appropriations of space and place, this ranging from the perceived need to defend traditional working-class communities from 'invasion' by newly arrived immigrants from the Caribbean and Indian subcontinent (Jefferson 1976) to a desire to *magically recover* a sense of working-class community as families were relocated from old housing stock to new post-war housing estates during the late 1960s and early 1970s (Cohen 1972). At this point, spatialization was read in terms of the symbolic appropriation of space and place according to the norms and values of a specific group, in this particular case, stylistically demarcated white, working-class (sub)cultures whose homological redefinition of space served largely as an exclusionary tactic. As work on spatialization developed and as urban societies became more culturally diverse, understandings of space was symbolically appropriated likewise became more sophisticated. Thus, it came to be acknowledged that to speak in terms of space and associated descriptors such as neighbourhood and locality invariably led to considerations of how the latter had grown over time to transcend aspects of class and traditional community to embrace a broader range of inhabitants, included transient inhabitants who temporarily accessed a place for specific purposes. This in turn led to a recasting of space as possessing not one but a range of different culturally constructed meanings, often distinct from one another, but in other cases overlapping or conflicting to create what Bennett defines as multiple narratives of the local. Thus he observes:

> [I]n referring to the 'local' we are in effect speaking about a place that is crossed by a variety of different collectives each of which imposes a different set of expectations and cultural needs upon that place. In doing so, such sensibilities also construct the local in particular ways, a process which ensures that that terms such as locality and local identity are always, in part at least, subjective elements, which begin by utilising the same basic knowledges about the local, its social and spatial organisation, but supplement such knowledges with their own collectively held values to create particular narratives of locality.
>
> (2000: 66)

The foregoing description accurately describes contemporary cities and cityscapes in a global context, the physical contours of the latter being overlaid with frequently intangible, yet intimately understood discourses that serve as mattering maps (Grossberg 1992) for individuals in the course of their everyday lives. The conflict and contestation that is frequently embedded in such multiple narratives of locality manifest in a variety of ways, including through aspects of musical taste and associated stylistic forms from clothing, through to street art and dance. An obvious example of this is hip hop culture which, as Rose (1994) comprehensively illustrates, from its origins in the inner-city United States to its evolution as a global phenomenon is inherently tied to collective appropriations of space and place. Such appropriations are both sonic and visual, the early desire to sonically populate the street setting with rap music having given rise to the DIY innovation of the early 'boombox' (Schloss and Bahng Boyer 2014), the latter facilitating a musical backdrop for other spatially focused forms of hip hop cultural practice, notably breakdancing (Rajakumar 2012) and graffiti (MacDonald 2001). The socially constructed nature of place is also evident through other forms of cultural practice of which music is a central focus. For example, 'postering' (illegally affixing posters for gigs, DJ nights and festivals to walls and the sides of buildings) has become a major source of contention resulting in both legal sanctions against those involved in the act and sparking turf wars between rival poster gangs. Here one sees a clear example of how multiple narratives of the local produce conflicting understandings of space, both between the police and the courts, who attempt to impose their authority over poster gangs, and between the gangs themselves for whom the battle for space is tied to self-ascribed notions of legitimate access to and use of space brokered on understandings of gang loyalty and livelihood.

Subcultures and scenes

In engaging with the connections between music, space and place there have been various attempts to theorize this. Two prominent conceptual models that are still in common use in social and cultural research are 'subculture' and 'scene'. Subculture assumed critical status during the 1970s as theorists at the Birmingham University-based Centre for Contemporary Cultural Studies (CCCS) applied it in studies of post-war working-class youth style and argo. As noted above, although the findings of this work constitute an early form of spatialization, the fact of space and place was largely used as a backdrop through which to situate the posturing and turf wars of stylistically unified youth gangs. In essence, the bomb-damaged, crumbling working-class neighbourhoods and new, yet soulless, housing estates, served as stages for the ongoing theatre of class struggle. With its quasi-empirical grounding in physical communities and neighbourhoods, during the 1970s subculture quickly gained momentum as a basis for conceptually articulating the cultural connectedness of music and fashion and its visible traces on the bodies of youth in the 'spectacular appropriation' of space and place (Hebdige 1979). And yet, in terms of its actual capturing of the spatial affects of youth belonging, subcultural theory also amounts in many ways to a series of missed opportunities. Unlike the Chicago School research on youth gangs and turf wars during the 1920s and 1930s, which formed a key inspiration for the CCCS work, there is no deep immersion in the physical spaces where the everyday dramas of youth subcultures unfold. Rather these spaces, like the subcultural actors who populate them, tend to 'flit across the screen' (Cohen 1987) in the CCCS literature. That said, purely through what was absent in this body of work, the CCCS importantly laid the groundwork for the deeper investigations that followed, while studies related to but not directly associated with the CCCS such as Paul Willis's (1978) *Profane Culture* and Iain Chambers's (1985) *Urban Rhythms* firmly pointed out the potential for a new body of work that engaged more intimately with the space and place and their bearing on the cultural landscapes of youth, and increasingly, post-youth. By dint of criticisms highlighting the metro-centric (Clarke 1990), UK bias (Brake 1985) of CCCS subcultural theory, it was also clear that future research would need to acknowledge that not all cities were equal in terms of the spaces and places they afforded for the growing of musical and associated cultural practices. Similarly, these critical studies also highlighted the fact that popular music and popular culture may have originated from metropolitan centres, their global development ranged across peri-urban and regional settings too.

It was with the emergence of music scenes scholarship, as the first of a series of what could be termed 'post-subcultural' perspectives on music and related cultural practices (see Bennett 2011), that a deeper engagement with the significance of space and place began to develop. Although Straw (1991) produced the first comprehensive theorization of scene as a conceptual device for the study of music, in vernacular sense scene had been in dominant used as a means of describing clusters of musicians, producers, promoters and audiences for a number of years prior (see Peterson and Bennett 2004). Indeed, such an understanding of scene was also implicit in some early sociological work on music, specifically Becker's (1951) celebrated study of jazz musicians. For Becker, the jazz musician's considered superiority to the jazz square (i.e. the average fan of jazz) turned on their deep absorption in and understanding of the music when compared to the square whose 'liking' of jazz was presaged around other activities, such as dating and dancing. Becker's opening up of debates concerning musical taste and 'status' through the prism of what he refers to as jazz spaces was in many respects a precursor to the emergence of scene theory several decades later. Becker's other critical insight, that music scenes were in effect eco-systems that clustered individuals – including musicians, promoters, writers, and of course audiences – in specific spaces at specific times of the day, was also an important precursor to the music scene studies that would emerge later in the twentieth century. In this sense, Straw's (1991) aforementioned essay on the scenes concept remains a critical cornerstone, shedding light on the highly complex dynamics at play between music, space and individual agency. Indeed, among other things Straw can be credited with drawing attention for the first time to the significance of music scenes as microcosms; scene spaces serving to nodal points for individuals who share common tastes in music and read off musical texts in complementary ways to foster collective bonds that relate as much, of not more, to their identities as fans of a particular genre, or genres, of music as to aspects of socio-economic background. According to Straw, although scenes are often organized around a bricks and mortar venue, or a series of venues within a particular part of a city, at the same time scene memberships frequently transcend particular localities 'reflect[ing] and actualiz[ing] a particular state of relations between various populations and social groups, as these coalesce around particular coalitions of musical style' (1991: 379).

Straw's original concept of scene has been subsequently modified by Peterson and Bennett (2004) who have added two further scene categorizations – 'trans-local' and 'virtual'. While each of these categorizations departs from the understanding of a music scene as an entity defined by and limited to a particular locality, both trans-local and virtual scenes continue to embody the local as a point of reference. Thus, trans-local scenes are connected by flows of musicians, DJs, fans and other scene identifiers who move between different local scenes. As Laing (1997) observes, such trans-local connections have become a defining feature of electronic dance music scenes while Kahn-Harris (2006) identifies similar trans-local connections among metal scenes around the world. Virtual scenes, while they rely on internet technology, also serve to connect fans from different local scenes and may also be anchored through a point of reference grounded in physical space. Such is the case of the Canterbury Sound (see Bennett 2002, 2004) a virtual scene that originated during the mid-1990s as a space for fans of Canterbury Sound bands including Soft Machine, Caravan and Gong who had been popular during the late 1960s and early 1970s English progressive scene and strong associations with the Cathedral City of Canterbury in the South East of England. In a later study, Bennett et al. (2008) revisit the concept of scene, noting that rather than existing as individual entities, local, trans-local and virtual scenes may often overlap and encompass elements of each other. Indeed, among Canterbury Scene fans, the virtual is used as a means of connecting trans-locally connected fans whose focus for discussing the significance of the Canterbury Sound is its groundedness in the physical spaces of the city of Canterbury. As Bennett notes:

> In the case of the Canterbury Sound, the internet and its various resources have performed a critical role in essentially 'backfilling' the history and, equally importantly, the spatio-cultural narrative of the Canterbury Sound to the extent that its phenomenological absence from the city is slowly but surely airbrushed from the collective memory of Canterburyism.
>
> (2021: 19)

Public and private space

Sociological research has also contributed significantly to understandings of how music's spatialization properties extend across both public and private space. Although acknowledgement of music's significance in defining the meaning of public–private space intersections pre-dates the digital era (see, for example, McRobbie and Garber 1976; Hosokawa 1984) the advent of digital media technology during the 1990s and its increasing sophistication in the early twenty-first century has provided significant new opportunities for the musicalized intersection of public and private space. Bull's (2005) work on the iPod, a popular mobile digital music sound carrier and playback device and successor to the walkman cassette player (see Bull 2000), examines how listeners are able to create their own personalized soundscapes as they move through public spaces. As Bull notes, iPod technology, due to its high storage capacity and playlist function, affords the listener a significant degree of choice in choosing music to suit a range of activities, from commuting, exercising or relaxing on a beach. In each case the phenomenological experience of the listener is self-modified through a soundtrack of their own creation. They are, in effect, simultaneously in both a public and private space, the latter being shaped by the private listening experience. Bird, in a study of flash mobs in Melbourne, Australia, illustrates how the public–private experience of iPod listening can be fashioned towards a subversive purpose. Thus she observes, flash mobs armed with iPods playing the same track congregate on pedestrian crossings when the lights are at red, dancing to a private, shared soundtrack inaccessible to onlookers. As such, the private soundscape made public through the flash mob performance disrupts and challenges the regulated terrain of everyday live. According to Bird:

> Playful performances such as flash mobs encourage onlookers and participants to question the rigidness of laws and norms that govern street behaviour… however, unlike the participants in a protest, the flash mob does not seek to provide answers of solutions… They merely throw out a possibility of change.
>
> (2014: 227)

A further insightful study of how the private and public musical soundscapes are linked through digital technology is Lincoln's (2012) study of teenage bedroom culture. Lincoln's work draws on an earlier study by McRobbie and Garber (1976) who conceptualized the bedroom of the teenage female teenybopper fan as a safe-space, within the family home and away from the male-dominated, street-based youth cultures, where young working-class girls could exchange fan magazines and posters and listen to music (on the radio or recorded from the radio or television on the then popular cassette recorder). Lincoln's work considers how digital technology has served to augment the closed, private space of the teen bedroom, creating in the process a portal between the private and the public as teens connect with others online, share music and information about parties and club events. According to Lincoln, a connection and continuity evolves between the bedroom (private) and party/club (public) as the former becomes a place in which to prepare for and anticipate the latter.

In early 2020, the emergence and rapid spread of the COVID-19 virus led to the world facing its first global pandemic in over a hundred years. As governments around the world sought ways of containing the spread of the virus, lockdowns and social distancing were imposed in many countries. This involved a banning of public gatherings, including sporting and live music/club events (van Leeuwen 2020). Amidst the deepening crisis and uncertainty about the future of live and recorded music events in public spaces, music artists, club and festival organizers resorted to online streaming of gigs and events (Howard et al. 2021). Although this was not the first time that music artists had streamed live concerts (Frenneaux and Bennett 2021) or that terms such as the 'virtual club' had been used (see Armour 2018) the use of such concepts as a means of addressing a global ban on the use of public space for music events was novel and challenging. While mainstream artists such as Neil Diamond adopted a streamed fire side performance format, the lyrics of his 1969 hit 'Sweet Caroline' being changed from 'touching hands' to 'washing hands' to suit the new health directives prompted by the pandemic (Lehman 2020) other artists and their audiences struggled with the forced switch to an online experience. Research conducted by the author and colleagues from Griffith University on young music-makers in Australia, one participant noted:

> It's kind of hard to have that social engagement through online comments and forum type thing from the show. It wasn't quite what, I don't know what we were really expecting, but there wasn't a huge amount of social interaction with us. But that's because we weren't playing a show and then talking to people. (John, 30, musician)[1]

The emergence of the pandemic has had major, and hard-hitting effects on the social life and well-being of communities throughout the world. In the specific context of a discussion about music and place, it demonstrates how even as digital technologies offer new ways for people to experience music, in both public and private spaces, the two domains of spatialized experience remain inextricably bound up. A telling reminder of this is found in a study by Green (2015) of peak music experiences. As Green notes, this feature of music consumption and the memories it generates can extend across both live and recorded music. However, even in the case of the latter, observes Green people will invariably flag memories of peak music experiences being generated through moments of collectivity, such as hearing a classic album for the first time at a party, or hearing a classic track on a car radio during a road trip. Similarly, Bennett (2013) notes in his discussion of affective music scenes, that is, scenes of individuals who no longer, or rarely, attend live shows (but remain emotionally attached through their memory of doing so), it is the collective experience of music in public spaces that inform their sense of connection to others through shared musical tastes.

Cultural memory and emotional geographies

Spatializations involving music have, until quite recently, been cast as something with tangible qualities, that is, something experienced in the present. However, as Green's (2015) aforementioned study illustrates, there is an increasing acknowledgement in sociological studies of music, place and affect that the past may also act as a frame of reference, not to say anchoring point, for how individuals envisaged music's significance as a place marker. Neoliberal economics have, since the latter years of the twentieth century changed the face of many cities. Old cultural quarters have been demolished and re-designated for business and/or private dwellings, while live music entertainment, such as it continues to exist as part of available urban leisure, has been corralled into designated night-time economy precincts (Burke and Schmidt 2013) that are heavily regulated and, in many cases undesirable and/or unsafe for individuals identifying with alternative and fringe cultural groups (Carah et al. 2020). Despite such patterns of change and renewal in the physical attributes of cities, emotional attachment remains to spaces and places that no longer exist in a tangible sense. Indeed, it is apparent from emerging research on music and cultural memory that much of what has been resigned to the past – demolished or repurposed buildings that once housed music venues, night clubs and record stores – continue to resonate as important local landmarks in the emotional geographies of those who remember them. According to Bondi and colleagues, emotional geography is defined by a 'concern with the spatiality and temporality of emotions, with the way they coalesce around and within certain places. Indeed, much of the symbolic importance of these places stems from their emotional associations, the feelings they inspire' (2007: 3). Although Bondi and colleagues focus on the significance of emotional geography as a means through which we can understand individuals' inscription of emotional meaning in the present, it follows that such an inscription may remain even as the place changes. At that point, the memory of the place as meaningful to the individual or group, assumes central importance as a means of preserving meaning invested in a place. Feldman-Barrett's (2017) study of Medusa's nightclub in the US city of Chicago is a pertinent case in point. The club has been defunct for a number of years but the building where the club was situated, on Sheffield Avenue, remains, serving as both a nostalgic landmark and an anchoring point for the memories of many former patrons for whom Medusa's was an iconic space for alternative music and culture during the 1980s and 1990s. Indeed, even in cases where the buildings that housed venues or other important spaces for music scenes have been demolished, thus removing all physical trace of their former presence, memories continue to resonate with such spaces such that emotional cartographies are created. An interesting example of this is seen on Australia's Gold Coast where, as Green and Bennett observe:

> [W]hile current debates focus on the lack of infrastructure to encourage a thriving local music scene, in a more retrospective sense a clear understanding exists among local musicians of the Gold Coast as a space that is particularly rich in cultural memory as far as live music is concerned.
>
> (2019: 22)

This cultural memory is frequently anchored in the personal experience of former venues such as Take Five, El Rancho, the Red Orb and the Summit, all of which were demolished and replaced with new buildings. Even for those too young to have such physical memories of the 'glory decades' of the Gold Coast music scene's past, acquired memories from older peers, parents and siblings work to a similar effect in assuring the tenacity of emotional narrative as a way through which people understand the space they live in as a musicalized space. Where a venue once stood is for many as important as where venues on the Gold Coast are located today. Like Liverpool's Cavern Club – a place demolished in the early 1970s but permanently ingrained in the minds of many (to the extent that it was later re-established in a different location, albeit at a ninety degree angle to the original Cavern[2]) – former Gold Coast venues such as the Jet Club and the Playroom continue to figure large in the way musicians and audiences continue to think of the Gold Coast and map the local music scene.

The foregoing example cogently illustrates the importance of emotional affect in the collective production of music scenes. In being part of a scene, individuals can construct their 'beingness' with reference to such patterns of affect and their connectedness with the nuances of space and place. Indeed, as contemporary work on scene histories is beginning to show, aspects of memory and emotion are also becoming key to the longevity of particular scenes as the discourses of preservation that are employed by scene members. Two examples of this are seen in Nicola Smith's (2012) work on Northern Soul and Zoe Armour's (2018) work on dance music clubs in the English midlands. In both cases, discourses of scene identity and belonging are critically narrated around discourses of what these scenes have achieved in the past – a cluster of largely unwritten, and often unwritable histories, that invariably rely on a word of mouth passing down among and between those who remember and who choose to share their memories with some, but not others. How these two scenes manifest in the present is very much based on shared memories of the past and the deeper emotive links to these scenes thus created.

Conclusion

This chapter has focused on mapping the connections between music and place as these have been conceptualized in the work of sociologists, cultural sociologists and researchers working in adjacent fields. The chapter began by considering the concept of space as a social construct and the significance of music as a cultural resource through which spaces and places are inscribed with meaning. Following this, a series of key areas were focused on, each having a particular bearing on how social and cultural researchers have considered music's significance in processes of spatialization. This began with a consideration of subcultures and scenes, concepts that have engaged with the musicalized appropriation of space, subcultures assuming a class-based, neighbourhood-focused approach while scenes assumes a more subcultural, cross-class and trans-local focus. The following section of the chapter considered the relation between public and private forms of musicalized spatialization, with a specific focus on how the intersection between the public and private is managed via the use of digital media. The final section of the chapter examines the value of cultural memory and emotional geography as more recent concepts in social and cultural research on music and space that have offered new perspectives on how defunct or demolished spaces and places of musical significance are remembered and inscribed with meaning even as they continue to exist in memory only.

Notes

1 This project, entitled, 'Youth, Music-Making and Well-Being During a Public Health Crisis' was conducted by the author along with Ernesta Sofija (School of Medicine and Dentistry – Public Health, Griffith University) and Ben Green (Griffith Social and Cultural Research, Griffith University). The project was funded by the Griffith Centre for Social and Cultural Research and was granted ethical clearance (Ref. no. 2020/359).
2 This repositioning of the new Cavern has resulted in changes to the original spatial flow of the original Cavern club, for example the fire exit for the new venue is positioned where the main exit of the original venue was located.

References

Armour, Z. (2018), 'Dedicated Followers of PaSSion (1995 – Present): Seasoned Clubbers and the Mediation of Collective Memory as a Process of Digital Gift Giving', in A. Hardy, A. Bennett and B. Robards (eds), *Neo-Tribes: Consumption, Leisure and Tourism*, 137–52, Basingstoke: Palgrave Macmillan.

Becker, H.S. (1951), 'The Professional Jazz Musician and His Audience', *American Journal of Sociology*, 57 (2): 136–44.

Bennett, A. (2000), *Popular Music and Youth Culture: Music, Identity and Place*, Basingstoke: Palgrave Macmillan.

Bennett, A. (2002), 'Music, Media and Urban Mythscapes: A Study of the Canterbury Sound', *Media, Culture and Society*, 24 (1): 107–20.

Bennett, A. (2004), 'New Tales from Canterbury: The Making of a Virtual Music Scene', in A. Bennett, and R.A. Peterson (eds), *Music Scenes: Local, Trans-Local and Virtual*, 205–20, Nashville, TN: Vanderbilt University Press.

Bennett, A. (2011), 'The Post-subcultural Turn: Some Reflections Ten Years on', *Journal of Youth Studies*, 14 (5): 493–506.

Bennett, A. (2013), *Music, Style and Aging: Growing Old Disgracefully?* Philadelphia: Temple University Press.

Bennett, A. (2021), 'The Canterbury Sound as a Local, Trans-local and Virtual Scene', in A. Draganova, S. Blackman and A. Bennett (eds), *The Canterbury Sound in Popular Music: Scene, Identity and Myth*, 13–22, Oxford: Emerald.

Bennett, A., Stratton, J. and Peterson, R.A. (2008), 'The Scenes Perspective and the Australian Context', *Continuum: Journal of Media and Cultural Studies*, 22 (5): 593–9.

Bird, S. (2014), 'Flash Mobs and Zombie Shuffles: Play in the Augmented City', in A. Bennett and B. Robards (eds), *Mediated Youth Cultures: The Internet, Belonging and New Cultural Configurations*, 213–31, Basingstoke: Palgrave Macmillan.

Bondi, L., Davidson, J. and Smith, M. (2007), 'Introduction: Geography's "Emotional Turn"', in J. Davidson, L. Bondi and M. Smith (eds), *Emotional Geographies*, 1–18, Aldershot: Ashgate.

Brake, M. (1985), *Comparative Youth Culture: The Sociology of Youth Cultures and Youth Subcultures in America, Britain and Canada*, London: Routledge and Kegan Paul.

Bull, M. (2000), *Sounding Out the City: Personal Stereos and the Management of Everyday Life*, Oxford: Berg.

Bull, M. (2005), 'No Dead Air! The iPod and the Culture of Mobile Listening', *Leisure Studies*, 24 (4): 343–55.

Burke, M. and Schmidt, A. (2013), 'How Should We Plan and Regulate Live Music in Australian Cities? Learnings from Brisbane', *Australian Planner*, 50 (1): 68–78.

Carah, N., Regan, S., Goold, L., Rangiah, L., Miller, P. and Ferris, J. (2020), 'Original Live Music Venues in Hyper-Commercialised Nightlife Precincts: Exploring How Venue Owners and Managers Navigate Cultural, Commercial and Regulatory Forces', *International Journal of Cultural Policy*, 621–35.

Chambers, I. (1985), *Urban Rhythms: Pop Music and Popular Culture*, London: Macmillan.

Clarke, G. (1990), 'Defending Ski-Jumpers: A Critique of Theories of Youth Subcultures', in S. Frith and A. Goodwin (eds), *On Record: Rock, Pop and the Written Word*, 68–80, London: Routledge.

Cohen, P. (1972), *Subcultural Conflict and Working Class Community*, Working Papers in Cultural Studies 2. Birmingham: University of Birmingham.

Cohen, S. (1987), *Folk Devils and Moral Panics: The Creation of the Mods and Rockers*, 3rd edn., Oxford: Basil Blackwell.

Feldman-Barrett, C. (2017), 'Medusa's on Sheffield, 1983 – 1992: Chicago's Alternative All-Ages Nightclub in History and Memory', *Popular Music and Society*, 41 (3): 319–38.

Frenneaux, R. and Bennett, A. (2021), 'A New Paradigm of Engagement for the Socially Distanced Artist', *Rock Music Studies*, 8(1): 66–75.

Green, B. and Bennett, A. (2019), 'Gateways and Corridors: Spatial Challenges and Opportunities for Live Music on the Gold Coast', *City, Culture and Society*, 17: 20–5.

Grossberg, L. (1992), *We Gotta Get Out of This Place: Popular Conservatism and Postmodern Culture*, London: Routledge.

Hebdige, D. (1979), *Subculture: The Meaning of Style*, London: Routledge.

Hosokawa, S. (1984), 'The Walkman Effect', *Popular Music*, 4 (4): 165–80.

Howard, F., Bennett, A., Green, B., Guerra, P., Sousa, S. and Sofija, E. (2021), '"It's Turned Me from a Professional to a "bedroom DJ" Once Again": COVID-19 and New Forms of Inequality for Young Music-makers', *Young: Nordic Journal of Youth Research*. DOI: 10.1177/1103308821998542.

Green, B. (2015), '"I Always Remember That Moment": Peak Music Experiences as Epiphanies', *Sociology*, 50 (2): 333–48.

Jefferson, T. (1976), 'Cultural Responses of the Teds: The Defence of Space and Status', in S. Hall and T. Jefferson (eds), *Resistance through Rituals: Youth Subcultures in Post-War Britain*, 81–6, London: Hutchinson.

Kahn-Harris, K. (2006), *Extreme Metal: Music and Culture on the Edge*, Oxford: Berg.

Keith, M. and Pile, S. (1993), 'Introduction Part 1 The Politics of Place…', in M. Keith and S. Pile (eds), *Place and the Politics of Identity*, 1–21, London: Routledge.

Laing, D. (1997), 'Rock Anxieties and New Music Networks', in A. McRobbie (ed.), *Back to Reality: Social Experience and Cultural Studies*, 116–32, Manchester: Manchester University Press.

Lehman, E.T. (2020), '"Washing Hands, Reaching Out" – Popular Music, Digital Leisure and Touch during the COVID-19 Pandemic', *Leisure Sciences*, 43 (1–2): 273–9.

Lincoln, S. (2012), *Youth Culture and Private Space*, Basingstoke: Palgrave Macmillan.

MacDonald, N. (2001), *The Graffiti Subculture: Youth, Masculinity and Identity in London and New York*, New York: Palgrave Macmillan.

Massey, D. (1993), 'Power-Geometry and a Progressive Sense of Place', in J. Bird, B. Curtis, T. Putnam, G. Robertson, and L. Tickner (eds), *Mapping the Futures: Local Cultures, Global Change*, 59–69, London: Routledge.

McRobbie, A. and Garber, J. (1976), 'Girls and Subcultures: An Exploration', in S. Hall and T. Jefferson (eds), *Resistance through Rituals: Youth Subcultures in Post-War Britain*, 209–22, London: Hutchinson.

Peterson, R.A. and Bennett, A., eds (2004), 'Introducing Music Scenes', in A. Bennett, and R.A. Peterson (eds), *Music Scenes: Local, Trans-local and Virtual*, 1–15, Nashville: TN. Vanderbilt University Press.

Rajakumar, M. (2012), *Hip Hop Dance*, Santa Barbara, CA: Greenwood.

Rose, T. (1994), *Black Noise: Rap Music and Black Culture in Contemporary America*, London: Wesleyan University Press.

Schloss, J. and Bahng B. B. (2014), 'Urban Echoes: The Boombox and Sonic Mobility in the 1980s', in S. Gopinath and J. Stanyek (eds), *The Oxford Handbook of Mobile Music Studies Volume 1*, 399–414. Oxford: Oxford University Press.

Simmel, G. (1957), 'Fashion', *American Journal of Sociology*, 62 (6): 541–58.

Smith, N. (2012), 'Parenthood and the Transfer of Capital in the Northern Soul Scene', in A. Bennett and P. Hodkinson (eds), *Ageing and Youth Cultures: Music, Style and Identity*, 159–72, London: Berg.

Stahl, G. (1999), '"Still Winning Space?" Updating Subcultural Theory', *Invisible Culture: An Electronic Journal for Visual Studies*, 2.

Straw, W. (1991), 'Systems of Articulation, Logics of Change: Communities and Scenes in Popular Music', *Cultural Studies*, 5 (3): 368–88.

Veblen, T. (1994 [1924]), *The Theory of the Leisure Class: An Economic Study of Institutions*, New York: Mentor Books.

Weber, M. (1919/1978), 'The Distribution of Power within the Political Community: Class, Status, Party', in G. Roth and C. Wittich (eds), *Economy and Society: An Outline of Interpretive Sociology*, 926–38, Berkeley, CA: University of California Press.

Willis, P. (1978), *Profane Culture*, London: Routledge and Kegan Paul.

van Leeuwen, M., Klerks, Y., Bargeman, B., Heslinga, J. and Bastiaansen, M. (2020), 'Leisure Will Not Be Locked Down – Insights on Leisure and COVID-19 from the Netherlands', *World Leisure Journal*, 62 (4): 339–43.

5
Ethnomusicology and place

Kimberly Cannady

This chapter explores ethnomusicology and its contributions to research on popular music and place. Ethnomusicology as a distinct discipline emerged in the mid-twentieth century with roots in related fields, such as comparative musicology, historical musicology, folklore studies, ethnology and anthropology. Defining ethnomusicology is notoriously tricky, and scholars have dedicated a large amount of writing to discussing the field and meanings of the term 'ethnomusicology' itself (Nettl 2010: xv).[1] For the purposes of this chapter, my own attempt to define ethnomusicology will only go so far as to say that today, in the early twenty-first century, ethnomusicologists work all over the world on nearly every conceivable type of music and draw from a wide variety of intellectual and cultural traditions. Tim Rice, an American ethnomusicologist who has written extensively on music in Bulgaria and the field of ethnomusicology, argued that '[e]thnomusicology has developed as an omnivorous intellectual arena for asking nearly every conceivable question about music' (Rice 2003: 151). Thus, it is not the genre or style of music, or the location, or even the time period of music under investigation that distinguishes ethnomusicological research from other related disciplines, but the methodological and theoretical approaches taken by scholars, as well as their engagement with the intellectual legacies of the field.

My focus here is primarily on English-language scholarship, although this is a practical decision rather than a value-judgement. One of the hallmarks of ethnomusicological research, including research on popular music, is the priority often placed on engaging with local-language scholarship. In my own area of research in the Nordic region, where scholars tend to have a strong command of English in addition to their native language(s), many choose to publish research in both English-language contexts and in Nordic-language contexts. In addition to being able to engage with local scholarship, fluency in local languages is often vital for understanding lyrics, press articles, and for engaging directly with the artists and related parties themselves. While outside the scope of this volume, there is a growing interest in translating academic research in ethnomusicology into and out of English to broaden our collective understandings and potential for truly international research.[2] As such, internationally focused research that does not inherently privilege Anglosphere popular music is one of the key contributions to research on popular music and place from ethnomusicology.

In the material that follows I return to a discussion of the field of ethnomusicology to further elaborate on the 'omnivorous' nature of the field specifically in relation to popular music studies. This is followed by an elaboration of the methodological contributions that ethnomusicology offers research on popular music and place. I then explore relationships between ethnomusicology and popular music studies more broadly, and studies of popular music and place more specifically. Together this material serves, in part, as a corrective for the still-common misperception of ethnomusicology as the study of 'non-western' and 'traditional' music, and positions the methodologies and approaches developed by ethnomusicologists as vital contributions to the study of popular music and place.

Ethnomusicology

As discussed in the introduction, the field of ethnomusicology encompasses a wide range of issues, theoretical models, musical genres and styles, geographic locations and overall approaches to the study of music. Without exception, each of the chapters in this volume discusses topics that ethnomusicologists have studied in one context or another. Despite the seemingly wide-open nature of the field, close readings of monographs in ethnomusicology series from publishers such as University of Chicago Press, Oxford University Press, University of Illinois Press, Indiana University Press, Routledge's SOAS Musicology Series, and from journals such as *Ethnomusicology, Yearbook for Traditional Music* and *Ethnomusicology Forum* show a, perhaps surprisingly, unified field in terms of research methodologies. This focus on ethnomusicology as being primarily defined by the research methodologies adopted by scholars has been discussed elsewhere, including by ethnomusicologist Ellen Koskoff in her argument that '[e]thnomusicology, still sometimes defined as the study of non-Western music, is, more accurately, the study of all musics currently existing in the world today, using methodologies derived mainly from folklore and cultural anthropology' (Koskoff 2005: 92). It is then tempting to argue that fieldwork, particularly sustained fieldwork in situ, is the defining feature of ethnomusicological scholarship. Yet emerging fields of virtual music ethnography, historical ethnomusicology, among others, challenge more traditional views of ethnographic fieldwork and the very nature of 'the field'.

This emphasis on fieldwork, including participant observation, in-depth interviews and other qualitative research methods, distinguishes ethnomusicological research from more common text-based readings of popular music. The growing interest among ethnomusicologists in studying popular music and popular media more broadly also contributes new understandings of the possibilities for fieldwork.[3] In the introduction to the Fall 2007 volume of the journal *Ethnomusicology*, the first volume of that journal to feature articles exclusively on popular music, the editor Timothy Cooley pointed out that the three articles dedicated to the study of popular music in the volume each took different methodological approaches – only Timothy Rommen's article on rock and cosmopolitanism in Trinidad was based on more traditional notions of fieldwork. Kiri

Miller's 2012 monograph *Playing Along: Digital Games, YouTube, and Virtual Performance* offered a reconsideration of what 'the field' is through her work in virtual ethnography. Miller argued that her fieldwork for her research on *Grand Theft Auto: San Andreas* was 'quite traditional' even though it focused on the virtual world of San Andreas (Miller 2012: 27). In the introduction to the volume Miller wrote that her text has methodological implications through its evocation of participant-observation and ethnographic fieldwork, and that while this might seem obvious for research on participatory culture,

> ethnographic studies of popular music and digital media remain outnumbered by analyses that treat all media products as 'texts', suitable for close reading according to the interpretive conventions of literary theory.... A performance-oriented approach grounded in ethnographic methodology brings different perspective to this burgeoning field of cultural production and criticism: that is, *the perspectives of players and producers*, as well as the analytical insights they inspire.
>
> (Miller 2012: 6)

Miller's emphasis on the perspectives of players and producers is mirrored in much ethnomusicological research in which the lived experiences of those involved, whether as the artists, producers, technology experts, listeners, fans and so on are of vital importance to research on popular music. This is not to say that ethnomusicologists avoid textual analyses of music and related phenomena, but there is a strong legacy of complementing textual analyses with consideration of lived experiences that do not overly privilege the perspective of the researchers themselves.

Ethnomusicology as methodology

What then are the methodological contributions that ethnomusicology offers scholars interested in popular music studies? In her review of Robert Walser's *Running with the Devil: Power, Gender, and Madness in Heavy Metal Music*, Deborah Wong identifies that despite the author's attempts to problematize 'a musicology that constructs bloodless, disembodied, dehistoricized, apolitical musics, he also reenacts the historiographical moves that bring him to this moment' (Wong 1998: 149). Wong goes on to argue:

> [T]he humanistic impulse, in cultural studies, toward ungrounded interpretation is sometimes all too evident and reminiscent of what used to be called armchair anthropology (before 'here', 'there', 'us', and 'them' were problematized).... The relationship of the techniques of cultural studies to those of ethnography is uneasy at best, especially since ethnographers themselves have thoroughly critiqued and problematized ethnographic premises.
>
> (Wong 1998: 150)

Despite Walser's use of interviews throughout his book, this was not enough to fully situate the book in the ethnographic realm.

Kevin Dawe argued that ethnomusicology's major contribution to popular music studies is that it 'provides fundamental data necessary for an understanding of not only the bigger musical picture, but also critical insights into the local nuances of the what, when, where, why and how of music-making at particular places and times' (Dawe 2015: 3). The from-the-ground contribution of much ethnomusicological research does indeed have much to offer more cultural studies-based approaches to the study of popular music. While sometimes-imperfect, ethnographic research often provides the best chance of understanding how and why certain people make or engage with certain types of music in different contexts. This is done through a commitment to long-term research that privileges the experiences of all involved in the research of 'being there', wherever there might be.

Methodology in ethnomusicology continues to expand and take in new ideas and approaches for other fields while also honing approaches grounded in the history of ethnomusicology and anthropology (Rice 2003). Ethnomusicology is inherently interdisciplinary and the research that is undertaken by ethnomusicologists almost inevitably draws on theories and methodologies that were also developed in other disciplines. A graduate seminar in fieldwork methods will most likely train students in certain skills-based approaches including how to conduct in-depth interviews and to transcribe and analyse those interviews, how to ethically document field experiences with video, film and audio recordings, and how to write an ethnographic text based on the research conducted. But such a seminar would also most likely include extensive training and discussion on the ethics of human-based research, the inadequacy of the insider/outsider binary, and questions of representation and positionality of the researcher. Such seminars are also likely to include discussions of how to conduct historical and virtual ethnographic research in addition to more traditional approaches. These methods are then combined with theoretical analysis and discussion of the material along with training in how to interpret, analyse and represent music and sound as part of the research process.

Ethnomusicology and popular music

The differences in textual approaches to popular music and ethnographic research have been discussed at length by scholars from both perspectives. In his seminal 1990 volume, *Studying Popular Music*, Richard Middleton argued that authenticity is a central area of concern in ethnomusicology and that 'most ethnomusicologists study the music of "primitive" societies, of the oriental high cultures and of "folk" cultures – popular music, let alone Western "art" music, has hardly been touched' (Middleton 1990: 146). Middleton also ascribed a structuralist 'scientific culture' to the field of ethnomusicology. A corrective discourse still ensues about Middleton's descriptions given the ongoing popularity of this text for popular music scholars who might not be familiar with the breadth of research in ethnomusicology. Even at the time of publication of Middleton's book, his arguments overlooked a significant output of ethnographic research on popular music.[4]

In a 2003 chapter exploring the sometimes-uneasy relationship between popular music studies and ethnomusicology, including Middleton's writing, Martin Stokes pointed out in a foot note that the real problem might be 'a persistent language gap which ensures that popular music scholars read little ethnomusicology, and vice versa' (Stokes 2003: 220). He notes that the journal *Popular Music* has been more likely to review ethnomusicological publications than *The Yearbook for Traditional Music* or *Ethnomusicology* have been to review British popular music scholarship. But he also noted that American-based ethnomusicologists published in Chicago University Press's ethnomusicology series were more likely to reference British popular music scholarship than the reverse.

This gap in reading across disciplinary lines was at the heart of Sara Cohen's 1993 article 'Ethnography and Popular Music Studies'. In this article Cohen argued:

> [P]articular emphases within popular music studies (e.g. upon music as commodity, media, capital and technology), and a reliance upon theoretical models abstracted from empirical data, and upon statistical, textual and journalistic sources, needs to be balanced by a more ethnographic approach. Ideally, that approach should focus upon social relationships, emphasizing music as social practice and process.
>
> (Cohen 1993: 123)

Cohen further argues that macro level studies of popular music that focus on 'globalization', 'the west', 'culture' and 'society' are often ethnocentric in their 'taken-for-granted Western sense of self and society' (Cohen 1993: 132). In more micro-level approaches to researching popular music, the researcher is very often trying to understand the musical experiences from the point of view of the musicians and fans of the music themselves. Recent examples of such research include Benjamin Teitelbaum's 2014 article on the Swedish nationalist singer Saga and the surrounding context of radical white nationalism in Sweden. Teitelbaum expanded this researcher into a book-length ethnography in 2017 on radical nationalism in the Nordic region and the use of popular music in nationalist political agendas. Teitelbaum's close ethnographic approach to this research resulted in nuanced and at times troubling scholarship on a network of individuals and musicians rarely studied in mainstream academia. But without the close relationships developed through ethnographic research, Teitelbaum would almost certainly not have gleaned the insider understanding of this network and its sometimes-surprising attitudes and uses of popular music.

Other scholars, such as Tia DeNora, have written more forcefully against the value of 'semiotic' or textual readings of popular music that tend to be prevalent in socio-musical studies most frequently devoted to the concept of the 'music itself' (DeNora 2000: 22). DeNora has argued against a 'culturology' approach, which she describes as a sociology devoted to 'reading' works to uncover or decode social content. In her book *Music in Everyday Life*, she introduced one of her studies designed 'to investigate musical practice in daily life, and to examine music as an organizing force in social life' for fifty-two American and British women (DeNora 2000: 48). This study was given as an example of how ethnographic research is required in order to truly understand how music functions for people in everyday contexts. Significantly, DeNora's own research background is in sociology, and she relies heavily on interviews for this research instead of extended fieldwork or participant observation. She also avoids a degree of self-reflexivity more common in ethnomusicological research. Adrian Renzo has cautioned against full-hearted adoption of Tia DeNora's demands for outright abandonment of textual analysis with ethnographic research as a more ethical research model for popular music studies (Renzo 2003: 5). Renzo offers examples of the potential inadequacies of relying solely on ethnographic research in the study of music, especially when the research focuses primarily on interviews. Combined, DeNora's text and Renzo's response to it demonstrate that ethnographic research is at its most valuable when multi-level methodologies are adopted.

Ethnographers have long been aware of the pitfalls of relying on interviews when conducting research. Peter Metcalf explored this topic at length in his book *They Lie, We Lie: Getting on with Anthropology* (2002). Metcalf explores how the very notion of storytelling differs based on cultural contexts, as does implicit understandings of what information is relevant and what might be more selectively revealed. But in popular music studies, the issues involved in interviewing can be even more complex. David B. Pruett discussed issues of interviewing and conducting research in mainstream American popular music at length in a 2011 article. He wrote that '[a]s a fieldwork-based discipline, ethnomusicology comprises numerous approaches to exploring musics of varying soundscapes. Fieldwork methodologies seem to equal the growing number of fieldwork opportunities available to ethnomusicologists, including those in popular music studies' (Pruett 2011: 1). Pruett goes on to suggest that scholars increasingly focus on studies that include fan-based communities, technoculture, and local or indie music scenes. Despite the seemingly overwhelming influence of mainstream Anglo music, Pruett points out that most research that is conducted on this type of research has been limited to distinctly outsider analyses that rely on secondary sources including commercial recordings and articles by critics or music journalists (Pruett 2011). Pruett goes on to discuss his own research with Nashville's 'MusicMafia' in the early 2000s and how, through considerable time and effort, he was eventually able to secure time and interviews with well-known musicians such as Kid Rock. In this same article, Pruett cautions against relying whole-heartedly on interviews published in mainstream music journalism outlets. He notes that the issues at play in such interviews, such as efforts to control the narrative by a press team, are well known in other fields but that ethnomusicologists tend to talk less about such problems (Pruett 2011: 12). Despite the known issues, both ethical and practical, with conducting interviews and ethnographic research in general, ethnography can often be a more equitable research approach to the study of popular music that welcomes individuals and groups who might otherwise not be directly heard from in mainstream research.

Ethnomusicology and place

Place has been a central issue in much English-language ethnomusicological research since the mid-1950s when the field of ethnomusicology was formally established. Even when scholars have not explicitly identified place in their research as a key theoretical concept, it often sits just under the surface of how ethnomusicologists have tended to approach their research. This supports Rodman's argument that the very 'meaning of place too often seems to go without saying' (Rodman 1992: 640). Rodman's work builds on Appadurai's earlier identification of 'problems of place' (Appadurai 1988a: 16). Wrazen, in her research on place-bound identities and music and memory in the context of diasporic Polish musicians, offers a compelling distinction between place, landscape and space (Wrazen 2007: 185). While Wheeler's observation that both place and music are polysemic in the growing body of literature that deal with these topics (Wheeler 2012: 77). Instead of trying to offer a definitive definition of place as it relates to the study of popular music, I explore how ethnomusicological research contributes to our understanding of dialogic relationships between place and popular music.

One of the great strengths of ethnographic research in matters of place and popular music is that this type of research is well-positioned to capture and explore the complexities and meanings of place from a local level. Popular music in various contexts throughout the world often simultaneously connects disparate populations sonically, while at the same time it can provide new opportunities for people to engage with their own local experiences of place and other factors. In the introduction to their 1996 volume, Feld and Basso argued that 'it is hardly surprising that anthropologists have come to worry less about place in broad philosophical or humanistic terms than about places as sites of power struggles or about displacement as histories of annexation, absorption, and resistance. Thus, ethnography's stories of place and places are increasingly about contestation' (Feld and Basso 1996: 5). In a similar argument, Rodman wrote that '(p)laces are not inert containers. They are politicized, culturally relative, historically specific, local, and multiple constructions' (Rodman: 641). Ethnographic research, then, provides an opportunity to combine theoretical approaches to studying popular music with lived experiences of people.

A recent example of this type of research is Catherine Appert's 2016 article on hybridity in Senegalese hip hop. In this research, Appert argued that popular genres have helped to ground musicians in local places worldwide as well as in Senegal and wider Africa. She explores the genre of Mbalax, a Senegalese style of popular music that combines the jazz and Cuban song of colonial nightclubs with Islamicized griot praise singing and indigenous rhythms. She argues that from the outside, such concepts as hybridity and syncretism have largely fallen out of favour with ethnomusicologists and scholars, but that from the ground, these concepts still prove quite useful for individuals and musicians around the world (Appert 2016: 281). In addition to demonstrating the important connections between place and genre, Appert's research also demonstrates how ethnographic research has the potential to avoid ethnocentric readings of popular music contexts by engaging directly with alternative viewpoints and understandings.

Scholars have also explored the relationships between landscape and place, two concepts which often closely overlap and yet have distinct meanings. This builds on Rice's argument that 'the "sense of place" varies from person to person, time to time, and narrative to narrative. Understanding this dimension as in flux, nested, dynamic, multiple and constructed is one way to deal with real-world complexity' (Rice 2003: 161). This is particularly important for scholars researching popular music within Indigenous communities. In a 2012 article on Samba in Brazil, Wheeler argued that research on popular, commodified music typically emphasizes the concept of place in terms of identifying a 'local' sound. But research in Indigenous contexts on popular music often reveals an essential relationship between certain musical practices and concepts of place, including landscape (Wheeler 2012).

Conclusion

Without going so far as DeNora to say that ethnographic research is the only ethical approach to researching music, ethnomusicological research on popular music and place has the potential to provide locally informed details of complex situations and musical practices. Acknowledging that truth is a murky concept and that, as Metcalf (2002) points out, everyone involved in the enterprise of ethnography is likely 'lying' in one way or another, getting on the ground and working directly with people involved in making and experiencing various popular musical styles and genres contributes a richer understanding of popular music practices around the world. Ethnomusicological research, at its best, combines rigorous social and cultural analysis with robust theoretical models and detailed descriptions of musical practices and sounds.

Music is one of the key ways that people around the world make sense of their own experiences and locations and places. Ethnomusicological research contributes to the opening up of popular music studies away from so-called armchair studies and contexts in which English-language commercial music might otherwise dominate. As discussed, it is not the topic, the location or even the style of music that defines ethnomusicological research; the approaches and methodologies that ethnomusicologists use to study music of all genres and locations are the hallmarks of the field now. This openness is combined with a deeply ingrained awareness of power and ethics in ethnographic research that leaves the researcher ever mindful of the relationships and responsibilities involved in such research.

Notes

1. In his 2010 book, Nettl offers a detailed discussion of this trend in ethnomusicology and an extensive discussion of the history of ethnomusicology and musicology more general. Nettl's long career goes back to the 1950s when the term 'ethnomusicology' came into use, and this book is an excellent resource for anyone wanting an in-depth history of the field.
2. See the 2016 volume *A Latin American Music Reader: View from the South* edited by Javier F. Leon and Helena Simonett and the Society for Ethnomusicology's *Ethnomusicology Translations* online open-access monograph series.
3. For a more comprehensive understanding of contemporary trends in fieldwork, see Barz and Cooley's edited volume *Shadows in the Field: New Perspectives for Fieldwork in Ethnomusicology*.
4. See Nettl (1972), Ridgeway and Roberts (1976), O'Grady (1979) and Waterman (1982) as only a few examples of ethnomusicologists publishing on popular music well before the 1990s.

References

Appadurai, A. (1988), 'Introduction: Place and Voice in Anthropological Theory', *Cultural Anthropology*, 3: 16–20.
Appert, C. M. (2016), 'On Hybridity in African Popular Music: The Case of Senegalese Hip Hop', *Ethnomusicology*, 60 (2): 279–99.
Barz, G. and Cooley, T. J., eds (2008), *Shadows in the Field: New Perspectives for Fieldwork in Ethnomusicology*, New York: Oxford University Press.
Cohen, S. (1993), 'Ethnography and Popular Music Studies', *Popular Music*, 12 (2): 123–38.
Dawe, K. (2015), 'The Many Worlds of Popular Music: Ethnomusicological Approaches', in A. Bennett and S. Waksman (eds), *The SAGE Handbook of Popular Music*, 15–32, London: SAGE Publications.
DeNora, T. (2000), *Music in Everyday Life*, Cambridge, UK: Cambridge University Press.
Feld, S. and Basso, K. H. (1996), 'Introduction', in S. Feld and K. H. Basso (eds), *Senses of Place*, 3–12, Santa Fe, NM: School of American Research Press.
Koskoff, E. (2005), '(Left "Out in") "Left" (the "Field"): The Effects of Post-Postmodern Scholarship on Feminist and Gender Studies in Musicology and Ethnomusicology, 1990–2000', *Women & Music – A Journal of Gender and Culture*, 9: 90–8.
Leon, J. F. and Simonett, H., eds (2016), *A Latin American Music Reader: Views from the South*, Champaign-Urbana, IL: University of Illinois Press.
Metcalf, P. (2002), *They Lie, We Lie: Getting on with Anthropology*, New York: Routledge University Press.
Middleton, R. (1990), *Studying Popular Music*, Milton Keynes, UK: Open University Press.
Miller, K. (2012), *Playing along: Digital Games, YouTube, and Virtual Performance*, New York: Oxford University Press.
Nettl, B. (1972), 'Persian Popular Music in 1969', *Ethnomusicology*, 16 (2): 218–39.
Nettl, B. (2010), *Nettl's Elephant: On the History of Ethnomusicology*, Champaign-Urbana, IL: University of Illinois Press.
O'Grady, T. J. (1979), '*Rubber Soul* and the Social Dance Tradition', *Ethnomusicology*, 23 (1): 87–94.
Pruett, D. B. (2011), 'When the Tribe Goes Triple Platinum: A Case Study toward an Ethnomusicology of Mainstream Popular Music in the U.S.', *Ethnomusicology*, 55 (1): 1–30.
Renzo, A. (2003), '"Nice Tune, but What Does It Mean?": Popular Music Studies, Ethnography and Textual Analysis', *Context*, 26: 5–16.
Rice, T. (2003), 'Time, Place, and Metaphor in Musical Experience and Ethnography', *Ethnomusicology*, 47 (2): 151–79.
Ridgeway, C. L. and Roberts, J. M. (1976), 'Urban Popular Music and Interaction: A Semantic Relationship', *Ethnomusicology*, 20 (2): 233–51.
Rodman, M. C. (1992), 'Empowering Place: Multilocality and Multivocality', *American Anthropologist*, 94 (3): 640–56.
Stokes, M. (2003), 'Talk and Text: Popular Music and Ethnomusicology', in Allan F. Moore (ed.), *Analyzing Popular Music*, 218–39, Cambridge: Cambridge University Press.
Teitelbaum, B. (2014), 'Saga's Sorrow: Femininities of Despair in the Music of Radical White Nationalism', *Ethnomusicology*, 58 (3): 405–30.
Teitelbaum, B. (2017), *Lions of the North: Sounds of the New Nordic Radical Nationalism*, New York: Oxford University Press.

Waterman, C. A. (1982), '"I'm a Leader, Not a Boss": Social Identity and Popular Music in Ibadan, Nigeria', *Ethnomusicology*, 26 (1): 59–71.

Wheeler, J. S. (2012), 'Rock, Refrain and Remove: Hearing Place and Seeing Music in Brasília', *Ethnomusicology Forum*, 21 (1): 77–103.

Wong, D. (1998), 'Review: Running with the Devil: Power, Gender, and Madness in Heavy Metal Music by Robert Walser', *Journal of the American Musicological Society*, 51 (1): 148–58.

Wrazen, L. (2007), 'Relocating the Tatras: Place and Music in Górale Identity and Imagination', *Ethnomusicology*, 51 (2): 185–204.

6

Political economies of urban music

Shane Homan

Introduction

In this chapter, I want to revisit the usual tensions evident in political economy debates and prescriptions of value – namely contestations between economic, social and cultural value in policy formation. Music activity – by musicians, critics, fans and a wider array of related industry workers – has always been present. As De Beukalaer and Spence (2019: 24) point out, the 'discovery' of such cultural industries by the state is itself a discursive act, embodied in particular values that shape understandings, practices and outcomes. For example, in a 2019 article for *The Guardian* newspaper, UK journalist Naomi Larsson explores the notion of the musical city and its relationship to politics, policy and representation:

> 'Music is in our DNA,' says Justine Simons, London's deputy mayor for culture and chair of the World Cities Culture Forum. 'There's punk in the 70s, and today you can think about grime and how that's projected London into the world stage.' She says there's a 'recognition that if you want to be a successful city you can't do it without culture'.
>
> (Larsson 2019)

More broadly, cultural policy involves internal and external pressures for governments: aspirations to 'excellence', 'innovation' and 'access' often also intersect with heritage, education, intellectual property and media policy formation (Throsby 2010: 42–9). These might also accord with broader fiscal, industry, labour market and trade policy (Throsby 2010: 50–3).

We are talking, then, of political economies of music. I am relying on Vincent Mosco's earlier definition of political economy as 'the study of the social relations, particularly the power relations, that mutually constitute the production, distribution, and consumption of resources' (Mosco 2009: 24). Within the context of the music industries, this involves not only relationships between the state and the 'cultural citizen' (Miller 1993), but also the forms, practices and discourses of industrial organization amidst shifting forms of capitalism. This includes examination of the industrial and social contexts of, for example, recording, consumption and live music. Revisiting Mosco, the mix of industry, government and citizen/consumer relations returns us to meanings and uses of power. And, like other political spheres, decisions about state funding and allocation of other resources (e.g. land use, zoning, labour) are made within the context of finite funds, ensuring a hierarchy of policies and values (Street 2012).

But how do we enunciate and pursue a political economy of music *spaces and places*? This involves, firstly, examining how spaces/places are deployed in urban contexts. Building on Hayden (1995), we might begin by exploring the specific ways in which music becomes part of discourses of place-making: particular clusters of capital and labour to produce distinctive areas of music production/consumption. I am not speaking here of music scenes (discussed elsewhere in this book), although they certainly are vivid examples of music-spatial formations, but deliberate or unwitting actions that provide for music 'precincts' that privilege recording, live music, music retail or other cultural/business forms.

Secondly, we need to examine music as a driver of economic growth. Governments and industries have often run joint tickets in arguing for music to recover declining urban areas. From Nashville (Wynn 2015) to Liverpool (Cohen 2007), the music industries are hailed for their ability to increase employment; increase the number of tourists; and/or related leisure/cultural industries benefits. In this sense, music has played a prominent role in wider discussions of culture's role in the life and economic health of towns and cities. In particular, inner suburban/Central Business District (CBD) areas are viewed as ripe for regeneration, where music can play a lively role in production and consumption. This in turn calls for an examination of the classed effects of regeneration:

> Gentrification takes older cities into a new organization of consumption based on cultural capital. One of the interesting aspects of this organization of consumption is that it is spatially specific: consumption markets (clubs, housing) are attached to places that claim to be unique.
>
> (Zukin 2010: 296)

Thirdly, in relation, a political economy approach would also include the forms of promotion and branding that make the uniqueness of music spaces and places seem self-evident. This might be the reinforcement of existing local/global narratives, or attempts to establish new ones. For example, the music industries have certainly played a role in how 'Toronto used arts and culture to *define* itself; and New York used arts and culture as a way to *redefine* itself' (Goldberg-Miller 2017: 213; emphasis in original). Most often, this has involved cities laying claim to a particular production/consumption strength: Austin as 'live music capital'; Kingston as reggae centre; or Berlin as techno city. The music industries – in this case, the popular music industries – can be regarded as ones that are increasingly regarded as providing cities with competitive advantage, to 'function as communal springboards facilitating the capacity of producers in the cognitive-cultural economy to contest national and global markets by means of uniquely configured products' (Scott 2017: 225). Further, the mix of music spaces – a venue, a retro retail shop, a festival – become powerful components evoking cultural spaces.

In the rest of this chapter, I examine political economies of space and place through further evaluation of the types of value placed upon music in urban contexts, and how they are measured; and the recurring issues and problems surrounding place-making/growth/promotional discourses. I also want to briefly look at the industrial, governmental and academic methods in mapping and evaluating political economies of music spaces and places. This has become important, not only for the obvious questions of methodological accuracy; the results themselves increasingly form part of particular discourses.

Economic and cultural value

While place-making arguments can be powerful, the primary discourse within industry and government policy-making remains the economic. Direct comparisons are made to other cultural or leisure industries. For example, a 2017 report revealed that the UK cultural industries 'contributed £8.5bn to the UK economy. More than double that of the Premier League [football]' (Arts Council England 2018). A similar comparison with sport was made for the Victorian live music industry in Australia, with a 2011 report stating that the live music sector was worth $AUD501 million, employing approximately 17,200 people – with Melbourne responsible for a significant component of this (Arts Victoria 2011: iv), and attendance at gigs reaching a higher number than attendance at Australian Football League matches (Arts Victoria 2011: 23). Basic ROI (Return On Investment) calculations reassure the taxpayer that funds are well spent, including 'indirect' and 'flow' arguments, explaining how cultural industries spending is returned to the national economy in different ways: 'Culture pays £2.6bn in taxes, £5 for every £1 of public funding' (Arts Council England 2018).

There is a heavy emphasis upon live music as sources of regeneration, employment and financial returns. Adelaide, minted as a UNESCO Music City in 2015, boasted that its live music sector provided $AUD264 million to the city's economy, a return of 3 to 1, with a related 4100 jobs (Bishop 2017) in a population of only 1.3 million. For larger cities, the economic contribution can be impressive:

> Indeed, New York City is home to one of the world's largest – if not the largest – and most influential music ecosystems, supporting nearly 60,000 jobs, accounting for roughly $5 billion in wages, and generating a total economic output of $21 billion (in business revenues and self-employment receipts).
>
> (New York City 2017: 3)

This supports the thesis of New York (along with Los Angeles and London) as a 'superstar' city, 'with the best hit-makers, the most complete support structures required to launch them, and the fast metabolisms needed to process many bets quickly and efficiently' (Florida 2017: 54). In flouting its economic power, New York cites its rich ecosystem of 'local artist communities, mass music consumption, the global record business, and infrastructure and support services' (New York City 2017: 3).

While Western cities build upon older genre and foundational legacies (e.g. Nashville as global 'home' to country music), others are exploiting more recent traditions. In Seoul, considerable effort is under way to establish 'music hub' policies based upon the ongoing success of K-pop. The establishment of 'Platform Chang-dong 61' entertainment district (in north-eastern Seoul) in 2016, incorporating music, fashion and food retail, and recording studios, workshop and exhibition spaces for musicians (Se-jeong 2016) is significant. The Seoul Metropolitan government has plans for a K-pop museum and a 20,000-seat Seoul Arena stadium for completion by 2020 (Se-jeong 2016). This is a good example of how K-pop is used locally to drive ancillary retail benefits and financial returns across fashion, cosmetics, tourism and sport industries.

The increasing number of reports commissioned by local music industries to reveal economic benefits to their city is not accidental. It reveals an ongoing shift from broader discourses of subsidy to discourses of investment. This is particularly the case in not simply stating bold arguments for direct ROI to central city funds, but emphasizing employment and related business benefits. There are parallels, too, in the accompanying rise in creative industries discourse that has allowed the music industries to argue other benefits of related industries' growth.

Austin, Texas, remains an interesting case study for its staged regeneration combining the creative, cultural, social and technological. Its self-proclaimed 'live capital of the world' status (see Grodach 2012) was accompanied by deliberative state and council government policy seeking comparative advantage in different music sectors (e.g. City of Austin 2015). Yet popular music has done more here than simply act as another inherent advantage. According to *The Economist*, Austin's revitalized music scenes also acted as symbolic reassurance ('we're back and we're now funky!') and attractor to growing industries, primarily IT, hospitality, tourism and media/gaming (Economist Intelligence Unit 2015). In addition, the perceived role of the city's flagship festival, South by Southwest, is typical of the heady mix of creativity, politics, economics and branding:

> What began as an ad-hoc music gathering in a sleepy university town has since grown into a massive conference-cum-festival that includes music, film and technology. According to a study by the consultancy Greyhill Advisors, in 2014 SXSW attracted more than 370,000 attendees and generated more than US$315m for Austin's economy. The event also strengthens the city's status as a trendsetter at the intersection of art, music and digital technology. Without SXSW, Austin's economy may have taken a different turn. Between 2000 and 2002, after the dotcom bubble of the late 1990s burst, the city lost more than 25,000 tech-sector jobs. Austin responded by moving aggressively to drive growth. Remarkably, until then, the city never had its own economic development office.
>
> (Economist Intelligence Unit 2015)

The symbiosis of industry and state has assumed renewed vision. However, further questions should follow such economic narratives: firstly, is financial return the sole rationale to play, listen to and produce music in urban contexts? Secondly, how does the primary economic rationale inform discourses and exercises of power within industries and governments? How to measure, and what is deemed valuable to measure, always seem contentious:

> [D]ebates over cultural policy and creative sector funding focus mostly on government-approved instrumental arguments and reasoning, thus leaving real and substantive issues of cultural value, access and justice under-explored and unchallenged.
>
> (Belfiore 2018: 2–3)

Within popular music, and the cultural industries more broadly, articulating cultural value has been notoriously difficult. Yet the live music experience – seeing and hearing music at the local pub, club, town square, shopping mall, concert hall or festival – remains a useful means of obtaining purchase between definitions, meanings and experiences. The live music experience adheres to Throsby's (2001) list of values (symbolic, aesthetic, social, authenticity, etc.) among much older ones (heritage, excellence, enlightenment/insight). Live music also provides a further range of cultural values if we further consider 'intrinsic' (the subjective, individual experience); 'instrumental' (ancillary effects that serve a wider social or economic purpose); and 'institutional' value (experiences and effects as a public good) (Holden 2006). Later studies have further acknowledged the differences (and tensions) between governmental, industry and consumer evaluations of 'public' value and culture (O'Brien 2015).

How are meanings of *place* understood here? Beyond individual experiences of pleasure and meaning, live music speaks to wider issues of access and the anchoring of culture within particular local spaces. This is most apparent when live circuits are threatened from without. The real or imminent loss of a favoured music venue produces much industry and media hand-wringing, where the sense of loss is firmly attached to the flow of local affects and effects. This perhaps reinforces the argument that values come into focus through lived experience; 'all talk about the value of artistic activity remains abstract until that art is experienced. When it is, the value ascribed goes well beyond the merely economic' (Behr, Brennan and Cloonan 2016: 416).

The United Kingdom's 'toilet circuit', 'defined by three core elements: historicism, distinguishable seedy aesthetics, and a compelling sense of community' (Schofield and Miller 2017: 139), is a vivid example. They are further defined by size, comprising small pub or club sites. The consistent loss of such venues – estimated for London to be 35 per cent of its 'grassroots' venues since 2007 (Greater London Authority 2017; see also Harris 2013) – is thus lamented for the accompanying loss of the intimate exchanges between punters and bands, and often, the loss of a potential social hub:

> There are different communities of users. The people who come for comedy, there's the mums, there's the dancers, there's the religious folks, there's the giggers, there's the drinkers and they can exist in harmony hopefully. They may bleed into one another.
>
> (Venue owner interviewee cited in Parkinson et al. 2015: 22)

The quote above derives from a Music Venues Trust report that epitomizes more recent strategies to address recurring political economy problems: working hard to provide more comprehensive data on the nature of the problem; re-aligning organizational power (in this case, the establishment of the Trust); and bringing the forces of the state to bear upon regulatory issues (in this case, the Mayor of London office). While 'cities may tout flashy new buildings and pedestrian-filled streets as signs of urban renewal' (Grodach and Ehrenfeucht 2016: 6), there is increasing evidence that attention must be paid to existing infrastructure that is not bright, new and shiny.

Policies and regulation

Of course, mapping industry/policy problems does not necessarily produce firm solutions; the problems themselves are often interconnected in their complexity; and intensely local conditions of governance and practice must be further taken into account. Noise regulations, council trading laws, zoning laws, gentrification/redevelopment and declining interest in the live gig are invariably cited as adverse factors (as was the case with the 'toilet circuit' debates). At the same time, UK Music pointed to the weight of business rates levied by the British government, and discrepancies in business rates in terms of scale: a Lexington venue in North London having to accept a 118 per cent rate rise in 2018, while football club 'Arsenal's 60,000 capacity Emirates Stadium nearby enjoyed a 7% cut in its rateable value' (UK Music's Michael Dugher cited in CMU 2018).

Consistent attention paid to (saving) existing venues also may obscure other debates. Local music industries point to the combination of factors prohibiting potential venue owners thinking about new venues. For New York, 'it costs upwards of $1 million to open a 100- to 300-person venue in New York City and as much as $5 million to open a 500- to 1,000-person venue, due to construction costs, license complexity, regulatory scrutiny, and the resources required to pass inspections' (New York City 2017: 17). Similarly, while liquor licence 'freezes' – either trading restrictions, or capping the number of late night trading venues, or both – can assist the viability of existing venues, they prevent new forms of venues and licences.

Liquor licensing policies reflect the recurring tensions in industries and governments seeking (and selling) vibrant night-time music experiences. The 'lockout laws' imposed on Sydney nightlife reveals how narratives of 'public safety' are inevitably part of more complex intersections of policy, statistical interpretations and media debate. After a series of 'one-punch' fatalities in 2012 and 2013, the New South Wales government imposed several changes for the CBD and nearby Kings Cross entertainment precinct. In 2014, the state premier established new mandatory sentencing for 'one punch' assaults; new mandatory or minimum sentences for alcohol or drug-related violence; a freeze on new liquor licences; and a redrawn entertainment precinct (New South Wales Government 2016). Patrons were to be 'locked out' after 1.30 am, with bar service ceasing at 3.00 am (bars with capacities of under 60 patrons were excluded); those venues with 3 am licences could remain open, but without the service of alcohol (New South Wales Government 2016). Surveying the various reports examining their effects, the director of the NSW Bureau of Crime Statistics and Research concluded that '[t]here is little doubt that liquor licensing law is a powerful tool when it comes to reducing alcohol-related violence', also noting that 'there is little information on which initiative, among the multiplicity undertaken since 2008 to reduce alcohol-related violence, has been most effective in reducing the incidence of assault' (Weatherburn 2016: 101).[1]

Unsurprisingly, the local music industries took a different view to the management of risk. Since the introduction of the 'lockout', Sydney's CBD had experienced a net loss of 176 licences (Taylor 2018). While the laws were abandoned in 2021 with the ability for venues to apply for 3.30 am closing, there is evidence that the state government was aware of the collateral damage to live music and other entertainment premises. The state government found the Sydney City Council, collecting society APRA AMCOS, advocacy body Music Australia and the federal Live Music Office collectively voicing the damage done to business, and the city's global reputation. A 2016 review recommended late night trading exemptions to those operating as bona fide music venues (Callinan 2016). A NSW Legislative Council Inquiry, *The music and arts economy in New South Wales*, published its findings in November 2018. Stopping short of winding back the lockout provisions, the Inquiry's final report contained many recommendations carving out live music exemptions across planning, noise law and licensing regulations (NSW Legislative Council 2018: xiii–vxiii).[2]

The Sydney case is also interesting for its wider marketing and branding consequences. A *Global Cities after Dark* annual forum was convened in 2017 by Sydney City Council, placing Sydney within global practices of city risk management and the creative industries. Presenting a range of night-time economy comparisons with international cities, a *Sydney as 24-Hour* report emphasized the economic and promotional losses (Committee for Sydney 2018). Similarly, a Deloitte Access Economics report, *Imagine Sydney: Play*, emphasized the lockout laws as part of broader management problems in Sydney attempting to achieve a diversity of night-time economy activities (Wade 2019).

A night mayor for Gotham

Sydney's problems return us to the original debates about the '24-hour city' and the 'cultural city' (e.g. Bianchini et al. 1988; Bianchini 1995; Lovatt and O'Connor 1995; Landry 2008) in how to simultaneously manage competing consumption and production cultural activities and visions across urban nightlife. One governmental solution is the emergence of the Night Mayor, a city manager of the night-time economy to mirror its day-time counterpart. The role is in part an acknowledgement of the increasing complexity of night-time economies, and local music industries have been prominent in seeing its benefits; it is not accidental that the foundational Night mayor in Amsterdam, Mirik Milan, had prior careers as a dance venue manager. Night mayor positions exist in a diverse range of cities including Paris, Mannheim, Washington, Prague and Cali.[3] While they could be viewed as higher profile variants to previous cultural/music development offices, they differ in important respects.

For New York, the Nightlife Mayor was created in 2017, situated within the Mayor's Office of Media and Entertainment. For London, a night czar position was created in 2016.

A 2018 email interview I conducted with Paul Broadhurst, Manager, Night Time and Music, Greater London Authority, outlined the interconnecting contexts:

> The Night Czar chairs [the Night Time Borough Champions network] which includes two representatives (one politician and one official) from all 33 of London's local authorities [who] hold significant powers over planning, licensing and community safety and are therefore key partners in making London a thriving city at night. In July 2017, the Mayor also published his Vision for London as a 24 Hour City, which set out ten principles to guide his work… The Night Czar is a Mayoral appointee. She reports to the Deputy Mayor for Culture and Creative Industries. She works closely with all of the Deputy Mayors and regularly meets with the Mayor. She is supported by a small core team of three officers in the Culture and Creative Industries Unit, plus other officers in a variety of teams across the organisation, including policing, transport, health, planning, economics, intelligence, regeneration, equalities and inclusion and the environment.
>
> (Broadhurst cited in Homan 2018: 24–5)

However, the 'value-added' nature of most of these positions raise various problems in questions of where power resides. The ability of night mayors to provide true independent oversight is difficult within any political/governance city structure, and intimately related to issues of precarity and funding structures: the positions are established and funded at the pleasure of city mayors or related structures (the original Amsterdam role was/is provided by industries, government and sponsorship providing a third each of the funding). In relation, none of the present roles possess regulatory powers. The primary benefits seem to remain in advocacy, in ensuring the cultural industries retain a presence within the regulatory machinery; and broadening contexts. Night Czar Amy Lamé 'has initiated responses to the negative impacts of gentrification on the city's gay bars and the facilitation of racism in regulatory procedures' (Wolfson 2018: 199), in keeping with Broadhurst's vision of the role as 'changing the conversation about London at night' and negating adverse law and order narratives (Broadhurst cited in Homan 2018: 26).

The rise of different forms of night-time economy managers forms part of wider policy networks. 'Creative industry coalitions' (Indergaard 2013: 196) have become more influential in shaping cultural city policies, and popular music is no exception; beyond establishing useful collaborations, such coalitions are also preoccupied with battling real estate interests as to best use of finite land (Indergaard 2013: 203). Different forms of clustering are also evident within local industries, where the city is increasingly host to clusters of innovation. In contrast to earlier, formalized business clusters, 'music accelerators' are designed to establish connections between individuals, companies and ideas. The Rattle, 'a collective of 100 artists, bands, producers, MCs, labels, composers and music entrepreneurs' based in London, provides a space for collaboration, recording and writing, with a daily 'guest expert' (The Rattle 2019). Director and co-founder Jon Eades views The Rattle as an 'incubator members club', asking participants to provide a fee (and not equity), with career sustainability as the central target (Eades 2019).

A promotional economy of popular music

I have argued for some of the ways that music – popular music in particular – can accommodate industry and state visions for urban culture, that flit across other cultural forms, and in forms that combine economic, social and cultural benefits. This is reflected in government, industry and academic attempts to formalize what should be measured, and more importantly, what is required in policy terms. While 'global music cities' (Watson 2008) is a useful term to denote the larger, historical agglomerations of capital, scenes and histories at the centre of the 'music business', it is useful to investigate how the 'music city' operates in different ways and contexts.

Within its wider Creative Cities Network of 180 cities – 'created in 2004 to promote cooperation with and among cities that have identified creativity as a strategic factor for sustainable urban development' – UNESCO have conferred Music City status upon twenty five, including Chennai, Auckland, Almaty, Salvador, Kansas City, Norrkoping and Glasgow. The central criteria for acceptance are a commitment to demonstrate long-term plans for creative/music activity (including education, infrastructure, festivals and other visible/audible forms of music life) and engaging with international debates through localized experiences (UNESCO Creative Cities Network 2019). In some cases, the title simply confirms existing status (e.g. Liverpool's 2015 award for its historic roles in pop and rock; Kingston awarded in 2015 for its status as international hub for reggae).

An International Federation of Phonographic Industries (IFPI) and Music Canada report, *Mastering of a Music City*, has also been influential in shaping historical and contemporary meanings. The music city must have '[a]rtists and musicians; a thriving music scene; access to spaces and places; a receptive and engaged audience; and record labels and other music-related businesses' (IFPI/Music Canada 2015: 13). The state is to play its part in providing 'music-friendly and musician-friendly policies; a Music Office or Officer; a Music Advisory Board; engaging the broader music community to get their buy-in and support; access to spaces and places; and audience development' (IFPI/Music Canada 201: 13–15).

The report offers a toolkit approach to constructing what is required, and by extension, assessing success through a stocktake of activities and policies on offer. IFPI/Music Canada 'does not attempt to establish a benchmark for Music Cities or otherwise codify success' (IFPI/Music Canada 201: 10). However, there is some evidence that this is precisely what industries, policy-makers and academics are undertaking, where the influence of Florida (2002, 2005, 2008) remains. For example, *The Great Music City* establishes four 'algorithms': Economy (A); (Florida's) '4 Ts'[4] (B); Heritage (C); and 'Music Cities Definition' (D) (Baker 2019: 15–21).[5] Leaving aside that 'algorithm D' appears to be simply an amalgamation of the other three, in its efforts to measure, define and compare (with case studies of Melbourne, Berlin and Austin), this form of research ultimately fails to see the ironies in warning of the 'Dubious nature of branding' while relentlessly producing the 'quantitative-driven political economy discourse' (Baker 2019: 305, 303) of who is in, and who is out.

In some instances, the 'music city' definition is in danger, like Florida's 'creative class' thesis, in becoming the ultimate in 'postmodern urban theorization' (Rossi and Vanolo 2012: 56), whose flexibility is such that its prescriptions (of music/creativity in this case) can apply to all urban contexts, histories and practices. The 'scene effect' – evaluation of US cities through different 'creative' modelling indicators – revealed the benefits of scenes to be highly contingent upon particular geographies, histories and legitimations; 'glamour and tradition can generate innovation and growth, just as can bohemia' (Silver, Clark and Graziul 2011: 254). Instead, attention should turn to the range of indicators that governments speak less about, including the scope of employment and wages offered in reality to local musicians, bar workers and songwriters; and the localized ways that Florida's original focus on amenities to attract the 'creatives' reinforced existing inequalities across labour, housing and industry markets (see, for example, Scott 2017: 143–6). In contrast to his previous work, Florida (2017: 213) now acknowledges that 'no top-down, one-size-fits-all strategy' can address new crises of inequality. The 'new urban crisis' is argued to be resolved through new clusters of land, housing and industrial uses to address gentrification (Florida 2017).

These older debates were brought into focus with the arrival of COVID-19. As the one most acutely dependent upon nightly receipts, the live music venue sector – and the range of related performance and hospitality jobs – has suffered greatly. One Australian report estimated a downturn in all live event entertainment of 65 per cent in 2020, from $AUD36.4 billion to $AUD12.8 billion (Challenor 2020). In the United Kingdom, the live music economy was predicted to record an 85 per cent downturn in 2020, down from the record £1.3 billion of 2019 to £300 million (Sweeney 2020). Similar sector reductions were recorded elsewhere, with most nations and larger cities responding with relief packages. For example, Germany provided a stimulus package of €50 billion for the cultural/creative sector (BYP Group 2020); Norway a NOK300 million scheme for the cultural industries (BYP Group 2020); and a UK government package of €1.57b was provided for cultural organizations (Brown 2020). In most cases, sector pleadings for assistance were based upon economic contributions, no doubt bolstered by the visible impact of shuttered high streets and the dire predictions of employment losses. In turn, the pandemic has provided an absence that has revealed its deeper roots within street life. This focus on the local may see renewed attention to domestic infrastructure needs and regulatory obstacles.

Conclusion

The increasing interest shown by the state in popular music policy since the 1980s is undeniable, driven in the main by promises of direct economic gain or at best, ancillary benefits. Questions remain, however, about just *how* the state should intervene; and *where* it should allocate scarce funding, legislative and regulatory resources. Even the continued preoccupation with music venue policies (such as building and planning; noise amelioration) raise other important questions: when should governments actively assist in the preservation of particular venues and scenes, and when should they allow their 'creative destruction'? This is further complicated by notions of the organic; and plausible arguments from their participants that they engineer more than simply promotional sites for bands, or for the alcohol industries.

The rise of the 'music city' term is a useful indicator of the success of popular music to be regarded as a valuable sector of urban culture for fans, industries and governments. The emergence, too, of the night mayor concept (with live venues an integral part of night-time management) is interesting, in being envisaged as an interventionist strategy that will, somehow, straddle both economic and social outcomes of a healthy urban culture. Yet local political economies of music share a sense that they are never settled. The examples discussed above indicate this. For New York, the abolition of 1980s racist cabaret licensing laws for its jazz bands was regarded as an important step to incorporating what music meant to New Yorkers, and for tourists seeking the 'New York' experience (Chevigny 1991). Yet its recovery from the loss of music venues in the late 1970s and 1980s is being fought again, due to the same problems: land use allocation, property prices and council/State regulation. For Sydney, the planning and licensing reforms in the 2000s designed to protect music venues were revisited with a Live Music Taskforce in 2013; and ongoing licensing, planning and branding debates as a result of the 'lockout laws'.

The 'music city' discourses have also been useful in broadening scope and approaches. A political economy of urban music should encompass both direct (such as planning and licensing) and indirect (such as labour laws, transport or education) policies in seeking 'an imprimatur of desirability' (Goldberg-Miller 2017: 68). This reinforces the fact that too often, urban music policies (for industries and governments) remain primarily live music city policies, with little consideration of other direct and indirect effects.

Cities will continue to expend significant resources in chasing favourable 'liveability' and 'cultural' or 'creative' city outcomes in annual indexes that may or may not produce economic benefits. However, continuing preoccupations with the size and scope of music's contribution to urban contexts – and, one would hope, cultural creativity – is a zero sum game. Both industries and governments have become more adept at evidence-based research, and harnessing stakeholder power to present economic evidence. Other questions remain in how to incorporate the social value – and costs – of urban music activity. The current 'toilet circuit' debates in the United Kingdom reveal not just the difficulties in landing on suitable policies for the 'indie' sector, but the very different discourses evident in place-making (and what is deemed to be 'organic' or 'authentic'). Similarly, in what ways can cities place social and economic value on new forms of networking, where entrepreneurial hubs are at the centre of formal/informal exchanges of financial and cultural capital? The dimensions of popular music in cities and towns remain complex, involving different mixes of the utilitarian, symbolic, traditional and the transgressive. The most interesting debates (and methodologies) will be entertained through finding the means to adequately assess and consider its less shiny forms and outcomes. Put simply, researchers, industries and punters alike must continue to fight for 'the opportunity for behaviour that transgresses social, cultural and even legal codes' (Sisson and Maginn 2018).

Notes

1. Conigrave (2016: 112) summarizes the effects: 'Assaults in Kings Cross fell by more than 30 per cent and in the CBD by 26 per cent without evidence of displacement of harms to neighbouring suburbs' (Menendez, Weatherburn et al. 2015). There was a comparable '25 per cent reduction in critically injured patients presenting to St Vincent's Hospital ED [Emergency Department] during peak drinking times (that is, from 6 pm Friday to 6 am Sunday; from 318 to 246 per year)' (Fulde, Smith and Forster 2015).
2. The government's Inquiry Chair noted in the Report's Foreword that Sydney was experiencing a 'live music venues crisis… Sydney is the gateway to Australia for international and domestic tourists and not having a vibrant music industry will cost us greatly and bring embarrassment to our beautiful global city' (NSW Legislative Council 2018: ix–xi).
3. Others have applied different titles with different duties and responsibilities. For example, in June 2018, a nightclub entrepreneur was appointed as 'night-time economy advisor' to lead a panel overseeing Manchester's nightlife (Heward 2018).
4. 'Technology', 'talent' and 'tolerance' were the original '3Ts' (see Florida 2002). 'Territorial assets', encompassing 'quality of place' characteristics, was added later (see Florida 2012).
5. There is no discussion about the decisions made in including various sectors within each 'algorithm'. For example, it is unclear how music education or 'music-making' is placed within understandings and practices of 'Heritage' (Baker 2019: 16).

References

Arts Council England (2018), *Contribution of the Arts and Culture Industry to the UK Economy: An Updated Assessment of the Macroeconomic Contributions of the Arts and Culture Industry to the National and Regional Economies of the UK*, London: Centre for Economics and Business Research.

Arts Victoria (2011), *The Economic, Soical and Cultural Contribution of Venue-based Live Music in Victoria*, Melbourne: Deloitte Access Economics / Arts Victoria.

Baker, A. J. (2019), *The Great Music City: Exploring Music, Space and Identity*, London: Palgrave Macmillan.

Behr, A., Brennan, M. and Cloonan, M. (2016), 'Cultural Value and Cultural Policy: Some Evidence from the World of Live Music', *International Journal of Cultural Policy*, 22 (3): 403–18.

Belfiore, E. (2018), 'Whose Cultural Value? Representation, Power and Creative Industries', *International Journal of Cultural Policy*, 1–15, DOI: 10.1080/10286632.2018.1495713.

Bianchini, F., Fisher, M., Montgomery, J. and Worpole, K. (1988), *City Centres, City Cultures*, London: CLES.

Bianchini, F. (1995), 'Night Cultures, Night Economies', *Planning Practice & Research*, 10 (2): 121–6.

Bishop, L. (2017), 'An Umbrella Over a Winter City of Music', *The Adelaide Review*, 10 July. Available online: https://www.adelaidereview.com.au/arts/music/umbrella-winter-city-music/

Brown, M. (2020), 'Boris Johnson Pledges £1.5bn Lifeline to Keep UK's Arts Sector Afloat', *The Guardian*, 6 July. Available online: https://www.theguardian.com/world/2020/jul/05/boris-johnson-uk-lifeline-arts-heritage-sector-afloat

BYP Group (2020), 'Government Responses to the Impact of COVID-19 on the Arts and Creative Industries'. Available online: https://www.bypgroup.com/blog/2020/3/21/government-arts-responses-to-covid-19?fbclid=IwAR2UyFZaxOm7Ejhlj92cdf115Jf75wYWUOElK0oAMWQDiMdu9cP5CRN7Do

Callinan, I. (2016), *Review of Amendments to the Liquor Act 2007 (NSW)*, 13 September.

Challenor, J. (2020), 'Damning New Report Details True Impact of COVID on Live Events', *The Music Network*, 14 October. Available online: https://themusicnetwork.com/ey-report-live-event-covid/

Chevigny, P. (1991), *Gigs: Jazz and the Cabaret Laws in New York City*, London and New York: Routledge.

City of Austin (2015), *Austin Music Census: A Data-Driven Assessment of Austin's Commercial Music Economy*, Austin: Titan Group/Economic Development Department, Music and Entertainment Division.

CMU (2018), 'UK Music Calls for Quicker Action on Business Rates', *Complete Music Update* website, 14 March. Available online: https://completemusicupdate.com/article/uk-music-calls-for-quicker-action-on-business-rates/

Cohen, S. (2007) *Decline, Renewal and the City in Popular Music Culture: Beyond the Beatles*, Aldershot: Ashgate.

Committee for Sydney (2018), *Sydney as a 24-Hour City*, Sydney: Committee for Sydney.

Conigrave, K. (2016), 'Last Drinks Laws: A Health Perspective', *Current Issues in Criminal Justice*, 28 (1): 111–16.

De Beukelaer, C. and Spence, K. (2019), *Global Cultural Economy*, Abingdon: Routledge.

Eades, J. (2019), Panellist, 'The Role of Music Accelerators', Ny: LonConnect 2019 conference, London, 22–23 January.

Economist Intelligence Unit (2015), 'Future Cities: Driving Growth through the Creative Economy', *The Economist*. Available at: http://creativecities.eiu.com

Florida, R. (2002), *The Rise of the Creative Class and How It's Transforming Work, Leisure and Everyday Life*, New York: Basic Books.

Florida, R. (2005), *Cities and the Creative Class*, London: Routledge.

Florida, R. (2008), *Who's Your City?* New York: Basic Books.

Florida, R. (2012), 'What Draws Creative People? Quality of Place', *Urban Land* magazine, 11 October. Available online: https://urbanland.uli.org/industry-sectors/what-draws-creative-people-quality-of-place/

Florida, R. (2017), *The New Urban Crisis: How Our Cities Are Increasing Inequality, Deepening Segregation, and Failing the Middle Class – and What We Can Do about It*, New York: Basic Books.

Fulde, G., Smith, M. and Forster, S. L. (2015), 'Presentations with Alcohol-Related Serious Injury to a Major Trauma Hospital after 2014 Changes to Liquor Laws', *The Medical Journal of Australia*, 203 (9): 366–72.

Goldberg-Miller, S. (2017), *Planning for a City of Culture: Creative Urbanism in Toronto and New York*, New York and London: Routledge.

Greater London Authority (2017), *Rescue Plan for London's Grassroots Music Venues Making Progress*, London: Greater London Authority.

Grodach, C. (2012), 'City Image and the Politics of Music Policy in the "Live Music Capital of the World"', in C. Grodach and D. Silver (eds), *The Politics of Urban Cultural Policy*, 114–25, Abingdon: Routledge.

Holden, J. (2006), *Cultural Value and the Crisis of Legitimacy: Why Culture Needs a Democratic Mandate*, London: Demos.

Indergaard, M. (2013), 'When Worlds Collide: The Politics of Cultural Economy Policy in New York', in C. Grodach and D. Silver (eds), *The Politics of Urban Cultural Policy*, 195–207, London and New York: Routledge.

Grodach, C. and Ehrenfeucht, R. (2016), *Urban Revitalization: Remaking Cities in a Changing World*, London and New York: Routledge.

Harris, J. (2013), 'Can the UK's "Toilet Circuit" of Small Music Venues Survive?' *The Guardian*, 23 February. Available online: https://www.theguardian.com/music/2013/feb/22/toilet-circuit-venues-john-harris

Hayden, D. (1995) *The Power of Place: Urban Landscapes as Public History*, London and Cambridge: MIT Press.

Heward, E. (2018), 'Parklife and Warehouse Project Boss Sacha Lord Appointed as Greater Manchester's First "Night Tsar"', *Manchester Evening News*, 6 June. Available online: https://www.manchestereveningnews.co.uk/whats-on/music-nightlife-news/manchester-night-tsar-sacha-lord-14746892#ICID=sharebar_facebook

Homan, S. (2018), *International Contexts, Victorian Conditions: Music and the Night Time Economy*, Melbourne: Music Victoria/Creative Victoria.

IFPI/Music Canada (2015), *The Mastering of a Music City: Key Elements, Effective Strategies and Why It's Worth Pursuing*, London and Toronto: International Federation of Phonographic Industries and Music Canada.

Landry, C. (2008), *The Creative City: A Toolkit for Urban Innovators*, Canada: Earthscan.

Larsson, N. (2019), 'Which Is the World's Most Musical City?' *The Guardian*, 2 May. Available online: https://www.theguardian.com/cities/2019/may/02/which-is-the-worlds-most-musical-city?CMP=Share_iOSApp_Other

Lovatt, A. and O'Connor, J. (1995), 'Cities and the Night-Time Economy', *Planning Practice and Research*, 10 (2): 127–33.

Menéndez, P., Weatherburn, D., Kypri, K. and Fitzgerald, J. (2015), 'Lockouts and Last Drinks: The Impact of the January 2014 Liquor Licence Reforms on Assaults in NSW, Australia', *Crime and Justice Bulletin* 183, NSW Bureau of Crime Statistics and Research.

Miller, T. (1993), *The Well-Tempered Self: Citizenship, Culture and the Postmodern Subject*, Baltimore: Johns Hopkins University Press.

Mosco, V. (2009), *The Political Economy of Communication*, London: SAGE.

New South Wales Government (2016), Alcohol and Drug Fuelled Violence Initiatives, 27 May. Available at: https://www.nsw.gov.au/news-and-events/news/the-nsw-government-is-acting-on-drug-and-alcohol-violence/

New York City (2017), *Economic Impact, Trends, and Opportunities: Music in New York City*, Boston and New York: New York City's Mayor's Office of Media and Entertainment and Boston Consulting Group.

NSW Legislative Council (2018), *The Music and Arts Economy in New South Wales*, Sydney: Portfolio No. 6 – Planning and Environment, New South Wales Government.

O'Brien, D. (2015), 'Cultural Value, Measurement and Policy Making', *Arts & Humanities in Higher Education*, 14 (1): 79–94.

Parkinson, T. and Hunter, M. and Campanello, K., Dines, M. and Dylan S. G. (2015), *Understanding Small Music Venues: A Report by the Music Venues Trust*, London: UK Music.
Rossi, U. and Vanolo, A. (2012), *Urban Political Geographies: A Global Perspective*, London: SAGE.
Schofield, A. and Miller, D. (2017), 'The "Toilet Circuit": Cultural Production, Fandom and Heritage in England's Small Music Venues', *Heritage & Society*, 9 (2): 137–67.
Scott, A. J. (2017), *The Constitution of the City: Economy, Society and Urbanization in the Capitalist Era*, Gewerbestrasse: Palgrave Macmillan.
Se-jeong, K. (2016), 'Seoul to Establish K-pop Complex', *The Korea Times*, 14 July. Available at: http://www.koreatimes.co.kr/www/news/nation/2016/08/117_209426.html
Silver, D., Nichols C. T. and Graziul, C. (2011), 'Scenes, Innovation, and Urban Development', in D. Emannuel Andersson, A. E. Andersson, and C. Mellander (eds), *Handbook of Creative Cities* 229–58, Cheltenham and Northampton: Edward Elgar.
Sisson, A. and Maginn, P. (2018), 'Sanitised' Nightlife Precincts Become Places Where Some are Not Welcome', *The Conversation*, 10 May. Available at: https://theconversation.com/sanitised-nightlife-precincts-become-places-where-some-are-not-welcome-95870
Street, J. (2012), *Music and Politics*, Cambridge: Polity Press.
Sweeney, M. (2020) 'UK Music Industry Will Halve in Size Due to Covid, Says Report', *The Guardian*, 18 November. Available at: https://www.theguardian.com/business/2020/nov/18/uk-music-industry-will-halve-in-size-due-to-covid-says-report
Taylor, A. (2018), '"What the Hell Is Going in Sydney?" 176 Venues Disappear', *The Sydney Morning Herald*, 27 May. Available at: https://www.smh.com.au/national/nsw/what-the-hell-is-going-on-in-sydney-176-venues-disappear-20180527-p4zhst.html
The Rattle (2019) The Rattle website. Available online: https://www.wearetherattle.com/ (accessed 7 July 2019).
Throsby, D. (2001), *Economics and Culture*, Cambridge: Cambridge University Press.
Throsby, D. (2010), *The Economics of Cultural Policy*, Cambridge: Cambridge University Press.
UNESCO (2019), Cities of Music Network. Available at: https://citiesofmusic.net
Wade, M. (2019), 'Sydney's Underdeveloped Night-Time Economy Means City Misses out on $16b, Report Finds', *The Sydney Morning Herald*, 12 February. Available at: https://www.smh.com.au/national/nsw/sydney-s-underdeveloped-night-time-economy-means-city-misses-out-on-16b-report-finds-20190211-p50x2r.html
Watson, A. (2008), 'Global Music City: Knowledge and Geographical Proximity in London's Recorded Music Industry', *Area*, 40 (1): 12–23.
Weatherburn, D. (2016), 'What Does Research Tell Us about the Impact of Recent Liquor Licence Restrictions on Violence in New South Wales?' *Current Issues in Criminal Justice*, 28 (1): 97–103.
Wolfson, P. (2018), *Sydney at Night: People, Places, and Policies of the Neoliberal City*, PhD thesis, Sydney: University of New South Wales.
Wynn, J. R. (2015), *Music/City: American Festivals and Place-making in Austin, Nashville and Newport*, Chicago: University of Chicago Press.
Zukin, S. (2010), 'Landscapes of Power: From Detroit to Disney World', in G. Bridge and S. Watson (eds), *The Blackwell City Reader*, 293–302, Oxford: Wiley-Blackwell.

7

Sensobiographic walking and ethnographic approach of the Finnish school of soundscape studies

Helmi Järviluoma

Introduction

The way one defines the beginning of Finnish soundscape studies is very much dependent on the person doing the defining. Someone might consider it relevant to call the founder of *Pure Geography*, J. Granö (1930), the first Finnish soundscape scholar. Whichever way we define the beginnings of this scholarly field, the situation in early 2019, when writing this essay, is such that almost daily, one tends to bump into the word 'soundscape' in prevalent media. The term is not only used by special journalists but also by ordinary regional and local media workers, who consider it self-evident that so-called 'ordinary' people understand the word *äänimaisema*. It is clear that, despite the critique against the use of the term soundscape (Ingold 2007), in the Finnish language the term manages to capture and bring to everybody's ears the mixture of subjectivity, inter-subjectivity and even the atmospheric-aesthetic aspect of the sonic environment. Soundscape is not a mechanical collection of traits of the environment, but there is a subject or a group of people interpreting, experiencing and producing the elements. In this chapter, the focus is on introducing one possible methodology for studying the ways in which sounds, music, the moving human being – as well as other senses – all relate in the creation of atmospheres, and experiences of places: namely, *sensobiographic walking*.

Finnish ethnographic and cultural analytic approach in soundscape studies

From my listening point, I argue that a distinctive ethnographic methodology of Finnish soundscape studies emerged in the late 1980s in Tampere as a fruitful crossbreeding of: (1) new efficient ethnomusicological field research training; (2) emergent popular music studies; and (3) ethnomethodological sociology. Firstly, the beginnings of soundscape studies in Finland connect to the vivid 1980s ethnomusicological community in Finland at that time. Ethnomusicology was then intensively developing its role as a kind of umbrella discipline of 'The Other Musics' – folk music, music outside Europe, music in everyday life, minority music and popular music – which, especially for a certain period in the 1960s, had been pushed to the margins of Finnish musicology. Elsewhere, I have argued (Järviluoma 2008) that ethnomusicologists in Finland, in their tireless questioning of relationships between the study of music, politics and power from the early 1970s onwards, were actually practising cultural studies as the first field of study in Finland, even before the sociologists.

Popular music studies, the second main root of Finnish soundscape studies, had started to rise vigorously as a branch of research in Finland in 1986 and 1987. I heard the word soundscape for the first time thirty-two years ago, when the concept was scholarly introduced in Finland by the popular music studies pioneer, Philip Tagg, in 1987.[1] After this, the adoption of soundscape studies by the large-hearted community of the Finnish ethnomusicologists happened quite naturally. That community was building professional ties with the University of Gothenburg where especially professor and then-rector, Jan Ling, had made sure that music-sociologists, semioticians (like Tagg) and music-ethnologists studied music in a very multifaceted and open-minded manner. Thirdly, it was in the 1980s, when the sociology of everyday life, along with the interesting ideas of the scholar of everyday culture, history and unconscious, Michel de Certeau, became well known in Finland. That was when I found myself with the Walter Benjamin researcher, Taina Rajanti and a fellow ethnomusicologist sitting in a Tampere café collecting observational data á la Certeau. I also got an ethnomethodological awakening along with a group of Tampere social studies professionals, who started to strongly advocate not only qualitative methodology but also the so-called 'naturally occurring data'. I became a kind of ethnomethodological preacher, being enthusiastic about the phenomenology-tinted methods converging with the postmodern questioning of grand narratives, and the linguistic turn in ethnographic research.

What would have been more suitable in this methodological turmoil than to study something you cannot even capture inside the strict category 'music'? Why not go really over the border and study all the sounds (of course including music) in our everyday environment; to study them as they emerge in the complex of other material and non-material elements of the environment, not even dreaming that one could ever create a 'complete' grand story or truth, or a whole?

Moulding soundscapes studies towards ethnography and cultural analysis

Canadian-led soundscape studies were innovative straight from the beginning of the 1970s. They were among the earliest humanities scholars articulating 'ecology' into their discourse already in the mid-seventies, promoting not only the diversity of biological ecosystems but bringing forth acoustic ecology, the idea of the importance of maintaining and promoting the many-faceted nature of sonic environments.

Also, one only needs to think about the recent keen interest towards the walking methodology (Grosz 1998; Collie 2013; Kusenbach 2003; Wylie 2005 Büscher et al. 2010; Fincham et al. 2010; Lee and Ingold 2006; Lund 2006; Pink et al. 2010) and the fact that in the 1970s the representatives of soundscape studies were ahead of their time with their mobile, dynamic methods of studying environment (Westerkamp 1974; Schafer 1977; see also Järviluoma 2002; Järviluoma 2022; Järviluoma and Vikman 2013; McCartney 2014). In its experimental methodologies when studying Five Village Soundscapes (FVS) in Europe in 1975, World Soundscape Project (WSP) researchers combined arts and sciences. Even if one of the most interesting methods then was walking, in FVS the method was not yet used to its full potential. Instead, researchers often ended up in quantitative listing of sounds while walking (see discussion on this in Järviluoma et al. 2009).

Finnish cultural analysis of soundscapes has aimed since the 1990s to develop more specifically the qualitative methodologies, pushing off from the basis described in the beginning of this chapter. According to the ecomusicologist Aaron Allen (2012), Finnish researchers' (Järviluoma et al. 2009) developmental work on ethnographic and qualitative approaches to acoustic ecology have been necessary. In the project that I led from the late 1990s, Acoustic Environments in Change (AEC), we returned to the WSP and studied five small towns and villages, adding one Finnish studying the changes in soundscapes from 1975 to 2000 in those villages. We did not want to replicate FSV as such, even if we borrowed some of its tests aiming at the possibility of doing some kind of comparisons. Mostly my perspective to methods was borrowed from Paul Feyerabend: there's no point in throwing the baby out with the bathwater. Why not use what is useful, and then, since replicating a study is never possible, go in new directions where necessary. All of our researchers had their own theoretical and methodological interests (see for instance Uimonen 2005; Vikman 2007; Hyvärinen 2007; Järviluoma and Wagstaff 2002; Järviluoma et al. 2009).

My own interest was, by the early 2000s, much directed to the problematics of sonic and sensory remembering (Järviluoma 2002, 2009a, b and c). When reading the book, *Five Village Soundscapes*, it struck me that bringing a person to a place, where they had heard and listened to interesting sounds, had an extraordinary effect on the quality of the interview. The person, in this case the solicitor and town clerk, David Graham, who was brought to the place that once was a vivid railway station in the Scottish village, Dollar, started to remember things hugely better when compared to an interview conducted at an office desk or living room. (See also Irving 2007; Murray and Järviluoma 2019.)

Mr David Graham was still alive and quite well when Heikki Uimonen and I had the chance to take him for a walk at the turn of the millennium in Dollar (Järviluoma 2002[2]). Slowly, from these developments and especially the work carried out in the Breton village, Lesconil, started the development of the method of *sensobiographic walking*, which I am focusing on in this article.

When carrying out the AEC project, listening and sound walking were developed into Sensory Memory Walking in the year 2000 (Järviluoma 2017: 191) in Lesconil with researchers from The Centre for Research on Sonic Space and Urban Environment (CRESSON in Grenoble) (Thibaud 2013; see also, Järviluoma and Vikman 2013; Järviluoma 2017: 191). Nicolas Tixier and Julien Oisans based their listening method, *ecoute située*, on commented city walks of the sociologist Jean-Paul Thibaud (2013), but the study of past sounds and remembering was not exactly the focus in that method. So, after adding the aspect of remembering to the method, I playfully called it *ecoute restituée*. It was exactly in Lesconil a few years later, Autumn 2004, that I realized the multimodality of the senses must be taken into account to a greater extent, when developing the walking method. Namely, it was impossible during the fieldwork to receive 'only' sonic memories – when taking people to the important places and paths of their childhood and youth, people tended to provide multisensory accounts, especially stories of smells and sounds. As an instruction, I started not only to talk about sounds but also about smells, and often the result was an overwhelming flow of sensory memories (see Järviluoma 2009a; Listen, also, Soundcloud Lesconil: Sonic memory walk in in *Quartier de Quatre Vents*).

Sensobiographic walking

By now, it is already clear to the reader that the method in focus in this article – sensobiographic walking – is a kind of culmination of a long line of attempts to chase the ever-escaping phenomena related to sensory remembering, together with my colleagues. To put it simply, sensobiographic walking is an ethnographic research method which offers a plethora of possibilities for researching the embodied and site-specific emergence of sensory remembering and experiences. Even if the method has a long history, this particular format was developed for the large European Research Council funded project, *Sensory transformations in Europe between 1950–2020* (SENSOTRA), which I am currently leading, studying transgenerational environmental relationships and engaging participant pairs composed of different generations.[3]

Basically, sensobiographic walking cannot be considered cumbersome. To start with, you have to ask a person or a group of persons to select a path significant to them in the past. The person/s are invited to talk about the sounds, smells and other sensuous memories they have from that path – in the case of SENSOTRA, we are interested especially in memories from childhood and youth. After the selection, you as a researcher are leading the walk, and walk this path with the person or group studied. In SENSOTRA, the walking is transgenerational (see Murray and Järviluoma 2019; Tiainen, Aula and Järviluoma 2019).

Sensobiographic walking helps to gather rich research material on sensory environmental relationships.

One might wonder why the word *biography* has to be included in the name of this method. A few decades ago, doing biographic research was considered as a quick way to ruin one's career as a young scholar not only as a historian but also, for instance, as a literary researcher. Things changed after the so-called biographic turn of the early 2000s (Caine 2010: 1–2, cit. Leskelä-Kärki 2012: 28).[4] It is quite illuminating that today in Finland the best-selling books come from the genre autobiography: indeed, it has been noted that the transition towards biographic elements does not only have to do with researchers, but there is a connection to the greater audience as well (Leskelä-Kärki 2012). In literature studies, new criticism bracketed out the author, and researchers focused on the 'text itself', sociology was quantitative, and structuralist philosophy and cultural studies proclaimed the death of the author (Hakasalo et al. 2014: 11).

There are different ideas about the reasons behind the new rise of biographical research. While the sociologist Liz Stanley (2001) has related this to an ontological turn, researchers including the cultural historian Maarit Leskelä-Kärki (2012: 28) hear in it the transformations in the discipline of history including the rise of microhistory since the 1970s. In any case, what all this means is that the locality and specificity of lives of subjects studied have been elevated, as well as careful analysis of the situations, processes and practices at the microlevel (2012: 29). Feminist researchers started to call for a qualitative reshaping of autobiographical research. It meant that the idea of a coherent narrative was abandoned, and the focus was moving towards the processes through which it is possible to interpret past lives (and their representations) from the present perspective (Stanley 1992: 3, 6–11, 17–18, 250–5; see also Järviluoma, Moisala and Vilkko 2003, Chapter 3; Leskelä-Kärki: 13–14).

When it comes to the inspiration behind sensobiography, I must say that even if microhistory and especially the everyday life school of history have been important to me ever since the mid-1980s, the idea got more flesh on its bones from humanistic geography and Pauli T. Karjalainen's concept of topobiography – the description of a life-course as it relates to lived places (Karjalainen 2009: 31). Karjalainen is a Finnish humanistic geographer, who, in the early 1980s, developed his existential geography, and whose colleagues call him 'a non-representational geographer before the term was even invented' (Paasi et al. 2013). As Karjalainen has said about topobiography, the ties that present themselves as memories construct and mould the self-hood or subject that each of us feels to be (Karjalainen 2006: 83). The name of Karjalainen's concept has changed as years have passed, from geobiography to topobiography, but the basic ideas have stayed almost the same since the early 1980s.

Karjalainen is a humanistic geographer, whose 'empirical material' comes from literary fiction from all over the world. In the SENSOTRA project, however, we have 'gone native' and are studying the sensobiographies of people currently living in three mid-sized European cities. Topo- and sensobiographic ideas can easily be intermingled with the current study of atmospheres (see Böhme 2017), and this is what we have done in the project (e.g. Tiainen, Aula and Järviluoma 2019). Already in the 1970s soundscape studies took seriously different kinds of materialities and rhytmicity. It is definitely worthwhile to link these developments to another 'turn' of the 2000s, namely new materialism (Järviluoma and Vikman 2013; Tiainen et al. 2019).

One of the good things in biographical research is, according to many commentators, the fact that it opens up into many directions and disciplines (Hakosalo, Jalagin, S. and Kurvinen 2014; Leskelä-Kärki 2012). It is almost impossible to find a working definition, or even a categorization of types which would be satisfactory to all. I quite like the idea of *relational biography*, concentrating on relationships between two or more people (Possing 2001: 1216) as well as *collective biography* (see also Leskelä-Kärki 2012: 34), both of which could be usable when we think about the 'nature' of sensobiographic walking, especially if we consider the relationality more broadly including also the aspects of environment as possible elements in the relational formation. And, in collective biography (Österberg 1996: 326–7), it could be interesting, not so much the writing of mini-biographies but presenting the subjects studied (Leskelä Kärki 2012: 36) in relation to each and as a group sharing characteristics and traits. This kind of approach might become useful in the analysis of sensobiographic walks, which we have indeed only recently begun.[5]

When we think about sensobiography, we need to accept the fact that even if we walk only a little way alongside the person we are studying, relating to the environmental elements that are meaningful to him/her, this is not a major problem. It was a major realization after the crisis of representation during the 1980s within anthropology and other human sciences that ethnographies are always partial (Clifford and Marcus 1986). So are sensobiographies, obtained through walking. Through walking, short reflective interviews and possibility of deep interviews afterwards, we can only obtain an unfinished, partial sensory biography, always co-constructed between the walkers, including the researchers' sensepoints.

Empirical example

Let us have a closer listening of one of the 'ordinary' sensobiographic walks on a sunny Spring day in Turku.[6] The walk was of the most common type for the Sensory Transformations project: the two walkers did not know each other beforehand; one represented the category 'ageing', that is, a seventy-two-year-old pensioner, and one represented the 'young' category, a twenty-four-year-old woman. I had received a tip about Mikko[7] from my friend, who knew that I was leading a research project and was interested in artists, and Mikko can be considered at least a semi-professional photographer. He had moved to Turku from another seaside town almost fifty years ago and worked for a long time in the city library, for instance, building exhibitions. He is bilingual, speaks fluently both Finnish and Swedish, is a Francophile, has loved the sea and sailing all his life and is a dedicated cyclist.

Marianne had lived in Turku for five years. She had moved from the Ostrobothnian rural seaside and after travelling a few years she settled on studying at health-related school. Her main hobby has to do with the circus, acrobatics, but she is also artistically oriented and often makes 'old-fashioned' cinefilm recordings while walking in the city+.

Two researchers were involved: I was in charge of the first walk with Mikko; then we had a coffee and conducted a short interview. After that, the other researcher, Juhana Venäläinen, was in charge of the walk with Marianne. But as usual, all participants are free to participate in the walking conversation.

Since sensobiographic walking does not distinguish between the senses, it is natural that the walks in SENSOTRA are quite different in the amount of bits and pieces of sounds and music that flow into conversation. Also, we researchers are different, and because I have a background in soundscape studies, I tended to bring sounds into the conversation: the past sounds, especially in the case of Mikko I asked about the sounds, smells and other sensual experiences, but also, when I heard a sound not mentioned by other walkers, I tended to draw attention to the sounds, or musical elements in the environment and ask questions about them.

Mikko chose his walking route right along the banks of the river Aura, starting from the old restaurant, Pinella, culturally and historically renowned for its Red Room, where the famous Swedish writer, August Stringberg, is said to have spent time. The walk was long, Mikko had a lot to tell and wished that we could end the walk with a cup of coffee at Göran, named after another writer, Göran Schild, whose famous sailing boat, Dapfne, found its destination inside the big cafe.

Among the first sounds heard when we commenced our walk was the pounding sound coming from a pile-driving boat, a loud hitting coming from the machine putting poles on the sides of the river on which people's boat could be kept during summer.

> MIKKO: (- -)This (sound) is a definite sign of Spring.
> MARIANNE: Oh, I see
> HELMI: Okay. It makes quite a noise.
> MIKKO: Yes, yes it makes a noise (- -)
> HELMI: Has the sound stayed the same as long as you have lived here?
> MIKKO: Erm, yes, yes, yes it has stayed the same. The thing is that these boat places have been diminished in the city centre because of vandalism.

This is very typical for Mikko's way of discussing sounds. He tends to move immediately from the sound and its qualities to its context, and actions that cause the sound. From explaining the illegal actions, he then immediately moves to explaining that, naturally, one of the reasons he chose the riverside for this walk was the fact that along it there are continuously all sorts of happenings, especially from Spring onwards, but even during the winter. The Aura riverside is a place for Turku citizens to meet friends and fellows. Every walker-talker has their own way of framing their story, and it is obvious that when I take the discussion to the past experienced sensory transformations, it is Mikko who always, one way or another, manages to make connections to changes in society. For example, early in the walk, I asked:

> HELMI: If you think about this place, and this bank, where we are walking now, so what was it like in the 60s, in 1969? And what kind of smells, fragrances were here, and what was here to be heard?
> MIKKO: (…) there were very few events (…) Pinella, where we just left from, has always stayed there, the restaurant life was started in fact from Pinella. Those piles, which we just

had a look upon, there were much more of them, and well, boats where mostly made of wood then (…) Erm, the atmosphere was much, much more peaceful if you compare to today. (–) So, the peacefulness that was here, it was much more striking, so that (all has) changed immensely during the last 40–50 years.

According to Mikko, there were definitely less sounds in the late 1960s, 'basically only the sound of motor boats could be heard' which was natural, since he would already then come by boat up the river from the sea towards this area. I asked Mikko to make a time jump and to think about himself in the late 1960s or early 1970s, on the bench, and to describe what he can hear around him. The thing that comes to his mind is drinking. At that time people drank heavily, and today people's drinking has become more civilized: 'The social behaviour or people have become much tidier, without doubt.'

Another important change was that the big restaurant boats that are now dominating the scenery, when we walked through the Aura riverbanks, were no longer there. The peacefulness in the late 1960s was made even more definite by the fact that there was so much more traffic than nowadays: 'We did not even know what a traffic jam means'. Cycling, however, was not particularly popular, not as popular as today; at that time, there were no cycling paths. Mikko connects many sensory transformations to the arrival of the so-called information society:

So nowadays, if one talks about sensory experiences, there are more and more of those, and all kinds of knowledge and… One can say that it has exploded. It is the biggest – no not the biggest but a problem that comes with too much of that knowledge, even an awful lot of unnecessary information. And people cannot really concentrate on anything properly. One example, erm, is reading a book. (… Very seldom when you walk on this bank, so very rarely do you see people reading books on the benches anymore. (- -) I have still tried to do that.

Mikko and also some other artists find a very clear difference when they compare life then and now. Before, after the theatre or other events everybody always went to one bar or the other, and there were extremely lively discussions, 'it was very much face-to-face action'. One sculptor, Timo, mentioned to me that this was to him the major change in Turku. He was not on Facebook and so he felt that he had lost connection with colleagues. Before, there were always bars where one would be sure to find people, and both Mikko and the sculptor stress in their talk that it was all kinds of people that came to the same bars: you could meet the town leaders as well as very ordinary people at the same place and discuss eagerly the theatre, art and everything between heaven and earth. 'This was the biggest thing, if you compare now and then…', Mikko says, stressing how important this societal, cultural and sensory transformation was.

These are typical moments in which Mikko and Timo the sculptor describe the past from the listening point of today. Even if the 'coherence' of the narrative may suffer from these paths that start directly from the observations about today's way of life and society, they give us clues for the interpretation of the process through which it is possible to have a glance to past sensory experiences. For me personally, it is also important to realize my own effect on the narrative, and the ways in which my own personal history weaves into the walking narratives (cf. Stanley 1992), as well as the histories and present endeavours of the other walk participants, making the borders between sensobiography and autosensobiography porous.

When talking about two theatre directors that in the leftist and radical times of the 1970s made Turku theatre famous (Kalle Holmberg, Ralf Långbacka), Mikko explains how equality and democracy reached even the face-to-face meetings in a sailor bar after the theatre:

> MIKKO: And well, anyone was welcome to talk to anyone, so to say. It was typical for the times, yes, that you didn't sneer at others, you didn't act like 'okay, you don't belong here'. So, everyone (…) who had something to say about theatre could come there, 'welcome'. We came (…) and discussed in a group (…) went to the tavern to discuss a theatre performance, any sort of art performance. Naturally, this does not exist anymore. (…) There was a strong spirit of excitement in the air.

When I tried to figure out the sensory experiences in that particular sailors' pub at Ursininkatu, which was one of the main gathering points of at least theatre folk in the early 1970s, and asked about music the answer of Mikko was:

> Erm, no (–), you mean, erm, the music actually ruined the atmosphere there so that (–) when we wanted to discuss we did not want any noise around. No, there was no music, but what was in every restaurant was the horrible smoke of cigarettes.

At that point, I wanted to get a glimpse of today's situation and asked the younger participant, Marianne, whether Mikko's account sounds familiar. She doesn't sound like she wishes to give a very firm answer, instead she says that what she can say is that it sounds that before it was extremely common, and now it is less common:

> MARIANNE: I believe that it is not common, at least not to that extent that it used to be, when, indeed, it has been extremely common.
>
> MIKKO: But we must also take into account that the times were different, erm (–) really it is the technology. We did not have mobile phones, we had nothing, so people were also forced to contact each other directly. This is probably the biggest thing [change±] if you compare it to today's time. Here and now.

Marianne brings up the Vegetarian restaurant Keidas: 'There are all sorts of discussions, game evenings and then some sort of music nights and…'. The younger walker's answer is very similar to the one that I received when walking with the sculptor Timo. The younger man walker during that walk, a student of humanities and an amateur musician accepts the claim in general, but not completely: sometimes even today the groups of friends go to a restaurant after an art or cultural event in order to share their experiences.

Towards the end of the walk, approaching Forum Marina and cafe Göran, we walked through a part of the river bank that used to be docks. In the 1960s and 1970s it was a closed area to Turku citizens and only after the mid-eighties the river bank was constructed in a way that people could move in the area. Mikko uses an interesting expression when we walk in the area that used to be a dockland:

> MIKKO: Just a moment. This was, *this place did not exist*. And well (- -) docks started from that spot and it was so that you could not even go there. It was such junk from that spot,

only a couple of hundred meters from that spot on. (…) it ended in a way (…) In the 80s, could it be in the middle, one started to build up to the harbour (…) It was wasteland (…) So straight to the river Aura, the land went straight to the river Aura.

When walking in this area now, researcher Venäläinen draws attention to the sounds of the dock:

> JUHANA: Could the sounds of the dock be heard towards the city at all?
> MIKKO: Erm, if the wind is blowing from the west, then one can hear something, when the wind brings the sound. So then, well, to a certain extent one could hear it but it was rattles and bangs. (…) I was living on the other side of town. I didn't hear them ever (…) one never heard those sounds except when visiting this place. But one must remember that this was only wasteland, not like it is now. Or, this all in all was an industrial district.

After passing a restaurant boat which brought the smell of tar to our noses, we discussed it, and all of us agreed that it was a commercial trick – tar was there to tempt customers with the nice smell. 'It is a trick, the smell brings nice memories', says Mikko, and then people think that this is a good place to have a beer. When passing the numerous restaurant boats on the Aura riverside, it is as well possible to hear – at this time of day, in the afternoon – only quietly different kinds of music from the boats. For example, from the Vaakahuone (owned by a famous all-round musician), stamped by Mikko as a tourist attraction, sounds of quiet mainstream jazz could be heard in the Springy air of the riverbank, when we walked past it. For me, it was almost a sign that I could have gone there, and we could have had our conversation there with a cup of coffee, but I also knew from experience, that the place was not the kind of coffee place that we were searching for, because people had gone there in order to really entertain themselves with music and food, perhaps even a bit of dancing.

It is indeed an interesting contrast when walking on top of the old industrial soil, which has been gentrified and was an area developing more and more expensive-looking apartments and sculptures, heading towards Forum Marina. The apartments, low blocks of flats with glass terraces look expensive. Mikko has deep personal memories of the area, since his sailing mate lived in the area. Both of them had looked at the plan for the restaurant Nooa before construction and immediately thought that 'no, no, not places like that':

> Immediately, a feeling came that at least I am not going to a place like that. It is meant for people, well, to put it straight, it is meant for people who have money and fancy boats and they are coming to that spot there. And it is not, erm (- -) it has no 'the spirit of being from Turku' – Turku people were not thought of at all (when building that).

When walking past Mikko's friends' flat, he gives us a short description of him. The friend died a short while ago, and we as listeners can tell that this has been a big loss to Mikko, so we give him our condolences. He remembers his friend in the following:

> MIKKO: He did not (- -) have a television or such things. He just had a mobile phone. And this whale [sculpture just under his window], when the sculpture is on, there's water coming from it. And when [you live here], and water is coming, which drops now and then, täp-täp-täp-täp-täp, dropping especially [- -] when it is 'pläkä', which means the wind is not blowing at all, the sound can be heard extremely well. And in the summer,

his terrace door was open, and he couldn't sleep because of the dripping noise klik-klik-klik-klyt (–).
HELMI: So that…
MIKKO: That I always remember, when I cycle past here, that oh yes.
HELMI: Yes, it means that the sound was meant to be even beautiful, but it did not give him pleasure.
MIKKO: Yes, it was like, like someone would have left the tap open (laughs).
HELMI: Exactly
MIKKO: (- -) could not stand it, so.
HELMI: Aha. But there was nothing to be done?
MIKKO: Nothing was to be done (–)

Mikko surely had a taste for music, art and the places he liked and the places he did not like – the flashy restaurant Nooa alongside the river bank was condemned by him completely to be a poshy, expensive yuppie place, as well as many of the sculptures were in his opinion 'art', not art.

Conclusion

Sensobiography is, in a way, mobile life writing, talking sensory life into being while moving and then the researcher writing about the biographical fractions captured by microphone and video devices. It can be interpreted as crossings, collectives of remembered experiences, touching each other, sharing family resemblances in a mid-sized city. Subjects are moulded in crossroads of larger processes and structures, as Florin (2014: 9) has put it, they reassemble bookmarks of history. It is important to 'reveal' how people saw, and I would say not only saw, but heard, smelled, tasted and experienced their world and their own actions (cf. Florin 2014: 27). It is based on a different understanding of a human being as a subject: a human being creates their world and understands their social being, persona, through constructing meaning and subjective identity in the discursive connections in which they are living (Florin 2014: 28).

When using this method, the subject is not seen as isolated from their environment, but in connection to different categories and developments. Sensobiography becomes a way to understand the converging of the personal into larger social contexts: the biographical can help us progress towards the transformational processes of the sensory environment, and help us to understand how subjects, different generations, groups and institutions interpret societal transformations.

Notes

1   When Philip Tagg was brought to Helsinki in the Spring of 1987 by IASPM-Norden, the Tampere chapter of the Finnish Ethnomusicological Society brought him to the

University of Tampere, where he gave a lecture mentioning soundscapes, and developing the ways in which it could be used in the analysis of popular music.

2   Listen also to https://soundcloud.com/akueko/dollar-sonic-memory-walk-with-david-graham?in=akueko/sets/acoustic-environments-in

3   This entry is part of research project SENSOTRA (*Sensory Transformations and Transgenerational Environmental Relationships in Europe, 1950–2020*), which received funding from the European Research Council (ERC) under the European Union's Horizon 2020 Research and Innovation programme (grant agreement No 694893). SENSOTRA is an Advanced Grant 2015 project led by Principal Investigator Helmi Järviluoma.

4   I am using the term 'turn' in spite of the many troubles that are inherent in it.

5   One thing worth pondering upon: Since, for example, Liz Stanley is much stressing the importance of different networks in the auto/biographical study. This was very much taken into account, for instance, in the walks that I made in the fishing village, Lesconil, with often members of the same family present on the same walk, or at least a group of friends. In SENSOTRA, however, the transgenerational pairs are not always parts of the same network, even if sometimes the pairs may be, for example, a grandchild and a grandparent. This is on the hand an interesting point in the study. We lose something from the 'natural' relationality but often this method creates new, fresh, interesting encounters and relations.

6   At the time of writing this article, we have almost finished the gathering of empirical data in Turku and Slovenia, however, Brighton material gathering is in its early phases. We are still processing the data, and my analysis here is based more on preliminary thoughts and impressions from the early phase of data analysis.

7   The names of the research subjects have been pseudonymized.

References

Allen, A. (2012), 'Ecomusicology: Music, Culture, Nature… and Change in Environmental Studies?' *Journal of Environmental Studies and Sciences*, 2 (2): 192–201.

Büscher, M., Urry, J. and Witchger, K. (2010), *Mobile Methods*, London: Routledge.

Böhme, G., ed. (Jean-Paul Thibaud). (2017), *The Aesthetics of Atmospheres*, New York: Routledge.

Caine, B. (2010), *Biography and History*, New York: Palgrave Macmillan.

Clifford, J. and Marcus, G. E. (1986), *Writing Culture. The Poetics and Politics of Ethnography*, Berkeley: University of California Press.

Collie, N. (2013), 'Walking in the City: Urban Space, Stories and Gender,' *Gender Forum*, 42: 3–14.

Fincham, B., McGuinness, M. and Murray, L., eds (2010), *Mobile Methodologies*, London: Palgrave MacMillan.

Florin, C. (2014), 'Biografia rajoja rikkomassa (Breaking biographical borders.). Kolme esimerkkiä ruotsalaisesta elämäkertatutkimuksesta', in H. Hakosalo, S. Jalagin, M. Junila and H. Kurvinen (eds), *Historiallinen elämä. Biografia ja historiantutkimus*. (Historical

life. Biography and historical research), 27–44, Historiallinen arkisto 141. SKS, Helsinki: Finnish Literature Society.
Grosz, E. (1998), 'Bodies-Cities', in S. Pile and H. J. Nast (eds), *Places Through the Body*, 42–51, London: Routledge.
Hakosalo, H., Jalagin, S., Marianne, J. and Kurvinen, H. (2014), 'Johdanto. elämää suurempaa. (Introduction. Larger than Life.)', in H. Hakosalo, S. Jalagin, M. Junila and H. Kurvinen (eds), *Historiallinen elämä. Biografia ja historiantutkimus.* (Historical life. Biography and Historical Research), 7–26, Historiallinen arkisto 141. SKS, Finnish Literature Society: Helsinki.
Hyvärinen, T. (2007), *Estetiikka, tiedonmuodostus ja Nauvon äänimaisema.* (Aesthetics, formation of knowledge and the soundscape of Nauvo), MPhil Thesis, University of Joensuu.
Ingold, T. (2007), 'Against Soundscape', in A. Carlyle (ed), *Autumn Leaves: Sound and the Environment in Artistic Practice*, 10–13, Paris: Double Entendre.
Irving, A. (2007), 'Ethnography, Art and Death', *Journal of the Royal Anthropological Institute*, 13: 185–208.
Järviluoma, H. (forthcoming), 'Transgenerational sensobiography as mobile and embodied life writing', in H. Järviluoma and L. Murray (eds), *Sensory Transformations*, London: Taylor and Francis.
Järviluoma, H. (2017), 'The Art and Science of Sensory Memory Walking', in M. Cobussen, V. Meelberg and B. Truax (eds), *The Routledge Companion to Sounding Art*, London: Routledge.
Järviluoma, H. (2009a), "Lesconil, My Home: Memories of Listening", in H. Järviluoma et al. (eds), *Acoustic Environments in Change*. Translation editor Bruce Johnson. Book + four CDs, 172–193. University of Joensuu, Faculty of Humanities Publications & Tampere University of Applied Sciences.
Järviluoma, H. (2009b), "Soundscape and Social Memory in Skruv", in H. Järviluoma et al. (eds), *Acoustic Environments in Change*, 138–53, Tampere: University of Joensuu and Tampere University of Applied Sciences.
Järviluoma, H. (2009c), "The Scythe-driven Nostalgia", in H. Järviluoma et al. (eds), *Acoustic Environments in Change*, 154–71, Tampere: University of Joensuu and Tampere University of Applied Sciences.
Järviluoma, H. (2008), 'Etnomusikologi kulttuurintutkijana – pakkoavioliitto vai aito romanssi. [Ethnomusicologist as a cultural researcher – a forced marriage or a true romance]', *Kulttuurintutkimus*, 25 (2): 11–24.
Järviluoma, H. (2002), 'Memory and Acoustic Environments: Five European Villages Revisited', in E. Waterman (ed.), *Sonic Geography Remembered and Imagined*, Toronto: Penumbra Press.
Järviluoma, H., Moisala, P. and Vilkko, A. (2003), *Gender and Qualitative Methods*, London: Sage.
Järviluoma, H., Uimonen, H., Vikman, N., Kytö, M. and Truax, B. (2009), *Acoustic Environments in Change*. Translation editor Bruce Johnson. Book + four CDs. University of Joensuu, Faculty of Humanities Publications & Tampere University of Applied Sciences.
Järviluoma, H. and Vikman, N. (2013), 'On Soundscape Methods and Audiovisual Sensibility', in C. Gorbman Claudia, J. Richardson and C. Vernallis (eds), *Oxford Handbook of New Audiovisual Aesthetics*, 645–58, Oxford: Oxford University Press.

Järviluoma, H. and Wagstaff, G. (2002), 'Soundscape Studies and Methods', Helsinki: The Finnish Society for Ethnomusicology Publ. 9 & University of Turku, Dept. of Art, Literature & Music Series A51.

Karjalainen P. T. (2009), 'Topobiography: Remembrance of Places Past', *Nordia Geographical Publications*, 38 (5): 31–4.

Karjalainen, P. T. (2006), "Topobiografinen paikan tulkinta" (Topobiographic Interpretation of Place), in S. Knuuttila, P. Laaksonen and U. Piela (eds) *Paikka: eletty, kuviteltu, kerrottu.* (Place: lived, imagined, narrated.), Yearbook of the Kalevala Society 85, Helsinki: Finnish Literature Society.

Kusenbach, M. (2003), 'Street Phenomenology: The Go-Along as Ethnographic Research Tool', *Ethnography*, 4 (3): 455–85.

Lee, J. and Ingold, T. (2006), 'Fieldwork on Foot: Perceiving, Routing, Socializing', in S. Coleman and P. Collins (eds), *Locating the Field: Space, Place and Context in Anthropology*, 67–86, Oxford: Berg.

Leskelä-Kärki, M. (2012), 'Samastumisia ja etääntymisiä. Elämäkerta historiantutkimuksen kysymyksenä', in A. Nivala, and R. Mähkä (eds), *Tulkinnan polkuja: Kulttuurihistorian tutkimusmenetelmiä*. Turku: K & H.

Lund, K. (2006), 'Seeing in Motion and the Touching Eye: Walking Over Scotland's Mountains', *Anthropological Journal*, 18 (1): 27–42.

McCartney, A. (2014), 'Soundwalking: Creating Moving Environmental Sound', in S. Gopinath J. Stanyek (eds), *The Oxford Handbook of Mobile Music Studies*, vol. 2, 212–37, Oxford: Oxford University Press.

Murray, L. and Järviluoma, H. (2019), 'Walking as Transgenerational Methodology', *Qualitative Research*, Online https://doi.org/10.1177/1468794119830533.

Paasi, A., Rannela, S. and Tani, S. (2013), *Matkalla. Pauli Tapani Karjalaisen 60-vuotisjuhlakirja*, Oulu: Multiprint.

Possing, B. (2001), 'Historical Biography', in *The International Encyclopedia of Social and Behavioral Sciences*, 1213–17, Oxford: Elsevier.

Pink, S., Hubbard, P., O'Neill, M. and Radley, A. (2010), 'Walking across Disciplines: From Ethnography to Arts Practice', *Visual Studies*, 25 (1): 1–7.

Schafer, Murray, R. M. (1977), *The Tuning of the World*, New York: Alfred A. Knopf.

Soundcloud Lesconil: Sonic memory walk in in *Quartier de Quatre Vents*.Qu https://soundcloud.com/akueko/sets/acoustic-environments-in

Stanley, L. (1992), *The Auto/biographical I. The Theory and Practice of Feminist Auto/biography*, Manchester: Manchester University Press.

Thibaud, J-P. (2013), 'Commented City Walks', *Wi: Journal of Mobile Culture*, 7 (1): 1–32.

Tiainen, M., Inkeri, A., and Järviluoma, H. (2019), 'Transformations in mediations of lived sonic experience. A sensobiographic approach', in Friedlind Riedel and Juha Torvinen (eds), *Music as Atmosphere. Collective Feelings and Affective Sounds*, 238–54, London: Taylor and Francis.

Uimonen, H. (2005), *Ääntä kohti. Äänympäristön kuuntelu, muutos ja merkitys*, Tampere: Acta Universitatis Tamperensis 1110.

Vikman, N. (2007), *Eletty ääniympäristö. Pohjoisitalialaisen Cembran kylän kuulokulmat muutoksessa* (The Lived Acoustic Environment: Cembra's Changing Points of Ear), Tampere: Acta Universitatis Tamperensis 1271

Westerkamp, H. (1974), 'Soundwalking', *Sound Heritage*, 3 (4): 18–27

Wylie, J. W. (2005), 'A Single Day's Walking: Narrating Self and Landscape on the Southwest Coast Path', *Transactions of the Institute of British Geographers*, 30 (2): 234–47.

Österberg, E. (1996). 'Individen i historien: En (o)möjilighet mellan Sartre och Foucault', in *Det roliga börjar hela tiden: festskrift till Kjell Peterson*, 321–33, Stockholm: Clio.

Section II

Space, place and consumption

8

At home with Sinatra

Keir Keightley

Introduction

One winter evening in 1958 – en route from your white-collar job in a downtown office building to your detached house in the suburbs – you spy something in the display window of your local record shop that makes you stop: a brand-new Sinatra album. He's been releasing so much music lately (this is at least his fourth new, high-fidelity, long-player in a year!) that you didn't even know there was another one until its full-colour cover caught your eye. Entering the shop, moving past the sheet music and instruments and boxes of phonograph needles, you request your copy of the new release. As the clerk hands it to you, you realize once more that the cardboard sleeve of the LP isn't just there to protect the vinyl within. It's also a big part of what you enjoy about these new 12" pop albums, what the trade press has been calling 'packages'. They certainly are packed with sound and vision, image and text, songs and personalities. On the front cover, Frank looks right at you, gesturing for you to Come Fly with Me – to join him on a musical journey and fly away via phonograph. The modern packaging pulls you into the world of the LP by promising pleasure, by producing meanings, perhaps even by providing plans for use (some LPs of late have been including diagrams telling you the perfect place to sit in relation to your speakers, in order to achieve the ideal home audio experience!).

As it turns out, this new Sinatra 'package' of songs about different places around the world does contain instructions for listening – liner notes inviting particular ways of approaching audition. The back cover includes an image of a spiral-bound 'flight log', recording a hypothetical listener's experience of the album. It encourages you, too, to imagine the LP as a vehicle for musical transportation. In this log, Sinatra's performances of individual songs ('Blue Hawaii', 'April in Paris', 'Brazil') are described in terms of an airline passenger's reactions to a global flight. You're excited to hear what Sinatra will do in these high-flying, high-fidelity versions of such old, familiar songs, thematically organized into a world tour. Added into the mix, you notice some brand-new songs, titles you don't recognize, like 'It's Nice to Go Trav'ling'. The packaging works its intended magic and so you hand the clerk five dollars. Now it's yours, this glossy parcel of star singer, superior recording quality, a dozen old and new songs – all bundled into an appealing concept: a musical trip to faraway locales. Arriving at your residence, you fire up your hi-fi system, and set the tonearm on its journey. As it moves from the perimeter of the slick black disk towards its spinning centre, the room in which you are sitting is saturated with sound and soon is sensually transformed. As Frank's powerful vocals take you somewhere else, the domestic becomes exotic, here becomes there, and home fades away for awhile. And then, as the album concludes and the tonearm returns to its resting place, you find yourself having been moved, both emotionally and virtually, from vinyl periphery back to domestic centre. You are home, once more.

Come fly with me

Listening at home defined a crucial epoch in the history of popular musical mediation. Developments in sound technologies altered long-standing relationships between music listening and ideas of space and place (Durant 1984; Connell and Gibson 2003; O'Brien 2004). This was keenly felt in the home, long a place of musical production, but increasingly now also a space of audio consumption. It is noteworthy, then, that musical conceptions of the 'home' consumed therein were themselves frequently constituted in contrast to fantasies of an 'away' – musical 'elsewheres' that helped highlight the 'here' of hearth and home (cf. Frith 1983). From popular sheet music played on a home piano to the rise of high-fidelity home audio equipment and beyond, music in domestic space often expounded, explored and exploited a productive tension between 'home' and 'away'. For instance, even before the advent of sound recording, 'Home Sweet Home' (1823), among the most-performed popular songs of the nineteenth century, contains a verse about roaming far away to distant 'pleasures and palaces', whose 'splendor dazzles', so that its refrain may better embrace the simple comforts of a 'lowly thatched cottage' as it concludes: 'Be it ever so humble, there's no place like home'.

A century later, the Tin Pan Alley song-writing team of Sammy Cahn and Jimmy Van Heusen updated that sentiment for an age of trans-Atlantic jets and hi-fi phonography on 'It's Nice to Go Trav'ling (But It's Nicer to Come Home)'. It appears as the concluding track of *Come Fly with Me*, a best-selling 1958 long-play (LP) album that attends explicitly to ideas of place and is thus the focus of this chapter. Beginning with Frank Sinatra's shouted imperative, 'let's fly away!', the album alludes to at least sixteen different countries: United States, Mexico, Bermuda, Brazil, Peru, Ireland, England, France, Spain, Germany, Italy, Egypt, Iraq, India, Burma and China. While the instrumentation is predominantly that of a large swing orchestra with string section, sprinkled throughout are sounds suggestive of the places lyrically described (mandolins on 'Isle of Capri', gong on 'On the Road to Mandalay', shakers on 'Brazil'). As an example of mid-century musical exotica (Hayward 1999; Taylor 2001), the album proposes a domestic Self driven by desire for elsewhere and defined by the Other. The 'exotic' is even made lyrically explicit on its tracks 'Autumn in New York' ('Dreamers, with empty hands/Make plans for exotic lands') and 'Come Fly with Me' ('If you could use some exotic booze/There's a bar in far Bombay'). Its liner notes describe

Sinatra 'personally guiding you on a high flying musical tour that spans three continents!', thereby helping orient auditors towards particular modes of musical consumption and conceptualization associated with sound recording and domestic listening. Released at the very peak of the United States' post-war economic expansion, not long before the Cuban Missile Crisis, just as leisure air travel was becoming more commonplace and as the LP format had become, far and away, the most profitable commodity in the history of the US record industry (Keightley 2004), this best-selling Sinatra record mixes and mingles musical stereotypes, fantasies of the exotic and the erotic and contemporary geopolitical concerns. Framed as a virtual voyage to exciting elsewheres, *Come Fly with Me* nonetheless places listeners firmly at the comfortable centre of an implicitly white, suburban, heterosexual, domestic space.

If its final track remodels 'Home Sweet Home', this 'theme' LP's packaging of musical tourism for the jet age also modernizes an even older mode of musical presentation with pronounced centring tendencies: the operatic pasticcio, in which a variety of arias would be pastiched or mixed together to produce a new work. Historically, the consumer of the pasticcio enjoyed the position of a privileged Self partaking of a pleasurable parade of musical Otherness. On *Come Fly with Me,* this older musical structure is amplified via high-fidelity, long-play, audio technology's powerful placement of the listener as master or mistress of a home audio universe. And Sinatra himself was of course renowned for his commanding personality and masculinist mastery of popular entertainment; his virtuosic vocals offer a model subjectivity that might temporarily be inhabited by listeners. Thus, three modes of powerfully placing listeners at a virtual-musical centre converge and overlap on *Come Fly with Me*: First, high-fidelity protocols of audition position listeners as the nucleus of the soundfield, in order to be fully immersed and virtually transported out of domestic space. Second, in mixing a variety of songs about different places in the world, the album draws on the ethnic pasticcio descended from operatic tradition, where listeners indulge in a global-musical panorama arranged just for them. Finally, the complex ideological elaborations of a superstar pop vocalist occupy the centre of the mix, offering a point of listener identification and interpellation. In each instance, listeners are placed at a virtual centre where feelings of privilege and power are sounded out and enjoyed in domestic space.

Listening to LPs at home

Listening to an LP at mid-century was typically predicated upon access to hi-fi equipment and an interior space. This in turn facilitated other kinds of access. When powerful sound waves washed across domestic spaces, listeners could be moved emotionally and transported elsewhere (Keightley 1996; see also Hoechner 2007). Peter Bailey (2004) uses the word 'envelope' to encompass both sound and its senses of belonging. As the virtual audio space of the sound recording is draped across the domestic space of audition, the latter is reconfigured by the former, effectively superimposing one aural space on top of another. While the common dismissal of background or mood music as 'musical wallpaper' (cf. Hesmondhalgh 2021) in the period was explicitly dismissive and implicitly misogynist, it nonetheless indexed a common-sense understanding of sound recording's capacity to envelope, and hence sonically redesign, domestic interiors. Due to its potential for higher playback volume, longer playback duration and wider frequency response, the high-fidelity LP was celebrated (and occasionally demonized) precisely because of this unprecedented new power to overwrite (and often overwhelm) domestic living spaces. In so doing, an LP played loudly on a hi-fi system could transform the familiar home into something else – something frequently imagined as a *somewhere* else. As Peter Doyle (2005) so beautifully elucidates, hi-fi recordings could 'reterritorialize' the space of listening, sonically mapping a musical 'there' on to the physical 'here' of audition. This might result in a hybrid or even liminal space of audition, an uncanny feeling of being 'here' and 'there', at the very same time, what Anahid Kassabian (2004) has transcribed as 't/here'. A facility inherent in all phonography, it was rendered most spectacularly in period hi-fi LP marketing (on hi-fi culture, see also Anderson, Barry, Björnberg, Bourdage, Jansson, Perchard, Robertson-Wojcik, Theberge et al, Western). The phonograph's virtual exoticization of domestic realities was articulated repeatedly with the period's complex geopolitical economic situation of suburbia, itself often dismissed as a 'non-place' and reliant upon daily travel elsewhere (i.e. commuting to urban workplaces).

Hi-fi listening protocols that fetishized audio immersion, virtual transportation and phonographic reterritorialization resonated particularly well with albums that promised musical voyages to distant places, like *Come Fly with Me*. In this first moment of LP culture, albums of the 1950s were regularly presented as packaged worlds to be accessed sonically and inhabited virtually (Keightley 2011). Thus, we find thousands of mid-century LP covers promising home consumers mediated access to other places via sound recording, whether *Night in Manhattan, Dinner in Rio* or *Other Worlds, Other Sounds*, or hundreds upon hundreds of album titles that included phrases like 'the world of', 'a musical trip to' or 'around the world' (for an excellent sampling, see Borgerson and Schroeder 2017). Among the more arresting of such musical trip discs is a 1956 LP, *Night Out Music for Stay-at-Homes*, that renders the home/away dynamic of this LP listening formation most graphically. Its cover features a photograph of a young suburban couple lounging on their living room carpet, which has been superimposed upon, and thus floats over, the glowing skyscrapers of a modern metropolis. It thus proposes the possibility of occupying two spaces at once, of being 'home' and 'away' simultaneously (a longstanding phonographic fantasy, as Lisa Gitelman's 2006 account of early phonograph marketing shows). Well into the 1970s, LPs continued to offer such trippy access to elsewheres, real or imagined, as on Pink Floyd's 1973 album *Dark Side of the Moon* (itself a theme album with mood music overtones that moves between being 'on the run' and 'home, home again'). In other words, hi-fi LPs like *Come Fly with Me* enabled, and indeed frequently made manifest, a reconfiguration of domestic audition contexts, mediating the mundane or homely with external, exciting or exotic spaces of audacious virtuality.

A powerful high-fidelity amplifier helped auditors virtually 'possess the world' on vinyl, just as the mid-century United States was occupying centre stage of post-war geopolitics.

Jonathan Sterne (2015: 21), discussing the stereo technology being launched on LP that very year, 1958, sees it offering 'a stable audioposition, one from which the entire world is available to be heard', a most pleasurable and privileged place to dwell indeed. The very month *Come Fly with Me* was released on Capitol, an ad campaign for rival Columbia Records promoted their hi-fi LPs as offering powerful access to a pastiche of global-musical difference:

> thrill to exotic places, faces, sensations… enchantment, romance, the magic of mysterious far-off lands and sounds… captured with flawless fidelity… In undulating rhythms you'll visit crowded bazaars of India… sparkling festive rodeo in colorful romantic Chile… be spellbound by the pulsating native Caribbean drums… and more! 'At home' evenings become more delightful, gay and enriched at the flick of a switch. The journey's price? A mere… $4.98. Take several!
> (Columbia Records ad, *New York Times* 26 January, 1958, p.88)

This ad, for an LP series called 'Adventures in Sound', encapsulates a dominant listening formation into which *Come Fly with Me* was released (note here that, even as stereophonic sound has arrived, the Capitol and Columbia LPs in question are monophonic, reminding us that stereo was as much a change in degree as one of kind). Whether affluent or aspirational, presumptive or privileged, what such commodities promised was a delectable musical experience of 'the world': in this case, the post-Second World War geopolitical landscape, in which US hegemony was ascendant, in which the affluent US consumer was encouraged to feel vindicated as the triumphant agent of history, in which technological innovations overcame obstacles of time and space – whether via missiles and jets or LPs and TV sets. That global position of power was of course underpinned not only by modern industrial empires but by the possibility of total annihilation via global thermonuclear war, with President Eisenhower's finger on the nuclear launch button. 'Enriched at the flick of switch' is thus ad copy poetry capturing period investments in cosmopolitan consumerism and 'action at a distance' – the very essence of globalization for Anthony Giddens (1994: 96).

The ethnic pasticcio

And yet both the Columbia ad and *Come Fly with Me* also remediated a much, much older structure of musical cosmopolitanism, related to the rise to global hegemony of Italian opera by the early nineteenth century. The operatic pasticcio gathered together diverse arias by different composers for a single stage performance. In the culinary realm, a pasticcio was a pasta or pastry containing a variety of different ingredients, like a stew, potpourri, hotchpotch. Such medleys of consumable variety were implicated in early movements in musical globalization. The eighteenth-century London pasticcios of the English composer and impresario G.F. Handel, for example, involved removing a variety of Italian-composed, Italian-language arias from their original operas and serving them up, rearranged, under an appetizing new title, to English-speaking audiences (Strohm 1985). This helped Italian opera achieve dominance outside Italy, making it an early form of world music – not yet the panoply of performers from around the world that would characterize many post-war audio spectaculars, but a musical boundary-crossing nonetheless. The pasticcio produced a sonic space that mixed different musical materials into a single package for cosmopolitan consumption (cf. Veit Erlmann's 1993 argument about 'pastiche' as the key principal of late twentieth-century 'world music').

This helps explain the successful migration of pasticcio form, from a Europhile world of opera to the Broadway stage, Hollywood movie and Tin Pan Alley album, culminating in the most famous ethnic pastiche number of all time, Disneyland's 'It's A Small World After All' (1964). Such combinations reduced difference to consumable variety, and produced musical concoctions that underscored an audience's powerful sense of Self, in contrast to the Others subordinated within the pasticcio's totalizing structure. As Richard Middleton (2000: 62) notes, such hierarchically stable musical structures help to contain 'potentially infinite difference' and thereby reassure their preferred listeners that music, hence the world, can indeed 'belong' to them. The controlling, centring impulse implicit in the pasticcio structure would in turn resonate smoothly with the 'stable audioposition' of the hi-fi listener, sitting in the hi-fi 'sweet spot' (Grajeda 2015) of perfect immersion, audio transportation and sonic omniscience.

As the Disney example makes crystal clear, such post-operatic ethnic pasticcios are ultimately focused not on their putative subjects – ethnic or national musical Others – but on the auditing Self of the US consumer, the centre around whom this musical periphery is made to revolve. As with its culinary ancestor, the musical pasticcio offers up difference for delectation, flattering the consumer palate with a flattened parade of performers representing stereotypical elsewheres and fantasized Others. In so doing, the ethnic pastiche reaffirmed powerful pleasures of the centre – once more, 'home' constituted through a long-standing contrast with the 'away'. Tim Taylor (2007: 52), for instance, notes how a seventeenth-century French opera ballet, *l'Europe galante* (Andre Campra, 1697), portrays 'touring the world' via 'four sections, moving from the French center to its peripheries' and contains a lyric in its final aria that could also describe Sinatra's album: 'fly to all parts of the world'. Richard Dyer (2007) suggests pasticcios thrive in times of imperial power, and certainly circa 1958 the United States is at an apex of its cultural and industrial empire. The power of mobility and the power of occupying the centre: these, too, were long the purview and privilege of those consuming the stage pasticcio, living in world capitals controlling global capitalism, but now amplified by hi-fi technology wielded by a master musician.

Sinatra's worldly personality

A final ingredient in *Come Fly with Me*'s cosmopolitan mix was the powerful personality of a popular vocalist who regularly sang, 'I've Got the World on a String' (1953). As David Buxton (1983) has argued, the rise of sound recordings as massively popular leisure commodities involved a novel welding together of song, sound and star. Purchasing a Sinatra disk like *Come Fly with Me* thus meant more than simply acquiring a recording of a song performed a particular way. It also asked consumers to buy into a personality, hence a lifestyle, hence an ideology of individualistic mass consumption. Anticipating today's 'influencers', Buxton views pop stars as singular models of ideal consumer behaviour, whose aspirational emulation is but disguised discipline. The lavish lifestyles of pop personalities made an older ethic of self-denial seem passé, and so helped hurry a foundational shift in the economies of the global north from production to consumption. In Buxton's view, the pop star who most effectively pioneered a public life of excessive consumption (whether of clothes, alcohol, golf or simply 'fun') was Bing Crosby, not coincidentally also the single biggest vocal influence on Frank Sinatra. Both were bon vivants who enjoyed a very public pursuit of the 'good life' – a lifestyle increasingly available to larger portions of the US population as the post-war economy boomed, leisure air travel grew, union membership peaked and income inequality dropped to historical lows in many nations. Both Crosby and Sinatra were characterized as 'crooners', singers who exuded a casual intimacy that was technologically facilitated by microphone, amplifier and loudspeaker. With their shared, relaxed vocal style, they made it look easy to have fun while making millions singing for millions. Sinatra's song, 'Come Fly with Me', for example, suggests that because 'we'll just glide', it will be very easy indeed to 'pack up and fly away' with him at the spur of the moment. Entitling other albums *Swing Easy* (1955) and *Nice 'n' Easy* (1960), Sinatra modelled a life of leisure. He played a major role in the formation of the post-war 'easy listening' mainstream (Keightley 2008) associated with a newly ascendant professional-managerial class, the key consumers of hi-fis and LPs (cf. Ehrenreich 1983). As Rebecca Leydon (2001) describes mid-century mood music, its packaged promise of 'effortless excess' could likewise apply to Sinatra's period image.

By 1958, what Andrew Goodwin would call Sinatra's 'metanarrative' emphasized a seamless integration of the onstage and the offstage. This amplified perceptions of him as embodying an entire way of life, a lifestyle charted across his LP albums of the period. A profile published the year *Come Fly with Me* was released insisted that Sinatra's star image was an authentic version of his lived reality:

> the picture he projected was also the songs he sang... When Frankie sang of life and love, he knew the meaning of the lyrics all too well... Sinatra the man became a living representation of the songs he sang. He grew as a symbol of romance as he loved and lost and loved again.
> (Reisner 1958: 66, 64)

Sinatra's art is repeatedly identified as a purchasable version of his 'life', and that life is singled out as especially exemplary. As a 1957 review of Sinatra's TV show put it: '[Sinatra's] acting and singing seem to speak intimately of a special view of life – life lived dangerously but honorably' (Fulford 1957: 22). Some period observers highlighted his 'special' conjunction of gentle 'romance' and aggressive 'danger' by calling him a 'tender tough' (Taves 1954). This alluded to Sinatra's embrace of rarely conjoined antipathies, to what period observers coded as his feminized, sad, suffering side and his masculinized, swingin', successful side – polarities typically segregated onto 'sad/downbeat' LPs and 'happy/uptempo' ones in this period.

This is one background against which *Come Fly with Me* – unusual insofar as it methodically conjoined slow ballads and fast swing numbers – and its pedagogy of post-war identity may be grasped: 'Frank is living proof that certain things can be done, that a certain kind of life can be lived...' (Coss 1957: 15). As an agent of heterosexual conformity whose rebellious indulgences were prominently both chided and celebrated, Sinatra's 'certain kind of life' revelled in passionate commitments, sensuousness and sentimentality, endless consumption, promiscuous mobility and a restless hyper-individualism at the edge of anti-sociality. *Time*'s 1955 cover story reminded readers that 'Sinatra is doggedly independent...', and framed this independence as self-centred and aggressive, ending its profile with an infamous quote that might have inspired the lyricist (Paul Anka) of his later hit, 'My Way' (1969): 'I'm going to do as I please. I don't need anybody in the world. I did it all myself' ('The Kid...' 1955: 55). Animated by autonomy, Sinatra's authenticity for listeners vouched for a kind of consumer liberation, one further amplified by *Come Fly with Me*'s combinations of high-speed flight and lighting out for the territories, of excitement, exploration and exoticism, of the conquest of sexual others *and* sincere attestations of deep feelings and enduring romantic commitment (including the pleasures of hearth and home). In other words, the LP also mixes contrasting sides of Sinatra's star image in rare fashion.

The liner notes seem to acknowledge Sinatra's complex conjunction of conventional opposites in describing this work as being his 'jaunty, romantic best'. A pastiche is likewise a mixture of quite different elements and, along with Sinatra's multifoliate identity, on *Come Fly with Me* we encounter a variety of potential modes of LP listening. While Sinatra's other LP-only releases on Capitol were renowned for their singularity of timbre and tempo, *Come Fly with Me* purposefully alternates softly moody ballads ('London by Night', 'Moonlight in Vermont') with brassy swing numbers ('Brazil', 'Come Fly with Me'). It can thus be approached variously: as a convenient collection of great songs sung by a great singer, as a means of creating a series of background moods or as a thematically unified work with a storyline, an elaboration of an artistic personality or concept to be contemplated. The album collates songs he had recorded as singles previously for other labels ('Autumn in New York', 'April in Paris', 'Let's Get Away From It All') with well-known standards ('On the Road to Mandalay', 'Brazil') and a recent chart hit for other artists (Victor Young and Bing Crosby's 'Around the World in 80 Days', whose protagonist, upon returning from global wandering, reprises the sentiment of 'Home, Sweet Home' in vowing, 'I have found my home in you'). Some of the arrangements are decidedly in the mode of background or mood music, as in the lush, string-driven 'Moonlight in Vermont', where a gentle Sinatra croons about 'this romantic setting.' The inclusion of specially composed opening and closing songs (side 1 track 1: 'Come Fly with Me' and Side 2 track 6: 'It's Nice to Go Trav'ling') encourages an overall conception of the album as comprising a storyline like a Broadway musical – itself a key place the ethnic pasticcio flourished (Mordden 1983). Going in several directions at once as it does, *Come Fly with Me* thus pastiches ideas of LP as collection, LP as mood machine and LP as narrative form, just as its constituent songs pastiche pre-existing national stereotypes and musical clichés.

Sinatra was among the earliest theorists of the LP, introduced in 1948 by his label at the time, Columbia (Osborne 2012). In 1949, he argued that the 'LP calls for new orientation and pioneering', such as 'script material', 'musical sketches, narrative, commentary', since the format 'open[s] new production vistas in recording' ('Sinatra's Pioneering... ' 1949). The geographical metaphors ('orientation', 'vistas') seem to anticipate *Come Fly with Me*'s musical narrativization of a global flight, now piloted by Sinatra himself. Increasingly in this period, Sinatra is being aligned by critics with ideas of artistry and auteurship derived from jazz and anticipating the status of the rock star (cf. Shumway 2014). On his 'theme albums', Sinatra crafted conceptually coherent LPs that sought to elaborate more complex artistic statements with stronger narrative dimensions. The story of Sinatra's star persona was consistently interwoven into this material: *Come Fly with Me* incorporates slang phrases associated with his vulgar, roistering side ('swingin' honeymoon', 'exotic booze', 'Burma broad'; a conspicuous diamond wedding ring becomes 'a lovely meatball on her finger') and references to contemporary celebrity hangouts like the Villa Capri restaurant or the corner of Hollywood and Vine. His inclusion of the title song of the recent blockbuster film, *Around the World in 80 Days* (1956), in which Sinatra makes a cameo playing a pianist, also reminds listeners of his centrality as a movie star in this period. In other words, the subject of the LP is never simply a musical-global tour, but always also the story of 'Sinatra' himself, as he embodies and enacts a cosmopolitan-consumer identity. As an avatar of 'a special view of life', Sinatra offers a fantasy subjectivity for listeners to inhabit as they sing along. Such placing of listeners is perhaps most apparent on the numbers that conclude side one and side two of the album. These complex tracks are themselves miniature pasticcios, one set in a nineteenth-century, colonial past ('On the Road to Mandalay') and one in the 'chrome' present of the United States' Cold War hegemony ('It's Nice to Go Trav'ling"). As each renders ideas of home/away, centre/periphery, pasticcio and listener placement most audibly, I will attend to them in some detail.

On the road to Mandalay

Based on a famous 1890 poem by Rudyard Kipling, the lyric of 'On the Road to Mandalay' portrays a 'British soldier', who had once been stationed in Burma, a colony occupied by British Empire forces at the time of the poem's composition. Now that he has returned home to London, the military man reminisces fondly about the pleasures of being a colonizer. Adopting this persona, Sinatra romanticizes Mandalay as a place of freedom, passion and irrationality. He sings of a temple's 'crazy bells', of how 'the dawn comes up like thunder/ Out of China', and of a 'Burma broad', who is quoted repeatedly pleading with him to 'come... back to Mandalay'. As an established piece of musical exotica (adapted into song in 1907), 'Mandalay' is a colonialist fantasy, a celebration of what Edward Said (1978) calls the 'underground self' of Orientalist ideology: once one is far away, over there, Occidentals can indulge in what must be denied back here, at home. This renders the peripheralized Other a key constituent of the centred Self. Sinatra's character praises its 'temple bells' and indulgent, non-Christian culture, where 'there ain't no Ten Commandments and a cat can raise a thirst', understanding it as a place of freedom *from* as well as a freedom *to*. Most explicitly, the colonial relation of master/slave is played out here across the axis of gender/sexuality: the chorus is sung in the ventriloquized voice of the Burmese camp follower, sex worker or perhaps just a local lover, who pleads, 'Come you back, you British Soldier, come you back to Mandalay.' As in a key theme of blackface minstrelsy, the dominated desire domination and thereby reassure the dominator of *his* authentic superiority.

The song opens with what are arguably humanity's two oldest musical instruments: a woodblock and a flute. These are quickly followed by a glockenspiel, crash cymbal, muted brass, kettle drum, gong. Foregrounding such instruments, the arrangement relies on Western ideas of what we might call percussive primitivism, a long-standing, European view of percussion as undeveloped, indeed unrefined or inferior musical instruments (Agawu 1995; Brennan 2020). Its sonic Otherness is here updated via high fidelity recording technology, now able to capture percussive transients with unprecedented accuracy. The late 1950s/early 1960s is sometimes described as the 'percussion era', since so many popular hi-fi LPs trafficked in explosive recordings of drums and other struck instruments (for e.g. there are at least five different period LPs entitled *Exotic Percussion*, part of the popular 'Exotica' sub-genre; cf. Hosokawa 1999). After the introduction lays out the track's fulsome instrumental menu, the opening verse is sung to a bare-bones backing that is among the most modest – and oddest – of Sinatra's recording career: just a stand-up bass and a tambourine, an arrangement at once minimalist and primitivist. A full orchestra (winds and strings, with trap drums high in the mix) eventually joins in. We will hear glockenspiel or celesta play a descending riff when Sinatra sings of the 'crazy [temple] bells' calling him back, while the melody of 'wind is in the palm trees' veers into chromaticism. At one point the rhythm section stops entirely in order to highlight the most over-codified of Orientalist musical stereotypes: a xylophone playing pentatonic fourths, accompanied by a gong, appears after the word 'China' (cf. Moon 2006; Sheppard 2019).

The lyric refers several times to listening ('the wind is in the palm trees and the temple bells they say/Come you back'; 'Can't you hear their paddles chunkin'/From Rangoon to Mandalay;' 'And the dawn comes up like thunder.'), as if the place itself is speaking to the hi-fi listener at home. Billy May's arrangement amplifies this through spectacular dynamic variations and word painting (a gong becomes thunder). It emerges as a song about sound's invocational power, summoning desire from sonic memory, placing the singer in the position of listener, just as the listener is invited to occupy the place of the singer. Thus, listeners at home may play Sinatra playing the 'British Soldier' hailed by the nameless Burmese woman (whose voice they also ventriloquize when singing along). Here he is in London, now in Burma, now in the Capitol Building in L.A.: standing in the studio singing, hearing those temple bells yet missing them and dreaming of return – his is a voice at once in the past and in our living rooms, alive yet gone, here yet there like us at home listening. All of this is placed inside a reterritorializing audio space facilitating an encounter with the periphery, an elsewhere, that yet feels centred, even homey – the lyric pleasurably inverts centre/periphery relations so that 'come you back' may be a return to an elsewhere. Ultimately, however, such staging enhances one's occupation of a commanding centre at home in the world.

At the track's climax, Sinatra deliberately stutters over the 'f' in 'f-f-flyin' fishes play'. At each audition, it is simultaneously identical and yet charged with the possibility that he may, one day, finally be free to utter the implied vulgarism (in a 1958 Monaco nightclub performance of the song, Sinatra alters another line to 'you *mother* soldiers', suggesting the f-word was on Sinatra's mind). Listening at home, we replay this perfect loop that yet promises presence, hence change, hence freedom. Likewise, freedom feels present in Sinatra's famous back phrasing, shifting his sung words slightly behind or ahead of the rhythm section's pulse, as with Sinatra's playing with pitch, microtonally moving away from, or back to, the expected melody note, taking his time sometimes to reach the home plate implied by the instrumental backing. Sinatra thus adjusts musical time and space to suit his 'jaunty, romantic' whims. Sinatra's vocalized place at the centre of the soundfield asserts his agency and autonomy against a background of hyper-rationalized musicianship, recording technology and the complex industrial infrastructures of advanced capitalism – all pleasures ours to consume safely at home.

Describing arranger Billy May 'going wild at the controls' during 'Mandalay', the liner notes seem simply to refer to his arrangement's dynamic and timbral contrasts and excesses: instruments appear and disappear, the song seems to stop and start as musical feels shift dramatically (even if the tempo remains constant, controlled), and quiet passages erupt suddenly into fortissimo blasts of brass. Such varied features of 'Mandalay' make it a micro-pasticcio, containing mainstream swing jazz, a national-anthem-like march, faux Chinese music, midtempo balladry and an unusually wide range of musical instruments (it is rare to hear gong, tambourine, woodblock and xylophone all combined on a Sinatra recording). Yet May 'going wild at the controls' more fully expresses exotica's paradoxical nature, its controlled wildness: a rationalized rendering and technological transmission of an unfulfillable desire for *un*civilization beating at the centre of the colonialist imagination (remember, the lyric's narrator is back in London, fantasizing that his 'Burma broad' is imploring him to 'come back to Mandalay' – *her* ventriloquized desire stands in for *his*). In this light, the track's lack of structural resolution at its conclusion – a suspended chord hangs over a now-missing lyric ('Out of China...') that had been sung by Sinatra in the first refrain – may reinforce primitivist fantasy in refusing return to the 'home' note of European tonality and lingering elsewhere instead. And yet, since this is the final track of Side 1, Sinatra's ambitions for 'pioneering... narrative' LP structures may still be unfolding, positioning such non-resolution rather as a segue to Side 2 – thereby encouraging listeners to flip over the vinyl and continue the journey home.

From pasticcio to pizza

The final word sung on *Come Fly with Me* is 'pizza', also an Italian-born pastry of multiple ingredients. Side 1 had begun with an invitation to pack up and 'Come Fly with Me' (whose arrangement also refuses full harmonic closure) and ended with 'Mandalay's' complex dialectic of longing and (unfulfilled) return. Likewise, Side 2 begins by imploring 'Let's Get Away From It All', but reaches the final destination of all tourists on 'It's Nice to Go Trav'ling (But Nicer to Come Home)'. This last track, too, suggests a miniature version of the album's overall pasticcio structure: it stops and starts, alternating gentler, string-driven, mid-tempo balladry with overblown brass swing and features a prominent xylophone riff working alongside the wind and string sections. Frequent Sinatra collaborator Sammy Cahn's bespoke lyrics contrast 'home' and 'away', at once celebrating the pleasures of global differences – framed as sexual difference – while reasserting the primacy (and power) of US patrimony. As with 'Home Sweet Home', it acknowledges the lures of the foreign, the freedom 'to play gypsy' and be 'footloose' with 'just a toothbrush and comb.' It briefly praises different sites and sights enjoyed overseas, both geographical ('The camel route to Iraq') and human ('The mam'selles and frauleins and the señoritas are sweet'). But the focus is more on those aspects of US life most missed by the (white, heterosexual, male) consumer-tourist: US women, US urban landscapes and US consumer/media goods. These include the female Californians standing in a 'sexy line…at Sunset and Vine' and the 'models…on Madison Ave.', as well as the Empire State['s]….view from Miss Liberty's dome', and "the latest flivver [automobile] that's simply dripping with chrome." "It's very nice" is clearly a statement of choice and privilege, admitting of options and alternatives. Male tourists are consistently afforded freedoms denied women, hinted at in the album's several songs in which a cosmopolitan man dallies with a locally bound female and then leaves her behind ("Brazil", "Isle of Capri", "Mandalay"). In "It's Nice to Go Trav'ling", patriarchal power parades alongside metonyms of U.S. cultural-imperial power: Hollywood and Capitol Records' exact address, 'Sunset and Vine'; the 'Madison Ave.' centre of the advertising industry; Detroit's massive auto industry.

As the list of global sites winds down, an ideal of 'home' as desired terminus arises ('But your heart starts singin' when you're homeward wingin' across the foam'). Sinatra sings a concluding list of the domestic delights he's looking forward to: 'No more customs/Burn the passports/No more packin'/And unpackin'/Light the home fires/Get my slippers/Make a pizza.' This lyrical chain links the stability of home and hearth and escape from bureaucracy with bedroom apparel and home cooking. On 'pizza', Sinatra's final note hangs in the air, and for a second the vamp outro is suspended both harmonically and rhythmically. Then, suddenly, all is resolved by a full-band fortissimo stab terminating song, album, journey. This moment of suspension/resolution, articulated with Sinatra's suggestively odd cadence in singing 'make a pizza', intimates something more than cooking. Sinatra's delivery gives it a slightly lubricious feeling, hinting at the unsingable (Dyer notes the realm of the culinary is as important as that of sexuality as reservoir of metaphor, and of course both have been historically contained, if not consumed, within domestic space). In the US context, pizza is both domestic and foreign, comfort food and a special treat, as American as apple pie and yet, still, a marker of Italian-American specificity. Sinatra himself is both an archetypal 'American' and an icon of Italian-American ethnicity. Just as a culinary pasticcio combines different flavours, a pizza is typically a hodgepodge of various ingredients (e.g. 'all-dressed'). Sinatra's inflection foregrounds singing, food, sex, ethnicity, national identity, patriarchy, power. The appearance, in the last instance, of the most American of ethnic foods, pizza, also echoes the globalizing imperatives of pasticcio. Pasticcio is no simple symptom of globalization but one of modern imperialism's innumerable scripts or scores – one now articulated with US media-consumer hegemony by Sinatra in hi-fi. It is indeed striking that, just as a jet-fuelled phase of the USA's international cultural and economic domination was taking off, various round shapes (globe, pizza, LP) met Sinatra's round tones on the round trip of *Come Fly with Me*.

The album's final track is thus about a hierarchy of desire and value and power – what is nice, what is nicer; how getting away from it all revalues the return home as the ideal, 'best of all possible worlds'; how using fantasies of global public space to virtually saturate private domestic space ultimately comforts a felt white superiority (and may overwrite female disenfranchisement therein; see Tyler-May 1988); how exoticism frames an aesthetic of reassurance – that the trip to Oz may be thrilling but in the end 'there's no place like home.' As I have argued, popular musical artefacts like *Come Fly with Me* worked on multiple levels to position historical LP listeners at the virtual centre of a global auditory-imaginary. This was a musical place deeply rooted in a white, suburban, heterosexual domestic space, shaped by exoticized elsewheres and imperialist adventures, and ultimately endorsing an unprecedented wave of globalization whose reverberations still resound.

References

Agawu, K. (1995), 'The Invention of African Rhythm', *Journal of the American Musicological Society*, 48 (3): 380–95

Anderson, T. J. (2015), 'Training the Listener', in P. Théberge, K. Devine, T. Everrett (eds), *Living Stereo: Histories and Cultures of Multichannel Sound*, 107–24, New York: Bloomsbury.

Bailey, P. (2004), 'Breaking the Sound Barrier', M.M. Smith (ed), *Hearing History*, 23–35, Athens, GA: University of Georgia.

Barry, E. (2015), 'Mono in the Stereo Age', in P. Théberge, K. Devine, and T. Everrett (eds), *Living Stereo: Histories and Cultures of Multichannel Sound*, 125–46, New York: Bloomsbury.

Borgerson, J. and Schroeder, J. (2017), *Designed for Hi-Fi Living: The Vinyl LP in Midcentury America*, Cambridge: MIT Press.

Bourdage, M. (2016), 'Beyond the Centerfold: Masculinity, Technology, and Culture in Playboy's Multimedia Empire, 1953–1972.' PhD. dissertation, University of Michigan.

Brennan, M. (2020), *Kick It: A Social History of the Drum Kit*, New York: Oxford University.

Björnberg, A. (2009), 'Learning to Listen to Perfect Sound: Hi-fi Culture and Changes in Modes of Listening, 1950–80', in D.B. Scott (ed), *Ashgate Research Companion to Popular Musicology*, (chapter 5 of e-book), London: Routledge.

Buxton, D. ([1983] 1990), 'Rock Music, the Star System, and the Rise of Consumerism', in S. Frith & A. Goodwin (eds), *On Record*, 366–77, London: Routledge.

Connell, J. and Gibson, C. (2003), *Soundtracks: Popular Music, Identity and Place*, London: Routledge.

Coss, B. (1957), 'Frank Sinatra: Mr. Personality.' *Metronome* (December 1957): 14–15.

Doyle, P. (2005), *Echo and Reverb: Fabricating Space in Popular Music Recording, 1900–1960*, Middletown: Wesleyan University.

Durant, A. (1984), *Conditions of Music*, Albany: SUNY.

Dyer, R. (2007), *Pastiche*, New York: Routledge.

Ehrenreich, B. (1983), *The Hearts of Men*, New York: Anchor.

Erlmann, V. (1993), 'The Politics and Aesthetics of "World Music"', *The World of Music*, 35 (2): 3–15.

Frith, S. (1983), 'The Pleasures of the Hearth', in *Formations of Pleasure*, 101–23, London: Routledge.

Fulford, R. (1957), 'Sinatra with Sweetening', *New Republic*, 18 November: 22.

Giddens, A. (1994), 'Living in a Post-Traditional Society', in U. Beck, A. Giddens, and S. Lash (eds), *Reflexive Modernization*, 56–109, Cambridge: Polity.

Gitelman, L. (2006), *Always Already New*, Cambridge: MIT Press.

Goodwin, A. (1992), *Dancing in the Distraction Factory*, Minneapolis: University of Minnesota.

Grajeda, T. (2015), 'The "Sweet Spot": The Technology of Stereo and the Field of Auditorship', in P. Théberge, K. Devine, T. Everrett (eds), *Living Stereo: Histories and Cultures of Multichannel Sound*, 37–63, New York: Bloomsbury.

Hesmondhalgh, D. (2021), 'Streaming's Effects on Music Culture: Old Anxieties and New Simplifications', *Cultural Sociology* June: 1–22.

Hayward, P., ed. (1999), *Widening the Horizon*, Sydney: John Libbey.

Hoechner, B. (2007), 'Transport and Transportation in Audiovisual Memory', in D. Goldmark, L. Kramer, and R. Leppert (eds), *Beyond the Soundtrack*, 163–83, Berkeley: University of California.

Hosokawa, S. (1999), 'Martin Denny and the Development of Musical Exotica', in P. Hayward (ed), *Widening the Horizon*, 72–93, Sydney: John Libbey.

Jansson, S. (2010), '"Listen to these Speakers": Swedish Hi-fi Enthusiasts, Gender, and Listening', *IASPM@ Journal* 1 (2). doi:10.5429/2079-3871(2010)v1i2.5en.

Kassabian, A. (2004), 'Would You Like Some World Music with Your Latte? Starbucks, Putumayo, and Distributed Tourism', *Twentieth-Century Music*, 1 (2): 209–23.

Keightley, K. (1996), '"Turn It Down!"She Shrieked: Gender, Domestic Space, and High Fidelity, 1948–1959', *Popular Music*, 15 (2): 149–77.

Keightley, K. (2004), 'Long Play: Adult-Oriented Popular Music and the Temporal Logics of the Post-War Sound Recording Industry in the U.S.A.', *Media, Culture and Society*, 26 (3): 375–91.

Keightley, K. (2008), 'Music for Middlebrows: Defining the Easy Listening Era, 1946-1966', *American Music*, 26 (3): 309–35.

Keightley, K. (2011), '*Un voyage via barquinho*...: Global Circulation, Musical Hybridization, and Adult Modernity, 1961-69', in J. Toynbee and B. Dueck (eds), *Migrating Music: Media, Politics, and Style*, 112–26, London: Routledge.

'The Kid from Hoboken' (1955), *Time*, 29 August: 52–7.

Leydon, R. (1999), 'Utopias of the Topics – The Exotic Music of Les Baxter and Yma Sumac', in P. Hayward (ed), *Widening the Horizon: Exoticism in Post-War Popular Music*, 45–71, Sydney: John Libbey.

Leydon, R. (2001), 'The Soft-Focus Sound: Reverb as A Gendered Attribute in Mid-Century Mood Music', *Perspectives of New Music*, 39 (2): 96–107.

Middleton, R. (2000), 'Musical Belongings: Western Music and Its Low-Other', in G. Born and D. Hesmondhalgh (eds), *Western Music and Its Others*, 59–85, Berkeley: University of California.

Moon, K. (2006), *Yellowface: Creating the Chinese in American Popular Music and Performance, 1850s–1920s*, New Brunswick: Rutgers University.

Mordden, E. (1983), *Broadway Babies*, New York: Oxford University.
O'Brien, G. (2004), *Sonata for Jukebox*, New York: Counterpoint.
Osborne, R. (2012), *Vinyl: A History of the Analogue Record*, Abingdon: Ashgate.
Perchard, T. (2017), 'Technology, Listening and Historical Method: Placing Audio in the Postwar British Home', *Journal of the Royal Musical Association*, 142 (2): 367–99.
Reisner, R. (1958), 'Sinatra: The Man with the Golden Charm Has Become the Love God of Our Time', *Playboy*, November: 62–4, 66, 84–8.
Robertson-Wojcik, P. (2001), 'The Girl and the Phonograph', in A. Knight and P. Robertson-Wojcik (eds), *Soundtrack Available*, 433–54, Durham: Duke University.
Said, E. (1978), *Orientalism*, New York: Random House.
Shumway, D. (2014), *Rock Star: The Making of Musical Icons from Elvis to Springsteen*, Baltimore: Johns Hopkins University.
Sheppard, W.A. (2019), *Extreme Exoticism: Japan in the American Musical Imagination*, New York: Oxford University
'Sinatra's Pioneering Thoughts on LP Pop Tune Production' (1949), *Billboard*, 31 December 13.
Sterne, J. (2015), 'The Stereophonic Spaces of Soundscape 1', in P. Théberge, K. Devine and T. Everrett (eds), *Living Stereo: Histories and Cultures of Multichannel Sound*, 65–83, New York: Bloomsbury.
Strohm, R. (1985), *Essays on Handel and Italian Opera*, Cambridge: Cambridge University.
Taves, E. (1954), 'Frank Sinatra... Tender, Tough Guy', *Woman's Home Companion*, June: 34–5, 60–2.
Taylor, T. (2001), *Strange Sounds: Music, Technology and Culture*, New York: Routledge.
Taylor, T. (2007), *Beyond Exoticism*, Durham: Duke
Théberge, P., Devine, K., Everrett, T., eds (2015), *Living Stereo: Histories and Cultures of Multichannel Sound*, N.Y.: Bloomsbury.
Tyler-May, E. (1988), *Homeward Bound*, New York: Basic.
Western, T. (2014), 'The Age of the Golden Ear': The Columbia World Library and Sounding out Post-war Field Recording', *Twentieth-century Music*, 11 (2): 275–300

Discography

Berlingeri and His Percussive Harpsichord with His Orchestra (ca. 1960), *Exotic International Percussion*, International Award Series AK-170.
Bing Crosby with Victor Young and his Orchestra (1957), 'Around the World (in Eighty Days)', Decca 9-30262.
Stanley Black and His Orchestra and Chorus (1961), *Exotic Percussion*, London SP 44004.
Martin Denny (1961), *Exotic Percussion*, Liberty LST 7168.
Disneyland Boys Choir (1965), *It's a Small World*, Disneyland STER-1289.
Robert Drasnin (1959), *Percussion Exotique*, Tops 9694.
Esquivel (1958), *Other Sounds, Other Worlds* RCA-Victor LSP-1753.
John Evans and the Big Band (1961), *Exotic Percussion and Brilliant Brass*, Directional Sound DS 5006.
Fafa Lemos (1955), *Dinner in Rio*, RCA-Victor LPM-1017.

Pink Floyd (1973), *Dark Side of the Moon*, Harvest SHVL 804.
Milt Raskin (1961), *Exotic Percussion*, Crown 5189.
Frank Sinatra (1953), 'I've Got the World on a String', Capitol 2505.
Frank Sinatra (1955), *Swing Easy*, Capitol W 587.
Frank Sinatra with Billy May and His Orchestra (1958), *Come Fly with Me*, Capitol W920.
Frank Sinatra (1958) 'On the Road to Mandalay,' Live at the Monte Carlo Sporting Club, June 14, 1958, https://www.youtube.com/watch?v=nspErUr4SPo
Frank Sinatra (1960), *Nice 'n' Easy*, Capitol SW 1417.
Frank Sinatra (1969), 'My Way', Reprise 0817.
Various Artists (1956), *Night Out Music for Stay-at-Homes*, Coral CRL 57040.
Lee Wiley (1951), Night in Manhattan, Columbia CL6169.

9

Music radio

J. Mark Percival

Music radio matters

In this chapter, I will introduce and discuss ideas around the ways in which music radio produces space and place and consider how some of these have played out at key moments in the broadcast radio history of two case study nation-states, Canada and the UK. Building on some of the discussions of popular music, space and place theory elsewhere in this volume, I will explore the ways in which music radio (and music *on* radio) is both constructed by and reconstructs imaginaries of space and place at the intersections of national identity, and notions of the national, the regional and the local. I will show that music radio's ability to be understood simultaneously as both somewhere and nowhere allows for a peculiar flexibility in accommodating apparently contradictory imperatives around relations with place and space. The key moments I will examine are in Canada the political and ideological context for the launch of the Canadian Broadcasting Corporation (CBC) in the early 1930s and how some of the same challenges were approached in Canadian music radio from the 1970s onwards. In the section on the UK I will briefly set up the historical, constitutional complexities of the UK as nation-state before moving on to consider the ways in which music radio has worked to reframe ideas of place, space and identity in the unique context of a broadcast history dominated by over fifty years of public service broadcast radio legal monopoly (1922–73). The key moments I will address are the first 'illegal' music radio broadcasts into the UK in the 1930; the arrival of US forces and Forces Radio in the Second World War; the mid-1960s offshore pirate radio stations; and the launch of legal commercial radio in the 1970s. I will finish with some observations on the perhaps unexpected ongoing health of music radio as a media business model despite the rapid growth and success of quasi-radio streaming services and spectacular growth of podcasting as audio media.

Theorizing radio, space and place – Canada

At the beginning of the twentieth century, as broadcast radio technology was shifting from being seen as a solution to communication on the battlefield towards becoming the first mass broadcast medium. Louise Benjamin shows that in 1916 David Sarnoff, then an employee of the Marconi Wireless Telegraph Company of America had suggested that an obvious development of radio technology was broadcast home entertainment in the form of a 'radio music box' (Benjamin 2002: 97). In other words, one of the very earliest proposed applications of one-to-many radio broadcasting was not news, politics or sport – it was music as entertainment. It became obvious very quickly that radio content could also be those other things too even if faced with resistance from existing interests. In the UK, for example, the newspaper industry lobbied hard to prevent the nascent BBC from broadcasting news and current affairs, seeing that potentially damaging to its market (Barnard 2000). Nevertheless, music in the form of either live performances or record has been central to radio texts for decades. Music radio matters to the radio industry, to the record industry, to radio audiences and to music fans. It matters socially, economically, sometimes politically and always culturally. Music radio is an entity *distinct* from the record industry – it is a product of the economic and cultural interaction of the radio industry and the record industry. In this chapter I will be exploring a specific consequence of music radio's ubiquity – its power to shape and be shaped by constructions of space and place.

Jody Berland's (1993) essential essay, *Radio, Space and Industrial Time*, develops the first really clear theoretical approach to the ways in which broadcast radio became part of an ongoing process that draws together notions of space, place, national identity and genre as expressed in broadcast formats. It is true that her ideas were developed in the late 1980s and early 1990s but what is particularly impressive is the continuing relevance of these ideas after three decades of increasingly rapid technological disruption to communication industries and consequent challenges to our understanding of radio itself. I will make some brief observations on digital disruption and radio in the final section of this chapter but at this point it would be helpful to lay out some of Berland's central arguments and the ways in which they frame any discussion of music radio, space and place.

Although Berland had been exploring some of these ideas in earlier work (e.g. Berland 1988) it is in her 1993 work (a revision of Berland 1990) that she fully engages with music radio. She frames her discussion of radio and space by revisiting Harold Innes's (1950) classification of time-binding and space-binding communication. The former works to maintain relations over time, including heritage, hierarchy, identity and memory (storytelling traditions, for example); the latter tends to collapse spatial distance by moving information increasingly quickly and so tends to erode both notions of the local and the capacity of marginal groups for self-determination. What is interesting about radio in general and music radio in particular is that it can be both of these in different times and in different places (and often simultaneously). National radio (especially, but not only public radio) has often been explicitly tasked with collapsing real geographical distance into an imagined space of national identity (Hutchison 1999), an idea to which I'll return shortly. Yet at the same time, national radio is often required to do the work of a cultural institution, celebrating regional and local diversity, building cultural archives and shared memory within the context of the nation-state (Hendy 2013).

The second key strand of Berland's thinking is the way in which commercial music radio operations that may have started with distinctively, often explicitly, local or regional agendas have over time become consolidated into an oligopolistic market where a small number of large national (or even transnational) companies own large numbers of locally branded stations. This allows music radio to become what Berland refers to as 'omnisciently local' (1993: 112), concealing market consolidation and standardized programming through advertising of locally available products and services. DJs fail to identify their locations in on-air talk and thus are both everywhere and nowhere, an idea I will develop later in my discussion of the 1960s UK offshore pirate radio stations. To anyone who values localness and diversity of culture more generally this may seem like a problem, and indeed a process that has accelerated into the twenty-first century beyond anything Berland might have predicted in 1993. However, other scholars have argued that in the Canadian context (and Berland is based in Toronto) a clear policy agenda around place, popular music and radio has contributed to the development of a 'national scene', a scene with demonstrably positive effects on domestic popular music production (Henderson 2008). Why then is Canada such a productive lens through which to examine these relationships between radio, space, place and popular music?

Canada as a nation-state has some significant and distinctive issues related to its geography and topography. It is big – Canada is the second largest country in the world by surface area after Russia, and marginally ahead of China (United Nations 2012). The population in 2021 was around 38 million, ranking Canada 37th in the world. This disparity means that outside of a handful of major urban centres on the coasts and close to the border with the United States the country is relatively sparsely populated (Statistics Canada 2021). There is significant variability in environments: from the Arctic north to the lakes in the south and the prairies of the Midwest; from the Rocky Mountains and Vancouver coast in the west to the very different world of the Maritimes on the east coast (CIA 2021). So, there are very many different places for living each with often very distinctive local or regional cultures, there are cultural and political tensions between First Nation Canadians and late-arriving Europeans, and in the Anglophone/Francophone distinctions (largely in Québec Province, but also in neighbouring New Brunswick to the east) (CIA 2021). All of this certainly makes Canada a great, multi-textured place for tourists but crucially for Berland's arguments it provides a wide variety of variables with which to test and develop those arguments. That is, the relationships between music radio, place and space are clearly exposed in the Canadian context and can be considered within a variety of related theoretical frameworks, including media policy, constructions of national and regional identity, and the perceived threat of both cultural and economic imperialism from the United States.

David Hutchison (1999) has observed that Canadian concerns about the integrity of a Canadian identity in a broadcast communications context date back to the launch of the Canadian Broadcasting Corporation (CBC) in 1933. As the CBC was signed into being, then Prime Minister Bennett issued a now-much-quoted statement regarding the political and ideological objectives of a publicly funded national radio network:

> This country must be assured of complete Canadian control of broadcasting from Canadian sources, free from foreign influence. Without such control it can never be the agency by

which national consciousness may be fostered and sustained, and national unity still further strengthened.

(R.B. Bennett, quoted in Hutchison 1999: 201)

Prime Minister Bennett is here clearly demonstrating concern about the economic and cultural threat posed by Canada's southern neighbour, as amplified by the explosive growth of radio broadcasting and its lack of respect for arbitrary political borders. Bennett saw radio, through the CBC as a way of uniting the very disparate Provinces of Canada, the urban and the rural, the coasts and the prairies, in the shared experience of becoming a *national* audience united in real time for the duration of a broadcast. The sense of 'national consciousness' to which Bennett alludes is about creating a unified notion, and indeed a celebration of 'Canadian-ness' out of which would emerge resistance to perceived pernicious US culture. Broadcast radio then simultaneously represents both an opportunity and a threat: an opportunity to build an imagined national identity *within* the borders of the nation-state and a symbol of a cultural–economic threat from *outside* those borders. This establishes radio as central to the ideological objective of creating a virtual place ('Canada'), an objective that arises from concerns about the political–cultural integrity of a 'real' place (the nation-state of Canada, with its geographically specific borders).

The formal translation of these conceptually distinct but related notions of national place-ness into a form that would have lasting consequences for music radio and popular music culture in Canada eventually happened almost forty years after the creation of the CBC (Sutherland 2002: 13). In 1971, the Canadian government introduced a radio broadcasting policy designed to promote the interests of its domestic popular music industries by developing a measure of Canadian-ness in pop. This assessment of levels of Canadian content (Cancon) produced a value that could be attached to commercially released records. Releases that were sufficiently 'Canadian' could then become part of a legally imposed quota of Canadian music in music radio station playlists. Sutherland argues that one of the most important reasons for the success of the Cancon initiative is its simplicity (Sutherland 2002: 14). There are four categories against which Canadian-ness is measured and all of them draw on geographical or legal relationship to a place (in this case, a nation-state) called Canada. The four categories are: Music (the nationality of the music composer); Artist (the nationality of the 'primary' performer); Production (the geographical location at which the recording was made – that is, whether or not it was in Canada); Lyrics (the nationality of the composer of the lyric). The acronym is then MAPL which of course works to reinforce an association with the symbolic place-ness represented by the Canadian national flag and its use of the maple leaf, itself a representation of Canadian-ness dating back to the 1700s (Minahan 2009: 17). If a commercially released recording (a single, EP or album) is 'Canadian' in at least two of the MAPL metrics, that release is considered sufficiently Canadian to be placed on a music radio quota playlist. There have been occasional glitches in applying the system, notably in 1991 when Canadian artist Bryan Adams briefly failed to qualify as sufficiently Canadian (Sutherland 2002: 14), but Sutherland's argument has held up remarkably well and the Cancon system is still functioning for music radio at the time of writing this chapter (mid-2021). Scott Henderson (2008) has observed that the Cancon system for popular music has also been, broadly speaking, successful in developing what he refers to as a 'national scene'. Henderson argues that it makes sense to extend Will Straw's (1991) notion of scenes as local or regional centres of popular music production, mediation and consumption, to the *national* and that this sense of a 'national' scene, as understood in terms of geographical place has emerged as consequence of decades of a CanCon policy based on arbitrary, imagined-but-definable metrics of Canadian-ness. Canadian music radio, in both commercial and public sectors works through the Cancon system to buttress the conceptual importance of place for popular music industry and culture – in this case, place-as-nation and well as nation-as-place. Canadian radio audiences hear more Canadian music than an unregulated music radio market would be likely to programme. Henderson suggests that a virtuous circle then emerges where the Canadian-ness of Canadian music radio programming works to increase production of new Canadian music and to allow new Canadian artists to develop a domestic audience through presence on a platform that might otherwise be denied to them. Music radio then becomes part of a project in which an imagined national-place is superimposed on the geographic reality of a Canada for whom domestic popular music production and broadcasting is part of the ongoing development of a national consciousness that understands music as connected to (national) place.

Theorizing radio, space and place – The United Kingdom

Canada is an excellent national–cultural petri dish in which to examine issues of music radio and the construction of national-space and place, but the UK provides both enough similarities and differences to be a second instructive case study. In common with many other industrialized countries in the post-First World War period, the UK was engaged in deploying broadcast radio as a nation-building tool through the launch of a national public radio service, in this case the British Broadcasting Corporation, in 1922 (Scannell and Cardiff 1991; Hutchison 1999). Despite obvious differences in geography, the British shared some of the challenges that were being experienced by their Canadian allies in the early twentieth century, principally that of reinforcing a national imaginary that would bring together very different local, regional and indeed national cultures (Hendy 2013). It is worth briefly noting the unique constitutional conditions at play here – since 1922 the full name of the UK is the United Kingdom of Great Britain and Northern Ireland. 'Great Britain' means the main island containing Wales, Scotland and England, an entity formed in 1707 following the Scotland and England Acts of Union. So strictly speaking 'Britain' is just England and Wales, but just in case that was not messy enough, in legal terms Wales had been fully integrated within the 'Kingdom of England' since the late sixteenth century (Lyon 2003). This barely scratches the surface of the historical context but it matters because it illustrates the complexities of establishing a sense of 'Britishness' in a legal entity internationally recognized as the UK but consisting of four 'nations', each of which has any number of additional internal divisions in terms of religion, language, culture and economy. So the work that the BBC was expected to do under the guidance of its first director general, John Reith (in post 1922–38) in fostering the development of a unified 'British' identity was significant (Hendy 2013). Popular music was frequently programmed on the main BBC radio service right from the start but there was no legal broadcasting of anything that, say a US citizen might recognize as 'music radio' until the early 1970s (Barnard 1989). Independent Local Radio (ILR) launched in 1973 with mostly pop music formats and stations organized initially around urban centres like London, Glasgow, Birmingham and Newcastle-Upon-Tyne. Their licences to broadcast placed significant emphasis on signifiers of localness that would have been familiar to radio audiences elsewhere in the world in earlier decades: local news, weather, traffic, politics, politics, community events and most importantly from the perspective of this chapter, local music (Barnard 1989). Place was embedded from the beginnings of UK commercial pop radio, so in these early years I would argue that place mattered to music radio just as much as music radio mattered to place. For Berland this would be part of the process by which music radio works to construct the local even as it is shaped by the local. For UK radio audiences this was the first time that imagined, constructed place in music radio coalesced with their lived experience of their own local environment. This was not however the first time that those audiences had experienced music radio programming and the associated imaginaries of space and place.

In the 1930s, non-BBC music radio programming arrived for listeners in the UK (and indeed in Ireland, depending on atmospheric conditions) as transmitters on the French coast carried commercial English-language programming from Radio Luxembourg and Radio Normandy (Scannell and Cardiff 1991). Luxembourg and Normandy are clearly 'real' places but despite the international place-ness of the point of origin of the broadcasts, content was largely created in England by British broadcasters with sponsorship from quintessentially British companies like Vernon's Football Pools (sports gambling) and Zam-Buk (a medicated skin treatment) (https://en.wikipedia.org/wiki/Radio_Luxembourg). In the UK context this is a clear and early illustration of Berland's contention that music radio can be simultaneously local, trans-local and in this case, international. Vernon's was based in Liverpool, Zam-Buk in Leeds (and both signify a diverse urban localness), the music content was predominantly British recordings contextualized by British voices (trans-local, national), yet the station branding and technological infrastructure was 'foreign'. While the BBC used music and other programming in the years before the Second World War to signify a particular form of audible Britishness, Luxembourg and Normandy pointed towards a version of musical British identity framed by a subtly transnational sensibility. The 'place' of those early commercial broadcasters transmitting music content *into* the UK from elsewhere (rather than from within the UK *to* the UK) was then simultaneously both 'there' and 'here'. And so these stations worked to construct an imagined, place-based notion of a British 'us', an alternative to BBC Britishness that was only possible because of the *non*-Britishness of the place from which the broadcasts emanated. The transmitters that serviced Radios Luxembourg and Normandy were closed down at the start of the Second World War and British music fans were once again dependent solely on the BBC.

The role of music on the BBC during the Second World War is explored in detail by Christina Baade (2012), in particular its role in supporting 'morale' and the war effort more generally. Much of this support was concerned with a complex of overlapping strategies designed to build on notions of Britain as a place (in this case, a place worth defending) and space where ideals of democracy were resisting the threat of fascist totalitarianism. Of note here are two moments when the BBC was struggling with perceived challenges to these objectives, both of which are related to American-ness and its contrast with the BBC's understanding of 'British' values. The first of these was the 1942 BBC ban on the US-originated singing style of crooning which was seen to be undermining 'British' values of strength, decency and stoicism with performances that were 'anaemic' or 'insincere' (2012: 139). Ironically, the ban disproportionately affected British records, with many American hits continuing to appear on air. So alongside US-dominated UK cinema, BBC radio became a virtual space in which music constructed idealized imaginaries of another, more glamorous, more optimistic place – the wide vistas of an America not directly touched by the War. The second moment crystallized in July 1943 with the launch of American Forces Network (AFN) radio, strongly opposed by the BBC but very quickly widely listened to by a British audience outside of its target demographic of US military personnel based in the UK (2012: 176). The BBC was no longer in monopolistic control of the airwaves and so therefore also no longer able to shape the constructions of place enabled by that monopoly control. Music on AFN was not just American (jazz, swing) – it was contextualized by US presentation voices that completed a construction of an Americanized space in the UK, and I would argue also helped to create an association for UK audiences between music radio and the American voice. This was happening both sonically (denotationally, accents) and conceptually (connotationally, 'American-ness'). Twenty years would pass before this association of radio sound with imagined place was revisited and revitalized by the arrival of illegal but quickly successful commercial competitors for the BBC.

In 1964, the first of the UK offshore radio broadcasters, Radio Caroline, started commercially funded broadcasting into the south and east of England, and was soon joined by a number other stations, notably Radio London – they were soon dubbed 'pirates' by UK print media, rather than by the stations themselves (Hind and Mosco 1985; Barnard 1989; Briggs 1995; Crisell 2002). Based outside UK territorial waters (legal jurisdiction ended at three miles from the coast) these stations were broadcast from converted ships or disused sea forts (defensive structures in the English Channel dating from the early 1940s). This approach to non-licenced commercial radio broadcasting allowed stations freedom to adopt and adapt top-40 formats from the United States and to be tacitly supported by a UK record industry that was more than happy to have new music-led outlets on which their new releases would be heard, and heard often (Chapman 1992). Like their 1930s predecessors, Radios Normandy and Luxembourg (the latter of which had restarted its English-language music programming after the Second World War) the 1960s pirate stations quite legally carried advertising from UK businesses and demonstrated the profitability of a commercial music radio model. For most British listeners, this was the first time they had heard informal, DJ-led music format radio during the day – Radio Luxembourg's output was evenings only, partly because of the requirement for evening atmospheric conditions to bounce the medium wave signal to the wider UK (Chapman 1992). In 1967 the British government passed the Marine Broadcasting Offences Act and closed the loophole that allowed the offshore pirates to work as businesses by making it illegal to advertise on the stations.

The offshore pirate music radio stations further complicate the process of producing imaginaries of space and place. There are four strands to this process, the first of these being whence the broadcast signal originates. BBC programming for the most part came from London and was distributed across the country via a network of transmitters. Even if they had never been there most British citizens knew where London was, what it looked like and why it was significant. So the place-ness of BBC broadcasts was anchored in perceptions of the real-world British capital city. Listeners to Radio Luxembourg were regularly reminded that the studios from which the DJ voices emerged were really in the Grand Duchy and therefore easy enough for the curious audience member to find on an atlas of maps, even if they were unlikely to ever go there in person. But the offshore pirates? They were *somewhere* in the English Channel – a vagueness that contributed not only to the mystique of pirates lost on the High Seas, but also to a construction of place that is both specific ('we're on a boat off the English coast') and general (the sea – in an island nation, most residents of Great Britain would be familiar with the coast and variety of ships and boats visible at seaside resorts and ports). So despite being outside of British territorial control (therefore legally, nowhere) and by virtue of broadcasting (mostly) English voices and transnational anglophone music *into* the UK, the pirates represented themselves, and were understood by audiences to be 'British' in a way that Radio Luxembourg (based in another sovereign country) could never be.

The second place-building process in 1960s pirate radio works through the format itself in which DJs play records back-to-back on two turntables and largely improvise their spoken contributions, or 'links'. This format would have been understood by audiences as American and many younger listeners in particular would have been familiar with what it *looked* like as represented (albeit often in a stylized form) in US TV programming and feature films, and in the widespread specialist and generalist print media coverage of the pirate station. Even if listeners didn't know or care about exactly where the boat hosting Radio Caroline's DJs and transmitter was floating in the English Channel, many would have had a reasonably accurate conception of the *space* of the music radio broadcast studio.

The third strand of place-building lies in the radio text itself, the mix of voice, records, advertising and station ident (branding) jingles. The sense of improvised energy and vitality in the pirates' music formats worked to signify something very different to the relatively staid contemporaneous music output of the BBC. It was both youthful and concerned with pop culture in ways that the BBC was not and at the same time it was a symbol of the perceived glamour of a brash and exciting American-ness. The latter was evident in the work of some DJs like Tony Blackburn and Johnnie Walker who championed American soul and R&B alongside the explosion of new British pop, then rock talent (Chapman 1992). I have already argued that the pirates both represented themselves and were understood as being British (none more so than Radio London with its explicit link to the capital). The music radio formats used by the pirates was, however, derived from American models and one of the more interesting consequences of that is that a number of British DJs adopted a US-inflected accent, sometimes referred to as mid-Atlantic or trans-Atlantic, and a tendency to American phrasing. One example of this is the aforementioned Tony Blackburn whose later work for BBC Radio 1 (launched in 1967) is discussed by Scannell and Brand (1991). The ultimate expression of American authenticity was Los Angeles-born Radio Caroline DJ, Emperor Rosko (real name Mike Pasternak) whose output was as close to a US-sounding show as was possible for a station floating around in the Thames Estuary (Barnard 1989) (for a fascinating case study of accent and identity on British radio, see Tessler 2007).

The second key element of the radio text here was the music itself. The leading pirate stations, Caroline and London played mostly contemporary pop from the United States and the United Kingdom and for the first time in post-Second World War UK daytime radio, British audiences were presented with a music space that integrated sounds from both sides of the Atlantic in the same programming stream. One of the consequences of this was a radio imaginary that consolidated pop music into an international (or strictly speaking, bi-national) space where geographic place-ness was acknowledged but was also part of an international pop space made possible for the first time in the UK by the pirates.

The third radio text element was advertising and sponsorship. This hadn't been heard in British daytime radio since the end of the 1930s and advertising of British products and services on the pirate stations partly fits with Berland's argument about the consequences of market consolidation for the construction of localness. The element of Berland's theory that works retrospectively here is the way UK advertising on the offshore pirates is part of the construction of the stations as 'British' in a way that obscures the placeless-ness of the studios themselves and their 'somewhere-but-nowhere' situation in international waters. Indeed, it might be reasonable to speculate that the combination of 'somewhere-but-nowhere', signifiers of Britishness in advertising and the majority of the DJs (mid-Atlantic accents notwithstanding) may have helped develop a sense that the pirates were British without being tied to the geographical place-ness of the BBC in London (with all the class and regionalist baggage that may have entailed). It wasn't until 1968 that the BBC launched its local radio services so until that point the Corporation remained a national broadcaster serving the UK for the most part from London (Briggs 1995).

The fourth and final textual element that the pirates brought to daytime radio in the UK was the station identifier (ident) jingle. This had been the key element of pop formats in the United States since the late-1950s and until around 1975 the majority of all American station jingles emerged from just one production house, PAMS in Dallas, Texas (Wasser 2012). The UK offshore pirates, and BBC Radio 1 after them used the same jingle producers, so the sonic identity of a station was part of a continuity of US broadcast pop cultural production, both contrasting with the Britishness of the pirates and constructing pop radio as an imagined transnational space informed by the DNA of American pop (it is worth noting that Radio Caroline was co-founded by Ronan O'Rahilly, a young Irish entrepreneur, based in London [Hind and Mosco 1985]).

Part of the UK government strategy around closing down the pirate radio station was to offer the British public a BBC-sourced national alternative (Barnard 1989). So, as part of a wider restructuring of its services the BBC launched BBC Radio 1 in September of 1967 (Barnard 1989), offering a youth-orientated pop music service to audiences disenfranchised by the disappearance of the pirates. The BBC employed a significant number of former pirate radio DJs, used jingle packages recorded in Dallas and perhaps reluctantly allowed space for the more improvisational approach to presentation, albeit constrained by BBC management structures and public service objectives (Hendy 2000). In terms of place and space, Radio 1 had absorbed and rebranded much of what the pirates had been doing but switched out the 'somewhere-but-nowhere'-ness of the pirates for the most definite place-ness of the BBC in Broadcasting House, London. The other significant difference in terms of producing music radio space was national UK signal coverage. Much of the UK that was geographically distant from the south and east of England was able to hear daytime pop radio for the first time, and so there was a new set of processes involved in creating a 'national UK' radio space, and much larger audiences, peaking in the early 1970s at over 20 million. Audience numbers remained high even after the arrival in late 1973 of fully licenced commercial radio in the UK in the form of Independent Local Radio (ILR), as I noted at the beginning of this section.

Concluding remarks

In this chapter I have used key moments in the broadcasting histories of Canada and the UK to illustrate the ways in which music radio creates, shapes and is shaped by space and place. I have shown how these processes are framed by political and cultural ideologies, and responses to perceived and real challenges to existing values and power relations. I have not been able to address other areas in which music radio has particular resonance, one of which is the very specific use of radio in automobiles – the means by which many of us navigate the non-spaces of highways that Geoff Stahl discussed in Chapter 1 of this volume. Given that literature on broadcast radio listening in vehicles dates back to the 1930s (e.g. Suchman 1939), this is a project for another time but I wanted to acknowledge music radio's historical significance in creating and manipulating spatial meaning in travel. The other aspect of change in music radio is the disruption to patterns of audio media use caused by the arrival of streaming services like Spotify. Much of the literature in this area is concerned with the consequences of digital disruption for the recorded music and distribution industries (e.g. Sun 2019). Literature on the quasi-radio attributes of streaming services is starting to emerge as I write in 2021 but I hope to return to an analysis of place-ness and streamed music media in the near future. Do most users of Spotify know or care that it is a Swedish company? In what ways does knowing or not knowing matter? Regardless, music radio, a concept that dates back to David Sarnoff's 1916 memo continues to represent a significant slice of popular music distribution and consumption in the UK (RAJAR 2021) and elsewhere. In that context, it continues to construct, reconstruct and itself become shaped by notions of space, place and identity.

References

Baade, C.L. (2012), *Victory Through Harmony: The BBC and Popular Music in World War II*, Oxford: Oxford University Press.
Barnard, S. (1989), *On The Radio*, Milton Keynes: Open University Press.
Barnard, S. (2000), *Studying Radio*, London: Arnold.
Benjamin, L. (2002), 'In Search of the Sarnoff "Radio Music Box" Memo: Nally's Reply', *Journal of Radio Studies*, 9 (1): 97–106.
Berland, J. (1988), 'Locating Listening: Popular Music, Technological Space, Canadian Mediation', *Cultural Studies*, 2 (3): 343–58.
Berland, J. (1990), 'Radio, Space and Industrial Time: Music Formats, Local Narratives and Technological Mediation', *Popular Music*, 9 (2): 179–92.
Berland, J. (1993), 'Radio, Space and Industrial Time: The Case of Music Formats', in T. Bennett, S. Frith, L. Grossberg, J. Shepherd and G. Turner (eds), *Rock and Popular Music: Politics, Policies, Institutions*, 105–18, London: Routledge.
Briggs, A. (1995), *The History of Broadcasting in the United Kingdom, Volume 5: Competition*, Oxford: Oxford University Press.
Chapman, R. (1992), *Selling the Sixties: The Pirates and Pop Music Radio*, London: Routledge.
CIA (2021), The World Factbook: Canada, https://www.cia.gov/the-world-factbook/countries/canada. (accessed 5 September 2021).
Crisell, A. (2002), *An Introductory History of British Broadcasting*, 2nd edn, Abingdon: Routledge.
Henderson, S. (2008), 'Canadian Content Regulations and the Formation of a National Scene', *Popular Music*, 27 (2): 307–15.
Hendy, D. (2000), 'Pop Music Radio in the Public Service: BBC Radio 1 and New Music in the 1990s', *Media, Culture and Society*, 22 (6): 743–61.
Hendy, D. (2013), *Public Service Broadcasting*, London: McMillan Education UK.
Hind, J. and Mosco, S. (1985), *Rebel Radio: The Full Story of British Pirate Radio*, London: Pluto Press.
Hutchison, D. (1999), *Media Policy: An Introduction*, London Blackwell.
Innes, H. (1950), *Empire and Communications*, Oxford: Oxford University Press, quoted in Berland (1993).
Lyon, A. (2003), *Constitutional History of the United Kingdom*, London: Cavendish.
Minahan, J. (2009), *The Complete Guide to National Symbols and Emblems: Volume 2*, Oxford: Greenwood Press.
RAJAR (2021), https://www.rajar.co.uk. (accessed 23 July 2021).
Statistics Canada (2021), *Population Estimates Quarterly*, https://www150.statcan.gc.ca/t1/tbl1/en/tv.action?pid=1710000901. (accessed 24 July 2021).
Scannell, P. and Brand, G. (1991), 'Talk Identity and Performance', in P. Scannell (ed), *Broadcast Talk*, 201–26, London: Sage.
Scannell, P. and Cardiff, D. (1991), *A Social History of British Broadcasting*, Vol. 1, Oxford: Basil Blackwell.
Straw, W. (1991), 'Systems of Articulation, Logics of Change: Communities and Scenes in Popular Music', *Cultural Studies*, 5 (3): 368–88.

Suchman, E. A. (1939), 'Radio Listening and Automobiles', *Journal of Applied Psychology*, 23 (1): 148–57.
Sutherland, R. (2002), 'Canadian Content at 32', *Canadian Issues*, June, 13–17.
Sun, H. (2019), *Digital Revolution Tamed: The Case of the Recording Industry*, London: Palgrave Macmillan.
Tessler, H. (2007), 'Dialect and Dialectic: John Peel's Stylised Scouseness and Contested Contexts of Englishness in Broadcast Radio', *Radio Journal: International Studies in Broadcast & Audio Media*, 4 (1–3): 49–67.
United Nations (2012), 'Demographic Yearbook – Table 3: Population by Sex, Rate of Population Increase, Surface Area and Density'. https://unstats.un.org/unsd/demographic/products/dyb/dyb2012/Table03.pdf. (accessed 24 July 2021).
Wasser, F. (2012), *The Not-So-Distant History of Radio Jingles*, Washington: NPR. https://www.npr.org/2012/07/28/156997028/the-not-so-distant-history-of-radio-jingles?t=1627245973776. (accessed 23 July 2021).

10

The record shop

Nabeel Zuberi

In the early 1990s, Paul Du Gay and Keith Negus (1994: 393) remarked that '[t]he record shop has been strangely absent from most histories of pop and neglected or merely mentioned in passing in accounts of its production and consumption'. Academic writing on the topic remains scattered and marginal in popular music studies, media studies and cultural studies. However, representations of the record store have proliferated in music histories for a general readership, journalism, memoirs, novels, films, television, video and trade publications, driven by the dialectic of decline and precarity on the one hand, and the vinyl revival on the other. A particularly knowing representation of the historical–cultural significance of the record store appears in the Amazon show, *The Marvelous Mrs. Maisel* (2017). In an episode that uses a real location (The Music Inn, on West 4th Street in New York City) to make a point about why record stores matter, the street-wise wannabe manager Susie Myerson takes 'Midge' Maisel to the Music Inn. Mrs Maisel is baffled. 'What is this place?' she asks. Myerson answers, 'Part store, part museum, part archive'.

In the twentieth century, the record store was at the frontline of music consumption, developing a plethora of techniques for the ordering, promotion and sale of recorded music and associated goods, 'a landscape with its own customs, language and ritual' (King 2015: 6). Record shops engendered peculiar practices around browsing and buying, as well as activities that included live performances, conversation and loitering. They were connected to concert venues, dance clubs, radio stations, record companies and the music press. They nurtured friendships and collaboration, and operated like 'access networks', those 'environments that nurture a relationship with music simply by making it available' (Durkin 2014: 295).

In the twenty-first century, record stores have not quite disappeared as media industries have shifted to digital distribution and subscription services that offer ubiquitous streaming music at a finger's touch on mobile devices. Music retail has been one of the hardest hit sectors in the 'new ecology of consumption' shaped by information technology businesses (Hesmondhalgh and Meier 2018: 1556). Declining sales of physical entertainment media have been compounded by a wider 'retail apocalypse', with 2019 a record year for store closures in the United States (Herbert and Johnson 2020).

The sense of doom for record stores was captured in the titles of several documentaries in the last two decades. The voice-over narration of *I Need That Record! The Death (or Possible Survival) of the Independent Record Store* (2008) often uses the past tense as if the American record store is already extinct. *Last Shop Standing* (2014) blames cheaply imported mail order CDs and mass retailers for the decline of independent shops in the UK; its ray of light is the annual Record Store Day (RSD), introduced in the United States and a few other nations since 2008 (Harvey 2017). *All Things Must Pass* (2015) tracks the rise and fall of US megastore chain Tower Records since the 1960s. Many record stores have shrunk and recorded music has taken up less space in their premises. Rising rents have forced many businesses to move or shut up shop. In 'The pain of losing a local record store', David Sax (2019) writes that June Records in Toronto 'meant the world' because 'it was a block from my house; the selection was eclectic and sweeping; the prices were fair; and its staff members were the kind of knowledgeable, highly opinionated music geeks that possessed a soulful recognition engine more powerful than any algorithm'. The documentary *Other Music* (2020) captures the last few weeks of its eponymous store in May 2016 after two decades in New York City's East Village. The release of the film by rental from independent record store websites during COVID-19 lockdowns around the world was a stark reminder that these spaces were even more vulnerable than usual.

However, in the midst of this mourning, the record store's association with music's past may help the institution to survive as both antique shop and museum. 'Fetishistic audiophilia' for the vinyl record (though not the currently unfashionable compact disc) keeps the record store sustainable (Corbett 1990: 85). Vinyl came to signify nostalgia in the CD-era of the 1990s (Anderson 2008; Chivers Yochim and Biddinger 2008; Garwood 2016). In films released during the MP3 noughties of digital downloading, characters associated with record stores were less likely to be socially inept vinyl junkies than what the video essay *Romance in the Record Store* (2018) calls 'eclectic hopeless romantic types, clinging on to beauty that is fading in the eyes of others'. That these fictional aficionados, collectors and outsiders are usually white, male, and flirting in the aisles, suggests that the record store will remain a valued market niche due to this influential demographic group. In the UK, since 2013 vinyl has appeared in advertising for pensions, beer, car, coffee, condoms, furniture and internet service providers (Jones 2018: 31). Books about records inevitably discuss record stores. But record store literature is broad enough to have its own subgenres: coffee table books of interiors and record covers (Jonkmanns 2016); tourist guides and travelogues (Barnes 2018); memoirs (Pettit 2008; Burgess 2016); and histories of music retail (Cartwright 2017).

In the age of digital music, vinyl and record store cultures aren't hold-outs against digital media, but strongly shaped and enriched by post-digital cultures that embrace the pleasures of the analogue (Palm 2019). Record stores may be hybrids of physical and online spaces that generate a steady stream of digital content, using their own websites, as well as social media platforms and the world's largest music database and marketplace Discogs to promote foot traffic and online business. The stores themselves and sites such as the Vinyl Factory feature a plethora of media forms, including audio samples of music for sale, album recommendations and reviews, videos of celebrity in-store selections, and short documentary profiles of particular stores. Facebook pages archive photographs and stories of active and long-gone record stores. Retailers and consumers have YouTube channels, Twitter accounts and Instagram feeds devoted to content about record stores and mythologies about vinyl.

The independent record store currently dominates media representations of bricks-and-mortar music retail. For the critical political economy of music, vinyl culture is one site of struggle for independence in production and distribution as small record labels and merchants negotiate how they might survive and flourish (Palm 2019). The independent record store is often regarded as more authentic for its idiosyncratic curation of records, whether a general or specialist store, selling primarily new or used recordings. It is valued for its close attachment to the music cultures in its urban location than the standardized spaces and more mainstream stock of corporate retailers and chain stores.

Some of the negative associations of record stores as intimidating and masculine spaces have been mollified as even if the snobbery and sexism have been challenged (Anderson 2020). Documentaries about record stores often include female staff and record buyers describing harassment and patronizing attitudes, and male staff that vouch the misogynistic environment has changed significantly. Nevertheless, a number of male record store archetypes persist. The nerdy staffer was satirized famously in *The Onion*'s (2003) story '37 record-store clerks feared dead in Yo La Tengo concert disaster' which exclaimed, 'It's such a shame that all those bastions of indie-rock geekitude had to go in their prime. Their cries of "sellout" have forever been silenced.' Barry at Championship Vinyl in Nick Hornby's novel *High Fidelity* (1995), amped up in Jack Black's performance in Stephen Frears's 2000 film, is the judgmental enforcer of taste. Margaret Smith gave a queer spin on this archetype as the caustic owner of Permanent Record in short-lived sitcom *That '80s Show* (2002). That these characterizations are part of record store lore and quite often parodic may signal that their toxicity and power to define this corner of retail culture have waned; though gender-diverse record shoppers still have many stories to tell. The reboot of *High Fidelity* (2020) as a TV series with African-American women and queer record store staff suggests this shift too.

The boosting of the independent record store's status, now less intimidating, but still local and idiosyncratic, may have resulted in scholars not giving sufficient attention to other kinds of music retail. An open-ended definition of the record shop should aim to do justice to the range of places in which recorded music has been sold, considering everything from department stores, chain stores, supermarkets, megastores, thrift stores, market stalls, pop-ups and pirate operations on the pavement. Music has been sold alongside many types of goods and services, including sheet music, playback equipment, musical instruments, zines, posters, books and t-shirts. Reputedly the oldest record shop in the world, Spillers in Cardiff, sold washing machines and bicycles when it opened its doors in 1894. The smells of records, coffee, garlic and pasta blend in the sensorium of City Country City in Tokyo. We should also acknowledge the temporary and fragile architectures of music retail: shacks where vendors provide music content for USB sticks and sound cards; hastily organized sales at storage facilities when a record collector has died or failed to pay fees; yard sales and car boots. Only focusing on bricks and mortar or online sellers misses these other significant parts of music retail culture, and the porous boundaries between many types of 'record store'.

The department store played a significant role in twentieth-century record shopping. William Kenney (1999: 96) writes that 'the large urban department stores of the nineteen teens and twenties created small female recorded-music cultures'. Their phonograph departments featured listening rooms decorated with furniture and rugs to simulate domestic settings, and young women sales clerks recommended, played and ordered recordings for mostly female customers. These relatively low-paid workers often had extensive knowledge about music and inventory, though 'they rarely managed or owned the music supply store' (Kenney 1999: 98).

The mass retail of the twentieth century brought large record sections to department store chains that stocked music in the popular charts, new releases, discounted albums and compilations for working-class shoppers and teenagers with less money to spend on albums. In Zadie Smith's novel *Swing Time* (2016), the narrator recalls a time in the 1980s when she and her best friend accompany her mother to buy a birthday present for a ten-year-old school friend: 'For the gift she suggested a record, a pop single, it could be from both of us, cheap but sure to be appreciated: she would take us down the high road to Woolworths to find something suitable' (Smith 2016: 74). Pharmacies and newsagent chains also had record departments. These kinds of record stores often appear in memoirs and novels, but in academic scholarship they appear to have contributed little to local and national music cultures in any positive way. The same might be said of the monster discount superstores such as K-Mart, Wal-Mart, Target and Best Buy that used cheap music as a loss leader and, in the case of Wal-Mart expanded music censorship by not carrying particular releases (Fox 2005). The necessary critical political economy approaches to these businesses may not shed sufficient light on how these retailers shaped music tastes and cultures in places that were less likely to have a hip independent store or vibrant music scene.

Music megastore chains such as HMV, Virgin and Tower Records came to prominence between the mid 1960s and 1990s, but have almost disappeared in the twenty-first century. Alongside the now extinct mall chains, they occupy an ambivalent position in record store discourse, disliked for their price-cutting competition with smaller independent retailers and their more generic inventory, but respected for their brand longevity and focus on recorded music and associated merchandise in comparison with discount superstores. Rob Drew (2002) describes the music megastore as a 'gulag' of sadistic salespeople and 'insular' consumers flipping through racks in 'quiet desperation' in contrast to the once convivial social friction of 'the little music store on the wrong side of town' that was 'something halfway between a record shop and a record hop 'in John Waters's film *Hairspray* (1988) set in Baltimore in the early 1960s. For Drew, the post-millennial megastore lacks the sociability of bookstores, with no place to sit and talk with anyone, only listening stations and endless aisles of recordings with too many choices. These feelings of alienation prefigure anxieties about the abundance of digital music. Music megastores in the age of the CD now seem like a stage in the development of the 'celestial jukebox' of the cloud and streaming music (McCourt and Burkart 2004). Their expansion of inventory is one factor in the rise of compilation scores in films since the late 1960s, according to Julie Hubbert (2014: 300), who points out that 'Tower Records pursued a model of "deep cataloguing" more aggressively than others, carrying not only a large variety of musical styles but also a large number of niche or obscure recordings in each style'. In the 1990s the music megastore anticipated and shaped the surveillance of consumption today with its point-of-sale electronic data processing technologies (such as SoundScan) that gave music retailers greater influence in the music industries (Du Gay and Negus 1994; McCourt and Rothenbuhler 1999).

The concept of *mediality* is useful here for understanding the record store, as Will Straw proposes in his discussion of the music chart (Straw 2015). Drawing upon Friedrich Kittler's definition of media as having the properties of processing, transmission and storage, Straw argues that mediality is understood as 'not a permanent and definitive property of objects or forms but as the occasional state of a wide variety of objects, including those not normally classed as "media"' (Straw 2015: 128). Straw cites the mediality of 1950s high school culture which as a container 'captures the profound layering of temporalities which existed within it, as some songs and musical styles moved quickly towards being forgotten while others lingered' (Straw 2015: 134). The record store, like the MP3 collection or the music chart, is 'an archival space engaged simultaneously in the remembering and forgetting of music' (Straw 2015: 133–4). Pete Paphides's description of the singles display in a Woolworths department store in the late 1970s in his childhood memoir exemplifies this process:

> Here you were greeted with a floor-to-ceiling gallery of seventy-five small wall-mounted records – every one of them corresponding to a position in that week's chart. A wall of sound. A pop share index – a rock exchange, if you like – charting the differing fortunes of the artists seeking to establish a surer foothold in the affections of the nation… Woolworths' chart wall allowed me to see what records were likely to remain unsold as they dropped out of the chart. If say, Blondie's 'Sunday Girl' was at number 70, and there were still copies in stock, I soon came to realise that the following Wednesday – the day after the new chart was announced – the display would be updated and any remaining copies would be moved to the 49p rack.
>
> (Paphides 2020: 168–9)

The chart of bestsellers or list of new releases processes the temporalities of the music industry in the space of the record store. At the start of the Slim Gaillard Quartette's 'Jumpin' at the record shop' (1945), Gaillard vocalizes: 'May I hear your new releases, I'm in the market for some brand new pieces. Let me read your record lists, there may be something I don't want to miss.' He then proceeds to recite the names of big band artists of the day, male vocalists, female vocalists, international stars, western swing band leaders and comedy recording artists, in clusters that come from the new release list, but could just as well be recommendations played in store, or titles that catch his eye while he flips through discs: 'Duke Ellington, Count Basie, the Dorseys; Frank Sinatra, Bing Crosby, they're the voices'. The artists' roll-call also suggests the different genre categorizations of the record store. Carmen Miranda and Xavier Cugat are together, as are Jack Benny and Bob Hope.

In the cover photo of a 2002 jazz compilation of the same title, Gaillard is in a record store staring at the label of a 78 RPM record, the cover of which looks like a generic illustrated company sleeve. In the background, records are lined up on a shelf in a store that doesn't appear to have yet fully transitioned to self-service. Initially self-service was a necessity due to a labour shortage, but after the Second World War, it was taken up by most US stores selling music. *The Billboard*'s *1944 Music Year Book* advocates growth in self-service stores with racks against the walls where 'disks group themselves' according to types of music, and there are 'island racks in the center aisles for the single sides'. Together with 'sound-proofed and air-conditioned listening booths' or 'half a dozen or so turntables' these will help to constitute 'your modern record store of today and certainly the store of tomorrow' (Billboard 1944: 159). Self-service dominates today, though some stores still keep the media behind the counter with customers browsing through packaging.

African-American comic artist Jay Paul Johnson's dynamic and bop-infused 'Hippitty hop to the record shop' from the *Home Folks* strip attests to the vibrancy of the record store by the early 1950s (Stapinski 2020). The visual allure of these spaces was heightened as the graphic design, photographs and illustrations that might have been found in promotional posters on walls and booklets on the counter migrated to record covers in the racks and on walls. Steven Heller (2011: 33) writes that at Columbia Records, 'Alex Steinweiss designed the first illustrated 78 rpm album package in 1940, and by 1948 had invented the paperboard 33 ⅓ LP container.' According to Will Burtin, art director at *Fortune*, Steinweiss's 'colorful album covers… took the record shop out of the library-like atmosphere and put it right back into competition, moved from the rarefied air of penthouse and museum back to Broadway and Main Street' (Heller 2011: 39).

The walls of the store appear significantly in Paul Gilroy's (1992: 136) discussion of 'the record shop as a popular cultural archive and repository of folk knowledge' for the African-Caribbean diasporas in London. The images of reggae, soul, funk and hip hop create 'an ever-changing and seemingly organic agglomeration of covers, posters and advertisements which complement the power of sound' in often cramped spaces. Self-confessed 'vinyl freak' John Corbett (2015: 304) advises that on stepping into any record store, one should 'hit the walls' first, where rarities and bargains unavailable in the racks are placed, alongside new releases and canonical recordings. In the unidentified London store in John Schlesinger's affectionate satirical short film *Hi-Fi-Fo-Fum* (1959) for the BBC's *Monitor* program, the voice-over narrator notes that customers walk 'down past a shining mosaic of record covers to join the mysterious ritual' in record stores that have become 'glossy cathedrals' with assistants who are like 'church wardens'. A memorable tracking shot moves along a line of listening booths described as 'confessionals' with solitary and paired listeners that test out their own preferred music (spliced together in an audio montage). Listening booths have long been replaced by turntables and open listening stations with headphones, though many record stores do not allow customers to listen to new or second-hand records before purchase.

The heart of any record store is the stock of music and its arrangement in racks, shelves, boxes, crates, and in some cases, piles on the floor. The categorizations of sections reflect a record store's generalist or specialist ethos, its approach to curating, and depth of inventory. Generalist stores build reputations for their curating skills in a broad cross-section of music, with reputed strengths in some genres or styles. Specialist stores reveal the volume of music within a type of music, and how deep they delve into subgenres and related styles. Usually combining these two models, record stores are 'key spaces of contact for learning about the canon, for receiving what might be dubbed "sacred aural texts"' (Bartmanski and Woodward 2015: 145).

The placement and labelling of sections reflect the hegemony of industrial and journalistic tags for music styles in a place, though store owners and staff often add their own idiosyncratic categories. The relative distribution of stock reflects national markets and local scenes. The placement of different types of music in relation to each other in the store presents a map of music based on categorizations and affinities that have ideological, racialized and gendered histories. In most stores, the subdivisions in each genre/style section are organized alphabetically by the last name of the artist, but other modes of dividing the inventory are common too: for example, historical periodization by decade for rock compilations; record companies or labels in many specialist jazz, soul and dance music stores; in Japan, some jazz sections are divided by the musical instrument of the recording artist; reggae sections may be divided by the names of Jamaican rhythms versioned by many artists and recordings. The layout of record stores encourages movement and attention that shapes the discovery of music and educates about genealogies. Lavinia Greenlaw (2007: 162–3) recalls that the organization of her local small record shop 'reflected the way in which music adds up and how it moves in cycles. The disco and prog rock relegated to the bottom shelf of the second-hand section would one day be rediscovered just as I was then following the Sex Pistols back to the New York Dolls and the Velvet Underground'.

The organization, recommendation and discovery of music in the record store have been remediated unevenly in their own online avatars, and those of digital-only stores and streaming services. Analog and digital recordings can now be cross-listed for easier searching of databases. The hunt for a recording is less protracted. Attention to the art of record covers is more fleeting in shrunken images. The descriptions of recordings on websites and apps owe something to the handwritten staff recommendation cards in record stores, as well as sleeve/liner notes, music press reviews and PR releases. Discovery may still be pleasurably serendipitous on streaming platforms with their invisible curatorial hands, algorithmic nudges and digital wormholes. Websites and apps like Discogs and Bandcamp have blogs and spaces for interaction that may be as convivial as the sociability of the bricks-and-mortar record store. Adam Harper (2019) has adroitly pointed that the mostly autobiographical literature celebrating the 'real' practices of vinyl and the record store, particularly around the holding and touching of vinyl, fall into a romantic trope that doesn't acknowledge listeners can have relationships with digital music in its various forms.

Even as we unpack this mythological struggle between the 'physical' and the 'virtual', we might still reflect on the body's relationship to specific places and objects. Recalling life behind the counter in Bristol, Richard King (2015: 6) writes that '[c]ertain body movements, such as the particular angle at which one crooks one's head to read the spine of an album, reminded me of being in Revolver' and he realizes that his memories of the store 'had undergone a process of reification'. This kind of muscle memory is even more visceral in Elizabeth Hardwick's (1976) essay about Billie Holiday and New York in the early 1940s: 'And for us, there were the blaring shops, open most of the night, where we could buy old, scratched, worn-thin jazz records – Vocalian, Okeh, and Brunswick labels. Our hands sliced through the cases until the skin around our fingers bled.' And of spatial memory, Alan Warner (2015: 45) reveals about the Scottish highland hometown record store he frequented as a teenager that 'to this day every few years I still dream a warped version of the shop and more specifically of the delicious feeling of anticipation with which I would approach it on Saturdays – the musical possibilities contained therein'.

The word 'consumption' subsumes encounters with the particular materialities of media goods, in spaces of visual spectacle and musical sounds, of solitary silent browsing and conversation, of learning and love for music. Maybe the greatest record store film, Jeanie Finlay's documentary *Sound It Out* (2011), set in austerity-hit Stockton-on-Tees in North East England, details the life of the working-class staff and mostly male customers in its eponymous shop: heavy metal friends and Status Quo superfans who feel 'saved' by its presence; the DJs and beat makers obsessed with Makina, a Spanish electronic dance music genre; a local musician who has 'made it' in London plays an in-store on a nervous return to her hometown; the owner who takes on a former employee laid off by Zavvi (Virgin). This owner does the research to find any recording a customer wants, and takes as many of the used records he can from people who want to exchange them for cash, describing the damaged ones declined apologetically as 'well-loved'; the middle-aged man who comes into the store after a visit to the pub and hits on the filmmaker as she interviews him on camera. These are glimpses of the record store as a relatively autonomous space built on relationships with recorded music, but also a place always imbued with the cultural ethos and political realities of its location.

The author would like to thank Erin Rogatski, Tim Anderson, James Gardner, Cian O'Donnell and Martyn William Pepperell.

References

All Things Must Pass: The Rise and Fall of Tower Records (2015), [Film] Dir. Colin Hanks. USA: Company Name.
Anderson, T.J. (2008), 'As if History Was Merely a Record: The Pathology of Nostalgia and the Figure of the Recording in Contemporary Popular Cinema', *Music, Sound, and the Moving Image*, 2 (1): 51–76.
Anderson, T.J. (2020), 'Female Treble: Gender, Record Retail, and a Play for Space', D. Herbert and D. Johnson (eds), *Point of Sale: Analyzing Media Retail*, 160–74, New Brunswick, NJ: Rutgers University Press.
Bain, M. (2019), 'Liquidation Nation: 2019 Saw a Dramatic Spike in US Retailers Closing Stores', *Quartz*, 20 December 2019. Available online: https://qz.com/1771909/2019-saw-a-dramatic-spike-in-us-retailers-closing-stores/. (accessed 15 May 2020).
Barnes, M. (2018), *Around the World in 80 Record Stores: A Guide to the Best Vinyl Emporiums on the Planet*, London: Dog 'n' Bone Books.
Bartmanski, D. and Woodward, I. (2015), *Vinyl: The Analogue Record in the Digital Age*, London: Bloomsbury.
Billboard, The (1944), 'Sock Sales Stimulant: Technique Is No Mere Experiment to Meet a Temporary Need: It's Here to Stay and Grow', in *The Billboard 1944 Music Year Book*, 158–9, New York: The Billboard.

Burgess, T. (2016), *Tim Book Two: Vinyl Adventures From Istanbul to San Francisco*, London: Faber & Faber.

Burkart, P. and McCourt, T. (2004), 'Infrastructure for the Celestial Jukebox', *Popular Music*, 23 (3): 349–62.

Cartwright, G. (2017), *Going for a Song: A Chronicle of the UK Record Shop*, London: Flood Gallery.

Chivers Yochim, E. and Biddinger, M. (2008), '"It Kind of Gives You That Vintage Feel": Vinyl Records and the Trope of Death', *Media, Culture & Society*, 30 (2): 183–95.

Corbett, J. (1990), 'Free, Single, and Disengaged: Listening Pleasure and the Popular Music object', *October*, 54: 79–101.

Corbett, J. (2015), *Microgrooves: Forays into Other Music*, Durham: Duke University Press.

Drew, R. (2002), 'Fear Itself: Cruising for Music', *Bad Subjects*, 59. Available online: http://bad.eserver.org/issues/2002/59/drew.html (accessed 28 February 2019).

Du Gay, P. and Negus, K. (1994), 'The Changing Sites of Sound: Music Retailing and the Composition of Consumers', *Media, Culture & Society*, 16 (3): 395–413.

Durkin, A. (2014), *Decomposition: A Music Manifesto*, New York: Pantheon.

Editors of *The Onion* (2002), '37 Record-Store Clerks Feared Dead in Yo La Tengo Concert Disaster', *The Onion*, 10 April. Available online: https://www.theonion.com/37-record-store-clerks-feared-dead-in-yo-la-tengo-conce-1819566399 (accessed 20 May 2020).

Fox, M. (2005), 'Market Power in Music Retailing: The Case of Wal-Mart', *Popular Music and Society*, 28 (4): 501–19.

Garwood, I. (2016), 'Vinyl Noise and Narrative in CD-Era Indiewood', in L. Greene and D. Kulezic-Wilson (eds), *The Palgrave Handbook of Sound Design and Music in Screen Media*, 245–60, London: Palgrave Macmillan.

Gilroy, P. (1992), 'Wearing Your Art on Your Sleeve: Notes towards a Diaspora History of Black Ephemera', in D.A. Bailey and S. Hall (eds), *Ten 8: Critical Decade: Black British Photography in the 80s*, 2 (3): 128–37.

Greenlaw, L. (2007), *The Importance of Music to Girls*, London: Faber & Faber.

Hairspray (1988), [Film] Dir. John Waters, USA: New Line Cinema.

Hardwick, E. (1976), 'Billie Holiday', *New York Review of Books*, 4 March. Available online: https://www-nybooks-com.ezproxy.auckland.ac.nz/articles/1976/03/04/billie-holiday/ (accessed 20 May 2020).

Harper, A. (2019), 'To Have and to Hold: Touch and the Vinyl Resurgence', *Tempo*, 73 (287): 52–61.

Harvey, E. (2017), 'Siding with Vinyl: Record Store Day and the Branding of Independent Music', *International Journal of Cultural Studies*, 20 (6): 585–602.

Heller, S. (2011), 'Visualizing Music', in S. Heller and K. Reagan (eds), *Alex Steinweiss: The Inventor of the Modern Album Cover*, 33–42, Cologne: Taschen.

Herbert, D. and Johnson, D., eds (2020), *Point of Sale: Analyzing Media Retail*, New Brunswick: Rutgers University Press.

Hesmondhalgh, D. and Meier, L.M. (2018), 'What the Digitalisation of Music Tells Us about Capitalism, Culture and the Power of the Information Technology Sector', *Information, Communication & Society*, 21 (11):1555–70.

Hi-Fi-Fo-Fum (1959), [TV programme] Dir. John Schlesinger, *Monitor*, 12 April, UK: BBC. Available online: https://www.bbc.co.uk/archive/hi-fi-fo-fum/zjt6kmn (accessed 20 May 2020).

High Fidelity (2000), [Film] Dir. Stephen Frears, UK/USA: Touchstone Pictures/Working Title/Dog Star Films.

High Fidelity (2020), [TV Series], USA: ABC Signature Studios/Midnight Radio/Hulu.

Hornby, N. (1995), *High Fidelity*, London: Victor Gollancz.

Hubbert, J. (2014), 'The Compilation Soundtrack from the 1960s to the Present', in D. Neumeyer (ed.), *The Oxford Handbook of Film Music Studies*, 292–318, New York: Oxford University Press.

I Need That Record (2008), [Film] Dir. Brendan Toller, USA: Brendan Toller Productions/Outre Films.

Jones, G. (2018), *The Vinyl Revival and the Shops That Made It Happen*, London: Proper Music.

Jonkmanns B. (2016), *Record Stores: A Tribute to Record Stores*, Berlin: Seltmann+Soehne.

Kenney, W.H. (1999), *Recorded Music in American Life: The Phonograph and Popular Memory, 1890–1945*, New York: Oxford University Press.

King, R. (2015), *Original Rockers*, London: Faber & Faber.

Last Shop Standing (2012), [Film] Dir. Pip Piper, UK: Blue Hippo Media.

McCourt, T. and Rothenbuhler, E. (1999), 'SoundScan and the Consolidation of Control in the Popular Music Industry', *Media, Culture & Society*, 19 (2): 201–18.

Other Music (2020), [Film] Dir. Puloma Basu and Rob Hatch-Miller, USA: Factory 25.

Palm, M. (2019), 'Keeping What Real? Vinyl Records and the Future of Independent Culture', *Convergence*, 25 (4): 643–56.

Paphides, P. (2020), *Broken Greek: A Story of Chip Shops and Pop Songs*, London: Quercus.

Pettit, E. (2008), *Old Rare New: The Independent Record Shop*, London: Black Dog.

'Romance in the Record Store' (2018), [Video] Dir. Jacob T. Swinney, USA: Fandor. Available online: https://www.youtube.com/watch?v=2ur0Dhh3Y7c (accessed 20 May 2020).

Sax, D. (2019), 'The Pain of Losing A Local Record Store', *New York Times*, 17 August. Available online: https://www.nytimes.com/2019/08/17/opinion/sunday/local-record-store.html (accessed 20 May 2020).

Slim Gaillard Quartette (1944), 'Jumpin' at The Record Shop', [10-inch shellac recording], USA: Atomic Records.

Smith, G. (2018), *The Vinyl Revival and the Shops That Made It Happen*, London: Proper Music Publishing Ltd.

Smith, Z. (2016), *Swing Time*, New York: Penguin Books.

Sound It Out (2011), [Film] Dir. Jeanie Finlay, UK: Glimmer Films.

Stapinski, H. (2020), 'Superheroes and Trailblazers: Black Comic Book Artists, Rediscovered', *New York Times*, 31 December. Available online: https://www.nytimes.com/2020/12/31/arts/design/black-comic-book-artists-racism.html (accessed 15 April 2021).

Straw, W. (2015), 'Mediality and the Music Chart', *SubStance*, 44 (3): 128–38.

That '80s Show (2002), [TV series], USA: Carsey-Werner-Mandabach/Fox.

The Marvelous Mrs. Maisel (2017), [TV programme], Season 1, Episode 4, USA: Amazon Studios/Dorothy Parker Drank Here Productions/Picro.

Various Artists (2002), *Jumpin' At The Record Shop*, [CD], UK: Acrobat.

Warner, A. (2015), *Tago Mago*, London: Bloomsbury.

11

The nightclub

Hillegonda C Rietveld

Introduction

I can hear the bass-heavy beat of the dance music while I wait in the queue. There is a security system to filter access to the club, depending on various parameters based on desired patronage. Passing by a ticket booth and cloakroom, I walk towards the door from which direction the muffled sound of the music seeps through. On opening, the damp heat of dancing bodies hits my face, and the amplified dance music hits my body. It's late at night and the room is crowded, making it almost impossible to reach the bar for a drink. I look around for the dancefloor, its dynamic lighting sweeping through the dark space. Finding the DJ booth is not always easy at an event that depends on forms of organized chaos. The dancers are feeling the music, swaying to the groove. I'm offered a drink – strangers adopt me into their party. I'm at the nightclub.

The discussion that follows addresses the nightclub as a private venue that offers dancing to music. Historically also known as a 'discotheque', 'dance hall,' or 'dancing', the nightclub initially developed in an urban nocturnal setting, as a members' club that can legally conduct its business of entertainment during opening times that may differ from public venues. As a contained cultural space, the nightclub is a venue in which music and alternative night-time identities play central roles that can be extended into the daytime. From a design perspective, '(s)ince the 1960s nightclubs have been epicentres of escape and experimentation, these sealed-off spaces of nocturnal leisure offering opportunities for artists, architects, and designers all over the world, and creating places for partygoers to design their experiences and identities' (Rossi and Eisenbrand 2018: 15). A description of Andy Warhol's 1960s club night, *Exploding Plastic Inevitable* (EPI), held at New York's venue Electric Circus, aptly summarizes the experience of such a space as 'a delirious yet illegible atmosphere crowded with discontinuous bits of sound, light, and flesh' (Lavin 2009: 101). This chapter will address elements – such as night-time, sensory dynamics and DJ engagement – that make up the concept of the contemporary nightclub as a dance club, an immersive 'total-environment', as leading New York club *Studio 54* was described in 1977 (Gifford and Wallace, cited by Schrager 2017: 29), in which one can abandon one's daily sense of self.

The rise in popularity of the nightclub as discotheque via the New York dance club scene in the 1960s and 1970s is well-documented (Goldman 1978; Fikentscher 2000; Lawrence 2003; Shapiro 2005) replacing 'former ballrooms, dance halls and cabaret clubs as the big bands and the dancing styles that went along with them went out of fashion' (Kronenburg 2019: 197). Arguably, such venues responded to a rapidly changing world, in which the nightclub became a place to celebrate a new-found sense of freedom marked by the paradoxical twin developments of neoliberalism and civil rights movements. Nightclubs have a historical connection to the illicit otherness of the night, yet as registered businesses, they are important drivers in the legislated night-time economy, and are recognized as such in policy reports, such as *The Music Cities Manual* (S. Shapiro et al. 2019). Economically and culturally, they act as hubs in creative networks that include music, fashion, design, advertising, alcohol and catering industries, as well as the international tourist industry; see, for example, the commercialization of countercultural nightlife on the Spanish island Ibiza (Armstrong 2004; Morrison 2010; Serra-Cantallops and Ramon-Cardona 2017) or the gritty experimental atmosphere of nightclubs in Germany's capital Berlin (Stahl 2014; Garcia 2016). The focus of published discussions of such venues vary widely, from the promiscuous, escapist and even life-changing pleasures of the insomniac dancer (Malbon 1999; Jackson 2004; Rietveld 2004a; Rief 2009; Morrison 2010; Raine et al. 2019), to DJ histories (Poschardt 1998; Brewster and Broughton 1999; Fikentscher 2000; Lawrence 2003; Farrugia 2012), fashion (Smith 2008) and graphic design (Rose 1991; Banks and Brewster 2018); and from club journalism (Benson 1997; Aletti 2009), club histories (Savage 1992; Cheren 2000; Rietveld 2004b; Shapiro 2005; D'Andrea 2006; Ligura and Langenbach 2007; De Wit 2013; Carpenter and Silva 2015; Hill and Nourmand 2015; Schrager 2017) and architectural design (Kelly 1982; Lavin 2009; Rossi and Eisenbrand 2018; Kronenburg 2019; Loben et al. 2020), to the strategies of urban regeneration as part of the night-time industry (Lovatt 1996; Kolioulis 2018; S. Shapiro et al. 2019).

The nightclub is marked by its nocturnal existence. Hodge and Kress (1988) observe how the syntax of our everyday values dissolve during the night. During a spoken word presentation in 2019, sound artist LaBelle described the night poetically as an ambiguous space, and a time of transformation, in which one can disappear and renew one's sense of self – erotic, monstrous, magical, liminal, criminal, the night takes us to 'the edges of being', to 'intensities of freedom' and into a 'zone of altered subjectivity'. Writing about the nocturnal city, Shaw (2018) observes how the night is a time-space of pre-modern myth and ritual. Music enhances this experience, and sound is simultaneously enhanced by lowered light-levels light during the night. While our vision is dimmed, our hearing sharpens, foregrounding sound in the process, which one could argue is ruined by amplifying sound in our electrified urban culture. Nevertheless, the darkness of the night encourages haptic aurality of amplified sonic vibration and its somnambulant character gives preference to musical repetition (Rietveld 2018) that enables the dancer to enter a realm of 'sonic oblivion' (Sword 2021). Henriques (2011) introduces the term 'sonic dominance' in a study of Jamaican sound system culture, in which music is viscerally amplified across the full range of hearing, with emphasis on outer, marginalized, frequencies.

Nightclubs cater for the transgression of, and an escape from, everyday realities and the exploration of other ways of being. Under the cover of night, in the relative safety of invisibility, away from the glare of day, marginalized groups, such as LGBT+ or migrant communities, are enabled to meet more freely than would be possible during the daytime. As Kolioulis (2018: 209) states, '(a) network of nightclubs shapes alternative geographies of affect, making urban night-time more conducive to social inclusion'. The nightly escape from the tyranny of daily life has created a lifestyle in its own right, leading Mel Cheren, business partner in New York's Paradise Garage, to observe that during the 1970s and early 1980s, '[d]isco denizens became the ultimate night people, and those who partied several nights a week found themselves living in a time zone of their own, the graveyard shift of dance' (Cheren 2000: 106). Yet, Stahl and Bottà (2019: 4–5) explain that although music cultures flourish particularly well at night, they do so in a paradoxical relationship to regulation determined by daytime values:

> Night is where social regulation meets social ritual, often doing so most powerfully and paradoxically around music. As an expanse set aside from the day when identities can be more fruitfully explored, boundaries blurred, social norms questioned or even upturned, night also exists as a place of fear and danger around darkened spaces and places, of certain noises/sounds that must be tamed, insulated or mitigated and, more pointedly, a zone marked by the policing, containment or neutralization of particular identities.

In addition, Shaw (2018: 30) writes that '[d]uring the 19th century era of industrialisation, the introduction of electric lighting changed the cultural relationship to the darkness of the night: cafés, bars, operas and theaters opened to unprecedented late hours'. By extensively lighting up the night, it can both be enjoyed and colonized by broader social and cultural groups, and values, eventually enabling daytime values to intrude on its opaque realm (Rietveld 2013). Taking such issues to heart, Berlin club Berghain, a huge converted industrial space that, initially, opened its doors to a queer clientele in 2006, took the initiative not to allow cameras in order to protect the privacy of guests within its otherworldly club environment (Pirozkhov 2017).

As a place for dancing, the nightclub usually offers a dancefloor, a space to dance, however small. When dancers abandon their daytime selves to the music, they respond musically by dancing out its rhythms, textures and sentiments. Mainly for logistical and economic reasons, since the 1940s, the nightclub gradually replaced live musicians by the DJ, or disc jockey, who selects music recordings. This led the French naming such a club a 'discotheque' during the 1940s (P. Shapiro 2005), or 'disco' in short. Whereas a *bibliotheque*, or library, is a place to engage with an archive of texts, the discotheque resembles a space where one can physically engage with an archive of music recordings. Fikentscher defines 'the disco concept' as 'denoting a particular performance environment in which technologically mediated music is made immediate at the hands of the DJ, and in which this music is responded to via dance by bodies on the dancefloor' (2000: 22). Due to parallel developments in the enhancement of music production technologies, from the 1970s onwards dance music often only existed as studio productions. As electronic music technologies became increasingly ubiquitous during the 1980s, this eventually led to development of the electronic dance music as generic term for most club music (Leloup et al. 2020). In this context the DJ, in combination with a powerful sound-system, has become a performative interface between the recorded sonic simulacrum and its dancing audience (Middleton 2006).

The disco concept may be applied to both nightclubs and dance parties. In an ethnographic study titled *Clubbing*, Malbon (1999) focuses on the space of the nightclub in London during the 1990s, yet his description of his participants' nights out dancing at the club could resonate as well with the experience of ravers, the participants of large dance parties that have been taking place in abandoned post-industrial workspaces as well as in rural settings since the late 1980s. Similarly, in Jackson's 2004 study *Inside Clubbing*, the experience of the club dancefloor sounds almost indistinguishable from an urban weekend rave in terms of dancing all-night long to DJ-led music selections, while under the enhanced influence of stimulating and psychoactive dance drugs (O'Hagan 2004). It is therefore not be surprising that the term 'clubbing' and notion of 'club culture' has been generalized as a term associated with DJ-led nocturnal dancing events, even though a more precise term would be 'electronic dance music culture', a term consistently used by the specialist journal in the field, *Dancecult*, or 'dance culture' as it has been known over the last three decades within the English-speaking realm. Even going to a dance festival is described by some as 'clubbing'. Both Thornton (1995) and Rief (2009) titled their monographs *Club Cultures*; yet, despite taking different approaches to the study of electronic dance music culture, both seem to neglect the boundaries between the nightclubs and rave dance events that existed at their respective times of writing. According to Rief (2009: 3):

> Clubbing may refer to dance and music events in nightclubs of variable sizes and capacities (up to several thousand); to go out in smaller, hybrid venues [...]; to dances in venues previously designated as discotheques; or to open-air parties in the open countryside, on beaches or in the mountains.

This is further illustrated in a 1997 collection of club writing from style magazine *The Face* (Benson 1997), which ranges from the spectacularly dressed Blitz Kids in early 1980s London, to English free dance parties of the late 1990s. Redhead et al. (1998) stretch the idea of clubbing further, using the term 'clubculture' to signify a range of post-subcultural youth cultures. Here, though, I narrow the definition of the club as a delineated space, with walls and social boundaries that are protected and enforced by door staff, 'the bouncers'. The night club normally requires a set of licences, to sell tickets; to allow dancing; to allow the selling and consumption of alcohol; to allow a certain number of people in at any one time; and to open its doors at a certain time of the day and week. Subject to surveillance, it is policed both internally and externally. A rave, by contrast, can be semi-legal. In the case of commercial dance festivals, the policing is a different story, as also their licenses are in place, keeping the event in check. However, as illustrated by Loben et al. (2020), some currently globally successful clubs attempt to simulate the darkly lit cavernous space of a warehouse rave, while others opt for a spectacular festival-style DJ stage, complete with theatrical set pieces, dancers and impressive lighting rigs.

Historically, a club's dining and socializing guests may have been seated around a dancefloor, entertained by professional entertainers on stage, including a band of musicians, singers and even dancers. Precedents of enclosed spaces for the purpose of social dancing may be found in the dancefloors of pleasure gardens that catered for the gentry of London, England from the seventeenth into the nineteenth century, followed by ballrooms and dancehalls that gained wider audiences during the nineteenth century (Kronenburg 2019), when major cities were first lit by gas lamps, and later by electric light (Shaw 2018). In contrast to such legitimate dance spaces, during the early twentieth century in Chicago and New York City, in the United States, the format of the nightclub as we recognize it now can be found in speakeasies, members clubs that illegally served alcoholic beverages, liquor, during the American alcohol prohibition of 1920 which lasted till, roughly, 1933. Many of these venues were literally underground, in basements and cellars. In the more upmarket New York establishments, cabaret and jazz music was offered as entertainment, while provocative social dance styles like the Charleston gained popularity (Smith 2008). Jazz and dance clubs owe some of their arrangement of space, including the bar, the stage, the dancefloor, the cloakroom, the membership system, the door staff (bouncers), to such diverse precedents. This illicit network of lucrative venues tightened the connection between nightclubs and an organized criminal underworld, which seemed to remain in control after the prohibition was lifted.

Not all dance clubs and club nights offer alcohol though, especially if they want to cater for a younger clientele for which an alcohol-serving licence cannot be obtained, as can be the case for gay dance clubs in the United States. Alcohol and all-night dancing do not necessarily combine well; alcohol can produce an initial energizing effect, but ultimately slows the drinker down. Despite an often-problematic relationship with local legislation, stimulating and psychoactive dance drugs are preferred to enhance the dance experience by dedicated all-night dancers, whether all-night Northern Soul dancers (Raine et al. 2019), queer underground clubbers (Lawrence 2003), jazz dancers or ravers. The resultant aesthetics resonate throughout purpose-made electronic dance music in the form of intense repetition, other-worldly textures, and simple drone-like chord progressions. Nevertheless, for licenced venues contracts with breweries can bring financial stability to a nightclub, while illegal drug use is suppressed; the alcohol industry is politically powerful, affecting legislation on intoxicating substances to maintain its economic position. Shaw (2018) even goes as far as to define the night-time economy as a 'late night alcohol and leisure industry'.

In addition to sonic dominance, sustained dancing, and possible intoxication, also the manipulation of the visual field could produce a fragmentation of the self-conscious gaze. A mirror ball is a classic tool to send the dancers spinning, and the dancefloor may possibly be filled with artificial smoke within which strobe lights bounce. Some underground clubs take more minimalist approach by offering a dark space with incidental lighting to emphasize the sound of the music, enabling dancers to lose themselves into the total assemblage of the dancefloor (Ferreira 2008; Rietveld 2013). The use of visual projections and dynamic lighting are part and parcel of dancefloor technologies, to enhance a ritual of escape from daytime subjectivities within a sensory environment that makes participants oblivious to the passing of time. Bespoke set design and projections of video clips may also be part of a club night identity. In high-end commercial settings, visuals switch into a marketing spectacle, blatantly emphasizing brand identity, as is the case at larger venues in Ibiza, Spain, a popular clubbing tourist destination.

During the 1980s, the art of visual projections gave rise to the VJ, the video jockey, who in collaboration with the DJ creates a total immersive mixed-media experience. An American precedent can be found in American happenings that took place during the economic boom of the 1960s, which combined music performance with visual projections. For example, the multimedia events of Ken Kesey's acid-fuelled parties with the Merry Pranksters (Wolfe 1968; Lee and Shlain 1992) were combined with a journey or trip under the influence of the psychedelic drug LSD, which effect on consciousness is to disable the controlling ego and thereby enabling awareness of details and of sensory impressions that are normally ignored (Nutt cited by Cormier 2016). Another example can be found in Andy Warhol's multimedia EPI events in New York City. These parties took place in nightclub and music venue the Electric Circus, musically supported by the band the Velvet Underground. Incidentally, EPI inspired media theorist Marshall McLuhan to develop the idea of *allatonceness* (all-at-onceness), 'a regenerative and revitalizing unity of mediums and experience' (Lavin 2009: 101), which summarizes mediated information overload as well as its commensurate experience of dancing within a hi-tech club environment. For the then young Italian architect Fabrizio Fiummi, the fluid use of space and 'pulsing mass' of participants at the EPI events was a revelation, regarding these as 'the irruptive… solution to an emerging architectural critique of monumentality and power' (Lavin 2009: 101). Such fluidity was not only a consequence of LSD and changes in media technologies, but also of a wider context that included an increasing interest in yogic and meditative practices, as well as the liberal gay, feminist and civil rights movements that gained momentum during the 1960s and 1970s.

Nomadic and promiscuous, the DJ's mix offers a corresponding act of sonic fluidity. The art of DJing was refined by David Mancuso during his late-night held at The Loft, his New York home, the first of which was held on Valentine's Day in 1970 under the motto of 'Love Saves the Day' (or LSD). For Mancuso, the transmission of energy or the vibe was central, through both music selection and sound quality, to produce an immersive sonic experience. As afterparties, the Loft parties were particularly influential as they were attended by young underground club DJs who set up their own leading clubs. Mancuso's ideas on how best to build the energy of a dance night with music were partly inspired by Timothy Leary's LSD-fuelled parties in at Millbrook's mansion in Upstate New York (Lee and Shlain 1992; Kabil 2017), which reinterpret yogic and Buddhist notions of vibrational energy. Explaining a psychic connection with participants through sharing a 'sonic trail' of music, Mancuso refers to the vibrations of the mantra 'Om': 'Om is the source of all sound – it's a Buddhist chant where voices gel together and vibrate – and I felt we had returned h-om-e' (in Lawrence 2003: 13). A well-tuned sound system at the relatively low volume of 100dB maximum loudness was assembled for The Loft by the innovative sound engineer Richard Long (Lawrence 2016) and the acoustically comfortable room was decorated with a mirror ball and festive balloons. Eventually, Long would also design the sound system of New York discotheque Paradise Garage, a trendsetting underground ethnically mixed LBGTQ members club that operated between 1977 to 1987. There, the sound was more forceful, particularly in the sub-bass frequencies, hitting the body as though attending an amplified live concert (Lawrence 2016: 192), even though it was possible to maintain, simultaneously, a conversation with a fellow dancer. Notably, neither venue sold alcohol; instead, both offered free fruit and water to their dancers, reminiscent of yoga events.

The Haçienda FAC 51, Manchester's flagship nightclub between 1982 to 1997, is a nightclub that I experienced closely at first-hand. Much inspired by the buoyant underground club scene of New York, it nevertheless offered a very different sound system in a challenging acoustic environment. Despite efforts to control the sound when devoid of an absorbent mass of bodies the music scattered into fragments against its glass industrial ceiling and hard walls. The Haçienda was an odd case in terms of its 1982 visual space as well; it was not a generic black box or a glamour disco by any means. Designed by Ben Kelly (Kelly 1982; Savage 1992), the club's included idiosyncratic use of diagonally painted yellow and black caution stripes on its load-bearing iron pillars situated on the dancefloor, and an overall bold industrial colour scheme. The club's consistent use of logos and fonts and overall graphic presentation that made use of the diagonal stripes gave the impression of a powerful company: 'The Haçienda was both trend-setting and avant-garde with a desire for what [graphic designer] Peter Saville has described as "educating the audience". It was a branding blueprint for the future' (Banks 2018: 2). Spin-offs of the design can be seen, for example, in Yamamoto's Y3 design of Adidas (Cooper 2007), as well as the 2019–20 away kit of Manchester City FC (Avelar 2019). Simultaneously, the club venue was versatile in its offerings and had a theatre lighting system installed, rather than the usual dynamic spotlights one would see in a discotheque. The stage was set in a recess at the side of the dancefloor, so as not to dominate the main club space. The DJ/VJ booth was initially set in a bunker at the side of the stage, with narrow windows to see the stage and the crowd, rendering it virtually dysfunctional (Wilson 2012); most dancers did not even realize a DJ was present. Eventually, the DJ and VJ and light technicians moved to their own respective booths on the mezzanine opposite the stage; a good position to oversee the space. By 1988, during its fifth year, the combination of acid house and the dance drug ecstasy (MDMA) broke old habits as dancers took to the stage during DJ-led club nights, making participants the centre of attention rather than the music bands (Rietveld 2004b) – although eventually dancers used the stage to look upwards to the DJs, as though gazing towards the pulpit of a church. Overcrowding during its popular dance nights led to condensed sweat raining down from the glass roof. According to one of its directors, Peter Hook (2009: xii), 'it was the scene of too many great nights and gigs to recall – not that you were in any state to do so'.

As the example of the Haçienda shows, the relationship between entertainers and their audience, between the DJ and the dancers, between all of the participants, depends on their relative position within the club space. Some clubs offer a stage for performers, including their guest DJs, but most clubs have a DJ booth somewhere to the side of the dance floor or just above it. In a discussion of Canadian clubs, Straw (1995) shows that a DJ booth by the side of the dancefloor enables requests, situating the DJ as a human jukebox, while a DJ in a closed-off space or in an elevated position above crowd emphasizes the role of the

DJ as auteur. In the latter role, the DJ is encouraged to attend to sound manipulation, and even bring in additional instrumentation and musicians. Taking creative control, some DJs create remixes of music recordings adapted to a specific club sound system, and to the taste of their crowd. According to Cheren (2000: 102), during the disco days in 1970s New York, '[a] dance floor was like a ready-made focus group, with an unforgiving and sometimes fanatical audience that was quick to vote with its feet.' Eventually, the DJ's role shifted from being an entertaining record collector and music archivist to that of the music remixer and, eventually, to the creative role of music producer. As digital DJ technologies and music production technologies have started to converge especially since the turn of the millennium, the difference between mixing, producing and performing is starting to blur (Butler 2014; Rietveld 2016). As DJ is increasingly placed in the spotlight, the DJ is no longer the hidden sonic enabler and more a marketable artist. What happened to the democracy of the 1970s disco dancefloor, one may ask though, 'where anyone could be a star, as long as they had the right attitude and flair' (Hillard 2015: 9)?

Nightclubs seem to have come a long way from places where one can hide in secrecy and melt into the crowd within the darkened haziness of a sonically dominant culture. As is the case across the night-time economy, the visual world of daytime culture is re-interpreting the once-opaque cultures of the night, exploiting yet regulating it (Kolioulis 2018; Shaw 2018; Stahl and Bottà 2019). The nightclub can provide a safe haven for marginalized identities and subjectivities, and to imagine that another world is possible; yet for many of its clientele, the nightclub offers a gated environment to let off steam, a safety valve for the pressures of everyday life. Although the disco concept already existed, for current successful nightclubs, the dance concept of raves, electronic dance music styles, and associated DJs were brought into the regulated club space during the 1990s, where its 'subcultural capital' (Thornton 1995) can be safely celebrated and commercially exploited. In turn, this adds value to economically deprived areas of post-industrial cities (Lovatt 1996), making the reclaimed sites of nocturnal dance events particularly attractive, not only to teenagers, as Thornton argues, but also to 'upper-income social groups', as Kolioulis (2018: 209) points out in a case study on London's club multimodal venue Printworks. A previous newspaper print factory, Printworks' large set of flexible spaces are not only utilized as a nightclub and can be hired for trade fairs and corporate events. Ultimately, what was once a deserted area becomes attractive for property investment, an example of harnessing nightclub culture to raise the economic value of a forgotten and run-down part of London. This is just one example of how nightclubs play a role in the processes of gentrification. Manchester's nightclub FAC 51 The Haçienda was part of an earlier process of gentrification; after it closed its doors in 1997, the building was replaced by a block of flats, proudly named 'Haçienda Apartments'.

The attraction of a successful nightclub can, eventually, be its undoing, as gentrification can result in the rise of rents and rates (for an Australian example, see Williams 2019), and followed by complaints about noise pollution. The actual club venue that underpins the international nightclub brand of Ministry of Sound was crucial in the gentrification of the area around Elephant and Castle in South London, yet battled for five years with a building development across the street in order to remain in its location (Hubzin 2014). After the past decade, there has been a trend for nightclubs and other music venues to close down, in London and elsewhere, partly due to gentrification, while simultaneously cities acknowledge the economic value of its nightlife, installing night mayors and equivalents. In Berlin, its nightclubs have gone further, though, gaining protected status equivalent to cultural venues such as theatres (Connolly 2020; Coney 2021). A more recent, and new, challenge is the lockdown of public social life during the COVID-19 pandemic of 2020 and 2021 resulting in club closures across Europe and elsewhere.

Not only has daytime society repeatedly entered night-time culture, in its commodified and hyperreal form, the nightclub has also entered daytime culture. Electronic dance music, which has dominated the dancefloors of nightclubs for over three decades now, has become the soundtrack of everyday life, heard in clothes shops and during broadcasts, while the hissing 'ch-ch-ch-ch' of its hi-hat sound gives away its presence in mobile headphones. Despite the homophobic, racist and misogynist 'Disco Sucks' slump of the late 1970s, DJ-led dance culture has carried on, summarized as 'disco's revenge' by house music DJ Frankie Knuckles (see Rietveld, 1998). The soundtracks of club nights are commercially available in imaginatively packaged CD-series, reconfirming the brand identity of particular clubs (see also Banks and Brewster 2018). Since the 1990s, dance DJs have extended their marketable visualization on stage and on the front covers of club magazines. They post their mixes online and make video appearances, performing their DJ sets in front of the camera for online platforms such as *Boiler Room*. This practice has intensified across social media platforms during the COVID-19 epidemic-related lockdowns, for example spearheaded in early 2020 by Berlin clubs as *United We Stream*, which developed rapidly into a global performance platform. Another example is *DJ Mag*'s 9-week Top 100 *Clubs Virtual World Tour*, launched in May 2021, with top clubs as far apart as China, Singapore, Kenya, Ibiza, Berlin, London, Ecuador, Brazil, Washington, revealing an intensification of global club culture (*DJ Mag* 2021). Club culture even appears in the ultimate venue of visual exposure: the exhibition gallery. For example, in 2007, exhibition space Urbis in Manchester, England, showcased The Haçienda Club, twenty-five years after it had opened, including perspectives from participants, images, flyers and directional speakers to illustrate the images with restrained audio (see Cooper 2007). In 2018, iconic nightclubs were featured from an architectural design perspective at the Vitra Design Museum in Weil am Rhein, Germany (Rossi and Eisenbrand 2018). And in 2019, Cité la musique-Philharmonie in Paris featured the exhibition *Electro, De Kraftwerk à Daft Punk* on dance culture, including night clubs. In 2020, this was repeated at London's Design Museum as *Electronic, From Kraftwerk to the Chemical Brothers* (Leloup et al. 2020) – a rare opportunity during that COVID year to share amplified dance music in London. Although one can be immersed in the space and exhibits, and appreciation and cultural gravitas is finally bestowed on the concept of the nightclub, this does not quite convey the experience of losing oneself into the haptic shared experience of the dancefloor. It is the secluded experience of the total environment that counts, the shared feeling of the music while the world whirls around in fragments of light, where everything, for a seemingly endless yet fleeting moment, is all right.

References

Aletti, V. (2009), *The Disco Files 1973–78: New York's Underground, Week by Week*, London: DJhistory.com

Armstrong, S. (2004), *The White Island: The Colourful History of the Original Fantasy Island, Ibiza*, London: Corgi Books.

Avelar, D. (2019), 'Haçienda Designer Says Man City away Shirt Is "beyond Appropriation"', *The Guardian*. https://www.theguardian.com/football/2019/oct/25/hacienda-designer-says-man-city-away-shirt-is-beyond-appropriation

Banks, R. (2018), 'Preface,' in R. Banks, and B. Brewster, *Clubbed: A Visual History of UK Club Culture*, 2, Bolton: Face37.

Banks, R. and Brewster, B. (2018), *Clubbed: A Visual History of UK Club Culture*, Bolton: Face37.

Benson, R., ed. (1997), *Night Fever: Club Writing in The Face 1980–1997*, London and Basingstoke: Boxtree (Macmillan).

Brewster, B. and Broughton, F. (1999), *Last Night a DJ Saved My Life: The History of the Disc Jockey*, London: Headline.

Butler, M. J. (2014), *Playing with Something That Runs: Technology, Improvisation and Composition in DJ and Laptop Performance*, Oxford and New York: Oxford University Press.

Carpenter, C. and Silva, G. (2015), *Nightswimming: Discotheques from 1960s to the Present*, London: Bedford Press/AA Publications.

Cheren, M. (2000), *My Life and the Paradise Garage: Keep on Dancin'*, New York: 24 Hours for Life.

Coney, B. (2021), 'Berlin to Officially Declare Nightclubs as Cultural Institutions: The Change in Legal Status Protects Nightclubs from Gentrification', *DJMag*. https://djmag.com/news/Berlin-officially-declare-nightclubs-cultural-institutions

Connolly, K. (2020), 'Berlin's Nightclubs Fight for Same Cultural Status as Opera Houses: Clubs Tell Parliament That without Protection, Gentrification Threatens Their Existence', *The Guardian*. https://www.theguardian.com/world/2020/feb/12/berlins-nightclubs-fight-for-same-cultural-status-as-opera-houses

Cooper, J. (2007), 'Fac51-Y3 Trainers,' *Cerysmatic.Factory*. https://factoryrecords.org/cerysmatic/fac51-y3.php

Cooper, J. (2007), 'hacienda_25_the_exhibition_fac_491: Review,' *Cerysmatic.Factory*. https://factoryrecords.org/cerysmatic/hacienda_25_the_exhibition_fac_491.php

Cormier, Z. (2016), 'Brain Scans Reveal How LSD Affects. Drug Researcher David Nutt Discusses Brain-Imaging Studies with Hallucinogens', *Nature: International Weekly Journal of Science*. https://www.nature.com/news/brain-scans-reveal-how-lsd-affects-consciousness-1.19727

D'Andrea, A. (2006), 'The Spiritual Economy of Nightclubs and Raves: Osho Sannyasins as Party Promoters in Ibiza and Pune/Goa', *Culture and Religion: An Interdisciplinary Journal*, 7 (1): 61–75. https://doi.org/10.1080/01438300600625457.

De Wit, J. (2013), *RoXY en de Houserevolutie*, Amsterdam: Fast Moving Targets.

DJ Mag (13 May 2021), 'Top 100 Clubs Virtual World Tour,' *DJ Mag*. https://djmag.com/news/top-100-clubs-virtual-world-tour-launches-weekend

Farrugia, R. (2012), *Beyond the Dancefloor: Female DJs, Technology and Electronic Dance Music Culture*, Chicago IL and London: Intellect/University of Chicago Press.

Ferreira, P. P. (2008), 'When Sound Meets Movement: Performance in Electronic Dance Music,' *Leonardo Music Journal*, 18: 17–20. http://www.leonardo.info/isast/journal/toclmj18.html

Fikentscher, K. (2000), *'You Better Work!' Underground Dance Music in New York City*, Hanover, NH and London: Wesleyan University Press.

Garcia, L.-M. (2016), 'Techno-Tourism and Post-Industrial Neo-Romanticism in Berlin's Electronic Dance Music Scenes', *Tourist Studies*, 16 (3): 276–95. https://doi.org/10.1177/1468797615618037.

Goldman, A. (1978), *Disco*, New York: Shpritzgun Productions, and Hawthorn Books.

Henriques, J. (2011), *Sonic Bodies: Reggae Soundsystems, Performance Techniques and Ways of Knowing*, London and New York: Continuum.

Hillard, J. (2015), 'Foreword', in D. Hill and T. Nourmand, (eds), *Disco: The Bill Bernstein Photographs*, London: Rare Art Press.

Hill, D. and Nourmand, T., eds (2015), *Disco: The Bill Bernstein Photographs*, London: Rare Art Press.

Hodge, R. and Kress, G. (1988), *Social Semiotics*, Cambridge: Polity Press.

Hook, P. (2009), *The Haçienda: How Not to Run a Club*, Long: Simon & Schuster.

Hubzin, V. (2014), 'Ministry of Sound Saved: London Superclub Reaches Agreement', *DJ Mag*. https://djmag.com/content/ministry-sound-saved

Jackson, P. (2004), *Inside Clubbing: Sensual Experiments in the Art of Being Human*, New York and Oxford: Berg.

Kabil, A. (2017), 'This Magical Drug Mansion in Upstate New York Is Where the Psychedelic '60s Took Off', *Timeline*. https://timeline.com/drug-mansion-psychedelic-60s-5116867d5041

Kelly, B. (1982), 'The Haçienda', *Ben Kelly Design* (BKD). http://benkellydesign.com/hacienda/

Kolioulis, A. (2018), 'More Day in The Night? The Gentrification of London's Night-Time through Clubbing', *Bollettino della Società Geografica Italiana*. Serie 14, 1 (2): 207–18. doi: 10.13128/bsgi.v1i2.536.

Kronenburg, R. (2019), *This Must Be the Place: An Architectural History of Popular Music Performance Venues*, New York and London: Bloomsbury Academic.

LaBelle, B. (2018), 'Night', Presentation at *Invisible Symposium* at IKLECTIK, London, Organised by Points of Listening, CRiSAP (Creative Research into Sound Art Practice), The London College of Communication (LCC, UAL).

Lavin, S. (2009), 'Architect™ – Or, a Funny Thing Happened on the Way to the Disco', *Log*, 15 (Winter): 99–110.

Lawrence, T. (2003), *Love Saves the Day: A History of American Music Culture, 1970–1979*, Durham and London: Duke University Press.

Lawrence, T. (2016), 'Remembering David Mancuso and the Loft', *Document Journal*. http://www.timlawrence.info/articles2/2016/11/30/remembering-david-mancuso-and-the-loft-1

Lee, M. A. and Shlain, B. (1992), *Acid Dreams, The Complete Social History of LSD: The CIA, The Sixties, and beyond*, New York: Grove Press.

Leloup, J.-Y., Curtin, G. and McLintock, M. eds (2020), *Electronic: From Kraftwerk to the Chemical Brothers*, London: Design Museum Publishing.

Ligura, P. and Langenbach, T. (2007), *Now & Wow: The Peepbox*, Amsterdam: Artemis.

Loben, C. et al., eds (2020), *100 of the World's Best Clubs*, London: DJ Mag/Thrust Publishing.

Lovatt, A. (1996), 'The Ecstasy of Urban Regeneration: Regulation of the Nighttime Economy in the Transition to a Post-Fordist City', in J. O'conner and D. Wynne (eds), *From the Margins to the Centre: Cultural Production and Consumption in the Post-Industrial City*, 141–68, Brookfield, VT and Aldershot: Arena.

Malbon, B. (1999), *Clubbing: Dancing, Ecstasy and Vitality*, London: Routledge.

Middleton, R. (2006), '"Last Night a DJ Saved My Life": Avians, Cyborgs and Siren Bodies in the Era of Phonographic Technology', *Radical Musicology*, 1: 1–31.

Morrison, S. (2010), *Discombobulated: Dispatches from the Wrong Side*, London: Headpress.

O'Hagan, C. (2004), *Comparative Dance Drugs Research in UK Garage Scene and Trance/Techno Scenes*, PhD Thesis, London: South Bank University.

Pirozhkov, S. (2017), 'No Photo Policy in Clubs', *Clubs Are Art*, https://clubs-are-art.medium.com/no-photo-policy-in-clubs-df5ed8198e08

Poschardt, U. (1998), *DJ Culture*, trans. Shaun Whiteside, London: Quartet Books.

Raine, S., Wall, T. and Watchman-Smith, N., eds (2019), *The Northern Soul Scene*, Bristol, CT and Sheffield: Equinox.

Redhead, S., Wynne, D. and O'Connor, J. eds (1998), *The Clubcultures Reader: Readings in Popular Cultural Studies*, Malden, MA and Oxford: Blackwell Publishers.

Rief, S. (2009) *Club Cultures: Boundaries, Identities, and Otherness*. New York, NY and London: Routledge.

Rietveld, H. C. (1998), *This Is Our House: House Music, Cultural Spaces and Technologies*, Aldershot: Ashgate.

Rietveld, H. C. (2004a), 'Ephemeral Spirit: Sacrificial Cyborg and Soulful Community', in G. St John (ed.), *Rave Culture and Religion*, 45–60, London and New York: Routledge.

Rietveld, H. C. (2004b), 'House Music: The Haçienda Must Be Built', in P. Lawrence and V. Howard (eds), *Crossfade: A Big Chill Anthology*, 119–40, London: A Serpent's Tail.

Rietveld, H. C. (2011), 'Disco's Revenge: House Music's Nomadic Memory', *Dancecult: Journal of Electronic Dance Music Culture*, 2 (1): 4–23. http://dj.dancecult.net

Rietveld, H. C. (2013), 'Journey to the Light? Immersion, Spectacle and Mediation', in B. A. Attias, A. Gavanas and H. C. Rietveld (eds), *DJ Culture in the Mix: Power, Technology, and Social Change in Electronic Dance Music*, 79–102, New York and London: Bloomsbury Academic.

Rietveld, H. C. (2016), 'Authenticity and Liveness in Digital DJ Performance', in Ioannis Tsioulakis and Elina Hytönen-Ng (eds), *Musicians and Their Audiences*, 123–33, New York and London: Routledge.

Rietveld, H.C. (2018), 'Machine Possession: Dancing to Repetitive Beats'. Levaux, C. and Julien, O. (eds), *Over and Over: Exploring Repetition in Popular Music*, 75–88, New York: Bloomsbury Academic.

Rose, C. (1991), *Design after Dark: The Story of Dancefloor Style*, London: Thames & Hudson.

Rossi, C. and Eisenbrand, J. (2018), 'Introduction,' in C. Rossi and J. Eisenbrand (eds), *Night Fever: Designing Club Culture, 1960-Today*, 14–23, Weil am Rhein: Vitra Design Museum.

Savage, J., ed, (1992), *The Hacienda Must Be Built!* Woodford Green: IMP.

Schrager, I. (2017), *Studio 54*, New York: Rizzolli

Serra-Cantallops, A. and Ramon-Cardona, J. (2017), 'Host Community Resignation to Nightclub Tourism', *Current Issues in Tourism*, 20 (6): 566–79. https://doi.org/10.1080/13683500.2016.1161604.

Shapiro, P. (2005), *Turn the Beat Around: The Secret History of Disco*, London: Faber & Faber.

Shapiro, S. et al. (2019), *The Music Cities Manual: Your Comprehensive Guide to Building Music Cities*, London: Sound Diplomacy.
Shaw, R. (2018), *The Nocturnal City*, London and New York: Routledge.
Smith, R. ed (2008), *Club Kids: From Speakeasies to Boombox and beyond*, London: Black Dog Publishing.
Stahl, G. ed. (2014), *Poor but Sexy: Reflections on Berlin Scenes*, Bern: Peter Lang.
Stahl, G. and Bottà, G., eds (2019), *Nocturnes: Popular Music and the Night*, Cham: Palgrave Macmillan.
Straw, W. (1995), 'The Booth, the Floor and the Wall: Dance Music and the Fear of Falling', in W. Straw, et al. (eds), *Popular Music: Style and Identity*, 249–54, Proceedings of 7th Biennial IASPM Conference, Montreal: Centre of Research on Canadian Cultural Industries and Institutions.
Sword, H. (2021), *Monolithic Undertow: In Search of Sonic Oblivion*, London: White Rabbit (Orion).
Thornton, S. (1995), *Club Cultures: Music, Media and Subcultural Capital*, Cambridge: Polity.
Williams, S. (2019), 'High Rents and Falling Patronage Force Many Gay Bars to Close', *Commercial Real Estate*, https://www.commercialrealestate.com.au/news/high-rents-and-falling-patronage-force-many-gay-bars-to-close-42629/
Wilson, G. (May 2012), 'The Haçienda DJ Booth', *Electro Funk Roots*. https://www.electrofunkroots.co.uk/the-hacienda-dj-booth/
Wolfe, T. (1968), *The Electric Kool-Aid Acid Test*, New York: Farrar Strauss Giroux.

12

The live venue

Robert Kronenburg

Introduction

In January 2011, quite by chance, I went to a live gig at The Cavern Club in Liverpool. The Cavern is famous as the 1960s setting for the Mersey Sound (The Beatles, The Big Three, Gerry and the Pacemakers, and others) and also important as a local rock venue where touring bands like The Kinks, The Rolling Stones, The Yardbirds, The Who and Queen played. The original nineteenth-century warehouse building in which the venue occupied the cellar was demolished in 1973, and this Cavern is a wholly new creation, though on the same site. Built into the basement of a multi-storey shopping and office development, the 'new' club is a recreation of the original one, constructed using the same bricks and the same plan as the old building, with an extended space at the rear not restricted to the old brick arch pattern. The rebuilt Cavern opened in April 1984 but, run by a celebrity footballer, it was not successful and closed again in 1989. Local music enthusiasts Dave Jones and Bill Heckle, with existing businesses linked to the city's musical heritage, took on the club's licence and reopened it in 1991, committed to reintroducing live music, although initially these gigs lost money compared to the DJ club nights. A pivotal moment happened on 14 December 1999 when Paul McCartney, complete with a backing band of other star musicians: David Gilmour, Ian Paice, Mick Green and Pete Wingfield, played a live version of his new album; the gig later being released on DVD (*Live at the Cavern*, 2003). McCartney had apparently looked at the recreation of the old Cavern stage, and the new bigger one that Jones and Heckle had introduced in the adjacent space (incidentally closer to the position of the original stage) and chose that, thereby legitimizing both the new Cavern club and the stage unburdened by 1960s nostalgia, as a fresh place for fan pilgrimage.

On that winter's night in 2011, the club was set out with a few dozen tables in front, the rest of the small crowd of about 200 standing to the sides and rear. Though no bigger than the recreated Cavern next door, this space still has an archetypal small club atmosphere with a low ceiling in front of the stage, which is lower still at the rear where two steps lead up to the bar area. This was a showcase gig by the singer/songwriter Adele, run as a publicity event by Smooth FM radio station, and for the artist it was a chance to promote her second album which would be released the following month. Though no one knew it in the Cavern that night, after a powerful performance of her single *Someone Like You* at the Brit Awards on 15 February 2011, she would shoot to number one in the UK record charts, and the album *21* would go into the top five as would her previous album *19*. When another single, *Rolling in the Deep* also went high in the charts, Adele became the first artist to have two albums and two singles in the top five of their respective charts at the same time since The Beatles in 1964. By December that year *21* was the best-selling record of the twenty-first century and the best-selling record ever by a female artist. But a couple of weeks before all this began, here she was in a small club performing to a small crowd, just a single acoustic guitarist for accompaniment – powerful, emotive renditions of great songs (despite complaining of bronchitis) interspersed with expletive-strewn chat that had the audience laughing along with her, totally immersed in the experience. In this setting Adele's talent as a composer and as a performer, her personality and identity, were all harnessed to communicate directly with her audience, some of whom were fans and knew and loved her first record – others like me, won over for the first time during a great live performance in intimate surroundings. This shared experience between audience and artist is a key component of the live gig: 'bringing people from all different backgrounds together with one shared collective love: the music (Mac 2017)'. This was a diverse group of individuals gathering together in one place at the same time, forming a transient 'community not defined in traditional terms of status' (Shuker 2013: 167). The passion generated by events like this is clear, creating powerful lasting memories for those who were there that is often reflected in published and social media, and in the fan forums which have become a rich source of information about live gig history (Cohen 2014: 143).

For The Cavern Club it was also an important moment, an indication of the venue's continuing relevance to contemporary popular music, a place where artists now come to debut new material including Oasis, Travis, Arctic Monkeys, as well as McCartney for a second album launch in 2018. To the city of Liverpool, it was another recognition that it is not simply a place of nostalgia for the 1960s but a place where contemporary popular music happens, of course not just in the Cavern but also in the many other clubs, pubs, halls, arenas and city spaces. Live performance of popular music is a crucial part of the urban identity of Liverpool (UNESCO City of Music since 2016), enhanced as a locale by its particular musical scene. This is so for uncountable other places around the world, which possess a musical 'marker of identity', even though all are not globally recognized (Shuker 2013: 180). It is a cultural activity that embodies and communicates the character of specific places both through the home-grown talent that performs in grass roots venues, and in the larger spaces that receive visiting touring artists and become the aspirational locations for those trying to work their way up the ladder of success. The live gig event is at the core of this experience, venues a vital part of the physical: 'Infrastructures of music exchange' that also include recording studios and music shops (Connell and Gibson 2003: 102). All art must have a place to be, and for music, the buildings and spaces in which live performances happen are that place. Popular music may begin in the home but for continued success it must transfer to more formal settings which range widely in size and type, from small bars and clubs like the Cavern through to the largest stadiums (Kronenburg 2019: 2–3). In between are the jazz and social clubs, dance halls and discotheques, theatres and auditoria, urban and rural festival stages which all vary dramatically in operation and style dependant on geographic and cultural location. These spaces of live music performance have a physical presence in cities and towns, adding to and affecting the distinctiveness of streets, neighbourhoods and locales. There is also an impact on some rural areas because of remote venues that audiences must travel to, or for temporary events such as festivals.

As can be seen from the example of these two performances by Adele, the live gig is strongly linked with other aspects of artists' careers, such as recording and media. Her Cavern gig was an acoustic warm-up promoted by a radio station (Smooth FM) for her forthcoming tour of larger venues, and one she valued, characteristically commenting that '[i]t sent chills down my spine! And the brick work… with all the names of who's played there made me dribble!' (Sanderson 2013). The intimate experience of working before crowds like this was the essential training that enhanced her ability to perform so well before the following month's dramatically larger 20,000 strong audience at the O2 Arena in London for the Brit Awards, a performance that would have a live television audience of 4.8 million (Osborn 2011). She engaged with other radio stations on this warm-up tour and of course television and digital media became more and more important as her career progressed. The gig itself was based around her forthcoming recording releases, and although important changes have taken place in musical artists' income from recording due to streaming platforms, this has only served to increase the importance of the live gig in developing and maintaining a successful career in the popular music business. As Lou Reed said, people need to 'view the body' if you want to make it in the music business (Byrne 2012: 44).

Live popular music performance can take place in a multitude of different environments, but there are certain characteristics that are common to all. The live gig is an authentic experience – each time an artist performs live it is a unique event (Radbourne, Johanson and Glow 2014: 58). This may be less so than in the past before technology made it possible to pre-record elements of the performance, when shows were not so complex that they could become a full entertainment package with projection, animation, complex stage sets and other theatrical effects. However, even if a show is fully rehearsed and performed in the same order each night there are numerous factors that remain unique. The circumstances surrounding the gig, such as its geographic location, obtaining the ticket, the journey to and from the venue, who you were with, what else had happened that day all feature in how the individual actually experiences the event and equally important, how they remember it – which might not necessarily be the same. Alice O'Grady draws attention to the fact that studies in environmental psychology have shown how outdoor and indoor space impact on how people feel and behave thereby, 'framing how we engage with the cultural event or experience for which we have paid' (O'Grady 2015: 115). However, the venue itself is perhaps the most important mutable element beyond that of the actual performance – its acoustics and the view it affords are obvious factors but there are many more environmental factors like smell, temperature and air quality. The building itself in terms of its architectural character is also crucial in creating what might be regarded as a good or a bad performance space. Many venues are set in older converted buildings, often those that have passed from one use to another, and often converted cheaply by the operators or even the musicians, with the minimum of specialist intervention. They may still be loved by artists and audiences alike, even though facilities and comfort may be minimal. Patti Smith said of the famous New York punk venue CBGB and OMFUG, which was situated in a long narrow room below a vagrant's flop house, that it was, 'the ideal place to sound the clarion call. It was a club in the street of the downtrodden' (Smith 2012: 115). The fact it was a pretty rough space made it even better because, 'The absence of glamour made it seem more familiar, a place we could call our own' (Smith 2012: 240). Byrne more pragmatically describes the club's uneven walls and scattered furnishings as ideal for providing a good acoustic space in which the music would be heard as the musicians intended it and small enough that physical gestures and expressions could be seen (Byrne 2012: 16–17).

These older buildings may provide the venue with a specific historic character that becomes part of its new identity. The Ryman auditorium in Nashville, Tennessee, was originally the Union Gospel Tabernacle completed in 1892, but it became the 'Mother Church of Country Music' when adopted in 1925 to become the venue for broadcasting the radio show that became the 'Grand Ole Opry' which continues today, still on 650AM WSM (and also internationally via a live stream). Seating 3,500, the Gothic Revival auditorium had been a place where Confederate Army Veterans meetings took place (in 1897) and the New York Metropolitan Opera visited (in 1901) as well as a place of worship. Minor changes took place over the years; the addition of a stage (for the Met's visit); a radio control room and ticket booth in the 1940s; and new toilets in the 1950s, until as with many historic buildings it passed through a period of uncertainty when the radio show (now on television too) moved to a new dedicated building across town in 1974. But in the late 1980s a seven-year refurbishment plan began with the venue reopening in 1994. The Ryman continues to be sought out by artists such as Bob Dylan, Robert Plant and Elvis Costello because if its history (a stage where Hank Williams, Patsy Cline, Johnny Cash and all the greats of country music played), but also because its architecture makes it a good place to play and listen to live music (Kronenburg 2012: 30–7).

In the past, new buildings designed especially for live popular music have been far less common than for other types of music (e.g. classical concert halls, opera houses, musical theatre and religious spaces such as churches), however, there have been periods in the history of the popular music industry when they have been built to meet new commercial trends, for example Music Halls and Variety from c.1850–1910 and dance halls in the 1920–1930s. Music Hall and Variety mixed comedy and novelty acts with a steady diet of popular songs creating huge stars, some of whom persisted into the era of radio and television like George Formby and Arthur Askey. Every city in the UK saw new buildings erected, often extravagantly decorated with sophisticated technical developments such as opening roofs, auditoriums capable of being flooded for water shows and giant 'sunburner' light fittings with up to 500 gas flames. Frank Matcham was the premier British architect of the era, designing more than 150 separate theatres, those that survive like Blackpool's Grand Theatre (1899) and the Hackney Empire, London (1901) now precious listed buildings. Preserved historic Vaudeville theatres in North America are treated similarly. In the UK the dance hall craze emerged as a result of more liberal social conditions in the wake of the First World War, with higher wages for working-class people, a more relaxed attitude to gender fraternization and the new jazz music imported from North America. Such was the dance craze that all kinds of buildings were pressed into service at weekends and on holidays: local village halls, sports halls, even swimming baths with the pool boarded over. However, between 1919 and 1925 an estimated 11,000 new halls were converted or built in Britain, a trend also seen in North America and Europe. The Hammersmith Palais de Dance in London opened in 1919 with a huge first night crowd of 7,000. The Original Dixieland Jazz Band from New York (famous for making the first jazz recordings on 26 February 1917) were resident there for nine months. This venue had a long and successful history, accommodating many popular music genres. All the top artists of the 1960s, 1970s and 1980s played there including The Beatles, The Rolling Stones, The Who, David Bowie, The Police, U2 and The Cure. The building's final concert was by The Fall on 1 April 2007, before it became yet another victim to development after a drawn-out application process to construct commercial student housing on its site led to the building deteriorating before demolition in 2012.

Since the 1980s the principal innovation in venue design has been the multi-purpose arena. Originally intended as a sports facility that could also put on other entertainments, the commercial need for pop and rock concerts to move out of theatres and halls to meet audience demand and increase revenues led to an architectural shift in emphasis to buildings designed specifically to work for the large touring music set. Beginning in the 1960s, the big-name popular music artists wanted to do less live gigs while their management wanted to get more paying customers through the door. In North America there was a legacy of large indoor sports arenas (for basketball and ice hockey) such as Madison Square Garden in New York, that could be readily adopted to prove the concept and although for many seats the sound and view was at best a compromise, these large sheds began to be used for rock and pop gigs. The Spectrum Arena in Philadelphia, USA (1967–2009), was one of the first built to specifically address the idea of a multipurpose venue. For more than forty years, as well as holding basketball and ice hockey games, it was the setting for virtually every major rock and pop music act to tour the United States, many returning repeatedly such as the Grateful Dead who played there fifty-three times, recording three live albums. Its features are those that have come to characterize the modern arena – flexibility in layout for different types and sizes of show, location at the hub of a large urban population with good transport links, easy access for artists' equipment enabling a quick set-up and take down. There are approximately fifty indoor arenas in the United States and seventeen in the British Isles, some extensive refurbishments of older indoor sports buildings but most are new. Contemporary arena design is the most visible sign that popular music venue architecture is continuously developing, with some recent buildings being ambitious responses to the entertainment industry's growing technical demands for larger scale shows with improved acoustics and views of the stage. The best buildings, such as the Dublin Arena (2008), located in the docklands area of the city in the completely rebuilt Point Theatre, which had in turn been converted from a Victorian railway goods terminus in 1988, are built as urban regenerators enabling local businesses such as bars, restaurants and hotels to benefit from the new development. Through careful space planning and detailed design they improve audience experience with reduced sight lines (at most 60 metres [197 feet] from the stage in Dublin), better acoustics, easier access and pre- and post-show facilities. They mitigate the environmental and urban design challenges of situating a large building close to centres of population, utilizing local public transport links to reduce environmental pressures and incorporating construction that prevents nuisance sound leaking to the surrounding area.

Another area where the live gig has been transformed through design development is the mobile stage. Transportable and temporary staging and equipment are crucial enablers for touring live performance acts, for special events and for festivals. The arena building type would not exist without the use of sophisticated visual and audio presentation systems as they are designed as flexible empty spaces that the performance production crew transform into a setting for their unique show over a period of a few hours – the rock musician Steve Miller describes it as 'creating a new venue' each night (Hale 2014). The first large-scale popular music events that began to address the problem of communicating the artists' performance to large audiences were festivals such as the Newport Jazz Festival held in Rhode Island, USA, beginning in 1954 and the Beaulieu Jazz Festival, Hampshire, UK, held between 1956 and 1961. Bill Hanley was an engineer who had developed the sound system for Newport in 1957 and also the system operating in the important rock venue Fillmore East, New York. For the Woodstock Music and Art Fair held on Yasgur's Farm in rural New York State in 1969 he was asked to create a suitable system for the expected 50,000 strong audience (though 186,000 tickets were sold and an estimated 400,000 turned up). Hanley created the most powerful, sophisticated sound system yet devised utilizing sixteen loudspeaker stacks, on-stage monitors for the performers, linked to new mixer boards specially designed for the event, all fed from a mobile industrial-scale electricity supply. The temporary stage itself was also an ambitious undertaking; 3.5-metre (10-feet) high, 30-metre wide (100-feet) built from reusable scaffolding and telegraph poles braced with cables. A suspended rain and sun canopy provided some protection for the performers and there were also towers for lighting and loudspeakers. Despite high winds and rain, and a relentlessly slipping schedule organizer Michael Lang later said: 'Everyone could hear, nothing blew up… ' so that when Jimi Hendrix took to the stage at 8.30 am on Monday 18 August he could still be seen and heard by the 30,000 or so who remained (Spitz 2014: 439). Woodstock and other festivals of the time like Monterey, USA (1967) and the Isle of Wight, UK (1970) set the template for the popular music festival, however, contemporary events vary widely in content and concept. Large festivals today habitually have multiple stages with associated entertainment such as theatre, cinema, dance and comedy. For artists at different stages in their career these are now crucially important live gigs. John Geddings, promoter of the 2017 Isle of Wight Festival observes, 'For acts at the top of the bill there is great money to be made… for less established acts there is the chance to reach new fans and establish reputations' (BBC 2018). Some festivals (e.g. Glastonbury) feature diverse music genres while others focus on a particular type of popular music (e.g. in the UK; Creamfields for dance; Download for rock; Wireless for hip-up and R&B). The actual stages are largely created by commercial companies who use standardized re-usable components (some in-house designed), for reliability and economy. The stage may be branded with the specific festival name, but it will be taken down and used on another site a few days or weeks later. Only occasionally does a festival stage require something unique as with Glastonbury's pyramid stage, a symbol of the event since its beginning in 1971 though the current steel structure is a permanent one that is fitted out with video screens, lighting and sound equipment in the weeks leading up to the event. Another special design is the giant sun-shade device that is built in the Colorado Desert for the Coachella festival each year. Known as the Sahara Tent it is not a tent at all but a modular parabolic compression structure that its creator, Andrew Gumper of AG Light and Sound describes as a self-climbing megastructure. This is a massive transportable concert space 111-metres (365-feet) wide by 43-metres (140-feet) tall that is assembled at ground level, being pushed up to its final height as each section is added from one side.

Festival stages are designed to accommodate multiple artists playing their sets consecutively, any individuality in the show comes from the performance itself or the graphic effects designed for the now-inevitable LED screens behind and to the side of the stage. The travelling shows, created to fit into arenas or for very successful acts, stadia, are usually created especially for the tour, which might be as long as three years in order to take in all the territories that the artist wishes to cover. The festival stage can be described as designed to present a concert: the travelling set is designed to present an experience, and major artists usually want them to be bigger and better than anything that has gone before. These grand popular music shows began in the 1960s with musicians looking to precedents in theatre, opera and film to create more visual experiences to accompany their more ambitious musical projects. Artists like Pink Floyd, Genesis, Yes seem unlikely precedents for Miley Cyrus, Taylor Swift and Beyoncé (which also owe a nod to traditional musical theatre); however, the same techniques and equipment are now used universally across all music genres. Specialist designers such as Stufish and Es Devlin not only create visual concepts but marry them to a practical construction system that can be reliably assembled and disassembled multiple times. As well as design consultants, specialist construction and road crew companies such as StageCo, PRG and Tait Towers provide mobile staging development and construction. Most large travelling stages are now geared towards arenas, vehicles driving right into the performance space to allow quick off-load and set-up. The designers work within a strict framework requiring an intimate knowledge of the standardized components that can be used to make up the structures, which as well as creating the look of the show must also carry all the technical equipment. The objective is to present something wholly original for each artist while still using as much of the standard components as possible. This is not an industry that stands still – new demands are always being made on both the designers and the construction companies so that new technology is being invented, trialled and put into practice. For example, for U2's 2017/18 *The Joshua Tree* Anniversary Tour at least three completely new technologies were created by Stufish and Tait Towers in order to satisfy Bono's vision of a giant screen in front of which the performers could perform while still being seen; the largest carbon-fibre LED 8k video screen ever made; an intelligent spotlight system that would follow performers across the stage; and a new ultra-lightweight speaker array capable of filling an entire football stadium with sound (Armstrong 2018). Shows like this, drawing literally millions of patrons (Taylor Swift's sold over 3-million tickets on her 2018 53-stadium *Reputation* tour) are the only way that these major artists now make substantial sums with streaming from sites like YouTube, Spotify, Amazon and Apple Music paying between $0.00397 and $0.00783 per play. And as well as the ticket prices the shows are carefully recorded for further sale, in Beyoncé's case now as a package with the online video streaming service Netflix, with whom she has agreed a three-project $60-million deal. The first film was *Homecoming* (2019), her 'big, bold and eminently streamable' 2018 Coachella performance (Bankare 2019). Roy Shuker describes these recorded live performances as, 'Pseudo-live [which] take place at one remove… from the original' (Shuker 2013: 47). These live shows are undeniably popular; audiences are competing to pick up tickets even at high prices and it is easy to understand why. Not only do they get to see their idol in the flesh (though the large video screens may be the best way to recognize them), the shows are undeniably spectacular events. As Kärki suggests, many of these shows (though not all) might be criticized merely as spectacles which are 'technological mediated, materialized and dominantly superficial' (Kärki 2015: 62). Nevertheless, it cannot be doubted that they create enduring experiences, indicated by the numerous lengthy anecdotes on fan forums about the overall event, specific incidents in the show and their resultant enhanced relationship with their favourite artists.

Though these large live gigs may be generating huge revenues, grassroots venues face significant challenges in a commercial environment that is hostile to independent operations, undermining both their operation and physical existence, which have been exacerbated by the COVID-19 pandemic. Across the world many live venues were forced to close and with limited resources to fall back on, have struggled to reopen as pandemic concerns in some areas have eased. Even before the recent lock-downs, the UK Live Music Census 2017 concluded that small venues face 'a "perfect storm" of issues which is affecting their long-term viability and sustainability' (Webster et al. 2018: 11). The homogenization of music management by companies such as Live Nation Entertainment (which is a part of the Ticketmaster group) and AEG Live can freeze out local venues from hosting some artists that are restricted to the venue chains they manage or with whom they have exclusive deals. Major threats also come from a number of other directions: local legislation that restricts the way they operate; increased operating costs from higher rents and rates applied by unsympathetic landlords and local authorities; and a situation in which their contribution to the attractiveness and viability of our cities is simply not recognized so that when they are threatened with closure there is a disinclination to help by those with the power to do so. Pre-COVID there were signs that a movement to change this situation was having some impact with the relaxing of some licensing rules for smaller venues enabling them to host live music more easily, in the UK the introduction of 'night czars' in London and Manchester to champion policies that will help the night-time economy, and learning from Australian experience by the introduction of an 'Agent of Change' principle that will put the onus on new developments to include adequate acoustic separation when locating them close to existing venues. The state government of Victoria, Australia. Nevertheless, despite a slight bounce back in subsequent years, statistics show that between 2005 and 2015 the number of nightclubs halved in the UK from 3,144 to 1,733 due to problems with obtaining licenses, planning permission and redevelopment removing their premises (ALMR 2015) a trend that has, without doubt, continued through the health emergency.

However, even in this challenging area of the live gig business there are some examples of high-quality new building design which show the potential for small local venues to not only be viable financially, but to provide new and valuable social benefits for the neighbourhoods in which they are located. Dutch architect Frits van Dongen has specialized in designing new popular music venues, mostly, though not exclusively in The Netherlands (Feddes and Jolles 2006). These small to middle-sized venues fulfil not only the traditional function of a place for live gigs such as the Heineken Music Hall (designed with practice Architekten Cie), a black box music venue in Amsterdam which opened in 2001, but also as cultural centres which engage with different age groups and social problems. Grenswerk (meaning Border Work) is a venue built in 2014 in the medieval town of Venlo on the Dutch/German border. It replaced an earlier venue; Perron 55, which was partly supported by a regional foundation to encourage well-being and cross-cultural activity. It was important that the new building stay in the existing location, a historic neighbourhood of old warehouses now converted to housing. By building new the venue could utilize the latest acoustic separation technology, but also envelope its main 500-capacity performance space with a second skin of other facilities: a café, bar, meeting spaces and in the basement rehearsal rooms and a recording studio. Instead of removing the club and its associated noise problems to another site (or simply closing it down as frequently happens), a new building was built in the same location that would sensitively reinforce the area's existing links to live music performance, with a contemporary external form that fitted in with the existing historic buildings, but using clever design and new technology to eradicate unwanted sound problems.

The live gig is an event that happens in dramatically varying forms and in many types of buildings and open spaces. It encompasses an equally wide range of musical genres and scenes, and artists who are content to perform for the pleasure of doing so, those at the beginning of professional careers, or at the peak of their fame and experience. It can be enjoyed by people from every walk of life, each having their own preferences and passions, willing to invest large sums of money in both tickets and travel for the experience, or happy just to drop in when a performance is convenient and affordable. It is an intrinsic part of the music business, with many people involved in making it happen, either directly in the performance process, or in one of the many associated activities that happen as a consequence. The music industry delivered £4.5billion to the UK economy in 2017 of which £991million was from live music. More than 28,000 people are directly employed in making live shows possible and there are over 91,000 people making a living as musicians (UK Music 2018). The live gig is a cultural and artistic phenomenon that is firmly embedded in the economy and society: 'music is and was a part of the fabric of everyday life' (Levitin 2006: 6). For young people it is particularly crucial for if you are standing at a cultural crossroads in your life, a young person unsure of yourself and your future, but passionate about something you have heard on the radio or the web; 'you're liberated if there's a venue where like minds gather, a venue that could open musical possibilities, and help you identify and define the person you are or the person you want to be' (Haslam 2015: 416). The live gig is an indispensable component in the crucial art form that is popular music, a fact that was accentuated by its forced absence from music lovers' lives during the pandemic.

References

ALMR (Association of Licensed Multiple Retailers) (2015), ALMR Christie & Co. Benchmarking Report, August 2015.

Armstrong, S. (2018), 'Inside the Amish Town That Builds U2, Lady Gaga, and Taylor Swift's Live Shows', *Wired*, 5 January 2018.

Bakare, L. (2019). 'Beyoncé Brings It Home: Why Concert Films Are Big Again', *The Guardian*, 19 April 2019.

BBC (2018), *Hits, Hypes and Hustle: An Insider's Guide to the Music Business*, 'Episode 2: On the Road' (Presenter: Colin Murray), Pacific Quay Productions BBC4, 19 January 2018.

Byrne, D. (2012), *How Music Works*, Edinburgh: Canongate.

Cohen, S. (2014), '"The Gigs I've Gone to": Mapping Memories and Places of Live Music', in K. Burland and S. Pitts (eds), *Coughing and Clapping: Investigating Audience Experience*, 131–46, Farnham: Ashgate.

Connell, J. and Gibson, C. (2003), *Soundtracks: Popular Music, Identity and Place*, Abingdon: Routledge.

Feddes, F. and Jolles, A. (2006), *Frits van Dongen: Designing for Culture*, Rotterdam: 010 Publishers.

Hale, J. (2014). *Born to Be Wild: The Golden Age of American Rock*, 'Episode 2: 1970s – School's Out', BBC4, 17 January 2014.

Haslam, D. (2015), *Life after Dark: A History of British Nightclubs and Music Venues*, London: Simon and Schuster, 416.

Homan, S. (2011), '"I Tote and I Vote": Australian Live Music and Cultural Policy', *Arts Marketing*, 1 (2): 96–107.

Kärki, K. (2015), 'Evolutions of the Wall: 1975–2015', in R. Edgar, K. Fairclough-Isaacs, B. Halligan and N. Spelman (eds), *The Arena Concert: Music, Media and Mass Entertainment*, 57–70, New York: Bloomsbury.

Kronenburg, R. (2012), *Live Architecture: Venues, Stages and Arenas for Popular Music*, Abingdon: Routledge.

Kronenburg, R. (2019), *This Must Be the Place: An Architectural History of Popular Music Performance Venues*, New York: Bloomsbury.

Levitin, D. (2006), *This Is Your Brain on Music: The Science of a Human Obsession*, London: Dutton.

Mac, A. (2017), Quote from *Annie Mac: Who Killed The Night?* BBC3, 18 January 2017.

O'Grady, A. (2015), 'Being There: Encounters with Space and the Affective Dimension of Arena Spectacle', in R. Edgar, K. Fairclough-Isaacs, B. Halligan and N. Spelman (eds), *The Arena Concert: Music, Media and Mass Entertainment*, New York: Bloomsbury, 111–122.

Osborn, M. (2011), 'Brit Awards: Verdict on the "New" Show', BBC News, Entertainment and Arts, 16 February 2011. Available online: https://www.bbc.com/news/entertainment-arts-12472422 (accessed 2 May 2019).

Radbourne, J., Johanson, K. and Glow, H. (2014), 'The Value of "Being There": How the Live Experience Measures Quality for the Audience', in K. Burland and S. Pitts (eds), *Coughing and Clapping: Investigating Audience Experience*, 55–68, Farnham: Ashgate.

Sanderson, C. (2013), *Someone Like Adele*, London: Omnibus.

Shuker, R. (2013), *Understanding Popular Music Culture*, Abingdon: Routledge.

Smith, P. (2012), *Just Kids*, London: Bloomsbury.

Spitz, B. (2014 [1979]), *Barefoot in Babylon: The Creation of the Woodstock Music Festival, 1969*, New York: Plume.

Webster, E., Brennan, M., Behr, A., Cloonan, M. and Ansell, J. (2018), *Valuing Live Music: The UK Live Music Census, 2017 Report Executive Summary*, Edinburgh: University of Edinburgh, ECA, Reid School of Music.

UK Music (2018), *Measuring Music 2018 Report*, London: UK Music.

13
Mobile listening cultures

Raphaël Nowak

Introduction

The phrase 'mobile listening cultures' refers to a range of practices of human mobility accompanied by the listening of music. It includes a range of different engagements with music while in mobility, such as listening to music while driving (see Bull 2004), while jogging, exercising or studying (DeNora 2000; Nowak 2016a), while walking in an urban area carrying a boombox and playing hip hop music (Schmieding 2011), or with earbuds in one's ears and an iPod in one's pocket (Bull 2005, 2007).

The advent of mobile listening cultures can be traced back to the introduction of the magnetic cassette tapes in the 1960s, which was accompanied with tape players that could be carried around. Since then, successive technological and cultural innovations have contributed in furthering the premises of agentic possibilities to privatize and individualize listening practices in social (and urban) spaces. In hindsight, three iconic moments can be identified in the history of mobile listening cultures, with a fourth one currently unfolding and developing with streaming services and algorithms. The first three historical moments can be described as follows: the advent of the portable cassette players in the 1960s; the advent of the Sony Walkman in 1984; and the advent of digital music portable devices in the early 2000s, and primarily the Apple iPod in 2001. A fourth cultural moment that marks the history of mobile listening cultures emerged in the late 2000s and started with the development of the Genius option on Apple's iTunes (see Beer 2009, 2010). It incorporates a new type of mobile listening culture, which is integrated within techno-cultural networks and processes of datafication. Mobile and private listening practices become increasingly connected via algorithms to a range of taste profiles and systems of recommendations, which constantly analyse the music content listened to, and the contexts within which the listening practices occur.

This chapter offers a brief overview of the history of mobile listening cultures by reviewing scholarly analyses that have aimed to seize and understand such phenomena, particularly in the 2000s and 2010s, when important techno-cultural shifts were taking place. It will draw on the different moments in the history of mobile listening cultures to identify particular trends. It opens with an analysis of the increasing agentic possibilities afforded to listeners by successive mobile music technologies. The second section analyses mobile listening cultures in the digital age of music technologies. A third section explores the materiality and iconicity of the iPod. The fourth and final section analyses the contemporary conditions of integration of mobile listening cultures within techno-cultural processes of datafication.

The increasing diffusion of music in private mobilities: a brief exploration of the history of mobile listening

Mobile listening cultures emerged after the Second World War with the advent of the magnetic cassette tape, and cassette tape recorders and players. Ancestor of the boombox, the first tape recorder player was easily transportable. It featured a built-in speaker that enabled users to listen to what they had recorded on cassettes, or to music cassettes they had purchased. However, it is the boombox from the late 1970s that started being used for mobile listening practices (see Schloss and Boyer 2014). These devices characterize the first moment of mobile listening cultures. Although practices of mobile listening were not greatly popular in the 1960s and 1970s, the cassette tape recorder and player and the boombox are technologies that afforded mobility while listening to music. The boombox later became an iconic instrument in the diffusion and affirmation of particular music styles, such as hip hop (see Schmieding 2011 for an example in Berlin). The problem associated with such practices lies in the high level of noise pollution they cause, which is often listed as one of music's main negative aspects (see Johnson and Cloonan 2009; Trotta 2020).

The launch of the cassette Sony Walkman in 1979 in Japan, and in 1982 in the rest of the world, privatized mobile listening cultures. The small device was more easily transportable than previous mobile devices. Working with magnetic cassette tapes, the Walkman had to be plugged to headphones, earphones or speakers, for the music to be listened to. The Walkman is described as a very iconic invention and opens the second moment of mobile listening cultures. Roy Shuker argues that it enables listeners to 're-appropriate place and time, with listeners regaining control of their auditory environments by blocking out undesirable surrounding noise (and people)' (2008: 43). Sushei Hosokawa (1984) writes that the Walkman opens the era of 'musica mobilis', which transforms the sensorial experience of urban spaces, thus providing the 'autonomy of the walking self'. He continues: 'De-territorialized listening induces an autonomous "head space" between his Self and his surroundings in order to distance itself from – not familiarise itself with – both of them. The result is the mobility of Self' (Hosokawa 1984: 175).

Hosokawa describes a process that places individuals in control of their experiences. The Walkman is in that regard the intermediary that enables individuals to increase their agentic control of the social. His account will later inspire other scholars in their approach to mobile listening cultures, primarily through its focus on individuals' agencies, as 'provided' by mobile music technologies.

Following the Sony Walkman, a range of objects were released and only furthered the possibilities for users to control their sonic environments while on the move. The Discman was commercialized in 1984 and the MiniDiscman in 1992. Listeners could more easily skip tracks, move back and forth, and repeat songs. After the emergence of online downloading of digital music files in the late 1990s, a number of USB stick devices devoted to music listening invaded the market. Containing between 64mb and 512mb of storage data, these devices enabled listeners to carry more music with them, 'fix' mp3 files downloaded online (legally or illegally), and eventually compile playlists. In the early 2000s, demand for a device that would allow listeners to interact with more of their music while on the move. This eventually led to the concentration of the market onto one device – the Apple iPod.

Mobile listening cultures in the digital age

The release of the Apple iPod in 2001 marked a third cultural moment in the history of mobile listening cultures. In over a decade, the device met an unprecedented global success. It also attracted quite a lot of scholarly attention over time, not only for its technical features, but also for its iconicity (see next section). Michael Bull published widely on the iPod (including 2005, 2006, 2007), after having explored uses of the Walkman (2001) and music listening in cars (2004). Bull sees in the iPod a device that transforms individuals' experiences of their daily, urban environments. The iPod in fact gives them unprecedented control over their own narrative. He writes:

> iPod use provides users with their own 'unique' regulated soundscape that mediates the experience of whatever space is passed through and regulates the flow of time as they wish [...] iPod users choose the manner in which they attend to these spaces, transforming space and time into their own personalised narrative.
>
> (Bull 2005: 351)

A number of concepts define Bull's approach to the iPod and help clarify how he sees the Apple object. Thus, he constructs a dichotomy between the 'coldness' of the open, social, urban spaces, and the 'warmth' sound bubble, or 'cocoon' that the iPod affords its users, by enclosing them within a sensory experience of their choosing, and with which they are familiar. For instance, Bull writes: 'Technologies such as iPods act as tools enabling the urban citizen to move through the chilly spaces of urban culture wrapped in a cocoon of communicative warmth whilst further contributing to the chill which surrounds them' (2007: 18). Focusing on the experiences of iPod users, Bull writes about the interactions between the mobile device, individuals' cognition and music selections, and the urban spaces within which these interactions occur. Bull's phenomenological account highlights the system of mediations that 'empowers' individuals who listen to music privately. The urban landscape is transformed through individuals' cognitions who experience 'filmic experiences' (Bull 2000, 2007).

The work of Bull is rather celebratory of the iPod, in that the technology is regarded as increasing the array of agentic possibilities that its users have in the social space. Miriam Simun (2009) develops a more critical account of mobile listening cultures, which is aimed at interrogating the social consequences of mobile listening practices. Drawing on Adorno (2003 [1967]), Simmel (2003 [1903]) and Lefebvre (1991), Simun explores the implications of private mobile listening cultures, and their increasing popularity. She argues: 'By engaging the MP3, users turn their "constrained time" into leisure – transforming, as they describe, their "boring" and "stressful" commutes into times of entertainment and relaxation' (Simun 2009: 926). A musical accompaniment during such 'constrained time' extends the reach of personalized entertainment. Simun adds:

> Crucially, for some users the MP3 enables them to avoid complete disassociation from the city by enabling them to enjoy musically mediated versions of the commute. Individuals enjoy shaping their experiences as they use the MP3 to navigate various levels of presence and reconfigure their commutes as personal and pleasurable spaces.
>
> (2009: 932).

Although she confirms some of Bull's findings, Simun focuses on the impact of the privatization of urban experiences as causing a form of de-socialization of listeners. She does not clearly refer to the iPod, but rather uses the generic phrase 'Mp3' to discuss Londoners' mobile listening practices. Ultimately, Simun defends a negative account of mobile listening cultures in the digital age, in that she sees in such practice a withdrawal from the very sociality of urban spaces. She writes:

> MP3 users emotionally, cognitively and even physically experience a private realm. And, by signifying absence with headphones, others they encounter may regard them as absent from the shared social space. But the illusion of solution through music remains – for problems of the urban space and of everyday life continue. In fact, for some MP3 users the unmediated urban space becomes unbearable. While the control the MP3 gives users does allow them to attend to their musically mediated environments in an enjoyable way, this very mediation prevents users' full participation in urban space – thereby negating the public nature of this space.
>
> (Simun 2009: 937)

What Simun interprets as a withdrawal from the social is expressed by Bull in a more neutral fashion along the lines of a 'retreat from an urban overkill of the senses' (2004: 244). The issue that emerges with Simun's account is that technological innovation (here, the 'Mp3') is identified as directly producing cultural changes. However, the author does not interrogate the greater social and cultural context that compels individuals to withdraw from the sociality of urban spaces in the first place. Simun's argument touches on technological determinism in that it assumes that individuals would be more participative to social spaces, were it for the use of the 'Mp3'.

In the end, Bull and Simun provide very opposed perspectives on the individualization and privatization of mobile listening cultures. However, they both identify a clear shift towards an increasing personal mediation of the social space, even though Bull tends to celebrate it whereas Simun regrets it. What I identify as the third cultural moment in the history of mobile listening cultures might be the most documented and discussed to date. Indeed, following a long history of increasing individualization and privatization of mobile listening practices, the advent of digital music technologies has long been seen as epitomizing the range of agentic possibilities that individuals enjoy with music in the social space. The iPod, the most successful mobile music technology, has been identified as the main facilitator of such cultural innovation.

Materiality, iconicity... and alienation?

As previously stated, the Apple iPod has attracted a lot of scholarly attention since its inception. Scholarship that specifically explores the iconicity of the object also deserves some attention. Besides the number of sales, the hype associated with the object, and Apple's constant renewal and remarketing of the object (which they now continue with the iPhone and other devices), publications on mobile listening cultures tend to highlight the technological and material features of the iPod as a key component to consider. The materiality of the Apple device is the focus point of many authors (see, for instance, Dant 2008; Jenkins 2008; Scott and Woodward 2011). Dant summarizes the iconicity of the device as follows:

> The iPod is culturally an iconic device in the sense that it is difficult not to know what one is or to recognise that it has cultural value – if only to other people. Clearly, not everyone owns an iPod but just about everyone owns and routinely uses many of the other devices in these series. The iPod is visible in advertisements, in media commentary and in people's possession and use familiar even to those who have no desire to use one.
> (2008: 12)

The iPod is described as 'iconic' by many (see, for instance, Bull 2005, 2006, 2007; Dant 2008; Jenkins 2008) because it is a technology that is 'embodied' by its users (Dant 2008), because it is designed for personal attachment (Scott and Woodward 2011; Beer 2012), because it is a hybrid technology (Nowak 2016b), or because it enables multiple and plural engagements (Simun 2009; Prior 2014).

Kathleen Ferguson is highly critical of how the iPod crystalizes the attention of many scholars. She points out that Apple has managed to saturate the market with its mobile device and that sensory experiences cannot be seen as liberating – contrary to what Bull argues (2005, 2007) – considering the material intermediary that 'enables' such experience. She writes:

> There is a quasi-religious underpinning to the tactile delights that are mentioned by Bull's iPod users: 'It's almost as if my iPod understands me' is a refrain that clearly wishes to go beyond Marshall McLuhan's suggestion of technology being an extension of our senses. This scenario would be relatively naturalized, in comparison with the machine that knows us better than we know ourselves. This projection of all our needs and desires is ennobled

through tools much greater, or at least more aesthetically pleasing, than the flawed mental and physical capacities of our selves, now seemingly inadequate to the task of living. In their place are machines that offer a model of an ideal self we could never be, a streamlined entity with preternatural instinct for coping with an environment that is comparatively underwhelming.

(Ferguson 2006: 362)

There is in Ferguson's account an underlying critical and Marxist perspective on technologies, in that she infers that the iPod – by definition – alienates individuals. She notes that the emancipatory experience described by Bull (2005, 2007), and later critiqued by Simun (2009), does not free individuals from private property, as Marx had predicted of any form of emancipation. Instead, the iPod enslaves its users within the consumption of an object, of a brand.

To Ferguson (2006), the playing of music becomes secondary in the ways in which authors write about the iPod. Instead, the use value of the device is the focus of attention. She concludes: 'As the value of commodities is jettisoned from their use value, to take on symbolic meaning, so too are social relations atomized – suggestive of their being secreted away in back pockets and stored away for a moment best fitting expenditure' (Ferguson 2006: 361). Other, less critical, accounts have attempted to explain the longevity of the iPod by exploring the multiplicity of practices that individuals engage with through the Apple device (see Prior 2014), or by highlighting its hybridity (see Nowak 2016b), thus explaining how the possibilities of the device have developed over time. However, another key element that explains the durability and iconicity of the iPod is its integration to other techno-cultural processes. The next section presents the shift that occurred from the third to the fourth moment of mobile listening cultures through the datafication of mobile listening practices.

The integration of mobile listening cultures

With the success of smartphones, and as the iPod is now phased out (Apple stopped the production of the 'classic' model in 2014), mobile listening cultures have entered a new era, characterized by the increasing integration of mobile listening practices within processes of datafication.

David Beer (2009, 2010) foresaw this shift from privatized and individualized mobile listening cultures towards more integrated and 'social' practices. From the first inception of algorithms within modes of distribution and consumption of music in the digital age, Beer has managed to identify the premises of a critical cultural shift. Focusing on the iPod, iTunes and the option Genius (launched in 2008), Beer (2010) first starts by stating that mobile listening devices are becoming more and more 'permeable'. He inscribes the iPod within a network of technological devices and options, which other authors such as Bull (2005, 2007) or Simun (2009) both fail to do. In that regard, Beer (2010) sheds light upon a particular 'circuit of practices' (Magaudda 2011) that is centralized around the iPod. He writes:

When docked into a networked computer the mobile music device may communicate this and other information about its use to external bodies – this may not just be recording musical taste in the traditional sense, it might also capture the way in which devices like the now famous Nike shoe sensor interact with iPods to construct playlists based on motion. The list of possibilities of this type of application are likely to expand.

(Beer 2010: 474–5)

Drawing on Martin Dodge and Rob Kitchin's (2009) notion of the 'logject', Beer describes how the iPod's permeability – or 'hybridity' (Nowak 2016b) – enables the development of new protocols and practices, by gathering data about the ways in which individuals use them. With the option Genius on iTunes, Apple developed new ways to provide individuals with recommendations about music content they ought to like and listen to, from the iTunes store, or from their own music library. Compiled by algorithms, these recommendations are based on what other individuals with similar taste profiles 'like'. The amount of data gathered about mobile listening practices (and other listening practices as well) only increases over time, with the aim of refining individuals' profiles and the recommendations provided to them. Beer comments:

> What is changing is that as the devices we use to consume music whilst on the move continue to become more permeable and networked so this information becomes real-time, locational and, most importantly, increasingly ambient and hidden. Admittedly, what this suggests is that the basic details about the type of information extracted is available but at the same time it again re-iterates the lack of insight that we currently have into how this technological infrastructure is operating.
>
> (2010: 478)

Beer locates his approach in opposition to Bull's (2005, 2007) argument of individualization. Through the increasing process of datafication that shifts mobile listening cultures, Beer sees a new form of socialization taking place: 'We can [...] no longer think of listening to music as being an individual practice that is somehow segregated off from something as important as the generation and use of transactional data' (2010: 475–6). Although there is an opposition that is constructed between Beer's argument and Bull's approach, they can both be thought as being complementary, as I have argued elsewhere (see Nowak 2016b). Indeed, Beer (2010) focuses on the techno-cultural processes of datafication that surround the experience of listening, whereas Bull's (2005, 2007) perspective clearly explores what happens in the interaction between the iPod, the music and the urban space where such interaction is said to be taking place. In other words, Beer looks at the framing of the mobile listening experience, when Bull disregards any other type of practice with the iPod than the listening experience itself.

Beer's contribution is critical in that it invites to think about a shift between moments in the historical development of mobile listening cultures. Indeed, the option Genius on iTunes, alongside music social media websites such as Last.fm, conducted the exploratory work of identifying the potential of algorithms in music listening practices. Since then, Spotify, Deezer, TIDAL, Google Play, Pandora, Apple Music and other similar streaming services have taken over as the dominant mode of distribution and consumption of music in the mid to late 2010s (see IFPI 2017). Smartphones have also largely replaced iPods in mobile listening practices. They are constantly harvesting data about the music that individuals listen to, and the contexts within which they listen to it, through the continuing connection to 3G, 4G, 5G or Wi-Fi networks. What Beer (2009, 2010) points out in the case of the iPod is much more performative and ubiquitous with smartphones and music streaming services. This potentially redefines our understandings of music listening practices and music tastes, in that it interrogates the role of intermediaries in how individuals interact with music content on a daily basis.

In the age of integrated and datafied mobile listening cultures, Bull's (2005, 2007) dichotomy between the 'private' and the 'public' certainly no longer holds. The 'cocoon of sound' is now fed by a new form of public input, mediated by algorithms. As Beer puts it, 'There is clearly an interplay at work between musical logjects and the predictive capacities of the related software, an interplay that could well be defining people's everyday soundscapes' (2010: 479). Beer's foundational perspective would certainly need to be followed up by further research into datafied mobile listening practices. However, the scholarly focus seems to have shifted towards broader cultural changes induced by algorithms and big data (see Beer 2013 for an example), while mobile listening cultures are no longer discussed per se, thus further proving their integration within contemporary techno-cultural processes of datafication.

Conclusion

This chapter has discussed the evolution of mobile listening cultures, with a particular focus on the latest techno-cultural developments in the 2000s and 2010s. I have argued that the history of mobile listening cultures can be divided into four moments, marked by particular technological innovations. Although it is possible to interpret the evolution and massification of mobile listening cultures through the lens of a greater privatization and individualization, or, 'autonomy of the walking self' (Hosokawa 1984), up until the integration of the iPod within algorithmic processes, the latest moment of mobile listening cultures is fully embedded within techno-cultural processes of datafication, which places mobile listening practices back into a social framework where individuals' practices feed into one another.

Of course, although presented here through overarching trends, and often interpreted in scholarly research through certain analogies ('filmic experiences' for instance) and interpretations ('withdrawal' from the social for instance), it is important to keep in mind that mobile listening cultures are multiple and mediated. This has been emphasized by Prior (2014) empirical investigation of individuals' various engagements with the iPod and acknowledged by Simun (2009: 935) with the phrase 'differing conceptualizations of MP3 listening'.

Finally, the evolution of mobile listening cultures tells us something about the history of recorded music as a whole, and about the role that music has come to take in our contemporary society. Indeed, mobile listening cultures ultimately bring music to new territories, and afford new possibilities to associate and define it with a range of everyday contexts, which has been essential to the development of certain genres of music over time (as with the case of hip hop and boomboxes for instance, see Schmieding 2011).

References

Adorno T. (1976), *Introduction to the Sociology of Music*, New York: Continuum.
Beer, D. (2009), 'Power through the Algorithm? Participatory Web Cultures and the Technological Unconscious', *New Media & Society*, 11: 985–1002.
Beer, D. (2010), 'Mobile Music, Coded Objects and Everyday Spaces', *Mobilities*, 5: 469–84.
Beer, D. (2012), 'The Comfort of Mobile Media: Uncovering Personal Attachments with Everyday Devices', *Convergence*, 18 (4): 361–7.
Beer, D. (2013), *Popular Culture and New Media. The Politics of Circulation*, Basingstoke: Palgrave Macmillan.
Bull, M. (2000), *Sounding out the City: Personal Stereos and the Management of Everyday Life*, Oxford: Berg.
Bull, M. (2001), 'The World According to Sound: Investigating the World of Walkman Users', *New Media & Society*, 3: 179–97.
Bull, M. (2004), 'Automobility and the Power of Sound', *Theory, Culture & Society*, 21: 243–59.
Bull, M. (2005), 'No Dead Air! The iPod and the Culture of Mobile Listening', *Leisure Studies*, 24 (4): 343–55.
Bull, M. (2006), 'Iconic Designs: The Apple iPod', *Senses and Society*, 1 (1): 105–9.
Bull, M. (2007), *Sound Moves: iPod Culture and Urban Experience*, London: Routledge.
Dant, T. (2008), 'iPod…iCon', *Studi Culturali*, 5: 355–73. Available Online: https://www.researchgate.net/publication/228787673_iPod_iCon, retrieved on 28 February 2018.
DeNora, T. (2000), *Music in Everyday Life*, Cambridge: Cambridge University Press.
Dodge, M. and Kitchin, R. (2009), 'Software, Objects, and Home Space', *Environment and Planning A*, 41 (6): 1344–65.
Ferguson, K. (2006), 'The Anti-pod: After Michael Bull's "Iconic Designs: The Apple iPod"', *Senses & Society*, 1: 359–66.
Hosokawa, S. (1984), 'The Walkman Effect', *Popular Music*, 4: 165–80.
IFPI (2017), 'IFPI Global Music Report 2017'. Available Online: http://www.ifpi.org/news/IFPI-GLOBAL-MUSIC-REPORT-2017?mc_cid=16de3d5cb0&mc_eid=[UNIQID], retrieved on 4 January 2018.
Jenkins, E. (2008), 'My iPod, My iCon: How and Why Do Images Become Icons?', *Critical Studies in Media Communication*, 25: 466–89.
Johnson, B. and Cloonan, M. (2009), *Dark Side of the Tune: Popular Music and Violence*, Surrey: Ashgate.
Lefebvre H. (1991), *Critique of Everyday Life*, London: Verso.
Magaudda, P. (2011), 'When Materiality "Bites Back": Digital Music Consumption Practices in the Age of Dematerialization', *Journal of Consumer Culture*, 11: 15–36.
Nowak, R. (2016a), *Consuming Music in the Digital Age: Technologies, Roles, and Everyday Life*, Basingstoke: Palgrave Macmillan.

Nowak, R. (2016b), 'The Multiplicity of iPod Cultures in Everyday Life: Uncovering the Performative Hybridity of the Iconic Object', *Journal for Cultural Research*, 20 (2): 189–203.

Prior, N. (2014), 'The Plural iPod: A Study of Technology in Action', *Poetics*, 42: 22–39.

Schloss, J. and Boyer, B. (2014), 'Urban Echoes: The Boombox and Sonic Mobility in the 1980s', in S. Gopinath and J. Stanyek (eds), *The Oxford Handbook of Mobile Music Studies*, 399–412, vol. 1, Oxford: Oxford University Press.

Schmieding, L. (2011), 'Boom Boxes and Backward Caps: Hip-Hop Culture in the GDR', in U. Balbier, C. Cuevas-Wolf, and J. Segal (eds), *East German Material Culture and the Power of Memory*, 67–86, Washington, DC: German Historical Institute.

Scott, A., and Woodward, I. (2011), 'Living with Design Objects: A Qualitative Study of iPod Relationship', *Design Principles and Practices: An International Journal*, 5: 499–508.

Shuker, R. (2008), *Understanding Popular Music Culture*, London: Routledge.

Simun, M. (2009), 'My Music, My World: Using the MP3 Player to Shape Experience in London', *New Media and Society*, 11: 921–41.

Simmel, G. (2003), 'The Metropolis and Mental Life', in M. Miles, T. Hall and I. Borden (eds), *The City Cultures Reader*, 12–19, London: Routledge.

Trotta, F. (2020), *Annoying Music in Everyday Life*, London: Bloomsbury.

Section III

Space, place, production and performance

14

In the city: Glasgow

Martin Cloonan

Introduction

Between 2000 and 2017 I was based in Glasgow, Scotland, and became active in the city's music scene(s). This chapter uses my experiences there to offer some critical reflections about the nature of the music industries within Glasgow and relate them to previous discussions of themes such as scene, mapping and policy. It falls into three main parts: Firstly it introduces Glasgow and its music scenes; secondly, it outlines my experiences as a researcher, teacher and band manager in Glasgow; and thirdly it relates all this to existing literature on music scenes. Some conclusions are also drawn.

Glasgow and its scenes

Situated on Scotland's west coast, in 2017 Glasgow's population was estimated at 621,000 (https://en.wikipedia.org/wiki/Glasgow), with the population of the greater Glasgow area being around 1.2 million (https://en.wikipedia.org/wiki/Greater_Glasgow). Historically Glasgow was characterized as being the Second City of the British Empire, and during the nineteenth century it had the fastest population growth in Europe. Between 1871 and 1914, its population doubled to around 1 million (Anderson 2015: 194), although it also experienced population declines in the 1950s and 1960s as large swathes of the population were moved out to the suburbs (Anderson 2015: 200). Today Glasgow can reasonably be described as being post-industrial, with the shipbuilding, coal and other heavy industries upon which much of the city was built largely being things of the past. By 2005, 89 per cent of its employment was in the service sector (Homan et al. 2015: 95).

The city has also carefully rebranded itself in recent years, via campaigns such as Glasgow's Miles Better (1983), Scotland With Style (2004) and, currently, People Make Glasgow (2013). The origins of this can be traced back to the establishment of the Scottish Development Agency in 1975 (Homan et al. 2015: 96). An important year for music was 1985 when the Scottish Exhibition and Conference Centre (SECC) opened as the first arena in the city. The Garden Festival in 1988 was another key stage in the rebranding of the city. Glasgow was European City of Culture in 1990, which also saw the opening of a new venue – the Royal Concert Hall. Overall Glasgow went from being a city which saw its razor gangs mythologized in the play *No Mean City* in 1935 to being a city of culture in 1990. However, it remains a city of extremes of wealth and poverty, variously being named a Europe's Murder capital in 2004 (Homan et al. 2015: 95), seen as Britain's most violent city in 2013 (Homan et al. 2015) and having the infamous 'Glasgow problem' which at one point saw male life expectancy in the city's Carlton area in being nearly 30 years lower than just outside the city – 54 as opposed to 82 (cited Gordon-Nesbitt 2006).

The city has a great deal of post-compulsory education provision, being home to three universities: Glasgow, Glasgow Caledonian and Strathclyde, as well as the SAE Institute which is a partner of Middlesex University and provides Popular Music degrees. It also hosts the Royal Conservatoire of Scotland (RCS) and Glasgow School of Art (GSA). The University of the West of Scotland is close by and runs a degree in Commercial Music. In addition, the city hosts three large further education colleges (City, Clyde and Kelvin) in the city. One of them, Glasgow Kelvin, is the home of the Electric Honey label which released early records by bands such as Belle and Sebastian, Snow Patrol and Biffy Clyro. Overall Glasgow has lots of students, as many as 130,000 according to the city itself (https://peoplemakeglasgow.com/discover/study).

The importance of this is that students have been found to be a vital force for music, providing players, audiences and entrepreneurs on a regular basis and that educational institutions can play a major role in local scenes. For example, much has been made of the Beatles' association with Liverpool Art School and, more generally, of the importance of art schools in 1960s British rock (Frith and Horne 1987). Barry Shank (1994) has shown the importance of the University of Texas to Austin's music scene, Alan O'Connor has shown the importance of art colleges in Toronto to the local 1970s punk scene (2002: 228) and in Glasgow Sarah Lowndes's work (2010) has drawn attention to the links between the local music and art scenes, something which Franz Ferdinand embodied. Overall Florida and colleagues (2010: 786) have noted that '[i]n recent decades music scenes have emerged in college towns where music talent is located, students have free time to form and play in musical acts, and there is considerable demand for live performance'. However, it should be noted that the sort of analysis provided by Florida has been noted to 'focus entirely on their subordination to economic development, and often ignore the democratic legitimacy of certain urban initiatives. In addition, they tend to fit the interests of global and neo-liberal concerns in constructing virtual and often unfulfilled urban promises' (Bottà 2009: 351).

Moving to music, since the early 1960s Glasgow's famous acts have included: Lulu, Alex Harvey, Orange Juice, Deacon Blue, Wet Wet Wet, Teenage Fanclub, Simple Minds, Primal Scream, The Delgados, Mogwai, Arab Strap, Franz Ferdinand, Snow Patrol, Travis, Texas, Emeli Sande, Hudson Mohawke, Glasvegas, Chvrches. Glasgow also hosts two orchestras and Scottish Opera. Five of Scotland's top music employers and half of Scotland's music workforce are located there and it has been cited as having the UK's largest music economy outside of London (https://en.unesco.org/creative-cities/glasgow).

In 2008 Glasgow became a UNESCO City of Music (GUCM). Since then, the GUCM has been subject to various stops and starts, mainly due to funding issues. It was certainly aspirational, with its application promising that it would 'function throughout the body of Glasgow's music to improve its health, maximize its performance and ensure that it seizes every opportunity' (cited Homan et al. 2015: 110). This was almost impossible to measure and overall local music journalist Keith Bruce (2014) has suggested that 'it is doubtful whether this City of Music has ever had so much music to choose from. But almost none of it can be associated with... the office of UNESCO City of Music'. Certainly, GUCM has not had any significant impact on the city's popular music scene.

That scene can be said to be subject to some ups and downs. Perhaps the most recent up was the success of the band Franz Ferdinand, when *Time* Magazine referred to the city as being as important at that time as Liverpool and Detroit were in the 1960s (Porter 2004). Franz Ferdinand also garnered critical acclaim, winning the Mercury Prize for Best British album in 2004, a year in which three of the twelve nominated acts came from Glasgow (Homan et al. 2015: 95). In 2006 Snow Patrol's 'Eyes Wide Shut' was the best selling UK album (https://en.wikipedia.org/wiki/Snow_Patrol) and in 2012 Emeli Sande's 'Our Version of Events' was the UK's top selling album (https://www.officialcharts.com/chart-news/the-official-top-40-biggest-selling-albums-of-2012-revealed-__2691/). More recently Chvrches have been the city's most commercially successful band. In 2010 the *Sydney Morning Herald* argued that 'Glasgow has produced some of the finest indie-rock bands of the past 30 years' (Phelan 2010) and it was reported that it was vying to be the UK's dance capital (Homan et al. 2015: 95). In 2018 the city's King Tuts Wah Wah Hut venue was named as the 70th best in the world (Ali 2018).

Such evidence suggests that Glasgow is a successful musical city, raising questions about why this is the case. Simon Frith, John Williamson and I (2009) have previously argued that Glasgow's success rests on it providing local musicians with the things they need, including resources, space and time. *Resources* include such things as music lessons, the passing on of musical values and traditions within families, access to performance opportunities and teachers and mentors. *Space* includes places to play and go to see music. We noted the importance of having a variety of venues, something which Glasgow has, with venue sizes ranging 50 to 50,000 capacities with most places in between. While new venues such as the SECC and Royal Concert Hall are a result of modern redevelopment, most venues are a legacy of Glasgow's industrial past which produced a large proletariat which needed entertainment spaces. Musicians also need rehearsal spaces and these are readily available, as is access to recording studios. In terms of *time*, musicians need time to learn their instruments and craft, to rehearse and to write. We noted that the rhythm of the student day can be particularly amenable to this as it can allow the necessary time to be a musician, something which can bolster the local scene – to which I now turn.

Being on a scene

During my time in Glasgow three things came together in mutually reinforcing ways – my academic research interests, my teaching activities and becoming a band manager. When I arrived in Glasgow in 2000 I began to *research* music industries politics at two levels – UK and Scottish. At the UK level a scheme called the New Deal for Musicians was running. In essence this was a government-funded advice scheme for young unemployed musicians which included them getting guidance from music industry insiders known as Music Industry Consultants (MICs). I researched the scheme via interviewing musicians involved in it and people who were working as MICs. One organization was coordinating the MICs. This was organized by former Deacon Blue tour manager Gill Maxwell, whom I came to know and via whom I met various key personnel in the Scottish music industries.

My arrival in Glasgow came just after the Scottish Parliament had been established in 1999. This was a particularly political time as everyone was expecting the new Parliament to do something for them. Within the Parliament a Cross Party Group on the contemporary Scottish music industry was formed in December 2000 and I began to attend their meetings, getting to know more music industries people. The Group was soon lobbying the country's main public economic agency, Scottish Enterprise, to have policies for developing Scotland's music industries.

To find out what it should do in 2002 Scottish Enterprise announced that it was tendering for a mapping report on the state of the Scottish music industry. I put a team together and won the bid. The subsequent mapping involved interviewing music industries personnel and so making further contacts, with much of the work being done in Glasgow (see Williamson et al. 2003). Thus overall my general research interests helped to get me known in the Scottish, Glasgow-dominated, music industries.

My *teaching* activities also helped. I was first employed in Glasgow in the Department of Adult and Continuing Education (DACE) and was soon teaching evening classes in popular music and, increasingly, the music business. As part of the New Deal research, I'd met John Williamson, a key figure on the Glasgow scene who had managed acts, promoted shows, written hundreds of reviews and went on to manage the band Belle and Sebastian. John began to teach with me and also undertook most of the research for the Scottish Enterprise report.

In 2006 I moved to the Music Department with a mandate to develop postgraduate provision. This included launching a postgraduate degree in Popular Music Studies which began in 2007–08 and eventually became an M.Litt in the Music Industries. My experience on the *Mapping* report had shown me that Glasgow was the hub for a lot of music industries activities and that most of the companies involved were very small, often one or two people. Such people often wanted to do new things, but lacked the resources to do so. So I designed a placement scheme whereby students would work in these companies for three months on research projects designed to develop the company's business.

Perhaps inevitably this had mixed results. However, it *did* give a lot of music industries students genuine music industries experience and produced some interesting projects. It also forged more links between myself and the local scene. I only worked with people I knew and that meant developing new links and new knowledge. Meanwhile students often chose to do research on Glasgow for their dissertation projects, which often entailed me coming in to contact with still more Glasgow music industries personnel via asking them for interviews. Some students went on to PhDs, including a history of Glasgow indie from

1979–2009, a critical history of the Glasgow International Jazz festival, a history of the Glasgow Apollo venue and one on the use of sectarian music in the city.

In 2006 I became the *manager* of a band called Zoey Van Goey, an experience about which I've written elsewhere (Cloonan 2015). Initially a three piece, they became four and released a couple of albums on Glasgow's Chemikal Underground label as well as touring widely, including a few European shows as guests of Belle and Sebastian.[1] My involvement stemmed from knowing of the band members, Michael John McCarhty, who had been around the Adult Education department, trying to organize a songwriting course. He had also met Matt Brennan, whom I knew through academic circles. The third member of the original band, Kim Moore, was a student in the Music Department whom I didn't know but who had attended some of my lectures. When the tria decided to recruit a bassist they first used various people for live shows, then eventually hired one of my former students, Adam Scott.

Becoming a band manager meant that I became more active on the scene and met more new people. It also gave me much more respect within the industries than when I was simply an academic, greatly increasing my cultural capital. Being a manager meant dealing with every aspect of the industries including musicians, fans, promoters, venues, record company personnel, merchandisers, film-makers and broadcasting people. I thus gained practical experience of working on the Glasgow scene, albeit at a relatively low level.

The band began by playing local gigs and the branching out. This meant that we got as good knowledge of smaller venues in Glasgow and the people who ran them. As we developed a fan base we were soon booking venues ourselves and learning about the good and bad sides of the local scene. We negotiated the time wasters and rip-off merchants and also met some of the nicest people I will ever meet. On the plus side while 'on the scene' I got to meet, and sometimes befriend, people whose music I had admired for years. Happily the band also enjoyed some success and by the time they disbanded in 2012 they could sell out 500 capacity venues in Glasgow and were getting offers from all over the UK and beyond. By the time of the split in 2012, the band were in credit and had a lot of fun. Their manager had also learned a lot.

Thus by 2010 I had an interest in music and politics which had brought me into contact with various music industries people and was reinforcing that via meeting people to provide placements on my Masters programme and managing a band which was attracting a lot of interest. Overall I was learning a lot about the musical life of the city I lived in. The need now is to critically examine all this.

Theorizing Glasgow

Local music scenes have been theorized seriously now for around thirty years, with landmark texts including Finnegan (1989), Cohen (1991), Shank (1994) and Straw (1997).

There are also numerous local histories, such as Allen's history of Portsmouth (2017), C.P. Lee's Manchester history (2002), Du Noyer's ode to Liverpool (2007), Stahl's edited collection on Berlin (2014) and the involvement of academics in the Birmingham Music Archive project (www.birminghammusicarchive.com). At the top of the theoretical tree sit Bourdieu's notion of fields of production and Becker's ideas of Art Worlds and the collective nature of art. Overall there is a range of literature to engage with. Space prevents a detailed analysis and I will thus limit myself to the discussion of some key ideas: scenes, mapping and policy to see how they help to understand my Glasgow experience.

The term 'scenes' can be seen as something of music industries term which became theorized to the extent that it now has its own academic journal, which proclaims itself to be 'dedicated to a critical examination of space and scenic production' (www.intellectbooks.co.uk/journals/view-Journal,id=206/). Straw is the first and major theorist of scene within Popular Music Studies and developed the following definition: 'A musical scene... is the cultural space in which a range of musical practices coexist, interacting with each other within a variety of processes of differentiation, and according to widely varying trajectories of change and cross-fertilisation' (Straw 1997: 494).

Importantly Straw links this to contemporary musical practice and the musical heritage which renders this practice appropriate (Straw 1997), going on to say that the point is to examine 'the ways in which particular practices "work" to produce a sense of community within the conditions of metropolitan music scenes' (Straw 1997: 495). Straw is less interested in the music per se than in 'the way in which such spaces of musical activity have come to establish a distinctive relationship to historical time and geographical location' (Straw 1997: 497).

Elsewhere Bennett and Peterson (2004: 1) have defined a scene as being 'the context in which clusters of producers, musicians, and fans collectively share their common musical tastes and collectively distinguish themselves from others'. For Silver and colleagues, scenes are 'modes of organizing cultural production and consumption (that)... foster certain shared values and tastes, certain ways of relating to one another and legitimating what one is doing or not doing' (2005: 6).

For Shank:

> The constitutive feature of local scenes of live music is their evident display of semiotic disruption, their potentially dangerous overproduction and exchange of musical signs of identity and community. Through this display of more than can be understood, encouraging the rational recombination of elements of the human in new structures of identification, local rock'n'roll... scenes produce momentary transformations within dominant cultural meanings.
>
> (Shank 1994: 122)

If this appears somewhat idealistic, O'Connor adopts a pragmatic approach, saying that he wants his definition to be based on what people on the Montreal punk scene mean by the term – viz. 'the active creation of infrastructure to support punk bands and other forms of creative activity' (O'Connor 2002: 226). For him it is important that this is made via active struggle against dominant norms (O'Connor 2002: 233) and so here scene is linked to notions of being alternative or non-mainstream), something which Straw also noted (1997: 496) and which Shank obviously embraces. In the case of Glasgow, that alternative is partly about rejecting the traditional music industries of having to move to London to have success and Anderson (2105), Hamilton (2005) and Lowndes (2010) are among those who have shown how Glasgow's musicians have sought to carve out such alternatives.

It is striking that all the definitions above place different emphases on what the scene is – and what its function is. Much is dependent here on whether the stress is on locality, musicians, audiences, industries, local media, organizations, political affiliation, etc. – and how these are affected by such things as geography, demographics, spaces and the general political economy. Thus, as soon as a scene is identified it is necessary to think about what it is comprised of, what its boundaries are and how it interacts with other scenes.

During my time in Glasgow, I certainly felt part of what might loosely be called an 'indie scene'. I hung out in independently owned venues and managed a band on an indie label who played various locally owned spaces. The Glasgow indie scene was independent – with a small 'i'. That is in terms of artistic and business practice, rather than necessarily political orientation (although it was also largely pro-independence in the 2014 referendum on Scottish independence). While some bands, notably Franz Ferdinand, enjoyed commercial success, most of the musical practice around me was done on minimal budgets and frequently on a barter basis. While that independence was often pragmatic – in the sense that there was often not much alternative to going it alone – labels such as Chemikal Underground (founded in 1995) were formed on the idea that local musicians didn't need to go to London to release records and have musical careers.

I also sometimes interacted with other Glasgow scenes such as dance, reggae, jazz, country, electro acoustic, folk, traditional and classical. Although certain forms of literate guitar rock did become associated with the city, the idea that there was such a thing as a Glasgow sound never really took hold. However, I *do* think that there was a Glasgow attitude – which I might describe as a spirit of social entrepreneurship. Musicians came together for various projects, with the music coming first and covering costs the main financial aim.

Overall, it was clear to me that the term 'scene' remains useful, if only simply because many people, including musicians, still use the term and have a sense of what it is. It thus retains at least some common-sense appeal.

Perhaps because I've been involved in such activities, I have also found *mapping* to be useful. In addition to the *Mapping* report in 2002, in 2016 I oversaw the Glasgow part of the UK's first live music census. This involved mapping all the live music events in Glasgow on one night (Thursday March 2017) and sending as many volunteers to as many as possible to gather information about who was playing, what, if any, admission price was charged, who was there, what they were spending, etc. Over eighty events were identified and around fifty visited. The result was a rounded picture of the state of the live music sector in Glasgow.[2]

The relevance here is that venues are places, places are the central part of scenes and thus mapping them can reveal a great deal about a scene. Venues are important and in the case of Glasgow this was recognized by the GUCM when it decided that the best way to celebrate Glasgow's music was via a book about its venues which was published as *Dear Green Places*[3] (Molleson 2015). Historical legacy is obviously important. Glasgow has long been a going out place.[4] Between 1862 and 1914, eighteen major theatres were built in the city, mainly music halls (Lowndes 2010: 17). By 1946 Glasgow had ninety-three dance halls, about three times as many as London in terms of population size (Lowndes 2010: 27). More broadly, simply looking at where venues[5] in a city were, for example, thirty years ago and where they are now can reveal a great deal about a city's musical – and broader – life. A number of questions immediately arise: Which venues have survived? Which have closed? Why? Which are/were publicly owned and which private? How many were sole-purpose and how many mixed? And so on.

When reflecting on Glasgow's venues it is apparent that they are comprised of a mixture of those which have received large-scale public investment (such as the SEEC, the Hydro, Royal Concert Hall and the Candleriggs complex), overtly commercial enterprises such as the Academy and 02 ABC and a range of smaller, independent, venues. As I noted elsewhere: 'Glasgow's live music economy remains a complex mixture of public and private investment, with the overall impact of the public investment on the city's musicians hard to gauge' (Homan et al. 2015: 102).

The O2 ABC and Academy venues are refurbishments of two large cinemas. The 1,300 capacity ABC was opened in 2005 and is on the city's main thoroughfare, Sauciehall Street. It boasted Europe's largest mirror ball until it was damaged by fire in 2018. At the time of writing it is closed and its fate uncertain. The Academy is located on the city's south side and owned by the Academy Music Group. It opened in 2003 and has a capacity of 2,500. These venues also provide competition for the 2,000 capacity Barrowlands Ballroom, a much-loved former dance hall which is in the city's east end and was Glasgow's immortalized in the film *Trainspotting*.[6]

Perhaps the most famous small venue is King Tuts Wah Wah Hut, a 300 capacity venue which regularly appears in the list of top small venues in the UK and which, as noted, in 2018 was declared to be one of the best seventy venues in the world. It is certainly an important venue not only for Glasgow – where playing there for the first time is a landmark event for all aspiring musicians – but also for the UK where it is a key venue for emergent acts on tour. However, it also reveals the sometimes complex nature of local scenes as it is owned by DF Concerts, a Scottish formed company which since 2008 has been part-owned by the world's biggest concert promoter, Live Nation in conjunction with Ireland's biggest promoter, Gaiety Investments. Thus this important part of Glasgow's indie scene is partly owned by international investors.

A contrast to such investment has been a series of venues operated by local activist Craig Tannock. At the time of writing this comprised five venues: Mono, Stereo, the Old Hairdressers, the 78 and the Flying Duck. All are vegan and all offer a mixture of music and other events. Mono also includes a record store. Such places have long been important for scenes as musicians hang out and work in them (Anderson 2015) and this remains the case here. The nearby 13th Note venue is also vegan and an important small venue, started by Tannock in 1997. A more recent edition has been the Glad Café, a 120 on the south side of the city, which opened in 2012 and is a not-for-profit company. Another vegan venue, the Hug and Pint, is named after an Arab Strap album. Located in the city's West End, its capacity is around 100.

Such venues are a vital part of Glasgow's indie scene, offering a more homely feel than some of the city's larger venues. Their importance is not only as venues, but also as parts of scenes. They represent cool places for musicians and scenesters to hang out in, whether or not there is a gig on. Because one is always likely to bump in to local musicians and scenesters in such places, they help to create a feeling of actually *being* on a scene, of being *part* of something. They can also be contrasted to the city's larger indoor venues which are almost entirely functional. When attending gigs at the Hydro or SECC, I went as late as possible and left as soon as possible. These were *not* cool places to hang out, they were functional places where, thankfully, I get to see some of the world's biggest acts. In economic terms they represent economies of scale, as an act can reach the same audience in one night as they could in a week at the Barrowland.

To note such things is not to set up a simple small = good, versus big = bad dichotomy. Things are more complex than that and, as I have noted elsewhere, successful music cities need a combination of the big and small (Frith et al. 2009). Because it has bigger venues (including three large football stadiums) Glasgow can attract the world's biggest names and because of this when resident in the city I got to see acts such as Bob Dylan, Madonna, Bruce Springsteen, The Rolling Stones, Girls Aloud and Radiohead in my hometown. That was pretty good and reinforced a sense of Glasgow being a musically cool place to live, a feeling reinforced by the city's venues.

The context for *policy* is that '[n]owadays, citizens, tourists or city officials increasingly understand popular music as a booster of local pride and a motor of the local economy' (Bottà 2009: 349). Within Glasgow policy can be considered at various levels – UK, Scottish government and local authority. Scotland remains a 'stateless nation' within the UK and it is the UK government which has responsibility for a number of key areas affecting musicians, including broadcasting, immigration, copyright and unemployment benefits. These have tangible effects on the local scene, while also feeling distant from it. At the Scottish-level bodies such as Creative Scotland – the country's main public arts funder – and its main public economic agency, Scottish Enterprise, have had various creative industries policies and their actions obviously affected local scenes. For example, the fact that Creative Scotland had a recording budget was very important for local bands – and studios.[7]

During twenty years in Glasgow I was unaware of Glasgow City Council having a music policy per se. Instead there were a series of ad hoc initiatives which included having a Music Development Officer (Belcher 2000), but nothing as formal as plans made in places such as Sydney (City of Sydney 2013) or London (Greater London Authority 2015). Overall Glasgow can be characterized as being a city where public money – and particularly local authority money – for music was mainly spent on high-profile projects. So, there has been City Council funding for the annual Celtic Connections festival which takes place every January (from 1994) and longer running, summer, Jazz Festival (2017). However, most of the major funding has been via investing in large-scale venues, something which really began with the investment in the Scottish Exhibition and Conference Centre (SECC). This opened in 1985 and is now owned by a company which is wholly owned by the Council. Its establishment can be seen as part of a wider movement within Glasgow whereby public investment is often undertaken by Arms Length External Organisations (ALEOs, Williamson 2017). The SECC was superseded in 2013 by the SSE Hydro venue, also owned by the same company and built with a mixture of public and private funding. It cost £125m and holds around 13,000 for gigs. Its success is such that it claims to be the fourth busiest venue in the world in terms of people attending (https://en.wikipedia.org/wiki/SSE_Hydro). Justifying the public expenditure involved here was done not in musical terms, but in terms of the tourists it would attract (Homan et al. 2015: 97). Overall, the message here was that Glasgow was a cool place to visit and live in because it could attract the best acts in the world (Homan et al. 2015: 98). This has also long been a concern. Thus in 1990 Glasgow evidenced its credentials as a City of Culture by attracting gigs by both Pavarotti and Miles Davis (Homan et al. 2015: 96).

Another manifestation of public investment has been getting high-profile events to come to the city. This has included the Commonwealth Games in 2014 and the European Games in 2018. In music it has included attracting the Music of Black Origins (MOBO) Awards in 2009, 2011, 2013 and 2016 and the MTV Europe awards in 2014. It is hard to see such things as much more than branding exercises with any effect on the local scene, something of a trickle down via such things as temporary employment. However, while there has been major public investment in high-profile projects such as these, there has been no noticeable investment at the lower end for such things as for rehearsal spaces or venues. Overall, policy remains important for Glasgow's musicians and their scenes in ways which have yet to be systematically explored in any depth.[8] Its major importance within the city has been to provide major venues which sometimes provide musical employment but more often provide the city's musicians and scenesters spaces within which they can see their musical heroes – the importance of which should not be underestimated.

Conclusion

When examining any local scene, it is important that observers remain dispassionate and that simply celebratory accounts are avoided. Any local scene will contain the bad as well as the good. Only by recognizing the bad can improvements be made – thus the importance of mapping and policy to any scene. In the case of Glasgow, poverty is still endemic in parts of the city and divides remain. Personal experience has shown me that the local music scene also has its share with charlatans and rip off merchants. There is also a virtual monopoly in large-scale promotion, and it is difficult to put on bigger shows without working with parts of Live Nation such as DF Concerts and Ticketmaster.

More broadly, my experience has shown me that the term 'scene' remains useful, that understanding how a location works via mapping can provide great insights and that that policy is vital in ways which are not always easy to unpack. In all this live music remains at the core. *That* is what makes 'the Glasgow scene'. Take it away and there would be no scene. If a music scene wishes to live forever, then it must be forever live.

Notes

1 See www.zoeyvangoey.com
2 For full details see Webster *et al* 2017.
3 Glasgow is known as the Dear Green Place, a term derived from the ancient Cumbric language.
4 See, for example, Forsyth and Cloonan 2008 and Kielty and Tobin.
5 For more on the importance of venues see Kronenberg 2012.
6 For more see https://m.facebook.com/groups/502179203162207?__tn__=CH-R. For Glasgow's great 'lost' venue, the Apollo, see Forbes 2015.
7 For more see Homan et al. 2015.
8 For an exception see Eales 2017.

References

Ali, A. (2018), 'King Tuts Wah Wah Hut Named among Best Live Music Venues – In the WORLD', 30 October. Available online: www.eveningtimes.co.uk/news/17188084.king-tuts-wah-wah-hut-named-among-best-live-music-venues-in-the-world/.

Allen, D. (2017), *Autumn of Love: How the Swinging Sixties and the Counterculture Came to Portsmouth*, London: Moyhill.

Anderson, R. (2015), 'Strength in Numbers: A Social History of Glasgow's Popular Music Scene (1979–2009)', PhD diss., University of Glasgow, Glasgow.

Belcher, D. (2000), 'Rock the City's Foundations', *The Herald* 21 April. Available online: www.heraldscotland.com/news/12192232.rock-the-citys-foundations-david-belcher-meets-a-man-with-bright-ideas-for-glasgows-music-scene/

Bennett, A. and Peterson, R., eds (2004), *Music Scenes: Local, Translocal and Virtual*, Nashville: Vanderbuilt University Press.

Bottà, G. (2009), 'The City That Was Creative and Did Not Know: Manchester and Popular Music, 1976–97', *European Journal of Cultural* Studies, 12 (3): 349–65.

City of Sydney Live Music and Live Performance Taskforce (2013), *Live Music Matters: Planning for Live Music and Performance in Sydney*, Sydney: City of Sydney Live Music and Live Performance Taskforce.

Cloonan, M. (2011), 'Researching Live Music: Some Thoughts on Policy Implications', *International Journal of Cultural Policy*, 17 (4): 405–20.

Cloonan, M. (2014), 'Making Glasgow a City of Music – Some Ruminations on an UNESCO Award', in A. Barber-Kersovan, V. Kirchberg and R. Kuchar (eds), *Music City: Musical Approaches to the 'Creative City'*, 121–38, Bielefeld: Transcript.

Cloonan, M. (2015), 'Managing The Zoeys: Some Reminiscences', in N. Beech and C. Gilmore (eds), *Organising Music: Theory, Practice, Performance*, 226–35, Cambridge: Cambridge University Press.

Cohen, S. (1991), *Rock Culture in Liverpool*, Oxford: Oxford University Press.

Du Noyer, P. (2007), *Liverpool: Wondrous Place*, London: Virgin.

Eales, A. (2017), 'Bunting and Blues: A Critical History of Glasgow International Jazz Festival, 1987–2015', PhD diss., University of Glasgow, Glasgow.

Finnegan, R. (1989), *The Hidden Musicians: Music Making in an English Town*, Cambridge: Cambridge University Press.

Florida, R., Mellander, C. and Stolarick, K. 2010. 'Music Scenes to Music Clusters: The Economic Geography of Music in the US, 1970-2000', *Environment and Plannig*, 42: 785–804.

Forbes, K. (2015), 'You Had to Be There? Reflections on the "Legendary" Status of the Glasgow Apollo Theatre (1973-85)', PhD diss., University of Glasgow, Glasgow.

Forsyth, A. and Cloonan, M. (2008), 'Alco-Pop? The Use of Music in Glasgow Pubs', *Popular Music and Society*, 31 (1): 57–78.

Frith, S., Cloonan, M. and Williamson, J. (2009), 'On Music as a Creative Industry', in A. Pratt and P. Jeffcutt (eds), *Creativity and Innovation in the Cultural Economy*, 74–89, London: Routledge.

Frith, S. and Horne, A. (1987), *Art into Pop*, London: Methuen.

Gordon-Nesbiit, R. (2006), 'A Brief History of Cultural Policy in Glasgow'. Available online: https://shiftyparadigms.wordpress.com/policy/a-brief-history-of-cultural-policy-in-glasgow/

Greater London Authority (2015), *London's Grassroots Venues Rescue Plan*, London: GLA.

Hamilton, H. (2005), *Franz Ferdinand and the Pop Renaissance*, Richmond: Reynolds and Hearn.

Homan, S., Cloonan, M. and Cattermole, J. (2015), *Popular Music Industries and the State: Policy Notes*, London: Routledge.

Kielty, M. and Tobin, E. (2010), *Are Ye Dancin'?*, Edinburgh: Waverley Books.

Kronenberg, R. (2012), *Live Architecture: Popular Music Venues, Stages and Arenas*, Oxford: Routledge.

Lee, C.P. (2002), *Shake, Rattle and Rain: Popular Music Making in Manchester*, Kilkerran: Hardinge Simpole.

Lowndes, S. (2010), *Social Sculpture: The Rise of the Glasgow Art Scene*, Edinburgh: Luath Press.

Molleson, K., ed. (2015), *Dear Green Places: Glasgow's Music through Time and Buildings*, Glasgow: Waverley Books.

O'Connor, A. (2002), 'Local Scenes and Dangerous Crossroads: Punk and Theories of Cultural Hybridity', *Popular Music*, 21 (2): 225–35.

Phelan, S. (2010), 'Soundtrack to Glasgow', *Sydney Morning Herald*, 18 June, www.smh.com.au/travel/soundtrack-to-glasgow-20100618-ylzb.htm (accessed 15 may 2011).

Porter, H. (2004), 'Glasgow: A Scene Gets Heard', *Time*, 22 August 2004.

Shank, B. (1994), *Dissonant Identities: The Rock n Roll Scene in Austin, Texas*, Hanover, NH: University Press of New England.

Silver, D., Clark, T. and Rothfield, L. (2005), 'A Theory of Scenes'. Available online: http://scenes.uchicago.edu/theoryofscenes.pdf

Stahl, G., ed. (2014), *Poor, but Sexy: Reflections on Berlin Scenes*, London: Peter Lang.

Straw, W. (1997), 'Communities and Scenes in Popular Music', in K. Gelder and S. Thornton (eds), *The Subcultures Reader*, 494–505, London: Routledge.

Webster, E., Brennan, M., Behr, A., and Cloonan, M. (2018), *Valuing Live Music: The UK Live Music Census 2017 report*. Available online. http://uklivemusiccensus.org/wp-content/uploads/2018/03/UK-Live-Music-Census-2017-full-report.pdf

Williamson, J. (2017), 'Where Local Scene Meets Geopolitics: The Strange Case of Glasgow as UNESCO City of Music', Communicating Music Scenes conference, Budapest.

Williamson, J., Cloonan, M. and Frith, S. (2003), *Mapping the Music Industry in Scotland*, Glasgow: Scottish Enterprise.

15
Bedroom production

Emília Barna

Introduction

This chapter explores the bedroom as a space for listening to, creating and performing music. The bedroom will be understood as a social, cultural, technological, as well as psychological space – a space within which household relations, family relations, gender and generational relations are being shaped and played out; a space wherein meanings are generated and appropriated; a material and technological space that is open to other spaces – whether through analogue media technology such as radio, or digital and online technology, such as online music platforms; and psychological space, a material extension one's identity, a storage of one's memories and feelings, as well as a technology for evoking these. It can function as a space for rest, a space for leisure and play and a space for work, and it may contribute to the blurring of the boundaries between these. It may be private and shared, individualized and collective, often each of these at the same time.

It needs to be stated at the beginning that the existence of a separate, and more or less private, bedroom – as some, though not nearly all, of the literature on bedroom and music point out – whether for parents or children, is strongly tied to a middle-class material reality, and pertaining more to a nuclear family setup. As Sibley observes, '[h]aving one's own space is important in developing autonomy and this distinguishes the middle-class child who is part of a small family from one with many siblings or living in poverty' (Sibley cited in Davies 2010: 103). Nevertheless, discussions around music and the bedroom also involve music making in home studios set up in single room apartments and could – and should – be extended to bedrooms shared by siblings or multiple generations, rooms in student halls, working-class homes or domestic spaces of people living under poor housing conditions. For instance, Wilson (2011) provides an excellent example of examining the do-it-yourself 'wardrobe studio' – set up in a small apartment – hip-hop production practices of Sudanese refugees resettled in Australia, practices which draw on the refugees' past experience of being forced to use limited space and material resources in refugee camps in a resourceful manner.

The chapter proceeds by exploring, first, the bedroom as a space for listening to music for teenagers in particular, for whom the bedroom, if they have one, is the first space where they are able to exert control (Lincoln 2005: 400). The bedroom for them acts as both private and collective space for the creation and representation of identities, of participation in subcultural activities, even acts of resistance, through music. This section revisits McRobbie and Garber's (1976) classic study, where the bedroom is described as the central space for young women's 'teeny bopper' subculture, as well as reflecting on more recent research on young women's use of the bedroom for engaging in cultural consumption and the formation and representation of individual and collective identities, increasingly with the augmentation of digital and online technology (Baker 2004; Lincoln 2005; Davies 2010, 2013). Taking a critical view of 'teeny bopper' culture as passive consumer culture primarily centred around the adoration of (male) stars, it also demonstrates how consumption and production are often practically inseparable social and cultural activities, as exemplified by teenagers singing along to music, practising dance routines and creating their own mixtapes. I then proceed to explore the bedroom studio as a location for cultural production embedded into broader social and economic structures; as a meeting point of musical practices, technologies – old and new – and social relations. Through referring to relevant studies, I also reflect on the changing function of the bedroom studio within the structure of the music industries. I invoke literature exploring the bedroom as a site for creating and recording music for women in particular and consider the question of whether, and in what ways, accessible and affordable technology has resulted in a democratization of music making, and whether it has opened up a space for change of the patriarchal power relations of the music industries. The fourth section examines the question of access and use of resources, focusing on bedroom music making as a DIY (do-it-yourself) practice, and the significance of this in the context of underground and mainstream relations.

The bedroom as a space for listening to music: girls and subcultures – revisited

In 'Girls and subcultures' (McRobbie and Garber [1976] 1991), which first appears in *Resistance through Rituals* (Hall and Jefferson [1976] 1991), a collection dedicated to the work of the 'Sub-cultures Group' of the Birmingham Centre for Contemporary Cultural Studies, Angela McRobbie and Jenny Garber start out by asking the question of why girls are apparently invisible from contemporary accounts of post-war youth subcultures.[1] They 'find' the missing young women in the space of their bedrooms, similarly engaged in activities around music and fashion to their male contemporaries. As part of what the authors termed 'Teeny Bopper' (sub)culture, served in part by pop magazines, some of which are particularly marketed at teenage girls, these girls can perform music fandom and engage in 'a quasi-sexual ritual' (220), typically in relation to the adoration of a male star such as Donny Osmond, in a protected female environment free from male threat. Such activity 'require[s] only a bedroom and a record player and permission to invite friends'

(220), which certainly held significance in a world where spending time in public outside of the home, let alone in gangs in the streets, was still very much limited for young women, not only with regard to their safety but also due to the obligations of helping out with housework. The authors suggest that the relative marginality of girls within subcultures can be understood with reference to women's general position of 'structured secondarity' in capitalist society: 'They are "marginal" to work *because* they are central to the subordinate, complementary sphere of the *family*' (211; italics in original). This draws our attention to a crucial aspect in relation to the bedroom as domestic space: it needs to be viewed in the structural hierarchy, developed with industrial capitalism, of the public space of productive labour versus the private, or domestic, space of – invisible and unpaid – reproductive labour (Mies 1986: 100–10). This structural division has symbolically strengthened the association between masculinity and paid work on the one hand, and, on the other, femininity and work performed within the space of the home – such as housework, the bringing up of children, care work and emotional labour (cf. Barna 2021).[2]

Although not exclusively focusing on the space of the bedroom, Helen Davies' (2010, 2013) ethnographic research conducted with girls in their early teenage years (around twelve) in the UK resonates with McRobbie and Garber's study, while also significantly extending the scope and providing the rich empirical data still lacking at the time of McRobbie and Garber's writing. Sarah Baker (2004) similarly draws on ethnographic research conducted with seven young girls (eight to eleven years) in Adelaide, Australia, while Sian Lincoln (2005) examines teenage boys' bedrooms as musical spaces in addition to those of girls. Common to the three studies is an agreement that '[y]oung girls' musical practices are often trivialized in contemporary cultural criticism' (Baker 2004: 75), and that one of the reasons behind this is the methodological difficulties of accessing the space of the bedroom for academic fieldwork, resulting in little data so far in comparison with other cultural spaces.

All three accounts emphasize the way the relationship between teenagers and music is characterized by increasing technological control – from a radio in the bedroom to mobile phones – over their autonomous cultural consumption within the domestic space. In Davies' study, all of the girls had some kind of technology for listening to music – often multiple – available to them either in their own bedrooms or at least in their home, whether this was a CD player, radio, computer and speakers, iPod, television, DVD player or their smartphones. For 71 per cent of the girls filling out Davies' school questionnaire, 'the bedroom was the place where they listened to music most' (Davies 2010: 102), although those girls who did not have a bedroom of their own also used the space of the parked family car to listen to music in private. And more than merely listening, bedrooms also served as locations of informal music exchange, such as downloading songs and albums from Napster, burning CDs, collecting and swapping music with friends (Lincoln 2005: 410).

Both Davies and Lincoln observe how family relations are played out, and shaped by, musical practices: music is shared with parents and siblings, for instance, but playing music loud can also be used to mark space, and whose music is played aloud can become a site of power struggle. The use of technology – in particular online social media – also complicates the extent to which the space of the bedroom is private: 'The blurring of public and private spaces is central to an understanding of contemporary teenage bedroom culture as through technology young people are able to "dip" in and out of each sphere at the touch of a button' (Lincoln 2005: 409). Teenage girls, moreover, reach out into other spaces in the sense that they may be talking about the music in a night club while preparing to go out, as well as what they will wear (Lincoln 2005), and they can strategically choose the music that assists them in getting into the mood of a night out. All three authors discuss the way adolescent selves and (social) identities are constructed with the help of music, with reference to Tia DeNora's (2000) important work on music and everyday life (Lincoln 2005: 401). Young people create 'soundtracks' to their lives, play out romances, manage and communicate moods and act out potential selves by experimenting with recordings and their own singing voices (Baker 2004: 86). The bedroom itself, with its objects and spatial organization, functions as an extension of the self, as well as the location of biographical memories (Lincoln 2005: 411): the twelve-year-old girls in Davies' study were already remembering their past musical selves through referring to pop posters they used to have on their bedroom walls (2010: 66).

The bedroom is often directly a site of creativity for teenagers. Music at times served as 'merely' background to other activities and was employed as a tool for mood management – Lincoln (2004) theorises this as zoning and argues that this is a creative technique that proves that teenage girls are active agents in choosing cultural forms, as opposed to being passive consumers. Nevertheless, music was also often brought into the foreground through singing, mastering dance moves, recording compilations or learning lyrics. Davies draws on Paul Wills' anti-elitist conceptualization of creativity as

> … the extraordinary symbolic creativity of the multitude of ways in which young people use, humanize, decorate, and invest with meanings their common and immediate life spaces and social practices – personal styles and choices of clothes; selective and active use of music, TV, magazines; decoration of bedrooms; the rituals of romance and subcultural styles; the style, banter and drama of friendship groups; music-making and dance. (Willis 1990: 2, quoted in Davies 2010: 134)

The focus on musical creativity for teenage *girls* in particular subverts the understanding of female bedroom cultures as opposed to passive adoration and the preparation for domesticity, for a married life. Singing and dancing, in settings that varied among private, social, as well as performative, were central activities for the girls. The subjects in Davies's study also expressed their preference for female singers – directly contradicting the boy idol adoration scenario described by McRobbie and Garber – because they are easier to sing along to: 'I don't mind boy bands but I like girl bands better cos you can sing along. You can't sing along to a boy band' (2010: 142). The girls thus used recordings as part of a musical learning process as well as experimenting with performing personas. Baker emphasizes that the musical practices her subjects engaged in were complex, highly nuanced and involving serious investment of time and meaning.

In general, it may be stated that the bedroom is an important space for individual and, in some cases, social musical learning, whether through practising an instrument, with the help of recorded music or digital and online technology, and any combination of these. Online video streaming platforms, YouTube in particular, can be utilized by young people in the learning process not only for accessing tutorial videos, but also for uploading musical content of their own and inviting feedback.[3] As a different example, the relatively new social media platform TikTok (and its predecessor Musical.ly), hugely popular at the time of writing among teenagers in many countries, is optimized for the creation and sharing of short – typically fifteen-second – playful and creative music or dance videos. Play, of course, may contain the potential for subversion – in the words of Baker, '[t]he concept of serious play is particularly powerful in a discussion of pre-teen girls' musical cultures in that it opens up a space that disrupts 'official culture' (Schechner 1995) and inserts the 'player' sensuously into the processes of production' (Baker 2004: 83). To what extent this experimentation remains contained by the consumer culture catered to by the cultural industries, and thus the capitalistic order, remains to be addressed. Musical.ly, for instance, was used by numerous pop stars, including Selena Gomez, Ariana Grande and Shakira, to promote their new releases through inviting response videos from fans, and TikTok continues to serve similar purposes.

As a final point, the aspect of class – understood as class relation and position – is present in McRobbie and Garber's work, in line with the CCCS' dominant understanding of subcultures in general as symbolic expressions of a class conflict and a generational conflict. However, it is lost in the more recent studies mentioned above, or only present to an extent that the authors make brief, albeit important, references to the class backgrounds of their subjects: for instance, Davies discusses how the parked car becomes the most important private space for teenagers from lower-than-middle-class backgrounds who typically do not have a private bedroom to themselves, but more often share with siblings, nevertheless observes that 'age and gender seem more significant' than social class. Both Baker and Davies refer to Sibley, who 'states [that] the notion of having a space of one's own "distinguishes the middle-class child who is part of a small family from one with many siblings or living in poverty" (1995: 133)' (Baker 2004: 84; cf. Davies 2010: 103). Baker also draws attention to the complicated ways in which class positions are lived, interpreted and understood, and that even though all the girls in her study may be classified as middle-class, family situations complicated this position. It would be worth looking, in a socialization – or Pierre Bourdieu's (1977) *habitus* – framework, at the ways in which class is enacted, communicated or subverted through musical activities taking place in the bedroom.

The bedroom as music studio

Bedroom recording and the music industries

Besides serving as a space for musical socialization, expression and identity formation for young people, with the help of digital and online technology – often complementing analogue technology – the bedroom is also utilized by musicians today as a professional recording space. Groenningsaeter (2017: 24) differentiates between the bedroom studio, which literally integrates functions of musical creation and relaxation; and the home studio – a professional studio set up in one's home but typically in a separate room. The bedroom as studio can be considered as a logical extension of the space of musical (instrument) practice and composition.[4] Before the availability of computer-based digital recording technologies, home recording typically meant the demoing of songs (11). The personal computer then 'graduated from a recording medium to a tool that could encapsulate the process of writing, recording, and mixing a song' (12) and, it should be added, the releasing, sharing or distributing, as well as communicating about, songs.

The constraints of the home or bedroom studio production model are identified by Groenningsaeter as those related to the potentially inferior acoustic qualities of home recording, and a potential lack of the skillsets typically associated with professional producers. He observes that bedroom producing lends itself more to EDM (electric dance music) and other electronic or sample-based music genres, which do not necessarily require more than a computer and a set of speakers or headphones, but of course any genre of music may be produced at home with the augmentation of more complicated – and more expensive – technology. The notion of the electronic music 'producer as composer' (Moorefield 2005; quoted in Groenningsaeter 2017: 25), who typically works individually, without other musicians, is itself closely linked to bedroom studio production practices.

Groenningsaeter understands the bedroom recording studio as a space for 'creativity, collaboration and place of rest', occupying 'a precarious role between "professional space" and "hobbyist space"' (3). The home is partly perceived by musicians as a more relaxed environment for musical creation (Kaloterakis 2013; quoted in Groenningsaeter 2017: 21), for instance, because time does not appear to cost money there – at least, we may add, not directly. On the other hand, many musicians find that for the same reason they are able to remain more focused in a professional studio (Ibid 2017: 21). Home recording requires the musician to combine the roles, as well as skill- and mind-sets of an art, engineer, producer and studio designer (9), not to mention the rest of the functions that are often present but do not directly belong to production, such as (self-)management, distribution, sales or communication. It can be argued that the difficulty of juggling these roles may, on the other hand, be balanced by the benefits of, and power involved in, taking control of production. Yet, from a more critical perspective, the flexibility of the boundary between work and leisure carries with it the dangers of self-exploitation, especially given the deep-felt engagement typically associated with creative work, such as music making (Hesmondhalgh and Baker 2011: 221; Gavanas and Reitsamer 2016: 2–3). From a creative labour perspective (e.g. Hesmondhalgh and Baker 2011), it may be observed that this trend is part of a broader process, namely a post-Fordist shift in the dominant forms of production and labour, within which the boundaries between home space and work space, work and leisure become increasingly blurred. The changing structure of the music industries from this aspect involves the 'outsourcing' of particular functions and costs to individual artists. Record labels, as Wolfe reports, increasingly expect artists to arrive 'fully formed' (Morley 2011 in Wolfe 2012: 3), with not only polished material but a reliable social media following established through digital labour. In the UK, DIY (Do-It-Yourself) self-production and self-promotion from 'the proverbial bedroom' are actively promoted (Wolfe 2012: 3) in the capitalistic spirit of digital, platform-based entrepreneurialism.

Women and the bedroom studio

The fact that Virginia Woolf's (1977 [1929]) famous concept of 'a room of one's own' has served as a popular metaphor for female musicians' use of the bedroom as recording studio or a space for practice and composition (Wolfe 2012; Barna 2017a; Wolfe 2020), or even for young women's musical learning and socialization (Björck 2013), points to the importance of the argument that for women a space that guarantees – not just metaphorical – insulation from the competitive masculine domain of the music industry and its patriarchal social relations may be crucial in the pursuit of musical paths and establishing satisfactory careers in the music industry. The parallel underlines the necessity of access to resources, both material and symbolic – 'a woman must have money and a room of her own if she is to write fiction', wrote Woolf in 1929 (Woolf 1977: 7). As Paula Wolfe observes, '[e]arly responses to digital technology saw some scholars taking a celebratory stance to the opportunities new technologies presented previously marginalized artists to distribute their music and connect directly to their fans (see: Fox 2004 and McLeod 2005), and so arguably an increase in women's self-production practices, facilitated by digital technology, might equally be seen to form part of that discussion' (Wolfe 2012: 2–3). 'The desire', she writes, 'expressed by all the women in this study to create in a private space (all the participants have a home recording facility with [one] exception [...]) resonates with early observations from Woolf' (6). This desire, however, is not necessarily met by the realities of the position of women in domestic spaces.

The forces pushing women towards the space of the bedroom are definitely real. In my own research (Barna 2017a), I have looked at the relationship between digital technologies and the leading role played by women in the lo-fi bedroom pop music scene in Budapest, Hungary, emerging in 2011–12. I observed how some of these female lo-fi artists contrasted the comfortable and free space of the home with the live performance environment. In the latter, some of them felt 'clumsy', and some of them had to endure unnecessary comments or 'assistance' from technicians, offered without asking on the presumption that women are less competent with technology, including their own instruments. The musicians consequently attributed these alienating experiences in the live music environment to the masculine relations dominating the industry. The traditional recording studio may be discouraging for female artists in similar ways (Bayton 1988).

Examining the rock music world from a gender socialization perspective, Clawson found that the average age at which women joined their first band was significantly higher than for men, meaning that boys' first experience of playing in a band was typically in high school, while for women, typically after graduation from high school, in their college years (1999: 105–6), with '[t]he masculine composition of early rock bands seem[ing] an almost incidental by-product of the interaction between a sex-segregated social life and the particular means by which rock musicianship develops' (107). This difference in socialization arguably means that the knowledge and skillset that come as second nature to men by the time that a large proportion of female musicians enter the music world have to be acquired by women at this later age, resulting in a false perception that they are 'naturally' less inclined to be good with technology, and so forth. Within their own bedroom, women then are able to 'circumnavigat[e] potential intimidation' (Wolfe 2012: 9) before emerging as a polished artist in public.

In a related narrative, Tara Rodgers (2010), author of the volume *Pink Noises: Women on Electronic Music and Sound*, shares her own experience of setting up a home studio towards the end of the 1990s, and later the website *Pinknoises.com*, precisely in response to spaces of musical socialization such as music stores and online discussion forums being dominated by men who were overly confident about their own technical skills, but unhelpful towards new entrants to the scene (Rodgers 2010: 2–3). The bedroom, in contrast to the live music environment and the commercial studio, appears as a safer environment in female artists' accounts, where they are free to experiment and develop their own musical identities – their own 'sound' – while also making mistakes along the process. 'Self-production practices have enabled these artists to progress to the starting point of a career, afforded by a recognizable "sound" which, as Théberge notes, "carr(ies) the same commercial and aesthetic weight as the melody or the lyric in pop songs" (Théberge 1997:195)' (Wolfe 2012: 7).

Wolfe argues that access to recording technologies in their own homes enables women to resolve the tension of motherhood and working as a recording artist (10) – a tension that otherwise provides a potential hurdle for women in the industry (as on the labour market in general). Yet the home, it is important to remember, is much less a place of leisure for women than for men due to the unequal division of household labour still characterizing the majority of households. Women are still primarily responsible for reproductive labour, including care work and household chores, in most places over the world – as Jenkins puts it, 'for some, mostly men, the home is a place of leisure; for others, mostly women, it is a place of labor' (Jenkins 2013: 57). The optimism regarding the democratizing potentials of digital technology and the possibility to work from home is thus complicated by gender relations within the household. As I argue based on more recent research conducted among musicians in Hungary in 2018–19, the household can be understood as a pool of various informal resources that contribute to musicians' careers – material as well as emotional and creative. At the same time, it is also a gendered social space where these resources and labour are allocated and provided according in a hierarchical structure (Barna 2021). As the COVID-19 pandemic and associated restrictions have recently highlighted worldwide, women often struggle with double or triple burdens of (formal) productive, reproductive, as well as, often, informal productive work – in the case of musicians, having a non-musical 'day job' in addition to creative and domestic tasks would be typical. These different types of labour may all be performed within the space of the home – especially, but not only during the pandemic – and exist in tension with one another.

Instead of this tension between reproductive and creative labour being resolved for women, it is rather creative labourers in general, both men and women, that are 'housewifed' (Mies 2014: 221) in the post-Fordist economy. In other words, structural parallels may be drawn between feminized, freelance or self-employed low-status cultural workers – standing opposed to the masculine entrepreneur-artist with prestige – and the 'housewife trap' originally described by Betty Friedan (1963) in relation to women in the post-war United States. '[F]or increasing numbers of people,' writes Stephanie Taylor, 'both male and female, working for yourself amounts to exclusion to an almost subsistence level of economic activity on the margins of the neoliberal economy' (Taylor 2015: 174).

Bedroom recording as do-it-yourself practice

An important set of questions relating to the technologies enabling bedroom recording today relates to two early promises, in societal terms, of digital technologies and the internet from the perspective of music as culture and as an industry. Firstly, the promise of democratization of cultural production and consumption through the extension, in geographical as well as social terms, of access to cultural products and resources, the tools and means for creating and distributing musical products. The idea of blurring boundaries between cultural producers and consumers – often conceptualized as the emergence of 'prosumers' (Ritzer and Jurgenson 2010) – however, had been a long-time purpose and ideal of so-called DIY cultural movements, most prominently the punk movement, appearing in the latter half of the 1970s. In punk music, the elimination of the distance between the band and the audience through a specific and subversive use of live music space, and the symbolic elimination of cultural – and ultimately, social – distance through an insistence on the lack of musical education and professional skills, were clear ideological and aesthetic goals. The celebration of bedroom music production and the technology enabling it from an access perspective may be viewed as a continuation of this ideology.

Secondly, the promise of the decentralization of the oligopolistic structure of the recording industry that had stabilized in the 1960s and had been based on the economic dominance of major labels. In an article that on certain accounts may appear naively celebratory today, Smith and Maughan (1998) explored the role of digital recording technology within the early 1990s' electronic dance music scene in the post-Fordist economic shift. This, according to the authors, took place through the founding of a large number of independent microlabels catering to a variety of niche tastes, releasing records by young home producer-entrepreneurs. In a more recent study concerning a much smaller music world (Barna 2017b), I have described the Budapest bedroom pop or lo-fi music scene as a digital and online underground scene, partly relying on the traditions and ethos of DIY going back decades both internationally and locally. Locally, it echoes the socialist-era (art) punk and underground world, even if the artists themselves make no explicit reference to this heritage. Throughout the 1960s to the '80s, the space of the home was utilized by informal collectives as a counter-cultural space of listening to, and playing music along with engaging in other forms of art (e.g. Pál Petrigalla's circle; *Artpool.hu* 2003). In international terms, the 2010s lo-fi scene is continuous with the traditions of both punk and indie, the latter emerging as a movement as well as style in the 1980s' UK, itself rooted in the punk movement through centring the ethos and practice of independence (Bannister 49–52; Hesmondhalgh 1999: 35–6). The so-called lo-fi sound, partly associated with indie, is based on the marked sonic distinction from a polished 'hi-fi' quality, and the making audible of the lack of technical and musical (such as musical instrument or singing technique) competence through a dirty, noisy sound. Although different in actual technical realization from the practices of the 1980s, this aesthetic principle predominated the Budapest lo-fi scene too, primarily through the use of home digital recording and editing software. The space of creation, that is, the bedroom that is extended into a translocal space through online platforms for distribution and interaction can be viewed as an effective means for the use of available resources. Yet this goes beyond the affordability of technology. As we have already seen, such use of technology also enables the circumvention of more traditional industry paths that typically lead through spaces dominated by men.

Finally, early promises of the internet also included a kind of 'placelessness' – but as Michael John Wilson's (2011) case study illustrates, bedroom music making can be a way of reinforcing a sense of locality. The case study is an intriguing example of 'place-making' after an experience of 'displacement and dispossession' through transnational migration and resettlement (48). The means of place-making is DIY music making by a Sudanese hip-hop group, resettled in Australia, in a small bedroom, through the creation and use of a 'sound-booth' from one side of wardrobe. Wilson connects 'the resourceful and, in some respects, anti-aesthetic appropriation of a seemingly banal, everyday domestic space' (49), such as the bedroom turned into a recording studio in Australia, with the subjects' previous experience in the refugee camp, where a similar resourcefulness had been a direct material necessity. Like Davies in relation to teenage girls, Wilson also refers to Paul Willis' theory, in particular the 'necessary work' (Willis 1990: 9) of symbolic creativity that, in this case, provides ontological security for the refugees and control over their physical environment (50). 'For the young Sudanese participants', he argues, 'the symbolic work of producing and reproducing their bedroom-recording studio reaffirms their "powers of the self" (Willis 1990: 12), and provides a material platform from which to effect cultural change among Sudanese and other migrant youth' (Willis 1990). Wilson asserts that recording hip-hop in their bedroom studio and sharing their music worldwide with the help of social media, reaching overseas fans and fellow hip-hop artists in Australia, Canada, the United States, as well as Kenya and their home Sudan, provide these young men with a sense of purpose that is crucial, even life-saving, given a link between the idleness of refugees in their new locations after resettlement and suicide and violence.

Far from enabling music to become 'placeless,' the bedroom as a space for music making may therefore serve to create and strengthen new localities and identities, to connect places through cultural activities, to create new paths by subverting existing hierarchical structures. The home in which the bedroom is located is never a neutral space, but rather a complex, layered social space – it is gendered and social in many other ways. It is, as we have seen, also an economic space, the location of reproductive as well as productive labour. It is, finally, increasingly a site of production deeply integrated into the structure of the music industries and platform capitalism.

Notes

1. Along with Frith and McRobbie (1978), the contribution of McRobbie and Garber played an important role in beginning a discussion of the role of gender in music subcultures, and popular music cultures in general.
2. In a study relevant to this point, Keir Keightley (1996) explores the way hi-fi music technology and sound was used in the construction of the post-war American home as a gendered space; in particular the ways music technology and the hi-fi experience of listening were used by men – aided by marketing and the media – to (re)claim space within the home and reaffirm masculine identities.
3. In an intriguing article, Schaap and Berkers (2014) explore women's use of video streaming platforms for 'vocal covers' of metal songs, providing valuable insights with regard to music making, gender, genre and the use of online social media.
4. As an 'analogue' example of the latter, one might think of a young Lennon and McCartney famously sitting together and playing their guitars face to face in their Liverpool bedrooms to compose the first Beatles hits.

References

Artpool.hu (2003), 'A harmadik típusú hely archetípusa: A kulturális magántér. Vécsey utca 3. III. 8.', retrieved from http://www.artpool.hu/harmas/petrigalla.html.

Baker, S. L. (2004), 'Pop in(to) the Bedroom. Popular Music in Pre-teen Girls' bedroom culture', *Cultural Studies*, 7 (1): 75–93.

Bannister, M. (2006), *White Boys, White Noise: Masculinities and 1980s Indie Guitar Rock*, Aldershot and Burlington, VT: Ashgate.

Barna, E. (2017a), 'A Translocal Music Room of One's Own: Female Musicians within the Budapest Lo-Fi Music Scene', in E. Barna and T. Tófalvy (eds), *Made in Hungary: Studies in Popular Music*, 47–57, Abingdon and New York: Routledge.

Barna, E. (2017b), 'Változás és kontinuitás egy budapesti underground zenei világban a műfaj-esztétika, ízlés, technológia és alkotómunka viszonyrendszerén keresztül', *Társadalmi Nemek Tudománya Interdiszciplináris eFolyóirat*, 7 (1): 1–21.

Barna, E. (2021), 'Between Cultural Policies, Industry Structures, and the Household: A Feminist Perspective on Digitalization and Musical Careers in Hungary', *Popular Music and Society*, 44 (5): DOI: 10.1080/03007766.2021.1984022.

Bayton, M. (1988), 'How Women Become Musicians', in S. Frith and A. Goodwin (eds), *On Record, Rock, Pop and The Written Word*, 238–57, New York: Pantheon Books.

Björck, C. (2013), 'A Music Room of One's Own: Discursive Constructions of Girls-Only Spaces for Learning Popular Music', *Girlhood Studies*, 11 (3): 11–29.

Bourdieu, P. (1977), *Outline of a Theory of Practice*, Cambridge: Cambridge University Press.

Clawson, M. A. (1999), 'Masculinity and Skill Acquisition in the Adolescent Rock Band', *Popular Music*, 34 (1): 99–114.

Davies, H. (2010), 'Music in the Everyday Lives of Young Teenage Girls', PhD diss., University of Liverpool.

Davies, H. (2013), 'Never Mind the Generation Gap? Music Listening in the Everyday Lives of Young Teenage Girls and Their Parents', *Volume!*, 10 (1): 229–47.

DeNora, T. (2000), *Music in Everyday Life*, Cambridge: Cambridge University Press.

Frith, S. and McRobbie, A. (1978), 'Rock and Sexuality', *Screen Education* 29: 5–18.

Fonarow, W. (2006), *Empire of Dirt. The Aesthetics and Rituals of British Indie Music*, Middletown, CT: Wesleyan University Press.

Fox, M. (2004), 'E-Commerce Business Models for the Music Industry', *Popular Music and Society*, 27 (2): 201–20.

Friedan, B. (1963), *The Feminine Mystique*. New York: W. W. Norton & Company.

Gavanas, A. and Reitsamer, R. (2016), 'Neoliberal Working Conditions, Self-Promotion and DJ Trajectories: A Gendered Minefield', *PopScriptum 12: Sound, Sex und Sexismus*, retrieved from https://www2.hu-berlin.de/fpm/popscrip/themen/pst12/pst12_gavanas_reitsamer.html.

Groenningsaeter, A. K. (2017), 'Musical Bedroom: Models of Creative Collaboration in the Bedroom Recording Studio', MA diss., Creative Industries Faculty, Queensland University of Technology.

Hall, S. and Jefferson, T. ([1976] 1991), *Resistance through Rituals: Youth Subcultures in Post-War Britain*, New York: Harper Collins Academic.

Hesmondhalgh, D. (1999), 'Indie: The Institutional Politics and Aesthetics of a Popular Music Genre', *Cultural Studies*, 13 (1): 34–61.

Hesmondhalgh, D. and Baker, S. (2011), *Creative Labour: Media Work in Three Cultural Industries*, London and New York: Routledge.

Jenkins, H. (2013), *Textual Poachers: Television Fans and Participatory Culture*, Abingdon and New York: Routledge.

Kaloterakis, S. (2013), 'Creativity and Home Studios: An In-Depth Study of Recording Artists in Greece', *Journal on the Art of Record Production*, 8, retrieved from http://arpjournal.com/creativity-and-home-studios-an-in-depth-study-of-recording-artists-in-greece/.

Keightley, K. (1996), '"Turn It down!" She Shrieked: Gender, Domestic Space, and High Fidelity, 1948–59', *Popular Music*, 15 (2): 149–77.

Lincoln, S. (2004), 'Teenage Girls' Bedroom Culture: Codes versus Zones', in A. Bennett and K. Kahn-Harris (eds), *After Subculture: Critical Studies in Contemporary Youth Culture*, 94–106, London: Palgrave.

Lincoln, S. (2005), 'Feeling the Noise: Teenagers, Bedrooms and Music', *Leisure Studies*, 24 (4): 399–414.

McLeod, K. (2005), 'MP3s Are Killing Home Taping: The Rise of Internet Distribution and Its Challenge to The Major Label Music Monopoly', *Popular Music and Society*, 28 (4): 521–31.

McRobbie, A. and Garber, J. ([1976] 1991), 'Girls and Subcultures', in A. Gray, J. Campbell, M. Erickson, S. Hanson and H. Wood (eds), *CCCS Selected Working Papers Volume 2*, 219–29, Abingdon and New York: Routledge.

Mies, M. (1986), *Patriarchy and Accumulation on a World Scale. Women in the International Division of Labour*. London and New York: Zed Books.

Mies, M. (2014), 'Housewifisation – Globalisation – Subsistence Perspective', in M. Van Der Linden and K. H. Roth (eds), *Beyond Marx: Theorising the Labour Relations of the Twenty-First Century*, 209–37, Leiden and Boston: Brill.

Moorefield, V. (2005), *The Producer as Composer: Shaping the Sounds of Popular Music*, Cambridge, MA: MIT Press.

Morley, T. (2011), Public interview recorded by P. Wolfe at http://norwichartscentre.co.uk/norwich-sound-vision-conference-day/ Norwich, 1 October.

Ritzer, G. and Jurgenson, N. (2010), 'Production, Consumption, Prosumption: The Nature of Capitalism in the Age of the Digital "Prosumer"', *Journal of Consumer Culture*, 10 (1): 13–36.

Rodgers, T. (2010), *Pink Noises: Women on Electronic Music and Sound*, Durham and London: Duke University Press.

Schaap, J. and Berkers, P. (2014), 'Grunting Alone? Online Gender Inequality in Extreme Metal Music', *IASPM@Journal*, 4 (1): 101–16.

Schechner, R. (1995), *The Future of Ritual: Writings on Culture and Performance*, London: Routledge.

Sibley, D. (1995), 'Families and Domestic Routines: Constructing the Boundaries of Childhood', in S. Pile and N. Thrift (eds), *Mapping the Subject: Geographies of Cultural Transformation*, 123–37, London: Routledge.

Smith, R. and Maughan, T. (1998), 'Youth Culture and the Making of the Post-Fordist Economy: Dance Music in Contemporary Britain', *Journal of Youth Studies*, 1 (2): 211–28.

Taylor, S. (2015), 'A New Mystique? Working for Yourself in the Neoliberal Economy', *The Sociological Review*, 63 (1): 174–87.

Théberge, P. (1997), *Any Sound You Can Imagine: Making Music/Consuming Technology*, Middletown, CT: Wesleyan University Press.

Willis, P. (1990), *Common Culture: Symbolic Work at Play in the Everyday Cultures of the Young*, Milton Keynes: Open University Press.

Wilson, M. J. (2011), '"Making Space, Pushing Time": A Sudanese Hip-Hop Group and Their Wardrobe-recording Studio', *International Journal of Cultural Studies*, 15 (1): 47–64.

Wolfe, P. (2012), 'A Studio of One's Own: Music Production, Technology and Gender', *Journal of the Art of Record Production* 7, retrieved from http://arpjournal.com/a-studio-of-one%E2%80%99s-own-music-production-technology-and-gender/.

Wolfe, P. (2020), *Women in the Studio: Creativity, Control and Gender in Popular Music Production*, Abingdon and New York: Routledge.

Woolf, V. ([1929] 1977), *A Room of One's Own*, London: Grafton.

16

The studio

Ruth Dockwray

Mountain Studios in Montreux, Switzerland, was the location of a recent trip, where one can stand with the Freddie Mercury statue and visit the 'place' where a number of tracks from classic albums such as *Lodger* and *Black Tie White Noise* by David Bowie, *Going for the One* by Yes and *Jazz*, *A Kind of Magic*, *The Miracle* and *Innuendo* by Queen – just to name a few – were recorded. Although the actual recording studios are no longer functioning, a small section of Mountain studios, located in the Casino building, accommodates *Queen: The Studio Experience* – an exhibition of Queen memorabilia (which opened in 2013), which enables a glimpse into the 'place'/location where they spent time recording several of their albums. Visitors, or rather fans like myself, on a quasi-pilgrimage are able to immerse themselves in the recording environment and interact with a multi-track recording of 'Mother Love' and 'Let me Live'. The studio is arranged to allow full access to the channel faders in order to manipulate the balance of sounds during playback of the songs. The multi-sensory and immersive experience that is achieved is somewhat mythical and hauntological, relying on the historical significance of these places. Being able to visit and be situated in the recording studio (or studio recreation) offers an insight into the place which captured the social, creative and unique auditory aspects, which all combined to shape the music with which we are familiar.

Although a very simplified notion of a recording studio can be defined as a space or facility designed for sound recording, there are many other aspects worth considering in terms of the changing concept of the recording studio and its continual shifts of social and technological practices. With this in mind, the main focus of this chapter will consider the recording studio, primarily within a popular music context, in the following areas: as a physical place where its function relies on social interactions to encourage creativity, as a place where virtual auditory spaces are created and as a place where music practice can ultimately ascribe unique identities.

The recording studio, according to Zak can be regarded as 'any place where sound is captured or manipulated, and it is often staffed, and all duties performed, by one person' (2007). With this quote, Zak presents a current definition of a recording studio or rather the notion of a 'project studio', which presents the concept of *mobile production* that is not reliant on being produced within a building specifically designed for recording sound.

Most recording studios are places that have been purposefully altered to house recording equipment and various technologies. The rise of the recording industry in the 1960s, due to 'new equipment and techniques for manipulating and altering sound – led to the creation of a specialised studio environment optimised for recording' (Massey 2015: 1). The recording studios from that era are considered to be important and relevant, representing important technological and sociological developments from a culturally significant period in musical history. Key British recording studios include: Abbey Road, Decca, Lansdowne, Olympic, Trident, AIR, De Lane Lea, Wessex, Chalk Farm, Sarm, Townhouse and The Manor, to name a few. A few key US recording studios include: Chess (Chicago), Muscle Shoals (Alabama), Sunset (Los Angeles), Motown (Detroit), Electric Lady (New York), Sun Studio (Memphis) and Capitol (Los Angeles). These studios generally consisted of separate spaces including; the studio or 'live room' where the sound for the recording is created; the control room, which allows for sonic recording and manipulation; and the machine room – all of which are designed to ensure the acoustical properties of the room support clarity and accuracy when recording sound. Drawing on Kirby's work (2015), these *professional* recording studios will be referred to as 'traditional' studios, highlighting these types of independent facilities as reflecting 'the division of labour found in the corporate studios with strictly demarcated job roles, such as producers, engineers, maintenance staff and front of house staff' (2015: 6). These traditional recording studios are different to DAW (Digital Audio Workstation) methods of recording sound, of which both present some interesting notions of 'the recording studio' and 'place'. Before focussing on various recording studios and their functions, it is necessary to clarify what is meant by 'place' within this context.

Agnew provides a useful starting point as his concept of 'place' ultimately refers to a 'meaningful location' (1987). In deconstructing what pertains to a meaningful location, his tripartite definition identifies key aspects including; location, locale and sense of place. The application of Agnew's definition to recording studios is particularly useful as it provides a starting point from which to discuss how recording studios function and their development (and later, their demise). For this chapter, we refer to the recording studio as a 'place' within which virtual spaces (both actual and metaphorical spaces (see Moore 2012: 30) are created through the recording and manipulation of sound. Another definition provided by Gieryn is that 'place is space filled up by people, practices, objects, and representations' (2000: 463) and has 'physicality' (465).

Recording 'spaces', where the term 'space' is 'regarded largely as a dimension within which matter is located' (Agnew 2011), are more commonly discussed with a view to aligning themselves with sonic characteristics. As Augé (1995: 82) discusses, the term 'space' can be considered to be an abstract construct, referring to distance 'between two things or points' or to a 'temporal expanse'. In a recording aesthetic, it can refer to the type of space within which recording takes place (the actual space) and the space created that is audible within the recording (the virtual space). The virtual space within which sounds can be located will be discussed later on in this chapter.

Conversely, Paul Théberge's use of 'non-place' (2004) to describe non-traditional workplaces highlights the individual and isolated nature of the practices associated with home studios and the potential view of some recording spaces as being temporary and non-fixed. Drawing on Augé's possibility of 'non-place', described as 'a space which cannot be defined as relational, or historical, or concerned with identity' (Augé 1995: 77–8), the recording of sounds in de-characterized spaces, which can be understood as being everywhere but nowhere, offers an alternative to 'traditional' recording studios that are very much concerned with identity. Nelson further reiterates this point by noting that, 'the distributed space of the commercial recording studio... acts as a sort of non-place, its artificially constructed resonances and reverberations producing the outward semblance of a place that does not correspond to any actual circumstance' (2015: 328). In the context of mobile production, aided by DAW and laptop computers, it is potentially worth describing this creative process as being 'de-spaced' rather than 'non-place'.

'Non-places' where sound recording has taken place may allude to one or more parts of Agnew's definition of 'place' (such as location), however, it seems that identifying a 'sense of place' is what distinguishes traditional recording studios from mobile production and their 'non-space' or 'de-spaced' mode. Through a deconstruction of Agnew's definition, it is possible to comprehend 'traditional' recording studios as 'place'. Firstly, location: this can refer to the position of the studio in terms of the permanency of the space's function and the architectural form of the 'concrete' space to utilize Lefebvre's (1991) term. Secondly, locale: this develops on from the place or position to include the setting – whether the studio is isolated in a countryside setting or city-based. Finally, a sense of place. This suggests that a personal and emotional attachment exists. For numerous musicians, specific traditional recording studios offer a distinctive character and sounds that create a unique identity. In many ways, this is due to aspects such as the architecture, the technology equipment or simply the historical significance of the place, which is reliant on past social and musical events. Augé explains that 'the space of non-place creates neither singular identity nor relations; only solitude, and similitude' (103) and therefore highlights the mobile production or post-digital studio as being devoid of any attachment that may be responsible for creating identity.

Functions of recording studios

Regardless of location, the function of the recording studio is to facilitate the capturing and manipulation of sound, and to create recordings which can be considered 'as sonic interventions in social space' (Wallach 2003: 46). Recording studios can be identified according to their key personnel (recording and maintenance engineers), physical features (including acoustic treatments) and key equipment (including mix consoles, monitors, microphones and outboard signal processors). Bates (2012) refers to recording studios as 'container technologies' within which he details the key functions, of which the following seem to be the most pertinent: affecting and effecting sound during tracking and mixing; isolating workers from the outside world; cultivating new practices and shaping social interactions. The social aspect of the *space* within recording studios presents an interesting perspective into the creative and collaborative nature of the recording process.

Historically, the recording process has been collaborative and relied upon the contribution and work of a number of personnel; the artist/ band, engineers, arrangers, producers and additional musicians. This team of personnel also recognized as a 'creative collective' work together to create a recording that is a product of 'a continuous exchange of views between the various members of the team, and the result is a fusion between musical objects and the needs of the public' (Hennion 1983: 161). More recently, however, the collaborative nature of the recording process has somewhat diminished and key roles in the recording process, such as defining what a producer is and does, have altered. Howlett's paper discusses the record producer as a 'nexus' acting 'as a means of connection between the artist, the technology and the commercial interest' (2012). Described as being someone who 'facilitates the creative process' (Burgess 2002: 81–2) to 'acting as a therapist in some way' (52), the producer is ultimately viewed as being able to steer the recording process to a successful outcome. The means by which this may occur, could see the producer take on other various roles such as arranger, engineer, creative director, project manager, psychologist and mediator (Howlett 2012). This has certainly influenced and impacted on project studios and DAW-based producers whereby most roles are assumed by one person.

Thompson and Lashua (2016) provide a detailed account of the myths of creative practices within recording studios. In their paper, they detail 'how mythic representations of studios often overlook or diminish the more mundane processes of music production and how these myths influenced some of the musicians' technical expectations of recording studio processes' (2016: 72). Indeed, the mythic beliefs that surround the studio's creative practices highlight some interesting discourses from both social and psychological perspectives, as outlined by McIntyre (2008). An example of types of constructed myths includes those regarding Abbey Road, which has been described as 'magical' (Bennett 2016: 414). Bates (2012) notes that 'Abbey Road never lost its surrounding mythology and in 2010 was granted English Heritage Grade II status' for its impact on British music, despite having undergone significant changes to the design and set-up of the rooms., despite having undergone significant changes to the design and set-up of the rooms. Indeed, Bennett's close examination of Abbey Road's mythological status highlights 'Notions of "magic" and sonic "alchemy", as well as ongoing religious analogy, pepper the marketing discourse' further noting that 'the intangible Abbey Road aura has become a lucrative commodity in its own right' (2016: 414). This notion of *aura* is an important consideration related to studio myths and will be discussed later on in this chapter. Another example of recording studio myth is one depicted in the film 'Bohemian Rhapsody' (2018) where scenes reconstruct the creative practices that developed songs such as 'We Will Rock You'. Whether accurate or not, these visual reconstructions emphasize the collective force of the group and spontaneous constructions of ideas that have taken place within the recording studio.

The recording context within which this collaborative process occurs is also important. In Hecker's examination of pianist Glenn Gould's studio practice, he summarizes the studio as 'a physical space, a field of social relations and a frame of musical consciousness, one that encourages aesthetic experimentation while providing the possibility of a life of solitude' (2008: 78). This definition provides an interesting dichotomy in terms of the recognized and often discussed social activity involved in studio practice and the solitude of DAW-based producers/musicians. What is more important, perhaps is the use of the term 'space' and the potential interaction between the studio as a creative tool and the musician/producer. There are a number of studios, however, that due to their *locale,* offer the musicians a place to work without distraction and isolated from potential distractions. Recording studios located in the countryside, removed from city locations, enabled a more focused place within which to work. Similarly, Zak notes that 'studios and ambient chambers contribute a particularity of place' (2001: 101) and gives the example of U2's use of an Irish castle for recording locations as being an important and influential environment for the creative process.

With studios therefore being seen as places for capturing sound, it is necessary to understand specific recording studios as being attractive in terms of their architectural qualities and technological set-up.

Technological set

Musicians (including engineers and producers) have chosen to record in a specific studio due to what they afford in terms of tangible and non-tangible qualities. The recording studio can be seen to be a keeper of a plethora of recording technology and perform an important role in the development of new sounds and ultimately new musical identities, whether generically or socially situated. The studio environment and the technologies utilized during the recording process, such as the types of microphones employed, dynamic treatments, equalization, are an important consideration for the creation of recordings.

As Horning (2002: 344 cited in Kirby 2015: 5) notes the 'development of the recording studio is an example of technological determinism, but of course mitigated by user choice, ingenuity and human aims'. This reaffirms the necessity of the studio to continually develop in order to continually attract new creative partnerships. In the late-fifties, Philips Studios, for example, was equipped with Philips Pro 75 (4-track) and Pro 50 (2-track and mono) tape machines, which were replaced in 1968 with an Ampex 9-track machine, later followed the Ampex 16-track and 24-track machines, which were later replaced by Studer A80 24-track models. Similarly, Abbey Road studios replaced the EMI BTR2 (mono) tape recorders and Studer J37 (4-track) recorders with the Studer A80 (see Massey 2015). Both studios illustrate the need to ensure that the latest technology is available and to be aware of key technological changes, such as the developments from mono to stereo recording. Trident for example, was one of the first 'operational 16-track studio in the UK, when an M56 was installed in 1969' (Massey 2015: 186). The commitment to replacing old technology and offering a very different 'place' to be creative was very much at the centre of the way studios such as Trident operated and identified themselves.

Despite the financial cost to studios, keeping up with current trends was one way of ensuring that it attracted key artists to its facilities. However, this was not to last as 'significant disruptive changes to the business models of both record labels and professional studios occurred in the twenty-first century due to the impact of digitization (Kirby 2015: 302) and many of the large-scale studios were closed. As Kirby (2015: 366) notes 'despite the closures of many large facilities, studios haven't died out, but they have evolved and in fact proliferated. The large-scale studio still has a role in the contemporary recording industry but is no longer the locus of the bulk of music recording and production'. Indeed, many recording facilities now utilize much smaller consoles such as the SSL XL-Desk or the SSL Matrix and this feeds into more efficient recording practices, impacting on the studio time required, which ultimately reduces the financial cost.

Of those 'traditional' recording studios that are still functioning as recording facilities, many conjure up notions of being places that hoard collections of various vintage and earlier recording technologies. There is a trend in certain recording contexts, such as professional studios, home studios and project studios, where 'facilities appear to be using their precursors and vintage systems as marketing tools'. The proliferation of the 'places' with vintage equipment seems to be tapping into the notion of 'technostalgia' (Bennett 2012). While this is not just simply a matter of nostalgia, vintage technologies afford the artists and producer to realize 'musical and recording aesthetic intention on the part of the musicians and recordist(s), sonic characteristics of chosen technologies' (Bennett 2012) and also feed into the cultural value and 'technological iconicity' (Bennett 2012). An example of this is Jack White's 2014 album *Lazaretto*, which was recorded utilizing two Studer A800 two-inch machines (Tingen 2014). For White, using analogue is the medium with which he achieves the desired sound and vibe for his work.

The identity of, or use of, vintage technologies as a marketing technique, offers a way of differentiating those recording facilities that rely on achieving a particular sonic aesthetic and to those that are representative of the standardized hardware set-up within the interior spaces of recording studios. Studios offering recording artists the opportunity to employ vintage equipment are utilizing the mythology surrounding such iconic systems and as a result, are able to attract musicians and producers. In addition to Jack White's studio 'Third Man Studios', which provided the recording location for his analogue-based albums, another example of a studio is 'The Kitchen Writing Studio', which is identified as a 'West London recording studio for writing, over-dubbing, editing, vocal recording and programming' (The Kitchen website 2018). It draws on the vintage technology aspect in its marketing noting that it is 'fitted out with an excellent Pro Tools rig and a comprehensive list of classic outboard gear, vintage guitars and amplifiers, as well as virtual instruments, the room offers a fantastic experience for a large range of projects'. The location and locale are also important as it also highlights on its website that 'The studio is based in the vibrant Stanley House, which is where Hugh Padgham's beautiful SSL recording and mix studio, Sofa Sound is based', ensuring that Padgham's name is mentioned, which alludes to associations as having worked as a producer with key artists such as Kate Bush, Genesis, David Bowie, Paul McCartney and Elton John, just to name a few. Padgham is perhaps a useful example that highlights the fact that 'places may be thought of as open articulations of connections' and 'identities of subjects and identities of places constructed through interrelations not only challenge notions of past authenticities but also hold open the possibility of change in the future' (Massey 1999: 288). A sense of place can therefore be created by way of association and the creative practices that have taken place, enabling a historical identity to enhance the sense of place, which is clearly important for artists and may enhance creativity.

While some musicians are owners of their own studios, many artists have built their own home studios, possibly as a consequence of the need for a sense of place. Additionally, building a studio within your own living space, or in a chosen location, provides an element of control, convenience, within a location already known. In this sense, the *locale* provides a necessary comfort within which to work and undertake creative practice. Returning to Mountain Studios in Montreux, it is possibly this reason of a sense of place, as a sense of home or specific *locale*, that Queen resided there while recording their albums. It provided a sanctuary for the final recording sessions of Queen and as such, the legacy of the recording studio is constructed on a combination of aspects such as the collective creative process of the band, significance of the album as a finale and the location that provided inspiration for a number of tracks and the setting for the album cover. Similarly, Peter Gabriel's 'Real World Studios' for example, is identified on its website as being 'embraced in its breathtaking natural environment, Real World inspires creativity. Conceived by Peter Gabriel as both a paragon of technical excellence and an idyllic artistic retreat' (Real World Studios, 2018). As a professional 'traditional' studio, the association with Gabriel is attractive for those wishing for creative inspiration through association with his output of work.

There are indeed financial and artistic advantages to building your own studio such as affording the musicians space for experimentation with no time constraints. Related to this is the 'project studio', which is 'essentially a home studio that takes in commercial work and often consists of little more than a well-equipped control room and perhaps a small booth for recording single instruments or vocals… ' (Théberge 2012: 84). Perhaps the most popular type of studio, running a 'project studio' on a commercial basis became a viable business model for many and with the rise of digital software, the accessibility and affordability of technology impacted its rise, while ultimately affecting the number of professional 'traditional' studios. However, what they are more associated with is the notion of 'non-place' and less with the sense of place and myths attached to the traditional studio.

Virtual spaces

Recording studios offer the means for aural construction, a place that facilitates the creation of virtual spaces. These virtual spaces never existed in a reality and were created for the track – with track referring to the song that is captured on a medium (see Moore 2012: 15). The way in which sounds are heard can be understood as occupying locations within a sound-box. The sound-box can be understood as a four-dimensional heuristic device within which sounds can be located according to laterality, frequency, depth and across time (Dockwray and Moore 2010). Indeed, the listener experiences captured sounds in terms of the actual auditory space created if listening through speakers and a metaphorical space if receiving the recording via headphones (Moore 2012: 30).

Recording studios, particularly where popular music production is concerned, represent a place where 'electrosonic aesthetics' are constructed and ultimately manipulated (Jones 1992; Théberge 1997; Zak 2001). As Wallach points out, studio technologies and techno-cultural practices manifest sonic materiality of which their properties 'have come under conscious control by music producers and employed as compositional strategies' (2003: 15). So, the artificial nature of the 'space' means that the 'place' is not related to any real or actual.

Eno, in his work 'Studio as a compositional tool' is concerned with key themes including 'space and materiality' and 'in-studio composition' (Albiez and Dockwray 2016: 148). He discusses recording music as a process of removing the sounds from a time dimension to a space dimension and constructing a sense of space through the creation of a virtual sonic environment. Moreover, it is the removal of the sounds from any geographical location 'and ambience and locale in which it was made' so that it can be 'transposed into any situation' that interests Eno. Again, this is related to the concept of 'non-place' and the idea of 'any-space'. The various creative and recording practices of constructing a recording in the studio, where any aesthetic associations with that 'place' are removed, emphasize 'the view that the studio' as a 'non-place' that affords the composer/arranger/musician/producer another perspective on the use of the studio.

Conversely, the importance of the studio as a *place* within which the *art* of music recording took place, emphasizes its historical importance as a place with a very specific function. Sterne highlights this point effectively;

> The studio was a necessary framing device for the performance of both the performer and apparatus: the room isolated the performer from the outside world, while crude soundproofing and physical separation optimized the room to the needs of the tympanic machine...
>
> (2003: 306).

Kun (2005) offers another perspective through 'audiotopias', described as the spaces 'within and produced by a musical element that offers the listener and/or musician new maps for re-imagining the present social world' (22–3). With this interdisciplinary approach, this allows the listener to consider the social, cultural and racial elements within recordings and challenges understandings of the recordings that have been created. Moreover, it considers itself within places identifying location (geographical) and the social production of space(s).

Identities of recording studio

The significance of audiotopias and the associated creative practices that occur within studios are important considerations when ascribing identities to studios. Nelson (2015: 2) discusses Lefebvre's work within a context that is linked to social practices and highlights the awareness 'that space is intimately connected to its inhabitants in ways that deeply affect our possible understanding of music and sound'. Lefebvre states that, 'Physical space has no "reality" without the energy that is deployed within it' (Lefebvre 1991: 13). The space, therefore, within which sounds is captured embeds a sense of both the place and the music makers; a soundscape is where 'a set of sonic-spatial practices, the metadiscourses that describe them, and the conditions of possibility for experiencing that space' occur simultaneously (Sterne 2015: 80). This virtual performance space or soundscape is better presented as what Sterne refers to as a 'stable audioposition' from which numerous sonic possibilities can be heard (2015: 79).

Indeed, it is not just the technologies that afford the music makers and producers to create these virtual performance spaces. The recording space, or rather the interior of the recording studios, can also influence the sonic qualities heard in the recordings. Mowitt's notion of 'the space is the grain' (Mowitt cited in Sterne 2015: 79) identifies the importance of the 'container' within which recording practices take place.

Zak discusses the principles of sound and the affect that architectural elements of recording studios and 'places' has on recorded sound, giving it an 'aesthetic dimension' (2001: 97). Room acoustics can offer a unique sonic property to the recorded sound and it is these sonic *identities* that can make certain recording studios attractive to musicians and producers. As Nelson explains, a recording studio,

> may be identified acoustically by its so-called impulse response: its moderation of a single sound containing, theoretically, an equal portion of every frequency. This impulse response can indeed be recorded, and used to print the qualities of that place onto other sounds. Thus space gets itself embedded in sound and music, not only through the experience of a particular place but also through the impact of that place on the sounds that inhabit it.
>
> (2015: 6)

Studios are both place-*specific* and *non-specific* places and various discourses surrounding the importance of space and place, with specific reference to notions and myths of space, are central to understanding the recording studio as place. Indeed, these myths can attract certain artists and producers to seek out a specific place to record, due to a combination of its acoustic properties and its association with previous artists, producers and albums. The unique identity of a particular recording studio affords many artists much needed inspiration for creative practice. This identity ascribed to particular recording studios can arguably be constructed around a combination of 'heritage, branding and aura' (Bennett 2016: 398).

The notion of aura is an interesting concept and can be linked to the architectural and acoustic properties that affect sound in a variety of ways in addition to the mythical, historical and hauntological associations, as previously mentioned. These 'places' may even be associated with a particular sound or as Bates points out they have 'a vibe' (2012). In this sense, studios can be considered as unique places, with aspects of *location*, *locale* and *sense of place* all influencing the way studios are presented and branded. Indeed, the 'vibe' and 'feel' of a recording studio can also account for those elements that attract many to record in that location.

Conclusion

The proliferation of commercial recording studios or 'non-spaces' continues to provide a way of creating virtual spaces that are experienced through listening to the recordings, however, what they lack is the social histories and the embedding of the 'impulse responses' and qualities of that space.

'One could say that sound recording has allowed the trading of space; as the acquisition and sharing of: actual locations, both current and historical; ambiences; social spheres, and constructed non-places' (Nelson 2015: 8). Regarding the studio as 'place' reinforces the associated ideologies of commercial processes, heritage and identities that make them attractive and sought after by creative music makers.

References

Agnew, J. A. (1987), *Place and Politics: The Geographical Mediation of State and Society.* London: Allen and Unwin.

Agnew, J. (2011), 'Space and Place', in J. Agnew and D. Livingstone (eds), *Handbook of Geographical Knowledge*, 316–30, London: Sage.

Albiez, S. and Dockwray, R. (2016), 'Before and after Eno: Situating the Recording Studio as Compositional Tool', in S. Albiez and D. Pattie (eds), *Brian Eno: Oblique Music*, 139–73, London: Bloomsbury.

Augé, M. (1995), *Non-Places: Introduction to an Anthropology of Supermodernity*, trans. John Howe, New York: Verso.

Bates, E. (2012), 'What Studios Do', *Journal on the Art of Record Production.* Available online: http://www.arpjournal.com/asarpwp/what-studios-do/ (accessed 5 November 2018).

Bennett, S. (2012), 'Endless Analogue: Situating Vintage Technologies in the Contemporary Recording & Production Workplace', *Journal on the Art of Record Production* [online] Available at: http://arpjournal.com/2199/what-studios-do/ (Accessed 5 November 2018).

Bennett, S. (2016), 'Behind the Magical Mystery Door: History, Mythology and the Aura of Abbey Road Studios', *Popular Music*, 35 (3): 396–417.

Bohemian Rhapsody (2018), [Film] Dir. Bryan Singer, UK: 20th Century Fox.

Burgess, R.J. (2002), *The Art of Music Production*, London: Omnibus Press.

Dockwray, R. and Moore, A.F. (2010), 'Configuring the Sound-box 1965–72', *Popular Music*, 29 (2): 181–97.

Gieryn, T.F. (2000), 'A Space for Place in Sociology', *Annual Review of Sociology*, 26: 463–96.

Hecker, T. (2008), 'Glenn Gould, the Vanishing Performer and the Ambivalence of the Studio', *Leonardo Music Journal*, 18: 77–83.

Hennion, A. (1983), 'The Production of success: An anti-musicology of the pop song', *Popular Music*, 3: 159–93.

Horning, S. (2002), 'Chasing Sound: The Culture and Technology of Recording Studios in America, 1877–1977', PhD, Cape Western University.

Howlett, M. (2012), 'The Producer as Nexus', *Journal on the Art of Record Production*. Available online: http://www.arpjournal.com/asarpwp/the-record-producer-as-nexus/ (accessed 9 November 2018).

'Introducing Kitchen Studios'. https://milocostudios.com/2014/01/introducingthe-kitchen-in-partnership-with-paul-draper/ (accessed 8 November 2018).

Jones, S. (1992), *Rock Formation: Music, Technology, and Mass Communication*, Newbury Park, CA: Sage.

Kirby, P. R. (2015), *The Evolution and Decline of the Traditional Recording Studio*, PhD Thesis, University of Liverpool.

Kun, J. (2005), *Audiotopia: Music, Race and America*, Berkeley: University of California Press.

Lefebvre, H. (1991), *The Production of Space*, Oxford: Blackwell.

Massey, D. (1999), *Power-Geometries and the Politics of Space-Time*, Hettner Lecture 1998. Heidelberg: University of Heidelberg, Institute of Geography.

Massey, H. (2015), *The Great British Recording Studios*, Milwaukee: Hal Leonard.

McIntyre, P. (2008), 'Creativity and Cultural Production: A Study of Contemporary Western Popular Music Songwriting', *Creativity Research Journal*, 20 (1): 40–52.

Moore, A.F. (2012), *Song Means: Analysing and Interpreting Recorded Popular Song*, Surrey: Ashgate.

Nelson, P. (2015), 'The Materiality of Space', *Organised Sound*, 20 (3): 323–30.

Sterne, J. (2003), *Audible Past: Cultural Origins of Sound Reproduction*, Durham, NC: Duke University Press.

Sterne, J. (2015), 'The Stereophonic Space of Soundscape', in P. Théberge, K. Devine, and T. Everett (eds), *Living Stereo: Histories and Cultures of Multichannel Sound*, 65–83, New York: Continuum.

Théberge, P. (1997), *Any Sound You Can Imagine: Making Music/Consuming Technology*, Hanover, NH: Wesleyan University Press.

Théberge, P. (2004), 'The Network Studio: Historical and Technological Paths to a New Ideal in Music Making', *Social Studies of Science*, 34 (5), 759–81.

Théberge, P. (2012), 'The End of the World as We Know it: The Changing World of the Studio in the Age of the Internet', in S. Zagorski-Thomas, K. Isakoff, S. Lacasse, and S. Stévance (eds), *The Art of Record Production: An Introductory Reader for a New Academic Field*. ProQuest Ebook Central. https://ebookcentral.proquest.com

Thompson, P.A. and Lashua, B.D. (2016), 'Producing Music, Producing Myth? Creativity in Recording Studios', *IASPM@Journal*, 6 (2): 70–90.

Tingen, P. (2014), 'Inside Track: Jack White: Secrets of the Mix Engineers: Jack White, Vance Powell and Joshua V Smith, in *Sound on Sound*. Available online: https://www.soundonsound.com/techniques/inside-track-jack-white. (accessed 11 October 2021).

Wallach, J. (2003), 'The Poetics of Electrosonic Presence: Recorded Music and the Materiality of Sound', *Journal of Popular Music Studies*, 15: 34–64.

Zak, A. (2001), *The Poetics of Rock: Cutting Tracks, Making Records*, Berkeley: University of California Press.

Zak, A. (2007), 'Recording Studio as Space/Place', ARP online Issue 01. Available online: http://www.arpjournal.com/asarpwp/recording-studio-as-spaceplace/ (accessed 12 November 2018).

Discography

Lodger, David Bowie. (1979) RCA BOW K1
Black Tie White Noise, David Bowie. (1993) Arista, BMG International, Savage Records DB002
Going for the One, Yes. (1977) Atlantic K 50379
Jazz, Queen. (1978) EMI EMA 788, 0C 064-61820
A Kind of Magic, Queen. (1986) EMI CDP 7 46267 2
The Miracle, Queen (1989) Parlophone PCSD 107
Innuendo, Queen (1991) Parlophone CDP 79 5887 2

17

The virtual studio

Martin K. Koszolko

The term 'virtual studio' encompasses a range of online solutions for recording and producing music in the cloud, commonly in the context of remote music collaboration. The area of music production in virtual settings has undergone a phase of unprecedented growth in recent years. Capitalizing on previous developments in the field of networked music collaboration, contemporary 'remote music collaboration software' (RMCS) enables interaction between global communities of musicians. The development of Web 2.0 combined with the emergence of innovative software platforms has opened new avenues for virtual collaboration as well as crowdsourcing (Koszolko 2015) of musical input and collective work in the cloud.

My research on virtual studio-based music production is grounded in my own creative practice. I have participated in remote music collaborations on multiple musical compositions with over forty participants located in various geographical locations on three continents: Europe, North America and Australia. In my work, I have extensively used platforms such as Audiotool, BandLab, Blend, Ohm Studio and SonoBus, each facilitating virtual music production in different ways.

The virtual studio platforms often incorporate several Internet technologies, such as World Wide Web, Transmission Control Protocol/Internet Protocol, HyperText Transfer Protocol and server-based data storage. In the case of Ohm Studio, a custom made, real-time online collaboration framework called Flip is also used. Central to the idea of music creation in the cloud is what Théberge refers to as the 'Network Studio', which 'extends and enhances the technical infrastructure of the "studio-as-node" by allowing for greater levels of coordination and connectivity, and at increased speed' (2004: 776).

For the purpose of defining the boundaries of RMCS-based work, it is important to distinguish between Internet-based music production and live performances over a computer network. The problem of latency is inherent to sending audio data via the Internet, and typically, virtual studio platforms should not be seen as facilitating or attempting real-time music performance (Guensche 2007). However, a growing number of contemporary virtual studio RMCS solutions enable synchronous collaboration which allows for the actions of project participants to be manifested in front of their collaborators with only a small time delay. However, the idea of jamming live over a computer network is not part of the design objectives of most virtual studio software.

A brief history of early, networked music

Early online collaborators utilized large and slow computers over the first networks that preceded what is now known as the Internet. The origin of web-based musical collaboration can be traced to a group of musicians called The League of Automatic Music Composers, operating in the San Francisco Bay Area between 1978 and 1983. Members of this group played interactively by allowing musical algorithms written for one computer to influence the output of other computers, connected via network during live performances. In 1986 some of the composers involved in the League formed The Hub, which operated until 1997. This group was responsible for conducting the first performance where two venues in New York were networked and could exchange data by using modems and a phone line. Even though the data bandwidth was very limited by today's standards, that first performance was considered a success and launched a decade-long career for The Hub. Despite constant developments in software and network technology, The Hub struggled with some substantial technical issues, and after a particularly problematic performance in 1997 the band admitted that 'the technology had finally begun to defeat the music' (Duckworth 2005: 65), which led to their disbandment.

In 1990 Craig Latta developed the 'Net Jam' system that allowed the exchange of MIDI data among multiple users. Net Jam users began experimenting with real-time collaboration and started exchanging MIDI files via dedicated servers allowing data synchronization and virtual jam sessions over the network. Net Jam sessions were conducted over slow networks and the real-time or near real-time aspect of music making was heavily compromised.

In 1993 Thomas 'Dolby' Robertson had started a venture called Headspace, which eventually was renamed 'Beatnik' in 1996. It was designed and maximized specifically for the web. Dolby's intention was to 'bridge the gap between composers and technicians and to facilitate a little more cooperation between the artists and the people with the technology' (Duckworth 2005: 74). At its core, Beatnik incorporated a General MIDI software synthesizer and also a Beatnik Editor facilitating the creation of custom samples.

A groundbreaking virtual studio development arrived in 1994 in the form of the Rocket Network, which started its life as the ResRocket website. The proprietary software was created as a collaboration between two British musicians – Tim Bram and Willy Henshall – and two software developers – Canton Becker and Matt Moller (Holloway 2000; Duckworth 2005). The project became a successful venture and by 1998 had 15,000 users, which increased the opportunities to network online and find musical collaborators around the world. The Rocket Network Corporation was successful in securing partnerships with audio companies such as Steinberg, Emagic and Digidesign, which in turn led to a close integration with their flagship Digital Audio Workstations (DAWs) – Cubase, Logic and ProTools (Duckworth 2005). The software associated with the Rocket Network was called Rocket Power and supported various operating systems as well as a multitude of sound file types, including MIDI, MP3, WAV and AIFF. Users could save their projects in the virtual studio's archives which serve as an example of an early cloud-based project backup system, an approach that is also in use in contemporary RMCS designs. Despite its popularity, the

Rocket Network struggled financially and its operations were closed in 2003. The closure took place after its acquisition by Avid Technology, Digidesign's parent company.

Contemporary virtual studio collaboration

At present, the field of virtual music production is relatively complex. It includes entry-level as well as advanced DAW platforms created from the ground up with remote collaboration in mind. Available are also project management systems such as Blend and Splice that turn, otherwise non-collaborative, established DAWs into virtual collaboration environments. Established, non-collaborative DAWs can also be connected with plugins that allow for streaming high-quality, low-latency audio between remotely located recording group members. Examples of such plugins include SonoBus and Source-Nexus. Collaborative DAW software includes standalone applications, for example Ohm Studio and Pro Tools, and web browser-based systems, for example Audiotool and BandLab. Most of these developments support macOS and Windows, although selected collaborative plugins and DAWs also support Linux and offer iOS and Android apps. Music creators have access to a varied set of production tools and features, and depending on the platform, to several types of memberships, including free and premium subscription models.

The developments of contemporary RMCS intersect with the emergence of Web 2.0, which is a 'term that describes the progression of the web away from static content to a dynamic platform enabling content to be created by anyone, and encouraging collaboration and community' (Donelan, Kear and Ramage 2010). The advent of mobile devices and wireless networks further enhanced the possibilities of networked computer music. Other technological advances responsible for the shape of the contemporary virtual music collaboration include the rising prevalence of broadband Internet and cloud-based data storage solutions combined with growing storage capacities. Looking at a broader context of how developments concerning computer networks impact on music production, the Internet has affected all levels of the music business, including the ability of music hobbyists to make studio-level recordings at home (Prior 2010; Rojek 2011).

Online storage of data generated in cloud-based platforms allows music producers to work on any computer with an Internet connection. If web browser-based DAWs are factored into the equation, then even the need for installing dedicated music software on a computer is eliminated, offering the ultimate flexibility to a mobile producer. Mobility is facilitated to a larger degree by tablet devices such as the iPad, with a selection of iOS RMCS apps that include BandLab, Endlesss and Soundtrap, among others. Mobile devices also afford a more flexible workflow, new ways of musical expression and controlling collaborative studio applications via touchscreen interfaces (Koszolko 2019).

Social networking is a crucial feature of almost all RMCS platforms. It facilitates access to a vast network of collaborators, who are part of a larger symbiotic system associated with a given platform. One of the defining characteristics of contemporary online music collaboration is the potential to contact and work with individuals we do not know and with whom we can form new creative relationships. There is also the potential to engage people known to us, for example to work with old musical friends who are based in remote locations. The realization of collaborative ideas by a small group of musicians working together is one of the key strengths of music production facilitated by the Internet (Föllmer 2005: 443). Furthermore, remote collaboration systems can be a solution to the displacement of musicians in time and/or space.

The notion of affordability of music-making tools, and advances in DAW and related production technologies, have had a major impact on the current music production landscape, where software is able to provide most of the essential tools which previously required hardware devices. This is highly relevant to RMCS, which is often offered as affordable or even free software. The virtual studio symbolizes further economic advantages in comparison to music production solutions that require on-site, face-to-face work. For example, musicians can limit expenditure on transport costs and instruments difficult to transfer can now be used from home. The arrival of the COVID-19 pandemic in 2020 has also highlighted that virtual studios offer a safe way of working for music makers who face pandemic-induced travel restrictions.

The last few years have seen a renewed interest within the music industry in collaborative, networked music making and established software manufacturers have started entering this field. In 2012, Steinberg introduced the VST Connect remote recording system and in 2018 a new collaborative, cross-platform application – VST Transit. In 2014, Propellerhead Software launched the Discover network, which eventually was transformed into Allihoopa – a collaborative, social networking platform for music makers. In 2015, Avid announced support for artist collaboration and content distribution with Avid Cloud Collaboration and the ability for Pro Tools users to invite new collaborators through the Avid Marketplace Artist Community. Many features that were made available to musicians using Pro Tools resembled various collaborative aspects of Ohm Studio introduced a few years earlier. Similar to other RMCS platforms, Avid and Propellerhead have attempted to create online communities of users with the idea of facilitating musical crowdsourcing and creative partnerships.

Given the growing competition in the field, it would be worth questioning how sustainable each of the platforms can be over time. The now dysfunctional Rocket Network, eSession, Indaba Music Mantis, Aviary Myna, Geisha Music, Digital Musician as well as Allihoopa platforms are examples of failing start-ups or discontinued collaborative ventures. Fortunately, there have also been several virtual studio solutions that seem to be thriving despite new collaborative products for music producers being introduced on an ongoing basis.

Music producers

In the context of RMCS, the roles of the performer, arranger, producer, recording engineer and mediator are typically performed by one person. This type of production activity is particularly applicable to many contemporary virtual studio projects where '[t]he designator *bedroom producer*, in common parlance, refers to an ideal-typical individual, making music in (it is usually taken to be) *his* bedroom' (Whelan 2008: 18, italics in original). The multiple roles undertaken by a bedroom producer engaged in online collaborative work are also reflected in Burgess's understanding of a producer as an auteur 'who is audibly the primary creative force in the production' (2013: 9). It could be argued that bedroom producers constitute a large portion of people using virtual studio platforms such as Audiotool, BandLab, Blend, Splice and Ohm Studio. The concept of bedroom production does not necessarily imply a level of amateurism and commercially successful artists sometimes publicly adopt the label.

I witnessed that RMCS is utilized primarily by amateurs rather than professional musicians. However, established artists like David Byrne also recognize the value of collaborating remotely on recording projects, particularly when the recording of a larger group of musicians at the same time is not required (Byrne 2012).

The role of the bedroom producer often involves a large amount of independent work, and therefore it can be a solitary or even isolating activity. Even in the pre-COVID-19 world, the cloud-based networks had been viewed as a way to solve the problem of musical isolation (Théberge 2004). RMCS plays a progressive role, changing the mainstream paradigm of individualistic music production. Music creation in the context of interconnected musical networks is an interdependent art form, where musicians often form groups featuring leaders and followers and are influenced by other group members' musical input (Weinberg 2005). Virtual studios and their online communities provide a platform where amateurs and professionals can share their experiences and learn from one another.

Virtual group work

The social networking features of contemporary RMCS provide opportunities for creative and technically savvy people to expand their networks and facilitate easier ways to collaborate. A critical aspect of RMCS is the large number of users registered with such platforms as Audiotool, BandLab, Ohm Studio and Soundtrap. Tens of thousands of people use social networking functionality built into RMCS and follow social media profiles of virtual studio platforms, participate in conversations and share their work on Facebook and Discord groups.

Effective group work in virtual studio settings depends on the ability to communicate effectively among the personnel involved in a project. Available communication tools vary depending on the RMCS platform and can include private and public text and video chat rooms, discussion forums, private messaging and posting comments on a user's project pages. Project participants also frequently use non-RMCS online communication tools such as email, third-party direct messaging and video conferencing tools as well as external user groups on Facebook or Discord.

My own collaborations provide evidence that communities of RMCS users consist of individuals capable of enriching one's musical projects and fulfilling specific skill gaps as identified by the music producer. However, perseverance is required to locate and engage suitable collaborators. If users take time to build relationships with members of RMCS communities and understand how to effectively use available communication tools, then successful musical outcomes are frequently achieved. Such results are aided by the status of a given user within the community which correlates to how many musicians are connected with a particular music creator. When considering which RMCS platform to work with, it helps if one understands their differences. These are characterized by such aspects as the features affecting music production, communication tools and approach to synchronicity, which all have an impact on the outcome of music production.

The increased amount of time that one needs to spend on navigating the large communities of users, locating and engaging with potential collaborators and building relationships with them might be challenging to RMCS users who need to work to a tight schedule. Hence why crowdsourced projects characterized by short production time frames might not be successfully executed within RMCS, as leading them to completion can be more difficult. The majority of my projects required more than one month of production time, and others took close to six months of production.

The experience of synchronous work facilitated by tools such as the chat enables connectivity between users that resembles face-to-face conversations. This experience makes it possible to feel thrilled by developments concerning the song because users can discuss it in real time and share the enjoyment coming from creative actions. Specific songwriting actions, such as creation of new musical lines, can have immediate impact on collaborators working in synchronous systems. This in turn permits a response that enables collaborators to shape the composition in a more interactive way than in asynchronous systems where users are unaware of the actions of the collaborator until he/she publishes the project. In addition, projects published on asynchronous systems such as Blend or Splice typically contain multiple new takes and modifications, so a collaborating party listening to this contribution is responding to a larger set of musical parameters than while working on specific tasks in real time within synchronous platforms.

RMCS facilitates various approaches to crowdsourcing. Depending on the platform, it might be more efficient to work on building a user's profile and eventually proceed to inviting selected users rather than hope for spontaneous participation in public projects. Such spontaneous participation is possible, although RMCS contributions are more often a result of actively engaging with other users and incorporating communication tools. Sometimes crowdsourcing can happen in the most passive way, and musical input can be received from strangers without any initial discussions. However, I learned that a proactive approach to crowdsourcing reflected in building one's profile within the community and direct messaging of users is required in order to maximize participation.

Successful crowdsourced virtual studio collaboration involves certain profile-building behaviours that are also common in face-to-face communication. These include building trust, as well as engaging in regular conversations with RMCS users in order to become known to them. All of this takes time and indicates that effective remote music collaboration is not a way of work that necessarily allows time saving, in comparison to face-to-face collaborative projects. In fact, my experience shows that RMCS music production is more time-consuming than face-to-face studio-based work. Therefore, the discussion on the benefits of virtual music collaboration should be focusing on the unprecedented ability to crowdsource international talent. This can be done successfully, provided that enough time is invested in specific community building actions and communication with the users of RMCS.

Project management challenges

The premise of using RMCS is not to make face-to-face interactions between musicians obsolete. It is to provide a viable alternative that allows crowdsourcing of musical talent and leads to an expansion of one's creative networks that extend far beyond the confines of the physical studio. RMCS-based interactions between remotely located collaborators can impact positively on music production by allowing them to fulfil musical objectives and benefit from skill sets of participating contributors. At the same time, remote music collaboration is not without its set of challenges affecting the outcomes of the production process. The stylistic bias of users can be a restrictive factor in relation to what projects can find traction within RMCS communities. Furthermore, even though the available communication tools are critical to establishing rapport with other users and discussing project direction, not all RMCS manufacturers have implemented them to a satisfactory level, which influences how users can connect and communicate ideas related to music production. Some of the other challenges are not dissimilar to what music producers face in non-collaborative DAW environments. For example, a lack of technical proficiency and inability to perform sound engineering tasks will negatively impact on the input of a user and his/her capacity to capture musical ideas while working remotely.

Another consideration is that cloud-based music production is being impacted by problems affecting all computer music production, such as viruses, hardware failures, software incompatibilities and crashes. The dependence of many virtual studio platforms on having an ongoing Internet connection adds a further layer of potential risk, as on a global scale servers can be down from time to time, and on a personal scale one's Internet connection can also fail due to various factors.

A unique challenge stemming from engagement in cloud-based interaction is related to managing complex projects. The possibility of easily finding and engaging multiple collaborators while working on a particular composition increases the complexity of the production process by necessitating information exchanges with multiple parties, often simultaneously. Managing this complexity is increasingly an issue now, as the tools are more multifaceted and technologically advanced. The higher number of people using RMCS platforms means that finding suitable collaborators often requires a trial-and-error approach. Furthermore, there are situations when overcoming technical problems can be challenging, for example, when multiple remote collaborators with varied technical skills and different types of equipment work on one project. A failure to effectively resolve project management challenges can render crowdsourcing efforts ineffective. Working in different time zones is also an issue associated with project management challenges. In relation to synchronous collaboration, time zone differences require discipline and planning, without which it can be difficult for users to meet, collaborate and discuss their projects in real time.

Working collaboratively can potentially lead to conflicts regarding the ownership of content created with various partners. To address this, RMCS offers various approaches to copyright and project ownership management. As with offline collaborations, these matters are best dealt with early on in a joint songwriting process. Determining a song's ownership can become a complex issue and it is difficult to predict all possible problems that can arise when co-writers engage in a lengthy creative process. Being a collaborative songwriter for many years, I am sensitive to the importance of protecting one's intellectual property. My discovery that several very skilled musicians whom I interacted with in RMCS were not members of Performing Rights Organisations (PRO) indicates that protecting their rights as authors was not of high importance to them. From a legal point of view, lack of PRO membership prevents composers from registering as co-authors of collaboratively created pieces. Despite these challenges, conflicts in RMCS are rare and if some disagreements emerge, they are typically not very significant. On rare occasions, participants in my projects simply withdrew early in the process as they lost interest in continuing the work. When creative obstacles or minor disagreements were encountered, instead of arguing, I turned my energy into finding solutions. This has proven to be an effective strategy, leading to successful completion of several projects. RMCS is an environment where one does not typically invest energy in conflict. Being online, often anonymously, means that collaborators are not as accountable as in face-to-face interactions so there is a limited likelihood of collaborators explaining themselves. In my experience they just leave if they are not satisfied. I conducted over a dozen interviews with musicians with whom I collaborated online asking about a range of their past collaborative experiences. Four of my interviewees referred to past conflict situations that included ego-based conflicts, lack of receiving due credit, incomparable musicianship and copyright violation. One of my collaborators also pointed out the responsiveness of RMCS management in addressing copyright violations.

Creative relationships formed while collaborating in RMCS start with great ease. This sometimes leads to the relationship being transient. For example, I encountered collaborators offering to contribute to specific parts of a song or proposing general songwriting input without ultimately delivering anything. It is also not uncommon to witness multiple RMCS users joining projects open to the public and leaving them without any communication. In addition, the level of loyalty of a collaborator that we have not met in person is sometimes harder to determine early on in the process, which necessitates stronger trust being placed on the prospective partners and their integrity.

Conclusion

Virtual studio platforms offer a democratic working environment where amateurs and professionals can collaborate, discuss ideas and learn from each other. The large and growing number of users, sometimes free access to advanced sound editing features and the availability of new forms of engagement contribute to the disruptive potential of RMCS. The inclusion of social networks increases the engagement of participants and is likely an appealing factor for users. The potential of RMCS lies in combining the collaborative user interface and technical solutions supporting collaborative music production within thriving online communities. The successful implementation of social networking and communication tools has a strong correlation to facilitating engagement of previously unknown musical partners.

Chat rooms, private messaging and commenting on work in progress have a critical influence on the effectiveness of communication implemented in crowdsourced projects. The stylistic inclination of users is a factor that can determine the crowdsourcing potential of a planned musical collaboration. Knowledge of this inclination within the community associated with a chosen virtual studio platform is required in order to execute an effective music production campaign. The technical sophistication of sound processing effects is not necessarily a major limiting factor as projects can be moved to other DAWs for final mixing; however, technical aspects of software certainly affect the creative result. The availability of a range of editing and sound production tools influences the sonic shape of the compositions, and accordingly, is an important consideration from the music production point of view.

In the COVID-19 pandemic climate, more than ever before, virtual studio platforms connect isolated and locked down musicians. Widespread physical isolation and remote work have led to virtual music collaboration becoming a necessity for international music production teams but also for many music and sound production students and teachers. This has led to a significant increase in the number of musicians using virtual studio platforms (Vitagliano 2021) as well as the development of new software solutions (Koszolko 2021).

Despite specific shortcomings of RMCS, collaborative methodologies facilitated by the virtual studio platforms represent a major leap forward in regard to the collaborative opportunities available to music producers. Social networking, communication tools and avenues for joint songwriting and remixing can foster musical understanding, and enable experimentation and the pooling of knowledge towards a common goal. Since anyone can join projects set up as public, cloud-based collaboration opens up one's studio to unforeseen musical guests who can contribute innovation, skills, instruments and studio equipment. In addition to contributing their musical knowledge, participants bring their unique sound. My experience of producing music on a semi-professional level in the past, without RMCS, resonated with the argument presented by Carson that working with a DAW in a home-based studio can be an isolating experience (2014). The use of RMCS led to changes in my compositional workflow. My songwriting process has become substantially more social and open. I have exposed my work to the input of other musicians with all its associated possibilities and unpredictability. My collaborative processes have shifted, as I am no longer restricted by geographical context. Earlier in my producing career, I often found that collaborators typically met offline before commencing an online exchange of ideas and sound files. It is apparent that there is a significant shift in this interaction in the sense that such offline meetings are no longer a prerequisite to building trust and achieving fulfilling musical outcomes.

Notwithstanding the global pandemic, the use of Internet cloud technology breaks down borders and reshapes music scenes, while also eroding or substantially reducing the time delay that is part of the workflow of musicians exchanging data files via the Internet without RMCS. This breaking down of borders also has cultural and cross-genre implications, allowing producers from different countries and musical backgrounds to collaborate without restrictions. At the same time it should be acknowledged that access to this technology is dependent on a number of factors, such as access to fast computers and the Internet.

Virtual studios allow music creators to overcome three key limitations: firstly, enabling work on music projects despite geographical boundaries and travel restrictions. Secondly, by implementing creative crowdsourcing they allow them to go beyond limited skill sets in various aspects of music composition, performance and production. Thirdly, collaborative studio spaces allow for the significant expansion of creative networks. Consequently, RMCS impacts on music production in a variety of ways. It is cost-effective and it empowers music producers to experiment and engage with a large, international community through the process of crowdsourcing. In addition, RMCS facilitates learning from others and receiving feedback on ones' work. Finally, it leads to successful musical outcomes that might not be possible to achieve with other means, particularly if the limitations mentioned above are considered.

Virtual studio tools are now mature and complex enough to allow for selecting from a range of music production approaches. If one is not prepared to use dedicated virtual and collaborative DAWs, it is possible to enhance existing software with plugins or project management solutions that facilitate virtual music collaboration. Engaging in RMCS-based music production is creatively rewarding. Significant shifts have developed in my practice, on both individual and collaborative levels. In order to successfully implement RMCS technologies into the work of a musician, an understanding of how to operate within the environment of various collaborative platforms is required. Music makers attempting to incorporate these tools in their workflow must skilfully utilize the social element of RMCS communities of practice. This requires understanding of how to build a profile within these communities in order to attract collaborators and gain desirable musical outcomes. The key to unlocking the potential of these communities is an effective and proactive use of the available communication tools. Looking retrospectively at all the collaborations I executed, I acknowledge that operating within RMCS necessitates some behaviour similar to what a music producer would do in face-to-face contact and this includes various forms of community engagement. The RMCS process can be slow and, perhaps, more suited to the amateur producer rather than to the professional needing to work to short deadlines. However, this concern exists primarily in relation to the process of crowdsourcing the input of strangers. If one would like to work with musicians previously known, as I also did in my projects, the technological tools available in various RMCS tools are absolutely sufficient to achieve satisfactory, high-quality recording and production results. During my virtual work on multiple compositions, I encountered the excitement also known to me from face-to-face studio practice. It was caused by receiving and responding to engaging musical and songwriting ideas, which frequently met and even exceeded my initial production objectives.

References

Burgess, R.J. (2013), *The Art of Music Production: The Theory and Practice*, New York: Oxford University Press.

Byrne, D. (2012), *How Music Works*, Edinburgh: Canongate.

Carson, E. (2014), 'Cloud Sounds: What the Latest Tech Revolution Means for the Future of Music'. *TechRepublic*. Available online: http://www.techrepublic.com/article/cloud-sounds-what-the-latest-tech-revolution-means-for-the-future-of-making-music/ (accessed 8 May 2019).

Donelan, H., Kear, K. and Ramage, M., eds (2010), 'Introduction to Part VII', in *Online Communication and Collaboration: A Reader*, 222–3, New York: Routledge.

Duckworth, W. (2005), *Virtual Music: How the Web Got Wired for Sound*, New York: Routledge.

Föllmer, G. (2005), 'Lines of Net Music', *Contemporary Music Review*, 24 (6): 439–44.

Guensche, R. (2007), *Real-time Remote Collaboration via NINJAM*. Available online: http://web.archive.org/web/20081210155201/http://www.prorec.com/Articles/tabid/109/EntryId/263/Real-time-Remote-Collaboration-via-NINJAM.aspx (accessed 12 May 2019).

Holloway, D. (2000), 'Collaboration on the Net', *Next Music* (9): 74–7.

Koszolko, M. K. (2015), 'Crowdsourcing, Jamming and Remixing: A Qualitative Study of Contemporary Music Production Practices in the Cloud', *Journal on the Art of Record Production* (10). Available online: https://www.arpjournal.com/asarpwp/crowdsourcing-jamming-and-remixing-a-qualitative-study-of-contemporary-music-production-practices-in-the-cloud/ (accessed 12 May 2019).

Koszolko, M. K. (2019), 'The Tactile Evolution – Electronic Music Production and Affordances of iOS Apps', in Gullö J.O. (ed), *Proceedings of the 12th Art of Record Production Conference Mono: Stereo: Multi, 187–204,* Stockholm: Royal College of Music (KMH) & Art of Record Production.

Koszolko, M. K. (2021), 'School of Music Collaboration live – Martin Koszolko in Conversation with Jesse Chappell (SonoBus)', *Philosophy of Sound-School of Music Collaboration*. Available online: https://youtu.be/3SkQ7UAm56I (accessed 1 September 2021).

Prior, N. (2010), 'The Rise of the New Amateurs: Popular Music, Digital Technology and the Fate of Cultural Production', in JR. Hall, L. Grindstaff, and L. Ming-Cheng (eds), *Handbook of Cultural Sociology*, 398–407, London: Routledge.

Rojek, C. (2011), *Pop Music, Pop Culture*, Cambridge: Polity Press.

Théberge, P. (2004), 'The Network Studio: Historical and Technological Paths to a New Ideal in Music Making', *Social Studies of Science*, 34 (5): 759–81.

Vitagliano, J. (2021), 'BandLab Founder Meng Ru Kuok Talks Reaching 30 Million Users, Outselling GarageBand and Empowering Music-Makers around the World', *American Songwriter*. Available online: https://americansongwriter.com/

bandlab-founder-meng-ru-kuok-talks-reaching-30-million-users-outselling-garageband-and-empowering-music-makers-around-the-world/ (accessed 7 July 2021).

Weinberg, G. (2005), 'Interconnected Musical Networks: Toward a Theoretical Framework', *Computer Music Journal*, 29 (2): 23–39.

Whelan, A. (2008), *Breakcore: Identity and Interaction on Peer-to-Peer*, Newcastle Upon Tyne: Cambridge Scholars Publishing.

18

The space of the record: Something happening somewhere

Simon Zagorski-Thomas

A common form of imagery used in advertising for early domestic high-fidelity phonographic playback equipment was the idea of bringing a public musical event into the comfort of your own home. For example a 1958 Magnavox hi-fi advert[1] claims that it seems 'the orchestra is in the room with you' and the image is of a couple at home sitting next to their gramophone with an orchestra in a concert hall floating above them. While the verbal imagery might be about the idea of bringing the musicians into your home, the sonic imagery is about transporting you to the concert hall. Despite the terminology, an audio recording is only a 'record' of an event in the sense that a photograph is a 'record' of a place: on the one hand it is partial and distorting in the way it captures what we perceive, and on the other there are aspects of the technology that allow us to manipulate, edit and construct elements of the 'record' such that it becomes a 'record' of something that never actually took place. The technology and its operators create a schematic representation of a real or constructed performance and that includes the space in which it took place. As Albin Zak puts it: 'Because we associate ambience with space, it provides the illusion that the recording exists in some unique place, the true world of the disembodied voice' (Zak 2001: 77).

In the same chapter, Zak (2001: 62) also distinguishes between the physical and rhetorical aspects of sound, a concept very similar to Middleton's (1993) distinction between gesture and connotation. The first term in each of these pairings relates to the cognitive process by which we mark some new experience as being categorically the same as some past experience – that there are certain invariant properties that appear in different contexts which we learn to categorize as 'the same'. Thus there are certain aspects of my sensory experience that I learn to categorize as 'the sight of an arm waving' or 'the sound of something happening in a large enclosed space (like a church or a concert hall)'. The details of these sensory experiences may be very different but certain invariant properties such as the topology of an arm and the way it moves allow me to categorize it as a waving arm even if the precise size, shape, distance, angle of view, lighting and context may be different each time. The second term in each of these pairings is more complex and relates to the implications or affordances that an experience suggests to us. These can take two forms. The most obvious of these forms relates to the linear chronological sequence of experiences that have been associated with this experience in the past. Thus, the sound of long reverberation times, a large space, might be most commonly associated in my past experience with church and with ritual activities or quiet mediation – and that recordings of music that employ long reverberation times therefore suggest that kind of associative meaning. The other form refers back to the schematic nature of recordings – a phenomenon I have described as *sonic cartoons* (Zagorski-Thomas 2014b). One of the key cognitive facilities that marks humans out as different from other species is the extent to which we can use a single feature of an experience to represent the whole experience – and, indeed, how we can deliberately use a feature of experience to represent another unrelated experience. Thus, we can use a long slowly fading homogenous audio signal to represent the spatial characteristics of large space even though it is only one of several invariant properties of large space that we experience in the 'real world'. We can interpret digital reverberation in a recording as indicative of the activity happening in a large space but we can also make more distant connotative or rhetorical 'leaps' such as the slowly fading audio envelope of a vibrating string like a guitar or a piano or a metal plate like a cymbal or a gong as creating a sense of space.

In a more general discussion of sound studies, albeit focused on stereo audio, Sterne says about techniques for placing a listener into a stereo soundscape: 'The practices all sound spatial at first blush, but they are ultimately perspectival, and in each case they construct a singularity of perspective and fixedness of perspective. As it were, they put the two ears on their listener's heads' (Sterne 2015: 80). In the end, the distinction between the physical and the rhetorical is a distinction between the descriptive and the analytical, between the technicalities of the spatial practices being utilized in the schematic representation and the types of interpretation that our perspective encourages us to engage in.

History of recorded space

All of the above indicates that we need to maintain a clear distinction between the 'space of the record' and the 'recording space'. Of course the sound of the recording space and the ways in which that space and the recording technologies are used contribute to the spatial characteristics of the recording. Peterson (1995) discusses the way that the sound and staging of music reflect social activity – that the intimate small space and close proximity of domestic music making traditions can be contrasted with the more distant public-facing sensibility of larger-scale communal music making. In a more general sense, recording practices and the spaces in which they occur have reflected, or at least been heavily affected by, the social contexts in which the musical styles developed. This can be seen in several of the studies which are to be found in Greene and Porcello's (2004) collection and which relate to styles as varied as Samba at the Rio carnival, Native American Pow Wow music, South African popular music, Indonesian Dangdut and Texan Country music.

In each of these instances the spatial characteristics of the recording are negotiated and constructed in relation to the ideas of authenticity that are embodied in the social practices of the musicians and their audiences. But there is an equally important influence from the industrial processes of studio design and the development of recording technology that have influenced notions of quality that are based on broader cultural discourses such as 'progress', 'modernity' and 'creativity'. Thus, for example, Schmidt-Horning (2013) on studio design and techniques that control ambience and Doyle (2006) on echo and reverberation have concentrated on the first half of the twentieth century while scholars such as Zak (2001, 2010) and Cunningham (1999) have examined more recent history when the representation of space in recordings moved away from the sound of the recorded spaces and towards mechanically and electronically constructed representations of acoustic spatial characteristics. I have also examined (Zagorski-Thomas 2012, 2016) how geopolitical and socio-economic factors have had a specific influence on the spatial characteristics of recorded music in particular places at particular times.

Staging

One of the key players in the theorizing of space in recorded music has been William Moylan (1992, 2007) who came at the 'problem' from the recording arts perspective, using the notion of staging to provide a theoretical framework that allowed aspiring sound engineers to get to grips with the problem. Moylan's approach was to see recorded stereo music as existing in a perceived performance environment in which the various elements could be staged: left to right through stereo panning and front to back through the illusion of depth created through relative volume, audio processing and the time-domain effects of echo and reverberation. The intuitive nature of this approach can be seen in the way that a great many 'how to' books for sound engineers and record producers use these ideas either explicitly or implicitly (see, for example, Owsinski 1999; Gibson 2005; Case 2007; Izhaki 2008). Expanding on Moylan's concept of spatial staging, Lacasse (2005) introduced the idea of staging as a timbral as well as a spatial process. Staging in the theatre goes beyond the construction of a set and the placing of actors within that physical space to include costume, make-up and lighting and Lacasse discusses the ways in which audio processing such as equalization, dynamic compression and harmonic distortion can be used to alter the character of the musical 'actors' (principally vocalists) and the atmosphere in a recording. More recently I have moved beyond the theatrical metaphor to include the notions of functional staging (Zagorski-Thomas 2010) and media-based staging (Zagorski-Thomas 2014c). Functional staging refers to spatial and timbral techniques that are chosen because of the social and/or cultural function for which the recording is designed. Thus, dance music mix techniques changed in the 1970s as the disco and club scene developed. In recordings that were being played back in large nightclub environments for the purpose of dancing, mix engineers started to compensate for the additional ambience that the large playback auditorium added by removing ambience from elements that were important for 'feeling' the beat. In particular, drums, percussion and bass were kept very 'dry' (i.e. without reverberation) to maintain maximum rhythmic clarity in the club while components with participatory associations (e.g. hand claps and chorus vocals) were given more reverberation as that placed them more firmly in the environment 'with' the audience. Media-based staging utilizes the sonic characteristics of various reproduction media to suggest cultural associations to the listener. This can be heard in the use of telephone voices, the suggestion of nostalgia through the sonic characteristics of old records or treatments that imitate megaphones, radio speakers or public address systems.

The sound box

While the concept of staging was initially developed as a teaching aid for the education of recording arts students and only later started to be used in musicological analysis, at around the same time in the early 1990s that Moylan introduced the term staging, Allan Moore first wrote about the *sound box* (Moore 1992, 2012) as a musicological tool for analysis. As implied in the name, Moore's 'box' represents recorded sound in three dimensions but these are not the physical dimensions of 3D space. While the left to right dimension in the model does correlate to physical space, the front-to-back dimension is more of a schematic representation of distance: it doesn't relate to the perceived performance environment of the staging model, but to subjective estimations of proximity and distance. Obviously the sonic characteristics of physical height are not represented or reproduced by normal stereo playback systems and in the sound box model, the low to high, vertical dimension relates to the approximate frequency content of the various sound sources, for example, bass guitars are low and cymbals are high. The two approaches of staging and the *sound box* are superficially very similar and, indeed, the diagrams generated in both frameworks are quite alike: both present images or representations of the musical instruments featured in a recording within a rectangular frame to represent aspects of their spatial position (or our perception of it in the recording). Moylan's staging diagrams look down on the 'stage' from above and represent the left-to-right stereo image on the horizontal axis and the perceived distance from the listener on the vertical axis. Moore and Dockwray's (2010) diagrams similarly present the stereo image on the horizontal axis but the vertical axis represents frequency or pitch. The *sound box* represents various aspects of recorded sound in ways that help us to visualize some of the spatial properties of a recording. Indeed, the vertical frequency axis is a deliberate metaphorical device aimed at representing an important aspect of abstract musical space – the density of sound in various frequency ranges. However, there are many complexities in musical and physical space that we hear in recorded music that cannot be represented through the *sound box*. Brøvig-Hanssen and Danielsen (2016), for example, despite using the *sound box* as a starting point in their analysis of Kate Bush's 'Get Out of My House' (1982), point to the many simultaneous layers of different spaces that exist in the track and the fact that several of them are 'impossible' in the sense that there is no possible physical environment that would produce these types of electronically generated ambience. Neither of these things can be represented in the *sound box* despite its obvious use as an analytical tool.

Hearing space

So how then does spatial hearing work and how can we use that sort of understanding to analyse the space of recorded music? Rumsey (2002) identifies the parameters of *width*, *depth/distance* and *envelopment* as being applicable to individual sound sources, ensemble groupings, the environment and to the scene as a whole. While these are very useful tools for thinking about spatial sound, they are based more on the science of sound than on cognition. Indeed, works on psychoacoustics and spatial sound such as Howard and Angus (1996) and Rossing et al. (2001) tend to focus on the minutiae of sonic spatial clues and the physiology of the hearing system rather than the way the mind interprets these sound waves and the nerve activity that they stimulate. Building on Gibson's (1979) ecological approach to visual perception, Clarke (2005) initiated a move to introduce those ideas to aural perception and musicology which has been quite widely adopted (see also, for example, Moore 2012; Windsor and De Bézenac 2012; Dibben 2013; Zagorski-Thomas 2018b). The ecological approach is built upon the idea that much of the logical structure of human thought flows directly from the nature of our environment. Our perception of the world is such that repeated patterns in our experience which arise due to the physical nature of that environment become ingrained in the mind through a mechanism which Gibson characterized as an *invariant property* paired with an *affordance*. For example, patterns of light moving rapidly from the centre of our retina to the edge (an *invariant property* of a rapidly approaching object) very often lead to experiences of impact and pain (an *affordance*) and that certain types of bodily action (jerking the head backwards or sideways and/or raising an arm in front of the face) can produce a less painful *affordance*. Thus the way in which objects that approach us at speed interact with our perceptual system creates a set of neural pathways in the brain that are not reliant on our generating an understanding of what might be approaching and which allow us to respond to a particular class of phenomena in any context. This is very different from other approaches to cognition which have worked on the basis of using perceptual information to build a cognitive model of what is happening in our world and planning action on the basis of that model. Another key feature of perception for which there is evidence from neuroscience and psychology is that the various modes of perception (sight, hearing, touch, etc.) interact at very low levels of cognition – before any 'decisions' are made about what we are perceiving. The ecological approach, when applied to spatial hearing, explains our understanding of space in terms of multi-modal patterns of *invariant properties* and *affordances*. Thus, my experience of loud noises in large spaces is constructed from my physical experience of the types of energy expenditure that make loud noises (e.g. the bodily sensation of shouting, hitting things hard etc., and the visual sensations of seeing others doing the same), my physical experience of large spaces (e.g. the potential for physical movements such as running around and the visual experience of high ceilings and distant walls) and my experience of high-energy activity in large spaces (e.g. the long reverberation tails, the disproportionate build-up of low frequency reverberation in comparison to high frequency). The *invariant properties* of the sound of loud noises in large spaces are connected through these pathways of experience in the brain with these associative (or in Middleton's term, connotative) experiences. We hear spatial sound in terms of *affordances* for different types of activity because spatial sound is never simply the sound of that space, it is always the sound of something happening in that space. And we are combining two sets of *affordances*: our prior experience of activities that share the *invariant properties* of this activity and our prior experience of places that share the *invariant properties* of this place. That takes us back to the idea of church-like sounds that I discussed in the introduction and the associative meanings we have for that kind of sound – meaning that is based on the types of activity that take place in churches.

Sonic cartoons

However, that also takes us back to the notion that representational systems like recording are schematic – they include, highlight or exaggerate some features and exclude, inhibit or distort other features. Not only that, but they can be used to construct representations of events that either didn't happen or even are not physically possible. The notion of sonic cartoons embraces the schematic nature of recordings (Zagorski-Thomas, 2014b, 2014c, 2014a, 2018a) and explores that schematic nature in terms of *invariant properties* and their *affordances* for interpretation. In particular the *invariant properties* of specific types of activity, the materiality of specific instruments and the acoustics of different types of space are exploited in the production and mixing process. As discussed above, a single *invariant property* of space might be used to represent the entire phenomenon – for example the length of the reverberation tail may be used to suggest the size of a space without the additional complexity of the frequency imbalance that reverberation adds. This type of strategy developed because, despite the narrative of equating better audio quality with greater realism that the Magnavox advert provides an example of, clarity became an equally important trope in the production of recorded music. And clarity is not about realism, it is about establishing a hierarchy of importance for different features and using some schematic distortion of realism to highlight features at the top of the hierarchy and inhibit features at the bottom (or which produce 'noise' that interfere with or obscure features at the top). In this respect, the history of recording is similar to the history of humanity's other schematic representational systems (language, science, visual art, cinema, literature, etc.) in that, on the one hand, we seek to represent reality, the messy complexity of the physical world and on the other hand we seek to represent what we think of as truth: schematic narratives and structures that we believe represent something more important than the undifferentiated chaos of empirical detail.

In the mundane practical world of making records this involves pop stars singing about love, instrumentalists trying to encourage us to dance or earnest composers trying to make apparent the brilliance of their complex ideas about structure. In any piece of music there is an agenda about what is important and the schematic nature of recording and mixing audio is part of the process of establishing and presenting that hierarchy of importance. As we have seen, the spatial characteristics of the recording are important in establishing the social and cultural frame in which the musical activity happens. Hall (1966) developed the notion of proxemics in relation to the sociology of architecture to discuss the way that perceived distance in interpersonal interaction contributes to social meaning and this has been used by scholars in musicology to explore notions of intimate and public space in recordings (see for example Moore 2012; Dibben 2013; Zagorski-Thomas 2014c; Brøvig-Hanssen and Danielsen 2016) A stadium rock band need to sound as if they are performing in a stadium even when you invite them to play through your living room speakers or in your headphones as you travel on the bus. However, there are many aspects about the reality of sound in a stadium that are unsatisfactory in terms of musical clarity and this is exaggerated by the multi-modal nature of perception when we listen to recorded music. When we listen to a record, any ambiguity that might exist in our aural perception is not being resolved through reference to our visual perception. When we can see a singer's mouth move we can understand the words better with a much less clear audio signal than we need when we only have a speaker to look at. Our stadium rock band recording therefore needs additional clarity as well as 'stadium-ness' (and, of course, other subjective aesthetic characteristics such as high energy and heaviness) and this is where the cartoon-like techniques of record production come into their own. A mix engineer might, for example, only add a long reverb to musical materials that lie in the higher frequency range (like vocals, snare drum and guitar) to prevent the 'muddiness' of low frequency reverberation on the kick drum and bass guitar. Or they might add reverberation to the whole ensemble and filter the low frequency sound out of the reverb. Or they might use shorter reverb tails on lower frequency sounds and longer reverb tails on higher ones. In addition they might provide some of the *invariant property* of exaggerated low frequency in large reverberant space by creating a partial impression of that phenomenon through equalizing and/or compressing the bass and kick drum to add more bass without the lack of clarity. They may stage the recording in a smaller space for rhythmically complicated sections and in a larger space for rhythmically simpler ones where issues of clarity may be less important than a sense of 'size'. All of these processes and the many more that are available to sound engineers and record producers when they are creating these schematic representations of 'something happening somewhere' have two types of perceptual and interpretative consequences. On the one hand we are using some subset of the *invariant properties* of space to create a representation of space but on the other hand that very lack of realism can become more recognizable as the *invariant properties* of the representational system – something that Brøvig-Hanssen has termed *opaque mediation* (Brøvig-Hanssen and Danielsen 2016). But, again this is a double-edged sword. In some instances the artificiality of the spatial (or other) processing might be seen as a bad thing – something which undermines the authenticity of the recording as a 'true record' of a performance event – and there is a substantial record of journalism that criticizes records for being overproduced (for a discussion of this see Frith 2012; Jarrett 2012). In other instances the opacity of the mediation may be part of the creative process. Our appreciation of Monet's representation of water lilies through the medium of oil paint on canvas balances between an understanding of how he represents water lilies and the visible beauty of the brush strokes. Likewise, our appreciation of Prince's 'Sign O The Times' (1987) is split between the musical activity being represented and the innovative way that the recording has been produced. Although most listeners won't notice the six different levels of spatial processing that are superimposed on one another in this recording, they will notice the artificiality and strangeness of the production – that it is a very unusual sounding record that creates a very sparse and odd-sounding spatial impression.

Indeed, the moments in that recording where we get the most significant impression of a change of space have not to do with reverberation or echo but with the entry of a keyboard pad in the background (between 1' 47" and 2' 06"). Camilleri (2010) discusses this kind of metaphorical space when he distinguishes between *localized space, spectral space* and *morphological space*. This notion of *spectral space* or what has also been described as musical space is related quite strongly to the vertical axis in Moore's *sound box*, that is, that denser 'patches' of frequency content in the audio spectrum create a metaphorical sense of fullness in the same way that the decaying vibrating tails of string and metal plate sounds create a metaphorical analogue of reverberation. Camilleri's category of *morphological space* relates to the way that a sense of space changes throughout a piece of music. This can be achieved through spatial processing in a track, such as the way that the Kings of Leon's *Sex on Fire* (2009) uses a much shorter reverb in the verses than the choruses so that the increased energy is enhanced through the use of a bigger space. It can also be achieved through musical metaphor such as in the Prince example where reverberation and echo create an overall sense of artificial spaciousness but where the musical pad keyboard sound changes our sense of space and place.

Within the world of electroacoustic music these issues have been addressed through the twin concepts of *spectromorphology* (Smalley 2007) and *landscape* (Wishart 1986) and there are very clear connections between the thinking behind the ecological approach to perception, *sonic cartoons* and *spectromorphology*. They are all concerned with the idea of understanding sound in terms of 'something happening somewhere' and of analysing it through perceived agency and energy expenditure and the nature of the environment in which that energy expenditure occurs.

Conclusion

Within popular music studies, the recording is far more often the 'text' that is analysed than a score. In some ways this reflects the different ideologies about creativity that exist within western art music and western popular music: the focus on the composer and the focus on the performing artist. While a score is a representational system that communicates a set of instructions about how to perform a composition, a recording is a schematic representation of musical performance (real or constructed) and, as such, it also provides a schematic representation of the place (real or constructed) in which the performance occurred. The development of ways of thinking about space in recorded music since 1992, when William Moylan and Allan Moore first made their important contributions to the debate, has in large part been about formulating ways of thinking about the abstract, schematic or caricature representations of space rather than the realistic. While the visual metaphors of staging and the *sound box* do provide useful ways of thinking about space in records they do also run the risk of encouraging simplification by being based on that notion of realism. The abstract, schematic and caricature-based nature of recorded music, especially popular music, is a hugely important factor in determining how we interpret it. Just as the ideology of classical music led to a musicology based on the score rather than performance and the sounds of the music, there is a danger that the ideology of popular music studies encourages us to treat the record as a transparent medium: as an unmediated performance. The notion of the *sonic cartoon* acknowledges the dualistic nature of recorded music, where the aesthetic lies in both the performance and the space being represented and in the artistry and the sophistication of the system of representation. To return to Monet, we are not just interested in the little corner of the world being represented in A Bridge over a Pond of Water Lilies (1899) but also in the way that light, form and texture have been represented through brush strokes and mixed or layered oil paint.

Note

1   https://www.pinterest.co.uk/pin/313633561533280193/

Bibliography

Brøvig-Hanssen, R. and Danielsen, A. (2016), *Digital Signatures: The Impact of Digitization on Popular Music Sound*, Cambridge: MIT Press.
Camilleri, L. (2010), 'Shaping Sounds, Shaping Spaces', *Popular Music*, 29 (2): 199–211.
Case, A. U. (2007), *Sound FX: Unlocking the Creative Potential of Recording Studio Effects*, Burlington, MA: Focal Press.
Clarke, E. F. (2005), *Ways of Listening: An Ecological Approach to the Perception of Musical Meaning*, USA: Oxford University Press.
Cunningham, M. (1999), *Good Vibrations: History of Record Production*. 2nd rev. edn, London: Sanctuary Publishing Ltd.
Dibben, N. (2013), 'The Intimate Singing Voice: Auditory Spatial Perception and Emotion in Pop Recordings', in D. Zakharine and N. Meise (eds), *Electrified Voices: Medial, Socio-Historical and Cultural Aspects of Voice Transfer*, 107–22, Göttingen: V&R University Press.
Doyle, P. (2006), *Echo and Reverb: Fabricating Space in Popular Music Recording, 1900–1960*, Middletown: Wesleyan University Press.
Frith, S. (2012), 'The Place of the Producer in the Discourse of Rock', in S. Frith and S. Zagorski-Thomas (eds), *The Art of Record Production: An Introductory Reader to a New Academic Field*, 207–21, Farnham: Ashgate.

Gibson, D. (2005), *The Art of Mixing: A Visual Guide to Recording, Engineering and Production*, 2nd rev. edn, artistpro.com LLC.
Gibson, J. J. (1979), *The Ecological Approach to Visual Perception*, London: Psychology Press.
Hall, E. T. (1966), *The Hidden Dimension*, London: Doubleday.
Howard, D. M. and Angus, J. (1996), *Acoustics and Psychoacoustics*, Oxford: Focal Press.
Izhaki, R. (2008), *Mixing Audio: Concepts, Practices and Tools*, Oxford: Focal Press.
Jarrett, M. (2012), 'The Self-Effacing Producer: Absence Summons Presence', in S. Frith, and S. Zagorski-Thomas (eds), *The Art of Record Production: An Introductory Reader to a New Academic Field*, 129–48, Farnham: Ashgate.
Lacasse, S. (2005), 'Persona, Emotions and Technology: The Phonographic Staging of the Popular Music Voice', *Art of Record Production Conference*, London. Available online: http://www.artofrecordproduction.com/content/view/143/ (accessed 30 June 2011).
Middleton, R. (1993), 'Music Analysis and Musicology: Bridging the Gap', *Popular Music*, 12 (2): 177–90.
Moore, A. F. (1992), *Rock: The Primary Text : Developing a Musicology of Rock (Ashgate Popular and Folk Music Series)*, 2nd edn., Farnham: Ashgate Pub Ltd.
Moore, A. F. (2012), *Song Means: Analysing and Interpreting Recorded Popular Song*, Farnham: Ashgate Pub Ltd.
Moore, A. F. and Dockwray, R. (2010), 'The Establishment of the Virtual Performance Space in Rock', *Twentieth Century Music*, 5: 219–41.
Moylan, W. (1992), *The Art of Recording: Understanding and Crafting the Mix*, Oxford: Focal Press.
Moylan, W. (2007), *Understanding and Crafting the Mix: The Art of Recording*, 2nd edn, Oxford: Focal Press.
Owsinski, B. (1999), *The Mixing Engineer's Handbook*, 001 edn. Artistpro.
Peterson, R. (1995), 'The Dialectic of Hard-Core and Soft-Shell Country Music', *South Atlantic Quarterly*, 94 (1): 273–300.
Porcello, T. and Greene, P. D. (2004), *Wired for Sound: Engineering and Technologies in Sonic Cultures*, Middletown: Wesleyan University Press.
Rossing, T. D., Moore, R. F. and Wheeler, P. A. (2001), *The Science of Sound*. 3rd edn, Boston: Addison-Wesley.
Rumsey, F. (2002), 'Spatial Quality Evaluation for Reproduced Sound: Terminology, Meaning and a Scene-Based Paradigm', *Journal of the Audio Engineering Society*, 50 (9): 651–66.
Schmidt-Horning, S. (2013), *Chasing Sound: Technology, Culture, and the Art of Studio Recording From Edison to the LP*, Baltimore, MD: Johns Hopkins University Press.
Smalley, D. (2007), 'Space-Form and the Acousmatic Image', *Organised Sound*, 12 (1): 35–58.
Sterne, J. (2015), 'The Stereophonic Spaces of Soundscape', in P. Théberge, K. Devine, and T. Everrett (eds), *Living Stereo: Histories and Cultures of Multichannel Sound*, 65–83, New York: Bloomsbury.
Windsor, W. L. and De Bézenac, C. (2012), 'Music and Affordances', *Musicae Scientiae*, 16 (1): 102–20.
Wishart, T. (1986), 'Sound Symbols and Landscape', in S. Emmerson (ed), *The Language of Electroacoustic Music*, 41–60, London: Macmillan.
Zagorski-Thomas, S. (2010), 'The Stadium in Your Bedroom: Functional Staging, Authenticity and the Audience Led Aesthetic in Record Production', *Popular Music*, 29 (2): 251–66.
Zagorski-Thomas, S. (2012), 'The US vs the UK Sound: Meaning in Music Production in the 1970s', in S. Frith and S. Zagorski-Thomas (eds), *The Art of Record Production: An Introductory Reader to a New Academic Field*, 57–76, Farnham: Ashgate.

Zagorski-Thomas, S. (2014a), 'An Analysis of Space, Gesture and Interaction in Kings of Leon's "Sex on Fire" (2008)', in R. Von Appen, et al. (eds), *Twenty-First-Century Pop Music Analyses: Methods, Models,* 115–32, *Debates,* Farnham: Ashgate.

Zagorski-Thomas, S. (2014b), 'Sonic Cartoons', in Schulze, H. and Papenburg, J. (eds), *Sound as Popular Culture: A Research Companion,* 403–10, Cambridge, MA: MIT Press.

Zagorski-Thomas, S. (2014c), *The Musicology of Record Production,* Cambridge: Cambridge University Press.

Zagorski-Thomas, S. (2016), 'The Influence of Recording Technology and Practice on Popular Music Performance in the Recording Studio in Poland between 1960 and 1989', *Polish Sociological Review,* 196: 531–48.

Zagorski-Thomas, S. (2018a), 'The Spectromorphology of Recorded Popular Music: The Shaping of Sonic Cartoons through Record Production', in R. Fink, M.L. O'Brien, and Z. Wallmark (eds), *The Relentless Pursuit of Tone: Timbre In Popular Music,* 345–66, New York: Oxford University Press, USA.

Zagorski-Thomas, S. (2018b), 'Timbre as Text: The Cognitive Roots of Intertextuality', in S. Lacasse and L. Burns (eds), *The Pop Palimpsest: Intertextuality in Recorded Popular Music,* 273–90, Ann Arbor, MI: University of Michigan Press.

Zak, A. J. (2001), *The Poetics of Rock: Cutting Tracks, Making Records,* Berkeley: University of California Press.

Zak, A. J. (2010), *I Don't Sound Like Nobody: Remaking Music in 1950s America,* Detroit: University of Michigan Press.

19
The live gig
Sam Whiting

Introduction

The concept of 'live music' is recent in human history. Before the invention of recorded sound, music could only be experienced 'live'. Since the early twentieth century, the term 'live music' has largely been used as a descriptor for those experiences where the audience is in physical proximity to the musical performance itself (Shuker 2012: 201). With the advent of jazz, blues and later pop and rock, this proximity took on connotations of intimacy and authenticity; what could be described as *liveness* (Auslander 2008). The experience of engaging with live music in a familiar, accessible context can be felt in small venues around the world, typified in the everyday performances carried out by working and amateur musicians in a diverse array of settings and contexts. These small-scale local performances are commonly referred to as 'live gigs', and it is their ubiquity, their *everydayness*, that defines them. Until recently the concert spectacle, audience consumption habits and questions of stardom were dominant in live music studies whereas research on live gigs has been relatively limited. However, since the early-2000s there has been increasing research on the role of music in everyday life (Bennett 2000; Bull 2000; Denora 2000). As the most ubiquitous of musical performances, the local gig serves as a pertinent case study for questions of live music in everyday life, and the significance of small-scale local performances for musicians, audiences and the venues that host them.

The 'live gig' describes those most accessible and intimate of performances, which take place in the local pubs, clubs and other small live music venues of a city. Gigs are localized and specific to time and place. They contribute to the ongoing musical activities of a city and provide the network of social actors participating in such activities – the 'scene' – with a place to congregate. Although the advent of the Internet and Web 2.0 has changed the way that music scenes function, with some scholars referring to the emergence of 'virtual scenes' (Kibby 2000; Bennett 2004, 2002; Peterson and Bennett 2004), local music scenes still primarily articulate themselves in relation to live gigs. These give them context, social and cultural events to organize themselves around, and opportunities to construct collective identity. Regular gigging opportunities provide musicians with exposure, income and the means to hone their craft in front of a live audience, while audiences who frequent gigs are able to participate in local music scenes on an accessible, everyday level, due to the ubiquitousness of gigs and their relatively low cost of entry.

The link between live gigs and place-based music scenes has led to the emergence of internationally recognized city-specific musical movements, such as the Seattle grunge boom of the early 1990s and the Madchester dance scene of 1980s Manchester. Such scenes relied on a sustainable live music culture of regular gigs, providing musicians with consistent performance opportunities and scene participants with the means to network and socialize. Without regular live gigs performed on a local and everyday level, music scenes would not flourish. The live gig is what simultaneously grounds music scenes in local processes of meaning-making and encourages their development into something bigger than the sum of their parts.

Within the context of this collection, previous studies on popular music and place have focused largely on cities and the relationship between the city, venues and the musicians that gig at such venues regularly. Research by Finnegan (1989), Cohen (2013, 1991), Shank (1994, 1988) and Bennett (1997) has considered how music scenes form around networks of venues in a geographically specific place, such as a city or town. The concept of 'scene' has also been identified and theorized by Straw (2001, 1991), Rogers (2008) and Bennett (Bennett and Rogers 2016a), and such discussions of scenes have been extended to include more nuanced understandings of live music and place, such as the 'live music ecology' (Behr, Brennan and Cloonan 2014; Behr et al. 2016). Relevant to research on the live gig are recent publications on popular music and *space*, rather than place (Gallan 2012; Gallan and Gibson 2013; Holt 2014; Kronenburg 2019, 2012, 2011; van der Hoeven and Hitters 2020). The ubiquity of local gigs and the small-to-medium spaces in which they take place make gigs identifiable as distinct phenomena within live music studies.

This chapter will provide a definition of the 'live gig' and how it differs from other live music events. This is followed by an overview of dominant themes in the field of live music and venue studies, such as music in everyday life and the role of small venues specifically, before moving onto a more focused consideration of how these themes play out in relation to cities, musicians, audiences and the live music experience generally. This chapter will examine the role that place and space – specifically small venues – play in influencing and facilitating live music, how gigs provide everyday opportunities to engage with live music, and how music scenes rely on live gigs for meaning-making.

The live gig

The live gig provides the means for music scenes to articulate themselves at the level of the local and the commonplace. Further, gigs are inherently shaped by the venues in which they take place. Although they are a key part of the day-to-day functioning of music scenes, with their ubiquity rendering them almost mundane, no two gigs are the same, and their differences are influenced largely by the spaces in which they take place.

In the context of popular music and place, gigs provide an insight into what makes live music ephemeral and unique. As Robert Kronenburg explains:

> Popular music is a creative form that is experiential and transient. Though it is marketed via the recorded medium and totally transportable in this form, it is also very definitely rooted in time and place… The immersive experience of the gig, as musician or as audience member, cannot be duplicated by any existing medium. Every performance is unique, shaped by a vast range of factors that can benefit or impair the event and the individual's experience of it.
>
> (2012: 4)

In contrast with the live concert, gigs are small-scale and defined by the size of the venue, along with the informality of the space and the performances therein. They are not replicable, as the idiosyncrasies of a live music experience are vast and difficult to measure and reproduce. The emphasis on *space* and transience here suggests a departure from most studies of live music, as most previous research, including this collection, have focused on *place* and its ongoing influence on popular music scenes. A gap in the literature is clear, along with an opportunity to address this with research on venue spaces themselves.

Kronenburg has written at length on the nuances of live music venues and their design, focusing on the architecture of performance spaces (2012), while creating a typology of venues[1] (2011) and analysing the cultural and social impact of these different types of spaces on the experience of popular music performance broadly (2019). Kronenburg argues that throughout the current literature on live music, *place* has taken precedence as a descriptor of cultural context, whereas small-scale live music events are more clearly defined by *space*:

> Place can mean the country, region, city, neighbourhood and the actual venue. In recent years there has been considerable recognition of the importance of place as a defining factor in popular music development… However, the vast majority of this illuminating research has dealt with geographical place rather than physical space – comparatively little has examined the location of popular music performance in terms of the building in which the experience actually happens.
>
> (Kronenburg 2012: 5)

The live gig is dependent on both place *and* space to give it meaning and to shape the experiences of those engaging with the live gig as a musical event. The size of the venue, its decor, its regular clientele, the way patrons move through the space and how closely audiences can interact with the musicians all contribute to an understanding of the live gig as accessible and commonplace.

The live gig further differs from the live concert in that gigs are of the 'everyday'. This is due to their ubiquity, their high rate of incidence in cities and their low thresholds for professional and operational needs. In contrast, live concerts require considerable planning, logistics, expertise, dedicated or highly adapted performance spaces equipped with quality audio-visual technology, plenty of staff and a revolving door of professional musicians. Gigs, on the other hand, are regular occurrences in small venues all over the world. The venues they take place in are often more informal or accessible than large-scale performance venues (Whiting and Carter 2016), production standards are generally lower and performers are usually either amateurs, hobbyists or semi-professionals who hold down day jobs and careers outside of musical performance. The relationship between the musicians and audience is also significantly different to concerts, as any distinction between the two groups is often blurred by hobbyism (Rogers 2012). Therefore, the accessibility and everyday nature of gigs is the key difference between them and live concert events.

The 'everyday'

The 'everyday' relates to both time and space. It refers to those events that take place both every day, week, month or year, and occur in a local setting that is accessible to those participating regularly (Hesmondhalgh 2002: 125). As Felski states, 'the everyday is, above all, a temporal concept' (1999: 18). We perceive the everyday as something that is commonplace and perpetual. Everyday events are part of the fabric of life and can be valued as much as they are taken for granted. This makes such events routine, and part of the larger process of 'getting through the day'. David Hesmondhalgh positions the 'everyday' in terms of ordinary life and the mundane, stating:

> ... the concept of the everyday needs to be expanded to cover the notion of routine more adequately: events that happen every night or every week, even every month and every year, are part of mundane, ordinary living, and might serve to remind us of lived experience 'beyond' structures of power.
>
> (Hesmondhalgh 2002: 126)

In the abstract, the local gig is one of many ordinary experiences that make up everyday engagement with music. Live gigs can be viewed as novel entertainment for those occasionally engaging with live music culture, or a 'way of life' for participants that are more entrenched within the scene. The lived experience of local music scenes is made up of gigs. Gigs give scenes coherence and the ability to construct and maintain collective identities, as well as a social functioning which brings participants together on a regular basis.

Until recently, gigs were often overlooked in studies of popular music due to their 'everyday' nature and mundanity. Local gigs lacked the spectacle of the concert and were too often bound up with issues of amateurism and hobbyism to warrant the kind of attention that 'spectacular subcultures' garnered in the mid-to-late twentieth century. However, since the early 1990s, local music scenes and the live gigs that populate them have received further attention in scholarly studies of popular music. This research has been strengthened by recent investigations into small venues and their musical cultures. David Hesmondhalgh articulated the impetus for this research in a call for a more nuanced consideration of time, space and the everyday in live music studies:

> ... what we need to focus on in providing a more adequate conception of ordinary experiences of music than in existing audience studies is not merely the idea of the everyday, but time and space. There has been too much focus within popular music studies on the concept of 'youth' and supposedly typical youth genres and experiences of music, at the expense of

other age groups, and other types of experience; and there has been too much attention to spectacular and supposedly rebellious uses of popular music, at the expense of the mundane and the banal.

(Hesmondhalgh 2002: 127)

This call seems to have been largely answered, given the numerous publications and research projects on local, small-scale live music events published in the following years (Bennett 2004; Cohen 2007; Bennett and Peterson 2004; Gibson and Homan 2004; Rogers 2008; Gallan 2012; Gallan and Gibson 2013; Behr, Brennan and Cloonan 2014; Holt 2014; Behr et al. 2016; Bennett and Rogers 2016a, 2016b). Such research has served to elucidate the importance of small venues and the gigs that take place within them as foundational to the live music ecologies of cities and regions. Small venues act as entry-level performance spaces for emerging artists and musicians, and live gigs provide an accessible opportunity for audiences to engage with live music on an everyday level.

The venue

The live gig almost uniformly takes place in a small venue, whether adopted, adapted or dedicated (Kronenburg 2011, 2012); licensed or unlicensed (Bennett and Rogers 2016a); official or unofficial (Bennett and Rogers 2016b). Small venues act as launch pads for emerging artists, providing them with a space to hone their craft in a live setting. Small venues also serve as social hubs for local music scenes; spaces where musicians and other live music enthusiasts can mingle and socialize, contributing to the cultural milieu of local music scenes. The informality and accessibility of these small venues make the live gig more attainable for both musicians that want to perform, and audiences that want to engage with live music away from large arenas and concert halls.

Small live music venues are nuanced, complex sites of cultural production and consumption. Previous ethnographies of small venues have relied on fieldwork and participant interviews to gather perceptions of place and space. Ben Gallan's work on Wollongong's Oxford Tavern uses the example of the Oxford as an opportunity to explore 'the peculiar character of the live music pub as quintessential Australian cultural infrastructure' (Gallan and Gibson 2013: 174). Gallan's research holds implications for the acknowledgement of pubs as sites of vernacular cultural history[2], regional meanings of what it means to play and support local music and the investment of a personal stake in a venue's distinct culture (Gallan 2012; Gallan and Gibson 2013). The small gigs that take place in local pubs and bars such as the Oxford code the space musically and connect with specific audiences who may find a sense of belonging in local associated scenes. As Kronenburg states, 'Musical performance, regardless of whether or not it is in association with a building, transforms the space, internal or external, into an identifiable "place", the boundary of which is limited by the aural and visual experience of being there' (2012: 5). The influence of the performance on the space and the space on the performance is essential to the meanings fostered and maintained by scene participants who patronize small venues regularly.

Gallan's work emphasizes the cultural and social stake Australians place in the idea of the 'local', both as a physical space – the 'local' pub/record store/music venue – and as a set of meanings tied to the musical and social practices of scene participants engaging with live music in a specific urban or regional centre. He explores this through an examination of the spaces and music scenes that are disconnected from the global music industry; enmeshed in other local and translocal contexts, such as regional pubs. This focus on local music and place is preceded by the work of Finnegan and Cohen, in which local forms of music are framed as tangible manifestations of music 'in its own right' (Finnegan 1989: 235). Similarly, Andy Bennett's research on northern English 'pub rock' emphasizes the everyday significance that these scenes hold for participants, and 'recognises the social function of scenes within a specific "local" context – regardless of competency or commercial viability' (Gallan 2012: 38). There is an implication of amateur and hobbyist musical practices here, with an emphasis on the everyday social relevance of these practices. The day-to-day of small live music venues hinges on the small gigs that take place therein, and an understanding of such minutiae provides further evidence towards each venue's social and cultural value (van der Hoeven and Hitters 2019).

Live gigs take place in local venues. Not only are they small, but these spaces are intrinsically connected to the wider constellation of performance spaces and cultural hubs that give form and function to music scenes. However, 'scene' as a term does not go far enough in accounting for the materiality of venue spaces, nor the interdependence between otherwise disparate social actors necessary for a live gig to occur.

In response to this, scholars in the UK have taken a more holistic approach to the study of live music, defining a network of venues in a localized place as being part of a 'live music ecology' (Behr et al. 2016). Whereas scene denotes a milieu of social actors that are loosely tied to music-making by way of participation and regular interaction, the 'live music ecology' emphasizes place and space. Moreover, it factors in the built environment of venue spaces – their materiality – alongside the influence of interdependent yet disparate social actors that operate outside of the scene (Behr et al. 2016: 6). These include the police, liquor-licensing bodies, policy-makers, building developers, the EPA (Environment Protection Authority) and any other groups or organizations that are not part of a local music scene yet still have a decisive impact and influence on its sustainability.

Scenes are built around the actions and agency of scene participants. A live music ecology, on the other hand, is dependent on the materiality of venue spaces, the cooperation of multiple insiders and outsiders and an ongoing live music culture to hold it together (Behr et al. 2016: 20):

> The value of a concept like 'scene' (as Straw, for example, defines it) for popular music scholars is that it describes a social process of music meaning-making which is not limited by the materiality of place, whereas it is precisely these constraints that interest us.
>
> (Behr et al. 2016: 6)

Although proponents of scene would argue that the term already accounts for the live music ecology, scene is more concerned with the fluidity of collective forms of identity than the rigid built environment of venue spaces or the roles of social actors outside of the scene. As Behr et al. state, '(a)n ecological study of live music means studying social agents which are not in any coherent ideological way members of the social networks that are described by Becker's art worlds, Bourdieu's cultural fields, or Finnegan's social pathways' (2016: 6). Such social agents impact the ecology despite not otherwise forming a part of the scene. Therefore, the 'live music ecology' (Behr et al. 2016) is a more holistic way of understanding the factors necessary for a live music event to take place, and the sustainability of live music venues and gigs by extension.

The city

The role of space and place should not be underestimated in the cultivation of music scenes. Many internationally recognized music scenes initially centred on a handful of venues operating in a geographically specific place. As Kronenburg states, '(t)he importance of the local venue cannot be underestimated in providing support for musical activity; however, it is only natural that some locations gain greater importance in terms of the development of distinct musical scenes that then expand into national and international recognition' (2012: 4–5).

Identifiable musical styles, sounds and genres have all found their birthplace in the social milieu and music scenes of specific cities:

> The performance of popular music endows places with special identities that create an international image for their host cities – the US cities of Nashville, Detroit and Seattle are, respectively, synonymous with Country, Motown and Grunge. Elsewhere in the world, Tamworth is styled the Country Music capital of Australia, Cologne the birthplace of Krautrock (in Germany known as *Kosmische Musik,* cosmic music), and Ibiza the centre for Dance and House (sometimes known as Balearic Beat).
>
> (Kronenburg 2011: 139)

The venues of these cities serve as incubators for distinctive musical styles, the melting pot of each scene and the live music ecology that fosters them. Each of the styles of popular music listed above is intrinsically tied to place. The small live gigs that contributed to their birth were organized and performed by working musicians, each looking for their next gig and opportunity to work a live room. The network of small venues – the ecology – that each of these cities housed facilitated an identifiable scene and culture that eventually rose to international recognition. Without the ability for these musicians to organize and perform on the grassroots level of the regular and local, many of these scenes and their associated styles may not have come to fruition.

The musicians

Gigging musicians are often locally based hobbyists who engage in performance primarily for enjoyment, creative fulfilment and self-actualization. The social experience of performing music is also often cited as a key reason for 'playing live'. The practice of 'keeping up appearances' is prevalent among musicians in local music scenes, and it is evident that bands that ascribe to regular socializing are often presented with more opportunities. This concept is further outlined by Ian Rogers (2008). Writing on the independent music scene in Brisbane, Australia, Rogers states:

> As Brisbane's venue infrastructure has shrunk and moved out of traditional spaces, it has become more highly regulated by the personal networks of the musicians who perform in the city… In this way, face-to-face informal networking gatekeeps and governs the indie live circuit. If an emerging band is to succeed in the scene, it must socialize with the established acts. The desire, among musicians, for a more stable social environment drives this process.
>
> (Rogers 2008: 644)

Here social capital is posited as the primary force behind a place-based music scene's administration and organization. Brisbane's hobbyist musicians are not guided by the pursuit of fame or money, but rather what Simon Frith (1992) calls a 'desired social experience' (p. 184). Soft forms of capital (such as social capital) are often prioritized above harder economic forms and are seen as more desirable to music scene participants: '[s]ubcultures [or music scenes] may be viewed through the Bourdieuian notion of "disinterest"[3] in artistic fields – the "economic world reversed" (see Bourdieu 1993), where the rewards of the field are credibility and authenticity rather than financial gain' (Threadgold 2015: 58). Local gigging musicians are often more interested in the social and personal experience of performing music rather than any commercial success. However, there is certainly an aspirational class of musicians that use small gigs to move through the live music ecology towards bigger stages and larger audiences. For these musicians, the live gig is an entry-level performance opportunity that aids them in establishing a following and asserting themselves within the broader live music scene of the city, providing further opportunities within and outside of the scene. In this context, live gigs are springboards towards full-time careers in the music industry.

The audience

Much has been written about the cultural and economic role of small venues in live music scenes: as social hubs (Gallan and Gibson 2013); as live music infrastructure (Behr, Brennan and Cloonan 2014), and as harbingers of gentrification (Shaw 2013, 2009). When compared to other types of venues, small venues offer an intimate atmosphere wherein patrons are more readily identifiable and therefore less anonymous. Fabian Holt observed that large venues do not accommodate for socializing as readily as smaller venues. Holt states that larger concert audiences don't seem to allow for the kinds of informal networking and spontaneous interactions that the 'local' small venue might enable (2014: 24–5). While discussing the increased dominance of mid-sized venues (e.g. 500–1500 capacity) in New York City and the impact of these on audience experiences, Holt states:

The big crowd in mid-size venues is generally drawn to a headliner and thus has a more targeted interest in the concert itself. Such a crowd is also too big for extensive socializing and informal networking inside and outside the building… Comparing The Bowery Ballroom with a small DIY show, an experienced insider found a higher degree of community ownership and trust in the latter: 'A DIY show feels more like a house party,' he said. 'You don't go up to someone at The Bowery [Ballroom] and say "Hey, how's it going?" (Ariel Panero, personal communication, 23 April 2010).'

(Holt 2014: 24–5)

Here an emphasis on the performance aspect of the concert experience undermines socializing and audience interaction, contributing to a sense of anonymity and impersonality. The congregational sensation of collective participation in large-scale concert events may enhance feelings of shared experience among audience members (Holt 2014), but this comes at the cost of individual personal responses and the opportunity for social contact between participants that such responses afford. This is not to say that large concert events lack a commonality of social experience, as each audience member is ostensibly there to participate in the same live music event. Rather, the sense of impersonality inherent in large crowds tends to override any potential feelings of communal belonging among individual participants. Small gigs offer more opportunities for these feelings, many of which are tethered to ideas of place and space.

In their research, Ben Gallan and Chris Gibson cast The Oxford Tavern as a 'haven' for Wollongong's music scenes, asserting that the sense of belonging that permeated the space during its time as a music venue was owed to the participatory and communal philosophy advocated by the venue's regular patrons. As Gallan and Gibson state '(t)he Oxford… was colonised by music scene participants as an alternative to homogeneity, imagining and constructing "otherness" in relation to the restrictive cultural norms of the commercial mainstream' (2013: 179). Gallan's work emphasizes the role that venue-booking agents play in regulating what kinds of bands perform in small venue spaces, and therefore the nature of the crowds that attend. Patrons and musicians that frequent and perform in small venues don't do so purely for want of cultural consumption or entertainment as is often the case in larger concert environments. Their reasons for participation are also associated with regional meanings of what it means to play and support local music, as these venues offer a space for patrons and musicians to drink, socialize, dance, mosh, sing and belong (Gallan 2012: 35).

Local live music audiences are often made up of creatives, hospitality staff, regular patrons and musicians themselves. The key difference between large concert performances and local live gigs is the informality of the space and the 'everyday' nature of the performance. Audience attendance at gigs depends on a number of factors other than the music, such as the opportunity to socialize with other live music enthusiasts, the social and cultural capital gained from regular participation in music scenes and the fun of a 'good night out'. The size of the venue space and its layout also have a significant effect on its social use.

Venues with an identifiable 'front bar', for example, are more accommodating to scene participants who are primarily there for a social experience. Locals meet to drink, relax and socialize, but also participate in live music experiences. A feeling of assumed common ground permeates the interactions at live gigs in small venues, as participants bond over their experience of the venue, the musical performances and other identifying traits. This contributes to the venue's sense of vernacular culture (Rahnema 1997; Shorthose 2004; Gallan 2012; Gallan and Gibson 2013). As Will Straw elaborates, '(s)cenes extend the spatialization of city cultures through the grafting of tastes or affinities to physical locations. Within scenes, tastes or affinities become organized as itineraries across a series of spaces' (2001: 254). In this way, small live music venues and the gigs performed therein facilitate distinct music scenes that bleed into neighbouring venues, bars and house parties; re-enacting and reifying the tastes and affinities that make up their vernacular culture. Space has a decisive impact on experiences of small gigs, both socially and musically, for musicians and audiences alike.

Conclusion

Mythmaking around live music scenes is fundamental to their existence. Narratives, cultural memory and vernacular culture play a role in this mythmaking, as do the everyday rituals or 'moments of seemingly purposeless sociability' (Straw 2001: 250) that make up these narratives. These rituals and moments are perpetuated in a local context among social actors that become more familiar and comfortable with each other as their engagement with the scene progresses. This feedback loop of participation, interaction and satisfaction is unique to the small gig experience in comparison to larger concert events, as it reinforces a culture of participation that is difficult to identify in the anonymous environment of arenas and festivals. The common understanding and experiences shared between participants in music scenes include an emphasis on the local aspects of the space (both in terms of the performers and the nature of the venue itself), a lack of barriers (whether social, cultural or physical) between the audience and the performers and the sense of accessibility inherent in such familiar spaces.

The live gig provides an opportunity to engage with, enjoy and perform live music in the context of everyday life. The relative accessibility, intimacy and proximity to daily routines that live gigs afford make them integral to music scenes and the networks of venues – the live music ecology – that scenes rely on for meaning and form. By providing authentic yet mundane opportunities to engage with the live music experience, gigs act as building blocks for live music ecologies and music scenes. Musicians, audiences and the venues that host them benefit from this process, which builds towards a sustainable live music culture.

As discussed throughout this chapter, space and the ubiquity of live gigs – their ordinariness – render gigs an essential component of local live music scenes internationally. However, despite the large amount of research on popular music and place referenced in this collection and elsewhere, research on live music *spaces* and the mundanity of small-scale musical performances remains a relatively small field. Live gigs, performance spaces and live music in everyday life remain important yet under-researched areas of popular music studies. Yet publications on grassroots live music culture position it as more vital to the cultural industries than ever (Behr, Brennan and Cloonan 2014; Behr et al. 2016). Any further research on popular music and place would be incomplete without a consideration of the live gig and its influence on the spaces that make up such places.

Notes

1. This typology identifies *adopted*, *adapted* and *dedicated* live music venues. *Adopted* spaces are not purpose-built for performance and are temporarily set up for music-making activities. *Adapted* spaces are altered from their original purpose for the continued and regular performance of music. *Dedicated* spaces are purpose built for musical performance (Kronenburg 2011: 140–1).
2. Vernacular culture is that which is collectively imagined, enacted and retold by those that participate in said culture. It is informed by the vernacular knowledge and experience of its participants, and the articulations of social identity to which such knowledge gives rise (Bennett 1997: 98). In the context of live music venues, vernacular culture implicates themes of cultural heritage (MacKinnon 1994: 66), musical memory (Cohen 2013: 580), small-scale musical activities (Homan 2008a: 253), street-level culture and traditions (Jayne, Holloway and Valentine 2006: 459) and the grassroots cultural industries that depend on these venues to give them meaning (Waitt and Gibson 2009: 1234). Vernacular culture consists of the everyday histories of ordinary people participating in local venue cultures and music scenes, continuing a culture of participation and contributing to a collective understanding of these spaces that is shared among participants (Rahnema 1997; Shorthose 2004; Gallan 2012; Gallan and Gibson 2013).
3. 'Symbolic practices… deflect attention from the interested character of practices and thereby contribute to their enactment as disinterested pursuits. Activities and resources gain in symbolic power, or legitimacy, to the extent that they become separated from underlying material interests and hence go misrecognized as representing disinterested forms of activities and resources. Individuals and groups who are able to benefit from the transformation of self-interest into disinterest obtain what Bourdieu calls "symbolic capital"' (Swartz 1996: 77).

References

Auslander, P. (2008), *Liveness: Performance in a Mediatized Culture*, London: Routledge.
Behr, A., Brennan, M. and Cloonan, M. (2014), 'The Cultural Value of Live Music from the Pub to the Stadium: Getting beyond the Numbers', in *Arts and Humanities Research Council*, The University of Edinburgh and the University of Glasgow.
Behr, A., Brennan, M., Cloonan, M., Frith, S. and Webster, E. (2016), 'Live Concert Performance: An Ecological Approach', *Rock Music Studies*, 3 (1): 5–23.

Bennett, A. (1997), '"Going Down the Pub!": The Pub Rock Scene as a Resource for the Consumption of Popular Music', *Popular Music*, 16 (1): 97–108.

Bennett, A. (2000), *Popular Music and Youth Culture*, Basingstoke: Macmillan

Bennett, A. (2002), 'Music, Media and Urban Mythscapes: A Study of the Canterbury Sound', *Media, Culture and Society*, 24 (1): 107–20.

Bennett, A. (2004), 'New Tales from Canterbury: The Making of a Virtual Music Scene', in Bennett and R.A. Peterson (eds), *Music Scenes: Local, Translocal and Virtual*, 205–20, Nashville: Vanderbilt University Press

Bennett, A. and Peterson, R.A., eds (2004), *Music Scenes: Local, Translocal and Virtual*, Nashville: Vanderbilt University Press.

Bennett, A. and Rogers, I. (2016a), *Popular Music Scenes and Cultural Memory*, London: Palgrave Macmillan

Bennett, A. and Rogers, I. (2016b), 'In the Scattered Fields of Memory: Unofficial Live Music Venues, Intangible Heritage, and the Recreation of the Musical Past', *Space and Culture*, 19 (4): 490–501.

Bourdieu, P. (1993), *The Field of Cultural Production: Essays on Art and Literature*, New York: Columbia University Press.

Bull, M. (2000), *Sounding Out the City*, Oxford: Berg.

Cohen, S. (1991), *Rock Culture in Liverpool: Popular Music in the Making*, Oxford: Clarendon Press.

Cohen, S. (2007), *Decline, Renewal and the City in Popular Music Culture: Beyond the Beatles*, London: Ashgate.

Cohen, S. (2013), '"From the Big Dig to the Big Gig": Live Music, Urban Regeneration, and Social Change in the European Capital of Culture 2008', in C. Wergin and F. Holt (eds), *Musical Performance and the Changing City: Post-industrial Contexts in Europe*, 27–51, New York: Routledge.

DeNora, T. (2000), *Music in Everyday Life*, Cambridge: Cambridge University Press.

Felski, R. (1999), 'The Invention of Everyday Life', *New Formations*, 39: 15–31.

Finnegan, R. (1989), *The Hidden Musicians: Music-Making in an English Town*, Cambridge: Cambridge University Press.

Frith, S. (1992), 'The Cultural Study of Popular Music', in L. Grossberg, C. Nelson and P. Treichler (eds), *Cultural Studies*, 174–86, New York: Routledge.

Gallan, B. (2012), 'Gatekeeping Night Spaces: The Role of Booking Agents in Creating "Local" Live Music Venues and Scenes', *Australian Geographer*, 43 (1): 35–50.

Gallan, B. and Gibson, C. (2013), 'Mild-mannered Bistro by Day, Eclectic Freak-land at Night: Memories of an Australian Music Venue', *Journal of Australian Studies*, 37 (2): 174–93.

Gibson, C. and Homan, S. (2004), 'Urban Redevelopment, Live Music and Public Space: Cultural Performance and the Re-making of Marrickville', *International Journal of Cultural Policy*, 10 (1): 67–84.

Hesmondhalgh, D. (2002), 'Popular Music Audiences and Everyday Life', in D. Hesmondhalgh and K. Negus (eds), *Popular Music Studies*, 119–30, London: Arnold.

Holt, F. (2014), 'Rock Clubs and Gentrification in New York City: The Case of the Bowery Presents', *IASPM@ Journal*, 4 (1): 21–41.

Homan, S. (2008), 'A Portrait of The Politician as a Young Pub Rocker: Live Music Venue Reform in Australia', *Popular Music*, 27 (2): 243–56.

Jayne, M., Holloway, S., and Valentine, G. (2006), 'Drunk and Disorderly: Alcohol, Urban Life and Public Space', *Progress in Human Geography*, 30 (4): 451–68.
Kibby, M.D. (2000), 'Home on The Page: A Virtual Place of Music Community', *Popular Music*, 19 (1): 91–100.
Kronenburg, R. (2011), 'Typological Trends in Contemporary Popular Music Performance Venues', *Arts Marketing: An International Journal*, 1 (2): 136–44.
Kronenburg, R. (2012), *Live Architecture: Venues, Stages and Arenas for Popular Music*, London: Routledge.
Kronenburg, R. (2019), *This Music Be the Place: An Architectural History of Popular Music Performance Venues*, New York: Bloomsbury.
Mackinnon, N. (1994), *The British Folk Scene: Musical Performance and Social Identity*, Buckingham: Open University Press.
Peterson, R.A. and Bennett, A. (2004), 'Introducing Music Scenes', in *Music Scenes: Local, Translocal, and Virtual*, 1–16, Nashville: Vanderbilt University Press.
Rahnema, M. (1997), 'Afterword: Towards Post-development. Searching for Signposts, A New Language and A New Paradigm', in M. Rahnema and V. Bawtree (eds), *The Post-development Reader*, 377–403, London: Zed Books.
Rogers, I. (2012), 'Musicians and Aspiration: Exploring the Rock Dream in Independent Music', PhD Thesis, The University of Queensland, Brisbane Qld.
Rogers, I. (2008), '"You've Got to Go to Gigs to Get Gigs": Indie Musicians, Eclecticism and the Brisbane Scene', *Continuum: Journal of Media and Cultural Studies*, 22 (5): 639–49.
Sardiello, R. (1994), 'Secular Rituals in Popular Culture: A Case for Grateful Dead Concerts and Dead Head Identity', in J.S. Epstein (ed), *Adolescents and Their Music: If It's Too Loud, You're Too Old*, 115–40, New York: Garland Publishing.
Shank, B. (1988), 'Transgressing the Boundaries of a Rock "n" Roll Community', Paper Delivered at the 'First Joint Conference of IASPM-Canada and IASPM-USA', Yale University, 1 October 1988.
Shank, B. (1994), *Dissonant Identities: The rock'n'roll Scene in Austin, Texas*, Hanover, New England: Wesleyan University Press.
Shaw, K. (2009), 'The Melbourne Indie Music Scene and the Inner-City Blues', in L. Porter and K. Shaw (eds), *Whose Urban Renaissance? An International Comparison of Urban Regeneration Strategies*, 191–201, New York: Routledge.
Shaw, K. (2013), 'Independent Creative Subcultures and Why They Matter', *International Journal of Cultural Policy*, 19 (3): 333–52.
Shorthose, J. (2004), 'Accounting for Independent Creativity in the New Cultural Economy', *Media International Australia*, 112: 150–61.
Shuker, R. (2012), *Popular Music Culture: The Key Concepts*, 3rd edn, London and New York: Routledge.
Straw, W. (1991), 'Systems of Articulation, Logics of Change: Communities and Scenes in Popular Music', *Cultural Studies*, 5 (3): 368–88.
Straw, W. (2001), 'Scenes and Sensibilities', *Public*, 22–23: 245–57.
Swartz, D. (1996), 'Bridging the Study of Culture and Religion: Pierre Bourdieu's Political Economy of Symbolic Power', *Sociology of Religion*, 57 (1): 71–85.
Threadgold, S. (2015), '(Sub) cultural Capital, DIY Careers and Transferability: Towards Maintaining "Reproduction" When Using Bourdieu in Youth Culture Research', in S. Baker,

B. Robards and B. Buttigieg (eds), *Youth Cultures and Subcultures: Australian Perspectives*, 53–64, Ashgate: Surrey, England.

van Der Hoeven, A. and Hitters, E. (2019), 'The Social and Cultural Values of Live Music: Sustaining Urban Live Music Ecologies', *Cities*, 90: 263–71.

van Der Hoeven, A. and Hitters, E. (2020), 'The Spatial Value of Live Music: Performing, (Re)Developing and Narrating Urban Spaces', *Geoforum*, 117: 154–64.

Waitt, G. and Gibson, C. (2009), 'Creative Small Cities: Rethinking the Creative Economy in Place', *Urban Studies*, 46 (5–6): 1223–46.

Whiting, S. and Carter, D. (2016), 'Access, Place and Australian Live Music', *M/C Journal*, 19 (3)[1] [SW2]. https://doi.org/10.5204/mcj.1085.

Section IV

Cities, suburbs, nations and beyond

20

Suburban breakout: Nomadic reverie in British pop

Andrew Branch

The protagonist in Michael Bracewell's (2001) novel *Perfect Tense* is deeply embedded in the placeness of London through the relentless daily grind of his life. He is, unsurprisingly, not an optimist: 'If the city is a machine for living,' he observes, 'then some people would think of our suburbs as a machine for dying' (Bracewell 2001: 34). In Bracewell's fictional account of a disaffected suburbanite, invested in popular music as an antidote to the anomie office work effects, the city's energy offers the possibility of temporary transformation. We learn that the narrator's proximity to place shapes his world view, spatially regularizing the inherited dispositional practices framing the psychic investments he makes.

In order to think through this relationship between popular music and the suburbs, I complete four objectives: (i) establish the hegemonic representation of suburbia since the commercial coming of age of British popular music in the 1960s; (ii) consider the status of this suburban imaginary in response to global demographic shifts and socio-economic trends reshaping twenty-first-century Britain; (iii) examine new forms of digital technology impacting where, when and how music is consumed in the context of emergent and connected 'smart cities'; (iv) make the case that 'suburban music', because of its terms of reference, is in thrall to logocentrism and sketch the implications of this for judging its transformative power. I thematically connect these objectives by questioning how suburbia has been legitimated as a source of academic interest, particularly for scholars concerned with the vexed issue of how social relations are shaped by powerful inequities. In positing class as being central to our understanding of the place of suburbia in the social imagination, I endorse Carey's (1992) definition of the suburbs as a signifier deployed by intellectuals to denigrate the people who live there, whom they read as devoid of radical thought, in thrall to conventional pursuits and tastes.[1] Taking this position allows me to identify the key tropes deployed by musicians vis-à-vis suburbia and to examine the extent to which their creative output either reproduces, or conversely resists, this reading.

In insisting on specificity of space and place, my argument will nevertheless resonate with those for whom the psycho-geographic mode of enquiry is paramount, defined in the Debordian (1955) sense of studying the effects of environment on the emotions and behaviour of individuals. While the occupation of specific suburban sites is necessarily an expression of uniquely experienced socio-economic conjunctural determinants, connections will be made by those interested in transnational spatial mappings of identity formation. What concerns us is the proximity of the suburb to a valorized urban *Other*. This is to ask, then, how the suburbs have been articulated as a key autobiographical reference point by musicians and to interrogate what purpose they serve. Working in dialogue with published research in this area – notably Frith (1997), Huq (2013) and Worley (2017) – I explore how the suburbs have been read as a cultural incubator of reactionary force and, contra, site of resistance. I also interrogate what we mean when we speak of those liminal spaces bordering urban centres or located along commuter journeys – neither densely populated built environment, nor bucolic utopia. How these spaces are defined tells us much about ourselves and the investments we make in framing who we are and who we are not; what we recognize as legitimated value and what we reject as moribund, reactionary and psychically damaging.

In developing this approach to understanding the centrality of the suburbs to most peoples' lives – they are, after all, where so many of us live – I draw on Bourdieu's (1977, 1990a, 1993) conceptual apparatus underpinning his theorization of human practice: habitus, capital, field. Utilizing these interconnected concepts allows us to bridge the objectivist/subjectivist divide by empathetically understanding human practice as neither the manifestation of unconscious impulses, nor rational computation. Thus, Bourdieu's insistence on empirically locating the origins of our world view in the dispositional practices we inherit, and through our day-to-day encounters with other field inhabitants renegotiate, has implications for understanding how human perception – in this case the aesthetic perception employed by musicians – is socially constituted (Bourdieu 1984: 3–4). Indeed, we might remind ourselves here that while his analysis of music was limited, what Bourdieu did write cuts to the core of the issue, '… nothing more clearly affirms one's "class", nothing more infallibly classifies, than tastes in music' (Bourdieu 1984: 18).

In drawing inspiration from Bourdieu's work, we are able to resist a naïve reading which disconnects how musicians and their audiences have historically chosen to classify the suburbs from their habitual engagement in the field of cultural production and, earlier, the fields of education and family. In short, we need to *denaturalize* aesthetic dispositions. This is important because exposing the classificatory strategies of human actors reveals the power claims they assert in particular fields of practice. Thus, the visions of suburbia expressed in the popular music examples we encounter in this account are always an imagined construction, derived from the aesthetic disposition of the imaginer. It is why art-school graduate Karl Hyde, migrant to Essex and co-founder of EDM specialists, Underworld, can proffer a reading of my birthplace Romford at odds with its reputation as a non-place, 'What I like about Romford and south Essex is that it has a can-do spirit. Nothing is impossible. I haven't left Essex since we first arrived here and I probably never will. Romford has got an energy about it. It's my New York' (McConville 2014). What is important to register here is who gets the power to name, to discursively define space and place in terms concordant with their habitual world view.

'Semi-Detached, Suburban Mr. James' Manfred Mann (Fontana, 1966)

Sitting here as I write, listening again to the tracks that seem to me, and others,[2] redolent of the suburbs, either through the biographical details of the performer/writer, title, lyrical preoccupation or, more challengingly, affective force,[3] persistent themes emerge: boredom; a yearning to escape; sneering rejection of the alleged material aspiration of those residing in suburbia, of their perceived homogeneity.

Blur's *There's No Other Way* (Food, 1991), and flipside *Inertia* ('Fear of being left behind' its opening line), is a prime example of British pop's aversion to non-urban spaces. The song's accompanying video, directed by label boss and ex-Teardrop Explodes' keyboardist David Balfe, articulates the feelings of boredom-bordering-on-despair that define the lyrical preoccupations of the band's singer, Damon Albarn: the opening shot providing a homage to the sequence introducing David Lynch's *Blue Velvet* (DEG, 1986), in which Lynch's camera shifts from framing the iconic white picket fence of American suburbia to recording the unexpected death-by-stroke of an elderly resident watering his garden. We then follow the camera as it descends into the grass blades and soil of the manicured lawn, accompanied by a shift in musical tone: lightness and order giving way to darkness and the molecular: the suburbs as facade. Albarn's cultural capital, an inheritance from his artist father, undoubtedly ensured that he would have endorsed Balfe's video treatment. Indeed, the remainder of the video is composed of a series of suburban clichés (dutiful but repressed housewife; soberly dressed children; ordered family home, with father overseeing the serving of the Sunday Roast, etc.), selected to reinforce the pessimism of *There's No Other Way*: 'all you can do is watch them play'.

I have selected this song because its release year resonates, marking as it does a period of significant social and economic change in the UK: since the early seventies, and exacerbated during the eighties as a consequence of the de-industrialization policies of consecutive Conservative governments, city-based British residents migrated to the suburbs.[4] That demographic trend reversed in 1991, marking the beginning of a gradual return to the urban, particularly among the newly educated offspring of those whose material aspirations had informed the earlier exodus from city centres.[5] Indeed, as Harris (2011) shows, this return, particularly in London, was instigated primarily by artists attracted by cheap rents and an environment that indulged their aesthetic outlook – one reliant upon fetishizing the urban poor, a sensibility Harris terms 'urban pastoral'; quoting Stallabrass, a term he defines as the, 'cultural celebration of urban debasement' (cited in Harris 2011: 227). In this respect, Britpop-era Blur, two members of whom studied at Goldsmith College during the same period as a number of subsequently famous YBAs, were merely expressing the 'suburban sensibility' that Simon Frith (1997) detected in the work and pronouncements of many of their contemporaries, notably Suede and Pulp. *There's No Other Way* is the work of a musician in thrall to the allure of the urban as antidote to the sedimented reactionary practices inculcated in the suburbia of their youth.[6]

Frith, writing at the tail end of Britpop, argues that this suburban sensibility *is* British pop in as much as the configuration of social classes in twentieth-century Britain, particularly in the post-war years of pop's adolescence, has ensured that class distinctions have always broadly mapped middle-class youth's fetishization of the urban, derived from the intoxicating myths it constructs about the city – figuratively and literally always just out of reach – as 'gritty' space, inhabited by an authentic (and deeply romanticized) working class. Huq (2013), in her own review of pop's complex relationship to suburbia, reads the period Frith covers – his account essentially takes us from the post-war birth of pop to the tail end of the twentieth century – as the one in which this sensibility dominated, shaping for so long how many English pop performers invested in their work an antipathy to the environment that often incubated their world view: from Richards and Jagger jettisoning their grammar-school educated, respectable background in order to reinvent themselves as (cod) urban bluesmen as they sneered at provincial women (Reynolds and Press 1995); via punk's ambivalent positioning of the suburbs as a culturally dead space in which either nothing much happens, or what does pass as cultural practice is too in thrall to respectability, aspiration and middle-class convention – saving for a new car, two-week family holidays[2]; to the meditations of late eighties/early nineties pop stars lamenting (again) the sheer monotony of life among the hedgerows and semi-detached homes of the Pet Shop Boys' *Suburbia* (EMI, 1986), an updating of the dream silos of vacuous consumer bliss captured in Roxy Music's *In Every Dream Home a Heartache* (Island, 1973).

This history of the suburbs in pop reads like one long patronizing diatribe by those who position their own mobility and what we might call 'aesthetic awakening' in contrast to the claustrophobic dullness they attribute to the environments they have moved on from. In this landscape, the socially mobile David Bowie is the 'quintessential suburban star' (Frith 1997: 271). As I have argued elsewhere (Branch 2012), Bowie's queerness was key to his success, especially among aspiring suburban youth infatuated with his *Otherness* – a self-conscious performance that allowed them to fantasize about their own self-reinvention, and one that Frith suggests can only come from the suburbs: 'As David Bowie… always understood, a suburban pop sensibility means a camp sense of irony, a camp knowingness, a camp mockery, a camp challenge: do they really mean it?' (Frith 1997: 272).

What to make of this antipathy in respect of suburbia? In Worley's (2017) account of how the suburbs were made sense of by youth between 1976 and 1984, the period he defines as capturing punk's birth and subsequent overt political impact, he argues that to rely on the reading of suburbia prominent in the cultural imagination, captured in my aforementioned account, is to lose sight of 'Britain's shifting demographic' (2017: 116) and its impact on how space and place are inhabited and made sense of. I agree with Worley here: to limit our reading of suburban angst to the indulgences of aspirational middle-class youth desperate to acquire an imagined set of pseudo-bohemian dispositions, as it selectively relinquishes the very privilege that has funded its mobility, is to lose sight of how the hinterlands of urban centres – and especially the new towns created in response to post-war slum clearances – have been experienced, for example, by displaced working-class youth. For the latter social group, the (enforced) journey to the suburbs has historically facilitated modest material improvement, while paradoxically engendering a sense of identity loss, as Cohen (1997) originally contended and recent ethnographic research supports (Branch 2013).[7]

In thinking about how suburbia has been discursively framed in popular music, then, we need to acknowledge the conflicting narratives alluded to in its representation: it is both a space devoid of difference, lacking 'edge' *and* a space in which working-class youth have had to negotiate a new identity in the absence of the cultural and social anchors its forebears experienced. These dialogic narrations of suburbia, discursively dominant during the post-war period until the 1990s, are exemplified, for Worley (2017: 115) in the divergent mobility and thus different lyrical preoccupations of The Cure's Robert Smith and Paul Weller of The Jam: suburbia as established middle-class hell (Smith) and suburbia as edge-land in which, yes, not much happens and the city is still eulogized, albeit through an anxious lens – The Jam's *Down in the Tube Station at Midnight* (Polydor, 1978); *Strange Town* (Polydor, 1978) – but proximity to the non-urban at least allows for an articulation of a negotiated identity, room to breathe. Put another way, for those musicians drawing on the suburbs for inspiration – especially those who spent their formative years living there – growing up in these spaces was read, at least in part, in terms of aspiration, itself shaped by divergent dispositions informed by social class.

'I need a bohemian atmosphere! I'm an artist, Mr. Turner. Like yourself.' Chas in *Performance* (Goodtimes Enterprises, 1968)

In the field of literature – source of inspiration for many suburban musicians accumulating cultural capital in their referencing of canonical texts – Virgina Woolf's sardonic put-down of the 'middlebrow' archetype – 'of middlebred intelligence... in pursuit of no single object, neither art itself nor life itself' (1945: 115) – provides us with critical context. Following Woolf, this is a class fixated on acquiring *prestige* and thus always seeking the approval of 'high culture' highbrows, while simultaneously patronizing the 'living-in-the-moment' lowbrows they erroneously position themselves as superior to. For Woolf – as for so many of the members of the dominant class fraction populating the field of cultural production – those seeking recognition, craving the approval of perceived superiors able to confer status, are incapable of truly living; too caught up in worrying about what others will think. Here, in Cammell and Roeg's *Performance*, the bohemian Turner and working-class criminal Chas act as countercultural representatives of the high/low brow complementary pairing Woolf valorizes.

In the light of Frith's account of suburban pop, we are invited to read its history as middlebrow dispositional practice *par excellence*: the 'suburban' musicians he focuses on, and those captured in Huq's and Worley's accounts, have their artistic expression primarily defined in terms commensurate with their middlebrow status: they are keen on literary references, often self-consciously so in the case of the working-class but mobile Weller, an artist who, as Taylor (2017) notes, thought himself 'really thick' on leaving school and whose output, particularly during a period of creativity between 1978 and 1982, is suffused with references to canonical, *popular* writers. In this regard, Weller's self-consciousness reminds us of Kureishi's quasi-Bourdieusian account of the role linguistic capital plays in distinguishing groups. In his popular-music themed, *The Buddha of Suburbia*, Kureishi notes, 'For Eleanor's crowd hard words and sophisticated ideas were in the air they breathed from birth, and this language was the currency that bought you the best of what the world could offer. But for us [migrant; working class] it could only ever be a second language, consciously acquired' (Kureishi 1990: 178).

Taylor convincingly argues, then that one strand of (suburban) British Pop – mostly white, lower middle-class and male as I read it – is best defined as possessing a 'buried literary sensibility'. Here I would argue that lyrics are foreground because their exchange value is more immediately identifiable. And thus one's desire to creatively express oneself can never be disentangled from one's sense of what is at stake, status-wise. To draw attention to what Woolf would presumptuously insist is the political conservatism of middlebrow culture, however, is to capitulate too readily to a way of reading cultural practice – and in our case a reading suburban popular music – that sees evidence of paradox as a de facto justification for rejection. Conversely, I would call for a more nuanced account of middlebrow taste. Here we must recall Bourdieu's own ambivalence in respect of the ways in which dominated groups either resist incorporation by nihilistically revelling in their domination (lowbrow), or capitulate by adopting, unconvincingly, the values, tastes and dispositional practices of their dominators (middlebrow) (Bourdieu 1990b: 155).

Genders (2017) has contended, by way of illustration, that in so many respects the period immediately following Punk's mid-seventies intervention was notable for the evident ambition of musicians seeking to embrace a *range* of artistic influences, especially but not exclusively literary ones. For Genders, the period is rife with self-educators, with Bowie and Ferry's Roxy Music as role models for post-punks like Mark E. Smith or Ian Curtis, equally likely to cite Ballard, Burroughs or Camus alongside Berry, Little Richard or Presley. Genders sees scant evidence of this tradition in recent decades – the decline of 'art school' institutions as a radical space for experimentation, noted by Frith and Horne (1987), one obvious explanation – and laments the fact: 'If you believe that popular music is at its best when it channels ideas and fantasies from outside its own confines – even risking accusations of pretentiousness in the process – this has to be considered a loss' (Genders 2017).

The idea of valuing pretentiousness is also addressed by Reynolds (2009), who makes a case for defining 'middlebrow' not as dilution (insufficiently avant-garde) or capitulation (placing commercial success before artistic) but as a sensibility in which, for certain musicians and their audiences, binaries are resisted, replaced by nomadic fluidity and the exercising of catholic taste. This position doesn't escape the Bourdieusian charge that all that is really happening is a redrawing of taste barriers by newly formed class fractions on the move, but I think if we factor in the self-reflexivity of the musicians Reynolds valorizes, we can concur with much of what he argues. By this I mean that if we acknowledge *how* an individual agent self-reflexively reacts to the change that an abrupt disruption between habitus and field gives rise to *matters* – and therefore allow for the possibility of agency – we can begin to formulate an account that Bourdieu himself seemed reluctant to countenance, even though his own fieldwork and indeed his own educational and career trajectory suggested that such an account was plausible. (Bourdieu 2007). Here, then, an example of the 'abrupt disruption between habitus and field' might be the moment that aspiring musicians grasp 'ideas and fantasies' beyond immediate comprehension. That is to say, when musicians, often through fortuitous error, embrace heterodox ideas, thus in part relinquishing orthodoxy, and incorporate them alongside more conventional musical motifs. Indeed, in 2016 Mark Fisher and his colleague Kodwo Eshun cited The Pop Group's *For How Much Longer Do We Tolerate Mass Murder?* (Rough Trade/Y, 1980) as perhaps the finest example of this heterodoxic practice in their public celebration of the record's reissue and the band itself, formed by middlebrow-educated Mark Stewart and Nick Shepherd. For Fisher, The Pop Group's embracing of free jazz and realization of 'febrile dance music', alongside their refusal to subordinate form to proselytizing lyrical content, exemplified an ambition and relevance not witnessed since the calls-to-arms of the counterculture, 'The Pop Group retained fidelity to the counterculture's demands for a total transformation of the world. They were still part of what Herbert Marcuse called "the Great Refusal": "the refusal of that which is"' (Fisher 2016). Reynolds (2009) defends this reading of middlebrow pop – middlebrow because it cannot entirely evade the form's commercial imperatives – by proposing that at its best – think Public Image Limited's *Metal Box* (Virgin, 1979) – it re-heterodoxizes the field and therefore:

> calls into question both the mainstream and the margins: pop, for its lack of risk and reach, and the unpop peripheries, for their pointless extremism, concealed macho, impotent inconsequentiality. At its best, middlebrow really does offer the best of both worlds. There's a sense too in which anything really good is going to end up in the middle zone, if not by intent then by acclamation: The Beatles and the Smiths, obviously, but also the Velvet Underground, Sonic Youth and My Bloody Valentine (all of whose achievement lay not in their noise – plenty of other people were dealing in that – but in the merger of melody and riff-structure with swarming textural chaos).

'That golden age from the voice of the suburbs, we're seeing the end of it now' (Anderson, 2018)

In my final section, I want to offer some concluding remarks about the status of 'suburban music' in the contemporary moment. My starting point here will be to think about how the suburbs themselves, specifically in twenty-first-century Britain, are in the process of being repopulated and redrawn in the context of global demographic shifts and emergent socio-economic trends. This redrawing is occurring to such an extent that, as Anderson suggests, the established 'voice of the suburbs' populating the scholarly accounts I have referenced has reduced purchase. In developing this line of enquiry, I shall comment on another key development, namely the centrality of new forms of digital technology and their impact on how, when and where we listen to music. This analysis will move us beyond the account of middlebrow taste and its classificatory judgement-making processes of music production and consumption that I have sketched out. In this regard, I want to ask whether suburban pop actually still *exists* and, if so, what are its determinants if its voice has indeed lost purchase? This will allow me to explore one key aspect of Reynolds' thesis above, namely the need to focus equal attention on music itself as a potentially transformative affective political force, rather than just lyrical content.

In their review of the ways in which the suburbs have been theorized across a range of disciplines, the geographers Vaughan et al. (2009) argue that while the complexity of cities as sites of human interaction with the built environment has been acknowledged repeatedly, too often the suburbs are essentialized as peripheral non-spaces, or are cited in different contexts – dependent on different conceptualizations – as specific case studies, which nevertheless fail to establish their *generic* relevance. Another geographer, Hudson (2006), details at length the ways in which region and place have historically informed the ways in which people identify with music. Hudson's concern here is not to explain how the transformative qualities of music might work, but to show how particular places (e.g. Liverpool, Manchester, Sheffield) have embraced the production and visibility of music cultures, often in an attempt to instigate regeneration policies in the context of responding to the prolonged effects of deindustrialization. Hudson is, in my view, rightly sceptical that such initiatives – establishing 'cultural quarters', etc. – are sustainable, although he does acknowledge that music nevertheless plays a vital role in bringing communities together and harnessing a sense of identity vis-à-vis place.

This work is important because, as Vaughan et al. (2009: 485) note, the spaces we identify as suburban, 'are a theme of universal significance, implicated in the growth of globalized "world cities" and the rapid development of the built environment in emerging economies.' In 2022 their thesis holds: the growth of cities like London and Manchester in a UK context, and their appeal for economic migrants seeking better material conditions, has been maintained, despite eight years of austerity-driven government policy. This has meant that the suburbs and satellite towns that constitute the conurbations of these global cities continue to undergo complex transformation in response: they are destinations not only for the upwardly mobile, but remain one for a now a more racially diverse working class.[8] Alexander Thomas' short film, *Beverley* (Easy Tiger Productions/Urban Edge Films, 2015) captures the 1980s iteration of this trend in its narrative focus on the racism and identity crisis experienced by a multi-racial girl when her parents move to suburbia, with the emergence of Two Tone providing the backdrop. They are also the forced destination of the disenfranchised and newly impoverished 'service class' that Richard Florida (2017) belatedly recognizes is the major casualty of the gentrification thesis he once exalted. Paradoxically, suburbia is also the destination of choice for the less well-off members of Florida's (2002) 'creative class', who nevertheless still have enough economic capital to leave the city, often by cashing in on their 'bijou' properties in order to relocate to a house in the suburbs and invest their energies in contributing to the setting up of burgeoning suburban 'cultural quarters', with their attendant art galleries, music venues and festivals.[9] To inhabit the British suburb today is to witness not the bland uniformity of a complacent middle-class – the dominant British suburban imaginary of the post-war years – but two adjacent worlds divided by property value.

Evidently, digital 'solutions' to the challenges such rapidly evolving forms of urbanization give rise to are grist to the mill for tech companies seeking to maximize profits by owning consumer-generated data – the panoptic city as reality. More specifically, the market dominance of the Smartphone has reshaped how, when and where we listen to music. Michael Bull's (2005) analysis of the ways in which this new technology (in his study the then innovative iPod) facilitated the creation of 'personalised soundworlds' and allowed for the aestheticization of our movement through space has proven to be prophetic: we can now listen to an almost infinite amount of music at the swipe of a thumb; compose or invest in playlists to soundtrack our promiscuous moods; and have music affect us as a by-product of our use of gaming apps, when we watch broadcasts or surf the web.

The implications of these technological innovations for youth cultural practice were spotted early by Bennett (2004), who invited us to consider the ways in which music and place were necessarily being re-conceptualized as a consequence: gone were the subcultures of old, patrolling the suburbs looking to cure their ennui; replaced instead by virtual tribes, whose members connected across increasingly meaningless national borders. Wither the suburbs? And indeed, wither the city itself when, for Sinclair (2008) such tech dependency means that digital natives are, 'now wedded to a kind of instant, dominant present tense of the electronic digital world where people no longer move around in the city but above the city. They're floating on their devices.' Sinclair's reading of current (primarily youth) practice is typically speculative and he has been criticized, with some justification, for selective vision in his flanuerial accounts of how Londoners engage with their city. Laura Oldfield Ford (2011: 14), for example, has argued that Sinclair's classed habitus explains these blind spots in her own politicized reading of the ways in which urban spaces are either privatized or discarded under neoliberalism. However, Sinclair is surely right to draw our attention to the impact new technologies are having on how we experience space and place in the contemporary moment.

> It's boring down there, oh my God... Hackney is just live – the police cars, you hear them on the hour. In Edmonton, you hear a police car once every five years or something, man. It is dead down there.
>
> (Hasted 2004)

Shystie, UK grime artist and, in 2004, newly identified suburbanite on the cusp of fame, reminds us in her commentary of an important caveat to the omnipotence of the virtual world thesis I have just sketched: the experience of it is uneven when filtered through the categorizing categories of class, gender and race: to be *visible* on (sub)urban streets is to be marked. What is interesting about Shystie's take on Hackney, her birthplace, is the value she attributes to the sounds of the street. Indeed, later in the same interview, she contrasts this with the scenario she envisages when it is put to her that a future grime star might be contemporaneously making music in their suburban bedroom: 'She'd be talking about cows and the sheep she sees across the road. Oh, that is dry, man.' Here, the city is marked by manifold possibilities, its value residing in the disparate and infinite noises its built environment and diverse inhabitants produce. Conversely, the suburbs remain a cliché: semi-pastoral, *silent* dead ends.

This emphasis on disruptive sound is, however, an idea that we should pursue. What we need is an understanding of how music taste operates affectively (DeNora 2000), or, specifically, consideration of taste as an activity as Prior (2013) conceptualizes it. In this reframing we can explore music's ability to affectively engineer transformation. How the suburbs feature in this respect – particularly when, as I have noted, they are being repopulated by a new generation of tastemakers – is the key question. Perhaps the answer is to propose that if music is at its most affectively powerful when experienced *collectively*, the contemporary *individualized* listener is always in a sense suburban, with digital technologies facilitating the reconstituting of the clichéd privatized bedroom from which bored youth long to escape. To be suburban here is less about actual physical environment and location, and more about isolation.

If, then, to be suburban is, in Deleuzian (1988) terms, to be sedimented and territorialized, what kind of music de-territorializes, or acts, in incremental ways, to shift schemes of perception, engineering the transformation essential if the world is to be experienced anew? Braidotti (2011) articulates this challenge by drawing on Deleuze and Guattari's use of the terms 'migrant' and 'nomad', the former fixated on borders and boundaries, the latter a non-sedentary subject, aware of its partiality. For Braidotti, new social imaginaries come into play when a nomadic spirit is embraced. But how do they come into play? The experience of drug users is a form of nomadism, of course – transformative flight an effect of momentary affective disruption of synaptic transmission. But what might be the lasting aural equivalent? I suggest that such equivalence is nomadic music that subverts genre, that which confounds rather than conforms.[10] More than this, it is music that works most *affectively* in a communal setting – where bodies interact – in order to achieve its transformative power. In this sense the conservatism of 'suburban music' might be its logocentric focus on articulating the hegemonic suburban imaginary of dead spaces and historically contextual orthodox views – too often we hear what we already intuitively know, which offers little beyond affirmation. Here, music is affectively experienced in isolation as it evokes doxic habit.

The irony here is that pop from and about the suburbs has too often been aesthetically predictable in its railing against perceived conformity. Here, the tragedy of Doyle (2015) hearing Eno's music for the first time – 'Another Green World for me is inextricably rooted in times of quiet isolation and contemplative solace in the subtopian landscapes of Chandler's Ford, Hampshire when I was between the ages of 16 and 18' – is that he *contemplated* it, as middlebrows are inclined to do, suggesting a quelling of emotional attachment and subordination of body to mind.[11] Suburban music's negation, by contrast, is music alive to new possibilities, confounding our expectations and reconfiguring our emotional energies by going against the grain and remaining unencumbered by lyrical prioritization. That the latter might indeed, contra to Shystie, be produced in suburbia, where 'it's boring', is a possibility we should allow for given that it is *how* people use and make music that increasingly matters. To paraphrase a famous musician from the suburbs: it's the concrete in our heads we need to dissolve. This can be increasingly realized in built environments in flux, reshaped by technological innovation and flows of people – now more ethnically diverse than the mono-cultural suburbanites of old – which undermine the increasingly porous borders of nations, cities and towns.

Notes

1 As Huq (2013: 1) notes, in many respects the suburbs are a peculiarly Anglo-Saxon phenomenon, bound up as they are with sedimented social class hierarchies.
2 I am indebted to those online members of the *Interdisciplinary Network for the Study of Subcultures, Popular Music and Social Change* who responded to my social media request for lists of their favourite 'suburban' tracks. Network details available here: https://www.reading.ac.uk/history/research/Subcultures/
3 One of the tasks facing popular music scholars is how to make sense of its power to inform human practice beyond that which can be captured via a semiotic reading. The work of Middleton (1993) provides a lucid account of why the non-verbal affects of sounds themselves are integral to accounts of music and its relations to the wider culture.
4 See Thomas, Serwicka and Swinney (2015) for an overview of these trends.
5 The early nineties also mark a period of sharp growth in student numbers in the UK higher education system (Office for National Statistics 2016).
6 Albarn left the London suburb of Leytonstone at the age of nine to live in the edgelands of Colchester, Essex until he returned to London to take up a university place at Goldsmiths College.
7 This research involved interviewing headteachers leading schools located in the new towns – like those referenced by Cohen (1972) – about the challenges their adolescent male pupils faced in establishing their geographical identity. While their grandfathers and fathers were able to invest in east London as a place central to their sense of who they were, these boys struggled, feeling neither 'a Londoner', nor 'Essex and proud'.
8 See Muir (2016) for a contemporary account of this trend and its implications.
9 While evidenced-based data is as yet unavailable, this is not mere assertion: my own experiences of undertaking a journey back to the suburbs and witnessing first hand these trends is important to register.
10 While this conceptual apparatus remains useful, it is worth remembering its limitations. As Best and Kellner (1991: 107) argue, in their measured appraisal of Deleuze and Guattari's philosophical legacy, habit and routine aren't *de-facto* unprogressive and in fact shape so much of what we productively do on a day-to-day basis.
11 See Gilbert and Pearson for a critique of the ways in which 'meaning' has been foreground in the Western tradition of music appreciation. As they note, 'this tradition tends to demand of music that it – as far as possible – *be meaningful*, that even where it does not have words, it should offer itself up as an object of intellectual contemplation such as is likely to generate much meaningful discourse' (1999: 42).

References

Anderson, B. and Goddard, T. (2018), 'Only Artists Series 5', *BBC Radio 4*. Available online: https://www.bbc.co.uk/programmes/b0b6p5zh (accessed 20 June 2018).

Bennett, A. (2004), 'Virtual Subculture? Youth, Identity and the Internet', in A. Bennett and K. Kahn Harris (eds), *After Subculture: Critical Studies in Contemporary Youth Culture*, 162–72, Basingstoke: Palgrave Macmillan.

Best, S. and Kellner, D. (1991), 'Deleuze and Guattari: Schizos, Nomads, Rhizomes', in *Postmodern Theory: Critical Investigations*, 104–10, London: Routledge.

Bourdieu, P. (1977), *Outline of a Theory of Practice*, Cambridge: Cambridge University Press.

Bourdieu, P. (1984), *Distinction: A Social Critique of the Judgement of Taste*, London: Routledge.

Bourdieu, P. (1990a), *The Logic of Practice*, Cambridge: Polity.

Bourdieu, P. (1990b), 'The Uses of the "People"', in Matthew Adamson trans. *In Other Words*, 150–5, Cambridge: Polity.

Bourdieu, P. (1993), *The Field of Cultural Production*, Cambridge: Polity.

Bourdieu, P. (2007), *Sketch for a Self-Analysis*, Cambridge: Polity.

Bracewell, M. (2001), *Perfect Tense*, London: Jonathan Cape.

Braidotti, R. (2011), *Nomadic Theory: The Portable Rosi Braidotti*, New York: Columbia University Press.

Branch, A. (2012), 'All the Young Dudes: Educational Capital, Masculinity and the Uses of Popular Music', *Popular Music*, 31 (1): 25–44.

Branch, A. (2013), 'Making of Modern Men Project', unpublished interview transcripts (funded by the University of East London).

Bull, M. (2005), 'No Dead Air! The iPod and the Culture of Mobile Listening', *Leisure Studies*, 24 (4): 343–55.

Carey, J. (1992), *The Intellectuals and the Masses: Pride and Prejudice among the Literary Intelligentsia, 1880–1939*, London: Faber and Faber.

Cohen, P. (1997 [1972]), 'Subcultural Conflict and Working-Class Community', in P. Cohen (ed), *Rethinking the Youth Question: Education, Labour and Cultural Studies*, 48–63, London: Macmillan.

Debord, G. (1955), 'Introduction to a Critique of Urban Geography', *Situationist International Online*. Available online: https://www.cddc.vt.edu/sionline/presitu/geography.html (accessed 5 September 2018).

Deleuze, G. and Guattari, F. (1988), *A Thousand Plateaus*, trans. B. Massumi, London: Athlone Press.

DeNora, T. (2000), *Music and Everyday Life*, Cambridge: Cambridge University Press.

Doyle, W. (2015), 'Brian Eno's Another Green World, Revisited By East India Youth', *The Quietus*. Available online: http://thequietus.com/articles/19387-another-green-world-brian-eno-review-anniversary (accessed 12 December 2015).

Fisher, M. (2016), 'The Great Refusal', *Fact Magazine*. Available online: http://www.factmag.com/2016/02/08/mark-fisher-the-pop-group-for-how-much-longer/ (accessed 21 February 2016).

Florida, R. (2002), 'Bohemia and Economic Geography', *Journal of Economic Geography*, 2: 55–71

Florida, R. (2017), *The New Urban Crisis*, London: Oneworld.

Friedman, S. (2016), 'Habitus Clivé and the Emotional Imprint of Social Mobility', *The Sociological Review*, 64 (1): 129–47

Frith, S. (1997), 'The Suburban Sensibility in British Rock and Pop', in R. Silverstone (ed), *Visions of Suburbia*, 269–79, London: Routledge.

Frith, S. and Horne, H. (1987), *Art into Pop*, London: Methuen.

Gender, P. (2017), 'Back When Pop Music Was Literary', *The Times Literary Supplement*. Available online: https://www.the-tls.co.uk/articles/public/literary-pop-music/. (accessed 20 March 2017).

Gilbert, J. and Pearson, E. (1999), *Discographies: Dance, Music, Culture and the Politics of Sound*, London: Routledge.

Hasted, N. (2004), 'Shystie: My life of Grime', *The Independent*. Available online: https://www.independent.co.uk/arts-entertainment/music/features/shystie-my-life-of-grime-45441.html. (accessed 11 June 2017).

Harris, A. (2011), 'Art and Gentrification: Pursuing the Urban Pastoral in Hoxton, London', *Transactions of the Institute of British Photographers*, 37 (2): 226–41.

Hudson, R. (2006), 'Regions and Place: Music, Identity and Place', *Progress in Human Geography*, 30 (5): 626–34.

Huq, R. (2013), *Making Sense of Suburbia Through Popular Culture*, London: Bloomsbury Academic.

Kureishi, H. (1990), *The Buddha of Suburbia*, London: Faber and Faber.

MacInnes, C. (1959), *Absolute Beginners*, London: MacGibbon and Kee.

McConville, D. (2014), 'Underworld Interview: Romford is My New York', *Time Out*. Available online: https://www.timeout.com/london/music/underworld-interview-romford-is-my-new-york. (accessed 25 August 2018).

Middleton, R. (1993), 'Popular Music Analysis and Musicology: Bridging the Gap', *Popular Music*, 12 (2): 177–90.

Muir, H. (2016), 'Black Flight: How England's Suburbs are Changing Colour', *The Guardian*. Available online: https://www.theguardian.com/commentisfree/2016/jul/08/black-flight-england-suburbs-ethnic-minorities-multiculturalism (accessed 20 October 2017).

Office for National Statistics (2016), 'How Has the Student Population Changed?' Available online: https://www.ons.gov.uk/peoplepopulationandcommunity/birthsdeathsandmarriages/livebirths/articles/howhasthestudentpopulationchanged/2016-09-20 (accessed 15 September 2017).

Oldfield Ford, L. (2011), *Savage Messiah*, London: Verso.

Prior, N. (2013), 'Bourdieu and the Sociology of Music Consumption: A Critical Assessment of Recent Developments', *Sociology Compass*, 7 (3): 181–93.

Reynolds, S. (2009), 'Stuck in the Middle with You: Between Pop and Pretension', *The Guardian*. Available online: https://www.theguardian.com/music/musicblog/2009/feb/06/simon-reynolds-animal-collective (accessed 11 February 2012).

Reynolds, S. and Press, J. (1995), *The Sex Revolts: Gender, Rebellion and Rock 'n' Roll*, London: Serpent's Tail.

Sinclair, I. (2008), 'Thinking Allowed', *BBC Radio 4*. Available online: https://www.bbc.co.uk/programmes/b00d0sjj (accessed 27 August 2008).

Taylor, D. J. (2017), 'Going Underground', *The Times Literary Education Supplement*. Available online: https://www.the-tls.co.uk/articles/public/the-jam-paul-weller/ (accessed 11 September 2017).

Thomas, E., Serwicka, I., and Swinney, P. (2015), 'Urban Demographics: Where People Live and Work', *Centre for Cities*. Availabe at: http://www.centreforcities.org/publication/urban-demographics/ (accessed 15 September 2017).

Vaughan, L., Griffiths, S., Haklay, M. and Jones, C. (2009), 'Do the Suburbs Exist? Discovering Complexity and Specificity in Suburban Built Form', *Transactions of the Institute of British Geographers*, 34 (4): 475–88

Woolf, V. (1945 [1932]), 'Middlebrow: Unpublished Letter to the Editor of the New Statesman', in *The Death of the Moth and Other Essays*, 113–19, London: Hogarth Press.

Worley, M. (2017), *No Future: Punk, Politics and British Youth Culture, 1976–1984*, Cambridge: Cambridge University Press.

Discography

Blur, 'There's No Other Way'. Food, Food 29, 1991
The Jam, *Sound Affects*. Polydor, POLD5035. 1980
The Jam, 'Down in the Tube Station at Midnight'. Polydor, POSP 8. 1978
The Jam, 'Strange Town'. Polydor, POSP 34. 1979
The Jam, 'Absolute Beginners'. Polydor, POSP350. 1981
The Kinks, 'I'm Not Like Everybody Else'. Pye, 7N.17125. 1966
Manfred Mann, 'Semi-Detached, Suburban Mr. James'. Fontana, TF757. 1966
Pet Shop Boys, 'Suburbia'. Parlophone, R6140. 1986
Public Image Limited, *Metal Box*. Virgin, Metal 1. 1979
The Pop Group, *For How Much Longer Do We Tolerate Mass Murder?*. Rough Trade, Y Records, Rough 9, Y 2. 1980
Roxy Music, 'In Every dream Home a Heartache'. *For Your Pleasure*. Island, ILPS9232. 1973

Broadcasts, Films and Music Videos

Balfe, D. (dir.) *There's No Other Way*. Food. 1991
Cammell, D. and Roeg, N. (dir.) *Performance*. Goodtimes Enterprises. 1970
Lynch, D. (dir.) *Blue Velvet*. De Laurentiis Entertainment Group (DEG). 1986

21

Sounding South African township life

Kathryn Olsen

Contemporary South African townships were developed as constructions of apartheid designed intentionally to keep Black people on the margins of a white-dominated mainstream economy. According to recent statistics, approximately 80 per cent of the South African population is identified as Black African[1] and most live in or have close connections to townships. The transformation process which began in 1994 with euphoric idealism has shifted into a state of anxious uncertainty. Positions of power and the relationship between dominant and subordinate participants in society are in a state of perpetual flux. Ideologies, existential ideals and moral imperatives are constantly being remade in order to accommodate the struggles of everyday survival where unemployment, illness and violence are an ever-present threat. The African National Congress, while celebrated as liberators from apartheid oppression are now often framed as exploitative managers of positions of power and wealth with little interest in the plight of the average black citizen – the people of the township.

Not all townships are the same – just like the areas that are referred to as suburbs, some sections are more prosperous or deprived than others. Hugging the townships and other lower income housing suburbs are informal settlements which consist of closely stacked shack dwellings with extremely difficult living circumstances and fewer basic amenities than those generally available anywhere else. The most widely known townships in the areas surrounding Durban are Umlazi, KwaMashu, Inanda and Clermont. There are also other less densely populated township areas such as KwaMakhuta, which is south of Isipingo inland from the Kwazulu-Natal southern coastline. Different areas have different dynamics, partly because of the terrain, access to amenities, the condition of roads, drainage and sewerage and also because of the people who live there. In KwaZulu-Natal the townships are generally regarded as Zulu spaces, where Zulu culture, tradition, ideals and music dominate. In the Western Cape the biggest townships are Khayelitsha and Gugulethu. The dominant language in these areas is Xhosa. The most famous South African township is Soweto. Soweto has now been incorporated into the Johannesburg municipality.[2] Johannesburg has a population of about 4.4 million and while Zulu is quite prominent here as the language of everyday life, other official South African languages such as Sotho are also spoken here. Soweto has a more diverse ethnic population than other townships in South Africa.

South African townships are represented most often as places of fear and deprivation where crime and brutality are accepted as a part of everyday life. Townships are, however, also places that people call home. 'The township in South Africa is not unlike inner city black ghettos of Philadelphia, the *favelos* of Rio, slums of Delhi, *barrios* of Caracas, the *banlieues* of Paris, council estates of Glasgow and are by definition, *physical locations* of crowded housing and meagre services for the poor' (Olivier 2015: 186). While this may be so, communicative strategies are coded differently in different township spaces. Poverty and deprivation do not automatically produce uniformity. The South African township can be understood through a dominant communicative system identified through the term *iKasi* – which refers not only to the township as a place, but also to the moral consciousness, hopes and ideals of the people living there (Swartz 2009). The average age of people living in townships is around twenty-seven. *IKasi* style is thus seen as a young person's style and similarly *iKasi* music is a young person's music. The South African township is thus dominated by, and indeed defined by, a youthful identity and, what is more, it is the male version of this identity that is most visible in the public domain.

In terms of economic and social capital, the black South African male often lives precariously. Historically, as a consequence of apartheid's prescriptive migrancy policies, the Black male has lived in a state of perpetual inbetween-ness. Working and living most of the year in township areas left him alienated from his rural home – the home most often of his wife and children. When he returned home he often felt redundant (Olsen 2014). Apartheid was an emasculating system for black men. Today many black men continue to live parallel to the women and children in their lives. The concept of a family of mother, father and children living together as a unit is not the norm. A recently released statistic put the percentage of black children growing up without a father at about 60 per cent (Stats SA General Household Survey 2019). While fathers are often present in affluent black families who now live in the suburbs, for many living in the townships fathers seldom live permanently at the homes of their wives and children. While the *iKasi* style is most often postured as male, there is marked rupture between imagined and lived experience.

Music has historically been both a resource and refuge for township dwellers. David Coplan's (2007) *In Township Tonight! Three Centuries of South African Black City Music and Theatre (Second edition)* offers a comprehensive account of music-making and its sociopolitical context primarily during the apartheid years. Coplan tells 'a story of black South Africa's performing arts' (2007: 10). The theme of this story Coplan says is 'the relation between social and cultural creativity, between performers and their total local contexts amidst the peculiar South African rules and states of play' (2007). In this second edition, Coplan expands the original text of this book to accommodate the shift in his own perspective of and relationship to music and performance in South Africa and the shift in the perspective of those who make music and performance. Thus, while this rich and informative text offers renewed insight into the past it also offers (albeit to a much lesser extent) some important observations of contemporary music-making, particularly in the sections that deal with kwaito. Coplan highlights the constraints that the apartheid 'prison' put on people's lives. He also reveals their initiative and creativity: 'Although Western cultural repertoires were associated with cultural domination, black people constantly searched for ways to master and reconfigure those repertoires to escape or to mitigate their subordination' (402). In a similar response to the domination of the local music scene by global music, musicians today play with repertoires from abroad to produce sounds and styles that are located here in South Africa and very often more specifically in the township. The broader discourses that tie cultural practice with identity and power underpin the responses of music makers to different cultural practices and styles, which are seen as markers of social status and social mobility (403). There is a long-standing interaction between Black American performers and South African performance styles. However, just as in the past when 'creative syncretism' (2007) was the consequence of this interaction, so too in a contemporary context black American influences such as Gospel, R&B and Hip Hop have contributed significantly to the development of contemporary performance practices that are widespread in the townships across the country. In South Africa, stylistic elements from many sources have been recomposed into new frameworks of expression, reflecting changing moral relations, systems of identity-making and value and realities of power. Coplan speaks of performers as 'cultural brokers' (404); as such performers are active in creating images of a changing reality. It is the performing artists who have been among the most visible cultural brokers in South Africa.

Although it does not focus on music, Sharlene Swartz's book, *IKASI: The Moral Ecology of the South African Township* (2009) offers insights into township life that are extremely useful when trying to understand some of the most popular musical practices that are created, performed and heard in these areas. In the process of her fieldwork, Swartz asks the question, what world is this? The soundscape of this world is in some ways a reflection of it. However, perhaps more profoundly it is also a response to this world – one that puts musical performance practice to work as a significant tool in the construction of this world. The complex social realities observed from the academic and analytical perspective (from the outsider's perspective) are perhaps not thought of or experienced as such by those embedded in township environments. For them instability is 'the way things are'. As Swartz points out, there are no 'safe' spaces – even schools can often be fraught with 'predatory teachers and temptation from substance-abusing peers... Township communities are dirty, street justice is deadly, and violence is normalized. While religious and traditional beliefs are part of community life it seems to perpetuate fear, jealousy and sometimes alienation (as in the case of born again Christians who separate themselves from their peers)' (Swartz 2009: 44). Work is frequently identified by the young people who were part of Swartz's study, as the key to a better life – to moral and material redemption; the prospect of being able to get work was seen as the 'key to leaving behind substance use and crime and to providing a better life for mothers and younger siblings. Ironically, two thirds might also sacrifice honesty in order to obtain a job' (Swartz 133). For many the idea of '*music as work*' (Swartz 2009) shapes their aesthetic perception of music – music is valued for what it offers in the marketplace. The hope held in music as a source of escape from poverty underpins many young people's desire to follow a career in commercial music. Indeed some aspiring musicians carefully track the careers of successful musicians and become masters of imitation hoping that their reproduction of an already successful formula will guarantee a place on the runway of fame and the fortune that is assumed to go with it. Being concerned with an esoteric sound ideal is a luxury they can ill afford.

The youth culture of the township takes shape in the streets of the township. Young people in townships have little supervision and lots of free time as school is often disrupted and adults are away trying to make a living. Young people are torn between preparing for the future and enjoying what is on offer in the present. While they usually want education they attend school erratically; they know about AIDS but engage in sexual relationships with multiple partners. They drink alcohol, take drugs and party. They live the way of the township – what they call *ikasi* style. 'The term i*kasi* featured prominently in young people's talk, not merely as a physical location but as a social representation… young people spoke of *ikasi* as a cool place, the reason for certain behaviour, and as an explanation for certain social aspects of life' (Swartz, 74). *Ikasi* style is understood in actions, behaviours and relationship which shape young people's experiences and offers some measure of immunity from doing what they might articulate as 'the right thing' in the face of 'an *ikasi* style morality of inevitability (where you are)' (Swartz 146). They are subject to external forces (sometimes thought of as witches) against which they consider themselves powerless.

The *iKasi*-style soundtrack is often named as Kwaito although currently the labelling of popular music in South Africa is often quite arbitrary and thus quite ambiguous. Kwaito is perhaps best understood in relation to the context that sparked its success:

'Local black popular music was in a slump in the 1990s even Brenda Fassie seemed to be losing popularity – International genres such as American "rhythm and blues" and rap dominated the youth market and the studios' call for a new home-brewed popular style was answered, as is so often the case, by the culture of the streets. This answer was kwaito' (Coplan 2007: 327). Today's youth in South Africa are often referred to as the Y generation or more colloquially 'born frees'[3]: 'In popular and academic literature, certain generalized features are usually associated with the Y youth. These are a perceived focus on partying, consumption, and "stylizing the self" (Nuttall 432). Kwaito, hip hop and house are the music of choice of the Y generation' (Pietilä 2013: 44). While in the early 2000s many saw kwaito as something of a betrayal by young people of the liberation ideals and struggles of their parents (see, for example, Steingro 2005), others recognized a more complex engagement with a newly acquired liberation seeing the overt displays of sexuality, gold and goods as part of a discourse that used the body as a powerful canvas upon which action could be made, imagined and relocated in the previously 'out of bounds' realm of middle-class privilege, namely, leisure and pleasure:

> Kwaito is often hedonistic, misogynist and morally degenerate. But it is the first black controlled commercial music in South Africa, and as such, constitutes an important exposition of post-apartheid economic empowerment. From a gender perspective, a similar interpretive tension exists. While on the one hand kwaito is criticized for being a guilelessly

demeaning of women, from another perspective, by acting out the very symbols of sexual objectification it has provided a medium through which a new set of young black women artists have been able to construct a commanding presence in the music industry.

(Impey 2001: 44)

Some believe that kwaito lost its currency some time ago and that the new sound called *Skhanda*, said to be a blend of rap and kwaito epitomized by the performer, KO (born Ntokozo Mduli) has taken its place. This style is well represented by the song 'Caracara' (released in 2014).[4] According to KO, it is with this song that *Skhanda* style came into being. The *Skhanda* music video situates the music in the township through images of working-class housing, and dusty street. The musical make-up of this song is indeed quite typical of a lot of music identified as kwaito. Kwaito is broadly understood as township music and in many ways whatever new sub-label is attributed to music of the township it all has quite similar structural features. There is a uniformity and persistence in the articulation of a relatively slow-moving synthesized bass sound which carries the entire song. The voice is often processed so that the individuality and emotions of the rapper are disguised. The songs have a spatial breadth and move in time without any sense of urgency or any disruption to the bass-driven foundations of the song. These musical characteristics stand in sharp contrast to the physical experience of township life. Township life is messy, chaotic, unpredictable and unstable. Fear of crime and being robbed of one's hard-earned wares are the 'bassline' of everyday life. The music offers a different discourse and as such it offers a reprieve from hardship, and an opportunity to imagine and experience oneself and one's situation differently. Like trance and house music it reconstitutes the location of experience. The criteria for the differentiation that musicians and audiences make between different styles are quite ambivalent; it seems that these differentiations are not really made on account of musical or stylistic features. Musicians move between different styles constantly trying to reinvent the combination of sounds that they hope is going to bring them fame and fortune. In speaking about the different styles in his own repertoire KO makes a distinction between *Skhand*a and *iKasi* style without really revealing what this distinction is. Thus while 'Caracara' is *Skhanda*, Teargas is *iKasi* which he identifies as a 'lot of kwaito, disco and South African golden oldies music' (https://genius.com/Ko-mr-cashtime-caracara-lyrics). The stylistic experimentations take place not really with some musical ideal in mind but rather with the hope of an escape from poverty. 'With regards to the production itself, I wouldn't say we paid too much detail in creating it. Whatever that we came across that we thought was dope, we just jumped on it' (2014). Much of the discourse in the township is 'about survival – it is not about making a better place but rather about keeping bad things away' (Olivier 2015: 153). The best way to do this is by engaging diversionary tactics like going to church and *playing music* (Olivier 2015).

Gavin Steingo (2016) gives an account of non-commercial music-making activity in Soweto. Here music-making is represented as a socializing mechanism that is an ordinary part of township life. In Soweto,

> thousands of unemployed men and women create music on a daily basis. For most of these people, music making is something that one simply *does* without any particular goal.......

Unemployed men and women gather at particular houses, huddle around a computer, and perform for each other... ... The basis for every musical performance is a short electronic substrate that is looped, often for hours at a time.

(Steingo 2016: 90).

People may bring a range of different instruments and engage their own personal musical sensibilities to participate in an action which Steingo calls 'revealing themselves to each other' (Steingo 2016). This action is the making of community in an otherwise hostile and alienating environment. This activity contrasts significantly with the self-conscious posturing and production of the self for commercial purposes.

Another development in the township music scene has its origins not in Soweto like kwaito, but in the townships of Durban. This music, named *Gqom*, has more recently become very popular and is often referred to by young people as *the* soundtrack of townships across the country. In general terms *Gqom* is a dance-driven style, the lyrics are generally limited to a few words articulated arbitrarily by a dehumanized electronically processed voice. *Gqom* is music made by and for young people. Like the processes of musical engagement that Steingro describes (2016: 90), *Gqom* often takes shape when young people gather in a small room in the township around a computer. It is seen as music that is owned by the people who make it – hence there is very little sense of prescription from outside. 'If you are alive and you grew up in the township Gqom is part of you – It makes you feel better – if you hear a kick... ... that's it!!'[5] There is an element of flexibility in *Gqom* which allows individuals to play with it according to their own creative impulse. 'Music is not about the instrumentation that you have but about creation in your head'.[6] That said, there is nevertheless a certain sound that is expected from *Gqom* and a certain response that goes with it. Primarily it is expected to inspire dance... *Gqom* is 'THAT sound that is only found from the people who dance to the music and mostly they are the people who come from the townships'.[7] In this documentary *Gqom* is described as being composed around the idea of people dancing, partying and enjoying themselves. *Gqom* is a sonic response to the dance moves that inspire it. The 'feel' of *Bhenga*, the dance style behind a lot of the music is foundational in the creation of a song. *Gqom* (like rave) is often linked to drugs. 'Ecstasy... it goes hand in hand with Gqom music... ... Back in Umlazi they said the guys that were doing Gqom were the people who were using drugs'.[8]

One of the interviewees in this documentary expresses scepticism about success in the commercial market. While music is believed to have the potential to bring economic reward in the face of rampant unemployment, there is a perception that already established artists *own* the production process and without connections it is difficult to get one's music into the marketplace. You have to know the right people in order to grow a career in music. Thus, while the production process might be seen as having been democratized – the money-generating process is believed to be monopolized by those who are already successful.

Gqom's popularity grew when it was dispersed once it was taken on as taxi music – the taxis took it out into a much broader reception area. It is essentially dance music, music for partying. Like the young people who love it, it is constantly changing. Perhaps this ever-changing characteristic of *Gqom* is also a consequence of young, unemployed people pushing the hope that they have the key to commercial success in their variation of the same idea that all *Gqom* has – music for fun, to dance to, to feel better and ultimately to transcend or escape the weight of everyday lived experience of crime, poverty, AIDS, unemployment; *Gqom* counteracts feelings of hopelessness.

Interestingly there are some very dynamic women performing under the *Gqom* category, such as Babes Wadumo and Busiswe (both have been named as the Queen of Gqom!). The ambivalence of genre naming is evident in the award given to Busiswe's album, *Highly Flavoured* as the best Kwaito album in the 2018 SAMA[9] awards. Busiswa Gqulu was born in Mthatha in 1988 but raised in Durban. She released her first album, *Highly Flavoured* in December 2017. While *Gqom* characteristically has very few lyrics, Busiswe has managed to insert herself, her ideals and her love of poetry into the *Gqom* domain, giving it a rather different and somewhat unexpected flavour. The inertia and neutrality of most *Gqom* are far from the narratives of Busiswe's three-tiered tale of female harassment and finally triumph over predatory males.[10] She speaks from a feminist perspective of her right to pleasure without having to pleasure the men in the club environment. She is in charge of her body and she asserts her right to be more than a 'meal' for the hyena (https://www.sowetanlive.co.za/opinion/2018-12-12-lyrical-analysis-of-busiswas-banomoya/).

Hip Hop and Rap both have a strong presence in the township soundscape particularly as both are played quite often on the Zulu radio station *Ukhosi FM*. Performers like Kwesta, one of the most popular rap artists in the country, often produce songs that glorify the consumerist obsessions of many young township dwellers. The popular song *Ngud'* features Casper Nyovest, another superstar in the South African arena. The visual imagery in the music video accentuates the social capital invested in fast cars, sexy women and flashy housing. The song is set in two contrasting locations: the first is a township location of dusty streets and shebeen,[11] and the second is on the verges of an affluent housing estate of the sort generally occupied by upwardly mobile young professionals and businessmen. The rapping that accompanies these images is just too cool for coherence! It is a lethargic expression of disconnected ideas alluding to hedonistic indulgence in women and beer. The title *Ngud'* refers to the expensive imported Heineken beer. While the consumption of this beer is celebrated so indeed is its wasteful disposal over bodies. This is reminiscent of the conflicted craze of the youth of Johanessburg's townships known as *i'khothane*:

> Originally a competition between dance crews, *i'khothane* has acquired an edgier intention; whereas incarnations of youth culture affirm the self through forms of conspicuous consumption, *i'khothane* has evolved into what we might call *conspicuous destruction*. As crowds of young people gather around participants in Pimville, Soweto, designer clothes and shoes worth thousands of rand are set alight in a display that asserts wealth through indifference to the commodity.
>
> (Jones 2013, 209; italics in the original)

My focus so far has been on the music most commonly designated as 'township music'. There are other musical activities that also have a significant place in the township soundscape. Many township schools have a strong choir culture. The young people who embrace *iKasi* style in the evenings and on the weekends when they are partying are very often the same young people who sing in school choirs. The repertoire of these choirs is often quite diverse including music from the western classical repertoire such as 'Let Thy Hand Be Strengthened' by G.F. Handel or 'Quoniam tu solus sanctus &Cum Santo Spiritu (Gloria RV 589)' by A. Vivaldi; arrangements of traditional songs, hymns and popular music usually from local repertoires including gospel. They would also most definitely learn the South African National anthem, Nkosi Sikelel' iAfrika.[12]

The township also remains home to many musicians who are passionate about neo-traditional musical genres like those that developed in the 1940s and 1950s in response to experiences of labour migrancy, namely, *isicathamiya* and *maskanda*, and indeed in my own experience of weekends in the township these musicians often get together to rehearse in their backyards. This music is markedly different from the *iKasi* style and for many it is regarded as the music of the older generation. While youthful *isicathamiya* groups like Young Mbazo who carry the Ladysmith Black Mambazo legacy into the future defy this perception, in general young people are far more enthralled by music that is transcendent; music that allows them to hope for something that is far from the reality of their lived experience. *Maskanda* has a strong presence in rural areas. Its commercial production particularly in studios around Johannesburg keeps it in township spaces, but again the common everyday soundtrack is more likely to be Casper Nyovest or Beyoncé than Khuzani, the maskanda star recorded and promoted by Izingane Zoma Music Productions.

With its already primed market, Gospel music has a strong position in the music industry as one of the popular and commercially successful genres. The promises emanating from widespread evangelical churches are not only of everlasting life but also promises of wealth, health and happiness in the here and now. The gospel-style music popular in these churches plays an important role in appealing to the congregation/audience's emotions in solidifying the belief in a better future and redemption from the pain, uncertainty and hardship that permeate their lived experience. Popular gospel artist, Andile KaMajola[13], like many others pairs his role as entertainer with that of pastor. An extremely successful commercial concept within the Gospel domain is the Joyous Celebration Series. Like kwaito, Joyous Celebration may be seen as a response to the euphoria that followed the first democratic election in 1994. The success of the first studio project launched by gospel producers, Lindelane Mkhize, Jabu Hlongwane and Mthunzi Namba, has seen it become a platform for the launch of many gospel artists' careers (e.g. Khaya Mthethwa). Gospel is seen as a ticket to success and is often mixed with other styles and genres like kwaito, hip hop, maskanda and isicathamiya in an apparent attempt to boost sales.

The syncretic mixing of genres offers the opportunity for South Africans to be more assertive and experimental in the making of their identities than they were in the past, and they do so with little reverence for the boundaries that encapsulated and separated musical practices. Hence young jazz musicians, choirmasters, maskanda and isicathamiya musicians interact, share and compete in ways that were unimagined in the past.

The township is dominated by dance motivated music set to inspire and empower in the imagination if not in reality. The South African township receives a lot of publicity usually because of all the bad things that happen there; it is however also home to some of the most successful soundtracks that themselves have transcended the boundaries of place and poverty to find resonance with other locations of experience across the globe. These global resonances suggest a sameness registered through musical experience which perhaps goes some way to demystifying the African other.

Notes

1. https://www.indexmundi.com/south_africa/demographics_profile.html
2. http://worldpopulationreview.com/world-cities/johannesburg-population/
3. 'Born-frees' and people born after 1994 when apartheid was disbanded.
4. '"Caracara" is a specific Volkswagen Carravelle, which was manufactured between 1993 and 1995. This is a popular vehicle in the township because of how expensive it used to be and how cool it looked once modified. It is needless to say this anthem was as cool as the car' (https://genius.com/Ko-mr-cashtime-caracara-lyrics).
5. https://www.youtube.com/watch?v=xgHxtE4uzdY
6. https://www.youtube.com/watch?v=xgHxtE4uzdY
7. https://www.youtube.com/watch?v=xgHxtE4uzdY
8. https://www.youtube.com/watch?v=xgHxtE4uzdY
9. SAMA: The South African Music Awards.
10. The three tiers to her story of female empowerment take shape in three songs: *Ngoku (2013), Lahla (2014) and Banomoya (2018)*.
11. Shebeen: the Shebeen in South Africa is a pub in a township setting. Historically shebeens were regarded as places that operated illegally and that sold potent home-brewed liquor.
12. Personal Interview with Bhekani Buthelezi a former choirmaster of Umlazi High School. Durban, November 2017.
13. Andile KaMajola received 2018 SAMA award in the category Best Traditional Faith Music Album https://www.thesouthafrican.com/samas2018-all-the-winners-at-this-years-awards/

References

Coplan, D. B. (2007), *In Township Tonight! Three Centuries of South African Black City Music and Theatre*, 2nd edn, Johannesburg, South Africa: Jacana Media.

Crudo Volta Radio and GQOM OH!. (2016), 'Woza Taxi: Secret Stash Out of the Locations', Available online: https://www.youtube.com/watch?v=xgHxtE4uzdY (accessed 14 December 2018).

Impey, A. (2001), 'Resurrecting the Flesh', *Agenda*, 49: 44–50.

Jones, M. (2013), 'Conspicuous Destruction, Aspiration and Motion in the South African Township', *Safundi: The Journal of South African and American Studies*, 14 (2): 209–24. Available online: http://dx.doi.org/10.1080/17533171.2013.776749 (accessed 12 November 2018).

Musicians who are defining Gqom. Available online: https://theculturetrip.com/africa/south-africa/articles/musicians-who-are-defining-gqom-the-sound-of-south-africas-townships/ (accessed 10 October 2018).

Olivier, A. (2015), 'Heidegger in the Township', *South African Journal of Philosophy*, 34 (2): 240–54.

Olsen, K. (2014), *Music and Social Change in South Africa: Maskanda Past and Present*, Philadelphia, USA: Temple University Press.

Peterson, B. (2003), 'Kwaito "Dawds and the Antimonies of Hustling"', *African Identities*, 1 (2): 197–213.

Phakathi, V. (2018), 'Lyrical Analysis of Busiswa's *Banamoya*', Available online: https://www.sowetanlive.co.za/opinion/2018-12-12-lyrical-analysis-of-busiswas-banomoya/ (accessed 13 December 2018).

Pietilä, T. (2013), 'Body Politic: The Emergence of a "*Kwaito* Nation" in South Africa', *Popular Music and Society*, 36 (2): 143–61

Sauphie, E. (2018), 'Tendance Gqom: naissance d'un phénomène', *Jeune Afrique:* Paris, France. Available online: https://www.pressreader.com/benin/jeuneafrique/20180805/282565903955507 (accessed 10 October 2018).

Stats sa, Department Statics South Africa, Statistical Release PO318, General Household Survey, 2019. Available on: http://www.statssa.gov.za (accessed 2 September 2021).

Steingro, G. 2005. 'South African Music After Apartheid: *Kwaito*, the "Party Politic", and the Appropriation of Gold as a Sign of Success', *Popular Music and Society*, 28 (3): 333–57.

Steingro, G. (2016), *Kwaito's Promise Music and the Aesthetics of Freedom in South Africa*, Chicago and London: University of Chicago Press.

Swartz, S. (2009), *iKasi: The Moral Ecology of South Africa's Township Youth*, Johannesburg, South Africa: Wits University Press.

South Africa demographics Profile 2018. Available online: https://www.indexmundi.com/south_africa/demographics_profile.html (accessed 10 October 2018).

22

Funk: A musical symbol of Rio de Janeiro's favelas

Vincenzo Cambria

Favelas (commonly rendered in English as slums, or shantytowns) can be seen as a result of a long struggle for the 'right to the city' (Lefebvre 2006) perpetuated, since the end of the nineteenth century, by masses from the lowest part of Rio de Janeiro's working class that could not wait for effective public housing policies from the state.[1] They are heterogeneous physical and social spaces that defy any simplistic attempt of definition, resulting from more than a century of intense fluxes of people and expressive cultural practices coming from both within and beyond the city. Some of Rio de Janeiro's favelas have accumulated many thousands of residents, therefore acquiring the dimension and complexity of towns (or, even, cities) on their own. The musics produced and circulating in these places reflect this diversity of backgrounds, the most heterogeneous influences coming from the national and global flows of more or less commoditized sounds and the creative solutions their residents have developed over time to deal with the pleasures and pains of everyday life. The way that these musics are perceived and experienced also need to be understood as a result of the social dynamics that have historically defined the city, its unequal spaces and the ways in which they relate to each other.

A quantitative survey carried out by the Musicultura Group[2] in 2006 well captured the great diversity of musical practices and experiences that characterize the soundscape of favelas. One of its most clear results is that when 929 respondents were asked about the kinds of music they liked most, 152 different answers were given. If not all the musical genres cited in this survey have developed a visible, live scene within Maré and other favelas of the city, a number of them – such as *forró*,[3] *pagode*,[4] rock, evangelical music, samba, funk and sertaneja[5] – are quite regularly performed. Given the limits of this chapter, it would be impossible for me to present, in a minimally satisfactory way, this variety of musical practices.[6] For this reason, I have chosen to discuss here only one of favelas' most well-known musical symbols: funk. This music and the practices related to it have gradually assumed the common-sense position of the most representative expression of, and almost a metaphor for favelas. Before *funk*, this position had been, for a long time, occupied by *samba*. Given their association to favelas and to the impoverished black population residing within them, both of these musical expressions have suffered a strong prejudice and repression. Before being transformed into one of the main symbols of the nation, *samba*, as is happening today with funk, had been pointed out as one of the best examples of the backward and barbarous habits characterizing the then (early twentieth century) emerging favelas, stigmatized as an assault to morality and, therefore, feared and repressed as a practice fostering social disorder and degradation. Once considered one of the most genuine Brazilian traditions, *samba* monopolized, for better or for worse, all kinds of representations of favelas.[7]

If the production of studies discussing the relations of *samba* to favelas has significantly decreased, an ever-growing literature from different fields is being dedicated to the analysis of the funk phenomenon.[8] Taken together, these heterogeneous works provide an excellent picture of the historical evolution of this genre, the stylistic elements and forms of sociability that developed around it, the imageries and issues that are dealt with in its lyrics and the ways it is being feared and repressed.

What today has come to be known as *funk* (pronounced 'funkee'), *funk carioca* or *baile funk*[9] is the result of a long process through which American Black popular music expressions have been first assimilated into Rio de Janeiro's Black youth counterculture, and then, once resignified and hybridized, transformed into a (initially local, but, increasingly, national) mass phenomenon.[10] This process has been directly linked to the history of dance parties (*bailes*) organized in peripheral areas of the city which, on each weekend since the 1970s, started to gather thousands of people dancing to recorded music imported directly from the United States by DJs and *equipes de som* (sound systems). At the beginning, the music played consisted basically of American soul and funk and the dance parties were usually known as *bailes black*. This movement assumed a significant role in the identity politics of the time. By identifying themselves and their movement as 'Black' (and repeating slogans such as 'Black power' and 'Black is beautiful'), thousands of Afro-Brazilians were going directly against the national ideologies of race(lessness). The identification of those youngsters with a foreign cultural expression many times displaying an oppositional and protest tone, instead of embracing local Afro-Brazilian practices – as samba – legitimated by the *status quo* through a discourse centred on the idea of an 'harmonious mixture of races,' provoked a great polemic and a certain fear.[11]

The 1980s represented a special moment for such dances (then, already commonly called *bailes funk*) and their music. The gradual decline of disco music fever and the arrival of American hip-hop styles such as electro-funk, freestyle and especially Miami bass, all grounded on drum machines and rhythmic loops with a dance tempo, and displaying a festive lyrical content, established the foundation for the forthcoming definition of an original local dance music style. The first step in this direction has been the creation of Portuguese lyrics for the American songs thriving in *bailes*. The original lyrics (many times, only the refrains) started to be replaced by Portuguese ones usually having different meanings but similar sounds. Such versions, called *melôs* (most probably coming from *melodia* – melody), were sung over the original tracks (or over their sampled grooves).

During the first two decades (1970s and 1980s) the music played in Black dance parties has been primarily recorded in America. The first Brazilian funk commercial production came in 1989, with the LP *Funk Brasil*, organized by DJ Marlboro,[12] in which some successful imported grooves (the most used being 'Volt Mix' and 'Hassan')[13] had been used together with Portuguese lyrics (Medeiros 2006: 16). This LP was the first of a long series of local productions presenting to the public young DJs and MCs from peripheral areas of the city displaying all their creativity and irreverence. A distinctive style made up of a peculiar way of dressing, specific haircuts and a characteristic slang language, began to be adopted by the young *bailes* frequenters who also began to aggregate in groups (*galeras*).

The 1990s represented the climax of funk success. From an obscure and almost unnoticed movement of marginalized sectors of Rio's society, it turned into a mass phenomenon, achieving high visibility in the media. Inspired by the first local commercial productions and stimulated by the growing number of competing *equipes de som*, which started to organize music festivals in different neighbourhoods, a great number of young people began to compose, sing and dance original songs. At that time, it was very common for MCs to operate in *duplas* (duos), usually composed of young males residing in the same favela or suburban neighbourhood (some of the most well-known being Cidinho and Doca from Cidade de Deus, Junior and Leonardo from Rocinha and William and Duda from Borel).[14]

During the second half of the 1990s Rio de Janeiro's funk music and the practices developed around it had been at the centre of public attention. In spite of the first mass commercial success of some of its more pop-oriented exponents (MC Latino and the duo Claudinho and Buchecha surely being the best examples), and of the increased interest of middle-class youth in frequenting its dance parties, funk has been highly visible within the media dedicated to crime news much more than in those discussing music and culture.

At the turn of the century, *funk* acquired new elements and stylistic features that, for better or worse, kept alive the attention on it. One of the novelties has been the appearance of *bondes* (literally, trams, meaning a group of people), a new format for the performances of funk music featuring one or a few MCs and a group of dancers. Following the example of the first group to reach a mass success, *Bonde do Tigrão* (Big tiger's tram), many other groups emerged proposing a new formula for their performances: light-hearted lyrics full of double-meanings and catchy new slang expressions (as, for example, *tchuchuca* – young pretty girl – *popozuda* – a girl with big buttocks – and *preparada* – an 'easy' girl); and a group of attractive dancers (boys and/or girls) displaying choreographies rich in sexual connotations. This formula proved to be very successful and marketable, still representing one of the most visible facets of the funk phenomenon.

In the same period, a funk sub-genre emerged with force in the *bailes* organized within the favelas of the city (commonly called *bailes de comunidade*, that is, community dances): *proibidão* (highly prohibited) also known as *funk de facção* (faction's funk). What defines this subgenre is that the lyrics of its songs praise a specific criminal faction, exalting the power and courage of its members, celebrating its successful 'war' actions and sending messages of derision and menace to its enemies (i.e. rival gangs and the police). Sonically, *proibidão* funk songs are characterized by the frequent use of sampled or midi sounds reproducing gunshots and crossfires.[15]

Another funk subgenre that gained force during the same period is commonly called funk *putaria* (whoredom funk). As its name suggests, this music is characterized by lyrics with a highly sex-oriented or, even, explicit pornographic content. In these songs, displaying a hyperbolic and lascivious sexual imagery, boys and girls present themselves as voracious and tireless lovers in search of casual and multiple sexual relations, when not, as it became extremely common during the year of my fieldwork (2008), proclaiming themselves as 'prostitutes'. As *proibidão*, funk *putaria* is mainly consumed in the *bailes* and other private parties held in the favelas of the city or downloaded from the internet. Sharing many traits and circulating mostly within the same circuit, *funk de facção* and *funk putaria* are many times considered to be a single thing or, better, two aspects of a single more general phenomenon (sometimes both are considered *proibidão*). An important difference between these two funk repertoires, however, is that, without the direct association to specific criminal factions, *funk putaria* performers (and their songs) can more easily circulate in various favelas, no matter what specific faction controls them.

At the turn of the century, Rio de Janeiro's funk scene clearly divided into two fronts: commercial funk and funk produced and consumed mainly within the favelas of the city. These two fronts are, however, clearly interconnected, with the second constantly feeding the first. MCs and DJs continue being predominantly favela or suburban residents, and many commercial hits are lighter versions of songs thriving in *bailes*.

The excessively crude sexual content in the lyrics and choreographies of funk groups has been met with strong criticism. They have been accused of praising and fostering casual sex, of propagating a degrading image of women (as sexual objects) and of exalting in their songs a preference for *novinhas* (i.e. young girls) as sex partners. This wave of male groups was followed by a number of female singers and groups that enjoyed increased visibility (some of the most successful being Tati Quebra-Barraco, Deize Tigrona, Mc. Sabrina and Gaiola das Popozudas), proposing an equivalent formula, but with inverted positions (i.e. depicting males as sexual objects). An interesting debate developed around these female funk performers, in which some saw their activity as replicating and assuming a male point of view, where others have interpreted their open and direct sexual discourse as a form of (neo-feminist) liberation for those women who can now freely express their own sexuality.[16]

The sound of Rio de Janeiro's funk has assumed a decidedly local 'taste' through another significant novelty that was introduced at the turn of the century and, since then, dominated the scene: the *tamborzão* (big drum) groove. The introduction of this pattern (and its variations), initially played with sampled conga-like hand-drums and, more recently, with all kinds of sampled sounds (including voices in a kind of beatbox technique), is particularly meaningful since it is a widespread element in various Afro-Brazilian traditional musical practices. This new groove has supplanted all other previous rhythmic bases coming to represent the very essence of this music today (no matter what funk subgenre you consider).

The association of this music to violent practices and to criminal groups and activities started to be repeatedly pointed out in the 1990s, quickly turning into common-sense knowledge. During that decade, the rivalry between different *galeras* (organized groups of *baile* funk frequenters) soon generated a singular practice that would shock society: *bailes de corredor* (corridor dances), also known as *Lado A – Lado B* (A Side – B Side). Those *bailes* consisted of the more or less ritualized fight (but even so, extremely violent) between two rival *galeras* (the membership to which was mainly defined by the place of residence of the youths). The dance floor functioned as a battlefield where the rival groups occupied opposite sides with a 'corridor' (actually, an empty space) separating them. At the *grito de guerra* (battle cry) coming from the DJ, the rival gangs started to confront each other, trying to capture some of the 'enemies' to beat them. Security agents occupied the corridor, trying to impede them to do so. This practice often resulted in many people seriously injured and, in some cases, death. The visibility the media gave to this extremely violent form of sociability greatly contributed to the negative reputation that funk culture as a whole received. *Bailes de corredor*, now an extinct practice, contrary to what many assume, never took place within favelas. The drug gangs controlling their territories, in fact, did not want to call attention to them with the inevitable repercussion of the troubles they would bring. They were instead commonly held within clubs of suburban areas of the city.[17]

Initially middle and upper classes saw the funk movement as a distant barbaric reality not affecting them. However, it did not take too long for them to start feeling uncomfortable when they perceived that their contact with it was inevitable. On the one hand, their children began to go to favelas to frequent *bailes funk* and, on the other, both funk music and the *galeras* of suburban youth were visibly entering their social and physical space. One particular episode, however, made funk and funkeiros (funk fans) from favelas and suburban neighbourhoods extremely visible for the middle and upper classes. In 1992, rival gangs of *funkeiros* were involved in a large fight on the Arpoador beach (in the wealthy and touristic area of the city) under a very ambiguous circumstances, which the media presented as an *arrastão* (literally, a drag-net – a popular expression used to define a form of mugging in which a group of delinquents run on the beach, frightening people they meet on their way and stealing the belongings they leave behind). Distorted and exaggerated by the mass media, this episode provoked a general panic and was assumed as a clear evidence of the danger represented by this musical culture and its followers.[18] As a result, funk started to be publicly demonized, *bailes* prohibited and some of their organizers imprisoned. This situation reached a critical dimension when, in 1999, funk music and its parties were the target of an investigation by a Parliament Inquiry Commission of the Legislative State Assembly. This was just the beginning of a very controversial series of legislative actions aimed at limiting and regulating this musical culture. While initially criminalized and submitted to many restrictions and requirements (Law 3410 of 30 May 2000; Law 4264 of 1 May 2004; and Law 5265 of 19 June 2008), funk music achieved the unprecedented deed to be later officially recognized as a legitimate 'cultural and musical movement' that cannot be discriminated against (Law 5543 of 22 September 2009).[19]

Repressed and stigmatized, *bailes* funk have found the most suitable ground to flourish within the favelas of the city where, besides being highly appreciated by the young residents, due to the absence of the state, they did not need to comply with the repressive requirements and limits imposed on them. *Proibidão* and *putaria* funk subgenres emerged within this context, almost as a provocative response to these restraints, showing that no limits would be accepted there.

Outsiders, who know these repertories mostly through their sonic and audiovisual products,[20] imagine the *bailes* taking place within favelas as extremely dangerous and violent. It is very rare, however, to hear about fights or aggressions of any kind happening within them. Despite the overbearing presence of gangsters showing off their firearms, the atmosphere in the *bailes* is always joyful and festive. The real risk at such parties is represented by the possibility that a rival gang or the police might invade them.

Many of the scholars that have studied *proibidão* funk music have analysed and discussed almost exclusively its lyrical content and the ways it relates to the violence of the drugs factions controlling favelas.[21] Some have emphasized its elements aimed at attracting the residents: the constant reference to and celebration of the local faction, its territories and allies (and the parallel denigration of those of the rivals) being a means for inducing the residents to identify with them. Others have pointed out its use to convey menacing messages: the detailed description of brutal episodes of torture and killing being a way to alert the residents, possible (or actual) betrayers, the police and the rival gangs of the consequences of challenging that gang. Many agreed that these songs would be a way of taking advantage of them as a privileged means of communication permitting a wider audience to be aware of, among other things, the rules to be followed, recent or future war actions, new alliances, the loss of fellow gangsters and changes in the faction's hierarchy.[22] These readings catch important elements of the meanings involved from the point of view of the local criminal factions. What they usually do not consider, however, is how these songs are received and seen by those frequenting the *bailes*, ending up implicitly assuming that the meanings and interests motivating the production of these songs would be also central elements in their local fruition. If those messages surely have an influence on some of the residents, my interlocutors in the field suggested that most of the partygoers are not really interested in them. They enjoy funk parties and, as in many other spheres of their daily life, have to accept things as the local gangs want them to be. It is not really a matter of choice or of identification.

Violence is a fundamental aesthetic ingredient of these songs that represent a crude poetic depiction of criminal life and its ethos. Its excesses, however, shock more the external occasional listener than those who experience its burdening effects first-hand. The latter, in fact, have learned to transcend and sublimate them and are able to better perceive their fundamental dimension of humour (excessively violent scenes and ideas expressed in those songs turning into something grotesque). The same thing happens in the case of the funk *putaria* repertoire which audiences do not really see as degrading or aggressive but, for the most part, as a way to creatively play with sexuality, and male/female relations in general, assuming caricatured characters (as a form of 'make believe'). Another aspect not considered by those analysing funk songs' lyrics is that, due to the distorted and crackly sound coming from the loudspeakers of most *bailes*, it is really difficult to understand the lyrics. For most of my interlocutors, the rhythm and the power of sound (i.e. high volume, and very deep bass frequencies), the 'engine' of dancing, were the main attractive elements. The power of sound is so central to funk musical practices that is clearly implied in the use of augmentatives in all the most popular names given to this music and its grooves: *batidão, pancadão, porradão* (three terms with the same meaning: a big stroke – alternative names for funk music), and *tamborzão* (big drum – the name of its most diffused groove).

Rio de Janeiro's funk music today can be many different things. In addition to the subgenres briefly discussed here, other specific styles and trends include: *funk melody* (a more romantic and melodious style influenced by American 'freestyle'), *funk consciente* (conscious funk, with lyrics approaching the inequalities and struggles of daily life in the favelas, making a social critique); *montagem* (assemblage of sampled vocal fragments used as rhythmic material over the funk groove, often with no direct semantic meaning); *funk evangélico* or 'gospel' (funk songs with a religious content composed by and for the evangelical community); *funk de raiz* (roots funk, old times funk songs and new compositions following their model); and, more recently, *funk ostentação* (show off funk, a strand of funk developed initially in the State of São Paulo, by reducing the strong references to criminal gangs and activities and focusing on the intensive consumption of luxury products (Trotta 2016).

Notes

1 This chapter derives from my doctoral dissertation (Cambria 2012) which focuses on the relationships between different forms of violence and different musical practices in Rio de Janeiro and, more specifically, within the context of its biggest favela complex, the Maré neighbourhood. I'm very grateful to CAPES (Brazilian Ministry of Education) and to the USA Fulbright Commission for the financial support I received.
2 The Musicultura Group is a participatory research collective, coordinated by Samuel Araújo and made up of university researchers and young residents working since 2004 in the Maré neighbourhood. I collaborated with Samuel Araújo starting the research activities in Maré that led to the creation of the group and conducted the fieldwork for my dissertation, in 2008, co-working with them. For more information on this ongoing project, its methodological challenges and some of the results of the work carried out by the group, see Cambria (2012), and Araújo and Cambria (2013).
3 *Forró* is a general designation for some northeastern dance music styles.
4 A samba-derived musical style.
5 *Musica sertaneja* (loosely translatable as country music) is a popular music style developed out of rural traditional genres from the central and southeastern regions of Brazil.
6 For a more comprehensive analysis, see Cambria (2012).
7 Despite the unquestionable importance of favelas in the history of this music, however, the main analysts of samba's history (among others: Moura 1995; Vianna 1999 and Sandroni 2001) have presented a much more nuanced picture in which it is seen as developing through a rich interaction among different social and cultural spaces of the city of Rio de Janeiro.
8 See, among many others, Vianna (1988, 2006); Herschmann (2000); Sneed (2003, 2007a and 2007b); Essinger (2005); Rodrigues (2005); Medeiros (2006); Russano (2006); Cabral (2007); Guedes (2007); Palombini (2010, 2011); Lopes (2010); and Trotta (2016).
9 The qualifier carioca – meaning from Rio de Janeiro – after the word funk, is sometimes added to distinguish this music from American funk. For the same reason, others refer to

this music as *baile funk*, which actually means 'a funk dance party.' Both expressions are rarely used in Rio de Janeiro's daily speech, being more common among foreign audiences.

10 More details on the influence of American black musics in Rio de Janeiro over the last forty years can be found in McCann (2002), Alberto (2009) and Palombini (2010). For a well-written history of Rio de Janeiro's funk music scene see Essinger (2005).
11 For good analyses of the political dimension of this cultural movement and of how it has been interpreted at the time see McCann (2002), Giacomini (2006) and Alberto (2009).
12 DJ Marlboro (a.k.a. Fernando Luiz Mattos da Matta) had a central role, both as a DJ and a producer, in the creation and establishment of *funk carioca*.
13 The groove Volt Mix has been taken from the music '808 Volt Mix' composed by DJ Battery Brain. The groove known in Rio as Hassan, came from the music 'Pump Up the Party' composed by Hassan (alternative name of the freestyle singer Stevie B) (Medeiros 2006: 16).
14 Cidade de Deus, Rocinha and Borel are the names of three Rio de Janeiro's favelas.
15 In the context of the *bailes*, it is quite common for the bandits to add the sound of real firearms' shots to those recorded in the music.
16 This debate has generated a great deal of academic literature. See, among others, Lyra (2006), Pinho (2007) and Amorim (2009).
17 For more details on this controversial practice see Herschmann (2000) and Cabral (2007). The fact that the author of the last book is a police officer is itself symptomatic of the kind of reputation this musical culture has acquired in Brazil.
18 More details on how the mass media contributed to associate funk music and its followers to the violence of *arratões* can be found in Herschman (2000).
19 A detailed analysis of this process and of other legal controversies surrounding this music and its musicians can be found in Palombini (2011).
20 If during the 1990s these repertories (first proibidão and, later, putaria) were diffused through bootleg CDs, they are being spread today mainly through videos posted on the internet. A visual aesthetic dimension is therefore being consolidated, assuming a central position. Recurrent elements in *proibidão* videos are, for example, powerful motorcycles, piles of money, golden chains, brand-name sneakers, different kinds of firearms stored in arsenals or exhibited by young men, pictures of fellow gangsters that have been killed and walls tagged with the initials of the drug factions. Videos of funk *putaria* are usually more monotonous, always exhibiting beautiful women in sensual poses or dancing.
21 See, among others, Rodrigues (2005), Russano (2006), Guedes (2007), Sneed (2003, 2007a) and Orlando Junior (2009).
22 For this reason, *proibidão* funk songs have been often used by the police as a source of sensible information on these matters.

References

Alberto, P. L. (2009), 'When Rio Was Black: Soul Music, National Culture, and the Politics of Racial Comparison in 1970s Brazil', *Hispanic American Historical Review*, 89 (1): 3–39.
Araújo, S. and Cambria, V. (2013), 'Sound Praxis, Poverty, and Social Participation: Perspectives from a Collaborative Study in Rio de Janeiro', *Yearbook for Traditional Music*, 45: 28–42.

Cabral, A.c. (2007), *Bala perdida: nos bastidores dos bailes funks e suas conseqüências*, São Paulo: Editora Resultado.

Cambria, V. (2012), *Music and Violence in Rio de Janeiro: A Participatory Study in Urban Ethnomusicology*, PhD dissertation in Ethnomusicology, Middletown, CT: Wesleyan University.

Da Costa, T. F. (2016), 'O funk no Brasil contemporâneo: Uma música que incomoda', *Latin American Research Review*, 51 (4): 86–01.

Da Silva, G. M. (2007), 'A música que toca é nós que manda': um estudo do 'proibidão', MA. thesis in psychology, Rio de Janeiro: Pontifícia Universidade Católica.

De Amorim, M. F. (2009), *O discurso da e sobre a mulher no funk brasileiro de cunho erótico: uma proposta de análise do universo sexual feminino*, PhD dissertation, Campinas: UNICAMP.

Dos Santos, R. F. (2005), *O funk enquanto narrativa: uma crônica do quotidiano*, Niteroi, MA thesis, Niterói: Universidade Federal Fluminense.

Essinger, S. (2005), *Batidão: uma história do funk*, Rio de Janeiro e São Paulo: Record.

Giacomini, S. M. (2006), *A alma da festa: família, etnicidade e projetos num clube social da Zona Norte do Rio de Janeiro, o Renascença Clube*, Belo Horizonte and Rio de Janeiro: UFMG/Iuperj.

Herschmann, M. (2000), *O Funk e o hip-hop invadem a cena*, Rio de Janeiro: Editora da UFRJ.

Lefebvre, H. (2006), *O direito a cidade*, São Paulo: Centauro.

Lopes, A. C. (2010), *Funk-se quem quiser. No batidão negro da cidade carioca*, PhD dissertation, Campinas: Unicamp.

Lyra, K. (2006), 'Eu não sou cachorra não! Não? Voz e silêncio na construção da identidade feminina no rap e no funk no Rio de Janeiro', in Everaldo Rocha et al. (eds), *Comunicação, consumo e espaço urbano: novas sensibilidades nas culturas jovens*, pp. 175–195, Rio de Janeiro: PUC-RJ/Mauad.

McCann, B. (2002), 'Black Pau: Uncovering the History of Brazilian Soul', *Journal of Popular Music Studies*, 14 (1): 33–62.

Medeiros, J. (2006), *Funk carioca: crime ou cultura? O som dá medo. E prazer*, São Paulo: Editora Terceiro Nome.

Moura, R. (1995), *Tia Ciata e a Pequena África no Rio de Janeiro*, 2nd edn, Rio de Janeiro: Secretaria Municipal de Cultura.

Orlando, J. J. (2009), *Batidão: um estudo da variação discursiva na música funk*, MA. thesis, São Paulo: Pontifícia Universidade Católica.

Palombini, C. (2010), 'Notes on the Historiography of *Música Soul* and *Funk Carioca*', *HAOL*, 23: 99–106.

Palombini, C. (2011), 'Funk proibido', in L. Avritzer, N. Bignotto, F. Filgueiras, J. Guimarães, and H. Starling (eds), *Dimensões Políticas da Justiça*, pp. 647–657, Belo Horizonte: Editora UFMG.

Pinho, O. (2007), 'A «Fiel», a «Amante» e o «Jovem Macho Sedutor»: sujeitos de gênero na periferia racializada', *Saúde Social*, 16 (2): 133–45.

Russano, R. (2006), 'Bota o fuzil pra cantar!' *O Funk Proibido no Rio de Janeiro*, M.A. thesis in music, Rio de Janeiro: Universidade Federal do Estado do Rio de Janeiro (UNIRIO).

Sandroni, C. (2001), *Feitiço decente. Transformações do samba no Rio de Janeiro (1917–1933)*, Rio de Janeiro: Zahar.

Sneed, P. (2003), *Machine Gun Voices: Bandits, Favelas, and Utopia in Brazilian Funk*, PhD dissertation, University of Wisconsin-Madison.

Sneed, P. (2007a), 'Bandidos de Cristo: Representations of the Power of Criminal Factions in Rio's Proibidão Funk', *Latin American Music Review*, 28 (2): 220–41.

Sneed, P. (2007b), 'Favela Utopias: The Bailes Funk in Rio's Crisis of Social Exclusion and Violence', *Latin American Research Review*, 43 (2): 57–79.

Vianna, H. (1988), *O mundo funk carioca*, Rio de Janeiro: Jorge Zahar.

Vianna, H. (1999), *The Mystery of Samba: Popular Music and National Identity in Brazil*, Chapel Hill: University of North Carolina Press.

Vianna, H. (2006), 'O Funk Como Símbolo da Violência Carioca', in G. Velho and M. Alvito (eds), *Cidadania e Violência*, pp. 178–187, Rio de Janeiro: Editora FGV.

23
Postcolonial noise: How did French rap (re)invent 'the banlieue'?

Christina Horvath

French rap emerged in the early 1980s and by the turn of the new millennium it has become one of the best-selling musical industries in the Hexagon. Its adoption belongs to a long tradition of US musical influence in France like the discovery of jazz in the 1920s and 1930s, the arrival of rock and roll in the 1950s and the Disco wave of the 1970s (Prévos 2001: 40). Rap rose to popularity simultaneously with French rock and raï, a stereotypically exotic musical genre primarily produced by Algerian immigrants and visitors. Yet, unlike the colourful raï, which was able to 'cross over' and seduce Parisian middle and upper-class world-music devotees (Swedenburg 2015: 110), rap has been since its beginnings associated with the urban margins, in particular with the bleak post-industrial housing estates or *cités* in working-class suburbs known as *banlieues*. Since the 1980s, these multi-ethnic neighbourhoods in the urban periphery have been constructed in the media as places of irreconcilable otherness and home to the new dangerous classes, France's postcolonial ethnic minorities. French rap seems to have capitalized on this reputation by turning the banlieues into its symbolic territory, in the same way as US rap appropriated and commoditized the Afro-American ghettos.

This chapter aims to critically examine the general belief that French rap is naturally rooted in, emanates from and gives voice to the working-class suburban housing estates. It will investigate the privileged links between rap artists and the urban periphery to explore whether rap is actually a product of the banlieue or its (re)inventor. After a short historical overview retracing how France has become the country with the second-largest hip-hop industry to date (Cannon 2003: 191), I will examine how rap has shaped the banlieue as a symbolic space of exclusion, exploited its vernacular language for innovation and stylistic distinction and used the periphery as a place of enunciation from which to challenge hegemonic concepts of French identity. I will argue that, by appropriating the post-industrial urban margins, rappers have attempted to hijack the myth of the banlieue constructed in media-political discourses since the 1980s, not only to disrupt hegemonic narratives but also to sell albums.

The emergence of a distinctively French rap

In *Black Noise* (1994: 1), Tricia Rose describes rap as a protest music, a 'confusing and noisy element of American popular culture' that prioritizes Black voices from the urban margins and criticizes American society for its perpetuation of racial and economic discrimination. Hip-hop culture brings together complex social, cultural and political issues in dialogue. It reimagines the experiences of life on the margins and 'symbolically appropriates urban space through sampling, attitude, dance, style, and sound effects' (1994: 22). The post-industrial urban context is central to its emergence and is inscribed in its sound, lyrics and themes. In the America of the 1970s, hip-hop attempted to negotiate 'marginalization, brutally truncated opportunity, and oppression within the cultural imperatives of African-American and Caribbean history, identity, and community' (1994: 21). It was adopted in a similar economic context in France when, in the early 1980s, a neoliberal turn announced the end of the welfare state and the decline of working-class cohesion, giving way to 'a territorialisation associated with the ethnicisation of social relations' (Bazin 1995: 90–1).

Unlike its American models, however, French hip-hop was not born in the street but was established by mostly white music professionals and DJs (Lapassade and Rousselot 1996:10; Provot 2007: 148) such as Sidney (Patrick Duteil), Lionel D (Lionel Eguienta), Phil Barney or Dee Nasty (Daniel Bigault). Rap music was first broadcast via the independent private radio stations that were legalized by President Mitterrand's Socialist government in 1981. The very first French artists to experiment with hip-hop were musicians of the mainstream like pop duo Chagrin d'Amour or singer Annie Cordy (Hammou 2012: 31). In 1982, a group of US rappers toured Europe and in the same year the first French-speaking rap recording, 'Change the Beat' by Fab Freddy, was issued in New York City. Two years later, Afrika Bambaataa established a faction of Zulu Nation in the Parisian suburbs, introducing suburban youths to US hip-hop culture. The television programme *H.I.P-H.O.P.*, presented by Sydney on the national TV channel TF1 in 1984–5, and the success of the anthology *Rapattitudes*, produced by Virgin Record's Labelle Noir in 1990, greatly contributed to legitimizing rap as a popular genre in France.

The first French rap formations from banlieues, Suprême NTM, Assassin and Ministère A.M.E.R, emerged in the late 1980s, inspired by American groups NWA and Public Enemy. Their rise was less an example of globalization and uniformization than an act of 'cultural reterritorialisation' in so far as cultural products were 'reinscribed with meaning, adapted and reworked to relate to local contexts' (Cannon 2003: 193). Most of the first generation of hard-core rappers developed strong local or regional identities entrenched in the urban periphery. They used rap music as a platform to voice discrimination, racism, police brutality and unemployment among other issues and were frequently criticized by authorities and the media for their outspoken and controversial lyrics. In 1995, the group Suprême NTM was sentenced for orally abusing the security forces present while performing their song 'Police' in La Seyne-sur-Mer. In 1997, members of Ministère A.M.E.R. were found guilty of 'provocation to murder' for their song 'Sacrifice de poulet' (a double entendre of 'chicken sacrifice' and 'cop killing') and after the 2005 banlieue uprising, further seven groups were accused of promoting incivility (Silverstein 2018: 131).

In the early 1990s, French hip-hop became increasingly diversified. A new, less political trend appeared with artists like MC Solaar, Doc Gyneco, Ménélik or Alliance Ethnik whose well-crafted wordplays and highly poetic lyrics were closer to the traditions of French chanson and poetry. Embraced by mainstream media and audiences beyond the banlieues, they helped establish rap music as a widely accepted genre and a blockbusting industry. In the late 1990s, the French rap scene exploded with the emergence of new artists and powerful labels. The number of albums released in France increased sharply: 'one album was produced in 1984, three in 1988, [...] nine in 1992 [...] twenty-three in 1995, fifty-three in 1996' (Prévos 2002: 14). The genre increasingly distanced itself from its American models and found its own personality with artists like La Cliqua, 113, Oxmo Puccino, Booba, La Rumeur, Rocé, Le Ministère des Affaires populaires, Casey, Kery James, Ärsenik, Sinik, Sniper or Abd Al Malik publishing highly acclaimed albums and marking generations of listeners (Ghio 2016: 13).

Various attempts have been made to classify this fast-growing production divided by issues of authenticity, co-optation and identity politics like its US counterpart. Bestselling artists known for their sophisticated lyrics and frequent borrowing from French chanson like MC Solaar in the 1980s (Prévos 2002: 6) or Abd Al Malik in the 2000s (Bourderionnet 2011; Silverstein 2018) have often been criticized by rappers with angrier and more subversive messages who have been backed less by non-specialist or elite media. Yet the distinction hardcore *vs.* gangsta styles seems less relevant in France where armed conflicts are exceptional and gangsta influences remain limited to poses and album cover art.

Another key difference with the United States is that French rappers and their audiences do not belong to a homogeneous ethno-racial group. French rap formations often bring together artists of different ethnic, mostly North- and sub-Saharan African but also Turkish, Italian or Caribbean origins. According to Isabelle Marc Martinez:

> What ties this multi-ethnic community together is the fact that they are aware of their different backgrounds because they have not been assimilated into the French mainstream even if they were born French. Their marginalised place in society is epitomised by the *cités* where they live or that they recreate in their texts.
>
> (2011: 4)

Speaking from these concrete but also symbolic margins, French rappers undertake to construct a new identity based upon socio-economic, ideological and historical rather than ethnic bonds, to which all audiences who feel socially or culturally dispossessed, can relate.

Inventing a territory

Tricia Rose explains the territorial rooting of US hip-hop by three key factors. Firstly, born from the New York urban terrain in the 1970s, hip-hop was an answer to stigmatizing representations which depicted black and Hispanic inner-city communities as a backdrop for crime, deviance and barbarism. It proposed Afro-American youths from dilapidated inner-city neighbourhoods an aesthetic experience which helped them build an alternative identity in relation to their environment. Secondly, it provided black and Hispanic communities with a means to appropriate public space in the increasingly divided postindustrial city where 'shrinking federal funds and affordable housing, shifts in the occupational structure […] meant that new immigrant populations and the city's poorest residents paid the highest price for desindustrialisation and economic restructuring' (1994: 30). New York's poorest areas, the South Bronx and neighbourhoods in Brooklyn, Queens and Harlem, featured in media, popular culture and films as negative local colour and were depicted as 'drained of life, energy and vitality' (1994: 33). Rap songs and videos opposed these stigmatizing representations of everyday life acknowledged and celebrated in rap music. Thus favourite street corners, playgrounds, parking lots, school yards or rooftops from black inner-city locations were brought into public consciousness as a 'local turf' occupied by rappers and their crew or posse. They were claimed as places of enunciation from which the young, mostly male rappers spoke for themselves and their community. Finally, local turf scenes simultaneously became a 'model of "authenticity" and hipness' in rap music and satisfied 'national fantasies about the violence and danger that purportedly consume the poorest and the most economically fragile communities of color' (1994: 11).

These predominant uses of marginal urban places have their equivalents in France also. Ghio (2016: 67–8) notes that references to working-class suburbs have been omnipresent in the universe of French rap since its consecration in the 1980s. Place names and postcodes appearing in titles, group names, music videos and cover art have stood simultaneously for appropriation of space and belonging, alternative identity formation and self-authentication. Numerous artists have developed identities with strong local ties like Ministère A.M.E.R. in Sarcelles, IAM in Marseille, 113 in Vitry-sur-Seine, NTM in Seine-Saint-Denis, Assassin in Paris' 18th district and NAP in the Neuhof area of Strasbourg. According to Ghio, mentions of these concrete neighbourhoods, cities or departments coexist with references to *the banlieue* as a concept or 'total territory' (2016: 68). Pierre Marti also confirms that in many rap songs the banlieue is fashioned as a broader, dematerialized territory equated with marginalization and exclusion. He concludes that 'if not all rappers are *banlieusards* strictly speaking, all of them are vociferous inhabitants of an imaginary banlieue which haunts the national consciousness by gathering within its phantasmagorical space the Republic's pariahs' (Marti 2005: 97). The production of this symbolic space of belonging enables hip-hop artists to become the voices of an imagined community brought together by the shared experience of exclusion and stigmatization, and conversely, it allows audiences to identify with rap's political acts of speech independently from whether they are actually from banlieues or not.

Silverstein sees in French hip-hop artists' appropriation of images from African-American popular culture an endeavour to draw on a transcendent ghetto heritage. Rappers convert a local belonging into a common *banlieue* culture overwriting racial, ethnic or national identification and promoting a transnational solidarity across ghetto spaces (Silverstein 2018: 132). They express this ghetto heritage by using a kinship idiom addressing audiences as 'brothers' and 'sisters' and the large community – whether a housing project, or the entire postcolonial France, as their 'family' (Silverstein 2018: 135). By adopting a 'ghettocentric' subject position, rappers constitute the French banlieue as a site for postcolonial hip-hop interventions. They borrow figures of street lore from US gangsta rap, such as the pimp, the drug dealer or the thug and refer to these types through self-presentation, dress, pose, boasts, gestures, images and sounds of violence in their songs, videos and covers. By broadening the *caillera* (backslang for 'racaille' or thug) personae to a proto-political figure and reinventing and re-aestheticizing everyday life in the cités, they politicize the banlieue as a site for collective action and individual fulfilment.

In recent years, however, critics have been cautioning against taking French rap's 'ghetto-centric' imagery at face value as a realistic depiction of banlieues. Taking a literary approach to rap, which she considers as part of French urban literature, Bettina Ghio explains that instead of faithfully reproducing banlieue life, rappers make aesthetic choices about rhetoric figures and non-standard lexis they use. These choices are only understandable when considered from an aesthetic rather than a purely social-science perspective (Silverstein 2018: 69). She affirms that the banlieue itself is a *topos* composed of a set of themes, situations and particular motives which are recurrent in the literary genre of banlieue narrative. Through a range of examples drawn from rap lyrics, Ghio illustrates how rappers evoke banlieues using metonymy (i.e. when they depict suburban housing estates by naming the construction materials used to build them), metaphors (i.e. when they equate banlieues to prisons) or hyperboles (the most salient example of this is the emotionally charged term 'ghetto', used as a warning and a reference to US models rather than a factual description).[1] Like literary banlieue narratives, rap songs prioritize stereotypical narrative postures, among others those of the first-person witness-narrator (95) and the angry youth narrator (89) and also tend to engage in intertextualilty/intermediality with other discourses such as political speeches, films or other cultural forms. By personifying marginal neighbourhoods opposed to state institutions and proposing alternative narratives about them, first-person narratives successfully subvert hegemonic discourses about banlieues (Germes et al. 2012).

Creating a language

Language in rap music fulfils multiple functions. It allows performers to show off their verbal dexterity and creativity, influence mainstream society and the dictionary, communicate with peers and the public, create personal styles and models of identification and express their identity and belonging. Rappers engage in different relationships with the addressees of their utterances depending on whether these belong to their in-group (family, crew or posse, networks of peers, the artists' imagined community) or to their out-group (middle-class listeners and 'the-greatest-possible-number-of-people' who constitute their broader audience) (Pecqueux 2001: 34). While the lexicon and prosody of Afro-American communities constitute an obvious linguistic resource for US rappers, French rap's primary audiences do not share a homogeneous ethnic background and a shared dialect. As a result, French artists had to rely on stereotypical and stigmatized varieties of French mostly spoken in multi-ethnic working-class suburbs. In his dictionary of urban slang, *Comment tu tchatches?* (How do you talk?) (1998), Jean-Pierre Goudaillier named this vernacular 'français contemporain des cités' (Contemporary Banlieue French) or FCC. He inventoried a series of borrowings from English, Arabic, Berber, Gipsy, sub-Saharan African languages and regional dialects that co-exist in FCC and are used by rap artists as an important resource for non-standard language (NSL).

Martin Verbeke's (2017) lexicographic analysis shows that rappers often deviate from the rules of standard language. He affirms that individual artists 'face the need to stand out and be recognized by their peers and the audience. […] Some artists will attempt to do so by "appropriating" certain NSL words and developing this type of language further' (288). Non-standard language shows significant changes over time and is indicative of the scope of rappers' linguistic capabilities and influence. Unlike standard language (SL) that is broadly used for communication in public spheres, NSL is made up of colloquial, vulgar and slang words including *verlan* (backslang), colloquialisms, foreign borrowings and abbreviations. According to Verbeke, the amount of NSL used by rappers is not only regionally and diachronically motivated but it has also significantly increased since rap achieved a higher level of legitimation beyond banlieue neighbourhoods and the generalization of Internet has established more regular contact between remote networks of artists and listeners. Prominent events bringing banlieue subculture to the forefront also impact on the evolution of NSL use. This was namely the case after the 2005 revolts which prompted a sharp increase in the amount of vulgarisms, vernacular lexis and non-standard tonality used in rap lyrics. As Fagyal suggests, such intensifications of NSL use may be interpreted as 'momentary acts of identity signalling the artists' solidarity and symbolic belonging' (2007: 135). Since NSL eventually loses its value by becoming accepted by mainstream populations, original users tend to adopt or invent new words or 'use this language in a more complex manner to mark their own use as different from the rest of the society' (Verbeke 2017: 290). Finally, throughout their careers the same artists can deliberately choose to resort more or less to NSL language, depending on their changing relation to social norms and their desire to achieve upward or downward social mobility, for example to look more or less hard-core.

Recent research in socio-linguistics has also nuanced our understanding of how rap artists influence the linguistic practices of (mostly teenage) speakers living in multi-ethnic banlieues. Fagyal (2007) has demonstrated that, by establishing and promoting linguistic styles, French rappers may prompt changes not only in vocabulary but also in prosody, for example a shift from the last syllable to another one. Fagyal and Stewart (2011) suggest that the strategic use of tonal patterns associated with multi-ethnic banlieue youth vernacular and rap is not only determined by speakers' socio-ethnic and geographic origins but primarily depends on their deliberate choice as well as their roles and conversational moves in particular exchanges. In other words, language associated with banlieues is an important stylistic resource which rap artists do not only borrow from but which they also continue to enrich by producing new NSL terms and disseminating linguistic styles both in banlieues and beyond.

Making political claims... while also selling albums

Finally, we have to consider the general belief according to which rap is the privileged expression of post-colonial banlieue youth. Rap is known for being provocative, challenging preconceptions and denouncing social injustice. This is also true in France where hip-hop artists' 'avowed distance from a sense of unified French identity is intricately interwoven with French colonial history, as well as the construction of *laïcité* and its careful delineation of a religious subject' (Dotson-Renta 2015: 355). Yet aggressive display of counter-presence, voice and resistance to hegemonic narratives are also characteristic in US rap, we can therefore consider these as consubstantial to the genre. Overlapping themes such as Afro-centrism or colonial history are nonetheless articulated differently by French artists for whom Africa is often a familiar rather than an idealized remote location, and the history of the French empire is just as important part of colonial legacy as transatlantic slavery (Béru 2008: 63).

Scholars have inventoried a high number of postcolonial themes in French rap. These include among others institutional racism, in particular in the form of police brutality, which is denounced by artists like Suprême NTM or Ministère A.M.E.R. as a direct consequence of slavery and colonialism. Assassin, Médine and Youssoupha also tackle French colonial history, deploring its absence from public debate and schools books; IAM discuss socio-economical marginality and geographic segregation, and Muslim rappers Kery James, Abd Al Malik or Médine challenge Republican secularism or *laïcité* represented in official discourses as the only legitimate avenue to Frenchness (Jouili 2014: 75). Lara Dotson-Renta suggests that French rappers claim *banlieue identity* as an affirmative identity marker and by perpetuating the traditions of literary engagement they attempt to refashion national imagery, reshape the concept of community and disrupt the silence of postcolonial amnesia. As she observes:

> What these artists undertake is the creation of an alternative space, highlighting a geography of 'Other' *dans la marge* of the French political and social landscape that nevertheless belies constant encounters and negotiations with the established national identity tropes.
>
> (2015: 356)

For Dotson-Renta, the complex space of the French urban periphery provides a 'fertile landscape in which to enunciate an evolving and hybrid French identity' (2015: 355). By mapping out new geographies of belonging, French rap may be seen as a narrative that collaborates closely with literature in creating new spaces of discourse. A similar claim is formulated by Bettina Ghio (2010) who considers rap as an essentially literary expression that responds to the narrative urgency of banlieue youth to voice the social exclusion and spatial segregation they experience. As a counter-narrative, rap tends to react to media-political discourses, often by directly referring to politicians' speeches. These is the case namely of Sadek, who quotes Chirac's infamous speech about the 'noise and smell' of postcolonial immigrants, or Keny Arkana or X Kalibur and Blood, who comment on Sarkozy's boastful claim of cleaning the cités with a pressure-cleaner.

But are rappers able to reverse the hegemonic discourses consolidated by politicians and media about the banlieues? While there seems to be a consensus about rap's ability to challenge narratives of urban marginalization and stigmatization and open up new, less conventional avenues to Frenchness than the ones recognized as legitimate, it can be objected that by selling their records to the largest possible audiences contributes to a commodification of postcolonial alienation and exclusion. Silverstein (2018) also suggests that, while rap racializes banlieue spaces, it also spatializes French racial otherness. By validating politicians', media's and urban planners' representation of the banlieue as a space of alterity, it consolidates a stereotypical opposition between the secular, Euro-centric and civilized Republic and its multicultural margins marked by the rise of Islam and various forms of violence and incivilities. As Germes et al. (2012) note, the simplifying binaries used by rappers such as 'banlieue vs. France' or a revolted 'us' pitched against a hegemonic 'them', may jeopardize their very denunciation of a sharp divide between the banlieues and mainstream society, all the more so as their popularity with middle-class concert audiences reveals the fragility of these constructs.

Pecqueux (2007) also reminds us that rap is not just a text but a complex practice rooted simultaneously in the musical industry, cultural and aesthetic practices and public policies. Thus no truth or message can be extracted from the songs to inform urban policies seeking to prevent urban violence or to control suburban youth. Drawing on Pecqueux's findings, Hammou (2015) highlights the shortcomings of studies that only focused on lyrics, form, message and content. He questions dominant interpretation of rap being the expression of French banlieue youth and denounces an exoticizing trend in earlier approaches which discussed rap predominantly in terms of its resistance, moral effects or aesthetics while its context, audiences, participation in cultural policies and industries remain largely ignored.

To conclude, by appropriating the urban margin as its symbolic territory, rap helped construct the banlieue as a homogeneous space of exclusion and inscribe it into a series of simplifying binaries opposing it to mainstream French society. Through its use of banlieue vernacular, it contributed to renewing linguistic practices both in the *cités* and beyond and by voicing diverse peripheral, postcolonial or Muslim identities, rap artists continue to produce and circulate alternatives to hegemonic concepts of Frenchness prescribed by political elites. However, rap songs are also designed to entertain and address the largest possible audience and therefore cannot be reduced to their 'message' and dissociated from the artists' participation in the music industry whose ultimate aim is to sell records. As the rapper Booba said in a 2008 interview with *Le Journal du dimanche*: 'I make music, not politics. My only mission is to entertain young people with good sound' (Pecqueux 2009: 91). It is therefore justified to affirm that rap is as much a key producer/reproducer as one of the principal consumers and beneficiaries of the strongly exaggerated media-political myth that depicts banlieues not only as places of cultural and symbolic otherness, situated at the margins of the French Republic, but also embodying its exact opposite in a binary system of characteristics and values.

Note

1. A direct reference to Grandmaster Flash's 1982 song 'The Message', which was widely popular when rap first arrived to the banlieues.

References

Bazin, H. (1995), *La culture hip-hop*, Paris: Desclée de Brouwer.

Béru, L. (2008), 'Le rap français, un produit musical postcolonial?' *Voume! La Revue des Musiques populaires*, 6 (1): 61–79.

Bourderionnet (2011), '"A Picture-Perfect" Banlieue Artist: Abd al Malik or the Perils of a Conciliatory Rap Discourse', *French Cultural Studies*, 22 (2): 156–61.

Cannon, S. (1997), 'Panama City Rapping: B-boys in the Banlieues and beyond', in A. Hargeraves (ed), *Postcolonial Cultures in France*, 150–66, London: Routledge.

Cannon, S. (2003), 'Globalization, Americanization and Hip Hop in France', in H. Dauncey and S. Cannon (eds), *Popular Music in France from Chanson to Techno*, 191–205, Surrey: Ashgate.

Dotson-Renta, L. (2015), 'On n'est pas condamné à l'échec': Hip-Hop and the *Banlieue* Narrative', *French Cultural Studies*, 26 (3): 354–67.

Fagyal, Zs. (2007) 'Syncope: de l'irrégularité rythmique dans la musique rap au dévoisement des voyelles dans la parole des adolescents dits "des banlieues"', *Nottingham French Studies*, 46 (2): 119–34.

Fagyal, Zs. and Stewart, C. M. (2011), 'Prosodic Style-shifting in Preadolescent Peer-group Interactions in a Working-class Suburb of Paris', in F. Karn and M. Selting (eds), *Ethnic Styles of Speaking in European Metropolitan Areas*, 75–99, Amsterdam/Philadelphia: John Benjamins.

Germes, M., Tijé-Dra, A., Marquart, N. and Schreiber, V. (2012), Ortsregister transcript, pp. 32–8, https://halshs.archives-ouvertes.fr/halshs-00790690 (accessed 24 December 2018).

Ghio, B. (2010), 'Littérature populaire et urgence littéraire: le cas du rap français', *Trans-*, (9): 2–14.

Ghio, B. (2016), *Sans faute de frappe. Rap et littérature*, Marseille: Le Mot et le Reste.

Goudailler, J. P. (1998), *Comment tu tchatches?* Dictionnaire du français contemporain des cités, Paris: Maisonneuve et Larose.

Hammou, K. (2012), *Une histoire du rap en France*, Paris: La Découverte.

Hammou, K. (2015), 'Rap et banlieue: Crépuscule d'un mythe?' *Caisse nationale d'allocations familiales*, 190 (4): 74–82.

Jouili, J. S. (2014), 'Secular Sounds and the Politics of Listening', *Anthropological Quarterly*, 87 (4): 977–88.

Lapassade, G. and Rousselot, P. (1996), *Le rap ou la fureur de dire*, Paris: Loris Talmart.
Marc Martinez, I. (2011), 'Intermediality, Rewriting Histories, and Identities in French Rap', *CLCWeb: Comparative Literature and Culture*, 13 (3): no page numbers.
Marti, P. A. (2005), *Rap to France. Les mots d'une rupture identitaire*, Paris: L'Harmattan.
Pecqueux, A. (2001), 'Common Partitions: Musical Commonplaces', in A-P. Durand (ed), *Black, Blanc, Beur: Rap Music and "Hip-Hop" Culture in the Francophone World*, 1–21, Lanham, MD; Oxford: Scarecrow.
Pecqueux, A. (2007), *Voix du rap: Essai de sociologie de l'action musicale*, Paris: L'Harmattan.
Pecqueux, A. (2009), *Le rap*, Paris: le Cavalier Bleu.
Prévos, A. M. (2001), "Le business du rap en France", *The French Review*, 74 (5): 900–21.
Prévos, A. M. (2002), 'Two Decades of Rap in France: Emergence, Development, Prospects', in A-P Durand (ed), *Black, Blanc, Beur: Rap Music and hip-hop Culture in the Francophone World*, 1–21, Lanham, MD; Oxford: Scarecrow.
Provot, K. M. (2007). *La France est sa banlieue: L'identité française et sa périphérie urbaine à travers le cinéma, les médias et la musique*. [Doctoral dissertation, University of Cincinnati]. OhioLINK Electronic Theses and Dissertations Center. http://rave.ohiolink.edu/etdc/view?acc_num=ucin1184688497 (accessed 24 December 2018).
Rose, T. (1994), *Black Noise*, Hanover, NH: Wesleyan University Press.
Silverstein, P. (2018), *Postcolonial France: Race, Islam and the Future of the Republic*, London: Pluto Press.
Swedenburg, T. (2015), 'Beur/Maghribi Musical Interventions in France: Rai and Rap', *The Journal of North African Studies*, 20 (1): 109–26.
Verbeke, M. (2017), 'Rapping through Time: An Analysis of Non-Standard Language Use in French Rap', *Modern and Contemporary France*, 25 (3): 281–98.

24
Music and the nation
Melanie Schiller

Music and the origins of nations

Music has been fundamental to the establishment of modern nations. Nearly all the nation-building movements across Europe in the nineteenth century find some of their most influential and lasting expressions through the art of nationalist composers, who took an active part in those movements (Curtis 2008). But not only composers were important for the consolidation of a national culture, as Cecilia Applegate and Pamela Potter for instance argue for the case of Germany, the national project was just as much advanced by writers, music critics, conductors, organizers, musical amateurs and singing organizations (2002: 12). Besides art music, folk music was equally important for establishing and consolidating ideas of nationhood when Johann Gottfried Herder for instance began to refer to songs associated with modern nation-states as *Volkslieder* (folk songs) (Bohlman 2015). Music, therefore, does not simply represent the nation; music is mustered for the making of the nation (Bohlman 2009: 83) and it has implicitly and explicitly made a fundamental contribution to imaginings of collective identity and nationhood.

In his seminal *Imagined Communities*, Benedict Anderson (1991) theorizes the emergence of the nation-state as dependent on its collective imagination and its rootedness in everyday life. By reading the daily newspaper, or collectively singing the national anthem on national holidays, people imagine themselves as forming a nation, and 'in the minds of each lives the image of their communion' (Anderson 1991: 6). It is in synchronized experiences like this, Anderson argues, in which the collective recognition (or imagination) of a community constitutes national identification. 'Nothing connects us all, but imagined sound', Anderson concludes his celebration of unisonality in collectively singing the national anthem: 'People wholly unknown to each other utter the same verses to the same melody. [...] If we are aware that others are singing these songs precisely when and as we are, we have no idea who they may be, or even where, out of earshot, they are singing' (Anderson 1991: 145). It is in this simultaneity of singing the anthem, Anderson argues, that the nation is manifested in the imagination of the people.

Popular music and everyday nationhood

Clearly, music and the history of nationalism are intrinsically intertwined, but the connection between national identity and (popular) music reaches beyond this historical dimension. As imagined communities, nations are social constructions imagined by the people who perceive themselves to be a part of it, articulated in narratives that are always open for reinterpretation (Bhabha 1990; Anderson 1991; Balibar 1991). These narratives are created and negotiated in culture, and, as Stuart Hall (1996) aptly reminds us, are of course also told and retold in the media and popular culture. National identity therefore is not only grounded in the realm of 'high culture' (Gellner 2006: 56), art music, political institutions, invented traditions (Hobsbawm 2012: 1) and folk culture, but also in the mundane, everyday life and experiences, routines and habits. Popular culture therefore provides an important resource for the production of social identity as 'the constant process of producing meanings of and from our social experience' (Fiske 2011: 1). 'Traditional' cultural forms and practices of the nation, Tim Edensor argues, are supplemented, and increasingly replaced in their affective power, by meanings, images and activities drawn from popular culture (2002: 12). The fundamental importance of mundane details of the everyday in creating and maintaining a collective sense of identity and feeling of national community, is what Michael Billig describes as banal nationalism (Billig 1995). Arguing that everyday representations of the nation build a shared sense of national belonging, Billig mentions weather forecasts, national emblems on bank notes and the flag, which hangs unnoticed outside a public building. International sporting competitions, for example, are often perceived through national perspectives with the respective teams or athletes representing a nation. Here also, it is music that 'flags' and announces the nation: the national anthem of the respective teams played at the beginning of the competition or to honour the victory of teams or individuals during award ceremonies.

Popular music can also fulfil the function of reproducing the nation in seemingly banal and innocuous situations; as everyday culture, popular music is closely connected to the lived experience of people, or as Andy Bennett argues: popular music has become a central means for the framing of discourses concerning national culture and identity (Bennett 2016: 6). Musicians for instance have become signs of the nation – as Bruce Springsteen in the United States, Björk in Iceland, ABBA in Sweden or the Beatles in the UK (McLeod 2016: 157), and popular music genres have been connected to notions of national identity. Brit pop of the 1990s, for example, was associated with a particular idea of Englishness, discussed in the language of nationalism (Cloonan 1997) and embraced by politicians like Tony Blair (McRobbie 1999: 4). Another example of the interconnection between seemingly banal popular music and the nation is the Serbian variant of a wider pan-Balkan musical phenomenon and pop-folk musical style: 'turbofolk'. The genre emerged in the 1990s and has been discussed as being a lever of the Milošević regime – an inherently nationalist cultural phenomenon which developed due to the specific sociopolitical conditions of Serbia in the 1990s (Archer 2012). The pervasiveness of nationalism, as Clifford Geertz has described (1973: 306), then lies in its ability of transforming pre-existing ties and identities into national ones and, as I will work out in more detail below, the nation remains a crucial but ambivalent category for understanding how cultural texts and practices function in the construction of personal and collective identities (Biddle and Knights 2007: 1).

Popular music and the collective performance of nationhood

Popular music is a central means for constructions of identity, both individually as well as collectively (Connell and Gibson 2003). With its strong affective potential, music is often linked to a personal experience and a private self, channelling emotions and offering a 'kind of self-recognition, [freeing] us from everyday routines, from the social expectations with which we are encumbered' (Frith 1996: 275). As such, music can function as a marker for personal taste, style and identification, an empowering tool for self-expression and – identity. However, the individual experience of music and its role as a resource for identity formation is never isolated and, as Tia DeNora points out, is always based upon reflexivity and on seeing the self in relation to another (2008: 155). Music, as a 'technology of the self' (DeNora 2000: 46) then also has a profoundly social function, and often plays an important role in constructing a collective sense of identity and feeling of community; it is at the heart of our most profound social occasions and experiences from sporting events to national celebrations and religious holidays (DeNora 2000; Turino 2008). Besides individual identification, music can therefore also create companionship, and invite collective identification: music makes us *feel* part of a community (Frith 2007, emphasis in original). Music is hence not only 'embedded in the creation of (and constant maintenance of) nationhood' (Connell and Gibson 2003: 117), but it is also an integral component of processes through which cultural identities are formed, and popular music is an important cultural sphere in which national identities are affirmed, challenged, taken apart and reconstructed (Connell and Gibson 2003: 18).

One illustrative case for the formative role of popular music as everyday culture and expression of banal nationalism is the popular German Carnival Schlager 'Trizonesien-Song', which first consolidated a post-war West-German identity in 1948. After the unconditional surrender in 1945, Germany was divided into four zones, occupied by the Allied forces. The 'Trizonesien-Song' mockingly refers to the Tri-zone: the combination of the American, British and French occupied zones, which collaborated and later, on 23 May 1949, became the Federal Republic of Germany, commonly known as West Germany. During those years of disorientation, no nation-state existed on German territory, and cultural life was heavily censored and regulated by the occupying forces. Popular music, however, was primarily ('apolitical') entertainment, and was hence almost ignored by the regulatory institutions (Thacker 2007: 23). When in 1948 the traditional local carnival celebrations in Cologne were permitted again for the first time after the war, Karl Berbuer's humorous 'Trizonesien-Song' became a major hit. The song – a catchy sing-along-march in B flat and two-two time signature – mockingly addressed the political situation at the time. Disguised in humour it criticized the allies as colonizers, it bemoaned a loss of national sovereignty, it denied guilt and performativity introduced and created a collective identification as West-Germans (the Tri-zone) against the Allied forces, excluding east-Germany from its national narrative. In fact, the song was so popular that, in lieu of an official national anthem (and the non-existence of a nation-state for that matter), the carnival Schlager was on occasion used as a substitute national anthem during sporting events (Schiller 2020: 64). The popular song consolidated an emerging West-German imagined community, by drawing on its 'banal' everyday-ness as a carnival sing-along Schlager, collectively sung and celebrated by the people in the streets of Cologne. Although, of course, only an 'unofficial' national anthem for the yet-non-existing nation, the 'Trizonesien-Song' was the first to unite the people under the new common denominator, and as such the song not only symbolically represented the newly imagined community but is also provided a context for the nation's people to participate and actively perform 'Trizonesianness' (West-German identity) (Schiller 2020). The 'Trizonesien-Song' therefore illustrates how popular music does not merely represent the nation, and citizens do not merely 'read' the nation in music; they 'see, hear, and participate in it' (Tuohy 2001: 124), but they also *produce* it through music (Schiller 2020). Popular music as everyday culture can therefore be understood as facilitating a collective experience, and music's affective quality offers 'a platform to negotiate questions of belonging or to challenge national […] identification' (Stehle and Kahnke 2013: 123).

Popular music and nation-state policy

Thus far I have discussed how (popular) music has been instrumental in building, shaping and representing nationhood as everyday culture, and I showed how music is an active participant in the formation of national identity discourses. However, it also needs to be noted that the relation between popular music and the nation is reciprocal, and the nation-state remains crucial in determining the construction of meaning in popular music (Homan et al. 2016: 2). The actions of nation-states are important factors in musical life: in the form of subsidies and other kinds of cultural policy, or in the form of sanctions and laws (Fornäs 2002). As Homan et al. point out, the range of popular music funding and activities facilitated by the state has increased in western nations over the past two decades (2016: 2). As national governments are increasingly interested in popular music (cf. Cloonan 2016: 3), state music policies are often developed to encourage greater local (national) musical activity (Connell and Gibson 2003: 118). Such state policy generally aims at protecting national music cultures and strengthening a national music market in the face of an increasingly global music industry. Extreme forms of such regulations may go as far as banning all non-national music from its airwaves, as was decided by the Iranian leaders in 1994 (cf. Cloonan 1999). A less radical measure employed by nation-states to ensure the presence of domestic music is the implementation of national quotas for radio stations, requiring public broadcasting to dedicate a certain percentage of airtime to recordings by domestic artists. Countries like Australia, France and Canada for instance have been relying on national radio quotas for decades (cf. Shuker 2008) and, as Shuker shows, the willingness of New Zealand's government to introduce a (officially voluntary yet de facto compulsory) radio quota[1] has had tremendous impact on the national music industry and contributed to the present success of both the mainstream commercial and the indie sectors in the country, primarily by creating a changed musical climate that has ensured the greater viability of 'the local' generally (Shuker 2008: 282).

Other important realms of influence for nation-state policies in relation to popular music are national legal systems like for instance censorship laws – and the ability and willingness to implement these (Cloonan 1999: 197). In the German Democratic Republic, for instance, GDR officials initially tried to exploit the apolitical nature of a new popular music genre in the 1960s – Beat music – by appropriating the new sound for their own political agenda: Beat was temporarily supported as 'socialist dance- and entertainment music' (Grabowsky 2005: 48) and the state-owned company Amiga released records by the Beatles in an effort to ideologically commit the youth to the state (Schildt and Siegfried 2009: 206). In 1965, however, state policy suddenly changed: fearing it was losing its grip on the youth to western values, the Socialist Unity Party of Germany's (SED) chair Erich Honecker declared that the 'detrimental factor of such music on the thought and actions of adolescents had been crudely underestimated' (Peters 2010: 162). This 'misjudgment' was henceforth rectified by a complete ban of Beat music in the GDR (Schiller 2020). Another instance of GDR state-policy affecting popular music was when in 1975 a purge of rock bands, including the popular Klaus Renft Combo, were forced to disband because they were considered to be a threat (Cf. Cloonan 1999: 198).

Another way for the nation-state to utilize popular music for its own ideological purposes is the development of cultural policies related to popular music heritage. In her discussion of the relationship between rock music, collective memory and local identity, Sara Cohen (2013) analyses Liverpool's status as European Capital of Culture 2008. While European nation-states have traditionally turned to classical and folk culture to promote national identity, Cohen describes a pan-European trend involving national policies designed to protect and promote local cultural traditions and identities within a context of globalization and shows that the development of popular music heritage industries is an important trend in cultural policy: the commercial selling of the local musical past within a global marketplace. Roberts and Cohen (2014) also highlight that the promotion of a national popular music legacy can function as symbolic affirmation of collective structures of national cultural memory and identity. Popular music heritage may for instance be promoted by the tourism industries and as part of commercial place-marketing initiatives, as illustrated by maps of popular music heritage sites such as England Rocks!, developed by the UK's national tourism body Visit Britain in 2007. The complex double move of simultaneously celebrating local cultural heritage as a means of protecting national identity in the context of globalization, and the effective rebranding of that heritage for global consumption, shows that discussions around national music policies exemplify the complex relationship of popular music and place: between local practices, national policies, international influences and global music industries.

Popular music and the nation: between local and global

Besides exemplifying the strong potential of popular music in processes of forging collective identities, articulating a symbolic sense of community and belonging and anchoring institutionalized representations of nation-state politics, Ian Biddle and Vanessa Knights refer to Hesmondhalgh and Negus in their influential edited volume Music, *National Identity and the Politics of Location* (2007) arguing that the nation also functions as 'a prime focus for understanding the relationship of popular music to places' (2007: 2). Popular music research, as Hesmondhalgh and Negus observe, is defined by a conceptual binarism focusing, on the one hand, on extreme local practices and micro-communities as 'authentic' scenes and emphasizing the increasing flow of transnational influences and international music movements of pop music as a global commodity on the other (Hesmondhalgh and Negus 2002: 8). Research on the former, in its extreme form, tends to celebrate 'local' engagements of musical communities, idealize place and romanticize their subversive, oppositional and dissident character (Biddle and Knights 2007: 3). The latter on the other hand, tends to stress international flows of cultural influences and capital. In this disjunctive syllogism, the national dimension can function as the missing middle ground, as space in which local and global are mutually imbricated, Biddle and Knights argue.

All popular music, Shuker (2008) argues, embraces a mix of the local and the global, which cannot be considered binary categories, but exist in a complex interrelationship. One illuminating example that teases out these tensions between local and global is Jeroen de Kloet's *China with a Cut: Globalisation, Urban Youth and Popular Music* (2010). In his study of rock music and youth culture in China from the 1990s to 2008, de Kloet addresses the – only apparently – mutually exclusive categories of local and global. Readings of rock in China often either stress that it is a copy of Western music or point out its specific Chinese characteristics. The paradox however, he concludes, is indeed that popular music in China, and elsewhere, is as local as it is global: 'The local and global are complementary rather than contradictory' (2010: 195). Another example of music's equivocal double bind between local and global, and the tension between non-Western and Western popular music is Keith Kahn-Harris' analysis of the Brazilian hard rock band Sepultura drawing on national identity in a globalized world (2006). Kahn-Harris shows that in its career trajectory from 1989 onwards, Sepultura needed to establish itself in the global Extreme Metal music scene by sonically distancing itself from its local context and musical traditions and adopting the English language in their lyrics, to be able to cater to an international market. Only after positioning itself as one of the most successful Death Metal bands in the world, musically and physically distanced from Brazil, the band could afford to increasingly incorporate 'Brazilian' elements into its music. The 'return' to national identity was especially marked by the release of the band's 1996 album called *Roots*, on which the band attempts to signify Brazilian-ness sonically through instrumentation, lyrically by commenting on national politics as well as by drawing on national cultural resources (2006: 132). In Kahn-Harris' discussion of the Extreme Metal scene it becomes clear that the national is indeed tightly interwoven with the global and the local.

Popular music and Nationalism-with-a-big-N

Music with its affective power can become a strong marker of national identity – pride, patriotism and what Anderson calls Nationalism-with-a-big-N (1991: 5). As mentioned earlier, music has been instrumental to the formation of modern nation states and has been used to mobilize the people in the name of the nation ever since. Although not in its mass-produced and mediated form as today, popular music was for instance important in forging nationalist sentiments and bellicoseness since the beginning of the nineteenth century, leading up to – and during – the First World War. Music production, entertainment music in music halls and cabarets in Germany for instance – but equally all over the Europe – readily subscribed to nationalistic jingoism and informal propaganda between 1914 and 1918 (Schiller 2019) and singing became a vector for patriotic support for the war (Mullen 2019). As one of the most popular forms of entertainment, cabarets in Berlin – either out of conviction or due to financial considerations – contributed their share to the war propaganda efforts of the military as they were caught between economic hardships, official encouragement for light entertainment, strict censorship supervision and a general sentiment of extreme nationalistic patriotism. That way, cabaret was an important factor in consolidating nationalist patriotism in society during the First World War, and its popular music and humour ideologically justified the war and emotionalized the German nation (Schiller 2019).

During the First World War, Music halls were submitted to censorship exerted by the military, precisely because of music's affective potential. John Street highlights that the urge to censor music is as old as music itself, and every century on every continent has seen those in authority use their powers to silence certain sounds or performers (Street 2017: 9). Political censorship of music is therefore widespread, he points out, but it remains associated with particular systems and ideologies (Street 2017: 11): both Stalin and the Nazis took music very seriously as a form of propaganda and as a form of oppression (Street 2017). Music that did not align with the political agendas, opposing dominant ideology or perceived as subversive or threatening, was denied public hearing and musicians subjected to any number of threats to life and liberty (Street 2017). While the Soviet Union, especially under Joseph Stalin, was very committed to realizing the potential of music in propagating communism's triumph over capitalism and the heroism of the Soviet people, the Nazi regime actively censored music and musicians for nationalist purposes and it used (popular) music to promote its racial politics. In line with the ideal of Aryan identity, German music was also expected to be free of 'other' influences or racial impurities. Music was considered to represent the 'proper' German-ness and expediting identification with the Nazi's ideology. The act of censorship was therefore not per se aesthetically motivated, but rather grounded in the notion that musical style conveyed political values (Street 2017).

Another instance of what Billig refers to as 'hot' nationalism (as opposed the earlier described 'banal' nationalism as everyday experience) connected to music is that some forms of popular music have become the voice of neo-Nazi subcultures or right-wing extremists. Tracing the history of racist skinhead culture and 'Nazi Rock' in England and Germany, Timothy S. Brown discusses the phenomenon as having become increasingly salient since the fall of Communism (2004), and as Fleischmidt and Pulay (2017) argue for the case of Hungarian nationalist music: music can function as a means of making the national imagination emotionally and ideologically appealing to new audiences (2017). As Futrell, Simi and Gottschalk show in their discussion of the US American White Power Music Scene (2006), participants in this musical culture of racist, militant nationalist white supremacy claim strong feelings of dignity, pride, pleasure, love, kinship and fellowship through their involvement with what they consider to be 'Aryan' music (2006: 275). Stylistically, this genre can vary from rock, and heavy metal, to country and western, while lyrics generally evoke notions of brotherhood, 'volk', 'white pride' and 'Aryan' heritage (2006: 281). As Futrell et al. highlight, the music of the White Power movement is what emotionally binds the participants and what continually reinforces collective identification with its ideology, mobilizes continued participation and motivates further actions (2006: 294). Similarly, albeit in a very different national context, Benjamin Teitelbaum traces in *Lions of the North* the importance of music in the establishment, rebranding and flourishing of radical nationalists in the Nordic countries. While this scene was also dominated by so-called White Power Rock, national populists now produce and consume a much wider range of genres from light pop, folk music and singer-songwriter balladry to techno and even rap and reggae (2017).

In recent years especially, the populist radical right and extreme right are increasingly drawing on popular music that explicitly avoids aesthetic associations with national 'radicalism', and instead produce and embrace popular music that can best be described as (aesthetically) 'mainstream'. In the United States, for instance, prominent neo-Nazi and White Supremacist websites like the Daily Stormer and Breitbart publicly embraced the likes of country-pop superstar Taylor Swift as supposedly representing an 'Aryan goddess' and turning her persona into alt-right memes (Prins 2020). This movement, prominently supported by president Donald Trump, also started producing its own popular music based on popular synthwave and vaporwave aesthetics labelled as fashwave. In their retro-futurist music productions, fashwave artists copy popular styles to overtly celebrate neo-Nazism, and fascism, while explicitly and strategically steering clear from sounding radical in their musical marketing strategy for White Supremacy: 'We want to hit the average. We want normal people. We have to be hip and we have to be sexy', Daily Stormer founder Andrew Anglin wrote in 2017 (Spitznagel 2020).

In turn, popular music culture in Europe has been increasingly marked by a rise of populist radical right discourses (Dunkel and Schiller forthcoming). In Austria and Italy, for instance, popular musicians like Andreas Gabalier and Giuseppe Povia have been described as performing populist discourses for a mainstream audience and thereby contributing to a social normalization of formerly radical politics (Dunkel, Schiller et al. 2021). In Germany, mainstream successful artists like Xavier Naidoo or prominent rappers like Kollegah actively participate in the spreading of populist and anti-Semitic conspiracy theories, and the South Tyrolian rock band Frei.Wild, who are known for promoting radical right populist and nationalist discourses in their music, not only sell millions of records but have also won the most prestigious German music awards. In Sweden, the popular singer Peter Jezewski has been supporting the populist radical right Sweden Democrats with his nostalgic rock'n'roll music and thereby successfully articulated rock culture with its associated 'authenticity' and the myth of subversion with populist and nativist discourses (Schiller, forthcoming). These new phenomena, again, highlight how popular music and nationalism interact in various ways across genres and aesthetic boundaries.

Popular music and alternative narratives of the nation

While some forms of popular music have become aligned with extreme forms of nationalism, others challenge normative narratives of the nation and offer competing notions of national identity. Especially in the current context of the rise of radical right populism all over Europe and beyond, investigations into the role of popular music in the maintenance of national identifications, as well as the formation of diasporic identities and alternative narratives of national belonging become increasingly important. Populist radical right parties in Europe like the Freedom Party of Austria, The Alternative for Germany and the Sweden Democrats, for example, are drawing heavily on the affective potential of popular music in their promotion of essentialist ideas of the nation and its history, claiming that 'true' nationals are white, Christian and of European descent (cf. Ginkel et al. forthcoming). Some leading politicians are active as musicians themselves, like Jimmie Åkesson of the Sweden Democrats, who plays in a band promoting patriotism, and others work closely with popular bands and well-known musicians, or appropriate existing popular songs that align with their ideological agendas.

On the other hand, musicians with migrant backgrounds – among others – are increasingly outspoken about their critique towards right-wing populist and nationalist rhetoric in and through popular music. In Sweden for instance, mainstream successful hip-hop artists like Erik Lundin or Silvana Imam use popular music to share their experiences of 'foreignness', racism and social exclusion to tell alternative narratives of Swedish-ness: they undermine populist 'us versus them' narratives (Mouffe 2016) by highlighting cultural hybridity and the multi-directional as well as processual character of culture (Hall 1990). Through these counter narratives, popular music remains an important cultural sphere of negotiating national inclusion and exclusion, as well as collective identity, spatial belonging and national heritage.

Note

1 Shuker notes that the quota was strongly 'encouraged' with the threat of license renewal being used as a tool to make it *de facto* compulsory: 'A voluntary NZ Music Code was negotiated (late 2001) between the Radio Broadcasters Association and the Minister of Broadcasting and began operating in 2002. While not mandatory, the new targets were "strongly encouraged" with the implicit threat of non-licence renewal, and in practice the quota was compulsory' (278).

References

Anderson, B. (1991), *Imagined Communities. Reflections on the Origin and Spread of Nationalism*, London: Verso.

Archer, R. (2012), 'Assessing Turbofolk Controversies: Popular Music between the Nation and the Balkans', *Southeastern Europe*, 36 (2): 178–207.

Applegate, C. and Potter, P. (2002), 'Germans as the "People of Music": Genealogy of an Identity', in C. Applegate and P. Potter (eds), *Music and German National Identity*, 1–35, London: Chicago University Press.

Balibar, E. (1991), 'The Nation Form: History and Ideology', in E. Balibar and I. M. Wallerstein (eds), *Race, Nation, Class: Ambiguous Identities*, 86–106, London: Verso.

Bennett, A. (2016), 'Music, Space and Place', in S. Whiteley, A. Bennett and S. Hawkins (eds), *Music, Space and Place. Popular Music and Cultural Identity*, 2–8, New York: Routledge.

Bhaba, H. (1990), 'Introduction: Narrating the Nation', in H. Bhabha (ed), *Nation and Narration*, 1–7, London: Routledge.

Biddle, I. and V. Knights (2007), 'Introduction. National Popular Musics: Betwixt and beyond the Local and the Global', in I. Biddle and V. Knights (eds), *Music, National Identity and the Politics of Location*, 1–15, Aldershot: Ashgate.

Billig, Michael (1995), *Banal Nationalism*, London: Sage.

Bohlman, P. V. (2009), 'Music before the Nation, Music after Nationalism', *Musicology Australia*, 31 (1): 79–100.

Bohlman, P. V. (2015), 'Music and Nationalism', *Wiley Online Library*, 30 December. Available online: https://onlinelibrary.wiley.com/doi/abs/10.1002/9781118663202.wberen454 (accessed 16 May 2019).

Brown, T. S. (2004), 'Subcultures, Pop Music and Politics: Skinheads and "Nazi Rock" in England and Germany', *Journal of Social History*, 38 (1): 157–78.

Cloonan, M. (1997), 'State of the Nation: "Englishness", Pop, and Politics in the Mid-1990s', *Popular Music and Society*, 21 (2): 47–70.

Cloonan, M. (1999), 'Pop and the Nation-State: Towards a Theorisation', *Popular Music*, 18 (2): 193–207.

Cloonan, M. (2016), *Popular Music and the State in the UK: Culture, Trade or Industry?* New York: Routledge.

Cohen, S. (2013), 'Musical Memory, Heritage and Local Identity: Remembering the Popular Music Past in a European Capital of Culture', *International Journal of Cultural Policy*, 19 (5): 576–94.

Connell, J. and Gibson, C. (2003), *Sound Tracks: Popular Music, Identity, and Place*, London: Routledge.
Curtis, B. (2008), *Music Makes the Nation. Nationalism Composers and Nation Building in Nineteenth- Century Europe*, New York: Cambria Press.
DeNora, T. (2000), *Music and Everyday Life*, Cambridge: Cambridge University Press.
DeNora, T. (2008), 'Culture and Music', in T. Bennett and J. Frow (eds), *The Sage Handbook of Cultural Analysis*, 145–62, London: Sage.
De Kloet, J. (2010), *China with a Cut: Globalization, Urban Youth and Popular Music*, Amsterdam: Amsterdam University Press.
Dunkel, M. and Schiller, M. (forthcoming), 'Popular Music and the Rise of Populism: An Introduction', in M. Dunkel and M. Schiller (eds), *Popular Music and the Rise of Populism in Europe*.
Dunkel, M., Schiller, M., and Schwenck, A. (2021), 'Researching Popular Music and the Rise of Populism in Europe', in K. Kärki (ed), *Turns and Revolutions in Popular Music: Proceedings from the XX Biennial Conference of IASPM, Canberra, Australia, 24th–28th June 2019*, 31–4, International Institute for Popular Culture.
Drewett, M. (2004), 'Aesopian Strategies of Textual Resistance in the Struggle to Overcome the Censorship of Popular Music in Apartheid South Africa', in B. Müller (ed), *Censorship & Cultural Regulation in the Modern Age*, 189–208, Amsterdam: Rodopi.
Edensor, T. (2002), *National Identity, Popular Culture and Everyday Life*, Oxford: Berg Publishers.
Feischmidt, M. and Pulay, G. (2017), 'Rocking the Nation: The Popular Culture of Neo-Nationalism', *Nations and Nationalism*, 23 (2): 309–26.
Fiske, J. (2011), *Reading the Popular*, Oxon: Routledge.
Fornäs, J. (2002), 'Limits of Musical Freedom', *Freemuse*: 1–18. Available online: http://freemuse.org/freemuseArchives/freerip/freemuse.org/sw3733.html (accessed 4 July 2018).
Frith, S. (1996), *Performing Rites*, Oxford: Oxford University Press.
Frith, S. (2007), 'Towards an Aesthetic of Popular Music', in S. Frith, *Taking Popular Music Seriously: Selected Essays*, 257–74, Farnham: Ashgate.
Futrell, R., Simi, P. and Gottschalk, S. (2006), 'Understanding Music in Movements: The White Power Music Scene', *The Sociological Quarterly*, 47 (2): 275–304.
Geertz, C. (1973), *The Interpretation of Cultures*, New York: Basic Books.
Gellner, E. (2006), *Nations and Nationalism*, New York: Cornell University Press.
Ginkel, K., Schwenck, A., Schiller, M., Doehring, A. and Dunkel, M. (Forthcoming), 'Populäre Musik als nationalistische Ressource? Vergleichende Schlaglichter auf AfD, FPÖ und die Schwedendemokraten (SD)', in M. Trummer and M. Spiritova (eds), *'Pop the Nation!'. Das Nationale als Ressource und Argument in Kulturen populärer Unterhaltung und Vergnügung*.
Grabowsky, I. (2005), '"Wie John, Paul, George und Ringo": Die "Beat-Ära"', in Stiftung Haus der Geschichte der Bundesrepublik Deutschland and Bundeszentrale für politische Bildung (eds), *Rock! Jugend und Musik in Deutschland*, 42–52, Bonn: Stiftung Haus der Geschichte der Bundesrepublik Deutschland/Bundeszentrale für politische Bildung.
Hall, S. (1990), 'Cultural Identity and Diaspora', in J. Rutherford (ed), *Identity, Community, Culture, Difference*, 222–37, London: Lawrence & Wishart.
Hall, S. (1996), 'The Question of Cultural identity', in S. Hall, D. Held, D. Hubert and K. Thompson (eds), *Modernity: An Introduction to Modern Societies*, 596–633, Cambridge: Blackwell.

Hesmondhalgh, D. and Negus, K. (2002), 'Introduction. Popular Music Studies: Meaning, Power and Value', in D. Hesmondhalgh and K. Negus (eds), *Popular Music Studies*, 1–9, London: Arnold.

Hobsbawm, E. (2012), 'Introduction: Inventing Traditions', in E. Hobsbawm and T. Ranger (eds), *The Invention of Tradition*, 1–14, Cambridge: Cambridge University Press.

Homan, S., Cloonan, M. and Cattermole, J. (2016), *Popular Music Industries and the State. Policy Notes*, New York: Routledge.

Kahn-Harris, K. (2006), '"Roots"? The Relationship between the Global and the Local within the Extreme Metal Scene', in A. Bennett, B. Shank and J. Toynbee (eds), *The Popular Music Studies Reader*, 128–34, London: Routledge.

McRobbie, A. (1999), *In the Culture Society: Art, Fashion and Popular Music*, Oxon: Routledge.

McLeod, K. (2016), *We Are the Champions: The Politics of Sports and Popular Music*, Oxon: Ashgate.

Mouffe, C. (2016), 'The Populist Challenge', *Opendecocracy.net*, 5 December. Available online: https://www.opendemocracy.net/democraciaabierta/chantal-mouffe/populist-challenge (accessed 16 May 2019).

Mullen, J. (2019), 'Introduction: Beyond the Question of Morale: Popular Music in the First World War', in J. Mullen (ed), *Popular Song in the First World War. An International Perspective*, 1–15, London: Routledge.

Peters, S. (2010), *Ein Lied mehr zur Lage der Nation. Politische Inhalte in deutschsprachigen Popsongs*, Berlin: Archiv der Jugendkulturen Verlag KG.

Prins, A. (2020), 'From Awkward Teen Girl to Aryan Goddess Meme: Taylor Swift and the Hijacking of Star Texts', *Celebrity Studies*, 11 (1): 144–8.

Robert, L. and Cohen, S. (2014), 'Unauthorising Popular Music Heritage: Outline of a Critical Framework', *International Journal of Heritage Studies*, 20 (3): 241–61.

Schildt, A. and Siegfriedited, D. (2009), *Deutsche Kulturgeschichte. Die Bundesrepublik von 1945 bis zur Gegenwart*, München: Hanser Verlag.

Schiller, M. (2019), 'Staging the Nation: Claire Waldoff and Berlin Cabaret before and during the Great War', in J. Mullen (ed), *Popular Song in the First World War. An International Perspective*, 152–67, London: Routledge.

Schiller, M. (2020), *Soundtracking Germany. Popular Music and National Identity*, London: Rowman and Littlefield.

Schiller, M. 'Populism, Subcultural Style and Authenticity: Popular Music, Rock Rebellion and the Radical Right in Sweden', in M. Anastasiadis and C. Goer (eds), '*The People vs. The Power Bloc*' (?) – *Interdisziplinäre Perspektiven auf Pop und Populismen*, Bielefeld: Transcript. Forthcoming.

Shuker, R. (2008), 'New Zealand Popular Music, Government Policy, and Cultural Identity', *Popular Music*, 27 (2): 271–87.

Spitznagel, E. (2020), 'How Far-right Groups Are Using Fashion Symbols to Recruit the Youth', *New York Post*, 31 October. Available online: https://nypost.com/2020/10/31/how-far-right-groups-are-using-fashion-symbols-to-recruit-youth/ (accessed 7 July 2021).

Stehle, M. and Kahnke, C. (2013), 'German Popular Music in the Twenty-First Century: Politics, Trends, and Trajectories', *Journal of Popular Music Studies*, 25 (2): 123–6.

Street, J. (2017), *Music and Politics*, Cambridge: Polity.

Teitelbaum, B. R. (2017), *Lions of the North: Sounds of the New Nordic Radical Nationalism*, New York: Oxford University Press.

Thacker, T. (2007), *Music after Hitler, 1945–1955*, Aldershot: Ashgate.

Tuohy, S. (2001), 'The Sonic Dimensions of Nationalism in Modern China: Musical Representation and Transformation', *Ethnomusicology*, 45 (1): 107–31.

Turino, T. (2008), *Music as Social Life: The Politics of Participation*, Chicago: University of Chicago Press.

25

Transnational music

Simone Krüger Bridge

Introduction

Transnationalism has become increasingly popular in contemporary scholarly and journalistic discourses, even though the term has fuzzy boundaries and often overlaps with the concept of diaspora.[1] Transnationalism resulted from the major changes brought on by global media and technologies, increasing (human) migration, modernization and Westernization, and commodification throughout the previous century – commonly referred to as globalization. Transnationalism refers to processes that transcend international borders, and is often used to refer to migrants' durable ties across countries, and to capture not only communities, but all sorts of social formations, such as transnationally active networks, groups, and organizations. Transnationalism connotes the everyday practices of migrants engaged in various activities, including reciprocity and solidarity within kinship networks, political participation in home and host country, small-scale entrepreneurship across borders, the transfer and re-transfer of cultural customs and practices, and others.

Transnationalism as a concept is relatively new, not only in public debates but also in academic analysis, and emerged in migration studies in the 1990s from previous scholarly work on the nation state and national identity (Anderson 2006 [1983]; Hobsbawm 1990), offering an alternative category to 'black' and 'white' in dominant Western discourses to refer to recent immigrant cohorts ('people out of place') entering industrial societies in North America and Europe. While transnationalism initially referred to migration as a one-way process, sociologists, historians, geographers, anthropologists and others gradually reconsidered its meaning to also include reverse, temporary, circular and other kinds of migration. The term also gradually expanded to include other groups of people, notably the capitalist class, as well as a whole array of cross-border activities, including tourism, marriage, cross-border activism, journalism, academic collaborations, criminal activity, news coverage, religious communities, social movements, mobility, communication media and so forth. Thus, while transnationalism is a facet of international migration, it is no longer restricted to immigrant groups, which has reconfigured the scholarly object of enquiry away from national society and towards *transnational social spaces* (Roudometof 2005) – the emerging spaces of human interaction, including spaces of popular music.

Music and transnationalism

Musicians represent some of the most mobile migrants in transnational culture and are thus a major focus on scholarly attention in transnational music studies. The proliferation of different levels of transnationalism across the globe has thus increasingly become the object of study in music studies, notably ethnomusicology, popular music and music sociology, where explanations of globalizing transnational trends are often made through the lenses of globalization, migration and diaspora, the transnational music business and capitalism, musical hybridization and cosmopolitanism (Garofalo 1993; Regev 2013; Taylor 2016; Krüger Bridge 2018). While much of this work focuses on the economic and financial dimensions of globalization and its mediation and facilitation by large-scale corporate transnational companies and organizations, research has increasingly demonstrated empirically the everyday life realities of the people involved in transnational networks and flows, recognizing the crucial role played by individuals within processes of globalization from below – the human dimension of globalization. Transnationalism thereby facilitates the study of migration as a dynamic process in which people travel readily between places of origin and resettlement and communicate on multiple levels across geographical boundaries via diverse media. Specifically, the work of ethnomusicologist Mark Slobin provides important foundations for theories of musical transnationalism by using the notion of 'scape' to explore the articulation of several musical translocal contexts, while adopting a sociological view on popular and secular music repertoires that have acquired a transnational dimension (1992, 1993). Such a sociological perspective is shared by others, including Nadia Kiwan and Ulrike Meinhof's study of musicians whose careers are part of transnational networks (2011), as well as some notable collections on music, diaspora, migration and cosmopolitanism (Aparicio and Jaquez 2003; Ramnarine 2007b; Kiwan and Meinhof 2011b; Toynbee and Dueck 2012; Krüger and Trandafoiu 2014).

Studies of musical transnationalism often pay attention to the ever-increasing migration of musicians and their routes, networks and (new hybrid) identities; the proliferation of new recording and other technologies; global power perspectives and disparities; the sense of belonging and imagined communities; and newer (online) and multi-sited research approaches. Indeed, the role of the internet in the creation and development of virtual communities is indeed highly relevant in transnational musical studies that seek to understand music's role played in transnational cultural development (e.g. Lysloff and Leslie 2003). Yet despite some pioneering work on music and transnationalism (e.g. Slobin 1992, 1993, 1994, 2012; Ramnarine 1996, 2001, 2007a, 2007b; Manuel 2000; Shelemay 2006; Um 2005; Stokes 2004, 2007; Solis 2005; Muller 2006; Baily and Collyer 2006; Martiniello and Lafleur 2008; Pistrick 2015; Zheng 2010), the interconnectedness between music and transnational social spaces still remains to be further explored. The following sections will contribute in three ways to existing studies of musical transnationalism: an ethnographic look at migrant experiences of hybrid identities in the local context of Liverpool; a historical analysis of reggae in the UK in the context of migration, memory and place; and a sociological view of the global music genre of hip hop as it has become inextricably linked to ideas of transnationalism.

Transnational identities in a local context: Migrant experiences in Liverpool

Salsa emerged from the rhythmic cultures of Africa and developed through the movement of people along transnational routes embracing the Caribbean, particularly Puerto Rico and Cuba, as well as the United States, Europe and other parts of the world. In its transformation to a hybrid and transnational dance practice, for example, in the Latin communities of New York where it was mixed with different South American and Caribbean music styles, as well as rock and jazz, salsa gradually transcended its original localized identity from a Hispanophone post-colonial imaginary to become a much wider Latino/a identifier, particularly in moments of collective pleasure experienced by dancers, which can unite migrants with very different histories and everyday life experiences. Indeed, diasporic migrant experience does not reflect one united sense of identity, but contradicted and fragmented identities united in a search for belonging.

That migrant identities are not fixed and static, but differentiated and heterogeneous, became clear to me when in 2009, during ethnographic research in Liverpool, I met Flor (female, twenty-four), Alan (male, twenty-three), Valessi (female, twenty-one) and Indira (female, seventeen), four siblings from Bolivia, who arrived in the UK about eight years prior to that, and who related to local salsa nights 'Noche Clandestina' at Liverpool's Latin venue El Rincon[2] in very unique ways. The salsa dance events were often attended by local Liverpudlians, who were attracted to salsa by a sense of exoticism and otherness; yet, Flor explained to me that in Bolivia, salsa dancing was about celebrating life and hope. Alan agreed that salsa represents their 'real' culture and triggered memories of 'who we really are'. Alan felt that due to their young age when migrating they hadn't yet learnt to cook Bolivian food, so music and dance became more central to them in evoking memories of homeland. The two oldest siblings, Flor and Alan, who were in their mid-teens upon arriving in the UK, had somewhat different experiences and felt Bolivian more strongly than Valessi and Indira, who also felt in tune with British identity. Salsa evoked strong memories in Flor and Alan: they spoke at length about the importance of salsa in Bolivia 'as a way of life', and how they grew up with salsa music and dance around them. Both Flor and Alan now lived with British partners and socialized mostly with British colleagues in their work places, so salsa music helped them to remember their homeland and to maintain a sense of Bolivianness. Flor even wished to return to Bolivia, which she referred to as 'my country', especially when starting a family, to give her children a similar upbringing to herself. Indira, who was nine years old when arriving in the UK, similarly explained that listening to salsa was integral to her identity, as listening to Western music would mean to 'pretend' and 'fake' to be someone she was not. She remembered people dancing salsa at home, and while she tried hard to fit into British culture at school, she felt increasingly confident to establish herself as Bolivian, while listening to salsa and other Latin music as a means to express her identity to herself and others – to be in touch with an essential part of herself.

Salsa events at El Rincon were thus important to the siblings in their confusion as to who they 'really are' and central for constructing and maintaining their Latin identity. Even so, there were some clear differences in how Valessi viewed and constructed her identity. On one occasion at El Rincon, I noticed that Valessi did not dance salsa with the rest of the family, and this was so since her memories were very different to her siblings'. As a child, while living in Bolivia, her family moved frequently, and this lack of attachment to a place and instability meant that Valessi felt a lack of attachment to Bolivia as a country. Valessi focused much on how she felt 'free' and does not need to be attached to a place to feel strong. After migrating at the age of eleven, Valessi tried hard to fit in with the Latin community in the UK, but always felt slightly out of place. Consequently, her relationship to salsa differed greatly from her siblings, and she clearly lacked her siblings' shared and idealized sense of Bolivian culture more generally. Moreover, Valessi believed to be a bad dancer while lacking rhythm, and so felt uncomfortable dancing in El Rincon. Indeed, rhythm has been used as a significant marker of Latinness in Western media, constructing the idea that dancing salsa comes 'natural' to Latin Americans (Román-Velázquez 2002: 220), which further impacted on her feeling inadequate and excluded, even non-Latin because of her lack of rhythm, especially in her teens. Only when Valessi grew older did she no longer feel the need to 'fit in', but that this 'doesn't make me any less Bolivian'. In her case, there was a sense of 'homing desire', which was not the same thing as a desire for returning to the homeland. While the Bolivian siblings expressed their identities in heterogeneous ways, I noted that none of them were 'naturally' Latin, but this was something they were all actively and consciously working on, driven by a desire to fix identity, to feel a sense of core identity. This was, at least to Flor, Alan and Valessi, found in their ethnicity, as identifying themselves in ethnic terms is indeed a basic human need to express social belonging (Simonett 2007: 88). Even so, it is important to remember that migrants may also have a contradictory relationship with this imagined belonging to an idealized homeland, and that individual experiences may indeed differ due to sociocultural circumstances.

Migration, memory and place: The case of reggae in the UK

Music in a migration context, which has become the everyday lived reality of people in many urban areas of the world, evokes collective memories and experiences of place, which is demonstrated by the post-war Caribbean migration to the UK and its impact upon the creation and dissemination of reggae music. While Caribbean migration to the UK was largely based on the post-war economic needs of British industries, it maintained the racialized appropriation of the African diaspora that was forcibly constructed through the slave trade and the forcible dispersion of people from their African homeland. Thus, while many migrants had preconceived idealistic ideas of job success, housing and social roles within British society, they found themselves in shock due to continuing racial segregation and prejudice, and the realization of being duped into the promise of a better economic standing in society (James 1993: 231; Hebdige 1987: 90). Coping with the hardships of this reality, many migrants took refuge in their own West Indian culture, including food and music. Post-war events such as Blues Dance that played reggae-precursors Blue Beat and Ska were popular, but these were gradually replaced by the 1960s phenomenon of the sound system, particularly in London areas heavily populated with Caribbean migrants, which successfully reproduced social events similar to those in Jamaica with toasters rhyming and talking over a bass-heavy sound system playing quintessential Rock Steady, Dub and Reggae.

To Caribbean migrants, the marginalization of Caribbean music in the British music industry at the time made these sound system events even more significant, further strengthened by the lyrical messages that echoed the social commentary in Jamaica, with themes including Rastafarian ideas of repatriation, rebellion against and emancipation from slavery, the mythologizing and idealizing of Africa as homeland, particularly Ethiopia, and the desecration of Babylon, as well as highlighting social issues in the UK such as unemployment, poor housing and racial abuse. In 1964, the first Notting Hill Carnival was held to enable West Indian and Afro-Caribbean migrants to emulate the annual Trinidadian carnival, which was originally conceived of to celebrate 'black' people's emancipation from colonial slavery. This event was the first of its kind in the UK in that it was both associated with and celebrated Caribbean (black) identity. Yet during 1976, the Notting Hill Carnival featured for the first time a particularly large sound system and so introduced reggae, which attracted half a million people and led to the culmination of increasing tensions that resulted in violence between West Indies youth contesting the oppression they had suffered in the UK and the British police force (Gutzmore 1993: 217). Thus, while music serves as a means to evoke collective memories and experiences of place, it also binds the politically opposing positions of people within a migrant culture.

In the late 1970s/early 1980s, second-generation socially conscious reggae artists, including bands like Aswad, Matumbi and Steel Pulse, continued to use themes of oppression, rebellion, Rastafarian themes and migrant culture in the UK in their lyrics,[3] but they also talked about displacement and Jamaica-as-homeland in their lyrics, thereby translating the Africa/Jamaica theme to a West Indies/UK enforced exodus (Bradley 2000: 431). The visual elements on vinyl sleeves of British reggae albums further reflect the glocalization of Caribbean cultural practices in the UK, while also providing stereotyped images to its fans and consumers. For example, album covers by Steel Pulse and Aswad signified Rastafarianism via images of dread-locked hairstyles, the colours of the Rastafarian flag (yellow, green and red) and the Lion of Judah as a Rastafarian religious symbol. By actively adopting writing styles similar to those produced in Jamaica by telling stories and relaying messages to both inform and influence social thinking, re-interpreting reggae music to adapt a rhetoric of oppression that makes sense beyond Jamaica, and absorbing Caribbean imagery in visual artwork to both evoke memory and a sense of place thus meant to add new meanings as these were shaped by the new sociocultural contexts in the UK (Daynes 2004: 32). Second-generation reggae lyrics and images thereby portrayed the social circumstances of second-generation Caribbean migrants, with reggae used to provide a strong link between the cultural idioms of the African diaspora and Jamaican one.

The clothing and fashion accessories of British reggae artists influenced subsequent music groups, as well as white working class youth, who had lived alongside and socialized with second-generation Caribbean migrants and attended sound system events, and felt similarly rejected by society and discriminated on the grounds of their appearance and beliefs. The punk subculture of the 1970s also turned to reggae, who similarly talked about Britain's crisis in much the same way as roots reggae artists dwelled on the decline of Babylon, which led to the ska revival by record label Two Tone mixing ska, reggae and punk elements. The Specials signified this social, musical and ethnic hybridity and transnationalism between Caribbean and English ethnicities and racial identities, building a new collective memory that blends elements from both place and time, while drawing on different traditions and harmonizing both old and new.

Transnational popular music: The global hip-hop phenomenon

Technology, corporate expansion, mediatization and commodification on a global scale have led to the diffusion and globalization of music, with some styles and genres spreading far and wide from their places of origin and becoming part of the expanding repertoire of transnational popular music. While salsa and reggae are clearly such examples (e.g. Savishinsky 1994), it is probably right to say that since the 1990s hip hop has diffused more widely, more intensely and more successfully than any other genre of popular music. Hip hop has thereby become linked to ideas of transnationalism as it has developed in different diasporic contexts and become the most widespread form of urban popular music since reggae, addressing many young migrants' search for identification that media corporations have gradually commodified globally. However, the cultural meanings of hip-hop music as a global commodity are often challenged and subverted in the streets of locally based rap cultures where it is re-used and re-interpreted stylistically. Initially seen as black music, rap music emerged in the late 1970s as part of a wider hip-hop culture in the South Bronx in New York and was quickly taken up by residents in other American urban neighbourhoods. Hip hop has increasingly been adopted by a much wider ethnic audience inside and outside of the United States, and was diffused across the world and appropriated by artists in all sorts of countries, especially those associated with more recent international migration. It is largely a product in cities of the diaspora, particularly among the more depressed urban groups with imagined links to distant 'sources' and roots in Africa. Hip hop was also appropriated in places without a history of international migration, but where there were significant ethnic minorities in urban settings. Existing in various locations around the world today, hip hop is a transnational musical form that uses black music and liberation theory as a base, and through which artists can resist the trappings of their respective cultures. It reflects that music in both the homeland and diaspora is never static, but a living product of synthesis and hybridity. Two examples of hip hop from France and China will illustrate some of the range of practices specific of migrant ethnic groups, in space and time, while linking the sociocultural, geopolitical and historical contexts to narratives of identities.

In France, hip hop developed in the outer suburbs (*banlieues*) of Paris and Marseilles among youths of West Indian, African or Maghrebi descent, and represents the separation of migrant groups from the music of their homelands. As elsewhere, rap lyrics have gradually been localized through the use of the French national language (with regional variants) and other languages, while resonating with the specific cultural, economic, and political issues and circumstances of particular migrant groups, to whom the genre has given a voice to express their identities and sensitivities, and to understand life in the inner-city *banlieues*. Two scenes dominate the French hip-hop scene: a US-influenced 'hardcore' gangsta-rap hip hop that addresses the issues faced by young people in France and is represented by the likes of Supreme NTM and Ministére Amer and a more localized 'cool', laid-back kind of rap music reflects the ethnic identities of its Central African and Maghrebi protagonists, inflected by local languages and represented by groups and rappers such as De la Soul, A Tribe Called Quest, Mc Solaar and Alliance Ethnik. Language is an important cultural and political signifier of national difference, especially since English dominates popular culture and music. The reasons for using local language are varied: they may be cultural, economic and/or political. In using their own language, including local forms of slang, rap artists emphasize local experience and localized subcultures, stressing difference and often marginality. Thus, over time, lyrics, styles and delivery become adapted to particular migrant circumstances.

While their adoption of Afro-American hip-hop props, including Nike trainers, has continued in both more hard-core hip-hop scenes and among middle-class kids as a form of resistance against the Parisian urban milieu, hip-hop crews often deal with French colonial and post-colonial history, factory exploitation, anti-immigrant policies and experiences of migration. For instance, Mc Solaar, one of the French hip-hop artists closer to the mainstream, raps in his first single 'Bouge de Là' (transl. 'Get Out of Here') about the arrival of a Senegalese immigrant to France – probably Mc Solaar's own alter ego and experience of cultural shock – and the movements of the migrant body in a desire to change and disguise his cultural identity, to let it disappear, in order to conform and reappear under a new hybrid transnational identity (Huq 2006). Dressed in the Senegalese *boubous* and a bohemian 'old-skool' urban style, connoted by the flat cap worn to the side, Mc Solaar's song represents musical narratives of transnational hybrid identity. Meanwhile, IAM (*Invasion arrive de Mars*; transl. Invasion from Mars [abbreviation for Marseilles]) from Marseille delivers a rap message of 'pharaoism' in the *verlan* dialect, a form of French slang that reverses letter orders and plays with syllables and represents a refusal of the nationalistic hierarchies reinforced by the *Loi Toubon* (transl. Toubon Law), which evokes Marseilles' Mediterranean inheritance via a mythical connection between the river Rhone and the Nile. Their album cover for *De La Planete Mars* (1991) uses Arabic fonts in the title to depict the Islamic identity of two of its members (Algeria and Mali), while the image depicts Marseille from a hill top to evoke their adopted 'in-between', hybrid identity.

French hip hop reflects elements of the heritage of transnational migrants – visually, linguistically, ideologically – thereby giving a voice to urban youths to make communitarian claims within their different sociocultural transnational environments, and critique racism and the growing gaps between suburbs and inner cities in French society, and with it the experiences of transnational multi-ethnic underclasses in the *banlieues*. It shows the ways that hip hop connects people across most of the African diaspora through a pan-African consciousness, whereby diasporic, transnational peoples are engaged in a dialectic of opposition and resistance to the hegemonic logic of multinational capital, reflexive of a certain liberatory character of global, diasporic practices. This use of transnationalism as a counter-hegemonic political space is found in the many musical practices of non-white and white hip-hop artists across the globe, and reflects the ways that transnational practices surrounding hip-hop culture are potentially counter-hegemonic, but not always resistant (see also Krüger Bridge 2018: 132–42).

In China, musicians from mainland China, Hong Kong and Taiwan had injected rap elements into rock and pop music already in the 1990s; however, hip hop did not really attract widespread attention at the time. Following the globalization of economies and cultures worldwide, hip hop began to become prominent in China during the 2000s and impacted on the youth born in the 1980s and 1990s, although the Golden Age of Chinese hip-hop is yet to come. Earlier hip hop was predominantly American, which contained strong negative emotions and was associated with violence, sex, drugs, and dissatisfaction with social status. Operating in a society of state cultural policy limitations that selectively backs state-approved musicians, the hip-hop scene has become increasingly difficult to navigate. Thus, hip hop in China became influenced by Sinicization and more concerned with socialism and 'Chineseness', and less with political resistance to comply with Chinese state regulations. Rapping in Mandarin became prominent in the noughties. During this decade, hip-hop artists and crews sprung up all over the country and began appearing on public occasions, with a nationwide growth in freestyle battles, hip-hop parties and music festivals. In 2017, Chinese hip hop went literally mainstream almost overnight due to *The Rap of China*, a talent show on the streaming platform iQIYI, which reflects Chinese commercialism and 'good' citizenship in the hip-hop music market. Indeed, Chinese hip-hop musicians need commodification and widespread popularity to support themselves financially. Mainstream record labels often utilize consumer psychology to create superficial hip hop that is intrinsically pop music and attractive for large audiences, so the state-backed record companies flood the market with their versions of hip hop by pushing pop artists like Jay Chou, the Justin Bieber of China, to look and sound like a rapper, which reflects an industry-wide trend across Taiwan, Hong Kong and the mainland. Many Chinese artists thereby turn to hip hop to aspire to enter the mainstream market, and commercialism and capitalist profitability is an indispensable part of the hip-hop trajectory in contemporary China.

While it is difficult to make enough money as an underground artist, many hip-hop artists willingly commercialize their music to make it 'acceptable', but there are also independent musicians who firmly reject commercialization. The Chinese hip-hop scene is thus divided into an 'official' state-promoted hip-hop scene that reflects a contemporary fashion trend in popular culture and lifestyle, and an underground hip-hop scene that reflects artists' counter-hegemonic practices in response to censorship of freedom of speech and capitalist tendencies in China. One of the most pioneering underground Chinese hip-hop bands, Yin Tsang, hailed from the capital city of Beijing, and their first album *Serve the People*, which was a groundbreaking success with its hit single 'In Beijing' going viral and receiving millions of downloads, television and radio play, reflects the harsh reality of expressing national identity with counter-hegemonic critiques. Yin Tsang was officially established in 2001 by MC Webber (Chinese), MC Jeremy (American), MC Sbazzo (Chinese-Canadian) and MC Hef (Irish-American). This pioneering joint Chinese-American-Canadian crew started to rap in Mandarin, the official Chinese language, and is localized by MC Jeremy via his rhotic accent, a phonological process that adds the r-suffix in standard Northern Mandarin (Beijing Mandarin). While influenced by American hip hop, Yin Tsang includes instruments like Chinese drums and *erhu*, a Chinese two-stringed traditional instrument, with video shooting locations in the most distinctive spots in Beijing: the Lama Temple, the Drum Tower and the Quadrangle, cultural symbols that challenge and subvert the stereotypical images of the hip-hop tradition and reflect the icons of Chinese national identity.

Yet the album title *Serve the People* (2003) is the same name as the well-known political slogan in Mao Zedong-era China, and in particular when, on 5th September 1944, President Mao Zedong gave a speech to commemorate the sacrifice of a soldier from the Chinese People's Liberation Army. His slogan 'Serve the People' represented national identity after the liberation and the establishment of P.R. China, and is still today capsuled as the tenet of the Communist Party. It is unclear whether Yin Tsang's album name demonstrates the same meaning, or whether it is a political statement; to a certain extent, it also reflects the aspirations of many Chinese hip-hop musicians to enter the mainstream state-controlled music market, although Yin Tsang received only $7,000 for sales and three years of touring. Indeed, before Yin Tsang released the album, the record label asked them to revise almost half of their lyrics in order to meet censorship conditions, which are reinforced and controlled by the Ministry of Culture and State Administration of Press, Publication, Radio, Film and Television. MC Webber even refused to perform on China-Central Television (CCTV) because it restricted his wearing of a baseball cap and colourful clothes containing English writing. Recently, the Ministry of Culture announced a 'blacklist' of 120 pieces of online music after analysing over 5,700 pieces of Chinese songs in the hip-hop ranking list (Zhou 2018), which contained content that promotes obscenity, violence, abetting crimes or endangering social morality, which violated the provisions of Article 16 of the Interim Provisions on Internet Culture Management and were removed from all streaming platforms. Most underground hip-hop musicians feel that Chinese hip hop should reflect counter-hegemonic opinions due to these political limitations; however, censorship of Chinese hip hop reflects the State's intention towards cultural protection and safeguarding of certain social and aesthetic values. Nevertheless, contemporary transnational musical activities such as hip hop are often a reaction against purist constructions of Chinese nationalism, reflecting the changes in political agendas and social and musical values that are more relevant to Chinese youths' current perceptions of the world and their position in it.

Conclusion

Musical interactions across nation-state boundaries are an everyday occurrence in today's interconnected world; thus, transnationalism has become an important concept in contemporary music studies. Transnationalism facilitates the meaningful study of local music scenes as socio-musically connected to other sites in the transnational scene, and how these connections impact local musical practices. Transnational music studies consider the multilocality of diasporic musicians and audiences, and their lifeworlds beyond hybridity, creolization, new performance contexts and cultural contact. With their focus on the transcultural production, performance and consumption of music, transnational music studies also acknowledge the intensity and simultaneity of multiple ties and interactions of individuals or institutions across nation states (Vertovec 1999: 447–8). Transnationalism allows us to think beyond old categorical ideas of geographic space and social identity, and importantly relates to the interactions of musicians, and it is these networks of social and cultural relations that are particularly important in contemporary studies of music and transnationalism. This chapter has focused on three case study examples of cross-cultural musical activities as an assertion of peoples' transnational identities, which are maintained and expressed through social and cultural relationships. The examples show the varied ways in which migrant and non-migrant people today make music useful and meaningful in their transnational lives, and how musicians collaborate, source new material, adopt musical instruments and market their music across geographical boundaries. By listening to music, appropriating music and creating hybrid glocalized fusions, people perform their ideal transnational social lives and relationships.

Notes

1   The term diaspora has often been used to denote religious or national groups living outside an (imagined) homeland. For further reading, see Rainer Bauböck and Thomas Faist, eds (2010), *Diaspora and Transnationalism: Concepts, Theories and Methods*, Amsterdam University Press.
2   El Rincon was opened by the company All Things Latin, now called One Latin Culture, which promotes contemporary Latin America, its people and its culture and to develop projects and presentations that represent different aspects of Latin America. OLC also works to advance the education of the communities of Liverpool and the UK and to

develop their understanding of Global education (see http://www.allthingslatin.co.uk/, accessed 26 April 2019).
3   A good example is provided by Steel Pulse's 'Handsworth Revolution' (1978), released by Islands Records.

References

Aparicio, F. R. and Jaquez, C. F. (2003), *Musical Migrations: Transnationalism and Cultural Hybridity in Latin/o America*, vol. 1. New York: Macmillan.

Anderson, B. (2006 [1983]), *Imagined Communities: Reflections on the Origins and Spread of Nationalism*, London: Verso.

Baily, J. and Collyer, M. (2006), 'Introduction: Music and Migration', *Journal of Ethnic and Migration Studies*, 32 (2): 167–82.

Bradley, L. (2000), *Bass Culture: When Reggae Was King*, London: Penguin.

Daynes, S. (2004), 'The Musical Construction of the Diaspora: The Case of Reggae and Rastafari', in S. Whiteley, A. Bennett and S. Hawkins (eds), *Music, Space and Place: Popular Music and Cultural Identity*, 25–41, Aldershot: Ashgate.

Garofalo, R. (1993), 'Whose World, What Beat: The Transnational Music Industry, Identity, and Cultural Imperialism', *The World of Music*, 35 (2): 16–32.

Gutzmore, C. (1993), 'Carnival, the State and the Black Masses in the United Kingdom', in W. James and C. Harris (eds), *Inside Babylon: The Caribbean Diaspora in Britain*, 207–30, London: Verso.

Hebdige, D. (1987), *Cut 'N' Mix: Culture, Identity and Caribbean Music*, London: Methuen.

Hobsbawm, E. J. (1990), *Nations and Nationalism since 1780, Second Edition: Programme, Myth, Reality*, Cambridge: Cambridge University Press.

Huq, R. (2006) 'European Youth Cultures in a Post-colonial World: British Asian Underground and French Hip-Hop Music Scenes', in Pam Nilan and Carles Feixa (eds.), *Global Youth? : Hybrid Identities, Plural Worlds*, pp. 14–31. London, UK: Routledge.

James, W. (1993), 'Migration, Racism and Identity Formation: The Caribbean Experience in Britain', in W. James and C. Harris (eds), *Inside Babylon: The Caribbean Diaspora in Britain*, 231–88, London: Verso.

Kiwan, N. and Meinhof, U. H. (2011a), *Cultural Globalization and Music: African Artists in Transnational Networks*, London: Palgrave Macmillan.

Kiwan, N. and Meinhof, U. H., eds (2011b), 'Music and Migration: A Transnational Approach', Special issue of *Music and Arts in Action* 3 (3).

Krüger, B. S. (2018), *Trajectories and Themes in World Popular Music: Globalization, Capitalism, Identity*, Sheffield, UK: Equinox.

Krüger, S. and Trandafoiu, R., eds (2014), *The Globalization of Musics in Transit: Music Migration and Tourism*, New York: Routledge.

Lysloff, R., and Gay, L. C. (2003), *Music and Technoculture*, Middletown, CT: Wesleyan University Press.

Manuel, P. (2000), *East Indian Music in the West Indies: Tān-Singing, Chutney, and the Making of Indo-Caribbean Culture*, Philadelphia: Temple University Press.

Martiniello, M. and Lafleur, J. M. (2008), 'Ethnic Minorities' Cultural and Artistic Practices as Forms of Political Expression: A Review of the Literature and a Theoretical Discussion on Music', *Journal of Ethnic and Migration Studies*, 34 (8): 1191–215.

Muller, C. A. (2006), 'The New African Diaspora, the Built Environment and the Past in Jazz', *Ethnomusicology Forum*, 15 (1): 63–86.

Pistrick, E. (2015), *Performing Nostalgia: Migration Culture and Creativity in South Albania*, New York: Routledge.

Ramnarine, T. K. (1996), 'Indian: Music in the Diaspora: Case Studies of "Chutney" in Trinidad and London', *British Journal of Ethnomusicology*, 5: 133–53.

Ramnarine, T. K. (2001), *Creating Their Own Space: The Development of an Indian-Caribbean Musical Tradition*, Jamaica: University of West Indies Press.

Ramnarine, T. K. (2007a), *Beautiful Cosmos: Performance and Belonging in the Caribbean Diaspora*, London and Ann Arbor: Pluto Press.

Ramnarine, T. K., ed. (2007b), *Musical Performance in the Diaspora*, New York: Routledge.

Regev, M. (2013), *Pop-Rock Music: Aesthetic Cosmopolitanism in Late Modernity*, Cambridge: Polity.

Román-Velázquez, P. (2002), 'Locating Salsa', in D. Hesmondhalgh and K. Negus (eds), *Popular Music Studies*, 210–22, London: Hodder Arnold.

Roudometof, V. (2005), 'Transnationalism, Cosmopolitanism, and Glocalization', *Current Sociology*, 53 (1): 113–35.

Savishinsky, N. J. (1994), 'Transnational Popular Culture and the Global Spread of the Jamaican Rastafarian Movement', *NWIG: New West Indian Guide*, 68 (3/4): 259–81.

Shelemay, K. K. and Kaplan, Steven, (2006), 'Diaspora', Special Issue *Creating the Ethiopian Diaspora: Perspectives from Across the Disciplines*, 15 (2).

Simonett, H. (2007), 'Banda, A New Sound from the Barrios of Los Angeles: Transmigration and Transcultural Production', in I. Biddle and V. Knights (eds), *Music, National Identity and the Politics of Location: Between the Global and the Local*, 81–92, Aldershot: Ashgate.

Slobin, M. (1992), 'Micromusics of the West: A Comparative Approach', *Ethnomusicology*, 36 (1): 1–87.

Slobin, M. (1993), *Subcultural Sounds: Micromusics of the West*, Hanover, NH: Wesleyan University Press.

Slobin, M. (1994), 'Music in Diaspora: The View from Euro-America', *Diaspora: A Journal of Transnational Studies*, 3 (3): 243–51.

Slobin, M. (2012), 'The Destiny of "Diaspora" in Ethnomusicology', in M. Clayton, T. Herbert, and R. Middleton (eds), *The Cultural Study of Music: A Critical Introduction*, 2nd edn, 96–106, New York: Routledge.

Solis, T. (2005), '"You Shake Your Hips Too Much": Diasporic Values and Hawai'i Puerto Rican Dance Culture', *Ethnomusicology*, 49 (1): 75–119.

Stokes, M. (2004), 'Music and the Global Order', *Annual Review of Anthropology*, 33 (1): 47–72.

Stokes, M. (2007), 'On Cosmopolitanism', The Macalester International Roundtable 2007. Paper 3. Available online: http://digitalcommons.macalester.edu/intlrdtable/3 (accessed 9 July 2019).

Taylor, T. (2016), *Music and Capitalism: A History of the Present*, Chicago: University of Chicago Press.

Toynbee, J. and Dueck, B., eds (2012), *Migrating Music*, New York: Routledge.

Um, H. (2005), 'Introduction: Understanding Diaspora, Identity and Performance', in H. Um (ed), *Diasporas and Interculturalism in Asian Performing Arts: Translating Traditions*, 1–14, London: Routledge.
Vertovec, S. (1999), 'Conceiving and Researching Transnationalism', *Ethnic and Racial Studies*, 22 (2): 447–62.
Zheng, S. (2010), *Claiming Diaspora: Music, Transnationalism, and Cultural Politics in Asian/Chinese America*, New York: Oxford University Press.
Zhou, W. (2018), 'Will There Still Be Hip-Hop in China after the "Main Melody" Crackdown?' [online] *BBC News*. Available online: https://www.bbc.com/zhongwen/simp/chinese-news-42855743 (accessed 11 April 2019).

Section V

Selling, celebrating, representing space and place

26
Music, heritage and place

Catherine Strong

Thinking about popular music as heritage is a relatively recent phenomenon. Bennett (2015: 18–19) notes that contemporary popular music and popular culture more generally were long denied the label of heritage because their 'mass-produced, commercial and global cultural properties... rendered them the antithesis of anything deemed to be of authentic historical and cultural value as this was conceived in conventional heritage discourse'. However this situation has changed over time, as popular music has aged and gained more of a 'historical' aspect, and as those invested in it in their youth have gained positions as cultural gatekeepers. The rise of popular music as an aspect of heritage is also connected to broader changes, including the breakdown of the 'highbrow/lowbrow' division in culture, and a widening conception of whose versions of the past are seen as worthy or authoritative. This has led to a situation where Brandellero et al. (2014: 219) argue that 'for generations born after 1945, popular music forms such as rock and punk may be as potent a symbol of national or local identity and heritage as more traditional representations, for example, national and regional insignia, food, drink and sport'. This chapter will explore the connections between place, heritage and popular music, beginning with an examination of what heritage is and how popular music has been incorporated into it, and moving to look at how place has been a factor that strengthens or complicates the relationship between these.

Place is always implicated to some extent in ideas about heritage, mostly because of the way it can help strengthen identity through making people feel as though they are 'from' somewhere. Branderello et al. (2014: 224) define heritage in the following way:

> Heritage is both a source of identity and a receptor of value attributed to it by communities, institutions and people. It encompasses a sense of time, providing a sense of one's own past... while at the same time becoming a 'resource for the present' (Graham 2002: 1004). Insofar as understandings of heritage are necessarily embedded in time and space... heritage is in itself a manifestation of culture, better understood in its representational sense, that is to say, in the meaning given to it.

As popular music has become more and more embedded in heritage discourses, it has become apparent that place is often central to the stories that are told about the music that is seen as the most historically significant. Since rock and roll first emerged in the 1950s, 'the placeness of music is often regarded as an important aspect of its "authenticity"' (Bennett 2015: 16). Increasingly, this connection between music, place and authenticity has been foregrounded in the ways nations, cities and smaller areas such as towns or suburbs talk about their past and create a sense of identity and importance for themselves. This is perhaps best exemplified in the rise of the 'music city'. Music cities are places that make a claim to, or are recognized as having, an unusually strong connection to music, through having high numbers of venues or live music activity, or musical infrastructure that is a key component of the city's economy (Homan 2018). Pivotal, though, to a successful claim to be a music city is an ability to demonstrate a strong history of music making, or better yet, an important place in the development of a musical genre. Some of the most widely recognized music cities, then, are places like Nashville, with its strong association with country music, or Liverpool, with its claim to the Beatles and the Mersey Sound. The narrative created around such places connects them to a wider history of the development of popular music, giving them a mythical status. This not only works to increase the sense of pride and belonging that can be experienced by the residents of such cities – particularly in places like Liverpool where music heritage has been deployed as a part of strategies to counter urban decay and the effects of deindustrialization – but has concrete economic outcomes in terms of tourism (Brocken 2015). Successful appeals to a musical heritage then become part of a suite of strategies that encourage investment in music, policies from the government that facilitate music making, and identification with the city as a catalyst for the creation of music. In this way, heritage helps form the conditions in the present that frame how music making happens in the future in these cities.

Theorizing music, place and heritage

The most influential theorization of popular music as heritage has been by Roberts and Cohen (2014, 2015), who developed the work of Smith (2006) and applied it to music. They discuss three different types of popular music heritage, in a way that is designed to complicate versions of heritage that take a straightforward 'top down' or 'bottom up' approach. This leads to 'a more nuanced discussion of popular music heritage that does not assess its perceived authenticity or status but conceptualises it as a social and cultural process and considers how it is practised or "performed" in specific situations and contexts, often for different ends' (2014: 3). First, there is 'official authorised' heritage. This is where 'an aspect of the past ... has been formally legitimised as heritage using structures of authority recognised and agreed on within a society (often governments and government-sponsored bodies)' (Strong 2018b: 60). Insofar as 'the foundation of heritage as it exists today was powered by the nation-state for the purpose of discovering and delimiting the idea of the nation and legitimating its right to rule' (Ashworth and Tunbridge 2004: 214), the use of popular music as official heritage has served specific goals. Aside from the tourism strategies mentioned above, institutions such as museums can deploy popular music as a source of national pride, as we have seen in places such as the Rock and Roll Hall of Fame in Cleveland (see Burgoyne 2003 for a discussion of nationalistic themes in this museum), the British Music Experience in Liverpool or the Australian Music Vault in Melbourne, Australia. This is in addition to 'national heritage institutions which concern themselves with assembling a public record of popular music history, including, for example, the National Sound Archive at the National Library of Israel and the British Library Sound Archive' (Baker 2016: 170). Significant ceremonies relating to the nation-state are also increasingly likely to incorporate popular music (see Roberts 2014 on the use of popular music in the 2010 London Olympics). When used in these ways, official authorized heritage can help to reinforce the idea of a positive common (imagined) identity that binds people within certain geographic confines together.

Second, Roberts and Cohen discuss 'self-authorised' heritage, created by people such as 'musicians, audiences, entrepreneurs and organisations who participate in particular musical cultures' (Roberts and Cohen 2014: 248), who lack official power but have enough clout to make claims that carry weight with others. The line between these first two types of heritage can often be quite blurry, and self-authorized heritage can become official heritage under the right circumstances. Self-authorized heritage can often take the form of do-it-yourself (DIY) institutions. The work of Sarah Baker, for example, has focused on 'popular music archives, museums and halls of fame that were founded by enthusiasts, run largely by volunteers and which exist outside the frame of authorized projects of national collecting and display' (Baker 2016: 173). These often have a focus on place similar to the more official institutions. DIY and other self-authorized heritage making allows for a greater inclusion of alternative perspectives and marginalized voices in the history of popular music. For example, Liverpool's very official celebration as a European Capital of Culture in 2008 had its focus on the Beatles and EDM challenged by residents who designed their own commemoration of a local venue that had been omitted from the authorized story (Cohen 2013). These alternative voices offered different accounts of what is important in Liverpool's music history. Similarly, the creation of feminist (Withers 2014; Reitsamer 2015) and queer (Cantillon et al. 2017) music archives preserves a record of the diversity in local, national and global music scenes. These alternative stories challenge the dominant narratives created by official accounts. This function is particularly important as nationalist or tourism-related imperatives can emphasize the telling of familiar stories that draw on already-accepted popular music canons, which are likely to over-represent white men playing guitars (von Appen and Doehring 2006). However, the very nature of DIY and self-authorized activities makes them more vulnerable than official institutions and practices. Baker (2016) notes the way DIY archives are often run on shoestring budgets and kept in places that can be run down or poorly located. Self-authorized heritage can also, it must be noted, contain its own biases and omissions.

Finally, Roberts and Cohen's framework includes heritage-as-praxis, or unauthorized heritage, which 'is a form of memory work encompassing everyday social, cultural and pedagogic practices, and a process of tracing influences, connections, and "inheritance tracks"' (Roberts and Cohen 2015: 235). This is heritage creation on a more day-to-day or individual level, which may not be recognized as heritage or could even contain anti-heritage impulses. Strong and Whiting (2018), for example, have documented how the gig posters on the walls in small venues in Melbourne help create a sense of the identity of these spaces, and how they fit into the larger Melbourne music scene, by acting as reminders of past events, and through their reinforcing of the idea of what the venues are. Slow, informal 'heritage-as-praxis' processes see posters replaced, preserved or in some cases revered, as staff and punters make use of the venues on a day-to-day basis. The posters are essentially ephemeral; the fact that some remain over time while most are lost speaks to a community deciding for itself what parts of its past are most important to its present without (for the most part) any conscious process of heritage making. Similarly, Duffett and Löbert (2015) have documented the circulation of 'offstage photos' (photos taken by fans) of Take That by fans of the group, and how the collections that resulted from this activity – by a group of people generally not taken seriously as music fans – came to acquire heritage value over time.

Music heritage and placelessness

The example of Take That fandom speaks to how, although popular music heritage is often connected to specific physical locations and used to build identity and community in relation to these, it can also have a 'placeless' aspect. This can relate to the globalized nature of popular music, noted by Bennett above as being one of the reasons it was denied a place in heritage for a long time. The way contemporary popular music developed and spread means it has taken on very similar forms worldwide. Motti Regev (2013: 3) has described this as 'aesthetic cosmopolitanism',

> a process in which the expressive forms and cultural practices used by nations at large, and by groupings within them, to signify and perform their sense of uniqueness, growingly comes to share large proportions of aesthetic common ground, to a point where the cultural uniqueness of each nation or ethnicity cannot but be understood as a unit within one complex entity, one variant in a set of quite similar – but never identical – cases.

In this way, the popular music traditions of countries will often be very similar to one another, something that detracts from their ability to be deployed as markers of unique heritage. Further contradictions and tensions can arise here because of the way heritage discourses can play out in a similar fashion, particularly as they are related to tourism. Strategies for increasing tourism will often mean replicating what has succeeded for drawing people in other places, meaning certain types of places are emphasized as being important, and the experiences people are offered will start to converge (Ashworth and Tunbridge 2004). The combination of an aesthetic cosmopolitan cultural form, in the shape of popular music, and an increasingly globalized heritage tourism industry can create unexpected outcomes. For example, internationally renowned band AC/DC have streets named after them in Madrid, Spain and Melbourne, Australia, neither of which are cities they have deep ties to, and statues and tributes to the Beatles have been put in place in locations such as Kazakhstan, Russia and Texas. These types of commemoration are a way to draw on the global heritage of popular music to create tourist attractions regardless of a strong or obvious connection between an actual physical site and an artist (Strong, Cannizzo and Rogers 2017). The forms these tributes take – street names, statues – also speak to conventional forms of heritage that are easily understandable across cultures and sites.

The increase in online communities and repositories for discussion or archiving of popular music's past raise a different set of issues around music, place and heritage. While numerous websites, Facebook pages and discussion groups exist for specific musicians, or musical eras, which could be considered as part of the 'placeless' aspect of the internet, there are also many others that are much more place-specific. These can perform important functions in terms of consolidating collective memories, or giving form to identities connected to music and places. For example, Bennett (2004) has documented how an online discussion board helped to define and rekindle interest in what came to be known as the 'Canterbury Sound'. Other websites and groups preserve the memories of record stores, venues or specific club nights (see Collins 2018). The self-authorized heritage practices of such groups, and the ability of almost anyone to set about bringing people together online to discuss a particular place they found important, are another example of the democratic potential in popular music heritage. However, Long (2015: 74) cautions that:

> … while the digital might offer a utopian vision of democracy and communality, any DIY – or for that matter any official preservation – activity online is also tasked with the perennial business of the archivist in evaluating what counts, what is to be stored and to what uses might be put such materials.

Online archives and heritage resources also have different preservation issues to material ones due to, on the one hand, their 'placelessness' because of their lack of physical form, and on the other to the nature of the places they can be found online. Historians and archivists have been drawing attention to the variety of ways in which online material is vulnerable. Despite the tendency to sometimes view the internet as a place where everything can be found and stored, data can be easily lost and websites can disappear (Rogers 2019). Guarding against digital loss is something that is still being grappled with by large institutions with considerable funding, and may be beyond the resources or remit of smaller, community based groups. Much of this online heritage work is also happening on sites such as Facebook, where the ultimate control of the material resides with that company rather than any of the individuals creating their pages. Using social media for heritage and memory work gives a certain amount of control to those sites in terms of content and how users interact with the content; for instance, users must abide by standards set by the sites, and this may influence what is shared and what is said about it (Shou et al. 2015). A site such as Facebook may offer more fleeting interactions with memories shared or artefacts being digitized, as they move through people's feeds, whereas dedicated archival websites may be organized more to make items accessible.

Losing heritage

The quote by Long above touching on what counts and what is to be kept raises another issue that is pertinent to all popular music heritage, and indeed all heritage: the question of the limits of preservation. A number of commentators, most notably Simon Reynolds in his book *Retromania* (2011), have argued that we currently exist in a culture that is overly fixated on its own past, resulting in a situation where

> nothing is too trivial, too insignificant, to be discarded; every pop-culture scrap, every trend and fad, every forgotten-by-most performer or TV programme is being annotated and auteur-ised. The result, visible above all on the Internet, is that the archive degenerates into the *anarchive*: a barely navigable disorder of data-debris and memory-trash. For the archive to maintain any kind of integrity, it must sift and reject, consign some memories to oblivion.

In terms of place, the most obvious issue that arises from a desire to keep as much as possible is to do with physical space. The material items associated with popular music's past take up space; even relatively small items such as vinyl records or CDs require large storage facilities when collected en mass, and bulkier items (instruments, costumes, items associated with artists that could include anything imaginable) can create significant problems for those dedicated to preserving them. While some organizations aim to keep everything relating to their area, this is rarely practical. A tension therefore arises between processes of discovery, preservation and saving valuable items 'under the bed' from becoming 'rubbish' (Baker and Huber 2013a), and maintaining practical and meaningful collections that do not become either too expensive to house or degenerate into an 'anarchive'.

This raises then a wider question of how loss and destruction become part of the processes of heritage. In traditional institutions that deal with heritage, the role of curators is to decide what is worth keeping or acquiring, and what is not. In DIY institutions with flatter hierarchies this is much less straightforward. These questions become much more complex again when the heritage is embedded in built environments. The structures that contain (current or past) venues, recording studios, clubs or places where musicians once lived can be seen as having heritage value on that basis. 'These are, however, always at risk because of the way that change is at the heart of processes of modernization' (Berman 1988). Development and gentrification, particularly in inner-city environments, mean structures associated with music are to some extent always under threat. At other times, neglect, particularly in economically difficult periods, has seen the disappearance of other iconic structures. On the one hand, there is a perception that physical items or locations anchor memories and protect against the continuous change of modern society, meaning their loss will lead to forgetting. On the other hand, however, some theorists have suggested that sometimes the opposite may be true – that loss can create new ways of remembering and increase the heritage value of something, regardless of its absence (Holtorf 2014; Strong 2018a). For example, Holtorf describes how the burning of the Fantoft Church in Norway by black metal musicians changed – and probably increased – the way the church was valued in the Christian community in that country, but also gave it a new and unusual type of heritage value for black metal fans who visit the reconstruction of the church. Loss can highlight the heritage value of places that might otherwise have gone unremarked upon, and can also be a catalyst that makes communities reflect upon what they value and take action to preserve other threatened places. However, these processes of loss can happen more organically, particularly in areas of unauthorized heritage (e.g. the gig posters mentioned earlier, most of which end up in the bin). The overwhelming quantity of mass-produced items associated with popular music means that ultimately most *must* be disposed of (a situation that speaks to the place of music in the environmentally unsustainable processes of capitalism; see Devine 2019). The question of what should be kept is answered differently in different places, meaning there is little consistency but possibly a sufficiently diverse array of artefacts and stories ultimately being preserved.

In conclusion, the heritage value of popular music is likely to continue to increase over time, as more of the material items and places associated with different genres, artists and scenes are incorporated into the stories people tell about what has been important in their lives. The questions raised in this chapter about who decides what heritage counts, where and how it will be stored, and who should have access to it will continue to become more complex. Tensions between representations of popular music constructed for tourist consumption and more local and unusual forms of heritage making will persist also, and the challenge for curators, historians and academics working in this field will be how to capture the full richness of activity in this area.

References

Ashworth, G. J. and Tunbridge, J. (2004), 'Whose Tourist-Historic City? Localizing the Global and Globalizing the Local', in A. A. Lew, C. M. Hall and A. M. Williams (eds), *A Companion to Tourism*, 210–22, Malden, MA: Blackwell.

Baker, S. (2016), 'Do-It-Yourself Institutions of Popular Music Heritage: The Preservation of Music's Material Past in Community Archives, Museums and Halls of Fame', *Archives and Records*, 37 (2): 170–87.

Baker, S. and Huber, A. (2013a), 'Saving "Rubbish": Preserving Popular Music's Material Culture in Amateur Archives and Museums', in S. Cohen, R. Knifton, M. Leonard and L. Roberts (eds), *Sites of Popular Music Heritage: Memories, Histories, Places*, 112–24, New York: Routledge.

Baker, S. and Huber, A. (2013b), 'Notes Towards a Typology of the DIY Institution: Identifying Do-it-yourself Places of Popular Music Preservation', *European Journal of Cultural Studies*, 16 (5): 513–30.

Bennett, A. (2004). 'New Tales from Canterbury: The Making of a Virtual Music Scene', in A. Bennett and R. A. Peterson (eds), *Music Scenes: Local, Trans-Local and Virtual*, 205–20, Nashville, TN: Vanderbilt University Press.

Bennett, A. (2015), 'Popular Music and the "Problem" of Heritage', in S. Cohen, R. Knifton, M. Leonard and L. Roberts (eds), *Sites of Popular Music Heritage: Memories, Histories, Places*, 15–27, New York: Routledge.

Berman, M. (1988), *All That Is Solid Melts into Air: The Experience of Modernity*, New York: Penguin.

Brandellero, A., Janssen, S., Cohen, S. and Roberts, L. (2014), 'Popular Music Heritage, Cultural Memory and Cultural Identity', *International Journal of Heritage Studies*, 20 (3): 219–23.

Brandellero, A. and Janssen, S. (2014), 'Popular Music as Cultural Heritage: Scoping Out the Field of Practice', *International Journal of Heritage Studies*, 20 (3): 224–40.

Brocken, M. (2015), *The 21st Century Legacy of the Beatles*, Farnham: Ashgate.

Burgoyne, R. (2003), 'From Contested to Consensual Memory: The Rock and Roll Hall of Fame and Museum', in K. Hodgkin and S. Radstone (eds), *Contested Pasts: The Politics of Memory*, 208–20, London: Routledge.

Cantillon, Z., Baker, S. and Buttigieg, B. (2017), 'Queering the Community Music Archive', *Australian Feminist Studies*, 32: 41–57.

Cohen, S. (2013), 'Musical Memory, Heritage and Local Identity: Remembering the Popular Music Past in a European Capital of Culture', *International Journal of Cultural Policy*, 19 (5): 576–94.

Collins, J. (2018), 'Citizen Archiving and Virtual Sites of Musical Memory in Online Communities', in S. Baker, C. Strong, L. Istvandity and Z. Cantillon (eds), *The Routledge Companion to Popular Music History and Heritage*, 247–58, New York: Routledge.

Devine, K. (2019), *Decomposed: The Political Ecology of Music*, Cambridge, MA: MIT Press.

Duffett, M. and Löbert, A. (2015), 'Trading Offstage Photos: Take That Fan Culture and the Collaborative Preservation of Popular Music Heritage', in S. Baker (ed), *Preserving Popular Music Heritage: Do-It-Yourself, Do-It-Together*, 151–64, New York: Routledge.

Holtorf, C. (2014), 'Averting Loss Aversion in Cultural Heritage', *International Journal of Heritage Studies*, 21 (4): 405–21.

Homan, S. (2018), 'The Music City', in S. Brunt and G. Stahl (eds), *Made in Australia and Aotearoa/New Zealand*, 179–89, New York: Routledge.

Long, P. (2015), '"Really Saying Something?" What Do We Talk about When We Talk about Popular Music Heritage, Memory, Archives and the Digital?' in S. Baker (ed), *Preserving Popular Music Heritage: Do-It-Yourself, Do-It-Together*, 62–76, New York: Routledge.

Reitsamer, R. (2015), 'Alternative Histories and Counter-Memories: Feminist Music Archives in Europe', in S. Baker (ed), *Preserving Popular Music Heritage: Do-It-Yourself, Do-It-Together*, 91–103, New York: Routledge.

Regev, M. (2013), *Pop-Rock Music*, Cambridge: Polity.

Reynolds, S. (2011), *Retromania: Pop Culture's Addiction to Its Own Past*, London: Faber and Faber.

Roberts, L. (2014), 'Talkin Bout My Generation: Popular Music and the Culture of Heritage', *International Journal of Heritage Studies*, 20 (3): 262–80.

Roberts, L. and Cohen, S. (2014), 'Unauthorising Popular Music Heritage: Outline of a Critical Framework', *International Journal of Heritage Studies*, 20 (3): 241–61.

Roberts, L. and Cohen, S. (2015), 'Unveiling Memory: Blue Plaques as In/Tangible Markers of Popular Music Heritage', in S. Cohen, R. Knifton, M. Leonard and L. Roberts (eds), *Sites of Popular Music Heritage: Memories, Histories, Places*, 221–38, New York and London: Routledge.

Rogers, I. (2019), 'Disappearing History: Two Case Studies on the Precarity of Music Writing', in L. Istvandity, Z. Cantillon and S. Baker (eds), *Remembering Popular Music's Past*, 112–21, London: Anthem.

Shou, J., Farkas, J. and Hjelholt, M. (2015), 'The Double Conditioning of Political Participation: Grassroots Politics on Facebook', *Conjuctions*, 2 (2): 30–49.

Smith, L. (2006), *Uses of Heritage*, Abingdon: Routledge.

Strong, C. (2018a), 'Burning Punk and Bulldozing Clubs: The Role of Destruction and Loss in Popular Music Heritage', in S. Baker, C. Strong, L. Istvandity and Z. Cantillon (eds), *The Routledge Companion to Popular Music History and Heritage*, 180–8, New York: Routledge.

Strong, C. (2018b), 'Popular Music and Heritage Making in Melbourne', in S. Brunt and G. Stahl (eds), *Made in Australia and Aotearoa/New Zealand*, New York: Routledge.

Strong, C., Cannizzo, F. and Rogers, I. (2017), 'Aesthetic Cosmopolitan, National and Local Popular Music Heritage in Melbourne's Music Laneways', *International Journal of Heritage Studies*, 23 (2): 83–96.

Strong, C. and Whiting, S. (2018), '"We Love the Bands and We Want to Keep Them on the Walls": Gig Posters as Heritage-as-Praxis in Music Venues', *Continuum*, 32 (2): 151–61.

von Appen, R. and Doehring, A. (2006), 'Nevermind The Beatles, Here's Exile 61 and Nico: "The Top 100 Records of All Time" – A Canon of Pop and Rock Albums from a Sociological and an Aesthetic Perspective', *Popular Music*, 25 (1): 21–39.

Withers, D. (2014), 'Re-Enacting Process: Temporality, Historicity and the Women's Liberation Music Archive', *International Journal of Heritage Studies*, 20 (7–8), 688–701.

27

Music and tourism

Leonieke Bolderman

Introduction

The death of Aretha Franklin in the summer of 2018 put the spotlight firmly on the city where she spent most of her life: Detroit. Detroit is a music city, as emphasized in the narratives surrounding Aretha's death and funeral. Detroit is and has been home to world famous artists as diverse as Aretha Franklin, Motown artists Diana Ross, Marvin Gaye and the Jackson Five; Madonna; Eminem; Kid Rock and The White Stripes, and the city has brought forth not one but two music genres – Motown and techno. This rich musical heritage and current musical prowess is what draws growing audiences to the city.

Aretha's grave will add another music tourism location to the city's already-impressive list of musical must-sees. A place such as Detroit attracts different kinds of visitors, whose presence is visible in various ways in the city. Whereas Motown tourism for example finds a place in the Motown Museum, Detroit's techno music scene lives in clubs and its yearly sold-out Movement festival, showing that genres that are considered to be more niche can also form an attraction to substantial audiences.

Especially for post-industrial cities such as Detroit, music tourism holds the promise of economic and thereby social development, as cities search for ways to differentiate themselves and attract new tourism flows, replacing traditional local (manufacturing) industries (Cohen 2007; Smith 2016). In the case of Detroit, music is one of the pillars of redeveloping the downtown area, alongside sports and entertainment. Moreover, in October 2016, the Motown Museum in Detroit announced extensive renovation and expansion plans, banking on the increased visitor numbers to create jobs and increase spending in the area. According to the museum, 'when completed, the new Motown Museum Campus will have a transformative effect on its surrounding Detroit neighborhood (…) The new development will also further raise the profile of the city as an international travel destination'.

Music tourism as a form of contemporary niche tourism is on the rise (Connell and Gibson 2003; Bolderman 2020; Walton 2018). Although Detroit's heritage and live music sectors attract substantial audiences, comparative numbers on the size and scope of music tourism in general remain scarce. Memphis Tourism estimated in 2007 that the impact of the music tourism industry around Graceland and Beale Street was huge, attracting 11 million visitors and 3 billion in spending. UK Music, a British industry lobby group, estimated that the 12.5 million music tourists to the UK in 2016, who visit famous music tourism places such as the Beatles' Liverpool and festivals such as Glastonbury, spent around 4 billion pounds (UK Music 2017).

Drawn by these success stories, city marketers and heritage industry professionals such as the ones in Detroit increasingly turn to music as a theme for development plans. The label of 'UNESCO City of Music' is now a hot commodity for cities worldwide to try and acquire (www.en.unesco.org/creative-cities), while recent years have seen the rise of consultancies that are focused specifically on music tourism and promoting music cities (examples currently include Sound Diplomacy and Music Tourist). There is also a notable increase in practitioner conferences dedicated to the topic, such as the Music Cities Summit in Canada, and the Music Cities Events in Liverpool and more recently Cologne.

The academic attention for music tourism seems to be on the rise as well. Due to the diversity of music tourism examples in practice, several research fields have picked up on the potential music tourism offers for the study of culture and society. As pointed out by several authors, music tourism delivers an aural perspective on global mobilities and inequalities (Gibson and Connell 2003; Kruger and Trandafoiu 2014; Rommen and Neely 2014), and offers a fresh perspective on the role of music in everyday life (Bolderman 2020).

In this context, the main purpose of this chapter is to advance music tourism as a research field by consolidating the existing interdisciplinary literature and by identifying a future research agenda. To this end, this chapter first offers an overview of the development of music tourism as a phenomenon and of the academic work on the topic. After that, three major themes and debates in the literature will be highlighted: the attention for music tourist motivations, including debates surrounding authenticity, heritage and pilgrimage; the convergences between music and tourism industries, specifically relating to the role of music tourism in urban and regional development; and the aural experience of (music) tourism, exploring contributions from sound studies.

Development and definitions

Music tourism is not a new or unique phenomenon; rather, as several authors suggest, it is embedded in a longer tradition of music-related travel. Gibson and Connell for example refer to travel to religious festivals as an example of music-related travel throughout the ages (Gibson and Connell 2005: 32), while the novice composers and musicians who travelled to the rich musical and cultural cities of seventeenth-century Germany, Italy and France to learn from famous maestros can be regarded as music tourists avant-la-lettre (Bolderman 2020). The troubadour movement of mediaeval Southern France is also an example of the involvement of music in early forms of mobility (Lashua, Spracklen and Long 2014).

Music tourism as a specific type of music-related travel is commonly identified as a phenomenon of modernity, bound up with the development of tourism as a leisure activity for the masses. Originally, leisurely travel was the provenance of eighteenth- and nineteenth-century elites, who would travel in search of adventure, venturing out to explore the yet unknown world, or going on a Grand Tour through Europe for reasons of personal development. Over the course of the nineteenth and twentieth centuries and closely connected to the development of industrialization, the means for travel increased. Middle classes slowly started to have expendable income and leisure time, while transportation options became increasingly accessible through developments in steam-driven technology and railroad expansion (Urry and Larsen 2011).

At the same time, Romantic sensibilities invoked a desire for travel, as it came to be regarded as important to get away from everyday life and to experience the emotions of gazing upon extraordinary sites (Adler 1989: 22; Urry and Larsen 2011: 14). As photography developed in the same period, seeing and being able to document visually what was seen contributed to turning vision into the primary organizing principle of tourism (Urry and Larsen 2011: 16): tourism became equivalent to sightseeing. In this context, John Urry speaks of the 'tourist gaze' as the defining characteristic of modern tourism.

As tourism developed over the course of the twentieth and twenty-first centuries, tourism started to diversify and fragment. Where once historical landmarks and exotic landscapes would incite the attraction and awe of the masses, currently narratives from popular culture 'authenticate' tourism destinations as much as remarkable natural landscapes or historical landmarks do (Reijnders 2011; Smith 2016). Therefore, music tourism today is seen as a form of cultural tourism and exists alongside other forms of niche tourism, such as film tourism and literary tourism.

Recognized as a growing niche in global tourism (Connell and Gibson 2003: 221; Lashua et al. 2014: 8), contemporary music tourism is defined and theorized in several ways. Key authors on the topic are cultural geographers Connell and Gibson, who define music tourism broadly as 'travel, at least in some part, because of a connection with music' (Gibson and Connell 2005: 1). Since music tourism often involves live music events, and since it has been argued that these events like festivals and concerts make music tourism economically viable (Roberts 2014) and account for its special feel or appeal, music tourism is also sometimes understood more narrowly as 'travel to hear music played' (Lashua et al. 2014: 8).

The convergences between music and tourism are characterized by the specifics of the medium involved: music. Theoretically, music poses a problem in relation to tourism: sound is invisible, and as pointed out by Connell and Gibson, the central notion of tourism – being there and gazing upon a site – 'has only the most tenuous connection with music' (Connell and Gibson 2003: 13). What is there to gaze upon and take holiday snapshots of, if a central element of what makes music 'music' is sound, and sound is vibrating air?

Gibson and Connell conceptualize this inherent tension through the idea of the 'fixity and fluidity' of music. A central concern in their work is how music is embedded in certain places, while moving across geographical locations at the same time (2003). On the one hand, music travels across the globe, bound up in flows of people, capital, commodities and money (Connell and Gibson 2003: 10). On the other hand, sounds become recognizable as they are connected to geographical space (location) and a sense of place. Music tourism is a consequence of the commodification of the local embeddedness of musical sounds.

Building on this work and exploring the connections between music and place in the context of tourism further, Bolderman (2020) identifies four specific ways music evokes associations with destinations that each in their own way is capable of inducing tourism. First, music can be connected to place through characteristic sounds, linked to instrumentation and/or musical structure. Second, other aspects of music – such as lyrics and album covers – can evoke associations with particular places. Third, locations linked to the biography of the artist can induce tourism. Fourth, music is associated with the places where it is or once was produced, distributed and/or consumed. According to Bolderman, taken together these four connections account for the varied forms of music tourism in practice.

Survey of the field

Academic attention for music tourism is of a quite recent nature, as noted in overviews of the field by Gibson and Connell (2005), Cohen (2007), Lashua et al. (2014), Krüger and Trandafoiu (2014), Rommen and Neely (2014), Bolderman and Reijnders (2017) and Watson (2018).

One of the first works specifically on music tourism is Kaeppler and Lewin's *Come Mek Me Hol' Yu Han'. The Impact of Tourism on Traditional Music* (1988). A decade later, music tourism is the topic of a special issue of *The World of Music* (1999). To date, the only book to offer a comprehensive overview of music tourism is *Music and Tourism: On the Road Again* by Gibson and Connell (2005), which is acknowledged widely as the key publication in the field. In journals across research disciplines, the attention for music tourism seems to pick up only in the late 2000s.

Both Rommen and Neely (2014) and Krüger and Trandafoiu (2014) discuss reasons why up until that time there has been such little work on music tourism. In tourism studies, music has been subsumed under broader notions of culture, which meant the specific role of music in tourism has remained unexplored for a long time. In popular music studies and ethnomusicology, a sentiment of 'anti-tourism' discouraged the interest in music tourism as a topic, as scholars were keen to separate the study of music from the superficial and commercial nature ascribed to tourism.

Currently, the work is diversifying and more disciplines venture into exploring music tourism and related topics – the field is growing. The examples of music tourism studied are becoming more diverse; where scholarly attention used to focus primarily on eye-catching examples such as the Beatles' Liverpool (Kruse 2003, 2005a, b; Cohen 2007; Fremaux and Fremaux 2013; Brocken 2016) and pilgrimages to Graceland (King 1994; Rodman 1996; Alderman 2002; Doss 2008; Drummond 2011), other research focuses on popular music heritage including AC/DC Lane (Frost 2008), Joy Division's Manchester (Otter 2013), blues tourism (Duffett 2014; Fry 2014), hip-hop tourism (Xie, Osumare and Ibrahim 2007), electronic dance music (EDM) tourism (Saldanha 2002; Bennett 2004; Sandvoss 2014; Garcia 2016), 'blackpacking' (Podoshen 2013) and Goth music tourism (Spracklen and Spracklen 2014).

There is a growing interest in the touristic experience of music on site – the travel to hear music played (Lashua et al. 2014). This concerns world music genres such as flamenco (Aoyama 2007 and 2009), Irish traditional music tourism (Kneafsey 2002; Morton 2005; Kaul 2014), Breton fiddle music (Feintuch 2004) and steelpan (Granger 2015), but is more prominent as an interest in concert-related travel (Cavicchi 1999; Cohen 2005; Ward 2014) and music festival experiences (Duffy and Waitt 2011; Duffy, Waitt, Gorman-Murray and Gibson 2011; Gibson and Connell 2011; Szmigin, Bengry-Howell, Morey, Griffin and Riley 2017).

Surveying this growing body of work, the central debates about the topic converge around three major themes: tourism motivations; convergences between music and tourism industries; and aural experiences of (music) tourism.

Motivations: Authenticity, nostalgia and pilgrimage

A dominant strand in the literature is concerned with understanding music tourism and the motivations for travel that inspire tourists to seek out places connected to music. Johansson and Bell (2009) point out that music tourism concerns a meaningful journey of some sort, in line with the way Connell and Gibson construct this meaning as being a form of authenticity. This authenticity is based in heritage and nostalgia: 'music tourism, like all cultural tourism, is about nostalgia, and involves a sense of heritage and authenticity' (Connell and Gibson 2003: 210).

In their work on music tourism, Connell and Gibson mainly focus on nostalgia because at the time of writing (Connell and Gibson 2003 and 2004; Gibson and Connell 2005 and 2007) they observed that the most successful examples of music tourism were eye-catching examples involving popular music from the sixties, such as Elvis' Graceland and the Beatles Liverpool (Gibson and Connell 2005: 260) – destinations that attracted a senior audience looking for places connected to the music of their youth. The analysis of music tourism as nostalgia industry has been followed up in other research, such as Henke (2005), Frost on AC/DC Lane (2008) and the similar way in which Johansson and Bell (2009) explain music tourism as a search for authenticity and nostalgia. The importance of places as 'lieux de mémoire' (DeNora 1989) of icons of popular music fits particularly well with the rise of the nostalgia industry and the contemporary 'retromania' of popular culture as analysed by Reynolds (2011) and Lizardi (2015). However, contemporary music tourism extends beyond examples of sixties popular music nostalgia, as also noted by Watson (2018) and Bolderman (2020).

Nostalgic explanations of music tourism often frame music-related travel as a modern version of pilgrimage. Tourism in general is compared frequently to pilgrimage, as a chosen journey to a significant place (Graburn 1983). This comparison is not surprising, as fan-tourists themselves often use pilgrimage as a metaphor to describe the importance of their experiences (e.g. pointed out by Cavicchi 1999 and Cohen 2007). Besides the metaphor, Cavicchi also notes structural similarities in his study of Bruce Springsteen fans (Cavicchi 1999): religious pilgrimages have a particular goal, they involve overcoming adversity to reach that goal, and during the pilgrimage, fans meet others trying to achieve the same goal. Drawing on the work of Turner and Turner (1978), in research on Graceland tourism and The Beatles, tourist practices have been connected to different stages of pilgrimage, from preparing to travel, to the liminal phase of being on location, to a post-liminal phase of returning home and sharing the experience (King 1994; Rodman 1996; Alderman 2002; Kruse 2003 and 2005b; Brocken 2016).

Despite these parallels, other researchers point out that music tourism diverges from religious pilgrimage in significant ways. As remarked by Cohen (2007: 173), musical journeys generally do not have religious significance in the sense that they are about a communal search for a future place in another world; instead, as also pointed out by Sandvoss (2005) in his work on fandom, fan travels are individual journeys aimed at seeking a sense of place in this world.

In this context, Whyton states that the 'truth' found in music is often a personal one (Whyton 2014) – as analysed for example by Xie et al. (2007) in relation to hip-hop tourism to the Bronx in New York: 'For some tourists, hip-hop travel is a rite of passage, which is akin to a pilgrimage – the search for a greater depth of meaning and personal understanding – and may even be frequently repeated. The hood becomes the site for tourists who are in search of a validating authenticity' (Xie et al. 2007: 457). This is why musical journeys are often called secular pilgrimages (e.g. by Kruse 2005b) that offer a replacement for the central role of religion in modern society (King 1994; Doss 2008; Margry 2008). As a secular pilgrimage, music tourism is supposedly aimed at healing and wellbeing (Connell and Gibson 2003), which connects to an active strand of research into the healing powers of music (e.g. by DeNora 2000 and Andrews, Kingsbury and Kearns 2014).

Still, as pointed out by Bolderman (2020) the question remains whether connecting music tourism so closely to pilgrimage, and treating pilgrimage as an etic concept, is analytically useful. Bolderman follows up with comments made by Martin Stokes in an afterword to an early, special issue on music tourism (Stokes 1999: 151), in which he remarks on the importance of context when seeing music tourism as pilgrimage. As Stokes points out, the comparison takes on a different meaning when used to describe journeys involving Irish traditional music in Catholic Ireland, where the enthusiasm for pilgrimages resurged with the start of The Troubles (Stokes 1999: 152), rather than when describing the enthusiasm for Beatles tourism to Liverpool. As both Stokes and Bolderman contend, tourists use pilgrimage comparisons in a complex context of values central to the music genre, discourses surrounding fandom and tourists' personal spiritual self-representations.

Therefore, going beyond authenticity, nostalgia and pilgrimage, Bolderman (2020) proposes 'musical topophilia' as the key concept to understand music tourism practices. Music tourism in this theory is a way to engage with the human need to find physical reference points for something intangible. Music often plays a key role in the personal and cultural 'story of self', and visiting places is a way to engage with these intangible aspects of music (Bolderman and Reijnders 2017). This results in a musical topophilia, the love for place with and through music.

Convergences between the music and tourism industries

A second theme connecting different strands and fields of music tourism research deals with the similarities, differences and interactions between tourism and music industries. Music tourism in this vein of research is analysed as a consequence of the commodification of successful music scenes and local sounds (Gibson and Connell 2003 and 2005; Cohen 2005), and, in a more recent turn, for its cultural, social and economic impacts on primarily urban regeneration processes (Watson 2018).

According to Connell and Gibson (2003, 2005) and Cohen (2005), music tourism is the consequence of the commodification of successful music scenes and local sounds. Music tourism is based on a process of 'place fetishization': places continue to give meaning to music, while music invests places with authenticity value (Gibson and Connell 2005). This process is what according to Bennett (2002) gives way to 'the musicalized tourist gaze'. Tourism is about gazing upon places that are in some way out of the ordinary, and music provides narratives that authenticate locations in 'a particularly seductive way' (Bennett 2002).

The commodification of the associations between music and place that happen in both tourism and music industries can have negative consequences for local scenes and sounds, as tourism can stifle and interrupt local traditions. However, as already pointed out by Kaeppler and Lewin (1988) in relation to world music genres, tourism can also be a source of local host creativity and preservation of music styles. Tourists actively partake in activities to get to know the host culture, creating a give and take: tourists play 'traditional' music and thereby keep rituals and certain musical styles and forms preserved, while these forms are often adjusted to fit with the attention span and taste or expectations of tourists.

A range of examples shows this dynamic relation between music and tourism in practice, such as the Balinese dance described and analysed by Dunbar-Hall (2001); flamenco has been able to develop into a national symbol and translocal success through tourism (Aoyama 2007 and 2009); and as described by Kenneth Bilby in an edited volume on music tourism in the circum-Caribbean (Rommen and Neely 2014), being part of the tourism industry has aided the economic survival and musical development of reggae artists, despite the commercial profits made from its surrounding tourism development (Bilby 2014).

This is why Rommen and Neely propose the concept of 'music touristics' to examine the dynamics between music and tourism industries. Rommen and Neely point out the ambiguities involved when music and tourism converge, involving music as sonic signifier of otherness and its consequent local and translocal consumption. For Rommen and Neely, 'music touristics' as a concept addresses the complexities and the dynamics of tourism contexts, especially relating to the service relationships involved.

In a more recent turn, there is a growing attention for the impacts of music tourism and the transforming potential of music tourism for the post-industrial city. As described in the introduction to this chapter, music tourism is increasingly seen as an opportunity for city marketing (Henke 2005). However, as discussed in several publications (Cohen 2007; Lashua et al. 2014; and Roberts 2014; Cohen, Knifton, Leonard and Roberts 2015), if a particular local 'sound' is promoted as unique heritage of a city, a problem arises when all cities become tourist hotspots with similar ways of selling that popular music heritage. What happens when different cities claim globalized popular music as localized heritage? The effort of the city of Hamburg to attract Beatles tourists is a case in point (Fremaux and Fremaux 2013). As also pointed out by Prentice and Anderson (2003) in relation to the Edinburgh Fringe festival and by Fry on the King Biscuit blues festival (2014), festival tourists stay within their 'tourism bubble' and do not interact much with the city or its inhabitants.

Furthermore, music and music-related events are increasingly called on to stimulate tourism and thereby jumpstart economic growth, urban regeneration and social development (Watson 2018). However, it is not clear at this moment how exactly to measure the social and economic impacts of music tourism (Lees and Melhuish 2015; Watson 2018), both because of a lack of research and because of the diversity of music tourism examples (Watson 2018).

Moreover, the consequences of music tourism are not only positive. Access to tourism is not equally distributed across the globe, as pointed out by Kruger and Trandafoiu (2014), who analyse music tourism from a mobilities perspective. Music tourism also relates to issues of environmental sustainability, to its social impacts relating for example to noise pollution and over-tourism issues, while as Quinn (2010) observes, it is unclear what the economic gains are in relation to its (public) cost.

The role of embodied experiences in music tourism

A final theme around which research on music tourism gathers is the connection between the experience of music and the touristic experience of place. Early research in this vein builds on criticism on the tourist gaze. 'The tourist gaze' as central notion in tourism theory has been criticized for its visual focus and passivity (Edensor and Falconer 2011; Chronis 2015; Trandberg Jensen, Scarles and Cohen 2015), giving rise to a conceptualization of tourism as embodied performance (Edensor 2001) involving all the senses (Veijola and Jokinen 1994).

As music stands in an ambiguous relation to gazing, Connell and Gibson speak of 'the tourist ear' – meaning that music tourism revolves around sound and music, and possibly involves gazing, but also involves other dimensions of tourism experience. As discussed by Waitt and Duffy (2009), music and sound shape the tourist experience, as music creates touristic spaces and adds an affective dimension to tourism experiences. Waitt and Duffy refer to this as the 'sonic knowledge' of places, which has a specifically embodied dimension (Waitt and Duffy 2009: 467).

Whereas this 'sonic knowledge' of place is not specific to music tourism experiences, in the literature music and tourism are shown to be particularly suited to each other: the touristic experience of place can create, maintain or stimulate the affective attachment to places through music (Bolderman 2020). Much travel, according to Urry and Larsen, stems from what they call a 'compulsion to proximity': the need to be bodily in the same space as a landscape or townscape, to be at a live event, or to be with one's friends, family or even in the company of like-minded strangers (2011: 21). Tourism is about the need to connect, the need to see for oneself and experience a place directly – Urry calls this 'co-presence'. Co-presence is especially felt during live events, as these create 'intense moments of co-presence' (Urry and Larsen 2011: 21). Or, as Auslander has discussed in relation to rock music concerts, at least there is a cultural belief in the value of intense co-presence, the culturally constructed value of 'liveness' (Auslander 2008).

Music as a particular embodied experience is especially suited to the notion of 'intense co-presence'. Music's rhythmic quality and temporal unfolding are seen to play a major role in inducing states of flow and even trance (Csikszentmihalyi 1990; Blacking 1973; DeNora 2000; Turino 2008) while travelling. Listening together to music in real time can create a collective social identification, frequently called a sense of 'communitas' in reference to Turner's anthropological work on ritual (Hesmondhalgh 2013). Waitt and Duffy describe how people who listen to music together are taken on an embodied 'aural journey' of music together (Waitt and Duffy 2009),

Music tourism offers these moments of flow and connection when listening to music on site in the presence of like-minded others. A key article describing how this works is Arun Saldanha's analysis of Goa dancefloors (Saldanha 2002), dealing with EDM tourism to Goa and the way music creates pleasurable spaces for inclusion of tourists and exclusion of locals on the dance floor through sound and movement. In other work on EDM, this line of reseasoning is taken up (Bennett 2004; Ward 2014; Garcia 2016), but also criticized (Sandvoss 2014).

Not only the work on EDM tourism deals with the role of embodied musical experiences in music tourism; it also involves concert tourism such as Bruce Springsteen (Cavicchi 1999), the Grateful Dead (Ward 2014), The Beatles (Cohen 2005) and festival tourism (Duffy and Waitt 2011; Duffy et al. 2011; Gibson and Connell 2011; Szmigin et al. 2017). Besides concerts, musical co-presence is also used to analyse and explain the popularity of music workshops (Morton 2005; Sarbanes 2006; Ellis 2011; Granger 2015; Bolderman

2020), while Cashman analyses the way music can create music bubbles aboard cruiseships (Cashman 2014, 2016).

As remarked by Sandvoss in a paper on Ibiza fans (2014), the question remains whether these concert and listening experiences fully account for the special experience of community that music tourism supposedly provides – attending live music events is only a small part of what tourists do on site, and sometimes it is not even part of music tourism practices at all. As Cohen (2005) observes, music is present in different stages of tourism travel: before departure in ideas and imaginations about the musical place; during travel through concerts, museum visits and analysed by for example Waitt and Duffy (2009) and Cashman (2014, 2016) as a soundscape; and after returning home, in the memories and in listening back to the sounds and songs encountered on site. Therefore, Bolderman (2020) advocates a holistic approach to music tourism, bringing together these different dimensions of music tourism experience.

Conclusion

At the time Gibson and Connell published their key publication on music tourism in 2005, they questioned whether music tourism would last, as it seemed a phenomenon governed by fad and hype, and the baby boomers and snowbirds would of course dry up at some point (Gibson and Connell 2005: 268). As music tourism has spread out across genres and practices, music tourism today is at the centre of debates around urban regeneration and heritage politics, as de-industrialized urban regions try to redevelop their inner cities. At the same time, the expectations of music tourism are also high outside of urban city centres, as for example the work of Rommen and Neely (2014) attests to.

Music tourism today is a growing form of niche tourism and a successful billion-dollar industry that up until now has been studied primarily through individual case studies. As briefly shown in this chapter, exploring the connections between music, place and tourism opens up ways to examine the creation, negotiation and celebration of personal and collective identities. Music tourism in this sense is a prism through which to study more wide-ranging sociocultural issues and themes, such as global inequalities and local identities.

More specifically, opportunities are there to expand the current growing research field by including more diverse cases, in terms of both music genres and geographical scope. The focus seems to be on urban examples of music tourism, although rural and regional issues do exist and can offer a surprising and deepening perspective (Connell and Gibson 2011, 2014; Duffy and Waitt 2011; Wagg, Spracklen and Long 2014). Moreover, what is needed is an extension of the current work to include theory building, since up until now the focus has seemed to be primarily on eye-catching case studies.

Finally, a critical perspective is called for in music tourism research. Music is often attributed to positive powers in bringing people together and creating mutual understanding across cultures and places. However, as pointed out by Kruger and Trandafoiu (2014) and

Bolderman (2020), an unequivocally celebratory view on music should be critically reassessed in a world that is increasingly characterized by technological, social and cultural mobilities and processes of de-territorialization and displacement. Music can potentially create music 'bubbles' for the affluent and nostalgic (Bull 2007), both through technology (iPods, mp3s) and through the social practices that are involved whenever music and tourism converge, as Saldanha (2002) already showed in his work on Goa trance. Music tourism as a phenomenon of mobility and the meeting of cultures therefore is a prime way to study these processes in practice: not all people have access to the same kinds of mobility and not all people have access in equal ways.

In this chapter, the various connections between music and place were explored that feed into contemporary music tourism. Music tourism in many respects is the setting of tensions between attitudes of tourism and anti-tourism, professed by both tourists themselves and researchers. In these debates, a dichotomy is created between mass tourism as superficial sightseeing and music-related travel as more than that – a more profound engagement with places and identities. The reasons for creating these dichotomies are related to the commodified image of mass tourism, as tourists and researchers alike want to signal they are in some way more serious or looking for more than hedonism (Bolderman 2020). As tourists seek to deepen their engagement with something that is very much part of and meaningful in their everyday lives, and with the expectations of music tourism by practitioners and policymakers, the topic should be taken seriously.

References

Adler, J. (1989), 'Origins of Sightseeing', *Annals of Tourism Research*, 16 (1): 7–29.

Alderman, D. H. (2002), 'Writing on the Graceland Wall: On the Importance of Authorship in Pilgrimage Landscapes', *Tourism Recreation Research*, 27 (2): 27–33.

Andrews, G., Kingsbury, P. and Kearns, R. (2014), *Soundscapes of Wellbeing in Popular Music*, London: Routledge.

Aoyama, Y. (2007), 'The Role of Consumption and Globalization in a Cultural Industry: The Case of Flamenco', *Geoforum*, 38 (1): 103–13.

Aoyama, Y. (2009), 'Artists, Tourists, and the State: Cultural Tourism and the Flamenco Industry in Andalusia, Spain', *International Journal of Urban and Regional Research*, 33 (1): 80–104. DOI: 10.1111/j.1468-2427.2009.00846.x.

Auslander, P. (2008), *Liveness: Performance in a Mediatized Culture*, 2nd edn London: Routledge.

Bennett, A. (2002), 'Music, Media and Urban Mythscapes: A Study of the "Canterbury Sound"', *Media, Culture and Society*, 24: 87–100.

Bennett, A. (2004), 'Chilled Ibiza: Dance Tourism and the Neo-tribal Island Community', in K. Dawe (ed), *Island Musics*, 123–36, Oxford: Berg.

Bennett, A. and Janssen, S. (2016), 'Popular Music, Cultural Memory, and Heritage', *Popular Music and Society*, 39 (1): 1–7. DOI 10.1080/03007766.2015.1061332.

Bilby, K. (2014), 'Preface', in T. Rommen and D. T. Neely (eds), *Sun, Sea, and Sound. Music and Tourism in the Circum-Caribbean*, 1–16, Oxford: Oxford University Press.

Blacking, J. (1973), *How Musical Is Man?* Seattle: University of Washington Press.

Bolderman, S.L. (2020), *Contemporary Music Tourism. A Theory of Musical Topophilia*, London: Routledge.

Bolderman, S. L. and Reijnders, S. (2017), 'Have You Found What You're Looking for? Analysing Tourist Experiences of Wagner's Bayreuth, ABBA's Stockholm and U2's Dublin', *Tourist Studies*, 17 (2): 164–81.

Bowen, D. S. (1997), 'Lookin' for Margaritaville: Place and Imagination in Jimmy Buffett's Songs', *Journal of Cultural Geography*, 16 (2): 99–108.

Brocken, M. (2016), *The Twenty-First-Century-Legacy of The Beatles. Liverpool and Popular Muisc Heritage Tourism*, Farnham: Ashgate Publishing.

Bull, M. (2007), *Sound Moves: iPod Culture and Urban Experience*, London: Routledge.

Burkholder, J. P., Grout, D. J. and Palisca, C. V. (2014), *A History of Western Music* (9th edn), New York: W. W. Norton & Company.

Cashman, D. (2014). 'Music and (Touristic) Meaning on Cruise Ships: The Musicscape of the MV Carnival Paradise as a Semiotic Tourism Product', *IASPM@Journal*, 4 (2): 85–102.

Cashman, D. (2016). '"The Most Atypical Experience of My Life": The Experience of Popular Music Festivals on Cruise Ships', *Tourist Studies*, 17 (3): 245–62.

Cavicchi, D. (1999), *Tramps Like Us: Music and Meaning among Springsteen Fans*, Oxford: Oxford University Press.

Chronis, A. (2015), 'Moving Bodies and the Staging of the Tourist Experience', *Annals of Tourism Research*, 55: 124–40.

Cohen, S. (2005), 'Screaming at the Moptops: Convergences between Tourism and Popular Music', in D. Crouch, R. Jackson, and F. Thompson (eds), *The Media and the Tourist Imagination. Converging Cultures*, 76–91, London: Routledge.

Cohen, S. (2007), *Decline, Renewal and the City in Popular Music Culture: Beyond the Beatles*, Farnham: Ashgate.

Cohen, S. (2014), 'Urban Musicscapes: Mapping Music-making in Liverpool', in L. Roberts (ed), *Mapping Cultures: Place, Practice, Performance*, 123–43, Basingstoke: Palgrave Macmillan.

Cohen, S., Knifton, R., Leonard, M. and Roberts, L. (2015), *Sites of Popular Music Heritage: Memories, Histories, Places*, London: Routledge.

Connell, J. and Gibson, C. (2003), *Sound Tracks: Popular Music, Identity and Place*, London: Routledge.

Connell, J. and Gibson, C. (2004), 'Vicarious Journeys: Travels in Music', *Tourism Geographies*, 6 (1): 2–25.

Connell, J. and Gibson, C. (2014), 'Mobilizing Music Festivals for Rural Transformation: Opportunities and Ambiguities', in S. Krüger and R. Trandafoiu (eds), *The Globalization of Musics in Transit. Music, Migration and Tourism*, 115–34, London: Routledge.

Couldry, N. (2005), 'On the Actual Street', in D. Crouch, R. Jackson, and F. Thompson (eds), *The Media and the Tourist Imagination. Converging Cultures*, 60–75, London: Routledge.

Csikszentmihalyi, M. (1990), *Flow. The Psychology of Optimal Experience*, New York: Harper Collins.

DeNora, T. (2000), *Music in Everyday Life*, Cambridge: Cambridge University Press.

Doss, E. (2008), 'Rock and Roll Pilgrims: Reflections on Ritual, Religiosity, and Race at Graceland', in P. J. Margry (ed), *Shrines and Pilgrimage in the Modern World. New Itineraries into the Sacred*, 123–42, Amsterdam: Amsterdam University Press.

Drummond, K. (2011), 'Shame, Consumption, Redemption: Reflections on a Tour of Graceland', *Consumption, Markets and Culture*, 14 (2): 203–13.

Duffett, M. (2014), *Popular Music Fandom: Identities, Roles and Practices*, London: Routledge.

Duffy, M. and Waitt, G. (2011), 'Rural Festivals and Processes of Belonging', in C. Gibson and J. Connell (eds), *Festival Places: Revitalizing Rural Australia*, 44–60, Bristol: Channel View Publications.

Duffy, M., Waitt, G., Gorman-Murray, A. and Gibson, C. (2011), 'Bodily Rhythms: Corporeal Capacities to Engage with Festival Spaces', *Emotion, Space and Society*, 4 (1): 17–24. DOI 10.1016/j.emospa.2010.03.004.

Dunbar-Hall, P. (2001), 'Culture, Tourism and Cultural Tourism: Boundaries and Frontiers in Performances of Balinese Music and Dance', *Journal of Intercultural Studies*, 22 (2): 173–87.

Edensor, T. (2001), 'Performing Tourism, Staging Tourism. (Re)producing Tourist Space and Practice', *Tourist Studies*, 1 (1): 59–81.

Edensor, T., & Falconer, E. (2011), 'Sensuous Geographies of Tourism', in J. Wilson (ed), *The Routledge Handbook of Tourism Geographies*, 74–81, New York: Routledge.

Ellis, S. R. (2011), 'Music Camp: Experiential Consumption in a Guitar Workshop Setting', *International Journal of Culture, Tourism and Hospitality Research*, 5 (4): 376–82. DOI 10.1108/17506181111174655.

Feintuch, B. (2004), 'The Conditions for Cape Breton Fiddle Music: The Social and Economic Setting of a Regional Soundscape', *Ethnomusicology*, 48 (1): 73–104.

Fremaux, S. and Fremaux, M. (2013), 'Remembering the Beatles' Legacy in Hamburg's Problematic Tourism Strategy', *Journal of Heritage Tourism*, 8 (4): 303–19.

Frost, W. (2008), 'Popular Culture as a Different Type of Heritage: The Making of AC/DC Lane', *Journal of Heritage Tourism*, 3 (3): 176–84.

Fry, R. W. (2014), 'Becoming a "True Blues Fan": Blues Tourism and Performances of the King Biscuit Blues Festival', *Tourist Studies*, 14 (1): 66–85.

Garcia, L. (2016), 'Techno-tourism and Post-industrial Neo-romanticism in Berlin's Electronic Dance Music Scenes', *Tourist Studies*, 16 (3): 276–95.

Gibson, C. and Connell, J. (2005), *Music and Tourism: On the Road Again*, Clevedon: Channel View Publications.

Gibson, C. and Connell, J. (2007), 'Music, Tourism and the Transformation of Memphis', *Tourism Geographies*, 9 (2): 160–90.

Gibson, C. and Connell, J. eds (2011), *Festival Places: Revitalizing Rural Australia*, Bristol: Channel View Publications.

Graburn, N. H. H. (1983), 'The Anthropology of Tourism', *Annals of Tourism Research*, 10 (1): 9–33. DOI 10.1016/0160-7383(83)90113-5.

Granger, C. (2015), 'Dwelling in Movement: Panorama, Tourism and Performance', *Contemporary Music Review*, 34 (1): 54–66. DOI 10.1080/07494467.2015.1077566.

Henke, L. (2005), 'Music-induced Tourism: Strategic Use of Indigenous Music as a Tourist Icon', *Journal of Hospitality and Leisure Marketing*, 13 (2): 3–18. DOI: 10.1300/J150v13n02_02.

Hesmondhalgh, D. (2013), *Why Music Matters*, Oxford: Blackwell Publishing.

Johansson, O. and Bell, T. S. eds (2009), *Sound, Society and the Geography of Popular Music*, Farnham: Ashgate.

Kaul, A. (2014), *Turning the Tune. Traditional Music, Tourism, and Social Change in an Irish Village*, Oxford: Berghahn Books.

Kaeppler, A. L. and Lewin, O. eds (1988), *Come Mek Me Hol' Yu Han'. The Impact of Tourism on Traditional Music*, Jamaica: Montrose Printery Limited.

King, C. (1994), 'His Truth Goes Marching on: Elvis Presley and the Pilgrimage to Graceland', in I. Reader, and T. Walter (eds), *Pilgrimage in Popular Culture*, 92–104, London: Palgrave Macmillan.

Kneafsey, M. (2002), 'Sessions and Gigs: Tourism and Traditional Music in North Mayo, Ireland. Extracts from a Field Diary (A Fictional Account Based on Actual Events, People and Places)', *Cultural Geographies*, 9: 354–8.

Krüger, S. and Trandafoiu, R. (2014), *The Globalization of Musics in Transit. Music, Migration and Tourism*, London: Routledge.

Kruse, R. J. II. (2003), 'Imagining Strawberry Fields as a Place of Pilgrimage', *Area*, 35 (2): 154–62.

Kruse, R. J. II. (2005a), *A Cultural Geography of the Beatles: Representing Landscapes as Musical Texts*, Lampeter: Edwin Mellen Press.

Kruse, R. J. II. (2005b), 'The Beatles as Place Makers: Narrated Landscapes in Liverpool, England', *Journal of Cultural Geography*, 22 (2): 87–114.

Lashua, B., Spracklen, K. and Long, R. (2014), 'Introduction to the Special Issue: Music and Tourism', *Tourist Studies*, 14 (1): 3–9.

Lees, L. and Melhuish, C. (2015), 'Arts-led Regeneration in the UK: the Rhetoric and Evidence on Urban Social Inclusion', *European Urban and Regional Studies*, 22(3): 242–260. https://doi.org/10.1177%2F0969776412467474.

Lizardi, R. (2015), *Mediated Nostalgia: Individual Memory and Contemporary Mass Media*, London: Lexington Books.

Margry, P.J. ed (2008), *Shrines and Pilgrimage in the Modern World. New Itineraries into the Sacred*, Amsterdam: Amsterdam University Press.

Mangaoang, A. and O'Flynn, J. (2016), *Mapping Popular Music in Dublin: Executive Report*, Dublin: Dublin City University.

Morton, F. (2005), 'Performing Ethnography: Irish Traditional Music Sessions and New Methodological Spaces', *Social and Cultural Geography*, 6 (5): 661–76.

Nora, P. (1989), *Between Memory and History: Les Lieux de Mémoire*, Paris: Gallimard.

Otter, J. K. (2013), '*Joy Devotion: Adventures in Image and Authenticity through the Lens of Kurt Cobain and Ian Curtis*', (Unpublished doctoral thesis), Goldsmiths, University of London, London.

Podoshen, J. S. (2013), 'Dark Tourism Motivations: Simulation, Emotional Contagion and Topographic Comparison', *Tourism Management*, 35: 263–71.

Prentice, R. and Anderson, V. (2003), 'Festival as Creative Destination', *Annals of Tourism research*, 30 (1): 7–30. https://doi.org/10.1016/S0160-7383(02)00034-8.

Quinn, B. (2010). 'Arts Festivals, Urban Tourism and Cultural Policy', *Journal of Policy Research in Tourism, Leisure and Events*, 2 (3): 264–79.

Reijnders, S. (2011), *Places of the Imagination. Media, Tourism, Culture*, Farnham: Ashgate.

Reynolds, S. (2011), *Retromania: Pop Culture's Addiction to Its Own Past*, New York: Farrar, Straus and Giroux.

Roberts, L. (2014), 'Marketing Musicscapes, or, the Political Economy of Contagious Magic', *Tourist Studies*, 14 (1): 10–29.

Rodman, G. B. (1996), *Elvis after Elvis: The Posthumous Career of a Living Legend*, London: Routledge.

Rommen, T. and Neely, T. D. (2014), *Sun, Sea, and Sound: Music and Tourism in the Circum-Caribbean*, Oxford: Oxford University Press.

Saldanha, A. (2002), 'Music Tourism and Factions of Bodies in Goa', *Tourist Studies*, 2 (1): 43–62.

Sandvoss, C. (2005), *The Mirror of Consumption*, Cambridge: Polity Press.

Sandvoss, C. (2014), 'I (heart) Ibiza. Music, Place and Belonging', in M. Duffet (ed), *Popular Music Fandom: Identities, Roles and Practices*, 115–45, London: Routledge.

Sarbanes, J. (2006), 'Musicking and Communitas: The Aesthetic Mode of Sociality in Rebetika Subculture', *Popular Music and Society*, 29 (1): 17–35. DOI 10.1080/03007760500142738.

Smith, M. (2016), *Issues in Cultural Tourism*, 3rd edn, Abingdon: Taylor and Francis.

Spracklen, K. and Spracklen, B. (2014), 'The Strange and Spooky Battle over Bats and Black Dresses: The Commodification of Whitby Goth Weekend and the Loss of a Subculture', *Tourist Studies*, 14 (1): 86–102.

Stokes, M. (1999), 'Music, Travel and Tourism: An Afterword', *The World of Music*, 41 (3): 141–55.

Szmigin, I., Bengry-Howell, A., Morey, Y., Griffin, C. and Riley, S. (2017), 'Socio-spatial Authenticity at Co-created Music Festivals', *Annals of Tourism Research*, 63: 1–11.

Trandberg J. M., Scarles, C. and Cohen, S. A. (2015), 'A Multisensory Phenomenology of Interrail Mobilities', *Annals of Tourism Research*, 53: 61–76.

Turino, T. (2008), *Music as Social Life. The Politics of Participation*, Chicago: Chicago University Press.

Turner, V. and Turner, E. (1978), *Image and Pilgrimage in Christian Culture*, New York: Columbia University Press.

UK Music (2013), *Wish You Were Here: Music Tourism's Contribution to the UK Economy*, London: UK Music.

UK Music (2017), *UK Live Music Attendance and Music Tourism 2017*, London: UK Music.

Urry, J. (1990), *The Tourist Gaze: Leisure and Travel in Contemporary Societies*, Los Angeles: Sage.

Urry, J. and Larsen, J. (2011), *The Tourist Gaze 3.0*, 3rd edn, Los Angeles: Sage.

Veijola, S. and Jokinen, E. (1994), 'The Body in Tourism', *Theory, Culture & Society*, 11 (3): 125–51.

Wagg, S., Spracklen, K. and Lashua, B. (2014), 'Afterword: Reflections on Popular Music, Place and Globalization', in B. Lashua, K. Spracklen and S. Wagg (eds), *Sounds and the City: Popular Music, Place and Globalization*, 317–19, New York: Springer.

Waitt, G. and Duffy, M. (2009), 'Listening and Tourism Studies', *Annals of Tourism Research*, 37 (2): 457–77.

Ward, J. V. (2014), 'Pilgrimage, Place, and Preservation: The Real and Imagined Geography of the Grateful Dead in Song, On Tour, and in Cyberspace', in S. Cohen, R. Knifton, M. Leonard and L. Roberts (eds), *Sites of Popular Music Heritage: Memories, Histories, Places*, 193–206, London: Routledge.

Watson, A. (2018), 'Music Tourism', in S. Agarwal, G. Busby and R. Huang (eds), *Special Interest Tourism: Concepts, Contexts and Cases*, 73–84, Boston: CAB International.

Whyton, T. (2014), 'Song of Praise. Musicians, Myths and the Cult of John Coltrane', in M. Duffett (ed), *Popular Music Fandom. Identities, Roles, Practices*, 97–114, London: Routledge.

Xie, P. F., Osumare, H. and Ibrahim, A. (2007), 'Gazing the Hood: Hip-hop as Tourism Attraction', *Tourism Management*, 28 (2): 452–60.

28
Festivals

Chris Anderton

Introduction

Music festivals, especially those held outdoors on greenfield sites over a number of days, may become intimately associated with the locations which host them. For a few days each year, these sites take on a life of their own, with their own accommodation, entertainments, social experience, retail opportunities and policing. They form temporary villages or towns that are constructed and annually re-constructed in their own image by festival organizers and attendees, and increasingly mediated through traditional and online media by organizers, sponsors, broadcasters and festivalgoers. Drawing primarily on British examples, this chapter examines the spaces and places of such events, which typically offer the spectacle of live music performance on one or more stages alongside onsite accommodation and a wide variety of other activities and audience interactions. I begin by defining and categorizing music festivals and providing an overview of a variety of academic research strands. I then explore a number of theories that have been proposed to describe the relationship between festivals, space and place, before introducing my own conception of music festivals as 'cyclic places'.

Defining and categorizing music festivals

The academic literature on music, arts and other cultural festivals remains rather fragmented and transdisciplinary in nature, despite growth in this area since the early 2000s. This leads to a wide variety of definitions of the term 'festival' and the lack of a broadly accepted typology relating to such events (Getz 2010: 2). Shuker has defined music festivals in straightforward terms as 'concert[s], usually outdoor, often held over several days' (1998: 122), though most studies employ more expansive notions of 'festival' which draw on social and anthropological ideas of celebration, worship, conviviality, community and playfulness, or on policy-based understandings of festivals as drivers of tourism and economic development. For instance, Falassi's (1987) definition of festival focuses on the excessive behaviours and temporary transgressions that may be associated with 'festival times' (see also Bakhtin 1984; Anderton 2008; Ravenscroft and Gilchrist 2009), while other authors stress the role of festivals in creating or maintaining a sense of local or regional community (see Hall 1992; Duffy 2000; Derrett 2003; Jepson and Clarke 2015). Tourism and event management academics are also interested in how festivals foster civic pride, but are more likely to examine how tourist numbers may be increased, how local and regional economic growth and regeneration may be stimulated, or how a festival's service offering may be enhanced or its environmental impacts reduced (Getz 1991; Bowdin et al. 2001). There is an increasing interest in crossovers between these different positions, though the nascent discipline of event studies (Getz and Page 2016) has yet to gain traction in its own right. Nevertheless, we have seen the development of research that is situated at the intersection between economic/regional development and community identity/belonging, especially in Australia where several such studies have been published (Gibson and Connell 2012; Duffy and Mair 2018), as well as in the development of cultural economic approaches that examine the influence of culture on the organization and meaning of festivals (Anderton 2008, 2011, 2019).

As noted above, there is no generally agreed typology of festivals; yet, the growing music festival literature allows us to distinguish a variety of (often intersecting) festival forms in terms of their purpose and organization. Some of these are discussed here, though it should be noted that this is by no means a comprehensive typology and is intended primarily to indicate the range of events that we see in the contemporary music festival market. First, we may recognize what might be termed 'organic' events, which emerge in local communities to celebrate local cultures (Duffy 2000), or begin as one-off charity events or open-air garden-party style concerts that may later turn into longer-running annual events (Anderton 2016). These organically created events can remain highly localized and almost unknown to those living outside the event's immediate location or to music fans who lie beyond the particular genre or subculture being catered to. However, they may also transform into larger events that attract visitors from further afield. For instance, Blissfields in the south of England and the Green Man Festival in Wales each grew from events initially attended by only a few hundred people to become larger-scale events attracting thousands.

Second, we may identify destination-focused events where the purpose of the festival is to attract people to a specific location or to make use of that location's specific attributes as a marketing tool. Such events may vary both in scale and organizational framework, with large-scale 'hallmark' events often created by local or municipal authorities to enhance the place-image and economic regeneration of their towns or cities (Hall 1992). Such events include one-off celebrations linked to important historic occasions and anniversaries as well as events aimed at raising awareness or funds for specific charitable causes (Rojek 2013). Country house estates, sports stadia, farms, tourist attractions, holiday complexes and publicly owned parklands also fall into the category of 'destination-focused', since the owners of such sites are seeking to 'animate' their otherwise static (and expensive to maintain) tourist attractions and amenities by staging music (and other) festivals themselves or renting their land and facilities to commercial promoters to do so. Commercial promoters are especially important because of the high levels of investment and risk that are present in the music festival market, which has led to an increase in national and international level companies, including Live Nation, AEG Presents and Superstruct Entertainment, consolidating control of the mid- to large-scale sector of the market (events with daily attendances in excess of 25,000) and adding non-camping (hence, lower expense and lower risk) events in urban parks (Anderton 2019).

Third, there has been an increase in smaller-scale 'boutique' events that are design-led in their approach, typically commercial in their organization, and often camping-based. This form of event was pioneered by independently owned festival promoters in the early- to mid-2000s, though major national and international promoters have since diversified their activities into this market as the competition and costs associated with larger-scale festivals have increased over the same time period (Anderton 2019; Robinson 2015a). Some events, such as Boomtown (in Hampshire, UK) and Beat-Herder (in Lancashire, UK), create immersive themed environments with stages built to resemble, for example, castles, churches and Inca monuments – eccentric spectacles that are moderated by these events' emphasis on participatory activities including fancy dress and opportunities to perform plus the ability for festivalgoers to customize their on-site experience. However, the 'popular theatricality' of the 'boutique' sector can encompass a wide variety of themes including superheroes, TV shows, outer space, decades and vintage (Robinson 2015b). What is at stake for these events is to find a theme that resonates with audiences and to transform their locations appropriately – in some ways a negation of the specificity of their places, though often making use of the potential of the natural environment to help frame the activities and creative spaces on offer.

Researching music festivals

In his extensive review of the festivals and events literature, Getz (2010) identified three over-arching research themes: the social and cultural meanings and impacts of festivals, festivals as tourism, and festival management. The first of these themes incorporates questions about place identity, community and belonging though, as Duffy (2005) notes, multiculturalism and diversity of opinion among festivalgoers and local populations and stakeholders mean that the sense of belonging and community created by a festival may not be shared by all. This has further consequences for policymakers trying to make use of festivals to create community cohesion and development or to re-invent the place-images of their host locations (Gibson and Connell 2012). Another strand of research within this first theme is that of liminality and the carnivalesque – of the social meaning of events that are ephemeral in nature and may be associated with transgressive or excessive behaviours (discussed further below). In addition, we may add two further research areas that are found within the narrower field of music festival studies. The first is principally historical in nature and focuses either on analysing the role of music festivals within broader social history or on documenting the emergence, style and significance of particular examples or types of festival, for example, work on the Glastonbury Festival (McKay 2000), the Woodstock Festival (Spitz 1979) and the Free Festivals of 1970s Britain (Worthington 2004, 2005; Martin 2014). The second turns attention to the role of mediation and mythology in the creation of images and meanings that have become associated with particular events, whether in the form of festival films or the use of internet archives and social media (Street 2004; Goodall 2015; Morey et al. 2014). The latter is particularly interesting in terms of how the festival experience may be extended beyond the day or weekend of the event itself, and how organizers and sponsors may make advantageous use of this (Morey et al. 2014; Anderton 2019).

The second main theme identified by Getz (2010) includes tourism studies-based research into place-marketing and into the motivations and opinions of festival attendees. It also incorporates the notion of 'festivalization', which has emerged as an important topic in its own right in recent years. Négrier argues that festivalization refers to the 'process by which cultural activity, previously presented in a regular, on-going pattern or season [for instance, a season of concerts], is reconfigured to form a "new" event' [a 'festival'] (2015: 181). This is similar to what Ronström (2016) has termed 'semantic' festivalization, where the term 'festival' is used as a short-hand way to indicate a particular type of experience that will serve, as Stoeltje puts it, 'the commercial, ideological, or political purposes of self-interested authorities or entrepreneurs' (1992: 261). This concurs with Roche's (2011) argument that festivalization is not about creating transcendent or transformatory experiences, but is part of the everyday public sphere and/or public policy. Hence, a village fête may be turned into a 'festival' to attract more interest and visitors, or a city may host a string of festival-like events during the summer months in order to transform its place-identity and benefit from the potential economic spill-over effects of increased tourism. Furthermore, numerous independent and corporate brands have festivalized their products and marketing in order to take advantage of the marketing opportunities and 'good times' that festivals promise by 'activating' their marketing through on-site and online activities and the creation of brand-specific experiential zones within festival arenas (Anderton 2008, 2011, 2015, 2019).

The final theme discussed by Getz (2010) is that of festival management, which includes strategic planning and evaluation and the role of design in the creation of festival settings. The latter is typically formulated in terms of event concepts, the marketing mix and the creation of unique selling points – whether in the form of high-profile or exclusive performances, the development of a sense of 'authentic' community or the provision of themed environments. Environmental and economic impact assessments are another strand of this theme, though there is a tendency within the event management literature to use quantitative methodologies and to downplay the social and cultural meanings attributed to festivals and events in favour of examining their more tangible impacts. Perhaps surprisingly, there has been little research into the decision-making of festival organizers (for an exception see Hagan 2022) though festival volunteers have been the focus of a small number of studies (Elstad 2002; Bachman et al. 2016).

Festivals, space and place

The music festival sector has grown markedly since the turn of the millennium and proliferated in terms of both content and form (Webster and Mackay 2016; Anderton 2007, 2019); yet, all festivals are rooted in the physical and human landscapes of their host locations. This sense of rootedness can increase as festivals are re-staged in the same locations each year, and they may develop a character or identity of their own that is both place-based and event-based. This place-based character is constructed through the activities and decisions of, among other things, each event's particular mix of organizers, sponsors, contractors, concessions, performers, audiences and local authorities. Yet, as will be discussed below, past theorizations of music festival spaces and places have tended to focus on their ephemerality and liminality where festivals are characterized as occurring in out-of-the-way places, and as offering experiences that are either socially transgressive or utopian in nature.

The anthropological and cultural-historical literature typically views music festivals as a subset of festivals in general, and relates them to a long history of cultural festivities that are tied to religious observances, including the Roman Saturnalia, the Celtic Beltane and the Christian Carnival. Of particular note is the work of the Russian literary critic Mikhail Bakhtin, who analysed the representation of the medieval carnival in the work of the French author François Rabelais. He described the time of the carnival as 'a world turned inside out' (1984: 11), as a short-lived period of time during which everyday authority and social norms were overturned and mocked – a time characterized by a flattening of class hierarchy, of conspicuous consumption and waste, and of grotesque masks, playful activity and religious irreverence (see also Stallybrass and White 1986: 189). He extended these characteristics to other festival-type events, describing them as 'carnivalesque' in nature, and this usage is prevalent in academic accounts of late-twentieth-century music festivals (see McKay 2000; Hetherington 2001; Worthington 2004). I refer to such work as embodying the 'countercultural carnivalesque', as it demonstrates a range of stereotypes and behaviours associated with the late 1960s hippie counterculture (nudity, free love, use of drugs and other socially transgressive behaviour), and their extension into post-hippie era alternative cultures such as that of the so-called New Age Travellers in the UK. The utopian narrative of the countercultural carnivalesque can also be seen in festival films such as *Woodstock – Three Days of Peace and Music* (1970). However, neither the carnivalesque nor the countercultural carnivalesque can be said to be explicitly spatial in nature, since the emphasis is on the temporal experience of festivals and the behaviours associated with them.

An alternative conception is that proposed by Victor Turner, whose theory of anti-structure bears many resemblances to Bakhtin's carnival, but demarcates not only the time of the festival, but also the space of the festival (Turner 1969). For Turner, festivals are societal rites of passage that occur in particular geographical settings – liminal spaces and times that are separate from everyday life and where, during festival times, normative social structures are temporarily inverted or reversed. Turner's ideas have been developed by authors such as Rob Shields (1991) and Kevin Hetherington (1998a, b), the latter using liminality as a framework for understanding the British 'free festival' movement of the 1970s and 1980s. These events were typically held in out-of-the-way rural locations such as the Rhayader Valley in Wales as well as at, or near, prehistoric sites such as Stonehenge and Avebury Ring in England – sites that held resonance and meaning for the post-hippie New Age Travellers who created the events, and which demonstrated their Arcadian and utopian understanding of rurality (Hetherington 1998b). The descriptions of these events owe much to the countercultural carnivalesque, but also characterize their locations as liminal – as existing on the margins of mainstream modern society (Shields 1991). However, the contemporary market for commercial music festivals is quite different from that of the free festivals of the past, and the locations chosen for commercial festivals are often far from liminal in nature, including the grounds of stately homes, parkland and amenities owned by local authorities, and city centre parks such as Hyde Park, Victoria Park and Finsbury Park in London. Similarly, festivalgoers themselves are far more mainstream and broad-based in their demographic and psychographic constitution than they were prior to the 1990s, and many festivals make use of commercial sponsorship and broadcast media tie-ins (Anderton 2008, 2011, 2019).

A final theory to consider here is Michel Foucault's conception of the 'heterotopia of deviance', where individuals who are 'deviant in relation to the required mean or norm are placed' (1986: 25). He refers to places such as psychiatric hospitals and prisons; yet, the theory has since been adapted by Graham St John (2001) to discuss music festivals such as Australia's ConFest. At this event numerous people and groups who follow a range of alternative lifestyles come together to celebrate their 'deviance' from mainstream culture and society, and to engage in 'hedonistic consumption practices' (St John 2001: 51). Of particular note is the emphasis given to Foucault's understanding of heterotopia as 'capable of juxtaposing in a single real place several places' (1986: 25). This suggests that a single site (or festival) may mean very different things to different people – that it has the potential for multiple interpretations. Furthermore, it suggests that the image, meaning and behaviours associated with festival sites are necessarily constructed and reconstructed from year to year through the interactions of multiple agents – from those on the production side (organizers, contractors, concessions, local authorities, media and so on) to those on the consumption side (festivalgoers). The deviance implied within both Foucault's and St John's work is less pronounced within the contemporary commercial music festival market as a whole; yet, it remains the case that festivalgoers may experience events in very different ways depending, in part, on demographics and psychographics, as well as on expectations related to music genre (see Wilks and Quinn 2016; Anderton 2019) – there is no singular experience or understanding of any particular festival place.

Cyclic place

The above discussions lead to my own conception of festival sites and events as 'cyclic places'. This conception recognizes that festivals may be regarded as sites of transgression and the countercultural carnivalesque, but that there is no necessity for this to be the case – that festivals can take on many forms and meanings, and that individual festivals can themselves be understood in differing ways by the individuals and groups who are attending them. In this sense, I draw not only on Foucault's conception of heterotopia, but also on the work of Doreen Massey. She has suggested that *spaces* are 'constructed out of the multiplicity of social relations', rather than being fixed and bounded areas with singular identities (1994: 4). Furthermore, she has characterized *places* as 'spatio-temporal events' that are formed of multiple narratives (stories, memories, beliefs, mediations) that become centred on particular geographical locations (Massey 2005: 130). In my view, her emphasis on the processual and relational nature of space undermines the lived experience and understanding of place that is found, for example, in music festivals, where relatively stable place-images do emerge over time. There is still room for variation in experience from year to year, dependent on the particular mix of attractions, performers, attendees and so on; yet, longer-lived events in particular may develop a recognizable sense of place and festivalgoers themselves feel a sense of belonging and familiarity in relation to that place (Anderton 2019; see also Relph 1976 and Tuan 1977 on the humanistic geography notion of 'sense of place').

Annual music festivals may, in my formulation, be defined as 'cyclic places' (Anderton 2019). This refers both to the sense of place that is constructed around such events (they feel like 'real' places that can be returned to each year) and to their cyclical yet temporary material existence. Such events are characterized by four interrelated aspects. First, and unlike the liminal conception of space discussed above, festival places are often intimately connected to the pre-existing meanings of the locations that play host to them. They are not necessarily placed on the margins of society or in out-of-the-way places, and despite occasional concerns about noise pollution, land damage/waste and traffic congestion, local people and authorities often actively support events due to the economic, tourism and social benefits they may bring. They can animate otherwise static tourist attractions, enhance the place-image of the host location and provide employment opportunities and other economic and social benefits to host communities.

The second aspect relates to the sense of place, belonging and familiarity that is engendered by regularly occurring events. They may exist only temporarily in physical form, but the provision of on-site services, entertainments, accommodation and other facilities in a familiar layout and with familiar branding fosters a sense of continuity. Such events develop their own histories, behaviours, landmarks and rules that are shaped through the interaction of organizers and festivalgoers and are re-created or re-enacted on an annual basis. Furthermore, this sense of place and belonging will vary between different groups of attendees, such that those attendees develop their own sense of place which is linked to their lived experience and memories of the event. Thus, multiple narratives (Massey 2005) or heterotopic understandings (Foucault 1986) may be recognized.

This leads to the third aspect of cyclic places, which is that they are necessarily mediated in formal and informal ways. Such mediation includes official marketing by festival organizers and sponsors; previews, reviews and other coverage in traditional and online media; and the activities of festivalgoers in discussing, anticipating and remembering festivals through a variety of social and online media. Together these form a virtual version of a festival that continues to construct expectations and place-images throughout the year. This is particularly important in the contemporary festival market where event saturation means that there are many hundreds of events catering to a variety of demographic and psychographic target markets. Mediation therefore helps such events to define themselves within the market, to gain new attendees and to reinforce a sense of place and brand image that also highlights and strengthens expectations regarding social norms and behaviours within the festival site.

The final aspect of cyclic place is the combination of continuity and change. This is constructed through the intersection of a festival's relatively stable sense of place (its place-image and brand) with the ever-changing social interactions, mediations and performances which are to be found at the event each year. The mix of people, music, activities and tastes changes over time, and while the festival's overarching sense of place may remain familiar to regular attendees, each year's event will feel slightly different. This allows festival organizers to avoid stagnation and to react not only to changes in regulation and legislation, but also to developments in the tastes and demographics of their audiences – to add new attractions or stages or to extend the styles of music on offer. A sense of difference and novelty is therefore added to the sense of familiarity and belonging, which keeps the event experience fresh, while maintaining its overall identity. Taken together the four aspects outlined here help to characterize music festivals as cyclic places. It moves the discussion of these events beyond utopian and transgressive understandings of space and place, yet also acknowledges how festivals may be constructed as *places* that hold significant social and cultural meanings for attendees, even though they are commercially managed and marketed. It also acknowledges the role of festival organizers in fostering this sense of place, so begins to bridge the gap so often seen between the event/tourism management literature on one side, and the cultural geography/anthropological literature on the other.

References

Anderton, C. (2007), '(Re)Constructing Music Festival Places', PhD dissertation, Swansea University, Swansea, UK.

Anderton, C. (2008), 'Commercializing the Carnivalesque: The V Festival and Image/Risk Management', *Event Management*, 12 (1): 39–51.

Anderton, C. (2011), 'Music Festival Sponsorship: Between Commerce and Carnival', *Arts Marketing*, 1 (2): 145–58.

Anderton, C. (2015), 'Branding, Sponsorship and the Music Festival', in G. McKay (ed.), *The Pop Festival: History, Music, Media, Culture*, 199–212, New York and London: Bloomsbury Academic.

Anderton, C. (2016), 'Musikfestivals als »zyklische Orte«: Fairport's Cropredy Convention', in J. Springer and T. Dören (eds), *Draußen: Zum neuen Naturbezug in der Popkultur der Gegenwart*, 119–38, Bielefeld: Transcript Verlag.

Anderton, C. (2019), *Music Festivals in the UK. Beyond the Carnivalesque*, London: Routledge.

Bachman, J. R., Norman, W. C., Hopkins, C. D. and Brookover, R. S. (2016), 'Examining the Role of Self-Concept Theory on Motivation, Satisfaction, and Intent to Return of Music Festival Volunteers', *Event Management*, 20 (1): 41–52.

Bakhtin, M. (1984), *Rabelais and His World*, trans. H. Iswolsky, Bloomington, IN: Indiana University Press.

Bowdin, G. A. J., McDonnell, I., Allen, J. and O'Toole, W. (2001), *Events Management*, Oxford: Butterworth-Heinemann.

Derrett, R. (2003), 'Making Sense of How Festivals Demonstrate a Community's Sense of Place', *Event Management*, 8: 49–58.

Duffy, M. (2000), 'Lines of Drift: Festival Participation and Performing a Sense of Place', *Popular Music*, 19 (1): 51–64.

Duffy, M. (2005), 'Performing Identity within a Multicultural Framework', *Social & Cultural Geography*, 6 (5): 677–92.

Duffy, M. and Mair, J. (2018), *Festival Encounters: Theoretical Perspectives on Festival Events*, Abingdon and New York: Routledge.

Elstad, B. (2002), 'Continuance Commitment and Reasons to Quit: A Study of Volunteers at a Jazz Festival', *Event Management*, 8 (2): 99–108.

Falassi, A. (1987), 'Festival: Definition and Morphology', in A. Falassi (ed.), *Time Out of Time: Essays on the Festival*, 1–10, Albuquerque: University of New Mexico Press.

Foucault, M. (1986), 'Of Other Spaces', *Diacritics*, 16 (1): 22–7.

Getz, D. (1991), *Festivals, Special Events, and Tourism*, New York: Van Nostrand Reinhold.

Getz, D. (2010), 'The Nature and Scope of Festival Studies', *International Journal of Event Management Research*, 5 (1): 1–47.

Getz, D. and Page, S. (2016), *Event Studies. Theory, Research and Policy for Planned Events*, 3rd edn, Abingdon and New York: Routledge.

Gibson, C. and Connell, J. (2012), *Music Festivals and Regional Development in Australia*, London and New York: Routledge.

Goodall, M. (2015), 'Out of Sight: The Mediation of the Music Festival', in G. McKay (ed.), *The Pop Festival: History, Music, Media, Culture*, 33–48, New York and London: Bloomsbury Academic.

Hagan, D. (2022), 'As Long as They Go Home Safe: The Voice of the Independent Music Festival Promoter', in C. Anderton and S. Pisfil (eds), *Researching Live Music: Gigs, Tours, Concerts and Festivals*, 31–43, London and New York: Routledge.

Hall, C. M. (1992), *Hallmark Tourist Events. Impacts, Management & Planning*, London: Belhaven Press.

Hetherington, K. (1998a), 'Vanloads of Uproarious Humanity: New Age Travellers and the Utopics of the Countryside', in T. Skelton and G. Valentine (eds), *Cool Places: Geographies of Youth Cultures*, 328–42, London and New York: Routledge.

Hetherington, K. (1998b), *Expressions of Identity: Space, Performance, Politics*, London: SAGE Publications Ltd.

Hetherington, K. (2001), *New Age Travellers: Vanloads of Uproarious Humanity*, London: Cassell.

Jepson, A. and Clarke, A., eds (2015), *Exploring Community Festivals and Events*, Abingdon and New York: Routledge.

Lefebvre, H. (1991), *The Production of Space*, trans. D. Nicholson-Smith, Oxford: Basil Blackwell Ltd.

Martin, G. (2014), 'The Politics, Pleasure and Performance of New Age Travellers, Ravers and Anti-Road Protestors: Connecting Festivals, Carnival and New Social Movements', in A. Bennett, J. Taylor and I. Woodward (eds), *The Festivalization of Culture*, 87–106, Farnham: Ashgate.
Massey, D. (1994), *Space, Place, and Gender*, Minneapolis: University of Minnesota Press.
Massey, D. (2005), *For Space*, London: Sage.
McKay, G. (2000), *Glastonbury: A Very English Fair*, London: Victor Gollancz.
Morey, Y., Bengry-Howell, A., Griffin, C., Szmigin, I. and Riley, S. (2014), 'Festivals 2.0: Consuming, Producing and Participating in the Extended Festival Experience', in A. Bennett, J. Taylor and I. Woodward (eds), *The Festivalization of Culture*, 251–68, Farnham: Ashgate.
Négrier, E. (2015), 'Festivalisation: Patterns and Limits', in C. Newbold, C. Maughan, J. Jordan and F. Bianchini (eds), *Focus on Festivals. Contemporary European Case Studies and Perspectives*, 18–27, Oxford: Goodfellow Publishers Ltd.
Ravenscroft, N. and Gilchrist, P. (2009), 'Spaces of Transgression: Governance, Discipline and Reworking the Carnivalesque', *Leisure Studies*, 28 (1): 35–49.
Relph, E. (1976), *Place and Placelessness*, London: Pion.
Robinson, R. (2015a), *Music Festivals and the Politics of Participation*, Farnham: Ashgate.
Robinson, R. (2015b), 'No Spectators! The Art of Participation, from Burning Man to Boutique Festivals in Britain', in G. McKay (ed.), *The Pop Festival: History, Music, Media, Culture*, 165–81, New York and London: Bloomsbury Academic.
Roche, M. (2011), 'Festivalisation, Cosmopolitanism and European Culture: On the Sociological Significance of Mega-Events', in L. Giorgi, M. Sassatelli and G. Delanty (eds), *Festivals and the Cultural Public Sphere*, 124–41, London and New York: Routledge.
Rojek, C. (2013), *Event Power: How Global Events Manage and Manipulate*, London: Sage.
Ronström, O. (2016), 'Four Facets of Festivalisation', *PULS Musik- och Dansetnologisk Tidskrift*, 1 (1): 67–83.
St. John, G. (2001), 'Alternative Cultural Heterotopia and the Liminoid Body: Beyond Turner at ConFest', *The Australian Journal of Anthropology*, 12 (1): 47–66.
Shields, R. (1991), *Places on the Margin: Alternative Geographies of Modernity*, London: Routledge.
Shuker, R. (1998), *Key Concepts in Popular Music*, London: Routledge.
Spitz, R. S. (1979), *Barefoot in Babylon: the Creation of the Woodstock Festival, 1969*, New York: Viking Press.
Stallybrass, P. and White, A. (1986), *The Politics and Poetics of Transgression*, New York: Cornell University Press.
Stoeltje, B. J. (1992), 'Festival', in R. Bauman (ed.), *Folklore, Cultural Performances and Popular Entertainments*, 261–71, Oxford: Oxford University Press.
Street, J. (2004), '"This Is Your Woodstock": Popular Memories and Political Myths', in A. Bennett (ed.), *Remembering Woodstock*, 29–42, Aldershot: Ashgate.
Tuan, Y.-F. (1977), *Space and Place: The Perspective of Experience*, Minneapolis: University of Minnesota Press.
Turner, V. (1969), *The Ritual Process: Structure and Anti-Structure*, London: Routledge & Kegan Paul.
Webster, E. and McKay, G. (2016), *From Glyndebourne to Glastonbury: the Impact of British Music Festivals*, Norwich: Arts & Humanities Research Council/University of East Anglia.

Wilks, L. and Quinn, B. (2016), 'Linking Social Capital, Cultural Capital and Heterotopia at the Folk Festival', *Journal of Comparative Research in Anthropology and Sociology*, 7 (1): 23–39.

Woodstock – Three Days of Peace and Music (1970), directed by Michael Wadleigh, USA: Wadleigh-Maurice/Warner Bros. [Available as an extended Director's Cut from Warner Home video, 2002].

Worthington, A. (2004), *Stonehenge: Celebration and Subversion*, Loughborough: Alternative Albion.

Worthington, A. (2005), *The Battle of the Beanfield*, Teignmouth, Devon: Enabler Publications.

29

Cinematic places: Popular music soundtracks and the charge of the real

Kate Bolgar Smith

Introduction

Cinema plays a crucial role in how we understand place, and in how we understand ourselves within place. Films create worlds for us to be immersed in. They tell new stories – or reproduce well-worn stories – of places we know but have never visited, or introduce us to unknown or imaginary places. Films show us the people who inhabit places, reveal how they live, the languages they speak, the way they interact, the relationships they have with one another and with the space around them. Through cinema we can encounter an unknowable place – a mega city so large it cannot be experienced in full by one person, or a village so remote it can only be known by a few – and immerse us into that world so fully that it becomes familiar. From New York at night in *Taxi Driver* (Scorsese, 1976) to the hustle of Ho Chi Minh City (then Saigon) in *Good Morning Vietnam* (Levinson, 1988), the built environment of West London in *Notting Hill* (Michell, 1999) to the eastern coast of New Zealand in *Whale Rider* (Caro, 2002), films present the world to us, and crucially, they mediate that world, filtering it through the stories of the film, the editing of the camera shots, and, as this chapter will detail, through music.

Films, like television and photography, are particularly powerful modes for the mediation of the world around us because of the qualities of the camera. The camera has cartographical capabilities, capturing images of the real world to be translated on screen. As such, cinematic worlds are often closely related to the places around us. Films present recognizable spaces of the world we inhabit: neighbourhoods we walk through; landscapes we holiday in; iconic buildings we visit; towns, cities, regions, oceans and countries that we talk about, read about and imagine. When these places appear on screen, they are sometimes clearly recognizable, sometimes just reminiscent, but they are always reimagined. Within cinema, these locations are both real and unreal. They are apparitions that document the world around us, and also allow the landscape to be altered, re-viewed, re-narrated. For this reason, Gilberto Perez describes film as a 'material ghost', 'a fiction made up of documentary details' (Perez 2000: 34). The medium of film, Perez argues, carries a 'charge of reality' because of the camera's involvement with actual things; yet, 'the images on screen are neither a reproduction of reality nor an illusion of it: rather they are a construction, derived from reality but distinct from it, a parallel realm' (Perez 2000: 17).

Cinema, then, appears to reflect reality, with most films reproducing images taken directly from the world around us. Films show us place, but they are not simple reflections of the world. Crucially they also narrate place. Geographical locations are seen through the filters of narrative and emotion, making the filmic representation of the world both concrete and symbolic. Giuliana Bruno suggests that the plotting of place that occurs in cinema results in what she terms 'filmic site-seeing' as the cinema spectator travels through the architectural montage presented on screen. This locational detailing of place on film is, Bruno argues, an 'emotional mapping' (Bruno 2007: 23–4). A film spectator, 'site-seeing' through the setting of the film, does so with emotion and with their own personal experiences. These ideas are mirrored in the work of Tom Conley who suggests that films are maps, and that both are viewed through subjective experiences. Just as the person who looks at a map works through both the geographical information held within it and their own fantasies and memories associated with the names, places and forms on the map, 'so also do spectators of a film… sift through souvenirs and images of other films and personal memories' (Conley 2007: 4). Conley and Bruno here highlight important features of film-watching and the documenting of place, mediated through emotion and memory. Yet they remain focused on the visual (site-*seeing*, *spectators* of a film). This focus on the visual and silencing of sound is a recurring theme of film scholarship and indeed of the general perception of cinema: we 'watch' a film, ask if we have 'seen' the latest movie. It should not be forgotten that film is an *audio*-visual medium. Sound, and particularly music, has a deeply influential role to play in how we interpret the film alongside what we see on the screen.

Film watching and the art of not listening

Cinema is replete with music. Music plays across almost every film, soundtracking the people, places and stories within it. This near constant presence of music often goes unnoticed. Soundtracks rarely have a source within the narrative – music floats across the visual elements of the film. Decades of film-watching, and theatre-going before that, have conditioned audiences to expect musical accompaniment. The 'naturalized arbitrariness' of film music, as Michel Marie argues, is 'revealing of the degree of convention the spectator will accept, and it structures all the rules that determine the functioning of filmic listening' (Marie, cited in Gorbman 1987: 52). Filmic 'listening' is, then, a misleading term, for traditionally, film music remains 'unheard', as Claudia Gorbman terms it in one of the most influential studies on film music (Gorbman 1987). In this analysis, in spite of its ubiquitous presence in cinema, audiences do not 'normally (consciously) hear the film score' (Gorbman 1987: 31). Music should remain in the background of a film, quietly underscoring the impact of the narrative and surreptitiously influencing the audience's emotional response to the story. There is no reason, for instance, for an audience to expect to hear the bassoons, clarinets, harps, drums and the rest of the orchestra that performs the rousing theme song of *The Good, The Bad, and The Ugly* (Leone 1966). The music played by these instruments is not meant to be paid attention to; it is the soundtrack to the American Southwest during the era of the Civil War, and pushes the audience to get caught up in the betrayals and violence of the plot as the protagonists search for gold. In many films, then, soundtracks are 'not meant to be listened to' (Gorbman 1987: 57). This is predominantly the case for scored soundtracks in classical narrative cinema, where 'the music stabilises the image and secures meaning while remaining as unobtrusive as possible' (Herzog 2009: 6). Fragments of theme songs float through the narrative, and music swells to tell us of heightened emotion or darkens to anticipate an approaching disaster. In this sense, music has an empathetic relationship with the visual and narrative elements of the film.

However, this is obviously not always the case. Music can also force itself into the foreground of a film and demand the attention of the audience. This happens when music is at odds with the visual, creating a jarring effect; when music becomes a focus within the film's narrative, when characters select a certain song to play, when they talk about music, sing along to it, or dance to it; and this is also the case when music features lyrics. The words of the song become a feature for the audience, they *listen* to the words and the lyrics can often act as a commentary on the events seen on screen. Frequently, these moments of musical dominance feature popular music. The use of popular music on soundtracks has become widespread since its emergence in the 1970s. Within film studies and film music studies, popular music has been seen as 'a challenge to the traditional function of music in film' (Carey and Hannan 2003: 162). Popular music, when heard in film, does not only serve to underscore the image and narrative, but it also opens 'out the film to all the various real-world connotations, and cultural and historical associations that this music brings in tow' (Yacavone 2012: 31). Popular music exists beyond the screen. It has its own context, its own social relevance. Whether a soundtrack features a well-known song or draws on an existing popular music genre, the music heard on screen comes from a particular time and place. When heard within a film, these cultural associations echo within the narrative, drawing the 'real world' into the filmic world. For this reason, popular music tends to be sidelined in critical discussions of film. With a few exceptions, most work on film music, as Anahid Kassabian notes, 'has accepted the received notion that pre-existing songs do not play significant roles in the film that houses them' (Kassabian 2005: 5).

Outside of film studies – in areas such as popular music studies, (ethno-)musicology and cultural studies – much scholarly attention has been focused on exploring the meanings of popular music, assessing how it affects the way we see ourselves and others, and the world around us. As demonstrated by the contents of this book, popular music and place are mutually constitutive, constantly interweaving and influencing each other. Yet, when popular music is heard within film, itself a crucial medium through which we interpret the world around us, this research often remains unconsidered. The music is heard only within the context of the film itself.

Film music, whether it passes by 'unheard' or is actively listened to, is not a neutral medium in film. It has an influential power and carries codes with it that affect the audience's interpretation of what they are 'viewing' (Gorbman 2000: 234). This is particularly the case for popular music and its wealth of cultural associations that it already holds within it. The combination of cinema and popular music, with its strong connection to the 'real', makes film a powerful medium for the depiction of place.

Critical listening

Rather than restricting the discussion of popular music in cinema to the immediate context of the film and the world that it creates, this chapter encourages us to reflect on how the real-world relevance of popular music enters into a discussion of film. Rather like the traces of the real world that remain on film due to the camera's ability to document what is placed in front of it, music, and particularly popular music, draws the cultural, social and political contexts of that music into the world of the film, leaving echoes of the real resonating within the narrative.

This raises the question, what are the consequences of these representations? And what is our own ethical implication in those representations? Vivian Sobchack explores the ethics of fiction films that become 'charged with the real'. When an audience is moved 'from fictional into documentary consciousness', Sobchack argues that there is always an ethical charge (Sobchack 2004: 284). The viewer of the film is implicated; if the 'fictional space becomes charged with the real, the viewer is also so charged' (Sobchack, 2004: 284).

A specific consideration of place as seen on screen and mediated through music complicates these ideas of documentary consciousness on two levels. Due to the camera's documentary qualities, films constantly 'document' place and narrate ways of being within those places. When popular music is layered over these images that document place, this pre-existing music is also 'charged with the real'. It contains the sociopolitical histories of the people and places that made it, held within its beats, its melodies and its words.

Philippa Lovatt has developed the work of Sobchack to consider the auditory dimension of films about incarceration and punishment and suggests ways in which ethical spectatorship may require cinematic auditors to listen more critically. By choosing to fill the soundtracks of films with music that already exists and has its own cultural associations, filmmakers draw these musical narratives and associations into the filmic world. The spectators may consciously notice the music or it may filter through their subconscious and spark indirect associations, but either way the film becomes attached to the people, places and histories that swirl through the music. As with the move from fictional to documentary consciousness, there is also an ethical charge that comes with the use of music that tells of places and the people who live there.

When it takes hold, as Conley argues, 'a film encourages its public to think of the world in concert with its own articulation of space' (Conley 2007: 1). Cinema's combination of real and fictional worlds, the concrete and the symbolic, means that, as Iain Chambers notes, film 'offers a moment in which the seen is fused with the lived, the known with the possible, the here with the elsewhere' (Chambers 1986: 78). But, Chambers continues, it is the spectator who 'activates and feeds' the language of cinema (Chambers 1986: 78). This chapter thus builds on Lovatt's argument that the spectator needs to listen more critically, to suggest that this is true not just in films where the documentary consciousness is clearly engaged, but beyond that. In all films, we should think through the ways that music works with film to narrate place, how it creates worlds and communities that relate to the world we live in, tells stories that often seem to inform us about the people around us.

This chapter will now explore examples of this interweaving of popular music and place in films. Moving between Paris and Jamaica, and with a focus on hip hop and reggae, this chapter listens critically to the soundtracks of *La haine* (Hate, Mathieu Kassovitz, 1995) and *How Stella Got Her Groove Back* (Kevin Rodley Sullivan, 1998). In doing so, this chapter asks what narratives the music tells of the people and places shown in the films and explores how the music influences our interpretations of the filmic locations.

Parisian soundtracks

Paris has a strong presence within the global imaginary. From the nineteenth to twentieth centuries, Paris established itself as the capital of the literary world, and with the arrival of cinema Paris became one of the powerhouses of cinematic production as well. Paris' prominent position in literature and in film resulted in myriad depictions of the city. It is one of the most frequently seen places on cinema screens. The visual qualities of this iconic city are famous: Hausmann's wide boulevards and uniform yellow-tinge of the limestone architecture; the Eiffel Tower and the Sacré-Coeur dominating the skyline; the wide Seine river with its bookseller stalls and ornate bridges. The 'city of light' is romanticized through the representations of it in films as it is in other media, such as tourist photographs, travel agents or novels. Woody Allen's film *Midnight in Paris* (2011) is one such example. In this film, Paris' contemporary boulevards, bars and bistros are the backdrop for a recreation of the 'golden age' of the city in the 1920s. The music used in *Midnight in Paris* both recalls this era and coats the city in a warm glow of nostalgia. The soundtrack features musicians and musical genres that are famously connected to the city: the slow, sliding, lollop of Sidney Bechet's clarinet-playing, the French-inflected exoticism of Josephine Baker's 'La conga Blicoti', and modern versions of the bouncing jazz swing made famous by Django Reinhardt the Hot Club in Paris.

While strongly romanticized, Allen's cinematic recreation of Paris feels like a familiar depiction of the city. And this version of Paris is both representative and misleading. While the iconic city exists, filled with monuments, brasseries and tourists, beyond the ring road that circles the city, Paris is strikingly different. Paris is a city with a stark divide between its centre and its suburbs. In his study on the Parisian suburbs, the French historian Tyler Stovall says that 'in few of the world's great cities is the contrast between urb and suburb so dramatic as in Paris' (Stovall 1990: 1). As Kristin Ross notes, 'Paris *intramuros*, people mostly by white upper class and middle classes, became in [the 1960s] what we now know it to be: a power site at the centre of an archipelago of *banlieues* inhabited by working class people, a large percentage of them immigrants. The centre of the city, so familiar to the big screen, is a hub of power. Ringing the edges of the city are the less familiar *banlieues*' (Ross 1996: 151–152). The *banlieues* are the suburbs of Paris that have become associated with the high-rise housing estates (*cités*). Positioned on the periphery of the city, these estates house isolated communities of diverse ethnicities and have a high number of low-income households, high unemployment and limited opportunities.

In spite of the fact that a significant proportion of the Parisian population lives in the *banlieues*, these areas are rarely depicted. In 1990, Stovall noted that the French suburbs 'have often remained beyond the boundaries of popular imagination' (Stovall 1990: 1). What little is heard of the *banlieues* tends to be filtered through the media. From the 1980s onwards, news reports positioned the *banlieues* as a problem, and their inhabitants 'mostly as ethnic minority youths linked to crime and violence' (Tarr 2005: 6). Frequently, the ethnicities of people living in the *banlieues* became a focus, with the idea – often implied, sometimes openly asserted – that differences in religion and skin colour positioned the populations of the *banlieue* as something other than 'French'.

Resounding the city

La haine was one of the first of a series of films to be made in the *banlieues*, talking back to the existing representations both of the *banlieues* and of Paris more broadly, making these fraught suburban areas of Paris a central focus in cinema instead. Intensely focused on the depiction of space, the *banlieue* film is 'the first category of film since the western to be primarily defined by its geographical location' (Higbee 2007: 38). These films are so interwoven with the places they are set in that *La haine*, the emblematic film of this place-based genre, came to represent not only the genre of the *banlieue* film, but often the *banlieue* itself, aided by the on-location filming and the realist, documentary-style aesthetic that Kassovitz cultivated for the film. The Paris seen in this film is an entirely different place to the romanticized versions of the city; its popular music soundtrack, filled with hip hop and reggae, both reflects and asserts that. This section investigates the complex connections between music, place and cinema through a discussion of two key scenes of *La haine*.

The representation of the *banlieues* is a key feature of *La haine*, and it is during a scene that is one of the clearest visual depictions of the *banlieues* that the film is at its most interesting sonically. The scene begins as the camera surveys the housing estates from a window in one of the tower blocks. The audience watches children play in the courtyard below as the stark, concrete buildings encircle them and tower over them. Interspersed with shots of this view are images of a man as he sets up a turntable in another room of the block, turning his speakers outwards towards an open window so that the music plays out over the courtyard. As the audience is presented with images of the inhabitants of the *banlieues* and of the imposing architecture that contains them, on the soundtrack we hear an imitation of a siren and the words 'that's the sound of the police' and 'nique la police' (fuck the police). The man performing this mixing of sounds is Cut Killer, a famous French DJ of Moroccan heritage. Cut Killer cuts together tracks from various rap groups including KRS-One and two contemporary Parisian rap groups – Suprême NTM and Assassin – all known for their socially critical, politically engaged and often violent lyrics. Cut Killer manipulates the records to insist on the anger and force of the initial lyrics, drawing one record back on itself to repeat the word 'nique' (fuck). As this forceful rap resonates through the estate, Cut Killer adds another sample, layering the voice of a French cultural icon into the mix. Into this aggressive, outspoken critique of the authorities comes the voice of Edith Piaf singing 'non, rien de rien, non, je ne regrette rien' (no, nothing, I regret nothing).

This act of cutting, splicing and mixing of different tracks is fundamental to the history of hip hop. Hip hop takes a respectfully irreverent approach to sonic archives, both verbal and musical. Voices from famous speeches and sections of other songs are regularly sampled to create new tracks that place incongruous elements together, playing their individual histories and sounds against each other. In *La haine*, the act of sampling introduces disparate musics to form a sonic argument that debates the very notion of French identity. This is particularly important in the context of the immigrant communities as their rights to be considered as French are continually debated and undermined in the media. This filmic moment focuses visually on the hostile built environment of the *banlieues* and the people who are trapped there. Aurally, it is dominated by the fury of the rap groups as they critique institutional racism and violence. Interwoven with this anger is a sound that is iconic to French cultural history. The voice of Piaf serves as an aural contrast to the protagonists of the film. While one of the dominant sounds in this moment is a sample from the American group KRS-One, through its repositioning this track – 'Sounds of da police' – is made to speak anew. The palimpsestic layering of voices and sounds creates glimmers of musical history that are re-heard within the specific context of the banlieues. The rap by KRS-One here becomes a pointed critique at the French state's institutional treatment of marginalized citizens.

This is film music that is not meant to go 'unheard'. As it layers over the images of the *banlieues*, the soundtrack here narrates the 'other' Paris, voicing the multicultural reality of the inhabitants of the *banlieue* while also ensuring that the global echoes of the localized situation in the *banlieues* is heard. The protagonists of La haine are French, specifically Parisian, and even more precisely, they grew up in the *banlieues* on the periphery of this global city. Yet they are also linked through their families and histories to France's former colonies in West Africa and North Africa. The identities of these protagonists are both rooted to the local French space depicted in the film and far beyond these streets within the transnational space of postcolonial connections. The blending in the soundtrack of music of French, Algerian and black American origin itself imagines a musical heterotopia, identifying as part of the black Atlantic diaspora. Yet it is also a specifically local sound, rooted to the sociopolitical particularities of the *banlieues*. As such, this musical moment is demonstrative of the diasporic experience of both location and dislocation; 'diasporas are both dispersed and physically located, and as such imagined as belonging to various places simultaneously as bounded and as point of origin' (Román-Velázquez 2009: 104).

Connecting Kingston to Paris

While the film is deeply concerned with the very specific spaces of the *banlieues*, this localized focus is deliberately exploded through the film's soundtrack to insist on the global resonances contained within this local space. Alongside the film's abundant use of hip hop, Kassovitz also draws on reggae, a 'rebel music' rooted in Jamaica but exploring the politics of pan-Africanism. Throughout the credit sequence of La Haine, the audience hears Bob Marley's 'Burnin' and Lootin'. Unusually for a film soundtrack where music often features in short clips, the song plays from start to finish and, apart from the typed credits, this music is the only accompaniment to the visual elements of the credit sequence. Alongside Marley's music, the audience sees newsreel footage from various protests and riots in Paris from 1986 to 1994, including protests that evolved in the wake of the deaths of young men in police custody. These images – posters denouncing police violence; footage of a medic trying to resuscitate a man dying on the roadside; a line of riot police, their shields and helmets forming an impenetrable block; a close up of a police man's hand on a truncheon – are moments of Parisian history. Floating over them is the well-known voice of Bob Marley.

The music here transforms the scene of *La haine*, making them speak to more than the specific moments of protest in the *banlieues* of Paris. The footage of the riots repeatedly mirrors the images created through the song's lyrics: the 'uniforms of brutality' in Marley's song become a commentary on the riot police, their truncheons, helmets and shields; the images in *La haine* of riot shields blocking the dancing protesters, shutting down their expressions of anger, are reflected in Marley's cry asking what has to happen before 'we can talk to the boss'. The similarity between the events described in the lyrics and the images seen on screen draws the two elements of the film – the audio and the visual – together in dialogue. The voice from Kingston, Jamaica echoes through the *banlieues* of Paris, with narratives that resonate in both situations. The riots, rather than being reduced to localized issues as they are in media reports, are considered here within the ongoing history of demonstrations and protests against the racism that frequently underlies police brutality around the world.

The inclusion of 'Burnin' and 'Lootin' here draws the narrative of *La haine* into a far more extensive political discussion than might otherwise be suggested if only the visuals of the film are experienced. The violence and frustration of the protests in the film are framed within the global history of inequality. Roots and culture, the genre of reggae that this song is associated with, are a music of social commentary. It is 'grounded in the unresolved questions of race, class, colour, slavery, imperialism, colonialism and neo-colonialism' (Edwards 1998: 22). Marley's song speaks to the history of slavery and colonialism that links his homeland of Jamaica to Africa and to Europe. In this new context, Marley's music echoes with haunting recognizability as similar scenes play out across the world. Hearing this song over the footage of the riots that alerted the French media to the racialized 'fracture' at the heart of the French society highlights the film's exploration of the ongoing effects of France's colonial history (Blanchard et al. 2006).

The decision to soundtrack footage from the suburbs of Paris with reggae music from Kingston creates a powerful representation of (dis-)located space. In *La haine*, the music contributes towards a deconstructing of the grand narratives of Paris, and by extension France, and it deliberately places a transcultural, transnational filter over its depiction of the capital city of this former colonial power. The very local space of *banlieues* of France is seen and heard within the context of a broader discussion of French and indeed global histories of colonialism, slavery and their present-day evocations in the peripheries of the global cities in the powerful countries of the West.

Hidden histories

As George Lipsitz argues in *Footsteps in the Dark: The Hidden Histories of Music*, there is a 'long fetch' of social and political histories that lead up to the creation of a piece of popular music that often remains beneath the surface. Exhorting us to read popular music critically, Lipsitz argues that popular music can be an archive of past and present realities, and can reflect and shape important historical realities (Lipsitz 2007). The hidden histories of popular music are held within the sounds and the lyrics of the music; yet, this does not necessarily mean that they are heard. In *La haine*, Kassovitz's choice of music and the manipulation of the soundtrack within the context of his film increase the chance for the hidden histories held within the music to be given full expression. In the style of hip-hop sampling, familiar refrains of popular music – be it by KRS-One, Edith Piaf or Bob Marley – are recognized as the originals, but here, encountered alongside the images and narrative of the film, they are also heard anew.

This, of course, is not always the case; the presence of popular music on film does not necessarily create these moments where the music's own history interacts meaningfully with the narrative and setting of the film in which it is heard. The commercially successful film *How Stella Got Her Groove Back* (Sullivan 1998) also features the music of Bob Marley but in Sullivan's film, the music is entirely emptied of its critical, political focus. Filmed on location in Jamaica, *How Stella Got Her Groove Back* uses the country as a backdrop for an island paradise, a place for American tourists to come to recharge, and to be loved. The film's protagonist is an overworked mother from California who goes on holiday to Jamaica where she has a relationship with a Jamaican man much younger than herself. As she arrives in Jamaica, the 'real world' of her home life in the United States slips away, and she is transported into a land of relaxation and fun, surrounded by Jamaican staff waiting to serve her or men waiting to woo her.

The soundtrack at this moment is, predictably, Bob Marley – the global icon of reggae music and the voice most commonly associated with Jamaica. As the camera pans across the island idyll of blue seas, white sands and lush green mountains from its standpoint in the luxury hotel where the protagonist is staying, the distinctive opening guitar riff of 'Could you be Loved' by Bob Marley and the Wailers is heard. Like so much of reggae, this song has an upbeat feel but Marley's lyrics remain political. The opening lines – *Don't let them fool ya/Or even try to school ya! Oh, no!/We've got a mind of our own* –would serve well as a commentary on the questionable politics of the film's narrative. But in *How Stella Got Her Groove Back,* the music enters the film quietly, allowing it to kindle associations that this song – so renowned across the world – and the reggae genre more broadly have come to typify: easy-going, ganja-hazed, sun-soaked beach days. This is a trope familiar to the Caribbean. In his Nobel Prize lecture, the writer Derek Walcott notes:

> In serious cities, in grey, militant winter with its short afternoons, the days seem to pass by in buttoned overcoats [...]; one has the illusion of living in a Russian novel. So visitors to the Caribbean must feel that they are inhabiting a series of postcards. Both climates are shaped by what we have read about them.

As Derek Walcott suggests, perceptions of place are strongly influenced by 'what we have read about them'. There is a continuous, symbiotic overlapping and interaction between the constructed imagination of a place and the geographical location itself. The meaning that we invest in the places around us is not fixed. As Emile Durkheim tells us, 'the past does not inhere in places but is infused and brought out by groups of actors and sequences of events.... The interplay of language and memory solidifies into buildings, lawns, and monuments' (Durkheim, cited in Jordan 2003: 44). That is to say, people imbue sites with meaning. This approach to space underlines the importance of film which is able to narrate the meaning of place, framing it within the context of the film's narrative, the emotions of its characters and filtering it through the music on the soundtrack.

Each of the films discussed here had effects that were felt far beyond the cinema hall. Following the release of *La haine,* its commercial and critical success prompted widespread media reports discussing police brutality and governmental neglect of public housing in the city, while the serving Prime Minister at the time, Alain Juppé, commissioned a compulsory screening of the film for the cabinet (Johnston 1995). In contrast, the paradise depicted in *How Stella Got Her Groove Back* prompted the Jamaica Tourist Board to screen the film for travel agents in the United States, promoting Jamaica as a lover's getaway, while the success of the film initiated a trend of women travelling solo from the United States to Jamaica for a holiday with love and/or sex (Faul 1999).

Cinema is a powerful medium through which to represent place. Films have the ability to mix the imaginary with the real, to map out spaces that are familiar while altering them, taking concrete spaces and re-narrating them and reconstructing them. When used in film, popular music brings its history with it, and layers over the cinematic images, influencing the stories that we tell of them. These properties of popular music soundtracks introduce an ethical charge to the film and the viewer alike. As shown in the examples here, soundtracks can contribute towards complex, critical and socially aware depictions of place, or they can be used to suggest that there is nothing more to a place than the tourist's dream of perfect beaches, sunny weather and compliant populations waiting to serve and give pleasure to those who are able to visit.

References

Blanchard, P., Bancel, N. and Lemaire, S. (2006), *La fracture coloniale*, Paris: Editions La Découverte.

Bruno, Giuliana (2007), *Public Intimacy: Architecture and the Visual Arts*, Cambridge, MA: MIT Press.

Carey, M. and Hannan, M. (2003), 'Case Study 2: The Big Chill', in Ian Inglis (ed), *Popular Music and Film*, 162–77, New York: Columbia University Press.

Carpenter, C. and Silva, G. (2015) *Nightswimming: Discotheques from 1960s to the Present*. London: Bedford Press/AA Publications.

Chambers, I. (1986), *Popular Culture: The Metropolitan Experience*, London: Routledge.

Conley, T. (2007), *Cartographic Cinema*, Minneapolis: University of Minnesota Press.

Edwards, N. (1998), 'States of Emergency: Reggae Representations of the Jamaican Nation State', *Social and Economic Studies*, 47 (1): 21–32.

Faul, M. (1999), 'Real Life Imitates the Movies in Jamaica', *Los Angeles Times*, 17 January. Available online: https://www.latimes.com/archives/la-xpm-1999-jan-17-mn-64231-story.html. Accessed 05 July 2021.

Gorbman, C. (1987), *Unheard Melodies*, Bloomington: Indiana University Press.

Gorbman, C. (2000), 'Scoring the Indian', in G. Born and D. Hesmondhalgh (eds), *Western Music and Its Others*, 234–53, Berkeley: University of California Press.

Herzog, A. (2009), *Dreams of Difference, Songs of the Same*, Minneapolis: University of Minnesota Press.

Higbee, W. (2007), 'Re-Presenting the Urban Periphery', *Cinéaste*, 33 (1): 38–43.

Johnston, S. (1995), 'Why the Prime Minister Had to See *La Haine*', *The Independent*, 18 October. Available online: https://www.independent.co.uk/arts-entertainment/why-the-prime-minister-had-to-see-la-haine-1578297.html. Accessed 5 July 2021.

Jordan, J. (2003), 'Collective Memory and Locality in Global Cities', in L. Krause and P. Petro (eds), *Global Cities: Cinema, Architecture, and Urbanism in a Digital Age*, 31–48, New Brunswick: Rutgers University Press.

Kassabian, A. (2005), 'Foreword', in M. Caley and S. Lannin (eds), *Pop Fiction: The Song in Cinema*, 5–8, Bristol: Intellect Books.

Lipsitz, G. (2007), *Footsteps in the Dark: The Hidden Histories of Popular Music*, Minneapolis: University of Minnesota Press.

Perez, G. (2000), *The Material Ghost: Films and Their Medium*, Baltimore: Johns Hopkins University Press.

Román-Velázquez, P. (2009). 'Latin Americans in London and the Dynamics of Diasporic Identities', in M. Keown, D. Murphy, and J. Procter (eds), *Comparing Post-colonial Diasporas*, 104–24. London: Palgrave Macmillian.

Ross, K (1996) *Fast Cars, Clean Bodies: Decolonization and the Reordering of French Culture*, Cambridge: MIT Press.

Siciliano, A. (2007), '*La Haine*: Framing the "Urban Outcasts"', *ACME*, 6 (2): 211–30.

Sobchack, V. (2004), *Carnal Thoughts: Embodiment and Moving Image Culture*, Berkeley: University of California Press.

Stovall, T. (1990), *The Rise of the Paris Red Belt*, Berkeley: University of California Press.

Tarr, C. (2005), *Reframing Difference: Beur and Banlieue Filmmaking in France*, Manchester: Manchester University Press.
Walcott, D. (1992), 'Banquet Speech', *NobelPrize.org*. Available online: https://www.nobelprize.org/prizes/literature/1992/walcott/facts/ (accessed 5 July 2021).
Yacavone, D. (2012), 'Spaces, Gaps and Levels: From the Diegetic to the Aesthetic in Film Theory', *MSMI*, 6 (1): 21–37.

Filmography

Films

Good Morning Vietnam (1988), [Film] Dir. Barry Levinson, USA: Touchstone Pictures Silver Screen Partners III.
How Stella Got Her Groove Back (1998), [Film] Dir. Kevin Rodley Sullivan, USA: 20th Century Fox.
La haine (Hate) (1995), [Film] Dir. Mathieu Kassovitz, France: Canal+.
Midnight in Paris (2011), [Film] Dir. Woody Allen, USA/Spain: Gravier Productions/Mediapro/Televisió de Catalunya (TV3)/Versátil Cinema.
Notting Hill (1999), [Film] Dir. Roger Michell, UK/USA: PolyGram Filmed Entertainment/Working Title Films.
Taxi Driver (1976), [Film] Dir. Martin Scorsese, USA: Bill/Phillips Productions / Italo/Judeo Productions / Columbia Pictures.
The Good, The Bad and The Ugly (1966), [Film] Dir. Sergio Leone, Italy/USA: Produzioni Europee Associate/United Artists.
Whale Rider (2002) [Film] Dir. Niki Caro, New Zealand/Germany: South Pacific Pictures/ApolloMedia/Pandora Film/New Zealand Film Production Fund/New Zealand Film Commission/NZ On Air/Filmstiftung Nordrhein-Westfalen.

Discography

Brian Eno (1978), *Ambient 1: Music for Airports*, Polydor AMB 001, 2310647.

Index

Abbey Road studios 206, 208, 209
Acoustic Environments in Change (AEC) 85, 86
Adelaide 69, 193
Adele 153–5
Adhitya, S. 24
'Adventures in Sound' 105
advertising 119, 123–5, 130, 140, 229
AEG Live 160
aesthetic awakening 260
aesthetic cosmopolitanism 334
affordance 230, 233, 234
African National Congress 271
Agnew, J. 206, 207
Åkesson, J. 309
Albarn, D. 259, 267 n.6
alcohol 72, 73, 77, 107, 140, 142, 143, 145, 274
allatonceness 144
Allen, A. 85
Allen, W. 373
Allihoopa 220
all-night dancing 142, 143
All Things Must Pass (2015) 130
amateurism 221, 244
Ambient 1: Music for Airports (Eno) 15
American Forces Network (AFN) radio 123
Anderson, B. 10, 263–7, 301, 307
Anderson, V. 348
Anglo-American hegemony 32
Angus, J. 233
Aotearoa/New Zealand 11, 14
Appadurai, A. 63
Appert, C. M. 63
Applegate, C. 301
armchair anthropology 59
Armour, Z. 53
Arms Length External Organisations (ALEOs) 186
Around the World in 80 Record Stores (Barnes) 108, 109

arrythmia 22, 27
Aryan music 307, 308
Assassin 292, 294, 297, 375
asymmetry 33, 40 n.2
A Tribe Called Red 14
audience 248–50
audiotopias 212
Augé, M. 15, 206, 207
aura 11, 89, 90, 92, 208, 213
Austin 68, 70
authenticity 14, 37, 60, 108, 125, 131, 155, 210, 231, 235, 241, 248, 250, 293, 294, 306, 309, 332, 342, 343, 345–7, 360
avant-garde 9, 145, 262
Avid Technology 219, 220

Baade, C. 123
bailes de corredor 284–5
Bailey, P. 103
Baker, S. 193–5, 333
Bakhtin, M. 361
Bambaataa, A. 292
banal nationalism 302, 303, 308
banlieue identity 297
banlieues 3, 272, 291–8, 299 n.1, 321, 322, 374–7
Barthes, R. 24
Basso, K. H. 63
Bates, E. 207, 208, 213
Baulch, E. 34–5
BBC 118, 122–6
Beatles, The 10, 153, 154, 157, 178, 201 n.4, 263, 302, 305, 332, 333, 335, 342–6, 348, 349
Beat music 305
Beatnik 218
Beaulieu Jazz Festival 158
Becker, C. 218
Becker, H. S. 49
bedroom producer 220–1

bedroom studio 191–2
    do-it-yourself (DIY) 199–200
    Girls and Subcultures 192–5
    recording 195–6
    women and 197–9
Beer, D. 170–2
Behr, A. 246–7
Bell, T. 13, 345
Benjamin, L. 118
Benjamin, W. 84
Bennett, A. 2, 9, 38, 47, 49–52, 182, 208, 242, 246, 265, 302, 331, 334, 335, 347
Bennett, N. 119, 120
Berkers, P. 201 n.3
Berland, J. 118–19, 122, 125
Berlin 11, 68, 75, 140, 141, 147, 166, 182, 307
Besse, J. 21
Best, S. 267 n.10
Biddle, I. 306
Bilby, K. 347
Billboard, The (1944) 134
Billig, M. 302, 308
Bird, S. 50
Blackburn, T. 124, 125
Black Noise (Rose) 292
Blair, T. 302
Blues Dance 319
Blue Velvet (Lynch) 259
bohemia 8–9, 76, 260–3, 321
Bohemian Rhapsody (2018) 208
Bolderman, L. 3, 10, 344–7, 350, 351
Bondi, L. 52
boombox 47, 165, 166
Botta, G. 141
Boulin, J.-Y. 26
Bourdieu, P. 3, 8, 182, 195, 247, 248, 251 n.3, 258, 262, 263
boutique events 359
Bowery Ballroom 249
Bowie, D. 260, 262
Bracewell, M. 257
Braidotti, R. 266
Bram, T. 218
Brandellero, A. 331
Brand, G. 125
Brisbane 248
British Broadcasting Corporation 121
broadcast radio 117–18, 120, 121, 126

Brøvig-Hanssen, R. 232, 235
Brown, T. S. 308
Bruce, K. 179
Bruno, G. 370
Buddha of Suburbia, The (Kureishi) 262
Bull, M. 16, 50, 167–72, 265
Burgess, R. J. 221
Burtin, W. 134
Buttimer, A. 24
Buxton, D. 106, 107
Byrne, D. 156, 221

Cahn, S. 102, 112
caillera 295
Camilleri, L. 236
Canadian Broadcasting Corporation (CBC) 117, 119, 120
Cancon system 120, 121
Canterbury Sound 49, 50, 335
Carey, J. 257
Carney, G. 12
Carson, E. 225
Cashman, D. 350
Cavern Club 53, 54 n.2, 153–5
Cavicchi, D. 346
censorship 132, 305, 307, 323
center-periphery model 32
Central Business District (CBD) 68, 72, 73
Centre for Contemporary Cultural Studies (CCCS) 48, 195
Certeau, M. de 24, 25, 84
Chambers, I. 372–3
Chemikal Underground 183
Cheren, M. 141, 146
China 3, 31, 34–8, 119, 306, 321–4
China-Central Television (CCTV) 323
Chua, B. H. 35, 36
cinema 369–70, 378
    critical listening 372–3
    film and listening 370–2
    hidden histories 377–8
    Kingston 376–7
    Paris soundtracks 373–4
    resounding 374–6
circulation 2, 21, 22, 26–8, 334
civil rights movements 140, 144
Clarke, E. F. 233
Clawson, M. A. 197

Index

clubbing 28, 142, 144
Clubbing (Malbon) 142
club culture 142, 147
Club Cultures (Thornton and Rief) 142
club nights 139, 143–5, 147, 153, 335
Clubs Virtual World Tour (DJ Mag) 147
Cohen, S. 13, 61, 246, 267 n.7, 305, 332, 333, 346, 347, 350
collective biography 88
Come Fly With Me 2, 102–9, 111–13
concrete modalities 22
Conigrave, K. 78 n.1
Conley, T. 370, 372
Connell, J. 342–5, 347, 349, 350
Connerton, P. 24
connotation 33, 229, 241, 283, 371
consumption 9, 15, 46, 51, 67–9, 73, 102, 103, 107, 129, 133, 136, 142, 170–2, 192, 193, 199, 241, 245, 249, 274, 277, 305, 348, 361, 362
Cooley, T. 58
Coplan, D. B. 272–3
Corbett, J. 134
COVID-19 1, 51, 76, 130, 147, 160, 198, 220, 221, 225
creative class (Florida) 76, 264
Creative Scotland 185
creative syncretism 273
Crosby, B. 8, 107, 108, 133
cross-fertilization 9
crowdsourcing 217, 220, 222, 223, 225, 226
cultural
    capital 68, 77, 181, 249, 259, 261
    identity 9, 15, 303, 321
    imperialism 14, 32, 36
    memory 52–3
    policy 67, 71, 298, 304, 305, 322
    spaces 10, 26, 68, 139, 182, 193, 199
    value 11, 69–72, 169, 210, 246, 331
culturology approach 61
Cunningham, M. 231
Cut Killer 375
cyclic places 362–4

Dakar women 27
Dancecult 142
dance/dancing 49, 50, 92, 139, 140–4, 194, 231, 276, 282, 286, 317, 318, 376
    clubs 129, 139, 140, 143

culture 142, 147
    hall 139, 140, 155–7, 184
Danielsen, A. 232
Dant, T. 169
Dark Side of the Moon (Floyd) 104
datafication 165, 166, 170–2
Davies, H. 193–5
Dawe, K. 59–60
Daynes, S. 11
Death Metal band 306
De Beukelaer, C. 67
Debord, G. 258
de Jong, A. 26
De Kloet, J. 34, 306
DeLanda, M. 38
Deleuze, G. 266
Deloitte Access Economics 73
de-materialisation 12
DeNora, T. 61–2, 64, 194, 303
Department of Adult and Continuing Education (DACE) 180
desired social experience 248
Detroit 112, 179, 206, 247, 341–2
Devine, K. 11–12
Diamond, N. 51
diaspora 37, 134, 315, 316, 318, 320–2, 324 n.1, 375
diasporic belonging 13
differential spaces 9
Digital Audio Workstation (DAW) 206–9, 218–20, 223, 225, 226
digital recording 135, 196, 199, 200
digital sublime 16
Discman 167
disco concept 141–2, 146
discotheque 139–42, 145, 155
DIY (do-it-yourself) practice 47, 192, 196, 199–200, 249, 333, 335, 336
DJs 2, 47, 123–5, 139, 141, 142, 144–7, 153, 285
Dockwray, R. 232
Dodge, M. 171
Dolby, T. 218
Dotson-Renta, L. 297
Dovchin, S. 39
Doyle, P. 8, 104, 231, 266
Drew, R. 132
Dublin Arena 157
Duffett, M. 334

Duffy, M. 349, 350, 359
Du Gay, P. 129
Dunbar-Hall, P. 347
Dunedin Sound 11
Durkheim, E. 378
Dyer, R. 106

Eades, J. 74
East Asia 2, 31, 35–8, 40 n.4
ecoute resituée 86
ecoute située 86
Edensor, T. 302
electric dance music (EDM) 196, 258, 333, 345, 349
electroacoustic music 236
electronic music 23, 37, 49, 136, 141–3, 146, 147, 196, 199, 345
electrosonic aesthetics 212
elevator music 15
El Rincon 317, 318, 324 n.2
emotional geography 52–3
Eno, B. 15, 212, 266
Environment Protection Authority (EPA) 246
ethnic pasticcio 103, 105–6, 108
Ethnography and Popular Music Studies (Cohen) 61
ethnomusicology 2, 26, 27, 57–9, 64, 64 n.1, 84, 316
   as methodology 59–60
   and place 62–4
   and popular music 60–2
Ethnomusicology 58, 61
eurythmia 22, 27
'everyday' 244–5
Exploding Plastic Inevitable (EPI) 139, 144

Facebook 90, 131, 221, 335
Fagyal, Zs. 296
Fairley, J. 32
Falassi, A. 358
favelas 281–7, 287 n.7
Feldman-Barrett, C. 52
Feld, S. 63
Felski, R. 244
Ferguson, K. 169–70
festival concert 22–3
festivalization 360
festivals 357
   category 358–9
   cyclic places 362–4
   definition 357–8
   research 359–60
   space and place 361–2
Fikentscher, K. 141
film 369–78
filmic site-seeing 370
Finland 84, 87
Finlay, J. 136
Finnegan, R. 13, 246
Finnish soundscape 2, 83–5, 87, 88
First World War 9, 121, 157, 307
Fisher, M. 263
Fiummi, F. 144
Five Village Soundscapes (FVS) 85
flash mobs 50
flat ontology 38, 40
flexibility 10, 76, 117, 157, 196, 219, 276
Flip 217
Florida, R. 75, 76, 178, 264
Florin, C. 93
Floyd, P. 104
Footsteps in the Dark: The Hidden Histories of Music (Lipsitz) 377–8
Forman, M. 13
Fornas, J. 25
forró 281, 287 n.3
Foucault, M. 362, 363
Fouquet, T. 27
France 3, 291–5, 297, 321, 377
Franklin, A. 341
Franz Ferdinand 179, 183
free festival movement 362
French
   hip-hop 35, 292, 293, 295, 321
   identity 291, 297, 375
   rap 291–9
Friedan, B. 199
Frith, S. 32, 179, 201 n.1, 248, 258–62
functional staging 231
funk 3, 281–3, 287, 287 n.9
   bailes 282–6, 288 n.9, 288 n.15
   proibidão 283–6, 288 n.20, 288 n.22
   putaria 283–6
Futrell, R. 308

Gabriel, P. 211
Gaillard, S. 133
Gallan, B. 245, 246, 249

Garber, J. 50, 192–5, 201 n.1
Garden Festival 1988 178
Geddings, J. 158
Geertz, C. 302–3
Genders 2017 262
Gendron, B. 8–9
genre 1, 3, 8, 11, 13, 14, 26, 34–7, 40 n.6, 45, 49, 57, 278, 293, 295, 297, 302, 305, 308, 309, 320, 321, 341, 350, 374
geocultural market 35
German Democratic Republic (GDR) 305
Germany 76
Germes, M. 298
gesture 22, 156, 229
Getz, D. 359, 360
'ghettocentric' subject position 295
Ghio, B. 294, 295, 297–8
Gibson, C. 249, 342–5, 347, 349, 350
Gibson, J. J. 233
Giddens, A. 105
Gieryn, T. F. 206
Gilroy, P. 134
Girls and Subcultures (McRobbie and Garber) 192–5
Glasgow 2, 75, 122, 177–86, 187 n.3, 272
Glasgow City Council 185
Glasgow Kelvin 178
Glenn Gould studio 208
globalization 2, 13, 31, 32–4, 39, 61, 105, 112, 113, 292, 305, 315, 316, 320, 322
Global Minstrels (Wald) 34
global music 2, 3, 27, 31–7, 39, 75, 306–7, 320–4
  and local 31–7
Global Noise (Mitchell) 34
glocal/hybrid 35
glocalization 34, 319
glocal rap 34
Gold Coast (Australia) 52, 53
Goodman, S. 26
Goodwin, A. 107
Gorbman, C. 370
gospel music 278, 287
Gqom 276–7
Gqulu, B. 277
Grand Ole Opry 156
Grateful Dead 157
Great Music City, The (Baker) 75

Green, B. 51, 52
Greene, P. D. 230
Greenlaw, L. 135
Grenswerk 161
Groening, S. 16
Groenningsaeter, A. K. 195–6
Grossberg, L. 13
Gumper, A. 159
Gwiazdzinski, L. 21, 22

Haçienda FAC 51, The 145–7
Hairspray (Waters) 132
Hall, E. T. 235
hallmark 57, 64, 358
Hall, S. 9, 302
Hammersmith Palais 157
Hammou, K. 298
Handel, G. F. 105
Hanley, B. 158
Hardwick, E. 135
Harper, A. 135
Harris, A. 259
Hayden, D. 68
Headspace 218
hearing space 233–4
Hecker, T. 208
Heckle, B. 153
Heineken Music Hall 161
Heller, S. 134
Henderson, S. 120–1
Hendrix, J. 158
Hennion, A. 9
Henriques, J. 140
Henshall, W. 218
heritage 331–4
  ghetto 295
  losing 336–7
  and placelessness 334–5
  popular music 305, 332, 334–6
Hesmondhalgh, D. 9–10, 32, 35, 244, 306
heterotopia of deviance 362
Hi-Fi-Fo-Fum (1959) 134
hi-fi music 8, 102–7, 110, 112, 200, 201 n.2
high-fidelity 2, 102–4, 110
High Fidelity (1995) 131
High Fidelity (2020) 131
Highly Flavoured (Gqulu) 277
Highmore, B. 23–4

hip-hop 3, 13, 14, 34, 35, 191, 200, 292–5, 320–4, 346
    Chinese 322, 323
    French 35, 292, 293, 295, 321
H.I.P-H.O.P. 292
hobbyism 244
Hodge, R. 140
Holland, M. 11
Holt, F. 248–9
Holtorf, C. 336
Homan, S. 304
Homecoming (2019) 160
home recording 196, 197
'Home Sweet Home' (1823) 102, 103, 108, 112
homogenization 34, 160
homogenous-hybrid 35
Hook, P. 145
Hornby, N. 131
Horning, S. 209
Hosokawa, S. 14, 166–7
Hosono, H. 14
Howard, D. M. 233
How Stella Got Her Groove Back (Sullivan) 377, 378
Hubbert, J. 132–3
Hub, The 218
Hudson, R. 264
Huq, R. 260, 261, 267 n.1
Hutchison, D. 119
hybridity 2, 14, 27, 34, 36, 63, 170, 171, 309, 316, 320, 321, 324

IAM 297, 321
IFPI/Music Canada 75
iKasi style 272, 274, 275, 277, 278
IKASI: The Moral Ecology of the South African Township (Swartz) 273
i'khothane 277
illusion 8, 168, 229, 231, 370, 378
Imagined Communities (Anderson) 10, 301
imagined community 10, 294, 295, 302, 304, 316
Imagine Sydney: Play 73
Independent Local Radio (ILR) 122, 126
Innes, H. 118
Inside Clubbing (Jackson) 142
internal rhythms 22
International Federation of the Phonographic Industry (IFPI) 31, 75

Internet 49, 50, 200, 217–20, 223, 226, 241, 316, 335, 336, 360
In Township Tonight! Three Centuries of South African Black City Music and Theatre (Coplan) 272–3
invariant property 229, 230, 233–5
iPod 16, 25, 50, 165–72, 265
isicathamiya 278
'It's A Small World After All' (Disneyland) 106
Iwabuchi, K. 35, 36

Jackson, P. 142
jazz 8, 13, 49, 63, 77, 92, 109, 111, 133, 135, 143, 155, 157, 158, 185, 241, 263, 291, 373
jingle 125, 126
Johansson, O. 13, 345
Johnson, J. P. 134
Jones, D. 153
Joshua Tree, The 159

Kaeppler, A. L. 347
Kahn-Harris, K. 37, 49, 306–7
KaMajola, A. 278
Karjalainen, P. T. 87
Kärki, K. 160
Kassabian, A. 15–16, 104, 371
Kassovitz, M. 374, 376, 377
Keightley, K. 2, 8, 201 n.2
Keith, M. 46
Kellner, D. 267 n.10
Kelly, B. 145
Kenney, W. 132
Kielman, A. 38
King, R. 135
Kingston 68, 75, 376–7
King Tuts Wah Wah Hut 184
Kipling, R. 109
Kirbort, K. 14
Kirby, P. R. 206, 210
Kitchen Writing Studio, The 210
Kitchin, R. 171
Kittler, F. 133
Kiwan, N. 316
Knights, V. 306
KO 275
Kolioulis, A. 141, 146
Koskoff, E. 58
K-pop 31, 36–7, 40 n.3, 70

Kress, G. 140
Kronenburg, R. 243, 245, 247
KRS-One 375, 377
Krüger, S. 344, 348, 350–1
Kun, J. 212
Kureishi, H. 262
kwaito 3, 273–8

LaBelle, B. 140
Lacasse, S. 231
La haine 373–8
Laing, D. 32, 35, 49
landscape 236
Lang, M. 158
language 39, 295–7, 321
    Chinese 323
    English 39, 57, 62, 64, 122, 123, 306
    Finnish 83
Larsen, J. 349
Larsson, N. 67
Lashua, B. D. 208
Last Shop Standing (2014) 130
Latta, C. 218
Laura Oldfield Ford 265
Lazaretto 210
League of Automatic Music Composers, The 218
Léfebvre, H. 2, 7, 9, 22, 24, 25, 27, 168, 207, 212–13
Leskelä-Kärki, M. 87
Lewin, O. 347
Leydon, R. 107
Lil Nas X 26–7
Lincoln, S. 50, 51, 193–4
Lindner, R. 11
Ling, J. 84
Lipshutz, J. 26
Lipsitz, G. 377
liquor licensing policies 72
live gig 72, 153–5, 158, 160–2, 241–4, 250–1
    audience 248–50
    city 247
    'everyday' 244–5
    musicians 247–8
    venues 245–7
live music 153–62, 241
    ecology 242, 246–8, 250
    experience 71, 242, 243, 250
    performance 22, 155, 161

    venues 52, 73, 77, 78 n.2, 147, 160, 161, 241, 243, 245–7, 250, 251 n.1, 251 n.2
liveness 241, 349
Liverpool 3, 10, 53, 68, 122, 153, 154, 179, 181, 305, 316–18, 324 n.2, 332, 333, 342, 344–6
Lizardi, R. 345
Loben, C. 142
Löbert, A. 334
local 2, 3, 32–40, 47, 49, 53, 64, 72–4, 246, 248, 306
    gig 181, 241, 242, 244–50
    live music 249, 250
lockout laws 72, 73, 77
lo-fi sound 2, 197, 199, 200
Long, P. 335, 336
long-play (LP) 2, 102–5, 107–9, 111, 113, 283
Long, R. 144–5
Lopes, P. 8
Lovatt, P. 372, 373
Lowndes, S. 178, 183
Lynch, D. 259

McCartney, P. 153, 154, 201 n.4, 210
McIntyre, P. 208
McLuhan, M. 144, 169
McRobbie, A. 9, 50, 192–5, 201 n.1
Madchester dance scene 242
Ma, E. K. -W 38
Magnavox 229, 234
Malbon, B. 142
Mancuso, D. 144
Manfred Mann, 'Semi-Detached, Suburban Mr. James' 259–61
manufactured pop 36
Mao Zedong 323
MAPL 120
mapping 9, 24, 45, 53, 69, 72, 104, 180, 182, 183, 186, 258, 297, 370
Marc Martinez, I. 293
Marie, M. 370
Marine Broadcasting Offences Act 124
Marley, B. 376–8
Marti, P. 294
Marx, K. 170
maskanda 278
Massey, D. 37, 46, 363
Mastering of a Music City 75
Matcham, F. 156

Material Ghost, The (Perez) 370
Maughan, T. 199
May, B. 110, 111
MC Solaar 293, 321
meaningful location 206
mediality 133
mediation 9, 102, 121, 136, 168, 169, 230, 235, 316, 360, 363, 364, 369
Medusa 52
Meinhof, U. 316
memory 45, 50–4, 63, 118, 135, 136, 250, 305, 316, 319, 320, 333, 335, 336, 378
Memphis Tourism 342
Mendivil, J. 15
Metal Box 263
Metcalf, P. 62, 64
microphone 8, 93, 107, 207
Middleton, R. 60, 106, 229, 267 n.3
MIDI 218
Midnight in Paris (Allen) 373
migrant experience 316–18
migration 27, 37, 106, 200, 315, 316, 318–21
Miller, K. 58–9
Miller, S. 158
MiniDiscman 167
Ministère A.M.E.R 292–4, 297, 321
Minyo Crusaders 14
mirror ball 143, 144, 184
Mitchell, T. 14, 33, 34
mobile listening cultures 16, 165–6, 172–3
    in digital age 167–9
    history of 166–7
    integration of 170–2
    iPod 169–70
mobile privatization 16
mobile production 205, 207
mobility 15, 16, 38, 106, 108, 165–7, 219, 260, 261, 273, 296, 315, 342, 348, 351
Moller, M. 218
Monet 236, 237
montagem 287
Moore, A. 232, 236, 237
Mori, Y. 38
morphological space 236
Mosco, V. 16, 67
Motown Museum 341
moulding soundscape 85–6
Mountain Studios 205, 211

Moylan, W. 231, 232, 237
MP3 130, 133, 167, 168, 172, 351
Mückenberger, U. 26
music
    analogy 24–5
    diffusion of 166–7
    festival 3, 22–3, 158, 283, 322, 345, 357–64
    industry 32
    measure of 25
    megastore 132–3
    and mobility 16
    and nation 301
    and non-place 15–16
    and place 12–15, 45, 51, 53
    producers 212, 219–21, 223, 225, 226
    production 2, 68, 119, 121, 141, 146, 199, 208, 212, 217, 219–23, 225, 226, 264, 307, 308
    significance 45, 50, 52, 53
    and space 7–12
    and transnationalism 316–17
    ubiquity of 15
Musical Cities (Adhitya) 24
musical topophilia 347
musical wallpaper 104
Music and Tourism: On the Road Again (Gibson and Connell) 344
musica sertaneja 287 n.5
Music Canada 75
music city 75–7, 332, 341
Music Hall and Variety 156
music hub 70
musicians 247–8
Music Industry Consultants (MICs) 180
Music in Everyday Life (DeNora) 61
music itself 24, 61, 125, 264, 307
MusicMafia 62
Music of Black Origins (MOBO) 186
music radio 117, 126
    Canada 117–21
    United Kingdom 121–6
Music Scenes: Local, Translocal, and Virtual (Peterson and Bennett) 38
Musicultura Group 281, 287 n.2
Music Venues Trust 71
muzak 15, 16, 27
mythmaking 250

national identity 117, 120, 297, 302, 304–7, 309, 315, 323
nationalism 3, 36, 61, 302, 303, 307–9, 324
Nationalism-with-a-big-N 307–9
national radio 118–20, 305
naturally occurring data 84
Nazi Rock 308
Neely, T. D. 344, 348, 350
Négrier, E. 360
Negus, K. 31, 32, 129, 306
Nelson, P. 207, 212, 213
neoliberal economics 52
neoliberalism 140, 265
Net Jam system 218
Nettl, B. 64 n.1
networked music 218–20
Network Studio 217
New Deal for Musicians 180
Newport Jazz Festival 158
New York City 68, 69, 72–4, 77
nightclub 52, 63, 111, 139–47, 161, 231
Night Czar 73, 74, 160
night mayor 73–4
Night Out Music for Stay-at-Homes (Various Artists) 104
non-place 7, 15–16, 104, 206–7, 211, 212, 214, 258
non-standard language (NSL) 296, 297
non-Western music 58, 306
nostalgia 130, 153, 154, 210, 232, 345, 347, 373
NSW Legislative Council 73

O2 ABC and Academy 184
O'Connor, A. 178, 182
O'Grady, A. 155
Ohm Studio 217, 219–21
Oisans, J. 86
Okinawa Sound 14
OLC 324 n.2
Old Town Road (Lil Nas X) 26–7
Onion, The (2003) 131
On the Road to Mandalay (Kipling) 109–11
opaque mediation 235
O'Rahilly, R. 125
Original Dixieland Jazz Band 157
Osmond, D. 192
Other Music (2020) 130

Padgham 210
Paphides, P. 133
Paradise Garage 141, 145
Paris soundtracks 373–4
Pecqueux, A. 298
Perez, G. 370
Perfect Tense (Bracewell) 257
Performing Rights Organisations (PRO) 224
Peterson, R. A. 37, 38, 49, 182, 230
Philips Studios 209
Pieterse, J. N. 34
Pile, S. 46
pilgrimage 153, 342, 346, 347
Pink Noises: Women on Electronic Music and Sound (Rodgers) 198
place 37, 52, 243
    cyclic 362–4
    ethnomusicology and 62–4
    fetishization 347
    music and 12–15, 45, 51, 53, 361–2
    popular music and 57, 58, 64, 242, 243, 250, 251, 305, 371, 373
    social construct 46–7
    space and 2, 46–8, 53, 361–2
placelessness 200, 334–5
place-making 68, 69, 200
Platform Chang-dong 61 70
Playing Along: Digital Games, YouTube, and Virtual Performance (Miller) 59
policy 2, 3, 67, 72, 119–21, 140, 182, 185–6, 264, 304–5, 322
political economy 27, 67–9, 131, 132
    and cultural value 69–72
    night mayor 73–4
    policies and regulation 72–3
    popular music 75–6
    problems 71
    of urban music 77
politics 3, 10, 13, 14, 25, 181, 282, 293, 298, 306, 307, 350, 378
polyrhythmia 22, 24, 25, 27
Pop Group 263
Pop Montreal 21–3, 28
pop music 34, 122, 125, 126, 157, 197, 306, 322
Pop-rock Music: Aesthetic Cosmopolitanism in Late Modernity (Regev) 39, 334

Index

popular music 1–4, 13, 77, 122, 243, 331–7, 348, 371–4, 377, 378
  East Asian 36
  ethnomusicology and 60–2
  globalization in 32–3
  live 155, 156
  local and global 306–7
  narratives of the nation 309
  and nationalism 307–9
  and nationhood 302–4
  and nation-state policy 304–5
  and place 57, 58, 64, 242, 243, 250, 251, 305, 371, 373
  political ecology of 11–12
  promotional economy of 75–6
  and suburbs 257
  transnational 320–4
Porcello, T. 230
postering 47
post-subcultural (Bennett) 48
Potter, P. 301
Pradel, B. 23
Prentice, R. 348
Prior, N. 172, 266
Production of Space, The (Lefebvre) 7
professional recording 195, 206
project management challenges 223–4
project studio 205, 208, 210, 211
Propellerhead Software 220
Pruett, D. B. 62
public and private space 50–1
pub rock 246

Quayson, A. 25
Queen: The Studio Experience 205
Quinn, B. 348

Rabelais, F. 361
Radio Caroline 123–5
Radio London 123, 124
Radio Luxembourg 122–4
radio music box 118
Radio Normandy 122, 123
Radio, Space and Industrial Time (Berland) 118
Rajanti, T. 84
rap music 3, 34, 277, 291–8, 320–2, 375
Rap of China, The 322
rappers 291–8, 309, 321

rebel music 376
recorded space 229–30, 236–7
  hearing 233–4
  history of 230–1
  sonic cartoons 234–6
  sound box 232–3
  staging 231–2
recording studios 3, 205–7, 214
  bedroom 196, 197, 200
  defined 205, 206
  functions of 207–9
  identities of 212–13
  technology 209–12
  traditional 197, 206, 207, 210, 211
  virtual spaces 211–12
record shop 9, 129–36
Redhead, S. 142
Reed, L. 155
Regev, M. 39, 334
reggae 3, 11, 13, 14, 38, 134, 135, 308, 316, 318–20, 347, 373, 374, 376–8
regional bloc 35
regional/inter-Asian 35–7
regionalism 2, 40 n.4
Régulier, C. 2, 22, 27
Reijnders, S. 10
Reith, J. 122
relational biography 88
remote music collaboration software (RMCS) 217–27
Renzo, A. 61–2
Retromania (Reynolds) 336
Return On Investment (ROI) 69, 70
Reynolds, S. 262–4, 336, 345
rhythmanalysis 7, 23–7
rhythmic unity 25
Rice, T. 57, 63
Rief, S. 142
Rio de Janeiro 3, 281–4, 287
Roberts, L. 305, 332–4
Robertson, R. 34
Roche, M. 360
rock and roll 291, 309, 332
rock band 197, 235, 305, 306, 309
Rocket Network 218–20
Rocket Power 218
rock music 34, 58, 135, 153, 157, 158, 183, 197, 241
Rodgers, T. 198

Rodman, M. C. 62–3
Rogers, I. 248
Romance in the Record Store (2018) 130
Rommen, T. 58, 344, 348, 350
Ronström 360
Rose, T. 47, 292, 294
Rossing, T. D. 233
Ross, K. 373–4
Royal Concert Hall 178, 179, 184
Rumsey, F. 233
Running with the Devil (Wong) 59

Said, E. 109
Saldanha, A. 349, 351
salsa 317, 318, 320
samba 281, 282, 287 n.7
Sandvoss, C. 346, 350
Sarnoff, D. 118, 126
Saville, P. 145
Sax, D. 130
scale-making 33
Scannell, P. 125
scenes 2, 3, 9–11, 37, 38, 45, 48–53, 76, 182, 183, 186, 241–2, 246
  being on 179–81
  Glasgow and 177–9
  subcultures and 48–50
  virtual 49, 241
Schaap, J. 201 n.3
Schiller, M. 3, 10
Schlager music 13, 15, 303, 304
Schlesinger, J. 134
Schmidt-Horning, S. 231
Schuilenberg, M. 26
Scottish Exhibition and Conference Centre (SECC) 177–9, 185–6
Seattle grunge 242
Second World War 46, 105, 117, 122, 123, 125, 134, 166
secular pilgrimages 346
self-authorised heritage 333
semantic festivalization 360
Senegalese hip hop 63
sensobiographic walking 2, 83, 86–8, 91, 93
  empirical study 88–93
  Finnish soundscape 84
  moulding soundscape 85–6

Sensory transformations in Europe between 1950–2020 (SENSOTRA) 86–7, 89, 94 n.3, 94 n.5
Sepultura 306
Serve the People (2003) 323
Sex On Fire (Kings Of Leon) 236
Shank, B. 178, 181, 182, 242
Shaw, R. 140, 141, 143
Shin, H. 2, 38, 39
Shuker, R. 160, 166, 305, 306, 310 n.1, 357
Sibley, D. 191, 195
Sign O The Times (Prince) 236
Silver, D. 182
Silverstein, P. 295, 298
Simmel, G. 46
Simun, M. 168–70, 172
Sinatra, F. 2, 101–3
  Come Fly with Me 2, 102–9, 111, 113
  ethnic pasticcio 105–6
  It's Nice to Go Trav'ling 101, 102, 108, 111, 112
  I've Got the World on a String 106
  LPs 103–5
  My Way 108
  Nice 'n' Easy 107
  pasticcio to pizza 111–13
  personality 106–9
  On the Road to Mandalay (Kipling) 109–11
  Swing Easy 107
Sinclair, I. 265
Skhanda 275
Slobin, M. 316
small gigs 245, 246, 248–50
small-scale live music 243
small venues 245, 248
smartphones 16, 170, 172, 193, 265
Smith, L. 332
Smith, N. 53
Smith, P. 156
Smith, R. 199
Smith, Z. 132
Smooth FM radio station 154, 155
Sobchack, V. 372
social capital 248, 272, 277
social construct 45–7, 53, 302
social dancing 143
social form 2, 7, 9
social media 9, 130, 147, 154, 171, 193, 195, 196, 200, 221, 335, 360

social networking 219–21, 225, 247
solipsistic aestheticization 16
sonic cartoons 234–6
sonic dominance 140, 143
sonic knowledge 349
sonic oblivion 140
Sonified Urban Masterplan 24
sound box 232–3
sound communities 26
Sound It Out (2011) 136
South Africa 271–5, 277–9, 279 n.12
Soviet Union 307
space 46, 206
 adapted 251 n.1
 adopted 251 n.1
 of cities 25
 cultural 10, 26, 68, 139, 182, 193, 199
 dedicated 251 n.1
 differential 9
 hearing 233–4
 morphological 236
 music and 7–12, 33
 music festival 361–2
 and place 2, 46–8, 53, 361–2
 public and private 50–1
 time and 22, 27, 28
 urban 16, 24, 27, 28, 46, 165–8, 171, 259, 265, 292
 virtual 3, 14
spatialization 3, 8, 11, 46, 47, 50, 52–4, 250
spatial production 7
spatial staging 231
spectromorphology 236
Spectrum Arena 157
speedtribes 26
Spence, K. 67
sponsorship 74, 122, 125, 362
Springsteen, B. 302, 346
stadium rock band 235
staging 231–2
Stahl, G. 46, 126, 141, 181–2
standard language (SL) 296
Stanley, L. 87
Steinberg 218, 220
Steingo, G. 275–6
stereo soundscape 230
Sterne, J. 105, 212, 213, 230

Stewart, C. M. 296
St. John, G. 362
Stoeltje, B. J. 360
Stokes, M. 60–1, 346
storage space 10–12
Stovall, T. 373
strategic ambiguity 15
Straw, W. 2, 9–11, 48, 49, 121, 133, 145, 181, 182, 242, 246, 250
Street, J. 307
Strong, C. 334
Studio 54 139
studios. *See* recording studios
Studying Popular Music (Middleton) 60
subaltern cosmopolitanism (Shin) 39
subculture 9, 45, 46, 48–50, 53, 192–5, 201 n.1, 265, 296, 308, 320, 321, 358
suburban sensibility (Frith) 259, 260
suburbs 3, 257–61, 263–7, 267 n.1, 271, 272, 291, 296, 321, 322, 332, 373, 374, 377
Sudanese hip-hop group 191, 200
Superorganism 40
Suprême NTM 292, 293, 297, 321, 375
Sutherland, R. 120
Swartz, S. 273
Swing Time (Smith) 132
SXSW 70
Sydney 77
Sydney as 24-Hour 73
Sydney City Council 73
Sydney Morning Herald 179
symbolic capital 251 n.3
syncretism 27, 63, 273

Tagg, P. 84, 93 n.1
tamborzão (big drum) groove 284, 287
Tannock, C. 184
Taylor, D. J. 262
Taylor, S. 199
Taylor, T. D. 33–4, 106
teenage girls 192, 194, 200
teenagers 132, 146, 192–5
teeny bopper subculture 192
Teitelbaum, B. 61, 308
territory 27, 46, 291, 294–5, 298, 303
That '80s Show (2002) 131
Théberge, P. 198, 206–7, 217

There's No Other Way (1991) 259
They Lie, We Lie: Getting on with Anthropology (Metcalf) 62
Thibaud, J. -P. 86
Third Man Studios 210
Thompson, P. A. 208
Thornton, S. 142, 146
Throsby, D. 71
TikTok 26, 195
Tin Pan Alley 102, 106
Tixier, N. 86
toilet circuit 71, 72, 77
tourism 103, 334, 341–2, 350–1, 358–60
    development and definitions 342–4
    embodied experience 348–50
    industry 347–8
    motivations 345–7
    survey 344–5
tourist gaze 343, 347–9
Toynbee, J. 32, 34
Trainspotting 184
Trandafoiu, R. 344, 348, 350–1
translocal 37–40, 49, 200, 246, 316, 347, 348
transnational identity 317–18, 324
transnationalism 2, 3, 36, 315–17, 320, 322, 324
transnational popular music 320–4
'Trizonesien-Song' 303–4
Tsing, A. 33, 37
Tunstall, J. 34
Turner, E. 346
Turner, V. 346, 361

UK 117–19, 121–6, 130, 154, 156, 158, 160, 161, 178–81, 183, 184, 317–20
UK Live Music Census 2017 160
UK Music 72, 342
UNESCO City of Music (GUCM) 178–9, 183, 342
UNESCO Creative Cities Network 2019 75
United Kingdom 71, 76, 77, 121–6
urban rhythms 24, 25
Urry, J. 349

van Dongen, F. 161
Van Heusen, J. 102
Vaughan, L. 264
Veblen, T. 46

venues 245–7
Verbeke, M. 296
vernacular culture 250, 251 n.2
vinyl 11, 104, 111, 130, 131, 134, 135, 319, 336
violence 10, 72, 73, 200, 271, 273, 286, 287 n.1, 294, 295, 298, 319, 322, 323, 371, 375, 376
virtual club 51
virtual scene 49, 241
virtual spaces 211–12
virtual studio 217, 224–7
    bedroom producer 220–1
    collaboration 219–20
    group work in 221–3
    history of 218–19
    Internet technologies 217
    project management challenges 223–4
    tools 226
VJ (video jockey) 144, 145
Volt Mix 283, 288 n.13
VST Connect remote recording system 220
VST Transit 220

Waitt, G. 349, 350
Walcott, D. 378
Wald, E. 34
Walker, J. 124
Walkman 16, 50, 165–7
Wallach, J. 212
Wal-Mart 132
Walser, R. 59
Warhol, A. 139, 144
Warner, A. 136
Waters, J. 132
Web 2.0 217, 219, 241
Weber, M. 46
Wee, C. W. -L. 36
Wheeler, J. S. 63–4
White Power movement 308
White Power Rock 308
Whiting, S. 334
Whyton, T. 346
Williamson, J. 179
Williams, R. 16
Willis, P. 200
Wilson, M. J. 191, 200
Wilson, O. 11

winning space 9, 46
Wolfe, P. 196–8
Wong, D. 59
Woodstock Music and Art Fair 158
Woolf, V. 197, 261, 262
World Soundscape Project (WSP) 85
Worley, M. 260, 261
Wrazen, L. 63

Xie, P. F. 346

Yin Tsang 323
YouTube 14, 131, 160, 194–5

Zak, A. 205, 206, 209, 213, 229, 231
Zoey Van Goey 181
zoning 72, 194

Milton Keynes UK
Ingram Content Group UK Ltd.
UKHW030147030224
437206UK00006B/163